Praise for
The Devil's Chessboard by David Talbot

An Amazon Best Nonfiction Book of the Year
A *Los Angeles Times* Holiday Book Recommendation
A *Kirkus* Best Book of the Year

"This year's best spy thriller isn't fiction—it's history. . . . *The Devil's Chessboard* . . . zooms out from JFK's murder to investigate the rise of the shadowy network that Talbot holds ultimately responsible for the president's assassination. This isn't merely a whodunit story, though. Talbot's ultimate goal is exploring how the rise of the 'deep state' has impacted the trajectory of America, and given our nation's vast influence, the rest of the planet. By the time *The Devil's Chessboard* eventually climaxes with the events that unfolded in Dallas in 1963, Talbot's argument that Dulles had both the power and temperament to execute such a plot is more than believable."
—Liam O'Donoghue, *Salon*

"[Talbot finds] in Dulles, a Cold War villain of realpolitik whose successes and blunders were unrivaled. As framed by Talbot, Dulles's extralegal interventions, coups, slush funds, and ex-Nazi collaborations were as much pro-corporate as anti-Communist, more Cheneyish than Nixonian. In other words, he'd fit right into our globalized, subcontracted, and hyper-surveilled era."
—Boris Kachka, *New York* magazine

"Dulles is unmasked as the backstage manipulator of US policy (foreign and domestic) from the Cold War up to his skillful defense of the highly suspect Warren Commission report. Those who scoff at conspiracy theories might have a change of mind after reading this book."
—*Boston Globe*, "Pick of the Week"

"Disturbing, compulsively readable. . . . At one and the same time a damning biography of the CIA's longest standing director, and an exposé of American politics. . . . One would be hard pressed to find a book that is better at evoking the strange and apocalyptic atmospherics of the early Cold War years in America, and the cast of characters that made the era what it was. . . . Neither le Carré nor Graham Greene could do any better."
—James A. Warren, *Daily Beast*

"This is the sort of nonfiction book that, inevitably, gets likened to a fast-paced spy thriller. While the comparison isn't wrong, *The Devil's Chessboard* is also a chilling psychological depiction of a man who seemed to operate outside the moral cosmos that most people inhabit. . . . The vast surveillance system so dramatically revealed to the world by Edward Snowden could never have come to pass without the culture of fanatical secrecy and habitual lawlessness handed down by Dulles and his loyal agents."

—Justyn Dillingham, *Bookslut*

"A frightening biography of power, manipulation, and outright treason. . . . The story of Allen Dulles and the power elite that ran Washington, D.C., following World War II is the stuff of spy fiction. . . . All engaged American citizens should read this book and have their eyes opened."

—*Kirkus Reviews* (starred review)

"This aptly titled book portrays CIA director Allen Dulles as the dark prince of the Cold War who manipulated the media, deceived presidents, helped stir up coups . . . [and might] have been involved in Kennedy's assassination. Readers who enjoy espionage's dark history will have a tough time putting this book down." —*Library Journal*

"A compelling read. Talbot tells the story with light-handed skill that masks a prodigious amount of research. He scours recently discovered US documents and personal journals (including of Dulles's wife and mistress), interviews intelligence sources across the Atlantic and children of CIA officials (including Dulles's daughter) to build a riveting portrait of one of the most unfathomable men in American public life."

—*Business Standard*

"The book is certainly explosive, linking former CIA Director Allen Dulles to the assassination of President Kennedy and uncovering the secret history of U.S.-led regime change under the Dulles brothers."

—*Washington Life*

"Essential reading." —*CounterPunch*

The
Devil's
Chessboard

Also by David Talbot

Brothers: The Hidden History of the Kennedy Years

Season of the Witch: Enchantment, Terror, and Deliverance in the City of Love

HARPER PERENNIAL

NEW YORK • LONDON • TORONTO • SYDNEY • NEW DELHI • AUCKLAND

The Devil's Chessboard

Allen Dulles, the CIA, and the Rise of America's Secret Government

David Talbot

HARPER PERENNIAL

A hardcover edition of this book was published in 2015 by HarperCollins Publishers.

THE DEVIL'S CHESSBOARD. Copyright © 2015 by The Talbot Players, LLC. All rights reserved. Printed in the United States of America. No part of this book may be used or reproduced in any manner whatsoever without written permission except in the case of brief quotations embodied in critical articles and reviews. For information, address HarperCollins Publishers, 195 Broadway, New York, NY 10007.

HarperCollins books may be purchased for educational, business, or sales promotional use. For information, please e-mail the Special Markets Department at SPsales@harpercollins.com.

FIRST HARPER PERENNIAL EDITION PUBLISHED 2016.

Designed by William Ruoto

Library of Congress Cataloging-in-Publication Data has been applied for.

ISBN 978-0-06-227617-9 (pbk.)

20 21   OV/LSC   20 19 18 17 16 15 14 13 12 11

To Karen Croft, who dared to know

And ye shall know the truth, and the truth shall make you free.

—THE INSCRIPTION CHOSEN BY ALLEN DULLES FOR THE LOBBY OF CIA HEADQUARTERS, FROM JOHN 8:31–32

The Colonel laughed unpleasantly. "My dear friend, Dimitrios would have nothing to do with the actual shooting. No! His kind never risk their skins like that. They stay on the fringe of the plot. They are the professionals, the entrepreneurs, *the links between the businessmen, the politicians who desire the end but are afraid of the means, and the fanatics, the idealists who are prepared to die for their convictions. The important thing to know about an assassination or an attempted assassination is not who fired the shot, but who paid for the bullet."*

—*A COFFIN FOR DIMITRIOS*, ERIC AMBLER

Contents

Part III

Acknowledgments

If books were movies, Karen Croft's name would be prominently featured, high in the credits, as executive producer. This book could not have been accomplished without her essential contributions. It was born out of our mutual desire to get to the bottom of this darkly fascinating pool of history and to seek some type of justice for those who escaped it or were denied it in their time. Along the way, Karen and I engaged in endless discussions and debates. She was my fellow investigator as we pursued sources and documents around the globe. She was the first to read the pages I wrote as they came out of my laptop. Through her obsessive dedication and unfailing support, I was allowed to keep those pages coming. This book is the fruit of our partnership.

Karen and I owe much to the generous assistance and intellectual camaraderie of many individuals, who are equally committed to enlightening the public about the crimes and sorrows of our past. We must thank, in particular, our mentor, Peter Dale Scott. It was during one of our many stimulating conversations with Peter that the idea for this book was born. We also feel a special sense of gratitude for the aid and fellowship of Jefferson Morley, James Lesar, Gary Aguilar, Vincent Salandria, Gerry Percy, Lawrence Meli, Adam Walinsky, Paul Schrade, Lisa Pease, Rex Bradford, James DiEugenio, Dick Russell, Marie Fonzi, Daniel Alcorn, Bill Simpich, Jerry Policoff, William Kelly, and Cyril and Ben Wecht. In addition, we benefited from insights, suggestions, and documents provided by William Gowen, Dan Hardway, Eve Pell,

John Loftus, Fabrizo Calvi, David Lifton, John Kelin, Leo Sisti, Carlo Mastelloni, Malcolm Blunt, Joan Mellen, John Simkin, and Brenda Brody. And we express our thanks to the generous contributors to the Open America campaign on Indiegogo.

We also relied on the skillful research assistance of Francoise Sorgen-Goldschmidt, Rhoda Newman, Margot Williams, Cliff Callahan, Antony Shugaar, Norma Tennis, and Ron Basich. We are equally indebted to the staffs of Princeton's Seeley Mudd Library, where Allen Dulles's papers are kept; Harvard's Schlesinger Library, which houses the papers of Martha Clover Dulles and Mary Bancroft; as well as the staff members of the John F. Kennedy Library, Dwight D. Eisenhower Library, the New York Public Library's archives department, the Hoover Institution, the University of California–Santa Barbara special collections department, and the George C. Marshall Foundation.

We are among the historians plumbing the depths of U.S. intelligence and national security, from World War II on, who have made vital discoveries by combing through the wealth of official documents released under "sunshine laws" such as the John F. Kennedy Assassination Records Collection Act and the Nazi War Crimes Disclosure Act. (Many JFK–related documents are archived at the essential Mary Ferrell Foundation website.) The American people have only gained access to this hidden history as a result of concerted political pressure, and agencies such as the CIA still remain defiantly opposed to fully disclosing the information they are required to under federal law. As the tyrannical regime in Orwell's *1984* understood, "Who controls the past controls the future." It is essential that we continue to fight for the right to own our history.

In addition to archival and documentary research, we also learned much from interviewing the sons and daughters, as well as former colleagues, of the secretive men who are the subject of this book. We are especially thankful to Joan Talley, the daughter of Allen Dulles, though she bears no responsibility for our views.

Authors who put the products of their hard labors in the hands of editors often do so with the trepidation of parents who place their offspring in the hands of surgeons. It was, therefore, an enormous joy and relief—after entrusting this book to Jennifer Barth at Harper-Collins—to witness the delicate precision of her editorial hand. She earned my trust and respect, page by page.

I am also indebted to my longtime agent, Sloan Harris of ICM, for his sound judgment, levelheaded demeanor, and keen literary and business sense.

Thanks once again to the indomitable Kelly Frankeny for her cover-design wizardry, as well as to Robert Newman.

And last—but far, far from least—I celebrate my wife, Camille Peri. Only someone blessed with her indestructible strength of character—and afflicted with her literary talent and destiny—could have empathetically stood by me these past few years, as I clawed my way to the finish line.

Prologue

That little Kennedy . . . he thought he was a god."

The words were sharp and wrong, like a curse shattering the civility of the soft evening air. They seemed particularly strange coming from the genial older gentleman strolling by Willie Morris's side. In fact, they were the only strident remarks that Morris had heard him utter in the past few days, as the graying spymaster regaled his young visitor with a lifetime of covert adventures.

And then the storm passed. The man was himself again—the chatty and amiable Allen Welsh Dulles, a man whose conviviality masked a world of dark secrets. The two men continued their walk on that Indian summer evening in 1965, ambling along the rust-colored brick sidewalks as the lampposts began casting their yellow light on picturesque Georgetown—home of Washington hostesses, martini-loving spies, influential newspapermen, and the assorted insiders who fed off the fizz and sizzle of the nation's capital. Turning the corner from the unassuming, two-story brick mansion on Q Street that Dulles rented, they now found themselves on R Street, straddling the vast greenery of the Dumbarton Oaks estate.

Dulles, the creator of America's sprawling intelligence empire, had summoned Morris—a rising young editor at *Harper's* magazine—to help him set the record straight on the most cutting humiliation of his career. He wanted to write his side of the story about the Bay of Pigs. The words alone still brought a spasm of pain and rage to Dulles's face.

It was just a spit of sand and scrubby palms along Cuba's southern coast. But it was the scene, in April 1961, of the biggest disaster in the CIA's history—a motley invasion that fell ignominiously short of toppling Cuba's dangerously charismatic leader, Fidel Castro. The failed invasion, Dulles said, was "the blackest day of my life."

In public, the newly minted president, John F. Kennedy, took responsibility for the fiasco and made gracious remarks about Dulles as he prepared to usher the aging spy out the door, after a half century of public service encompassing eight different presidencies. But in private, a vicious war had begun between the Kennedy and Dulles camps, with the two men and their advocates working the press and arguing not just the botched mechanics of the invasion, but the past and future of U.S. foreign policy.

The Bay of Pigs came after a long string of Dulles victories. Given free rein by President Eisenhower to police the world against any insurgent threat to U.S. dominion, Dulles's CIA overthrew nationalist governments in Africa, Latin America, and the Middle East, and even targeted troublesome leaders in allied European countries. Dulles called himself "the secretary of state for unfriendly countries"—which had an ominous ring when one took note of what happened to unfriendly countries in the American Century. Meanwhile, his brother John Foster Dulles—Eisenhower's official secretary of state—brought the gloom of a doomsday-obsessed vicar to his job, with his frequent sermons on Communist perfidy and his constant threats of nuclear annihilation. John Foster Dulles needed Communism the way that Puritans needed sin, the infamous British double agent Kim Philby once remarked. With his long, dour face topped by his ever-present banker's homburg, the elder Dulles always seemed to be on the brink of foreclosing on all human hope and happiness.

By 1959, John Foster Dulles was rapidly succumbing to stomach cancer. It was as if the bile building up inside him all those years over the fallen state of the world had finally devoured him. And by then Eisenhower himself was heart-troubled and weary of his job. Only Allen Dulles still stood firmly at the top, past retirement age at sixty-six, but still determined that the ancient regime must continue.

When President Kennedy began his vigorous new reign in 1961, he decided to keep Allen Dulles as CIA chief, despite the obvious differences in their world outlooks. With his brush mustache, wire-rim glasses, tweed suits, and beloved pipe, Dulles could have been one of the elderly dons that young Jack Kennedy had studied under at Harvard. As a young senator, JFK had broken from the Eisenhower-Dulles regime over the older men's nuclear brinksmanship—a game that Kennedy felt courted the abyss. Kennedy had also signaled an eagerness to dramatically change America's hostile relationship to the developing world, expressing a sympathy for the national liberation movements in Algeria, the Congo, Vietnam, and elsewhere that he saw as historically inevitable. While President Eisenhower viewed the onrush of anticolonial independence in the Third World as a "destructive hurricane," Kennedy recognized it as the future.

Though their visions for how the United States should navigate the globe were profoundly far apart, Kennedy was loath to completely overturn the old ruling order that had been presided over by a popular World War II hero. Keeping Eisenhower men like Dulles and other Republican pillars of power like Wall Street banker and statesman C. Douglas Dillon, whom JFK named his Treasury secretary, was the new president's way of assuring the nation that he would be leading an orderly transition to the New Frontier. But Kennedy soon realized that when it came to men like Dulles, his political calculation was a grave mistake.

Allen Dulles was one of the wiliest masters of secret power ever produced by America. And his most ambitious clandestine efforts were directed not against hostile governments but against his own. While serving in multiple presidential administrations, he learned to manipulate them and sometimes subvert them.

In the view of the Dulles brothers, democracy was an enterprise that had to be carefully managed by the right men, not simply left to elected officials as a public trust. From their earliest days on Wall Street—where they ran Sullivan and Cromwell, the most powerful corporate law firm in the nation—their overriding commitment was always to the circle of accomplished, privileged men whom they saw as the true seat of power in America. Although Foster and Allen did not come from the same wealthy families who dominated this elite club, the brothers' shrewd talents, missionary drive, and powerful connections firmly established them as top executives in this rarefied world.

As younger men, the Dulles brothers were obsessive chess players. When they faced each other over a chessboard, everything else faded away. Even during his whirlwind courtship of Martha Clover Todd, a free-spirited beauty from a prominent family to whom he proposed after a three-day siege, Allen could not be distracted from a lengthy joust with his brother. The Dulleses would bring the same strategic fixation to the game of global politics.

John Foster Dulles would rise to become the chief counsel for American power, a man destined to quietly confer with kings, prime ministers, and despots. He liked to think of himself as chess master of the free world. His younger brother would become something more powerful still—the knight-errant who enforced America's imperial will. As director of the CIA, Allen Dulles liked to think he was the hand of the king, but if so, he was the left hand—the sinister hand. He was master of the dark deeds that empires require.

The Dulles brothers were not intimidated by mere presidents. When President Franklin Roosevelt pushed through New Deal legislation to restrain the rampant greed and speculation that had brought the country to economic ruin, John Foster Dulles simply gathered his corporate clients in his Wall Street law office and urged them to defy the president. "Do not comply," he told them. "Resist the law with all your might, and soon everything will be all right."

Later, when Allen Dulles served as the United States' top spy in continental Europe during World War II, he blatantly ignored Roosevelt's policy of unconditional surrender and pursued his own strategy of secret negotiations with Nazi leaders. The staggering sacrifice made by the Russian people in the war against Hitler meant little to Dulles. He was more interested in salvaging the Third Reich's security apparatus and turning it against the Soviet Union—which he had always regarded

as America's true enemy. After the war, Dulles helped a number of notorious war criminals escape via the "Nazi ratlines" that ran from Germany, down through Italy, to sanctuary in Latin America, the Middle
East, and even the United States.

Allen Dulles outmaneuvered and outlived Franklin Roosevelt. He
stunned Harry Truman, who signed the CIA into existence in 1947,
by turning the agency into a Cold War colossus far more powerful and
lethal than anything Truman had imagined. Eisenhower gave Dulles
immense license to fight the administration's shadow war against Communism, but at the end of his presidency, Ike concluded that Dulles had
robbed him of his place in history as a peacemaker and left him nothing
but "a legacy of ashes." Dulles undermined or betrayed every president
he served in high office.

Dulles would serve John F. Kennedy for less than a year, but their
briefly entwined stories would have monumental consequences. Clearly
outmatched in the beginning by the savvy spymaster, who beguiled
Kennedy into the Bay of Pigs disaster, JFK proved a quick learner in the
Washington power games. He became the first and only president who
dared to strip Dulles of his formidable authority. But Dulles's forced
retirement did not last long after Kennedy jettisoned him from the CIA
in November 1961. Instead of easing into his twilight years, Dulles continued to operate as if he were still America's intelligence chief, targeting
the president who had ended his illustrious career. The underground
struggle between these two icons of power is nothing less than the story
of the battle for American democracy.

Walking through Georgetown on that warm September evening,
Willie Morris was perplexed to hear Dulles erupt with such
scorn at the mere mention of Kennedy's name. But there was a reason
that—nearly two years after JFK's bloody end—Kennedy's hold on the
public's imagination still disturbed Dulles. He knew who the real "god"
was—and it was not Jack Kennedy.

After their stroll, the two men returned to Dulles's home for drinks
and dinner, and then more work on his article, which was to be titled

"My Answer to the Bay of Pigs." There was a sad stillness to the Dulles residence: Clover was away, at the family's summer retreat on Lake Ontario; their son, Allen Jr., a brilliant young man who had suffered a grievous head wound in the Korean War, was in and out of sanitariums; their grown daughters Joan and Toddie had their own worries and misfortunes. There was nothing to distract Morris and Dulles besides the fleeting presence of one or two servants. Morris proved a good companion, a son of Mississippi who knew how to keep up his end when the bourbon and conversation began flowing. And he was the most touted magazine editor of his generation, on his way to becoming the youngest editor of the venerable *Harper's* at age thirty-two. Under his leadership in the late '60s, *Harper's* would glow with the vibrant writing of Norman Mailer, William Styron, and David Halberstam.

But, in the end, even with Morris's expert hand, Dulles could not wrestle his manuscript into shape, and the old spook withdrew it from publication. By the time Dulles finally gave up, after months of toil, the article had gone through multiple drafts, adding up to several hundred coffee-stained pages. The drafts, now stuffed into boxes at a Princeton library where the Dulles papers are housed, are a window into Allen Dulles's tortured relationship with the young president. In finally abandoning the massive project, which one historian later called "The 'Confessions' of Allen Dulles," the old spymaster seemed to conclude that he was saying both too much and too little about what he had been through with Kennedy.

By writing the article, Dulles had set out to rebut charges made by JFK loyalists Theodore Sorensen and Arthur Schlesinger Jr. that Kennedy had been tricked by his intelligence advisers into the disastrous Cuban adventure. But instead, the spymaster's scribblings—in between angry eruptions at Kennedy and his White House circle of "doubting Thomases" and "Castro admirers"—revealed the myriad ways that Dulles's CIA had indeed contrived to lure the young president into the Cuban sand trap.

When the Bay of Pigs operation was under way and "the chips were down," Dulles wrote, he was confident that JFK would be compelled to do the right thing and send in the awesome power of the U.S. military to rescue the invasion. That's the way the CIA game was played: there was a certain amount of hoodwinking and massaging of White House anxieties, and then the president fell in line. But this time, the president, despite his youth and the collective browbeating of his gray-haired national security ministers, stood his ground. Kennedy said no to expanding an operation that he had felt all along was sordid. And the long reign of Allen Dulles came crashing down.

At least, that's the way Dulles's story is told in biographies and CIA histories. The truth is that Dulles's reign went on, deeply cloaked, toward an even more catastrophic conclusion.

In the first days and weeks after his ouster, Dulles's world caved in. Suddenly unmoored from the daily routines of power he had known ever since he was a budding young spy in the service of Woodrow Wilson, Dulles seemed "a very tragic man," in the words of one CIA colleague. He shuffled around his Georgetown home, with his gout-ridden feet softly coffined in bedroom slippers. But Dulles's "tragic" period did not last long. He soon began meeting with a surprising range of CIA officers—men from the top rungs of the agency, as well as agents from the field. They paraded in and out of the brick manor on Q Street, huddling with him in his book-lined study and on sunny days quietly chatting on his walled-in terrace. His day calendar was filled with yet more meetings at his favorite Washington retreats, the Alibi Club and the Metropolitan Club, where he dined with the same generals and national security wise men with whom he had done business at the CIA. It was, in fact, as if he had never left the spy agency.

Dulles would turn his Georgetown home into the center of an anti-Kennedy government in exile. As time went by, the Dulles circle became ever more disenchanted with JFK's foreign policy, which they considered appeasement of the Communist enemy. Dulles grew bolder in his opposition. He met with a controversial Cuban exile leader named Paulino Sierra Martinez, a former henchman for the deposed dictator Fulgencio Batista. Sierra, whose anti-Castro activities were underwritten by the Mafia and U.S. corporations with a stake in

Cuba, later fell under Secret Service suspicion in a conspiracy against President Kennedy. The topic of Sierra's meeting with Dulles in April 1963 remains a mystery.

By October 1963, Dulles felt confident enough to speak out against Kennedy's foreign policy in public, ignoring the Washington etiquette that deemed it bad form to criticize a president whom you recently had served. Dulles declared that the Kennedy presidency suffered from a "yearning to be loved by the rest of the world." This "weakness" was not the mark of a global power, insisted Dulles. "I should much prefer to have people respect us than to try to make them love us."

In the weeks leading up to the assassination of President Kennedy on November 22, 1963, the flurry of meetings at Dulles's home intensified. Among the CIA men coming in and out of Q Street were several who later came under investigation by the House Select Committee on Assassinations and other probes for their possible connection to the president's murder. And on the weekend of the assassination, Dulles hunkered down for unexplained reasons at a secret CIA facility in northern Virginia known as "the Farm," despite the fact that he had been removed from the agency two years earlier. Such was the odd swirl of activity around the "retired" Dulles.

After Kennedy's assassination, Dulles would again push himself into the Washington spotlight, lobbying President Lyndon Johnson to appoint him to the Warren Commission. Dulles was so actively involved in the official investigation of Kennedy's murder that one observer remarked it should have been called the Dulles Commission. He worked carefully behind the scenes with his former CIA colleagues to steer the inquiry away from the agency itself and toward "lone gunman" Lee Harvey Oswald.

How did a bitter political enemy of President Kennedy wind up playing a lead role in the official investigation into his death? It was just one more mystery in a lifetime full of enigmatic twists and turns. Just as puzzling is why the American press never troubled itself to explore this intriguing question.

Over half a century later, many questions about JFK's violent end remain "unspeakable," in the words of Kennedy biographer James W. Douglass—at least in the carefully controlled arena of media discourse. It is even more unthinkable in these circles to explore the suspicion that Allen Dulles himself—a towering pillar of the U.S. establishment—might have played a role in the epic crime against U.S. democracy that took place in Dallas. But this is just one of many taboo and top secret areas of Dulles's life explored in this book.

The Allen Dulles story continues to haunt the country. Many of the practices that still provoke bouts of American soul-searching originated during Dulles's formative rule at the CIA. Mind control experimentation, torture, political assassination, extraordinary rendition, massive surveillance of U.S. citizens and foreign allies—these were all widely used tools of the Dulles reign.

Dulles was capable of great personal cruelty, to his intimates as well as his enemies. Underneath his twinkly-eyed personality was an icy amorality. "Our faults did not often give us a sense of guilt," remarked Eleanor Dulles, who followed her two brothers into the Washington arena. Allen was less troubled by guilt or self-doubt than any of his siblings. He liked to tell people—and it was almost a boast—that he was one of the few men in Washington who could send people to their deaths.

But Dulles was not a rash man; he was coldly calculating. As the chairman of cloak-and-dagger America, he would never initiate a high-stakes operation unless he felt he had the support of the principal members of his "board"—the Washington and Wall Street men of influence who quietly dominated the nation's decision-making.

What follows is an espionage adventure that is far more action-packed and momentous than any spy tale with which readers are familiar. This is a history of secret power in America.

We often forget how fragile a creation democracy is—a delicate eggshell in the rough-and-tumble of history. Even in the cradle of democracy, ancient Athens, rule by the people could barely survive for a couple of centuries. And throughout its brief history, Athenian democracy was besieged from within by the forces of oligarchy and tyranny. There were plots led by generals to impose military rule. There were secret clubs of aristocrats who hired squads of assassins to kill popular leaders. Terror reigned during these convulsions, and civil society was too intimidated to bring the assassins to justice. Democracy, Thucydides tells us, was "cowed in mind."

Our country's cheerleaders are wedded to the notion of American exceptionalism. But when it comes to the machinations of power, we are all too similar to other societies and ones that have come before us. There is an implacable brutality to power that is familiar throughout the world and throughout history. And no matter where power rules, there is the same determination by those in high places to keep their activities hidden.

The Devil's Chessboard seeks to shine a torch down the well of "deep politics," as Peter Dale Scott—an important scholar of American power—has termed this underworld of unaccountable authority. Until we have a full reckoning of the Dulles era and its high crimes, the country cannot find its way forward.

In the course of researching this book, I came to know Joan Talley, one of the three children of Allen Dulles. When we met in her Santa Fe cottage, in a room cluttered with books and artifacts, Joan was nearing ninety and, after a long career as a Jungian therapist, devoting herself to editing the searingly intimate diaries of her mother. Our conversations at times took on a therapeutic character, as we wrestled with the painful legacy of her father and, more broadly, the American soul. In an effort to understand her family, and her own life, Joan had delved deeply into the historical literature on the Cold War and the CIA. She had read all about the coups and trench coat mayhem. "It seems we just went wild," she told me. "And the CIA was leading the way."

But as she pored through her mother's diaries, Joan also was seeking a deeper understanding of her father than mere history can provide. One afternoon, she invoked Jung's *Red Book*, the master's night journey into his own tortured soul. "Jung says you must embrace the dark, as well as the light, to understand life," remarked Joan, sitting in the passenger seat as I drove her dusty Prius through New Mexico's high-desert chaparral.

The next morning, we spoke again over the phone. Joan was still agitated by our conversations about her father the previous day. She was trying to make sense of how she could have been so oblivious to this violent rush of history as a younger woman, even when it roared right through her own living room.

"Life sweeps you along—you see people floating by. Everyone is so busy and in the moment. It's only later that you realize what happened and how alarming it all was. You read books and you finally try to put it all together, and you don't know what to believe.

"But it's very important to understand it all—the dark and the light."

Part I

The Double Agent

Allen Dulles went to war on November 9, 1942, crossing into neutral Switzerland from Vichy France, just minutes before the Nazis closed the border. He later told the story of his border crossing with pulse-racing, dramatic flair. But, in reality, it went surprisingly smoothly, especially considering the forty-nine-year-old Wall Street lawyer's high international profile. After presenting his passport to the French gendarme at the border station near Geneva, Dulles paced the train platform while the policeman made a phone call to Vichy authorities. Then, after a hovering Gestapo agent conveniently disappeared, the gendarme obligingly waved Dulles through. It was almost as if Dulles was expected.

There was nothing undercover about Allen Dulles's wartime exploits in Switzerland. Afterward, he made much of his espionage adventures, with a sympathetic press and then equally credulous biographers dutifully repeating his beguiling tales. But, in truth, there was little daring involved—for a very simple reason. Dulles was more in step with many Nazi leaders than he was with President Roosevelt. Dulles not only enjoyed a professional and social familiarity with many members of the Third Reich's elite that predated the war; he shared many of these men's postwar goals. While serving in his Swiss outpost, Dulles might have been encircled by Nazi forces, but he was also surrounded by old friends.

After crossing the border, Dulles wasted no time in settling into

Bern, the scenic Swiss capital where he had begun his espionage career a quarter century earlier as a junior member of the U.S. legation during World War I. The medieval city—built on cliffs overlooking the glacial-green Aar River, as it flowed down from the white-capped Alpine peaks on the horizon—held a treasure of memories. During the earlier war, there had been embassy parties and rounds of tennis—with balls arriving in diplomatic pouches from back home, courtesy of his brother Foster. There was an international parade of mistresses—young secretaries from the consulates that filled the city's diplomatic quarter as well as free-spirited women from the local art colony. He met his conquests for drinks and pleasure at the Bellevue Palace Hotel, the elegant Art Nouveau fortress that dominated the Old City's skyline. Dulles affected the look of a dashing Continental cavalry officer in those days, with a waxed mustache, slim waist jacket, and high starched collar.

One of his affairs during the First World War had a brutal ending. She was a young Czech patriot who worked alongside Dulles in the U.S. legation offices. British agents concluded that she was using her position to pass information to exiled Czech leader Jan Masaryk as well as to the Germans. When the British confronted Dulles with their suspicions, the ambitious young diplomat knew he was in an awkward spot, and he quickly complied with their plans. One night Dulles took the woman to dinner, and afterward he strolled with her along the cobblestone streets to an agreed-upon location, where he handed her over to two British agents. She disappeared forever.

When Dulles returned to Bern in 1942 for the Office of Strategic Services (OSS), America's World War II spy agency, he set up his base of operations in his residence—the ground-floor apartment of a handsomely renovated fourteenth-century mansion at 23 Herrengasse, near the city's majestic cathedral. Dulles later insisted that he had carefully chosen the location with security in mind, since the street ended in a cul-de-sac. He prevailed upon municipal authorities to extinguish the lamplight outside his building, giving late-night visitors a measure of anonymity as they slipped in and out. Guests seeking more confidentiality could enter Dulles's apartment from the rear, climbing an ancient flight of stone steps that rose steeply to his back terrace from the grape arbors and dark river below.

But all this cloak and dagger was a bit of a charade. As soon as Dulles showed up in Bern, his arrival was reported in one of Switzerland's leading newspapers, which announced him—to the spy's great delight—as "the personal representative of President Roosevelt." This afforded Dulles a status that would be very useful as he pursued his various intrigues.

After arriving at 23 Herrengasse with such great fanfare, Dulles found himself under intense scrutiny. Although the newly arrived American spy had enjoyed long friendships with many in the enemy camp, each side trusted the other only up to a point. From across the street, Nazi agents kept close watch on the Dulles residence twenty-four hours a day. The Germans also infiltrated his staff—his cook turned out to be a spy and his janitor stole carbon copies of his documents out of his trash. Meanwhile, Swiss intelligence agents, who worked closely with their Nazi counterparts, eavesdropped on Dulles's phone conversations. There was little that was secret about the American spy's life in Bern.

None of this seemed to disturb Dulles, who wandered openly through the streets of Bern in a rumpled raincoat and a fedora cocked carelessly on the back of his head. He did not have a bodyguard and he did not carry a gun. He met openly with informers and double agents in cafés and on the city streets. "Too much secrecy can be self-defeating," he observed.

This strategy of hiding in plain sight did not make much sense from an espionage point of view. And it confounded and angered Dulles's counterparts in the local office of MI6, the British spy agency, who dismissed the American as a rank amateur. But Dulles was involved in something far more ambitious than mere spy games. He was running his own foreign policy.

William "Wild Bill" Donovan, director of the OSS, originally wanted to station Dulles in London. But Dulles insisted on Bern and he prevailed. Donovan was a legend—a World War I combat hero and self-made Wall Street millionaire lawyer who had charmed FDR and outmaneuvered powerful rivals like J. Edgar Hoover to build the country's first international intelligence agency. Undaunted by Washington bureaucracy, Donovan had recruited an impressively eclectic array of talent for his new spy agency—from Ivy League adventurers and society girls to safecrackers and professional killers. But Dulles, who moved in the same social circles as Donovan and competed aggressively with him on the tennis court, was not awed by his boss. He thought he could do a better job than Donovan of running the show. Dulles knew that the isolated splendor of Bern would afford him free rein to operate as he chose, with only tenuous supervision from back home.

Dulles also positioned himself in Bern because the Swiss capital was the center of wartime financial and political intrigue. Bern was an espionage bazaar, teeming with spies, double agents, informers, and peddlers of secrets. And, as Dulles knew, Switzerland was a financial haven for the Nazi war machine.

The Swiss demonstrated that they were masters of duplicity during the war. Banks in Zurich and Basel allowed the Nazis to stash the treasure they were looting from Europe in secret accounts, which Germany then used to buy the essential products from neutral countries that fueled the Third Reich—tungsten from Spain, oil from Romania, steel from Sweden, beef from Argentina. Swiss bankers promised the Allies that they would block Germany's stolen assets, but all the while they reaped huge profits from their behind-the-scenes deals with the Nazi Reichsbank.

Dulles knew many of the central players in the secretive Swiss financial milieu because he and his brother had worked with them as clients or business partners before the war. Sullivan and Cromwell, the Dulles brothers' Wall Street law firm, was at the center of an intricate international network of banks, investment firms, and industrial conglomerates that rebuilt Germany after World War I. Foster, the law firm's top executive, grew skilled at structuring the complex merry-go-round of transactions that funneled massive U.S. investments into German industrial giants like the IG Farben chemical conglomerate and Krupp Steel. The profits generated by these investments then flowed to France and Britain in the form of war reparations, and then back to the United States to pay off war loans.

Foster Dulles became so deeply enmeshed in the lucrative revitalization of Germany that he found it difficult to separate his firm's interests from those of the rising economic and military power—even after Hitler consolidated control over the country in the 1930s. Foster continued to represent German cartels like IG Farben as they were integrated into the Nazis' growing war machine, helping the industrial giants secure access to key war materials. He donated money to America First, the campaign to keep the United States out of the gathering tempest in Europe, and helped sponsor a rally honoring Charles Lindbergh, the fair-haired aviation hero who had become enchanted by Hitler's miraculous revival of Germany. Foster refused to shut down the Berlin office of Sullivan and Cromwell—whose attorneys were forced to sign their correspondence "Heil Hitler"—until his partners (including Allen), fearful of a public relations disaster, insisted he do so. When Foster finally gave in—at an extremely tense 1935 partners' meeting in the firm's lavish offices at 48 Wall Street—he broke down in tears.

Foster still could not bring himself to cut off his former Berlin law partner, Gerhardt Westrick, when he showed up in New York in August 1940 to lobby on behalf of the Third Reich. Setting himself up in an opulent Westchester County estate, Westrick invited influential New York society types for weekend parties, taking the opportunity to subject them to his pro-Hitler charm offensive. Westrick's guest lists were dominated by oil executives because he was particularly keen on ensuring the continued flow of fuel supplies to Germany, despite the British embargo. The lobbyist finally went too far—even by the hospitable standards of the New York society set—when he had the gall to throw a gala party at the Waldorf-Astoria on June 26, 1940, to celebrate the Nazi defeat of France. Westrick's shameless audacity created an uproar in the New York press, but Foster rushed to the Nazi promoter's defense, insisting he had "a high regard for his integrity."

Until late in the day, Foster harbored sympathy for the devil himself, Adolf Hitler. Even after the Nazi regime pushed through the anti-Semitic Nuremberg Laws of 1935 and unleashed waves of terror against Germany's Jewish population, Foster clung to a sympathetic view of the Führer. He could not help being impressed by a man "who from humble beginnings . . . has attained the unquestioned leadership of a great nation," Foster told a friend in 1937. By 1939, Eustace Seligman—a Jewish senior partner at Sullivan and Cromwell—had become so fed up with Foster's position on Nazi Germany that he confronted his boss, telling Foster he was hurting the firm's reputation by publicly suggesting "that Germany's position is morally superior to that of the Allies."

Like his brother, Allen Dulles was slow to grasp the malevolence of Hitler's regime. Dulles met face-to-face with Hitler in the Führer's Berlin office in March 1933. He was ostensibly on a fact-finding mission to Europe for President Roosevelt, but Dulles was particularly interested in determining what Hitler's rise meant for his law firm's corporate clients in Germany and the United States. As Dulles subsequently informed Foster, he did not find Hitler particularly alarming. And he was "rather impressed" with Joseph Goebbels, remarking on the Nazi propaganda chief's "sincerity and frankness." After Dulles and fellow U.S. statesman Norman Davis returned to the Adlon, their luxury hotel across from the Brandenburg Gate, Davis was unnerved to find the word "*Juden*" scrawled crudely on the door of his room, even though he was not Jewish. "The conditions are not quite as bad" as anxious reports about Hitler would indicate, Dulles nonetheless wrote Foster from Germany.

By the late 1930s, Dulles's views finally shifted and he came to dismiss Nazi leaders as "those mad people in control in Germany." He grew increasingly certain that the United States must prepare for an inevitable showdown with Hitler. But, out of deference to Foster, Allen was reluctant to make his opinions public. He also continued to do business with the Nazi financial and industrial network, joining the board of J. Henry Schroder Bank, the U.S. subsidiary of a London bank that *Time* magazine in 1939 called "an economic booster of the Rome-Berlin Axis." And Allen and his wife, Clover, continued to socialize with the Lindberghs, who were their neighbors on Long Island's Gold Coast shore. (Lindbergh, enamored of Hitler, noted in his diary that he and Dulles "have somewhat similar views in a number of instances.")

Even after Dulles was recruited into the OSS by Donovan in October 1941, his loyalties were still questioned by some administration officials, including Roosevelt himself. Dulles's various financial connections to the Nazi regime prompted FDR to place the Wall Street lawyer under close surveillance when he began working in the OSS's thirty-sixth-floor suite in Rockefeller Center. Monitoring Dulles proved an easy task since he shared office space with a massive British spy operation run by legendary Canadian secret agent William Stephenson, who would become famous as the "Man Called Intrepid." At one point, Stephenson's Rockefeller Center operation—which was tucked away under the colorless name British Security Coordination—grew to as many as three thousand employees. It was a remarkably ambitious covert enterprise, particularly considering that England was operating on friendly soil.

Stephenson had been sent to the United States in 1940 by his enthusiastic patron, Winston Churchill—Britain's newly elected prime minister—after the evacuation of British forces from the beaches of Dunkirk. With Hitler's forces overrunning Europe and turning their gaze toward an increasingly isolated England, Churchill knew that his nation's only hope was to maneuver the United States into the war. Roosevelt was a strong supporter of the British cause, but with as much as 80 percent of the American public against entering the European war and Congress equally opposed, both FDR and Churchill realized it would take a major propaganda offensive to sway the nation.

The British government and the Roosevelt White House faced not only a deeply wary American public with understandable concerns about the costs of war, but a well-financed appeasement lobby with strong links to Nazi Germany. With the fate of nations at stake, the shadow war in America grew increasingly ruthless. Churchill made it clear that he was quite willing to engage in what he euphemistically called "ungentlemanly warfare" to save his nation—and he enjoyed Roosevelt's firm support.

Stephenson—Britain's point man in the underground war against Nazi Germany on American soil—was a suave operator, with a flair for hosting lively cocktail parties at his penthouse suite in midtown Manhattan's Dorset Hotel. But, like James Bond—the fictional spy partly modeled on Stephenson by his colleague Ian Fleming—Stephenson was also willing to do the dirty work of espionage. The slim, slight Stephenson, who arrived in New York at the age of forty-four, had the springy step of the boxer he once was—and the smooth self-assurance of the self-made millionaire he had become. He proved an adept practitioner of the black arts of espionage, working his far-flung press contacts in America to expose Nazi front companies—including some of the Dulles brothers' corporate clients—and pressuring Washington to deport Nazi lobbyists. Stephenson's operatives also undertook a variety of black-bag operations, such as breaking into the Spanish embassy in Washington, where they stole the secret codes for diplomatic messages flowing between General Francisco Franco's fascist government and Berlin.

Stephenson was even authorized to kill members of the Nazi network in the United States—including German agents and pro-Hitler American businessmen—using British assassination teams. One of the men considered for elimination was none other than Dulles business partner Gerhardt Westrick. (The big-spending Hitler lobbyist was eventually simply deported.) It was this decidedly ungentlemanly Stephenson tactic that inspired Fleming to grant his hero "the license to kill."

Fleming was a great admirer of Stephenson, whom he called "a magnetic personality" and "one of the great secret agents" of World War II. The novelist, who worked with Stephenson's operation as a British naval intelligence agent in Washington, also praised the spymaster's martinis—which he served in quart glasses—as "the most powerful in America." But as Fleming himself observed, even his fictional hero James Bond was "not in fact a hero—but an efficient and not very attractive blunt instrument in the hands of government."

Years later, when James Jesus Angleton and William K. Harvey—two legends of U.S. counterintelligence—were searching for assassins to kill Cuban leader Fidel Castro, they sought advice from a British colleague named Peter Wright. "Have you thought of approaching Stephenson?" Wright suggested. "A lot of the old-timers say he ran this kind of thing in New York during the war."

President Roosevelt was well aware that the Dulleses were at the center of Wall Street and Republican Party opposition to his presidency. The brothers, as top legal advisers to America's business royalty, were the very symbols of the "plutocracy" that the president railed against when giving vent to his populist passions. The fact that they were also linked to Nazi financial interests only deepened Roosevelt's suspicions.

While FDR himself was adept at hiding his true political feelings behind a mask of charm, there were some New Deal loyalists who openly expressed the deep enmity between the Roosevelt and Dulles camps. One such firebrand was William O. Douglas, the progressive young lawyer President Roosevelt put in charge of the Securities and Exchange Commission, the newly formed Wall Street watchdog agency, and later appointed a justice of the Supreme Court. As FDR's top Wall Street regulator, Douglas had more than one occasion to cross swords with Foster. Years later, Douglas's hatred for the "unctuous and self-righteous" senior Dulles brother still reverberated in the New Dealer's memoir. Foster carried himself like a "high churchman," observed Douglas. But in reality, he was the kind of "predatory" Wall Street shill "who for a fee would stand for almost anything." If the John Foster Dulleses of America were destined for heaven—as men of his ilk were always utterly certain—then Douglas would rather end up in hell. "I could perhaps endure [men like Foster] for an evening. But to sit on a cloud with [them] through eternity would be to exact too great a price."

Though FDR shared the Dulles crowd's privileged background, the president felt much more in tune with men like Douglas, the product of a hardscrabble childhood in Washington's Yakima Valley, where he had grown up picking fruit to help support his family. Brilliant and hard-driven, Douglas worked his way through Columbia University Law School. One of the talented law school graduate's first job interviews was with Foster Dulles at Sullivan and Cromwell. But Foster was so "pontifical" that Douglas decided against joining the firm. "In fact," he recalled, "I was so struck by [Foster's] pomposity that when he helped me on with my coat, as I was leaving his office, I turned and gave him a quarter tip."

After joining the Roosevelt administration at the age of thirty-five, Douglas quickly developed a reputation as a rising New Deal star, taking over as chairman of the Securities and Exchange Commission from Joseph P. Kennedy in 1937 and becoming a fixture in the president's inner circle. A frequent weekend guest at Camp David, the presidential retreat that was widely known in those years as Shangri-la, Douglas solidified his position with the president by learning to perfect a dry martini, FDR's favorite cocktail.

Roosevelt grew so fond of Douglas that in 1944, while pondering running mates for his fourth presidential run, he briefly considered his young SEC chairman. Douglas was an energetic New Dealer, FDR reminded a group of Democratic Party bosses who had gathered in the White House to advise him on the decision. Besides, he noted, Douglas played a stimulating game of poker. But the political bosses were not as enamored of Douglas as the president. They were well aware that announcing a Roosevelt-Douglas ticket would set off a bombshell on Wall Street.

While serving with the SEC, Douglas had become a scourge of the financial industry. Bankers and lawyers accustomed to the hushed privacy of wood-paneled suites and private dining rooms were yanked before public hearings presided over by Douglas and his sharp young staff and forced to account for their business practices. Even Robert Swaine of the white-shoe law firm Cravath—who had once been Douglas's boss—got the full treatment. "You stood me on my head and shook all the fillings out of my teeth," he later told Douglas.

With his craggy Western good looks and lean, outdoorsman's build, Douglas seemed cut out to be a populist hero—an everyman Gary Cooper taking on pompous big shots like the ones played by Edward Arnold in Frank Capra movies. And stuffed-shirt John Foster Dulles was his perfect nemesis. Douglas once put Foster on the witness stand for two full days, grilling him about the fortune that he had reaped for his law firm by managing a sketchy bankruptcy procedure that had fleeced a multitude of creditors. The high and mighty Foster had squirmed on the stand like a pontiff forced "to do business with the underworld," recalled Douglas.

By siccing men like William O. Douglas on men like John Foster Dulles, President Roosevelt drove the plutocracy mad. J. P. Morgan Jr. was so incensed by the "class traitor" FDR that his servants had to cut out the president's picture from the Wall Street titan's morning newspaper for fear that it would spike his blood pressure. The class hatred against Roosevelt even resulted in at least two abortive coups against his presidency. In 1934, a group of Wall Street plotters—financed by wealthy Roosevelt enemies (and Dulles clients) like the Du Ponts— tried to recruit Marine war hero General Smedley Butler to lead an armed march on Washington. In 1940, newspaperman and socialite Cornelius Vanderbilt Jr.—one of FDR's few friends in the New York club set—tipped off Eleanor Roosevelt to another anti-Roosevelt plot he had heard being hatched in his Fifth Avenue circles, involving tycoons as well as army officers.

The First Lady was among those who wondered about the wisdom of allowing someone like Allen Dulles to set up spy operations in wartorn Europe, where he was certain to open lines of communication to Nazi interests. But Dulles was not the only master chess player involved in this high-stakes game. FDR apparently had his own reason for allowing Dulles to establish himself in Bern. "He was a dangle," said John Loftus, a former Nazi war crimes investigator for the U.S. Justice Department. "The White House wanted Dulles in clear contact with his Nazi clients so they could be easily identified."

One of Dulles's most important contacts in Europe was Thomas McKittrick, an old Wall Street friend who was president of the Bank for International Settlements. BIS had been created by the world's leading central banks to administer German reparations payments after World War I, but it soon took on a life of its own, transforming itself into a pillar of the emerging global financial system. Lodged in a former hotel next to a chocolate shop in Basel, Switzerland, BIS was so secretive that nobody was permitted to peer inside its boardroom, even when it was empty. By 1940, when McKittrick arrived in Switzerland to oversee the bank, it was effectively controlled by Hitler's regime. Five of its directors would later be charged with war crimes, including Hermann Schmitz, the CEO of IG Farben, the chemical conglomerate that became notorious for its production of Zyklon B, the gas used in Hitler's death camps, and for its extensive use of slave labor during the war.

Schmitz was one of the many Dulles brothers' law clients and business associates who were involved with BIS. It was a close-knit circle of men whose relationships smoothly weathered the storms of war. Even as his company was stockpiling poison for Hitler's exterminators, Schmitz would send cheery Christmas and birthday greetings to his American business friends.

The secretive BIS became a crucial financial partner for the Nazis. Emil Puhl—vice president of Hitler's Reichsbank and a close associate of McKittrick—once called BIS the Reichsbank's only "foreign branch." BIS laundered hundreds of millions of dollars in Nazi gold looted from the treasuries of occupied countries. Some of the gold was torn from the mouths of concentration camp victims or melted down from Jewish families' candleholders, cigarette cases, and other personal belongings.

Dulles connected with McKittrick as soon as he set foot in Europe, meeting with the BIS president in Lisbon, even before he reached Switzerland. McKittrick, a well-tailored, pink-cheeked man with a high-domed forehead and prematurely snowy hair, later described the meeting as a happy coincidence. But both men were clearly eager to talk business. As soon as he walked into the lobby of his Lisbon hotel, the banker recalled, "Somebody grabbed me from behind and said, 'Is that you Tom McKittrick? Well, my gosh, I've got to see you. You're the first man I wanted to see in Switzerland.' And it was Allen Dulles, on his way over [to his OSS station in Bern]." The two men stayed up all night at the hotel, in deep conversation, until McKittrick had to leave for his five o'clock plane.

Dulles was eager to pump McKittrick for inside information about the Reich, since the banker had good connections in Berlin. But the two men also wanted to discuss another issue that was of paramount concern to both of them: how to protect the assets of their German and American corporate clients in the tumultuous war climate.

Like Dulles, McKittrick was not popular with Roosevelt and his inner circle. FDR's Treasury secretary, Henry Morgenthau Jr., developed a deep loathing for McKittrick, whom Morgenthau's aide, Harry Dexter White, called "an American [bank] president doing business with the Germans while our American boys are fighting the Germans." The Roosevelt administration moved to block BIS funds in the United States, but McKittrick hired Foster Dulles as legal counsel, who successfully intervened on the bank's behalf.

Morgenthau was outraged when McKittrick made a business trip to the United States in winter 1942 and was warmly feted by Wall Street. Dozens of powerful financiers and industrialists—including the executives of several corporations, such as General Motors and Standard Oil, that had profited handsomely from doing business with the Nazis—gathered for a banquet in McKittrick's honor at New York's University Club on December 17.

Morgenthau tried to prevent McKittrick from returning to BIS headquarters in Switzerland on the grounds that the bank was clearly aiding the Nazi war effort. The banker later sniffed about the "nasty crew in the Treasury at the time. . . . I was very suspect because I talked to Italians and talked to Germans—and I said that they had behaved very well. I [refused to denounce them as] villains of the worst sort." Allen Dulles came to McKittrick's rescue, deftly pulling strings on the banker's behalf, and in April 1943 he finally boarded a transatlantic flight to Europe.

Dulles and McKittrick continued to work closely together for the rest of the war. In the final months of the conflict, the two men collaborated against a Roosevelt operation called Project Safehaven that sought to track down and confiscate Nazi assets that were stashed in neutral countries. Administration officials feared that, by hiding their ill-gotten wealth, members of the German elite planned to bide their time after the war and would then try to regain power. Morgenthau's Treasury Department team, which spearheaded Project Safehaven, reached out to the OSS and BIS for assistance. But Dulles and McKittrick were more inclined to protect their clients' interests. Moreover, like many in the upper echelons of U.S. finance and national security, Dulles believed that a good number of these powerful German figures *should* be returned to postwar power, to ensure that Germany would be a strong bulwark against the Soviet Union. And during the Cold War, he would be more intent on using Nazi loot to finance covert anti-Soviet operations than on returning it to the families of Hitler's victims.

Dulles realized that none of his arguments against Project Safehaven would be well received by Morgenthau. So he resorted to time-honored methods of bureaucratic stalling and sabotage to help sink the operation, explaining in a December 1944 memo to his OSS superiors that his Bern office lacked "adequate personnel to do [an] effective job in this field and meet other demands."

McKittrick demonstrated equal disdain for the project, and his lack of cooperation proved particularly damaging to the operation, since BIS was the main conduit for the passage of Nazi gold. "The Treasury [Department] kept sending sleuth hounds over to Switzerland," he complained years later. "The only thing they were interested in was where was Hitler putting his money, and where [Hermann] Goering was putting his money, and [Heinrich] Himmler, and all the rest of the big boys in Germany. But I, myself, am convinced that those fellows were not piling up money for the future."

While Allen Dulles was using his OSS post in Switzerland to protect the interests of Sullivan and Cromwell's German clients, his brother Foster was doing the same in New York. By playing an intricate corporate shell game, Foster was able to hide the U.S. assets of major German cartels like IG Farben and Merck KGaA, the chemical and pharmaceutical giant, and protect these subsidiaries from being confiscated by the federal government as alien property. Some of Foster's legal origami allowed the Nazi regime to create bottlenecks in the production of essential war materials—such as diesel-fuel injection motors that the U.S. military needed for trucks, submarines, and airplanes. By the end of the war, many of Foster's clients were under investigation by the Justice Department's antitrust division. And Foster himself was under scrutiny for collaboration with the enemy.

But Foster's brother was guarding his back. From his frontline position in Europe, Allen was well placed to destroy incriminating evidence and to block any investigations that threatened the two brothers and their law firm. "Shredding of captured Nazi records was the favorite tactic of Dulles and his [associates] who stayed behind to help run the occupation of postwar Germany," observed Nazi hunter John Loftus, who pored through numerous war documents related to the Dulles brothers when he served as a U.S. prosecutor in the Justice Department under President Jimmy Carter.

If their powerful enemy in the White House had survived the war, the Dulles brothers would likely have faced serious criminal charges for their wartime activities. Supreme Court Justice Arthur Goldberg, who as a young lawyer served with Allen in the OSS, later declared that both Dulleses were guilty of treason.

But with Franklin Roosevelt gone from the arena, as of April 1945, there was not enough political will to challenge two such imposing pillars of the American establishment. Allen was acutely aware that knowledge was power, and he would use his control of the country's rapidly expanding postwar intelligence apparatus to carefully manage the flow of information about him and his brother.

FDR announced the Allied doctrine of "unconditional surrender" at the Casablanca Conference with British prime minister Winston Churchill in January 1943. The alliance's third major leader, Soviet premier Joseph Stalin, was unable to attend the conference because he was still contending with the horrific Nazi siege of Stalingrad. The Red Army would finally prevail at the Battle of Stalingrad, and the epic victory shifted the war's momentum against the Third Reich. But the costs were monumental. The Soviet Union lost over one million soldiers during the struggle for Stalingrad—more than the United States would lose during the entire war.

The Casablanca Conference, held January 12–23, 1943, at a barbed wire–encircled hotel in Morocco, would sorely aggrieve the missing Russian leader by concluding that it was too soon to open a second major front in France. But Roosevelt's unconditional surrender declaration, which took Churchill by surprise, was FDR's way of reassuring Stalin that the Americans and British would not sell out the Soviet Union by cutting a separate peace deal with Nazi leaders.

The Casablanca Conference was a major turning point in the war, sealing the fate of Hitler and his inner circle. As Roosevelt told the American people in a radio address following the conference, by taking an uncompromising stand against the Third Reich, the Allies made clear that they would not allow Hitler's regime to divide the antifascist alliance or to escape justice for its monumental crimes. "In our uncompromising policy," said Roosevelt, "we mean no harm to the common people of the Axis nations. But we do mean to impose punishment and retribution in full upon their guilty, barbaric leaders."

With his close ties to Germany's upper echelons, Dulles considered the unconditional surrender declaration a "disaster" and was quick to let his Nazi contacts know what he thought about it. Shortly after the Casablanca Conference, Dulles sat down one wintry evening with an agent of SS leader Heinrich Himmler, an oily Mittel-European aristocrat who had flitted in and out of Dulles's social circle for many years. Dulles received his guest, who was known as "the Nazi prince," at 23 Herrengasse, treating him to good Scotch in a drawing room warmed by a fire. The Casablanca Declaration had clearly unnerved Himmler's circle by making it clear that there would be no escape for the Reich's "barbaric leaders." But Dulles took pains to put his guest's mind at rest. The Allies' declaration, Dulles assured him, was "merely a piece of paper to be scrapped without further ado if Germany would sue for peace."

Thus began Allen Dulles's reign of treason as America's top spy in

Nazi-occupied Europe.

Maximilian Egon von Hohenlohe, the Nazi prince, was a creature of Europe's war-ravaged landed aristocracy. Prince Max and his wife, a Basque *marquesa*, had once presided over an empire of properties stretching from Bohemia to Mexico. But two world wars and global economic collapse had stripped Hohenlohe of his holdings and reduced him to playing the role of Nazi courier. The prince had first met Dulles in Vienna in 1916, when they were both young men trying to make a name for themselves in diplomatic circles. During the 1930s, after he fell into the less refined company of the SS thugs who had taken over Germany, Hohenlohe popped up as an occasional guest of Allen and Clover in New York.

Hohenlohe was just one more member of the titled set who saw advantages to Hitler's rise, and was quite willing to overlook its unpleasant side, which the prince explained away as rank-and-file Nazi Party excesses that would inevitably be sorted out. The Hohenlohe family was filled with ardent Nazi admirers. Perhaps the most bizarre was Stephanie von Hohenlohe, who became known as "Hitler's princess." A Jew by birth, Stephanie found social position by marrying another Hohenlohe prince. In the years before the war, she became one of Hitler's most tireless promoters, helping to bring British press magnate Lord Rothermere into the Nazi fold. Stephanie took Hitler's handsome, square-jawed adjutant Fritz Wiedemann as a lover and laid big plans for their rise to the top of the Nazi hierarchy. But it was not to be. Jealous of her favored position with Hitler, SS rivals plotted against her, spreading stories about her Jewish origins. Her aunt died in a concentration camp, and Stephanie was forced to flee Germany.

But Prince Max suffered no such fall from grace. He roamed Europe, feeling out British and American diplomats on a possible deal that would sacrifice Hitler but salvage the Reich. Wherever he went, Hohenlohe got a brusque reception. British foreign secretary Anthony Eden warned against even speaking with the prince: "If news of such a meeting became public . . . the damage would far exceed the value of anything the prince could possibly say." American diplomats in Madrid, who were also approached by Hohenlohe, dismissed him as a "flagrant" liar and a "totally unscrupulous" schemer whose overriding concern was "to protect his considerable fortune."

Dulles brushed aside these concerns; he had no compunctions about meeting with his old friend. The truth is, he felt perfectly at ease in the company of such people. Before the war, Dulles had been an occasional guest of Lord and Lady Astor at Cliveden, the posh couple's country home along the Thames that became notorious as a weekend retreat for the pro-Nazi aristocracy. (There is no getting around this unwelcome fact: Hitler was much more fashionable in the social settings that men like Dulles frequented—in England as well as the United States—than it was later comfortable to admit.)

Royall Tyler, the go-between who set up the Bern reunion between Dulles and Hohenlohe, was cut from similar cloth. Born into Boston wealth, Tyler traipsed around Europe for most of his life, collecting Byzantine art, marrying a Florentine contessa, and playing the market. The multilingual Tyler and his titled wife led a richly cultured life, with Tyler haunting antique shops and private collections in search of Byzantine treasures and restoring a château in Burgundy where he showed off his rare books and art. "Traveling with Tyler," noted London OSS chief David Bruce, "is like taking a witty, urbane, human Baedeker as a courier." The contessa, who was equally sophisticated, moved in artistic and literary circles. She was at the bedside of Edith Wharton in 1937 when the novelist expired at her villa outside Paris.

Tyler was another one of those refined men who glided smoothly across borders and did not think twice about doing business with Nazi luminaries. During the war, he moved to Geneva to dabble in banking for the Bank for International Settlements. Tyler's virulent anti-Semitism made him a congenial colleague when the Reich had business to conduct in Switzerland. Well connected in the enemy camp, Tyler was among the first people whom Dulles sought out after arriving in Switzerland.

Now Dulles and Hohenlohe, and their mutual friend Royall Tyler, were gathered amiably around the OSS man's fireplace at 23 Herrengasse. Dulles broke the ice by recalling old times with Prince Max in Vienna and New York. Then the men quickly got down to business—trying to determine whether a realpolitik deal could be struck between Germany and the United States that would take Hitler out of the equation but leave the Reich largely intact. As they spun out their visions for a postwar Europe, there was much common ground. Dulles and Hohenlohe clearly saw the Soviet Union as the enemy, with a strong Germany as a bastion against the Bolshevik and Slavic menace. The two old friends also agreed that there was probably no room for the Jewish people in postwar Europe, and certainly they should not return to positions of power. Dulles offered that there were some in America who felt the Jews should be resettled in Africa—an old dream of Hitler's: the Führer had once fantasized about sending the pariah population to Madagascar.

The two men were too worldly to engage in any emotional discussion about the Holocaust. Dulles put the prince at ease by telling him that he "was fed up with hearing from all the outdated politicians, emigrants and prejudiced Jews." He firmly believed that "a peace had to be made in Europe in which all of the parties would be interested—we cannot allow it to be a peace based on a policy of winners and losers."

Instead of Roosevelt's "unconditional surrender," in which the Nazi leadership would be held accountable for their crimes against humanity, Dulles was proposing a kind of no-fault surrender. It was a stunningly cynical and insubordinate gambit. The pact that Dulles envisioned not only dismissed the genocide against the Jews as an irrelevant issue, it also rejected the president's firmly stated policy against secret deal making with the enemy. The man in the White House, clinging to his anti-Nazi principles, was clearly one of those "outdated politicians" in Dulles's mind. While boldly undermining his president, Dulles had the nerve to assure Hohenlohe that he had FDR's "complete support."

The fireplace meeting was, in fact, a double betrayal—Dulles's of President Roosevelt, and the Nazi prince's of Adolf Hitler. Hovering over the tête-à-tête at 23 Herrengasse was the presence of Heinrich Himmler. He was the Reich's second most powerful man, and he dared to think he could become number one. With his weak chin, caterpillar mustache, and beady eyes gazing out from behind wire-rim glasses, Himmler looked less an icon of the master race than an officious bank clerk. The former chicken farmer and fertilizer salesman inflated himself by claiming noble heritage and was given to explorations of the occult and other flights of fantasy. But Himmler was a steely opportunist and he ruthlessly outmaneuvered his rivals, rising to become Hitler's indispensable deputy and the top security chief for the Nazi empire.

It was Himmler whom the Führer had entrusted with the Final Solution, their breathtaking plan to wipe the Jewish people from the face of the earth. It was Himmler who had the nerve to justify this plan, standing before his SS generals in October 1943 and assuring them that they had "the moral right to destroy this people which wanted to destroy us," to pile up their "corpses side by side" in monuments to the Reich's power. As Hannah Arendt later observed, Himmler was the Nazi leader most gifted at solving the "problems of conscience" that sometimes nagged the Reich's executioners. With his "winged words," as his diligent administrator of death, Adolf Eichmann, put it, Himmler transformed his men's gruesome work into a grand and secret mission that only the SS elite were capable of fulfilling. "The order to solve the Jewish question, this was the most frightening an organization could ever receive," Himmler told the leaders of his killing teams. He knew how to appeal to his men's sense of valor and vanity, telling them, "To have stuck it out and, apart from exceptions caused by human weakness, to have remained decent, that is what has made us hard. This is a page of glory in our history which has never been written and is never to be written."

And, in the end, it was Himmler who—despite his long enchantment with the Hitler cult—had the brass to consider replacing his Führer when he realized that the war could not be won militarily. Prince Max was only one of the emissaries Himmler dispatched across Europe to seek a separate peace deal with the United States and England. At one point, Himmler even recruited fashion designer Coco Chanel, bringing her to Berlin to discuss strategy.

Himmler knew he was playing a very dangerous game, letting Hitler know just enough about his various peace feelers, but not enough to arouse suspicion. Dulles, too, understood that he was playing with fire by defying presidential orders. After receiving a warning from Washington about the perils of fraternizing with Hohenlohe, Dulles sent back a cagey reply, cabling that he realized the prince was a "tough customer and extreme caution required," but he might prove "useful." Dulles did not find it necessary to inform his superiors just how deeply involved he was with Himmler's envoy.

Dulles and Tyler met with Hohenlohe on several other occasions over the next few weeks, from February into April. And even as late as November 1943, Dulles continued to forward to Washington Prince Max's reports on Himmler's frame of mind. Dulles regarded the prince as a serious enough collaborator to give him a secret OSS code number, 515.

In the end, Dulles's machinations with Hohenlohe went nowhere. President Roosevelt was very much in control of the U.S. government, and his uncompromising position on Nazi capitulation was still firmly in place. When OSS chief Wild Bill Donovan informed the president about the Himmler peace initiatives, FDR made it clear that he remained adamantly opposed to cutting any deals with the Nazi high command. As long as that was presidential policy, there was nothing Dulles could do but bide his time and maintain his secret lines to the enemy.

Despite Heinrich Himmler's elusive quest to cut a deal with the Allies, he never lost faith in Dulles. On May 10, 1945, just days after the war ended, Himmler set out from northern Germany with an entourage of SS faithful, heading south toward Switzerland—and the protection of the American agent. He was disguised in a threadbare blue raincoat and wore a patch over one eye, with his trademark wire-rims stashed in his pocket. But Himmler never made it to his rendezvous with Dulles. The SS chief and his retinue were captured by British soldiers as they prepared to cross the Oste River. While in custody, Himmler cheated the hangman by biting down on a glass capsule of cyanide.

Even if Himmler had made it to Switzerland, however, he would not have found sanctuary. He was too prominent a face of Nazi horror for even Dulles to salvage. But the American spy would come to the rescue of many other Nazi outlaws from justice.

Human Smoke

Neither Allen, Foster, nor their three sisters were ever as devout as their father, the Reverend Allen Macy Dulles, who presided over a small Presbyterian flock in Watertown, New York, a sleepy retreat favored by New York millionaires near Lake Ontario. But the siblings always regarded the family's summer vacations on nearby Henderson Harbor as some kind of heaven. The huge lake and its sprinkling of islands held countless adventures for the children. The boys would rise early in the morning and, in the company of a lean, laconic fishing guide, set off in a skiff, stalking the waters for the lake's delicious smallmouth black bass. At noon, they would ground their little sailboat on one of the islands and cook their catch over a driftwood fire. The fish was fried in crackling pork fat, served with corn and potatoes, and washed down with black coffee. Years later, they would recall these summer feasts as among the best meals of their lives.

Reverend Dulles was not a man of means, and he had difficulty supporting his family on his modest churchman's salary. His illustrious father-in-law, the luxuriantly bewhiskered John Watson Foster, who had served briefly as secretary of state under President Benjamin Harrison and then established himself as one of Washington's first power attorneys, was a beneficent presence in the family's life. Reverend Dulles sometimes resented his dependence on the old man's generosity. But the whole family thrived during their summer idylls on Lake Ontario, cozily squeezed into a big, red, clapboard cottage that had been built by Grandfather Foster. Their lakeside life was rustic—the house had no electricity and they had to pump their water. But it all seemed enchanted to the children.

There were picnics and moonlight sails, and on the Fourth of July the children would put small candles in paper balloons and set them floating in the air, watching as the golden lanterns drifted over the glittering water toward Canada. In the early evenings, Eleanor—the next oldest sibling after Allen—liked to sit on the family's dock and watch the clouds gather over the lake, casting red and pink shafts on the darkening water. "I never feared hell and I thought heaven would be like Henderson but more so," she mused in her later years.

Eleanor was exceedingly bright and curious, and she refused to resign herself to the prim, petticoat world to which girls of her generation were supposed to confine themselves. When the boys and men would go fishing, she would sometimes plunk herself down in the middle of the boat. When robed Chinese dignitaries and other exotic figures from her grandfather's diplomatic forays would pay visits to Henderson Harbor, she would be certain to listen in on their conversations. Eleanor's intelligence and determination would take her far, as she followed her brothers into the diplomatic corps, where she would eventually take over the State Department's German desk during the critical years after World War II. But, as a brainy woman in a thoroughly male arena, she was always something of an outsider. Even her brothers were often perplexed about how to handle her. With her dark, wiry hair and thick eyeglasses, she considered herself the ugly duckling in the family. Her slightly askew status in the Dulles constellation seemed to heighten her powers of observation, however. Eleanor often had the keenest eye when it came to sizing up her family, especially her two brothers.

Allen loomed large in her life. She attached herself to him at an early age, but she learned to be wary of his sudden, explosive mood shifts. Most people saw only Allen's charm and conviviality, but Eleanor was sometimes the target of his inexplicable eruptions of fury. Her infractions were often minor. Once Allen flew into a rage over how closely she parked the car to the family house. His moods were like the dark clouds that billowed without warning over Lake Ontario. Later in life, Eleanor simply took herself "out of his orbit to avoid the stress and furor that he stirred in me."

Allen was darker and more complex than his older brother, and his behavior sometimes mystified his sister. One summer incident during their childhood would stick with Eleanor for the rest of her life. Allen, who was nearly ten at the time, and Eleanor, who was two years younger, had been given the task of minding their five-year-old sister Nataline. With her blond curls and sweet demeanor, Nataline—the baby in the family—was usually the object of everyone's attention. But that day, the older children got distracted as they skipped stones across the lake's surface from the family's wooden dock. Suddenly, Nataline, who had retrieved a large rock to join in the game, went tumbling into the water, pulled down by the dead weight of her burden. As the child began floating away toward the lake's deep, cold waters, her pink dress buoying her like an air balloon, Eleanor began screaming frantically. But Allen, who by then was a strong swimmer, was strangely impassive. The boy just stood on the dock and watched as his little sister drifted away. Finally, as if prompted by Eleanor's cries, he, too, began yelling. Drawn by the uproar, their mother—who was recovering in bed from one of her periodic, pounding migraines—came flying down the dock and, plunging into the water, rescued little Nataline.

Throughout his life, Allen Dulles was slow to feel the distress of others. As a father, his daughter Joan would recall, Dulles seemed to regard his children with a curious remoteness, as if they were visitors in his house. Even his son and namesake Allen Jr. made little impact on him when he excelled in prep school and at Oxford, or later, in the Korean War, when the young man was struck in the head by a mortar shell fragment and suffered brain damage. Clover Dulles called her cold and driven husband "The Shark."

Allen did not take after his father. Reverend Dulles, a product of Princeton University and Germany's Göttingen University, was a scholarly, meditative type. While his children explored the wilds of Lake Ontario, he was likely to be sequestered in his upstairs study with his

Sunday sermon. The minister was a compassionate man. While walking home one frigid day, he took off his coat and gave it to a man shivering in the street. On another occasion, he risked expulsion from the Presbyterian Church for performing a marriage for a divorced woman.

It was her mother, Eleanor would recall, who ran the family. Edith Foster Dulles was "a doer," the kind of woman who "believed in action." Eleanor would remember her cracking the whip on her father. "Now, Allen," she would tell her husband, "you've been working on that book for five or six years. Don't you think it's good enough? Let's publish it."

The reflective pastor was less of an influence on his sons than their mother and grandfather. The Dulles boys were drawn to the men of action who called on Grandfather Foster, men who talked about war and high-stakes diplomacy, men who got things done. Foster and Allen both lacked their father's sensitive temperament. Like Allen, Foster felt little empathy for those who were weak or vulnerable. He understood that there was misfortune in the world, but he expected people to put their own houses in order.

Foster's callousness came into stark relief during the Nazi crisis in Germany. In 1932, as Hitler began his takeover of the German government, Foster visited three Jewish friends, all prominent bankers, in their Berlin office. The men were in a state of extreme anxiety during the meeting. At one point, the bankers—too afraid to speak—made motions to indicate a truck parked outside and suggested that it was monitoring their conversation. "They indicated to him that they felt absolutely no freedom," Eleanor recalled.

Foster's reaction to his friends' terrible dilemma unnerved his sister. "There's nothing that a person like me can do in dealing with these men, except probably to keep away from them," he later told Eleanor. "They're safer, if I keep away from them." Actually, there was much that a Wall Street power broker like John Foster Dulles could have done for his endangered friends, starting with pulling strings to get their families and at least some of their assets out of Germany before it was too late.

Throughout her life, Eleanor wrestled with her brothers' cold, if not cruel, behavior. A family loyalist to the end, she generally tried to

give her brothers the most charitable interpretation possible. But sometimes the brothers strained even her sisterly charity. The same year that
Foster sidestepped the urgent concerns of his Jewish friends in Berlin,
Eleanor informed him that she intended to marry David Blondheim,
the man she had been in love with ever since meeting him in Paris in
1925. Blondheim was a balding, middle-aged linguistics professor at
Johns Hopkins University—with "a very sensitive mouth," in Eleanor's
estimation, "and clear, brown eyes." He was also a Jew. Eleanor's parents had given Blondheim their approval, calling him "charming," after
meeting him and Eleanor for dinner during a visit to Paris. But by 1932,
Reverend Dulles was dead and Foster was head of the family. And he
had a different perspective on the mixed marriage that his sister and her
fiancé finally felt brave enough to attempt.

Foster wrote Eleanor a letter, asking her if she realized "the complications of marrying a Jew"—and helpfully pointing out a dozen such
problems. Her brother's letter stunned and infuriated Eleanor, who by
then was in her midthirties and not in need of her brother's counsel in
such matters. She promptly replied, but, not wanting to directly defy
her imposing brother, she sent the letter to his wife, Janet. In her letter,
Eleanor made it clear that Foster need not trouble himself with her life's
"complications" and that, in the future, she would simply "go my own
way."

Years later, Eleanor tried to explain away her brother's behavior. He
was not motivated by anti-Semitism, she insisted. He was just a product
of his social and professional milieu. In his circles, she explained, people
would say, "We can't have too many Jews in this club" or "We can't have
too many Jews in this firm." Foster simply saw this attitude as a fact of
life, Eleanor observed—"just like the climate."

In 1934, the fragile Blondheim, distressed by the growing cataclysm
in Europe and private demons, sunk into depression and killed himself,
sticking his head into the kitchen oven. Reasserting himself as paterfamilias, Foster swept back into the deeply shaken life of his sister and
took charge. The suicide must, of course, be hushed up. And Eleanor
must instantly shed the dead man's name, or she would be haunted by

it in years to come. Eleanor dutifully complied with Foster's direction and the name Blondheim was purged from the Dulles family record, as if the brilliant man with the sensitive mouth and clear, brown eyes had never existed. The fact she was about to give birth to Blondheim's son was a bond that Foster could never make disappear.

In early June 1939, the German transatlantic ocean liner *St. Louis* cruised slowly up the coastline of Florida. The ship, carrying more than nine hundred Jewish refugees from Europe, had been turned away from its original destination, Havana, after days of increasingly frantic negotiations with the Cuban government. Now the black-and-white ocean liner, towering eight decks high and flying a swastika flag, had become a ghost ship, with dimming hopes of finding a safe harbor. While the ship was anchored in Havana Harbor, relatives of the *St. Louis* passengers crowded onto motorboats and circled the ocean liner, desperately crying out to their loved ones. As the tension-filled days went by, one passenger grew more and more agitated, convinced that he was about to be seized by Gestapo agents on board and bundled off to a concentration camp. He slashed his wrists and jumped into the harbor, where he was rescued and sent to a hospital. He was one of the few allowed to stay in Cuba.

As *St. Louis* captain Gustav Schroeder guided his ship along the Florida shore, his passengers could see the sparkling lights of Miami in the near distance. Schroeder had ordered his German crew to treat the refugees just like any other passengers. While the ocean liner had steamed across the Atlantic from Hamburg, the captain asked his stewards to serve ice cream to the children and to play movies in the evening. But after the ship was turned away from Havana—where Nazi agents had stirred up anti-Semitic feelings among the local population and demagogues had fanned fears that the Jews would steal jobs that were ever scarcer in the declining economy—the festive mood on board the *St. Louis* had quickly dissipated. Now Captain Schroeder hugged the U.S. coastline in the dim hope that the Roosevelt administration would come to his passengers' rescue.

The doomed voyage of the *St. Louis* would become a symbol of the Jewish people's terrible predicament. While the ship plowed the seas with its human cargo, the governments of the world—from Washington, D.C., to London to Buenos Aires—debated its fate. In Washington, FDR's Treasury secretary, Henry Morgenthau Jr., maneuvered strenuously to win permission for the ship to dock in an American port. Morgenthau, who had established himself as the conscience of the administration on the Jewish refugee crisis, dispatched U.S. Coast Guard ships to follow the *St. Louis* as it journeyed north along the Eastern Seaboard, so he could keep track of the ghost vessel in case the government allowed it to land.

Morgenthau was so integral a member of Roosevelt's inner circle that he was known as "the assistant president." He was of German Jewish ancestry and Democratic Party royalty. His father, New York real estate mogul Henry Morgenthau Sr., had been one of President Woodrow Wilson's major financial backers and served as Wilson's ambassador to the Ottoman Empire. Henry Jr., who ran a Hudson Valley farm near the Roosevelt family's Hyde Park estate, would develop a long personal and political relationship with FDR. When Franklin's privileged life was suddenly turned upside down by the ravages of polio, Morgenthau was one of the few political advisers who remained close to him, keeping his spirits up with games of Parcheesi.

After he was elected to the White House in 1932, Roosevelt—who was the first presidential candidate to campaign against anti-Semitism—appointed Morgenthau and several other Jews to prominent positions in his administration. Fifteen percent of FDR's top appointees were Jewish, at a time when Jews represented less than 3 percent of the population. Bigoted enemies of the New Deal enjoyed a ditty about Franklin and First Lady Eleanor—who was known as a champion of African American civil rights—that went, "You kiss the niggers/and I'll kiss the Jews/and we'll stay in the White House/as long as we choose." There were even rumors that Roosevelt himself was Jewish.

Morgenthau was acutely sensitive about the anti-Jewish sentiments that prevailed in the country, not least in the nation's capital, where private clubs would restrict membership to white Christians until well into the 1960s. And despite his wealth, political status, and deep history with the president, he always remained somewhat insecure with Roosevelt, who was not immune to some of the prejudices of his day. Looking back on his long service with the president, Morgenthau later said, "He never let anybody around him have complete assurance that he would have a job tomorrow. . . . The thing that Roosevelt prided himself the most about was, 'I have to have a happy ship.' But he never had a happy ship."

One of the least happy aspects of the Roosevelt presidency was the bitter internal battle over the plight of European Jews. FDR was a man of conscience but also an intensely political creature. The president— who was briefed from time to time in the White House by longtime supporters such as Rabbi Stephen Wise of New York and other Jewish leaders—was keenly aware of the imminent danger facing the Jewish population in Hitler's increasingly hostile dominion. In the spring of 1938, a year before the voyage of the *St. Louis*, Roosevelt began discussing a plan to rescue millions of German Jews and resettle them in ten sympathetic countries. He vowed that he would request $150 million from Congress to implement the plan.

But Roosevelt found himself ensnared in political complications. He faced powerful nativist and anti-immigration sentiments in Congress, which reflected the mood of the country—feelings that had only hardened in the Depression's savagely competitive job market. The president, who knew that he was widely perceived as a friend of the Jews, wanted to avoid appearing too beholden to them. This became particularly urgent as the 1940 presidential election neared, with FDR aiming for an unprecedented third term. In the final analysis, the president believed that the only way that the people facing Nazi persecution might be saved was through U.S. military intervention against Hitler. And with prominent isolationist crusaders like Charles Lindbergh labeling the looming European conflict a Jewish war, FDR realized that this was another reason not to appear too impassioned about the refugee crisis.

As the debate raged within the administration, millions of lives hung in the balance, including those on board the *St. Louis*. If Henry Morgenthau was the voice of moral imperative in Roosevelt's government, then Breckinridge Long, the assistant secretary of state in charge of immigration, was its avatar of cynicism. Long used his bureaucratic wiles to frustrate Roosevelt's efforts to ease the restrictive immigration policies of the Depression era. In June 1940, he circulated a memo among his department officials, proposing that they delay for an "indefinite length [of time] the number of immigrants [allowed] into the United States. We can do this by simply advising our consuls to put every obstacle in the way and to require additional evidence and to resort to various administrative devices which would postpone and postpone and postpone the granting of the visas."

As a result of Breckinridge Long's delaying tactics, 90 percent of the quota places reserved for refugees from Hitler's and Mussolini's dark realms were never filled. This meant that another 190,000 souls who could have escaped were trapped inside Europe's burning building.

One Morgenthau aide later called the Long cabal within the State Department "an underground movement . . . to let the Jews be killed." At one point, Morgenthau himself—who always tried to restrain himself in these debates so as not to appear a "special pleader" for the Jews— felt compelled to confront Long directly. "Breck, we might be a little frank," began the gentlemanly Treasury secretary. "The impression is all around that you are particularly anti-Semitic."

Long was convinced that he was being persecuted by "the communists, extreme radicals, Jewish professional agitators [and] refugee enthusiasts." He was part of the State Department's deeply entrenched, high-born culture—a WASP aristocracy that regarded immigrants, particularly those non-Christian newcomers from central and eastern Europe, as socially offensive and potentially subversive. Anti-Jewish attitudes in this insular club were so deeply ingrained that they were reflexive.

Perhaps not surprisingly, then, when young Allen Dulles was serving in the U.S. embassy in Turkey, his first overseas posting after World War I, he fell for the most notorious anti-Jewish fabrication in history.

One day the young American diplomat was given a copy of *The Protocols of the Elders of Zion* by a British reporter who had fished the scurrilous document out of a secondhand bookstore in Istanbul's old European quarter. *The Protocols* purported to offer a secret plan for Jewish world domination, and included tales about Christian children being sacrificed for Passover feast rituals and other lurid fantasies. By the time Dulles got his hands on the book, which was the creation of the Russian czar's anti-Semitic secret police, the document had been widely denounced and discredited. But Dulles took it seriously enough to send a coded report about the secret Jewish "plot" back to his superiors in Washington.

Atavistic ideas about exotic Jewish "outsiders" were still widely prevalent in the State Department in June 1939 as the *St. Louis* lingered along the Eastern Seaboard, its food and water supplies running low. In the end, the Long faction in the Roosevelt administration would prevail in the debate over the ship. Captain Schroeder was forced to turn his ocean liner around and return to Europe, docking in Antwerp, Belgium, on June 17 after a month at sea, and disgorging the men, women, and children on board to their fates. Less than three months later, Hitler invaded Poland, and Europe went to war. More than 250 of the *St. Louis*'s passengers would be swallowed by the Holocaust.

As the war began, the struggle to save Europe's Jews was far from over. President Roosevelt continued to be pushed and pulled by both sides of the increasingly tumultuous refugee debate. Initial reports about the mass evacuations of Jews to death camps in the German and Polish countryside were vague. The State Department bureaucracy bottled up much of the information, so there was a great deal that Roosevelt never saw. Humanitarians like Rabbi Wise desperately sought solid evidence of the Nazi extermination machine, which they knew was essential in order to convince FDR to take decisive action.

This was the desperate situation as Dulles began monitoring European developments—first from his OSS office in Rockefeller Center and later from his post in Bern. Among Dulles's confidential sources was a German industrialist who was the first prominent figure inside the Nazi domain to provide credible information about the early stages of the Final Solution. The stories that the industrialist brought across the Swiss border were almost too monstrous to believe. The information that began flowing into neutral Switzerland, the listening post for war-torn Europe, should have helped force drastic Allied action. But it did not.

On July 17, 1942, Heinrich Himmler's luxurious private train— equipped with a dining room, shower, and even a screening room—pulled into Auschwitz, a backwater town in the swampy flatlands of southern Poland. Word quickly spread about the Reichsführer's unusual visit, soon reaching Eduard Schulte, the chief executive of a major German mining company with property in the area. What had brought Himmler to this forlorn destination? Schulte reckoned that it must have something to do with the rapidly expanding prison camp outside town, where IG Farben had built a factory to utilize the camp's slave labor.

It is not widely recognized that the Nazi reign of terror was, in a fundamental way, a lucrative racket—an extensive criminal enterprise set up to loot the wealth of Jewish victims and exploit their labor. The chemical giant Farben was at the forefront of integrating concentration camp labor into its industrial production process, with other major German corporations like Volkswagen, Siemens, and Krupp following closely behind. Himmler's SS empire moved aggressively to cut itself in on the spoils, extracting sizable payments from these companies for providing them with a steady flow of forced labor. Schulte, who was afraid that the rapidly expanding Auschwitz complex would begin to intrude on his own company's mining properties, immediately took a wary interest in Himmler's visit.

Schulte himself was not a Nazi, but he had good contacts in those circles. His deputy at the mining firm belonged to the Nazi Party and, in fact, knew Himmler. To ingratiate themselves with the party, the firm's board of directors had loaned the local Nazi chief a company-owned villa that was located in a nearby forest. It was here that Himmler and his entourage were to be entertained that evening.

When Himmler arrived for the party at the company villa, Schulte was still unaware of the horrific reason he had come to Auschwitz. Himmler was there to witness one of the camp's new gas chambers, a white brick cottage known as "Bunker 2," in action. That afternoon Himmler watched as a group of 449 Jewish prisoners, recently transported from Holland, were marched into Bunker 2 and gassed with Zyklon B, the pesticide produced by IG Farben. The execution process took a full twenty minutes, and the victims' frantic death cries could be heard even through the chamber's thick walls. Afterward, the bodies were dragged from the building by camp orderlies wearing gas masks and thrown into nearby incinerators. One of the triumphs of German engineering was to devise a convenient incineration process whereby the burning of the corpses provided the heat for the furnaces. Fritz Sander, the engineer who invented the system, later lamented the fact that he could not patent his creation because it was considered a state secret.

Himmler observed the grotesque procedure unfold that afternoon in "total silence," according to Auschwitz commandant Rudolf Höss. Later on, at the villa, he showed little strain from his day's chores. The Reichsführer broke from his austere routine by enjoying a cigar and a glass of red wine. In deference to the female guests, the details of his camp tour were not discussed.

Eduard Schulte was sickened when, a week and a half after Himmler's visit, he finally learned what had occurred during the Reichsführer's tour of Auschwitz. It confirmed his deepest fears about the Third Reich, a regime he had observed from its earliest days with a growing sense of dread. Schulte had met Hitler in Berlin back in February 1933 at a gathering of industrialists whom the Nazis wanted to shake down for political contributions. After listening to his rambling diatribe, Schulte concluded that Hitler was a dangerous lunatic who would lead Germany to ruin.

There was nothing rebellious or offbeat about Schulte. He was, in nearly every way, a typical specimen of the German bourgeoisie—a hardworking, conservative family man whose only indulgence was a passion for hunting. But he was the type of man who resented the steady encroachments of the Nazi state on his private life. In order to keep his position with the mining firm, he had been forced to join the Nazi-run German Labor Front. Even to maintain his hunting habit, he needed to belong to a state-run hunters club. He fumed when his two boys came home one day in Hitler Youth uniforms, though his wife reminded him it was compulsory and said he was making mountains out of molehills. But in Schulte's mind, the "brown poison," as he called it, was seeping everywhere.

It pained Schulte, who had a close Jewish friend while growing up, to see Jews being made scapegoats. He was a tall, outgoing, assertive businessman, but he had a feeling for the underdog that might have been reinforced by his own physical disability. At the age of eighteen, while going to the aid of some railroad workers, Schulte's left leg was crushed under the wheel of a freight car and had to be amputated. Outfitted with an artificial leg, he continued to get around with vigorous determination for the rest of his life, although with an obvious limp.

When Schulte heard about the unfolding horror at Auschwitz, he knew he had to act. From what he could piece together, the macabre display of German efficiency overseen by Himmler that day was part of an official policy of mass extermination that was now under way in the Nazi empire. The policy had been formally approved earlier that year by the Nazi high command at a conference held on January 20, 1942, in an SS villa on Lake Wannsee in suburban Berlin. The Wannsee Conference, run by Himmler's ambitious deputy Reinhard Heydrich, laid out a plan for the elimination of Europe's Jewry through a network of death factories. By lending the proposal a legal veneer, Heydrich assured the complete administrative cooperation of the German bureaucracy. Even the title assigned to the program of mass butchery—the Final Solution—conjured a civil servant's dream of a job well done.

Heydrich, who called himself "the chief garbage collector of the Third Reich," saw his gas ovens as a humane solution to the "Jewish problem." He considered himself a cultured man. The night before he was assassinated by Czech partisans, who threw a bomb into his open car as it slowed for a hairpin curve, Heydrich attended a performance of a violin concerto written by his father, Richard Bruno Heydrich, a highly regarded German opera singer and composer.

The Final Solution was meant to remain secret, with most of the death camps located in remote outposts of the Nazi empire. But as the systematic killing got under way, many people became aware of the mounting barbarity. One day in early 1942, an IG Farben official named Ernst Struss was returning home on a train after inspecting the company's factory that was affiliated with Auschwitz. A German worker also riding on the train began talking loudly about the nightmare at the camp. Great numbers of people were being burned in the compound's crematoria, he said. The smell of incinerated flesh was everywhere. Struss jumped up in a rage. "These are lies! You should not spread such lies." But the worker quietly corrected him: "No, these are not lies." There were thousands of workers like himself at Auschwitz, he said. "And all know it."

Eduard Schulte was not one of those men who could deny or hide from such a truth. On July 29, 1942—within twenty-four hours of learning about the assembly line of death at Auschwitz—the mining executive was on a train to Zurich, determined to put the information in the hands of the Allies. The trip across the border carried a high degree of risk. And Schulte, a prosperous, fifty-one-year-old businessman with a wife and family back in Breslau, had much to lose. But the revelations about Auschwitz and the Final Solution that Schulte was carrying to Zurich filled him with an overriding sense of urgency.

After arriving in Zurich, Schulte kept to his normal routine when doing business in Switzerland, checking into the Baur-au-Lac, a luxury hotel on the lake where he was an honored guest. He then phoned Isidor Koppelman, a Jewish investment adviser he knew whose services his company had used. Schulte was determined to get his information in the hands of international Jewish organizations, which he thought could prevail on the Allied governments to take action. The next day, meeting in his hotel room, Schulte gave Koppelman his shocking report. The investment adviser sat in silence, taking it all in. Schulte said he realized what he was reporting seemed too outrageous to believe, but it was absolutely true. And if the Allies failed to act, there would be few Jews left in Europe by the end of the year. Schulte discussed the next steps that Koppelman should take to get the word out, then checked out of the hotel and returned to Germany.

The circuitous and troubled route that Schulte's critical message took over the next several weeks through diplomatic and political channels reveals much about the failure of this bureaucratic labyrinth to confront the war's soaring humanitarian crisis. And, once again, at the core of this failure was the poisonous culture of the U.S. State Department.

Through Koppelman's efforts, Schulte's message was delivered to Gerhart Riegner, the young Geneva representative of the World Jewish Congress. Riegner, in turn, was intent on relaying the information to the president of the World Jewish Congress in New York—none other than Rabbi Stephen Wise, FDR's confidant and the leading voice of alarm in the United States about the Jewish crisis. The problem for Riegner was that he was compelled to use the services of the American Legation in Bern to dispatch the confidential cable to Wise. The U.S. diplomats in Switzerland thought young Riegner seemed to be in a state of "great agitation" as he related Schulte's story. U.S. minister to Switzerland Leland Harrison, an old colleague of Dulles's who was soon to be reunited with him in Bern, took a decidedly skeptical view of the account; in his dispatch to Washington, Harrison dismissed it as nothing more than "war rumor inspired by fear"—although he did concede that some Jews were dying due to "physical maltreatment . . . malnutrition, and disease."

The State Department later sent the OSS a summary of the report that had originated with Schulte. Allen Dulles, still working out of the OSS offices in New York at the time, was one of those who received the message. The State Department flatly refused to believe Schulte's account, calling it a "wild rumor inspired by Jewish fears." Even Harrison's concession that some Jews were dying as a result of the "privations" of war was stripped out of the State Department memo.

The State Department decided not to notify Rabbi Wise—whom Foggy Bottom officials considered a thorn in their side—about his Geneva deputy's efforts to reach him. It took a full month for Rabbi Wise to receive Riegner's report. When the telegram finally arrived in New York on August 28, it came not through U.S. diplomatic channels, but British. The State Department also did not see fit to pass along the Schulte revelations to President Roosevelt.

In frustration with the information bottleneck, Rabbi Wise finally held a press conference two days before Thanksgiving, announcing that Hitler had already killed about two million European Jews and had plans to exterminate the rest. *The New York Times* buried the story on page 10, *The Washington Post* on page 6. The press was reluctant to highlight such an explosive story since it lacked official government sources.

Dulles, who was soon headed to Switzerland, could have been one of these sources for the U.S. press. While still stationed in New York, he began sending out veteran reporters—under diplomatic cover—to gather intelligence in various forward posts in the European war zone. One of these reporters, a thirty-seven-year-old, Berlin-born, multilingual, former NBC correspondent named Gerald Mayer, was sent to Bern in April 1942. Soon after Schulte's report began circulating, Mayer also began filing stories about the Final Solution with the New York OSS office. "Germany no longer persecutes the Jews," began Mayer's first stark dispatch. "It is systematically exterminating them."

But Dulles did nothing to publicize Mayer's reports. They, too, remained buried in the government bureaucracy. Along with the Schulte bombshell, these alarms would have made a loud noise, particularly in the New York echo chamber. They might have finally blown apart Washington's institutional inertia on the refugee question. But this was not part of Dulles's agenda.

History would give Dulles one more chance to alert the world to the ongoing genocide. In Switzerland, he would hear directly from men like Schulte and others who had risked their lives to save the Jews. In Bern, the evil was not so remote—it was all around.

After arriving in Switzerland, Dulles took his time setting up a meeting with Eduard Schulte. When the two men finally did come together in spring 1943 for a furtive meeting in Zurich, it was an amiable enough occasion; they had met fifteen years earlier, they realized, in the New York offices of Sullivan and Cromwell, which represented Anaconda Copper, a partner of Schulte's mining firm.

The fate of the Jewish people was still of great urgency to Schulte— likely made even more urgent by the fact that during his trips to Switzerland, he had fallen in love with a younger Jewish woman who lived in Zurich. But Dulles expressed little interest in Schulte's information about the Final Solution. More intrigued by the political and psychological mood of the German people and how they could be won over by the Allies, Dulles asked Schulte to write up a memo on the state of the German nation. It was Hitler's people, not his victims, whom the intelligence official thought important to understand.

This was characteristic of Dulles's meetings with German informants while he was stationed in Bern. Fritz Kolbe, an efficient foreign service official who kept rising to higher posts in the German government despite his stubborn refusal to join the Nazi Party, was another mole who risked his life to give the United States rare insights into the operations of the Reich. One night, with documents stuffed down the front of his pants, Kolbe crossed into Switzerland and made his way to Dulles's residence in Bern. Like Schulte, Kolbe was well aware of the risk he was taking. After this first meeting with the American spy, Kolbe drew up his will. He also left Dulles a letter for his young son in case he was caught and executed. Dulles was untouched by Kolbe's request. The OSS agent sized him up as "somewhat naïve and a romantic idealist," which was not good for Kolbe, since Dulles always regarded these types as expendable.

But Kolbe had important information to impart, and he kept risking his life to smuggle Nazi documents across the border. During another meeting with Dulles, in April 1944, Kolbe handed over a thick sheaf of Nazi cables revealing that Hungary's Jews, who had remained secure late into the war, were about to be rounded up and deported to the death camps. Dulles's report on this meeting was one of the few from Bern that ended up on the president's desk in the White House. But there was nothing in Dulles's communiqué about the imminent fate of Hungary's Jews. And there was nothing about the possibility of bombing rail lines to the death camps—and even the camps themselves—as informants like Schulte were urging the Allies to do.

Instead, Dulles chose to focus the president's attention on another topic that he had discussed with Kolbe over glasses of Scotch in his drawing room. Underground Communist organizing seemed to be gaining strength in Germany as the Nazi war effort faltered, Kolbe had informed the U.S. agent. *This* was the emergency that Dulles thought the White House needed to hear about.

Dulles continued to receive Nazi documents about the fate of Hungary's Jews from Kolbe over the next seven months. One German cable reported that 120,000 Jews in Budapest, including children considered unfit for work, were soon to be "taken to the Reich territory for work in the labor service." The Nazis were always careful to use euphemisms like "labor service" in their communications. By this date, Washington was well aware that Hungary's Jews were headed to Auschwitz. And yet Dulles's communiqués to OSS headquarters used the same banal language as the Nazis, referring blandly to the "conscription" of Hungary's Jews.

When Dulles's communications from Bern to Washington were declassified decades later by the government, scholars were able to decipher his wartime obsessions. Dulles's interest was absorbed by psychological warfare tricks, such as distributing counterfeit stamps behind enemy lines depicting Hitler's profile as a death's skull, and other cloak-and-dagger antics. He was also deeply engaged with mapping out grand postwar strategies for Europe. But few of his more than three hundred communiqués mentioned the killing of Jews—and none carried a sense of urgency about the Final Solution.

This glaring blank spot in Dulles's wartime record continues to confound academic researchers decades later, though they remain reluctant to pass judgment on the legendary spy. "Why did Dulles choose not to emphasize the Holocaust in his reports to Washington?" wondered World War II historian Neal H. Petersen in his edited collection of Dulles's OSS intelligence reports. Petersen clearly struggled to answer his own question. "Whatever his reasoning," Petersen concluded with scholarly restraint, "his reticence on this subject is among the most controversial and least understandable aspects of his performance in Bern."

In April 1944, Rudolf Vrba, a nineteen-year-old Jew from a village in Czechoslovakia who had survived for nearly two years in Auschwitz, escaped from the camp with Alfred Wetzler, a childhood friend, by hiding in a pile of wood planks for three days and nights without food or water. They tied rags across their mouths to muffle the coughs that would have betrayed them to the SS patrols that were methodically searching the camp for them. On the third night, when they finally felt it was safe to make their escape, Rudi and Fred emerged from the pyramid of wood and began crawling under the moonless sky across a muddy field toward a cluster of birch trees in the distance. The two friends were determined to return home, not just to save their own lives but to bear witness to what was happening inside Auschwitz.

Their journey was harrowing. At one point, they were chased up a mountainside by a German patrol, with dogs snarling and bullets flying behind them. Along the way, they were helped by Polish peasants, who fed the famished teenagers potatoes and coffee and guided them toward the Slovak border. Two weeks after crawling out of the woodpile in Auschwitz, they were home and—after being put in touch with Oskar Neumann, the chairman of the local Jewish Council—they began telling their horrific tale. While the fundamental facts about the death camps were widely known by then, Rudi and Fred's forty-page report was the most thorough and specific to emerge from Auschwitz up to that point. It described the management and daily routine of the camp, and included haunting details about how the prisoners were killed: "The unfortunate victims are brought into Hall B, where they are told to undress. To complete the fiction that they are going to bathe, each person receives a towel and a small piece of soap issued by two men clad in white coats."

In mid-June, nearly two months after the escapees wrote down their account, the Vrba-Wetzler report was finally smuggled into Switzerland. A British correspondent named Walter Garrett got his hands on a copy, which he took to Allen Dulles on June 22. While the journalist sat with Dulles in his apartment on Herrengasse, the spy read the entire report. "He was profoundly shocked," Garrett later recalled. "He was as disconcerted as I was and said: 'One has to do something immediately.' "

Dulles's pantomime of concern clearly convinced the British reporter. But in fact Dulles had begun receiving reports about the mass extermination of Jews over two years earlier, before he even left the United States for Switzerland. Authoritative reports on the Holocaust had continued to flow into his hands ever since his arrival in Bern, from informants like Schulte and Kolbe.

"One" should indeed have finally taken drastic action. At that point, many of Hungary's Jews might still have been saved if Allied will had been sufficiently marshaled. Instead, Dulles sent off a routine cable on the Vrba-Wetzler report to Secretary of State Cordell Hull, a man Dulles knew would not lift a finger to help the Jews, even though he was married to a Jewish woman. It was Hull who had advised FDR to reject the ill-fated passengers of the *St. Louis*. And it was Hull who had blocked Schulte's report from getting to Rabbi Wise through State Department channels.

Through the efforts of an exiled Jewish businessman in Geneva and a group of students he recruited to make fifty mimeograph copies of the Vrba-Wetzler report, the eyewitness account of life and death inside Auschwitz finally broke in the Swiss press and was then picked up by *The New York Times* and the BBC. In the ensuing uproar, President Roosevelt and other world leaders successfully pressured the Hungarian government to stop the deportations of its Jewish citizens. But the reprieve didn't last long; in October 1944 Hitler ordered a Nazi takeover of the government in Budapest and the death trains soon began rolling again.

In the final months of the war, as the United States and Britain finally opened a second front in the war, and Hitler's forces were caught in an inexorable vise between the Red Army in the east and the Anglo-American military machine in the west, Roosevelt and close advisers like Morgenthau began contemplating the Nazi regime's postwar fate. The glory that was European civilization had gone up in "human smoke," in Nicholson Baker's words. But FDR was determined to keep the vow that he made repeatedly throughout the war. He would bring to justice the perpetrators of this unprecedented degradation of life. The Third Reich would be put on trial and its reign ground to dust.

Once again, however, Allen Dulles and his allies had other plans.

Ghosts of Nuremberg

Nuremberg was a haunted city in November 1945 as teams of Allied prosecutors and the world press converged on its bombed-out ruins for the first in a series of historic war crimes trials. The Allies had chosen Nuremberg to put the Third Reich on trial for its aggression and crimes against humanity because the city had been the main stage for Hitler's pageantry, playing host each year to the Nazi Party's extravagant propaganda spectacles. Film director Leni Riefenstahl memorialized the 1934 Nuremberg festival in *Triumph of the Will*, her paean to Hitler's highly choreographed militarism. In Riefenstahl's film, the city of medieval spires and cobblestone streets was transformed into a fascist fairyland. Every building was draped with exquisite precision in Nazi bunting. Every golden youth in the teeming crowd was filled with adoration as Hitler rode by, standing erect in his open car and returning the lusty cheers with his own rather limp salute.

But by 1945, Nuremberg had been reduced to rubble. On January 2, Royal Air Force and U.S. Army Air Force bombers swarmed over the city and destroyed the glories of its medieval center in just one hour. More raids followed in February. And then, in April, U.S. infantry divisions attacked the heavily defended city, finally taking it after fiery building-to-building fighting.

When Rebecca West arrived in Nuremberg that fall to cover the war crimes trial for *The New Yorker*, she found only a ruined landscape and hordes of scavengers. Making her way over the rubble one day, she was forced to hold her breath against "the double stench of disinfectant and of that which was irredeemably infected, for it concealed 30,000 dead." There was little food or fuel to buy in the shops—and no money for transactions, only cigarettes. At night, a Stygian blackness fell over the ghost city, relieved only by an eerie constellation of flickering candles in shattered windows.

That November, twenty-one prominent representatives of the Nazi regime that had brought Europe to this ruin faced their own moment of retribution as they sat in the defendants' galley in Nuremberg's Palace of Justice, one of the few official buildings left standing in Germany. Hitler and Himmler were already gone, as was the Reich's master propagandist Joseph Goebbels, escaping the executioner by their own hands. But the Nuremberg prosecutors had managed to assemble a representative spectrum from Hitler's glory days, including Reichsmarschall Hermann Goering, at one time the second-highest-ranking member of the Nazi Party and Hitler's designated successor. Goering was joined in the dock by dignitaries such as Rudolf Hess, Hitler's half-mad deputy who had flown to Scotland in 1941 in a wild bid to cut a peace deal with Britain; Ernst Kaltenbrunner, Himmler's grim, scar-faced executioner, the highest-ranking SS leader to be tried at Nuremberg; Hjalmar Schacht, the brilliant and arrogant international banker who had financed Hitler's military rise; Albert Speer, the architect of Hitler's imperial dreams and master of his weapons assembly line; and Julius Streicher, the unhinged politician and publisher who had parlayed his virulent brand of anti-Semitism into a thriving media empire based in Nuremberg.

Nuremberg, which enshrined the legal principle of personal responsibility for one's actions, even in war, was a showcase of Nazi denial. When Hitler's wily foreign minister, Joachim von Ribbentrop, was asked by an interrogator whether he was aware that millions had been murdered in the Nazi death camps, he had the gall to exclaim, "That . . . is an astounding thing to me . . . I can't imagine that!" It was as if he were suddenly waking from the bad dream of his own life. The defendants had long before abdicated all of their will to the Führer. As defendant Wilhelm Frick, the Reich's minister of the interior, declared in 1935, "I have no conscience; Adolf Hitler is my conscience."

The most egotistical defendants, like Goering and Schacht, struck defiant poses. At times, Reichsmarschall Goering mugged for the courtroom, laughing at the prosecutors' mispronunciation of German names and puffing his cheeks indignantly when they made errors about the Nazi chain of command.

The Reichsmarschall had not even bothered to run from the advancing American troops in the war's final days, convinced that he would be treated as the eminent representative of a defeated but noble people. His first hours in captivity surely encouraged his optimism, as the U.S. 36th Infantry Division soldiers who came for him at his quarters in southern Bavaria chatted amiably with him and treated the well-fed Nazi to one of their chicken and rice dinners from a tin can. Goering had no idea that he would be tried as a war criminal. At one point he blithely asked an American commander, "Should [I] wear a pistol or my ceremonial dagger when I appear before General Eisenhower?"

But the Reich's crimes would not be easily dismissed at Nuremberg. The very name of the city conjured not only Nazi triumphalism, but the race laws that Hitler ordered to be written in 1935—laws that, by criminalizing Jewishness, led inexorably to the butchery that followed. The city and its Palace of Justice had long been drenched with blood.

Nine days into the trial, the dead would make a dramatic appearance in the courtroom, conjured in a twenty-two-minute documentary called *Death Mills*. The documentary was made by Hollywood director Billy Wilder, an Austrian-born Jew who had fled Hitler, who compiled it from scraps of film taken by U.S. Army Signal Corps cameramen during the liberation of several Nazi concentration camps. In his opening statement, Robert Jackson, the chief U.S. prosecutor at Nuremberg, warned the courtroom that the film "will be disgusting and you will say I have robbed you of your sleep."

But nothing could prepare those who viewed the film for what they would see that day: the piles of shriveled corpses and the walking skeletons that greeted the stunned and sickened American liberators, the mangled remains of someone who had been experimented on by Nazi doctors ("This was a woman," intoned the narrator), the mounds of human ash to be sold as farm fertilizer, the pyramids of human hair and boxes of gold dental fillings to be sold for wigs and jewelry—the final value extracted from the victims of the Reich. One of the most punishing images was not grisly, but it would stay fixed in the mind's eye—a close-up shot that lingered on a bin of children's shoes, well worn from play.

As the film unreeled in the darkened courtroom, low lights were aimed at the defendants so the courtroom could see their reaction. From this point on, there was no place to hide. "The hilarity in the dock suddenly stopped," noted one courtroom witness. While the terrible images flickered on the screen, one criminal mopped his brow; another swallowed hard, trying to choke back tears. Now one buried his face in his hands, while another began openly weeping. ("These were crocodile tears. They wept for themselves, not for the dead," observed a British prosecutor.) Only the most arrogant remained impervious, with Schacht, Hitler's banker, turning his back to the screen, and Goering "trying to brazen it out," in the words of assistant U.S. prosecutor Telford Taylor.

Afterward, Goering complained that the film had ruined the show he was putting on for the courtroom: "It was such a good afternoon too, until they showed that film. They were reading my telephone conversations on the Austrian [annexation] and everybody was laughing with me. And then they showed that awful film, and it just spoiled everything."

The Nuremberg trial was a moral milestone, the first time that top government officials were held accountable for crimes against humanity that in earlier days would have likely been dismissed as the natural acts of war. During the war, Allied leaders had issued a "full warning" that Nazi war criminals would be pursued "to the uttermost ends of the earth . . . in order that justice be done." But it took a heated debate within Allied diplomatic circles before the international tribunal was finally established in Nuremberg. And even after it was up and running, the process was fraught with political maneuvering.

President Roosevelt and Prime Minister Winston Churchill were so intent on meting out a fitting punishment that they originally favored taking the law into their own hands and summarily shooting Hitler's top military, ministerial, and party ranks—Churchill estimated the number would be somewhere between fifty and a hundred men. The prime minister thought that once the proper identifications were made, the killing could be completed within six hours. In one of history's deeper ironies, it was Joseph Stalin who insisted that the Nazi leaders be put on trial, lecturing his Western allies on the merits of due process. "U[ncle]. J[oe]. took an unexpectedly ultra-respectable line," Churchill wrote Roosevelt after meeting with Stalin in Moscow in October 1944. The Soviet premier told Churchill that "there must be no executions without trial; otherwise the world would say we were afraid to try them."

Roosevelt finally came around to the idea of an international war crimes tribunal. But once again he had to face stiff opposition from within his own State Department. Future foreign service legend George Kennan, who was a junior diplomat in the U.S. embassy in Berlin when war broke out, was one of those who took a strong stand against punishing Nazi war criminals. Purging these leaders from German society would not only be greatly unpopular with the German people, Kennan argued, it would be hugely disruptive. "We would not find any other class of people competent to assume the burdens [of leading postwar Germany]," he insisted. "Whether we like it or not, nine-tenths of what is strong, able and respected in Germany" carried the taint of Nazism.

It was not until late 1943 that a small, underfunded international commission began the urgent work of trying to define the barbaric new crimes emerging from World War II and compiling a list of war criminals for prosecution as soon as peace permitted. FDR appointed an old friend named Herbert Pell as the U.S. representative to the United Nations War Crimes Commission. (The United Nations was yet to be founded, but this is how the Allies sometimes referred to themselves during the war.) Pell, a fellow New York Brahmin and ardent New Deal supporter, quickly found himself in a political vortex, besieged by State Department bureaucrats who did not consider an international tribunal necessary and were determined to sabotage Pell's efforts.

At six feet five inches and 250 pounds, Pell was a towering man— and, raised in the rarefied societies of Tuxedo Park and Newport Beach, he had more than enough self-confidence to hold his own among his Washington foes. The Pells had inherited a tobacco fortune, their forefathers had been granted the land that would become the Bronx and Westchester County by the British crown, and there was no need for "Bertie" Pell to do a thing with his life if he had so chosen. Indeed, with his waxed mustache and pince-nez glasses, he seemed like a throwback to the Gilded Age. But inspired by the rambunctious reformism of Teddy Roosevelt, Pell leaped into the grubby fray of American politics, albeit in Manhattan's silk stocking district on the Upper East Side, which, despite its long aversion to Democrats, briefly elected him to Congress. By the time his old Harvard classmate Franklin Roosevelt ran for president in 1932, Bertie Pell was a full-on renegade from his class, which he dismissed as a sybaritic and selfish lot whose "piglike rush for immediate profits" had brought ruin to the country in the crash of 1929.

Those who snubbed him at the clubhouse in Tuxedo Park—a rolling estate of woods, lakes, and citadels for America's gentry located in Orange County, New York, some forty miles outside of New York City—were too stupid, in Pell's not-so-humble opinion, to realize that Franklin Roosevelt was trying to save their bacon from a revolution that was rumbling right outside their gates. "I am almost the last capitalist who is willing to be saved by you," Pell wrote Roosevelt in 1936 in a letter beseeching the president to draft him for the New Deal cause. The following year, Pell wrote again, praising FDR's accomplishments: "Your administration has made possible the continuance of American institutions for at least fifty years. You have done for the government what St. Francis did for the Catholic Church. You have brought it back to the people."

Roosevelt finally did put Pell to work, sending him to Portugal and then to Hungary as U.S. ambassador in the late 1930s, from where he watched with growing alarm the rise of fascism. By the time Pell was chosen for the war crimes commission in June 1943, he knew the full depths of the evil that had taken hold of Europe. He was eager to get to London, where other commission members were already beginning to meet, but Pell found himself ensnared by State Department bureaucracy. His principal nemesis was the State Department legal adviser, a fussy and officious man named Green Hackworth.

The two men clashed immediately, on a personal as well as political level. "Hackworth was well named," Pell recalled later. "He was a little, legal hack of no particular attainments. He was manifestly not born a gentleman and had acquired very few of the ideas of a gentleman on his way up in the world. His manners were bad, his fingers were dirty [and] he was clearly unused to good society."

More important, Pell's mission abroad was strongly opposed by Hackworth, who took a narrowly legalistic approach to the war crimes question. War was not subject to a moral calculus, in the eyes of State Department officials like Hackworth, who rejected the very idea that the international community might hold heads of state responsible for atrocities against their own people. This traditional view was rendered obsolete by the Nazi inferno in Europe, but men like Hackworth seemed oblivious to the new world around them.

Pell, in contrast, was intent on bringing to justice not just Nazi Party high officials, but also the German business elite who had profited from Hitler's rule and even the rank-and-file Gestapo men who, unless they were severely punished, Pell feared, would go home to their villages and brag about what they had gotten away with. "The first thing is to make clear to every last German in the world that war is not a profitable business," Pell wrote to Secretary of State Hull in 1943. Pell's zeal for justice—and his broad definition of German guilt—sent alarms through the U.S. Foreign Service and Wall Street circles, where the primary concerns were related to postwar German stability.

Green Hackworth and his colleagues successfully conspired to hold up Pell's departure for months. Finally, after FDR intervened on his behalf with Hull, Pell was able to set sail for London on the *Queen Mary* in December 1943—a full six months after his appointment to the war crimes commission. Pell arrived in a frigidly cold, war-torn London, where heating fuel was in short supply. Fortunately, he had sent word ahead to his English tailor, who was able to supply him with woolen long underwear that fit his large frame.

Pell was shocked by London's widespread war damage: every block seemed to have at least one demolished building. Three of the friends in his small London social circle were killed by German bombs. One was blown up, along with the rest of the congregation, while attending Sunday church. Only the minister survived. Pell toughed it out during air raids, staying aboveground instead of descending into the crowded, badly ventilated shelters. At age fifty-nine, he thought he was more likely to die from catching the flu than by being blown up by a German bomb or a Doodlebug, as the British called the V–1 flying bombs whistling overhead. When the Luftwaffe bombers roared over London, they dropped huge flares to illuminate their targets, and the city was cast in a spectral glow just before the explosions began. As the president's man in London, Pell thought it was important to carry on with his life in the same plucky manner as the Brits. One afternoon, he took a visiting cousin for tea at the exclusive Athenaeum Club. Although every one of the club's windows had been blasted out, the waiters still made their rounds with the same crisp and aloof manner as they had before the war.

As the war crimes commission went about its work through 1944, Pell, despite his lack of legal experience, took a leadership role, developing prosecutorial guidelines for the postwar tribunal that would try Germany's war criminals. While some commission members were uncertain how to categorize the Nazi brutality against the Jews, Pell vehemently argued that this violence, even if conducted away from the battlefield, must be regarded as a prosecutable war crime, and the commission came to agree with him.

But Pell was unable to finish his work with the war crimes commission. In December 1944, he returned to America for the wedding of his only son—future U.S. senator Claiborne Pell—and to consult with the State Department. Once they had him back in Washington, his political enemies were determined to never let him return. Again, Pell appealed to his old friend in the White House to help him overpower the State Department hacks. But this time, Roosevelt's health was failing and he could not muster the energy to rescue Bertie. On February 1, the State Department announced Pell's dismissal.

In early April 1945, Henry Morgenthau went down to the presidential retreat in Warm Springs, Georgia, where FDR was convalescing, to urge him to directly confront the State Department cabal that seemed hell-bent on appeasing the country's German enemies and antagonizing its Soviet allies. Sitting down for cocktails with the president, Morgenthau was shaken by the president's "very haggard" appearance. "His hands shook so that he started to knock the glasses over. . . . I found his memory bad and he was constantly confusing names." After drinks and dinner, Roosevelt seemed to rally and he asked Morgenthau what he had in mind. The Treasury secretary told him it was time "to break the State Department" and replace the old guard with loyal New Dealers. FDR assured Morgenthau he was with him "100 percent." The next afternoon, April 12, Roosevelt died after suffering a massive cerebral hemorrhage.

That same day, Pell was scheduled to meet in Washington with the new secretary of state, Edward Stettinius Jr., to discuss being reinstated on the war crimes commission—a meeting that had been brokered by FDR. After he had been fired, Pell had fought on, working the Washington press and stirring up outrage over his treatment at the hands of the State Department. The public controversy put Pell's enemies on the defensive. But in the wake of Roosevelt's death, Pell was politically isolated, and by September 1945 he finally admitted defeat.

There were two reasons he was targeted for political destruction, Pell told a group of sympathetic lawyers who had rallied around him: "One is anti-Semitism, which is, to a large extent, prevalent in the State Department." He also antagonized his powerful enemies, he explained, by going after "German industrialists whose plight arouses the class loyalties of their opposition numbers in Great Britain and the United States. We cannot forget [for example] that one of the big war factories in Germany was the Opel Company which was owned and financed by the General Motors Corporation, a company in which Secretary Stettinius had a great interest. The biggest electric company in Germany was owned and financed by the General Electric Company of New York. We have here very potent reasons why a large and important group in this country is trying to pipe down on the serious investigations of [corporate Germany's collaboration with the Nazis]."

In the end, Pell would triumph. Because of the uproar in the press over his dismissal, the State Department was finally forced to recognize the inevitability of a war crimes trial. In a statement released in the midst of the Pell melee, the department acknowledged that President Roosevelt had repeatedly made clear his intention. As the first war crimes trial got under way in Nuremberg in November 1945, the spirit of FDR and the president's justice warriors—men like Pell and Morgenthau—hovered over the legal forum.

But the political foes who had opposed Roosevelt's day of reckoning for the Nazis did not fully surrender. They remained determined to control the proceedings at Nuremberg and to protect valued members of Hitler's hierarchy.

In May 1945, Allen Dulles and OSS chief Bill Donovan met in Frankfurt with Supreme Court associate justice Robert Jackson, who had just been named chief U.S. war crimes prosecutor by the new president, Harry S. Truman. During their meeting, Dulles underlined the various ways that he could be of use as Jackson prepared his case, including providing German witnesses for the prosecution as well as secret enemy documents. Jackson was delighted by Dulles's offer of assistance, noting in his diary that it was a "God send." Donovan further reinforced the relationship with Jackson's team by putting a number of OSS agents on his staff. But as the weeks went by, Jackson developed the sinking feeling that he had fallen into an OSS "trap." It became clear to the Nuremberg prosecutor that Donovan and Dulles harbored ulterior motives and agendas that did not always mesh with the interests of justice at Nuremberg.

The tensions between Donovan and Jackson began to grow in July when the OSS chief moved to take over what Nuremberg prosecutors referred to as the trial's "economic case." As Wall Street lawyers, Donovan and Dulles considered themselves uniquely equipped to take charge of the case against the industrialists and bankers who had financed Hitler's regime. But such a role would have given the two OSS men the ability to control the legal fates of German business figures who had strong ties to their own Wall Street circles—including infamous former clients of the Dulles brothers.

Robert Jackson was a strong New Dealer who had risen through FDR's Justice Department, where he had taken on powerful corporate interests like the Mellon family and fought tax evasion and antitrust battles. Well aware of the corporate conflicts of interest that Donovan and Dulles brought to the Nuremberg case, Jackson stunned the OSS chief by informing him that he would not be leading the prosecution of Hitler's financiers at Nuremberg.

Jackson quickly discovered that his concerns had been well founded. As the trial's start date approached that fall, Donovan began communicating with Goering and Schacht, whom he recognized as the two most financially astute men among the accused. Goering had amassed huge economic power under Hitler's regime, organizing state-run mining, steel, and weapons enterprises and taking control of heavy industries in the countries overrun by the Nazis. And Schacht, for his part, had remained a well-respected figure in New York, London, and Swiss banking circles even after selling his soul to Hitler. (Schacht later fell out with the Führer and spent the final days of the war in the VIP section of Dachau, where prisoners received relatively lenient treatment.) The banker knew where much of Nazi Germany's assets were hidden, which continued to make him a valued man in global financial circles.

Behind the scenes, Donovan took the shameless step of working out a deal with these two prominent defendants, offering them leniency in return for their testimony against the other accused Hitler accomplices.

When the OSS chief informed Jackson and his legal team that he had cut a tentative deal with Schacht and with—of all people—Goering, the prosecutors were aghast. Telford Taylor, Jackson's assistant prosecutor, later called Donovan's actions "ill conceived and dangerous . . . Goering was the surviving leader and symbol of Nazism. To put him forward as the man who could tell the truth about the Third Reich and lay bare the guilt of its leaders, as Donovan appeared to expect, was nothing short of ludicrous."

On November 26, a few days after the trial began, Jackson wrote a letter to Donovan, making it clear that their views were "far apart" and there was no role for the OSS chief on the Nuremberg team. By the end of the month, Donovan was gone.

But Allen Dulles was a more subtle practitioner of the art of power than Wild Bill Donovan. He would continue to play a crafty role in the dispensation of justice—or its opposite—not only during the first trial but through the eleven subsequent Nuremberg trials, which stretched from 1946 to 1949. In all, some two hundred accused German war criminals were prosecuted at Nuremberg, and hundreds more would be tried in military and civilian courts over the following decades. But due to Dulles's carefully calibrated interventions, a number of Europe's most notorious war criminals—men who should have found themselves in the dock at Nuremberg, where they almost certainly would have been convicted of capital crimes—escaped justice. Some were helped to flee through "ratlines" to Franco's Spain, the Middle East, South America, and even the United States. Others were eased into new lives of power and affluence in postwar West Germany, where they became essential confederates in Dulles's rapidly growing intelligence complex.

Near the end of 1945, Dulles returned home to New York, where, on December 3—a few days before leaving government service—he was asked to talk about postwar Germany at a meeting of the Council on Foreign Relations. He felt at home in the council's headquarters in the historic Harold Pratt House on Park Avenue, and his remarks were frank and unfiltered that day. The first Nuremberg trial had just begun and Winston Churchill's "Iron Curtain" speech was months in the future, but Dulles was already sounding the themes of the future Cold War era.

The United States must not go too far in its efforts to cleanse Germany of its Nazi past, Dulles told the meeting. "Most men of the caliber required to [run the new Germany] suffer a political taint," he said. "We have already found out that you can't run railroads without taking in some [Nazi] Party members."

Dulles went on to explain why it was essential to ensure a strong West Germany. Signs of Soviet perfidy were already glaringly apparent. In Poland, he warned, "The Russians are acting little better than thugs. . . . The promises at [the Allied leaders'] Yalta [conference] to the contrary, probably eight to ten million people are being enslaved."

For Dulles, the wartime alliance that had defeated Hitler was already dead. In fact, he had been planning throughout the war for this moment when the Western powers—including elements of the Third Reich—would unite against their true enemy in Moscow.

On October 1, 1946, after nearly a yearlong trial, the fates of the twenty-one Nuremberg defendants were finally read aloud in the stuffy courtroom. Three were acquitted, including the well-connected Schacht. Seven received prison sentences ranging from ten years to life. Like many convicted Nazi criminals in the early Cold War years, a number of the Nuremberg defendants sentenced to prison were later the beneficiaries of politically motivated interventions and early releases; few of the some five thousand convicted Nazis were still in prison after 1953. A number of the interventions on behalf of fortunate war criminals could be traced to the quiet stratagems of Allen Dulles.

Eleven of the original Nuremberg defendants did face swift and final justice, sentenced to hang by the neck until dead. Among them was Goering, whom not even Bill Donovan had been able to save. The Reichsmarschall had predictably proclaimed his innocence to the end. "The only motive which guided me was my ardent love for my people," he told the court in his bombastic final statement. This proved too much even for one of his fellow defendants, Hitler's former vice chancellor, Franz von Papen, who angrily confronted Goering later during a court lunch break: "Who in the world is responsible for all this destruction if not you? You haven't taken the responsibility for anything!" Goering simply laughed at him.

Goering feared death by the noose, and he requested a soldier's honorable exit by firing squad. When this last request was denied, Goering resorted to the favorite Nazi means of self-annihilation, cracking a glass capsule of cyanide with his teeth. (For men who had callously dispatched millions to their deaths, the Reich's high officials proved exquisitely sensitive about their own methods of departure.) According to Telford Taylor, it was likely one of Goering's American guards, a strapping Army lieutenant named Jack "Tex" Wheelis, who smuggled the poison capsule into the condemned Nazi's cell. Years after Tex Wheelis's own death, his widow showed a visitor a small trove of treasures, including a solid gold Mont Blanc fountain pen and a Swiss luxury watch, both inscribed with Goering's name, that had been bestowed upon the American soldier by his German "friend."

Goering's evasion of the gallows proved wise. The following morning, the ten remaining men who had been sentenced to death filed one by one into a gymnasium adjacent to the courtroom, where three black-painted wooden scaffolds awaited them. With its cracked plaster walls and glaring lighting, the gymnasium—which had hosted a basketball game just days before between U.S. Army security guards—provided a suitably bleak backdrop. The chief hangman, a squat, hard-drinking Army master sergeant from San Antonio named John C. Woods, was an experienced executioner, with numerous hangings to his credit. But, due to sloppiness or ill will, the Nuremberg hangings were not professionally carried out.

The drop was not long enough, so some of the condemned dangled in agony at the end of their ropes for long stretches of time before they died. Field Marshall Wilhelm Keitel, Hitler's war minister and the second-highest-ranking soldier after Goering to be tried at Nuremberg, suffered the longest, thrashing for a full twenty-four minutes. When the dead men were later photographed, they looked particularly ghoulish, since the swinging trapdoors had smashed and bloodied their faces as the men fell—another flaw, or intentional indignity, in the execution process.

Julius Streicher, defiant to the end, screamed a piercing "Heil Hitler!" as he began climbing the thirteen wooden steps of the scaffold. As the noose was placed around his neck, he spat at Woods, "The Bolsheviks will hang you one day." The short drop failed to kill him, too, and as Streicher groaned at the end of his rope, Woods was forced to descend from the platform, grab his swinging body, and yank sharply downward to finally silence him.

After the first executions, the American colonel in charge asked for a cigarette break. The soldiers on the execution team paced nervously around the gymnasium, smoking and speaking somberly among themselves. But after it was all over, Woods pronounced himself perfectly satisfied. "Never saw a hanging go off any better," he declared.

The hangman never expressed any doubt about his historic role at Nuremberg. "I hanged those ten Nazis . . . and I am proud of it," he said after the executions. A few years later, Woods accidentally electrocuted himself while repairing faulty machinery at a military base in the Marshall Islands.

The sectors of Germany occupied by the United States and its allies tried to quickly forget the war. Hollywood musicals and cowboy adventures—and their escapist German equivalents—flooded the movie theaters in West Germany. But in the Soviet-controlled East, there was a cinematic effort, though generally party-directed and heavy-handed, to force the German people to confront the nightmare and its consequences. In the early postwar period, there was a barrage of such dark movies, known as *Trümmerfilme*, or "rubble films." One of the more artful rubble films, *Murderers Among Us*, grappled disturbingly with the Nazi ghosts that still haunted Germany. Produced in 1946 by DEFA, the Soviet-run studio in East Berlin, *Murderers Among Us* was directed by Wolfgang Staudte, a once-promising young filmmaker who had made his own moral compromises in order to continue working during Hitler's rule. Staudte's film reverberates with guilt.

In the film, Dr. Hans Mertens, a German surgeon who had served with the Wehrmacht, returns to Berlin after the war. The city is a monument to rubble; it seems to have been deconstructed stone by stone, brick by brick. Staudte needed no studio back lot or special effects. Demolished Berlin was his sound stage. Dr. Mertens, who wants to forget everything he has witnessed during the war, wanders drunk and obliterated through the city's ruins. But his past won't release him. He comes across his former commander, Captain Bruckner, a happily shallow man who, despite the atrocities he ordered during the war, has returned to a prosperous life in Berlin as a factory owner.

"Don't look so sad," Bruckner tells the doctor as the two men pick their way through the rubble one day in search of a hidden cabaret. "Every era offers its chances if you find them. Helmets from saucepans or saucepans from helmets. It's the same game. You must manage—that's all."

Dr. Mertens's bitterness deepens as he observes Berlin being profitably revived by the very men who destroyed it. One day, fortified by drink, he comes across a lively nest of vermin, scurrying about in the rubble. "Rats," he says to himself. "Rats everywhere. The city is alive again."

By the end of the film, Mertens has emerged from his drunken anesthesia and has begun to consider a path of action. How do you make a better world after a reign of terror like Hitler's? Should he kill a man like Bruckner? Should he try to bring him to justice?

Murderers Among Us ends on a hopeful, if fanciful, note. Mertens imagines Bruckner behind bars—no longer looking smug, but stricken. "Why are you doing this to me?" he screams, as images of his victims float ghostlike around him.

When the movie was produced, the first Nuremberg trial was still under way, and it looked to the world as if justice would indeed prevail. But as the years went by, a surprising number of men like Bruckner not only escaped justice but thrived in the new Germany. Thanks to officials like Dulles, many Bruckners shimmied free from their cages. The rats were everywhere.

Sunrise

Allen Dulles's most audacious intervention on behalf of a major Nazi war criminal took place in the waning days of the war. The story of the relationship between Dulles and SS general Karl Wolff—Himmler's former chief of staff and commander of Nazi security forces in Italy—is a long and tangled one. But perhaps it's best to begin at a particularly dire moment for Wolff, in the still-dark early morning hours of April 26, 1945, less than two weeks before the end of the war in Europe.

That morning, soon after arriving at the SS command post in Cernobbio, a quaint town nestled in the foothills of the Italian Alps on the shores of Lake Como, Wolff was surrounded by a well-armed unit of Italian partisans. The partisans had established positions around the entire SS compound, a luxurious estate that had been seized by the Nazis from the Locatelli family, a wealthy dynasty of cheese manufacturers. With only a handful of SS soldiers standing guard outside his villa, Wolff had no way to break through the siege and his capture seemed imminent. As chief of all SS and Gestapo units in Italy, Wolff was well known to the Italian resistance, who blamed him for the reprisal killings of many civilians in response to partisan attacks on Nazi targets, as well as for the torture and murder of numerous resistance fighters. If he fell into the partisans' hands, the SS commander was not likely to be treated charitably.

At age forty-four, the tall, fair-haired, blue-eyed Wolff carried himself with the supreme self-confidence of a man who had long been paraded around by the Nazi high command as an ideal Aryan specimen. A former advertising executive, Wolff understood the power of imagery. His climb through the Nazi Party ranks had been paved by his Hessian bearing, his imperial, hawk-nosed profile, and the erect figure he cut in his SS dress uniform. Himmler, the former chicken farmer, drew confidence from Wolff's suave presence and fondly called him "Wolffie." The SS chief made Wolff his principal liaison to Hitler's headquarters, where he also quickly became a favorite.

Hitler enjoyed showing off Wolff at his dinner parties and made sure that the SS-Obergruppenführer was by his side during the war's tense overture, when German forces invaded Poland and Hitler prepared to join his troops at the front. "To my great and, I openly admit, joyful surprise, I was ordered to the innermost Führer headquarters," Wolff proudly recalled as an old man. "Hitler wanted to have me nearby, because he knew that he could rely on me completely. He had known me for a long time, and rather well."

But in April 1945, encircled by his enemies at the Villa Locatelli, Wolff was far from these glory days. The desperation of his situation was underlined the following day when Benito Mussolini, Italy's once all-powerful Duce, whose status had been reduced to that of Wolff's ward, was captured by partisans at a roadblock on the northern tip of Lake Como while fleeing with his dwindling entourage for Switzerland. Taken to the crumbling but still grand city hall in the nearby lakeside village of Dongo, Mussolini was assured he would be treated mercifully. "Don't worry," the mayor told him, "you will be all right."

A horde of partisans and curious townspeople crowded into the mayor's office, to fire questions at the man who had ruled Italy for over two decades. Mussolini answered each question thoughtfully. In the final months of his life, he had grown increasingly reflective and resigned to his fate. He spent more time reading—his tastes ranged from Dostoyevsky and Hemingway to Plato and Nietzsche—than dealing with governmental affairs. "I am crucified by my destiny," Mussolini had told a visiting Italian army chaplain in his final days.

When his captors asked him why he had allowed the Germans to exact harsh retributions on the Italian people, Mussolini mournfully explained that it was beyond his power. "My hands were tied. There was very little possibility of opposing General [Albert] Kesselring [field commander of the German armed forces in Italy] and General Wolff in what they did. Again and again in conversations with General Wolff, I mentioned that stories of people being tortured and other brutal deeds had come to my ears. One day Wolff replied that it was the only means of extracting the truth, and even the dead spoke the truth in his torture chambers."

In the end, Mussolini found no mercy. He and his mistress, Claretta Petacci, who insisted on sharing his fate, were machine-gunned and their bodies were put on display in Milan's Piazzale Loreto. Mussolini's body was subjected to particular abuse by the large, frantic crowd in the square; one woman fired five shots into Il Duce's head—one for each of her five dead sons. The bodies were then strung up by their feet from the overhanging girders of a garage roof, where they were subjected to further indignities. When he heard about Mussolini's grotesque finale, Hitler—who, near the end, had told the Duce that he was "perhaps the only friend I have in the world"—ordered that his own body be burned after he killed himself.

General Wolff knew that he, too, faced a merciless end if he fell captive at Villa Locatelli. But unlike Mussolini, the SS commander had a very dedicated and powerful friend in the enemy camp.

At eleven in the morning on April 26, Allen Dulles received an urgent phone call in his Bern office from Max Waibel, his contact in Swiss intelligence. Waibel reported that Karl Wolff was surrounded by partisans at Villa Locatelli and "there was a great danger they might storm the villa and kill Wolff."

The SS general was the key to Dulles's greatest wartime ambition: securing a separate peace with Nazi forces in Italy before the Soviet army could push into Austria and southward toward Trieste. With the Communists playing a dominant role in the Italian resistance, Dulles knew that blocking the advance of the Red Army into northern Italy was critical if Italy was to be prevented from falling into the Soviet orbit after the war. Dulles and his intelligence colleagues had been secretly meeting with Wolff and his SS aides since late February, trying to work out a separate surrender of German forces in Italy that would save the Nazi officers' necks and win the OSS spymaster the glory that had eluded him throughout the war.

The negotiations for Operation Sunrise, as Dulles optimistically christened his covert peace project, were a highly delicate dance. Exposure could spell disaster for both men. According to Wolff, during their diplomatic courtship, Dulles identified himself as a "special representative" and "a personal friend" of President Roosevelt—neither of which was true. In fact, by negotiating with the SS general, Dulles was clearly violating FDR's emphatic policy of unconditional surrender. Just days before Wolff was trapped at Villa Locatelli, Dulles had been expressly forbidden by Washington from continuing his contacts with Wolff.

Meanwhile, the SS commander's secret diplomatic efforts both dovetailed and competed with the numerous other Nazi peace initiatives coming Dulles's way, including that of his boss, Heinrich Himmler, who was also shrewd enough to realize that the German war effort was doomed and he along with it, unless he managed to cut his own deal. Even the Führer himself was toying with the idea of how he might save the Reich by splitting the Allies and winning a favorable peace settlement. In his backroom dealing with Dulles, Wolff at times found himself an emissary of the Nazi high command and at other times a traitorous agent working at cross-purposes to save his own skin.

But with Wolff now surrounded by Italian resistance fighters at Villa Locatelli, his end seemed near—and with it, all the painstaking and duplicitous efforts undertaken by the two men over the previous two months on behalf of Operation Sunrise. Dulles had too much at stake to let his happen. Alerted to Wolff's predicament, he flew into action, mounting a rescue party to cross the border and reach the villa before it was too late.

Dulles knew that risking brave men to save a Nazi war criminal's life—in the interests of his own unsanctioned peace mission—was an act of brazen insubordination that could cost him his intelligence career. So, to give himself cover, Dulles arranged for his loyal subordinate, Gero von Schulze-Gaevernitz, to oversee the rescue.

Dulles later related the story with typical bonhomie—but, as was often the case, his glib delivery masked a darker tale. "I told Gaevernitz that under the strict orders I had received, I could not get in touch with Wolff. . . . Gaevernitz listened silently for a moment. Then he said that since the whole [Operation Sunrise] affair seemed to have come to an end, he would like to go on a little trip for a few days. I noticed a twinkle in his eye, and as he told me later, he noticed one in mine. I realized, of course, what he was going to do, and that he intended to do it on his own responsibility."

When it came to saving Wolff, Gaevernitz shared his boss's zeal. Gaevernitz was the handsome scion of an illustrious European family and a relative of the Stinnes family, whose fortune had helped finance Hitler's political rise. The Gaevernitzes had broken from the Nazis early on, and Dulles helped funnel their money to safe havens outside of Germany, as he did for many wealthy Germans, including those who remained loyal to the Nazi regime, before and during the war. Dulles and Gaevernitz were also tied together by their political views—they both believed that "moderate" members of Hitler's regime must be salvaged from the war's wreckage and incorporated into postwar plans for Germany. By the extremely generous standards of Dulles and Gaevernitz, even Karl Wolff qualified as one such redeemable Nazi.

After being dispatched by Dulles, Gaevernitz, accompanied by the Swiss secret agent Waibel, jumped on an Italy-bound train, arriving at the Swiss border town of Chiasso late that evening. There they met one of Dulles's top agents, Don Jones, a man well known to the Italian resistance fighters in the border area as "Scotti." Gaevernitz thought that Scotti, a man who risked his life each day fighting SS soldiers, would balk at the idea of saving the general who commanded them. But Scotti gamely agreed to lead the mission.

And so, as midnight approached, a convoy of three cars set off toward the western shore of Lake Como. One vehicle carried OSS agent

Scotti and three Swiss intelligence operatives, the second was filled with Italian partisans, and the third conveyed two SS officials Dulles had recruited to ease the convoy's passage through German-controlled areas. It was one of the most bizarre missions in wartime Europe: a joint U.S.-German rescue effort organized for the benefit of a high-ranking Nazi general.

As the convoy crawled through the dark toward the lake, partisans opened fire on the cars. Scotti bravely jumped out of his vehicle and stood in the headlights, praying that the resistance soldiers would recognize him and stop shooting. Fortunately, one did. There was more gunfire and even a grenade attack as they continued their journey, but finally, the odd rescue team arrived at the Villa Locatelli. After talking their way past the partisans' blockade as well as the SS guard, they entered the villa and found General Wolff in full SS uniform, as if he had been expecting them all along. He offered the rescue party some of the vintage Scotch he kept for special occasions, volunteering that the whiskey had been expropriated from the British by Rommel during the North African campaign.

It was after two in the morning when the caravan arrived safely back in Chiasso with their special passenger, who had changed into civilian clothes for the journey and was slumped low in the backseat of the middle car. Gaevernitz was anxiously awaiting the rescue team's return in the dingy railroad station café. He had no intention of greeting Wolff in public. But when the SS general heard that Dulles's aide was there, he bounded over to him and shook his hand. "I will never forget what you have done for me," Wolff declared.

Dulles and Gaevernitz would learn that the SS man had a strange sense of gratitude. In the coming years, Wolff would become a millstone around their necks.

Later that morning, an exhausted Gaevernitz, who had not been out of his clothes all that night, took a train to his family's lovely villa in Ascona, on Lake Maggiore, so he could enjoy a long sleep. At the railway station in Locarno, where he stopped for breakfast, he listened to the 7:00 a.m. radio broadcast, which was filled with news of

Mussolini's capture and other dramatic bulletins from the Lake Como area. Gaevernitz kept expecting to hear news of General Wolff's rescue by a U.S.-led team of commandos; he was determined that his boss's name must be kept out of the story.

"It would have made a lovely headline in the papers," Gaevernitz later mused in his diary. "'German S.S. General Rescued From Italian Patriots by American Consul'!!! Poor Allen!! I really felt I had to spare him this [embarrassment]."

It took Wolff several more days of high-stakes diplomacy before his maneuvers finally resulted in the surrender of German forces on the Italian front on May 2, 1945. By then, Hitler was dead, the German military machine had all but collapsed, and it was just six days before the capitulation of all Axis forces in Europe. In the end, Operation Sunrise saved few lives and had little impact on the course of the war. It did succeed, however, in creating a new set of international tensions that some historians would identify as the first icy fissures of the Cold War.

The Dulles-Wolff maneuvers aggravated Stalin's paranoid disposition. While he was still alive, Roosevelt, whom Stalin genuinely liked and trusted, was able to reassure the Soviet leader that the United States had no intention of betraying an alliance forged in blood. But after FDR's death, Stalin's fears of a stab in the back at Caserta—where the surrender on the Italian front was signed by German and American military commanders—only grew more intense. His suspicions were not unfounded. After the separate peace was declared at Caserta, some German divisions in Italy were told not to lay down their arms but to get ready to begin battling the Red Army alongside the Americans and British.

Even Roosevelt's successor, Harry S. Truman, who would become a dedicated Cold Warrior, took a dim view of Operation Sunrise and tried unsuccessfully to shut it down. Truman later wrote in his memoir that Dulles's unauthorized diplomacy stirred up a tempest of trouble for him during his first days as president.

Operation Sunrise would become Allen Dulles's creation myth, the legend that loomed over his entire intelligence career. For the rest of his life, the spymaster would energetically work the publicity machinery on "the secret surrender," generating magazine articles and more than one book and attempting to turn the tale into a Hollywood thriller. It was, according to the story that Dulles assiduously spun throughout the rest of his life, a feat of daring personal diplomacy. *Time* magazine—which, under the ownership of his close friend Henry Luce, could always be counted on to give Dulles good press—trumpeted Operation Sunrise as "one of the most stunning triumphs in the history of secret wartime diplomacy." The reality, however, was far from triumphant.

Karl Wolff was Allen Dulles's kind of Nazi. Like Hitler and Himmler, Dulles admired Wolff's gentlemanly comportment and found him "extremely good-looking." He struck Dulles as a man with the right sort of pedigree, the type of trustworthy fellow with whom he could do business.

Wolff liked to present himself as a high-level administrator who was unsullied by the more inhumane operations of his government. He was not one of the Nazi Party's vulgar anti-Semites, he would later insist. He took pride in rescuing the occasional prominent Jewish prisoner from the Gestapo dungeons—a banker, a tennis celebrity, for instance. Eichmann sneeringly referred to Wolff as one of the "dandy officers of the SS, who wore white gloves and didn't want to know anything about what's going on."

Wolff was a financially savvy fixer, a man whom the Nazi hierarchy could rely on to get things done. After serving with distinction as a young army officer on the western front during World War I, Wolff originally pursued a career in banking, before going into advertising. But his ambitions in both fields were thwarted by Germany's postwar economic crash. His decision to join Hitler's rapidly growing enterprise, where he rose quickly through the ranks, was more of a professional decision than an ideological one. There were unlimited opportunities in the Nazi movement for a polished blond warrior like Wolff.

His business background gave Wolff cachet in the SS, where such skills were in short supply. It was Wolff who was put in charge of Himmler's important "circle of friends," a select group of some three dozen German industrialists and bankers who supplied the SS with a stream of slush money. "Himmler was no businessman and I took care of banking matters for him," Wolff later recalled. In return for their generosity, the corporate donors were given special access to pools of slave labor. They were also invited to attend high-level government meetings and special Nazi Party ceremonies. It was said that Wolff took such good care of the wealthy contributors at the 1933 Nuremberg rally that they were pampered more than the Führer himself. On other occasions, the privileged circle of friends was even taken on private tours of the Dachau and Sachsenhausen concentration camps, escorted by Himmler and Wolff. Presumably the SS shut down the camps' crematoria during the distinguished guests' visits to spare them the unpleasant stench.

In pursuing the Sunrise peace pact, Dulles and Wolff harbored similar political motives. Both viewed the Soviet army's advance into Western Europe as a catastrophe. But they also shared business interests. Throughout the war, Dulles had used his OSS command post in Switzerland to look out for Sullivan and Cromwell business clients in Europe. Stopping the war before these clients' manufacturing and power plants in industrial northern Italy were destroyed was a priority for both men.

Under the terms of Operation Sunrise, Wolff specifically agreed not to blow up the region's many hydroelectric plants, which generated power from the water roaring down from the Alps. Most of these installations were owned by a multinational holding company called Italian Superpower Corporation. Incorporated in Delaware in 1928, Italian Superpower's board was evenly divided between American and Italian utility executives, and by the following year the power company was swallowed by a bigger, J. P. Morgan–financed cartel. The ties between Italian Superpower and Dulles's financial circle were reinforced when, toward the end of the war, the spymaster's good friend—New York banker James Russell Forgan—took over as his OSS boss in London. Forgan was one of Italian Superpower's directors.

Dulles concluded that Wolff was, in effect, a member of his international club—a man with similar views, connections, and willingness to do business. Neither man was particularly interested in the clash of ideas or human tragedies associated with the war. They were fixed on the calculus of power; each understood the other's intense ambition. Operation Sunrise was for both of them a bold, high-wire career move.

After he decided that Wolff was a dependable partner, Dulles went to great lengths to rehabilitate the SS commander's image. In his reports back to OSS headquarters, he framed Wolff in the best possible light: he was a "moderate" and "probably the most dynamic [German] personality in North Italy." Although some U.S. and British intelligence officials suspected that Wolff was serving as an agent of Hitler and Himmler and trying to drive a wedge between the Allies, Dulles insisted that the German general was acting heroically and selflessly to bring peace to Italy and to spare its land, people, and art treasures from a final, scorched-earth conflagration.

Dulles knew from the beginning that working with Wolff was an extremely risky proposition—not just because of the Allies' strict prohibition against a separate peace deal but because Himmler's right-hand man was certain to be placed high on the list of Nazi war criminals. Even many years later, when the evidence against Wolff had grown to utterly damning proportions, the old spy refused to pass judgment on him. "The conclusions [about Wolff] must be left to history," wrote Dulles in his carefully calibrated Operation Sunrise memoir. He was delaying a judgment that, for many, had long since been obvious.

When Wolff was later confronted with the obscenity of the Nazi leadership's war crimes, he would inevitably plead ignorance, claiming he occupied such a lofty perch in the Reich's clouds that he did not learn about the death camps until the final days of the war. When this tactic failed, he would claim that he had been powerless to stop the mass slaughter, or he would fall back on legalisms and other technical evasions. But the stains on Wolff were not so easily erased.

Karl Wolff, who would go down in history as "one of the unknown giants of Hitler's Reich," was content to operate in the shadows. While little known by the public, however, he played a prominent administrative role in Hitler's lethal assembly line. He was, as *Time* magazine later branded him, the "Bureaucrat of Death."

The Nuremberg trials would firmly establish the principle that administrators of murder—not just the actual executioners—could be found guilty of war crimes. Although he was not a central cog in the daily operations of the Holocaust like Adolf Eichmann, Wolff, as Himmler's top troubleshooter, frequently intervened to ensure the smooth efficiency of the extermination process.

During the Nuremberg trials, a highly incriminating letter written by Wolff would emerge that made it clear how important his intervention could be in keeping the trains rolling to the death camps. In July 1942, after the trains hauling Polish Jews to the Treblinka gas chambers were temporarily halted because of the German military's demand for railcars, Wolff appealed to a Nazi transportation official for help. After the rail shortage was successfully resolved, Wolff sent off a heartfelt letter of thanks.

"I was especially pleased," Wolff wrote the transportation minister in a chillingly bureaucratic note, "to receive the information that, for the last 14 days, a train has been leaving daily for Treblinka with 5,000 members of the chosen people, and that in this way we are in a position to carry out this population movement at an accelerated tempo."

Wolff also played a key administrative role in a series of medical experiments on human subjects at the notorious Dachau camp from 1942 through 1943. The research was conducted by Luftwaffe doctors who were intent on increasing the survival rates of German pilots, and was strongly supported by Himmler, who fancied himself a man of science. In the first round of experiments, human guinea pigs culled by the SS from Dachau's ranks of the damned were forced inside special low-oxygen chambers to determine how long Luftwaffe pilots could fly at high altitudes before passing out. Inside the chambers, victims gasped for air, frantically cried out, and finally collapsed. It was up to the Luftwaffe doctor in charge of the experiments, a sadist named Siegmund Rascher, whether the victims would be revived in time or allowed to die. Rascher oversaw about 150 such high-altitude experiments, of which at least half resulted in death.

A subsequent round of medical experiments at Dachau was aimed at finding the best ways to revive German aviators who were rescued after crashing into the frigid North Sea. Camp inmates were forced to stand naked in freezing weather for up to fourteen hours. Others were submerged in tanks of iced water for three hours at a time. The subjects of the initial freezing experiments all died. But then the doctors added a new twist to their experiments. They "rewarmed" their victim in a hot bath and then revived him further with "animal heat" provided by four female Gypsies. The victim, after being nearly frozen to death, suddenly found his naked body warmly embraced by four women who brought him back to life.

Wolff should have been sitting in the dock at Nuremberg as part of the first round of defendants. But it was the cruder and less-connected executioner Ernst Kaltenbrunner who would hang for the sins of the SS. Nor was Wolff in the dock the following year, when the Doctors' Trial began, though he would be singled out by prosecutors as one of the principal "masterminds" behind the Dachau experiments. Throughout the Nuremberg proceedings and the legal challenges that confronted him in later years, Wolff was watched over by his twin guardian angels—Dulles and Gero von Schulze-Gaevernitz. They made sure that the sword of justice never came down with its full might on SS-Obergruppenführer Karl Wolff. Among the few lives saved by the Operation Sunrise peace gambit, as it turned out, was that of Wolff himself and those of the SS officers who conspired with him.

On May 13, 1945, shortly after the Operation Sunrise surrender, Karl Wolff celebrated his forty-fifth birthday at the villa of the Dukes of Pistoia in Bolzano, the royal estate he had requisitioned as his final SS command post. Before his lunch party began, Wolff relaxed on the villa's terrace with his SS aide and Sunrise partner Eugen Dollmann, who had served as the interpreter for Hitler and Himmler in Italy. "It's really rather pleasant here, Eugenio," remarked the SS-

Obergruppenführer, using his affectionate name for the Italy-besotted Dollmann as the two men gazed at Wolff's children and Dollmann's Alsatian hound gamboling in the rose garden. But Dollmann, who could hear American tanks rumbling nearby, could not let himself enjoy their idyll. "I have a feeling that this is going to be your last birthday in sunny Italy, Herr General," he remarked. Dollmann's grave mood brought a burst of laughter from Wolff. "My dear Eugenio! You're not going to get the wind up in these lovely surroundings? And on my birthday too!"

Shortly afterward, Wolff's wife, Ingeborg, a tall, blond beauty and former countess, who had left her aging, aristocratic husband for her perfect Aryan match, came onto the terrace and announced that lunch was ready.

Dollmann's instincts, as usual, proved correct. As Wolff and his guests—staff officers of the Wehrmacht in dress uniform—sipped champagne in the villa's flower-adorned entrance hall, they suddenly heard the growl of tanks outside. "The Americans," Wolff said in a deflated voice, as he looked out the windows. Soldiers in the white helmets of military policemen burst through the doors, carrying machine guns and herding Wolff's children in front of them. One of their officers, chewing a wad of gum, unceremoniously approached the SS commander and announced that he was under arrest.

Wolff was aghast, protesting indignantly that Allen Dulles, the president's personal representative in Switzerland, had promised him "honorable treatment." But the military police officer was unimpressed. "Put your things in a small case," he snapped at Wolff, still working his Wrigley's. "Go on, get a move on."

As the Obergruppenführer bid farewell to his wife and children outside the villa, a mob of Italians gathered to also send the SS officers on their way, pelting Wolff and Dollmann with rocks and rotten eggs as the MPs stood by laughing. The two Nazi VIPs were then stuffed inside an American jeep and whisked away—first to a gloomy Bolzano dungeon and then, more hospitably, to Cinecittà, the sprawling film studio in Rome that the Allies had transformed into a POW camp.

Wolff began invoking the name of Allen Dulles to anyone who

would listen as soon as he was behind bars. The question of whether Dulles had promised Wolff immunity from war crimes prosecution in return for his Sunrise collaboration would nag the intelligence chief for many years. Dulles would repeatedly insist that Wolff had never asked for such protection and he had never offered it. According to Dulles, the SS commander had maintained all along that he was no war criminal and "he was willing to stand on his record."

In truth, Wolff's growing confidence as he successfully dodged prosecution over the following years derived from the fact that Dulles had indeed offered him immunity. Two of the Swiss intermediaries involved in the Sunrise negotiations would later confirm that such an arrangement had been made. Dulles's negotiating team went so far as to promise Wolff that he and other "decent" and "idealistic" members of the Nazi high command would be allowed to participate in the leadership of postwar Germany. Wolff was even given to believe that he might be awarded the minister of education post.

Dulles threw his cloak of protection over Wolff from the very start. The SS general spent the first days of his confinement as a privileged guest of the U.S. military. He had been warned by Gaevernitz that he might have to spend some time behind bars, to deflect any criticism of preferential treatment. But Wolff enjoyed VIP treatment, receiving better food than other prisoners and even being allowed to wear his full uniform, complete with sidearm. In August, he was transferred to a small U.S.-run POW camp near Gmunden, Austria—a lakeside resort known for its health spas, featuring pinecone and salt-bath treatments. According to a highly embarrassing article that ran in the *New York Herald Tribune*, Wolff enjoyed a pleasant summer idyll on the lake, where he was reunited with his family and even asked for his yacht to be delivered to him.

That summer was the period of greatest jeopardy for Wolff, as the Nuremberg prosecutors selected their first list of defendants and the world outcry for justice was at its peak, on the heels of the appalling revelations about the Final Solution. Justice Robert Jackson and the Allied legal staff considered Wolff to be a primary target, circulating a list that named him one of the "major war criminals." With Hitler and Himmler both dead, Wolff was among the highest Nazi officials to survive the war, clearly outranking most of the defendants who were subsequently put on trial at Nuremberg.

Determined to keep Wolff out of the defendants' dock, however, Dulles went so far as to bury incriminating evidence, including one particularly damning OSS report that blamed the Nazi general not only for the "wholesale slaughter of populations" and "the collective reprisals" against Italian civilians, but also for the torture and murder of OSS agents in his Bolzano SS headquarters. The feelings against Wolff were running understandably high in some OSS quarters, where the SS general was suspected of personally interrogating American intelligence officers. But Dulles betrayed his own men, blocking the OSS report on Wolff from ever reaching the Nuremberg staff. Instead, it was Dulles's portrait of Wolff as a "moderate" and a "gentleman" that was sent to the Nuremberg legal team, along with a recommendation that he not be prosecuted for SS crimes.

Dulles succeeded in keeping Wolff off the Nuremberg defendants list. The general would appear at the trial only as a witness, testifying on behalf of his fellow war criminal Hermann Goering. But as Nuremberg prosecutors prepared for new rounds of trials, and as war crimes tribunals were organized in Italy and other countries that had fallen under the boot of Nazi occupation, Wolff still found himself behind bars. Realizing that the SS general was still not safe from prosecution, Dulles arranged for Wolff to be diagnosed with a nervous disorder, and in spring 1946 he was transferred to a psychiatric institution in Augsburg, Austria.

Wolff knew that Dulles had engineered his psychiatric diagnosis to shield him from prosecution, but he also suspected that it was a way "to prevent me [from] talking." The general knew that he continued to have great leverage over Dulles: if he revealed the immunity deal that the two men had worked out, the spymaster's career would be jeopardized. Wolff was also privy to another Sunrise dirty secret: the extent to which the separate peace pact was a cold betrayal of the United States' and

Britain's wartime Soviet allies. In fact, Dulles was so concerned about what Wolff might be telling his interrogators behind bars that he began to have his conversations secretly taped.

As Wolff's imprisonment stretched on, he grew increasingly frustrated and began talking more freely about the "mutual understanding" that he and Dulles had struck and about the way he had been double-crossed. Wolff's increasingly vocal behavior was not lost on Dulles and the other American and British authorities involved in the Sunrise deal. At one point, his jailers quietly offered him an open door to his freedom. But Wolff did not want the life of a rat on the run, hiding out in Argentina or Chile. He was determined to hold the Sunrise cabal to their deal; he wanted to be fully exonerated and allowed to regain a prominent position in the new Germany.

In February 1947, Wolff played his trump card, writing a letter to President Truman in which he boldly revealed the terms of the Operation Sunrise agreement. Wolff informed Truman that, in return for his cooperation on the secret surrender, "I received from Mr. Dulles and his secretary, Mr. Gaevernitz, an explicit promise" of freedom for himself and his fellow "meritorious" SS collaborators on the Sunrise deal. It was now time, Wolff informed Truman, for the United States to honor the bargain made by Dulles.

The German POW followed up his letter to Truman with an equally emphatic note to Dulles, in which he managed to strike a tone at once courtly and threatening. Wolff insisted that Dulles must come to his aid, and that of his "entire [Sunrise] squadron," to win their "honorable release from captivity." His direct appeal to Dulles, wrote Wolff, "is not only my right but my knightly duty"; by negotiating secretly with the U.S. spymaster, Wolff reminded him, he had "saved your honor and reputation . . . at the risk of our lives."

Wolff stirred the pot further by sending a similar letter to Major General Lyman Lemnitzer, who had worked closely with Dulles as the U.S. Army's point man on the Sunrise negotiations. Lemnitzer shared Dulles's strong anti-Soviet sentiments, and he had colluded with the OSS official to keep the secret talks with Wolff going forward, even after President Roosevelt and the Allied command thought they had pulled the plug on Sunrise. After the German surrender, the ambitious Lemnitzer had also worked with Dulles to promote Sunrise in the press as an espionage triumph. When Wolff's letter reached Lemnitzer, he was stationed at the Pentagon, where he had been appointed to a prestigious position with the Joint Chiefs of Staff. Lemnitzer would ultimately rise to become the Army chief of staff under President Kennedy, where once again his career would be fatefully linked with that of Dulles.

As soon as Lemnitzer received the letter from Wolff, who appealed to him "as one general to another" to make sure the Sunrise deal was honored, Lemnitzer smelled trouble. As with his letter to Dulles, Wolff's appeal to Lemnitzer melded obsequious German courtesy with a flash of steel. Wolff signed off with a clear warning, telling Lemnitzer that he was hoping to resolve the situation "as a comrade" before he was forced to air his grievances "publicly." Lemnitzer fired off a letter to Dulles, who was in Switzerland at the time, telling him that he was "anxious to discuss this matter with you" as soon as Dulles returned home.

Thus began a series of carefully worded letters and private discussions between the two most prominent Americans who were associated with the Sunrise deal. Dulles, who was savvy enough to never put his agreement with Wolff in writing, warned Lemnitzer to be "very careful" in communicating with Wolff. "He has proved to be a clever, tricky and wily customer," Dulles cautioned Lemnitzer. The spymaster appeared to have a certain amount of professional respect for the way the Nazi military man had played him.

The circumspect communications between Dulles and Lemnitzer led to a flurry of behind-the-scenes efforts on Wolff's behalf. The last thing anyone wanted was a "sensational trial," as Dulles put it, where Wolff would undoubtedly spill the entire Sunrise story.

In March 1948, Wolff was transferred to a detention center in Hamburg, and instead of being tried for war crimes, he was put through a much less threatening "denazification" hearing in a German court. Dulles supplied Wolff's defense team with a glowing affidavit that was read aloud in the courtroom and concluded, "In my opinion, General

Wolff's action . . . materially contributed to bringing about the end of the war in Italy." The ever-loyal Gaevernitz showed up as a character witness, testifying for over an hour about Wolff's Sunrise heroism and insisting, falsely, that the SS general had never "demanded any special treatment after the war."

The German court was impressed by the defendant's influential friends. Found guilty of the relatively minor charge of "being a member of the SS with knowledge of its criminal acts," Wolff received a four-year sentence. Through Dulles's lobbying efforts, the sentence was reduced to time already served, and in June 1949, Wolff walked out of the men's prison at Hamburg-Bergedorf a free man. Gaevernitz and other Sunrise intermediaries were there to celebrate the war criminal's release. "It seemed like old times and we missed you greatly," he wrote Dulles.

One of the first actions taken by the newly liberated Wolff was to, once again, demand special treatment. He insisted that the U.S. government owed him at least $45,000 for an itemized list of clothing and family belongings that he claimed were looted by U.S. military police from his SS palace in Bolzano after his arrest. The demand for reparations by Himmler's former right-hand man was, at last, even too much for Dulles. "Between you and me," an exasperated Dulles wrote the following year to his Swiss intelligence comrade Max Waibel, "KW doesn't realize what a lucky man he is not to be spending the rest of his days in jail, and his wisest policy would be to keep fairly quiet about the loss of a bit of underwear, etc. He might easily have lost more than his shirt."

Wolff's journey now came full circle, as the middle-aged SS veteran returned to the advertising field he had abandoned two decades earlier for a career with Hitler. Landing a job as an advertising sales manager with a weekly magazine in Cologne—courtesy yet again of Dulles, who had helped pave the return to civilian life by ensuring he was not subjected to an employment ban—Wolff quickly proved to be a man on his way up. With the "circle of friends" he had made as Himmler's banker, Wolff found it easy to establish contacts with the advertising departments of the leading German companies. As his sales soared, so did his commissions. By 1953, he was prosperous enough to buy a manor for his family on Lake Starnberg in southern Bavaria, complete with a dock and bathhouse.

Wolff's success emboldened him. He began talking more openly about his past to friends and even journalists. He revealed that ten days before Hitler's suicide in a Berlin bunker, the Führer had promoted him to the rank of senior general of the Waffen-SS, the military wing of Himmler's empire.

The general wanted it both ways: he wanted to be seen as one of the clean and honorable Germans, but his pride also had him crowing about his grand and loyal service to Hitler's Reich. Wolff's ambivalence was highlighted again when he told a newsletter published by an SS veterans club that Hitler had known about and "completely approved" of his Operation Sunrise machinations, presumably as a tactic for buying time and splitting the Allies. Wolff, regarded with disdain by his former SS colleagues for his role in Sunrise, might have been trying to ingratiate himself with his old Nazi brethren. But it was a dubious claim. Eugen Dollmann undoubtedly came closer to the truth when he wrote in his memoir that a fading Hitler—pumped full of drugs during their final meeting in the bunker—gave Wolff "a vague sort of permission to maintain the contact he had established with the Americans."

In the mid-1950s, the increasingly self-assured Wolff, convinced that Germany needed his leadership, became politically active again. In 1953, he took a lead role in establishing the Reichsreferat, a neofascist party, and in 1956, he began organizing an association of former SS officers. The old ideas came slithering out once more: the demonization of non-Germanic races and the Bolshevist menace, the glorification of power.

Karl Wolff was eager to return to center stage, and who better to help his quest than his powerful American patron? Wolff had stayed in touch with Dulles through the U.S. occupational authorities stationed in Germany, passing him notes and books related to Operation Sunrise that he thought the spymaster might find interesting. After his release from prison, Wolff had developed a side business with U.S. intelligence agencies, selling information to a notorious espionage freebooter named John "Frenchy" Grombach, who had served in Army intelligence. Grombach gathered information from a far-flung network of SS old boys and other ex-Nazis in Europe, peddling it to the CIA, State Department, and corporate clients. But Wolff knew that his best connection in the American intelligence world was Allen Dulles himself, who by 1953 had become chief of the CIA.

On May 20, 1958, Wolff marched confidently into the U.S. embassy in Bonn and asked to see two CIA officers he knew. Informed that those agents were no longer in Bonn, Wolff was escorted into the office of the CIA station chief. As usual, Wolff thoroughly charmed his host, who later reported that he "was most polite, almost ingratiating for a former General." Wolff, the station chief added, was "sporting a tan which looked as though it had been acquired south of the Alps and exuded prosperity." Wolff informed his CIA host that he wanted to visit the United States. He wanted to see his daughter, who was married to an American, and his son, who was also residing there. He did not mention the other person he wanted to see, but it was obvious to the station chief. Everyone in the agency's upper ranks knew about the CIA director's long and intricate history with Wolff.

Chatting with the Bonn station chief, Wolff soon got to the point. He wanted assurances that he would have no trouble securing a visa for his visit to the United States. Informed about his old wartime collaborator's wishes, Dulles pulled strings on his behalf in Washington. But the two men were never to be reunited in America. Karl Wolff's name still stirred too much unease in the bowels of Washington's bureaucracy. Some foreign service functionaries began asking awkward questions about the general's wartime activities. There were some specters from the past, realized Dulles, that were best left in the past, to be conjured only in one's smoothly crafted memoirs.

Ratlines

Karl Wolff was not the only prominent SS officer who greatly ben-efited from Dulles's Operation Sunrise. In the fall of 1945, former SS colonel Eugen Dollmann, Wolff's principal intermediary during the Sunrise negotiations, found himself living in a gilded cage in Rome. The apartment, which was located on Via Archimede, a quiet, horseshoe-shaped street in the city's exclusive Parioli district, contained few distractions for the bored Dollmann. But he did discover an exten-sive sadomasochistic literary collection left behind by the former tenant, a German mistress of Mussolini, and he whiled away the hours reading about feverishly inventive ways to mortify the flesh. Dollmann was not an entirely free man, since he was a guest of U.S. intelligence officers. But, even though he remained under close surveillance, compared to his accommodations after he and Karl Wolff were arrested in May, the colonel's Parioli lifestyle was sublime.

Before he was spirited off to Rome by the Strategic Services Unit, the agency that replaced the disbanded OSS after the war, the Nazi diplo-mat had been installed in a temporary cell at Cinecittà Studios. Spoiled by years of the best Italian cuisine, Dollmann found the rations at Ci-necittà so distasteful that he considered joining a hunger strike started by fellow POW Gudrun Himmler, the late Reichsführer's daughter. Then he was transferred to a POW camp in Ascona, on picturesque Lake Maggiore, where the daily fare—consisting mainly of watery pea soup—was even more objectionable, and the inmates were forced to sleep in tents that floated away in heavy downpours. Dollmann later had the nerve to compare Ascona to Dachau. "At least in Dachau they had wooden huts," he observed.

Relief for Dollmann came when he was transferred to a low-security prison camp run by the British military in Rimini, on the Adriatic coast. One night, Dollmann found it remarkably easy—one American intelligence agent would call it "suspiciously" easy—to cut through the wires encircling Rimini and flee to Milan, where he knew he would find sanctuary. Here Dollmann presented himself to the well-connected cardinal Alfredo Ildefonso Schuster in the prelate's palazzo adjoining the enormous Gothic cathedral. Dollmann, known as one of Rome's more elegant peacocks during his SS glory days, now sat before the eminent cardinal in a filthy raincoat, looking the worse for wear after his frantic trek from Rimini.

As they sipped liqueur from long-stemmed glasses, Dollmann reflected on how the cardinal always put him in mind of "a delicate alabaster statue." But Schuster, who had worked with Wolff's SS team on the Sunrise deal, was not as refined as all that. The wily cardinal was part of the Vatican elite that had collaborated with Mussolini's fascist regime—and, out of self-interest, he was inclined to help Dollmann now, to avoid an embarrassing war crimes trial. Besides, Schuster thought that men like Dollmann might still play a useful role in postwar Italy; he hoped to recruit the former SS officer in the campaign against the Church's nemesis, the Italian Communists, who had emerged from the war as a powerful political force.

Dollmann, who was conniving by nature but not political, was uninterested in the cardinal's plot, but he was in no position to quibble. He allowed himself to be safely hidden away in a Church-run asylum for wealthy drug addicts, where his fellow inmates included a fading Italian film diva and an emotionally fragile duchess. As he languished among the *delicato* junkies, Dollmann decided to sample some of the forbidden fruit that the screen siren kept stashed in her room, snorting a snowy mound of heroin. For a time, Dollmann—who had much to forget in his life, but was plagued by a detailed memory—seemed in danger of disappearing among the lotus eaters.

Salvation came in the form of James Jesus Angleton, a rising young star in U.S. intelligence who had run the X-2 branch (OSS counterintelligence) in Italy during the war and had stayed behind to use his wiles against the Communists. After tracking down Dollmann in the Milan asylum, Angleton sent a big U.S. Army Buick with a chauffeur to pick him up and drive him to the Eternal City, where he installed Dollmann in the Via Archimede safe house in the Parioli district.

Counterintelligence was the spy craft's deepest mind game—it was not just figuring out the enemy's next moves in advance and blocking them, but learning to think like him. Not yet thirty, Angleton was already being talked about in American and British intelligence circles as one of the masters of the field. He had been educated in British prep schools and at Yale, where he had edited the avant-garde poetry magazine *Furioso* and courted the likes of Ezra Pound and e.e. cummings as contributors, and he seemed to bring an artist's intuition to his profession. But he could get lost in the convolutions of his own fevered mind, which drove him to prowl the streets of Rome late at night in a black overcoat so big it looked like a cape, on the hunt for clues about the growing Communist menace, and to crawl around on his office floor at 69 Via Sicilia in search of hidden bugging devices.

Angleton was as gaunt as a saint. (His wife, Cicely, would rhapsodize about his "El Greco face." His colleagues called Angleton "the Cadaver.") He smoked incessantly, and his bony frame was wracked by consumptive fits of coughing. When he introduced himself to Dollmann, Angleton must have struck the colonel as yet another strung-out soul. But Angleton's addiction was of a more ideological nature.

As Angleton sat with Dollmann in the comfortable, five-room apartment on Via Archimede, the young spy explained his vision for the new world. Dollmann felt bound to listen politely, since Angleton had gone to the trouble of plucking him from Cardinal Schuster's madhouse. But Dollmann had heard it all before—with even more fervor—from the Führer himself and his SS overlords: how Bolshevism must be crushed for the new world to be born, why there must be no rules in a clash like this between civilization and barbarity.

Angleton, however, was lost in his own passion. He had found strong support for his views from Allen Dulles in the months after the war, as Dulles lingered in Europe, hoping that President Truman would anoint him commander of the shadow war against the Soviet Union. In October 1945, Dulles visited Rome with Clover, ostensibly to revive their marriage after the strains of separation during the war. But he had another mission as well: to organize the Italian front in the new Cold War. Angleton, who was wired into the Vatican, helped arrange a secret meeting for Dulles with Pope Pius XII, who had maintained a mutually beneficial arrangement with Mussolini's regime and was a determined foe of Communism.

Angleton looked up to Dulles as a mentor—a powerful figure in the mold of his adored father, James Hugh Angleton, an international businessman who had paved his son's path into the spy trade and continued to play an influential role in the young spook's life. Dulles would remain a strong, paternal figure for Angleton junior throughout their deeply entwined intelligence careers. In Rome, the two men conferred about the growing "Red challenge" and "the drastic, sub-rosa measures required to meet it," as a colleague put it. These extreme measures included recruiting agents "without overscrupulous concern for [their] past fascist affiliations."

Dollmann was high on their list of such recruitment targets. With his continental sophistication and network of contacts, Dollmann might prove a valuable espionage asset on the strategic front lines in both Italy and Germany. As Angleton sat with the well-groomed colonel in the Via Archimede safe house now, the American opened a bottle of Scotch whisky that he had brought along and carried on with his enthusiastic recruitment pitch. But as he listened, sipping the good Scotch, Dollmann was filled with utter contempt for his guest. "He was talking like a young university lecturer who dabbled a bit in espionage in his spare time," mused the colonel. His views struck the world-weary German as typically American—naïve and overblown.

As for Dulles, Dollmann had only contempt for his benefactor, whom he later called "a leather-faced Puritan archangel . . . [the type] who had fled from the European sink of iniquity on the *Mayflower* and now returned to scourge the sinners of the old world." He would ridicule the way that Dulles had misrepresented himself at their secret Sunrise meetings in Switzerland as President Roosevelt's personal emissary, delivering little speeches to Wolff and Dollmann about how "delighted" FDR supposedly was about the SS officers' selfless mission for peace. "Wasn't that nice now?" sneered Dollmann. "Such manly, upright and heartening words from President Roosevelt and his special representative in Europe, Mr. Allen W. Dulles!"

While Dollmann was unimpressed with Angleton's political lecture, he did appreciate the fake identity card the young spy gave him. The document—which identified him as an Italian employee of an American organization—afforded Dollmann the confidence to venture into the streets of his beloved Rome without fear of being molested by the authorities. Sprung from his apartment, the colonel found himself drawn to some of his favorite old haunts. He strolled through the fashionable Via Condotti shopping district, where he paid a visit to the Bulgari jewelry shop.

In the old days, he had been treated like royalty by the Bulgari brothers, who would take him on tours of their vaults beneath the Tiber River, where there was a red room for rubies, a blue room for sapphires, and a green room for emeralds. The Bulgaris would pour him Napoleon brandy as they showed off the crown jewels of the late czar and other dazzling treasures. But those pleasant days were long gone. This time, when he suddenly appeared in the luxury shop, Giorgio Bulgari greeted him as if he were a ghost. "We were all afraid you had been killed," the jeweler told Dollmann, after he recovered from his shock.

During the war, Giorgio Bulgari had been so revolted by the deportation of Rome's Jews—an order stamped by Dollmann's boss, Wolff—that he and his wife hid three Jewish women in their own home. Now, gazing at the resurrected SS colonel, the jeweler undoubtedly wished Dollmann *was* dead. And Dollmann knew it.

Afraid he'd been killed? That was rich. Bulgari's false concern infuriated Dollmann, but he adopted his usual droll manner. "How very amusing. People like me don't just disappear forever like that."

Dollmann always liked to give the impression that he was too cosmopolitan to indulge in the Nazis' anti-Jewish mania. But now he felt offended by Bulgari's forced courtesy; Bulgari "sickened" him—he was a "corpulent Levantine . . . [with] fleshy lips [and a] greasy smile." Dollmann turned abruptly and fled the shop.

Once upon a time, Dollmann had had a love affair with Italy, and he was certain that his sunny "arcadia," as he called it, returned his ardor. But now he was no longer certain. Dollmann had arrived in Italy two decades earlier, long before the war, as a young graduate student in Renaissance history. The young German was well educated, fluent in Italian, and boasted some sort of connection to the doomed Habsburg dynasty. He was also gay and charming, and he quickly shed as much of his stolid German upbringing as he could in favor of la dolce vita. With his slickly groomed hair, sleek Italian suits, and year-round tan, Dollmann went completely native, becoming Eugenio instead of Eugen.

Dollmann had been embraced by the German diplomatic set in Rome, who appreciated his nuanced grasp of the local language and customs, and by the Italian aristocratic set, who found him an amusing decoder of all things Deutsch. His binational skills were increasingly in demand as the two countries' fates grew more closely linked. He was sought out by a *principessa* named Donna Vittoria, who was the reigning queen of Roman salons. Her soirees, held at her otherworldly palazzo in the imperial ruins of Teatro Marcello, were frequented by Mussolini's daughter Edda and her husband, Count Ciano, as well as the leading Italian film stars of the day. She very much hoped to have Hitler, too, as an honored guest someday, the *principessa* confided to Dollmann.

In Naples, he was invited to the midnight entertainments at Duchess Rosalba's decaying mansion, festivities so lavishly debauched that they could have inspired a young Fellini. One night the lady of the house greeted Dollmann as she reclined on a divan and was attended to by two slyly grinning female dwarves and a well-built retainer packed into a form-fitting suit. The dwarves later appeared on a stage with a troupe of other diminutive performers, who enacted a long and baroque melodrama for the amusement of Duchess Rosalba's guests. Dollmann was haunted not just by the odd performance but by the strange smile that his hostess fixed on him. The duchess, he noted, had "a simultaneously charming and inhuman mouth." He later learned the story of her deformity. The duchess liked to prowl Naples's rough waterfront bars for her handsome henchmen, replacing them in quick succession with one rugged seaman after another. One night she was attacked with a knife by one such jealous sailor, who left the mark of his fury on her once beautiful face.

But not even this decadent world could prepare Dollmann for the life he began when he joined the SS, where he would rise to become the link between the courts of Hitler and Mussolini. Dollmann later tried to make sense of why he had enlisted in Himmler's death's-head corps. It wasn't political ambition that drove him—he insisted that he had none. And it wasn't monetary reward. "I [already] lived well and comfortably, and my life, after I had yielded to my so-called motives, was no better than before, only more arduous." Was it the way he looked in his trimly tailored SS uniform? Vanity was always a factor with Dollmann. Years later, he proudly displayed photos of himself standing in the very center of history, between Hitler and his visiting Italian dignitaries, gazing into the Führer's magnetic eyes, ready to translate his every momentous word. Dollmann, always up to date on the latest Rome gossip, became a court favorite of Hitler. He was at the Führer's side whenever Hitler and his retinue descended on Italy, and he was there whenever Mussolini or his top ministers trekked to summits in Germany.

By serving as the essential diplomatic link between Germany and Italy, Dollmann ensured that his sojourn in his adopted land would not be interrupted by the coming war. Dollmann would point to this as the primary reason why he made his Faustian bargain. Italia was the great passion of his life. "I loved Italy with the doomed love of all German romantics."

It was the most peculiar of ironies, and one that Dollmann and his intimates no doubt privately relished. The man who kept the Axis partners smoothly aligned, with his impressive language and social skills, was a highly educated, arts-loving homosexual who enjoyed trading in the most salacious gossip about the personalities who ruled Germany and Italy. Dollmann was, in short, precisely the type of person the Nazis sent to the gas chambers. But instead, Hitler's interpreter was free to attend gay and lesbian orgies in Venice, a city whose shadows offered some protection from the authorities' prying eyes. And he had the pleasure of going on shopping safaris with Eva Braun, Hitler's companion, during her Italian holidays.

Braun was mad for crocodile shoes and accessories. "She loved crocodile in every shape and form, and returned to her hotel looking as if she had come back from a trip up the Congo rather than along the Tiber."

Dollmann was fond of Braun, a sweet and simple young woman who confided her sad life to him. She was known throughout the world as the German strongman's mistress, but, as she confessed to Dollmann, there was no sexual intimacy between her and the Führer. "He is a saint," Braun told Dollmann wistfully. "The idea of physical contact would be for him to defile his mission. Many times we sit and watch the sun come up after spending the whole night talking. He says to me that his only love is Germany and to forget it, even for a moment, would shatter the mystical forces of his mission."

Dollmann strongly suspected that the Führer had other passions besides Germany. On Christmas Eve 1923, when he was a university student in Munich, Dollmann had been invited to an extravagant, candlelit party at the home of General Otto von Lossow, who had helped put down Hitler's Beer Hall putsch in November 1923. During the evening, Lossow took Dollmann and some of his other guests into his parlor, where he entertained them by reading selections from Hitler's thick police dossier. "In a café near the university on the evening of, Herr Hitler was observed . . ." Lossow's voice was matter-of-fact as he read through the depositions and eyewitness reports about Germany's future leader. The general's small audience listened in rapt silence, transfixed by the portrait of a Hitler who was more interested in boyish men than in national politics.

These were the sorts of tales that Dollmann kept tucked away— stories that would help the consummate survivor navigate what he called the "witches' cauldron" of Rome as well as Berlin's dark labyrinth. As the Nazis' main fixer in Rome, it helped to know everything he could about the dangerous men with whom he was dealing.

The Nazi official Dollmann most dreaded escorting around Italy was Reinhard Heydrich, Himmler's top executioner. "Now there was a man clearly meant to be murdered by someone or other," Dollmann observed years later. "He was a daemonic personality, a Lucifer with cold blue eyes." One night, Heydrich demanded that Dollmann take him to Naples's finest brothel. Two dozen half-naked women representing the full spectrum of the female form—from "slim gazelles to buxom Rubenesque beauties"—were arranged for Heydrich's inspection in the brothel's ornate lobby, with its gilt-edged mirrors and frescoes of rosy nymphs. Heydrich gazed at the women on display with his blank, shark eyes. Considering the SS butcher's reputation, Dollmann did not know what to expect next. Suddenly Heydrich flung a fistful of shiny gold coins across the marble floor. "Then he jumped up, Lucifer personified, and clapped his hands. With a sweeping gesture, he invited the girls to pick up the gold. A *Walpurgisnacht* orgy ensued. Fat and thin, ponderous and agile, the [women] scrambled madly across the *salotto* floor on all fours."

Afterward, Heydrich looked pale and spent, as if he himself had joined in the frenzy. He coolly thanked Dollmann and disappeared into the night. The interpreter was glad to see Heydrich go. He was, said Dollmann, "the only man I instinctively feared."

History has come to judge Eugen Dollmann as "a self-serving opportunist who prostituted himself to fascism," in the words of legal scholar Michael Salter, but not a fanatic like the men he served. Nevertheless, as war criminal proceedings got under way in Nuremberg in the fall of 1945, Dollmann knew that he was at high risk of prosecution. The Nuremberg trials, where Foreign Minister Joachim von Ribbentrop and Ambassador Franz von Papen were both convicted, firmly established that diplomats like Dollmann who moved in rarefied Nazi circles were not immune from judicial reckoning.

Dollmann was perhaps at even greater risk in Italy, where passions ran high regarding Nazi massacres of Italian civilians, such as the infamous slaughter of 335 prisoners in the Ardeatine Caves near Rome in March 1944. Although Roberto Rossellini modeled the effeminate, sadistic SS captain Bergmann on Dollmann in his postwar film *Rome, Open City*, Dollmann was not directly involved in the Ardeatine atrocity; in reality, the colonel had no taste for brutality. After the war, Dollmann claimed that he had once even rescued several Italian partisans who were being burned alive by fascist thugs. Regardless of his degree of guilt or innocence, however, Dollmann was the most visible symbol of the Nazi occupation of Rome. Italians were all too familiar with the numerous newspaper photos of his slim, *ben vestito* figure taken at social events in Mussolini's Palazzo Quirinale or the Vatican. In the fall of 1945, as he strolled around Rome with his fake ID card, Dollmann was acutely aware that if he fell into the wrong hands—particularly those of Italian Communists—he could be lynched.

Dollmann's anxieties were heightened when American agents installed two former SS colleagues in his Rome apartment—including the notorious Colonel Walter Rauff, who had served as Karl Wolff's second-in-command in northern Italy—because he knew that the hideout might now attract increased interest from Nazi hunters. Dollmann, who regarded Rauff as "one of my most disagreeable acquaintances," was well aware of his new roommate's past. In 1941, Rauff had overseen the development and operation of a fleet of "Black Raven" vans, in which victims were sealed inside and asphyxiated with exhaust fumes. As many as 250,000 people on the war's eastern front were murdered in Rauff's vehicles, which were eventually replaced by the gas chambers of Auschwitz and Dachau. "In my opinion," Dollmann mordantly remarked, "he was quite certainly due for the high jump [at Nuremberg] when they got round to him." But Rauff had managed to save his neck by prudently jumping on board the Operation Sunrise bandwagon with Wolff.

Weary of his roommate's baleful presence, Dollmann often fled the Via Archimede apartment to go to the movies. As he sat in the dark day after day, he began getting the prickling sensation that he was being followed. One afternoon in November 1946, as the colonel watched a trifle titled *Kisses You Dream Of* at his neighborhood cinema, Dollmann felt a firm hand on his shoulder and heard a voice of authority: "Kindly leave the cinema with me." He was taken into custody by a plainclothes detective who was accompanied by two armed carabinieri and then whisked away to a nearby police station.

Dollmann and his fellow SS escapees had been tracked for months by the 428th U.S. Army Counterintelligence Corps (CIC), a detachment of Nazi hunters based in Rome. Major Leo Pagnotta, the Italian American who was second-in-command of the CIC unit, was a sharp investigator. He figured out that Dollmann, who knew it was unwise to show his face too much on the streets, would sooner or later reconnect with the Italian chauffeur who had driven him around during his SS days. Dollmann did indeed contact the chauffeur, but Pagnotta had gotten to him first, making him an offer he couldn't refuse. "If you see Dollmann and you don't tell me," Pagnotta had told the driver, "I'll arrest you and you'll be shot." The chauffeur quickly gave up Dollmann, pinpointing when and where he would be dropped off at the cinema.

Now, as Dollmann sat waiting in the police station holding room, the door suddenly opened and Major Pagnotta walked in. The two men took an immediate dislike to each other. Dollmann was predisposed to look down on Americans, whom he found in general to be a crass, illiterate, and mongrelized people. To make matters worse, this one was "rather fat"—a cardinal sin with Dollmann—and the American didn't bother with any social niceties, treating the Nazi fugitive like "a pretty low sort of criminal."

The situation appeared bleak for Dollmann—his next stop could well be Nuremberg. But he knew that he had an ace up his sleeve, and he immediately played it. Dollmann took a piece of paper from his pocket and handed it to Pagnotta. "Please call this number," he told him. "Ask for Major Angleton. He knows who I am."

Major Pagnotta was quite familiar with Major Angleton. In fact, Pagnotta's team of Nazi hunters was headquartered in the same building on Via Sicilia as Angleton's rival intelligence operation, the Strategic Services Unit's X-2 branch. Pagnotta's CIC unit was on the first floor, Angleton was on the second, and British intelligence was on the third. Pagnotta and his men didn't trust Angleton—they thought he was "a devious and arrogant son of a bitch," in the words of Pagnotta's aide William Gowen. Angleton seemed to work more closely with the British spies than with his U.S. Army colleagues, and the British treated him like one of their own. Before transferring to Rome in 1944, Angleton had been stationed in London, where his X-2 unit was overseen by British intelligence.

The espionage scene in postwar Rome was rife with rivalries and competing agendas. Some U.S. intelligence units, such as Leo Pagnotta's, were determined Nazi hunters. But other operatives, such as Angleton, had very different objectives. This spy-versus-spy atmosphere made Pagnotta's investigative work extremely complicated.

As Pagnotta tracked top Nazi fugitives in Italy, many of whom had escaped from the British-run prisoner-of-war camp in Rimini, it became clear to him that he was often working at cross-purposes with Angleton and British intelligence. One of the most notorious fugitives, SS captain Karl Hass, who had overseen the Ardeatine Caves massacre, mysteriously escaped every time Pagnotta's team tracked him down and turned him over to British occupational authorities in Italy. Finally, after his fourth arrest, Hass escaped for good. It was not until many years later that Hass was tracked down in Argentina and extradited to stand trial in Italy for his role in the massacre. Hass received a life sentence, but by then he was an old man, and his failing health kept him out of prison.

Unsurprisingly, after capturing Dollmann, Pagnotta decided to hang on to him, placing him in a U.S. military prison in Rome instead of handing him over to the British. In the beginning, Dollmann was a cooperative prisoner, readily revealing the address of his apartment on Via Archimede. When Pagnotta's team raided the apartment, they narrowly missed catching Dollmann's infamous roommate Walter Rauff, who managed to flee to Bari, on the Adriatic coast, where he boarded a ship for Alexandria, Egypt—the next stop in the Nazi exterminator's long and winding ratline. Rauff would cap his bloody career in Chile, where he became a top adviser to DINA, military dictator Augusto Pinochet's own Gestapo. When Rauff died in 1984—at age seventy-seven, after successfully rebuffing years of extradition attempts—hundreds of aging Nazis flocked to his funeral in Santiago, where he was laid to rest amid loud salutes of "Heil Hitler!"

Pagnotta did snare another fugitive who was living in the Via Archimede apartment, SS officer Eugen Wenner, who had also played a part in the Operation Sunrise maneuvers. It soon dawned on Pagnotta's team that Angleton was operating a safe house on Via Archimede for a stream of Nazi fugitives who were connected to Sunrise and other Dulles operations. They even traced the car driven by Dollmann's chauffeur to Angleton's father, who kept a villa nearby in Parioli.

Nobody would get to know the deeply clever ways of Angleton in Rome better than William Gowen, who, at age eighteen, was one of the youngest members of Pagnotta's crew of Nazi hunters.

It was only a matter of time before Jim Angleton—who made it his business to meet the important people in postwar Rome—crossed paths with Bill Gowen, who, despite his youth, was known to be well connected. Gowen's father, Franklin, was a career diplomat who had served under Ambassador Joseph P. Kennedy in London and was currently the assistant to Myron C. Taylor, the former U.S. Steel chairman whom FDR had appointed as his special representative to the Vatican during the war. Gowen's family had money—one of his ancestors had been president of the Philadelphia Stock Exchange—but they were by tradition Democrats. Roosevelt was fond of Franklin Gowen, whom he regarded as one of the few blue-blooded members of the diplomatic corps he could trust.

The younger Gowen brought a special sense of mission to his Army counterintelligence job. His family owned property in Italy and had deep roots there. His grandfather Morris was living in Florence when war broke out. Although he was Episcopalian, Morris Gowen was denounced as a Jew and put on a train for Auschwitz. When the Germans realized he was American, he was taken off the train in northern Italy and put in an SS encampment, where the seventy-seven-year-old man died in July 1944 of what his death certificate stated was "exhaustion." Bill Gowen's family had a number of Jewish family friends in Italy who suffered similar fates. "When I got to Rome in 1946 as a young soldier," he later remarked, "I didn't need to read about the Nazi terror. My family had been touched by it."

All in all, young Bill Gowen had a pedigree that Angleton clearly found both appealing and threatening. Gowen's dedication as a war crimes investigator posed a distinct problem for Angleton, who viewed Nazi fugitives like Dollmann and Rauff in more pragmatic terms. And the Gowen family's Italian background also infringed on Angleton's turf. "I think that between the father and son, the Angletons thought they had a lock on Italy, and on the Vatican," Gowen observed. "Jim Angleton was very jealous of my family, because he wanted to have a monopoly on Italy. And anything that might threaten him had to be taken care of."

Angleton made a point of keeping Gowen close in Rome. In early 1947, Gowen and his father were invited to the Italian wedding of Angleton's sister, Carmen, where Angleton chatted up the younger Gowen and insisted they meet for lunch someday. They got together soon afterward at Angleton's favorite spot, a Jewish restaurant near Rome's once thriving ghetto. Angleton was fond of the restaurant's house specialty—*carciofi fritti*—and he took charge of ordering when the waiter arrived at their table. To Gowen's surprise, however, Angleton—who presented himself as an expert on all things Italian—displayed so little mastery of the language that his younger lunch companion had to take over communication with the puzzled waiter. Gowen, who was born in his family's Livorno villa, was impressively fluent in the local tongue. It was yet another thing that Angleton found irritating about Gowen.

Lunch companions like Bill Gowen always made Angleton uneasy. Gowen—whose family was filled with bankers, lawyers, diplomats, and Episcopalian ministers—had a solid Social Register background. And, despite his tender age, he was already a man of the world, having shuttled around Europe's diplomatic posts with his father. With his cheery mid-Atlantic accent and his continental sartorial flair, Gowen seemed born and bred for the top tier.

Angleton was also raised in wealth. But his father, Hugh, was not the Main Line type. He was a swashbuckling, self-made man who had swept up his future wife, Carmen, when she was a teenager in Mexico, after he joined General John "Black Jack" Pershing's 1916 expedition to capture Pancho Villa. Despite young Angleton's British affectations, his face would always carry traces of his south-of-the-border heritage. Even as he rose to the top ranks of the U.S. intelligence establishment, he remained something of an outsider in that thoroughly WASPy world, marked not just by his brilliant, idiosyncratic personality but by his mixed ethnicity. Angleton was, in short, what his Nazi associates would call a mongrelized American.

Gowen might have been Angleton's social superior, with much better connections to the Roosevelt and Truman administrations, but in the end it was Angleton who prevailed in the spy games. In May 1947, after Dollmann had spent several bleak months in prison in Rome, Angleton succeeded in outwitting Pagnotta and Gowen and getting the former SS colonel transferred to a U.S. military prison in Frankfurt, where he was safe from the wrath of Italian political enemies and prosecutors. The clever Angleton had Dollmann smuggled out of his Roman cell on a stretcher. In Germany, Dollmann was soon switched to even more agreeable accommodations: a cozy guesthouse in the lush Main countryside that he shared with other former Nazi VIPs, such as the notorious propagandist "Axis Sally," and Otto Skorzeny, the scar-faced Waffen-SS colonel who was famous for a daring glider raid that rescued Mussolini from mountaintop captivity. By November, after the U.S. military released him from incarceration, Dollmann was a completely free man.

There was sharp disagreement over suspected war criminals like Dollmann within the U.S. military command overseeing the occupation of Germany. General George Price Hays, a decorated officer who led the 10th Mountain Division's assault on Monte Cassino during the Allies' Italian campaign and commanded the 2nd Infantry Division's artillery on Omaha Beach during D-day, was angered by the kid-glove treatment given Dulles's Sunrise Nazis. Hays, who became high commissioner for the U.S. occupation zone in Germany, tartly pointed out in a November 1947 memo that it was the U.S. Army that was responsible for the surrender of Nazi troops in Italy, not Dulles's secret maneuvers. Hays was adamantly opposed to granting amnesty to "possible war criminals or war profiteers" like Dollmann, which, he observed, would "condone their crimes without proper examination." Nonetheless, by 1947, many in the American military hierarchy shared the Dulles-Angleton view that fighting Communism was a bigger priority than prosecuting fascist war criminals.

Even after securing Dollmann's release, Angleton remained nervous about Bill Gowen. The young man knew too much about Angleton's string-pulling on behalf of Dollmann and the other Nazi fugitives who had been harbored on Via Archimede. Angleton suspected that Gowen's CIC unit kept extensive files on the ratlines that had allowed Sunrise collaborators like Dollmann and Rauff to escape justice. He was determined to see what was in those files—an interest undoubtedly shared by Angleton's mentor, Dulles, as well as their allies in the U.S. intelligence complex.

In November 1947, as Dollmann walked free, the U.S. military moved to shut down its Nazi-hunting operation in Rome. That month, Bill Gowen hopped a train for Frankfurt, which was to be his new base of operations. By the time the slow-moving train crawled into the Frankfurt station, it was after midnight. A jeep driven by a hulking soldier with CIC insignia on his uniform was waiting for Gowen, who threw his duffel bag into the vehicle and jumped in.

Frankfurt was still pulverized from the war. One of the few buildings left miraculously untouched by Allied bombing was the massive

IG Farben complex, which now served as the headquarters of the Supreme Allied Command. The city's demolished landscape was illuminated only by scattered pinpoints of light, and the darkness closed in on Gowen and his driver as the jeep pulled away from the train platform.

"I guess you're tired," the driver said. "You'll want to go to a hotel."

Gowen, exhausted from the long train ride, nodded emphatically. But instead of heading toward a hotel, the soldier drove deeper into the city's ruins. Now the only light came from the jeep's headlamps.

"Where are we going?" asked Gowen.

"I just want to show you something," said the soldier. There was nothing to be seen, only dark piles of rubble.

"I've been to Germany before—I just want to go to bed," Gowen said.

But the jeep kept creeping slowly through the night shadows. Suddenly the driver came to a halt, jumped out, and told Gowen to follow him. Gowen didn't like his situation. "He was armed and I wasn't. I was alarmed, and I'm normally not scared." Gowen cautiously followed the soldier, walking slowly behind him into the gloom. Gowen didn't know how far they had walked when the soldier abruptly turned around and headed back to the jeep. When they got to the vehicle, Gowen immediately realized that his duffel bag was missing.

"I wasn't dumb enough to ask him where my bag was," Gowen recalled years later. "I knew what had happened. I knew what they were looking for." As it turned out, there were no intelligence files in Gowen's stolen bag. But the story wasn't over.

In January 1948, while Gowen was still stationed in Germany with Army intelligence, he received a transatlantic phone call from syndicated columnist Drew Pearson. The influential Washington journalist told Gowen that he was working on a hot scoop and that Gowen was at the center of it. Pearson was going to report that Ferenc Vajta, a fugitive from war crimes charges in Hungary, where he had worked as an anti-Semitic propagandist for the fascist Arrow Cross Party, had slipped into the United States illegally—with the help of young Nazi hunter Bill Gowen. Pearson claimed he had proof: documents that showed Gowen had worked closely with Vajta on various covert missions. As he listened to Pearson, Gowen was so flabbergasted that he didn't know what to say. Pearson's exclusive story ran in newspapers across America on January 18 and was amplified further by his coast-to-coast radio broadcast.

There was some truth to Pearson's report. Gowen did indeed know Vajta from his days in Rome, when he had used the Hungarian as an informer to help track the notorious Croatian fugitive Ante Pavelić, the fascist leader of the Ustaše movement who led a genocidal campaign in the Balkans during the war that was so extreme he had to be restrained by German authorities. With the help of Ferenc Vajta, Gowen had traced Pavelić to a villa atop the Aventine Hill. Pavelić was under the protection of Croatian officials in the Vatican and other fascist sympathizers. From his villa, Pavelić was able to sneak into nearby safe houses through a series of secret passageways that honeycombed the Aventine.

Gowen was perfectly willing to rely on lesser criminals like Vajta to locate much bigger targets like Pavelić. But he had had nothing to do with providing Vajta a special State Department security clearance and slipping him into the United States. That sleight of hand was likely performed by Frank Wisner, a close collaborator of Dulles's from their days in the OSS who had recently been appointed head of the State Department's clandestine operations unit, the Office of Policy Coordination.

But it was Gowen who would take the fall for the Vajta escapade. It did not take him long to figure out who was responsible for setting him up. Pearson had been fed the false story by Raymond Rocca, Angleton's deputy in Rome.

Pearson's exposé effectively ended Gowen's budding intelligence career. Gowen never stopped trying to clear his name. At one point, he managed to get an appointment to see Dulles after Dulles became CIA director, but when Gowen showed up at the agency's headquarters in Washington to plead his case, he was told that the spymaster had been called overseas.

Years after both men returned to America, Angleton continued to keep an eye on Gowen. Back in Washington, where he eventually became the all-powerful chief of CIA counterintelligence, Angleton invited Gowen to lunch at the Army-Navy Club and even to his home in Virginia. "You know, he was a very devious character," Gowen said, "but he wanted to give me the impression that he was very friendly. He introduced me to his wife, Cicely, and their children, who were very young at the time." Angleton's betrayal of Gowen hovered silently in the air. "I never discussed it openly with him, I never trusted Angleton enough to do that." Both men knew who had won the power struggle in Rome. But they also knew that the secret history they shared had the power to undo Angleton's grand career and expose the underside of Sunrise.

Intelligence reports do not normally make for entertaining reading. Few station chiefs come close to having the literary touch of one-time spies like Graham Greene, David Cornwell (John le Carré), or Ian Fleming. But, following his release from U.S. military detention in 1947, Eugen Dollmann's espionage career became such a flamboyant mess that he inspired some of the most colorful memoranda ever produced by the U.S. intelligence bureaucracy. Reading through these declassified CIA documents fills one with awe for Dollmann's endless powers of reinvention, and a sense of wonder as to why men as knowing as Dulles and Angleton ever saw him as spy material.

U.S. surveillance of Dollmann began getting interesting in 1951, when he was located in a suite at the posh Hotel Paradiso, overlooking Lake Lugano in Switzerland, near northern Italy. By then, the colonel's high life was beginning to catch up with him. He was reported to be in financial distress and looking for ways to make some quick cash. Among the schemes he was pondering was writing his memoirs—which he was promising would be dishy—and hustling various Nazi documents he claimed were authentic, including some supposedly written by Hitler. The colonel was shaking down the CIA for 200,000 lire in return for the "exclusive" rights to examine the documents.

Dulles and the CIA knew that there was great potential for embarrassment with Dollmann. As the years passed, the agency's memos on the colorful SS veteran revealed rising levels of anxiety and exasperation.

In November 1951, Dollmann was reported to be in "close contact" with Donald Jones, which was an intriguing twist, since Jones was the OSS daredevil whom Dulles had asked to rescue Karl Wolff from the Italian partisans during the war. Jones was "still presumed to be an agent of U.S. intelligence," but the memo made clear that Dollmann's contact with him was not strictly professional. "The two are now divided because of a quarrel, presumed to have originated over a question of money, or perhaps jealousy, since both are suspected of being sexual perverts." The memo concluded that Dollmann's value as "an agent or informer" was "uncertain . . . he is not the man he was in 1940–45."

Dollmann, no doubt, would have readily agreed. For one thing, he had less money. And he was stuck in purgatory in Switzerland rather than enjoying the sweet life in his beloved Italy because U.S. agents had warned him they still could not guarantee his safety there.

Nonetheless, Dollmann would soon find himself in Italy—at least briefly—after he outstayed his welcome in Switzerland. According to a U.S. intelligence report, Dollmann was expelled from Switzerland in February 1952 after he was caught having sex with a Swiss police official. In desperation, Dollmann appealed to his old fascist friends in the Italian church, and he was spirited across the border and given temporary sanctuary at a Franciscan monastery in Milan. Dollmann's savior this time, Father Enrico Zucca, was famous for his role in raising Mussolini's body from the grave on Easter 1946 in preparation for the day when Il Duce would be reburied with full honors on Rome's Capitoline Hill. The abbot had less spectacular plans for Dollmann. He slipped a monk's habit on him and smuggled him onto a boat in Genoa, from where Dollmann was shipped to General Franco's fascist paradise in Spain.

In Madrid, Dollmann came under the protection of former Nazi commando leader Otto Skorzeny, who had put together a wide-ranging racket, trading in arms and helping SS fugitives flee justice. Skorzeny was joined for a time in Spain by Hjalmar Schacht, who had been acquitted at Nuremberg and would parlay his reputation as Hitler's banker into a postwar career as an international financial consultant.

Schacht knew where much of the wealth plundered from Europe by German corporations and Nazi officials had been hidden, and Skorzeny used this inside knowledge to help finance his SS ratlines. Angleton also found Skorzeny's services useful, and he kept in regular touch with the entrepreneurial ex-Nazi.

Dollmann undertook errands for Skorzeny's international neo-Nazi circuit. But Dollmann was no good at the freelance espionage game. In October 1952, he flew to Germany on some sort of political mission to make contact with German youth groups. His plans were betrayed and he was arrested at the airport as soon as he landed. The authorities accused him of traveling on a false passport, and he didn't bother denying it. Even in his native Germany, Dollmann was a man without a country. No government wanted to claim him—at least not openly.

A November 1952 CIA memo reported that Dollmann was back in Rome. He started haunting his favorite cinemas again, but this time it nearly proved fatal when "he was noticed by certain Communist elements" in the theater and had to be "rescued by the police from a threatening mob."

Still desperate for cash in Rome, Dollmann again tried his hand at selling Hitler documents that he insisted were genuine. This time he was dangling an Operation Sunrise angle that Dulles certainly found compelling. Among the papers in his possession, Dollmann swore, was a letter from Hitler to Stalin proposing a separate peace between Germany and Russia. Such a letter would have put Dulles's own Operation Sunrise deal in a much better light. If Hitler and Stalin really did discuss their own pact near the end of the war, it made Dulles look like a brilliant chess player instead of an insubordinate troublemaker. Dulles's friends at *Life* magazine let it be known that they would pay a staggering $1 million for such a letter. But Dollmann apparently never produced it.

Dollmann's moneymaking schemes grew more frantic. In December 1952, he quietly reached out to Charles Siragusa, a federal narcotics agent in the U.S. embassy in Rome with close ties to the CIA. Siragusa had proved very useful to Angleton over the years, as a bagman for political payoffs and as a link to the criminal underworld when the agency required the Mafia's services. Dollmann had his own interesting offer for Siragusa. He proposed becoming a paid informant for the narcotics agent and infiltrating the neo-Nazi movement in Vienna, which he claimed was financing its activities by dealing cocaine.

Dollmann's offer smacked of desperation, but, in fact, he was already spying on other ex-Nazi colleagues for the CIA. At the same time, in true Dollmann fashion, he was also hiring himself out to these neo-Nazi groups and reporting back to them about U.S. intelligence activities. As if this web of competing loyalties was not complicated enough, while Dollmann was living in Madrid by the grace of the Franco government, he was also working as a British spy.

By 1952, CIA station chiefs in Europe had grown deeply leery of Dollmann. That spring, an agency memo circulating among the field stations in Germany, Italy, and Spain warned "against [the operational] use of Dollmann . . . because he had already been involved with several intelligence organizations in Western Europe since 1945; his reputation for blackmail, subterfuge and double-dealing is infamous; [and] he is homosexual." At one point, CIA officials even raised the possibility that Dollmann had sold himself to Moscow and was a Soviet double agent.

But it was not until 1955 that the CIA finally severed its ties to Dollmann. It took one last brazen blackmail attempt to persuade Dulles that he had to cut the cord. Dollmann had finished his memoirs that year, and, as promised, the book was rife with salacious details, including unflattering observations about Dulles and Angleton. Before the book went to the printers, Dollmann sent a message to Dulles through the U.S. consulate in Munich, letting it be known that he was eager "not to offend [my] great good friend" Dulles, and politely asking the CIA director to flag anything he found objectionable in the excerpts mailed to him. The implication was clear: They were men of the world who understood each other. They could certainly work out an appropriate arrangement.

After this, Dollmann abruptly disappeared from the CIA documentary record. The astute colonel undoubtedly realized that he had pushed his luck with the agency as far as he should, and, for his own good, it was time to retire from the spy game. He lived on for three more decades, trading on his notorious past to get by. He was a good storyteller, and his two colorful memoirs sold briskly in Europe. His astonishing tales even proved, for the most part, to be true. Dollmann also made frequent appearances on European television, and dabbled a bit in his beloved cinematic arts, writing the German subtitles for Fellini's *La Dolce Vita*.

In 1967, an American writer named Robert Katz, who was working on a book about the Ardeatine Caves massacre, tracked down Dollmann, finding him in the comfortable residential hotel in Munich where he would live out the rest of his days. At sixty-seven, the silver-haired and still trim Dollmann seemed quite content with his life. His sunny garret in the blue-painted hotel was cluttered with photos, books, and memorabilia that recalled his former life. He was perfectly happy to live in the past, Dollmann told his visitor—after all, he had begun his career as a historian, until he was kidnapped by history.

At one point, Dollmann brought up Allen Dulles, his old American benefactor. Dulles had recently published *The Secret Surrender*, his Operation Sunrise memoir, and Dollmann was upset to read the spymaster's description of him as a "slippery customer."

"From the little English I know," Dollmann told Katz in his perfect Italian, "'sleeperee coostomer' is not exactly a compliment. Is it?"

Katz explained that it meant someone who was shrewd, cunning, Machiavellian.

The colonel broke into a radiant smile. "Oh! That is a compliment—for me."

Part II

Useful People

Allen Dulles's wife, Clover, and his wartime mistress, Mary Bancroft, were both patients of Carl Jung. Mary began treatment with the man who was the second pillar of modern psychology in the 1930s, after moving to Zurich with her new husband, a Swiss banker. Clover entered analysis with Jung after reuniting with Allen in Switzerland in the final months of the war. The extroverted Mary got an electric charge from her connection to the great man, intellectually sparring with him, swapping gossip, and, although he was nearly three decades older, openly flirting with him. Clover, whom Jung quickly sized up as a classic introvert—sensitive, reticent, dreamy—had a more troubled reaction to him, and she terminated their relationship after a few sessions in favor of one of his disciples, a brilliant Jewish female analyst named Jolande Jacobi, who had fled the Nazi invasion of Vienna. After twenty-five years of marriage to Allen Dulles, Clover had had her fill of domineering men. Jung clearly was much more in touch with his female "anima" than her husband. But, still, the imposing figure struck her as "arrogant" and made her feel small in his presence. With his gray mustache, rimless spectacles, and ever-present pipe, Jung even bore some resemblance to her husband.

Despite their striking personality differences—and their awkward romantic triangle—Clover and Mary developed a unique friendship that would last the rest of their lives. With her keen intuition, Clover sized up the situation soon after arriving in Bern in January 1945.

Finding herself alone with Mary one day, she reportedly told her rival, "I want you to know I can see how much you and Allen care for each other—and I approve." This story gives Clover an authority over Allen's amorous adventures that, in reality, she sorely lacked. In truth, no woman in Dulles's life enjoyed this type of leverage over him. Even Mary Bancroft—who was allowed to participate in some of his secret life as his wartime courier, translator, confidante, and bedmate—would struggle for years to decipher her relationship with Dulles, which she called "the most complex and overwhelming" connection of her life.

Clover and Mary were bound by their mutual fascination and bewilderment with Dulles. But the two women's joint effort to understand the puzzle that was Allen Dulles was a doomed enterprise. On the surface he was full of a charm and gaiety that promised entry into a world of fascinating dignitaries and dazzling conversation. His air of mystery only seemed to add to his allure. But as the women in his life sought more from him, Dulles only revealed a deeper and deeper emotional impenetrability. Even in the life-and-death throes of wartime espionage, Dulles seemed untouched by the intense human drama swirling around him. Mary would always remember "those cold, blue eyes of his" and "that rather peculiar, mirthless laugh."

In her effort to find out more about the man at the emotional center of her life, Mary sought enlightenment from the great Jung. She made her way down the long, tree-lined path to his home on Lake Zurich, above whose elaborate stone portal was etched in Latin: *Vocatus atque non vocatus deus aderit* ("Called or uncalled, God will be present"). Jung was alive to the potential of the supernatural. He believed in demons and angels. The inscription reminded Jung, who said he always felt "unsafe," that he was "in the presence of superior possibilities."

Jung enjoyed discussing men of power and action like Dulles. Analyzing the dictators of his era who held the fate of Europe in their hands, he had developed various power "archetypes." Jung deemed Hitler a "medicine man" who ruled more through magic than political power. Whereas Mussolini projected the brute strength of a tribal chief, Hitler seemed to lack not just physical potency but basic human qualities. His power came from his uncanny "mystical" ability to tap into the German people's deeply troubled unconscious.

Before the war, standing near the two leaders at a Berlin military parade, Jung once had the occasion to observe Hitler and Mussolini together. Jung recalled the revealing experience for an interviewer in October 1938. While Mussolini greeted the goose-stepping troops and trotting cavalry horses "with the zest of a small boy at the circus," Hitler showed no emotion. He appeared to Jung like "a mask, like a robot, or a mask of a robot. . . . He seemed as if he might be the double of a real person, and that Hitler the man might perhaps be hiding inside like an appendix, and deliberately so hiding in order not to disturb the mechanism.

"What an amazing difference there is between Hitler and Mussolini!" Jung exclaimed. "I couldn't help liking Mussolini. . . . You have the homely feeling with Mussolini of being with a human being. With Hitler, you are scared."

Jung's portrait of Hitler is as chilling a picture of psychopathology as you will find. Dulles was fascinated by his insights into the German leader, and he urged Mary to keep seeking more such wisdom from Jung.

The esteemed psychoanalyst was happy to oblige. The two most powerful men in Mary Bancroft's life were intrigued with each other, though they had little direct communication. Jung had a hard time figuring out Dulles. He did not fit neatly into the Jungian system of power archetypes. One could see in Dulles the same disturbing mix of magnetism and ruthlessness that Jung observed in the dictators of his day. But there was also an impenetrable blankness that made him hard to read. Jung warned Mary that her lover was "quite a tough nut."

Dulles, for his part, approved of his wife and mistress's submitting to Jung's treatment. He told Mary that he realized analysis could be "useful" for others, but he was convinced that he himself had no need for it.

Throughout his life, Dulles was drawn to creative, intelligent, neurotic women like Clover and Mary—women who were under constant siege from their unconscious, as Joan Dulles described her mother's emotional plight. For a man as emotionally numb as Dulles, women like this were his essential link to the rest of humanity. They translated human feeling for him. They were, in short, "useful"—that favorite word of his. It was a word, recalled Mary, which "was constantly on his lips." If Dulles could use a person, that person was somehow real for him. If not, that person didn't exist.

Allen Dulles first laid eyes on Martha Clover Todd in the summer of 1920 at a party of fashionable young people at a lakeside resort near the Dulles family home in upstate New York. Before the week was out, he had proposed to her. She later spoke of her blitzkrieg courtship and marriage to Dulles with a sense of wonder. She couldn't quite explain why she had agreed to marry the headstrong young man. "I married Allen," she told a curious nephew years later, "because he was attractive, and doing interesting things." This commonplace observation was the best she could offer. Clover had other suitors at the time, including a perfectly acceptable young doctor who was particularly eager to win her. That courtship became entangled in her indecision. But Allen Dulles gave her no room to ruminate or reconsider. He had made the decision for both of them—she was the girl for him.

At twenty-six, Clover was a year younger than Dulles, and she radiated an ethereal beauty that set her apart from the other debutantes in her social set. She had sensuous lips and wide-set, almond-shaped green eyes that seemed to hint of deep sadness. She spoke in a breathy voice that made men lean closer to her. In photographs of Clover at the time, she always seemed to be looking away from the camera, as if her thoughts were somewhere else and too melancholy to be shared. She had an air of fragile mystery that undoubtedly appealed to Dulles.

But she also possessed some of the feisty "flapper" spirit of her generation of liberated women. She looked sexy and self-possessed in the masculine fashions of the day, posing for one photo in a trim suit, businesslike tie, and a wide-brimmed hat jammed down over her tightly coiffed curls.

Once, on holiday from her Connecticut boarding school, Clover was invited by an eccentric New York society queen to an evening in honor of "some poor convicts" recently paroled from Sing Sing prison. The evening was grinding on with excruciating stiffness until Clover broke the ice by challenging the ex-cons to a game of poker. In later years, she made prison reform a passionate personal commitment. Clover's affinity for convicts was fueled by the fact that she often felt like a prisoner of her own life. During World War I, she volunteered as a canteen girl in a Paris officers' club. She sometimes wandered the streets of the war-tattered city dressed as a beggar, just to feel what it was like to be someone else, someone who had to plead for bread.

Clover's own childhood was rich in material comfort. Her mother came from a wealthy Baltimore manufacturing family whose foundry had produced the metal plates for the USS *Monitor*, the famed ironclad Civil War vessel. Her father, Henry Todd, was a distinguished professor of romance languages at Columbia University. She and her sister and two brothers grew up in a tastefully furnished house near Central Park filled with books and music. Their father would take his children on long strolls through the city, discoursing at length on its history and architecture. Her mother would make "fairy circles" from tiny white stones in the park, where, she insisted, the sprites would gather for dances on moonlit nights. Clover grew up with her mother's fey spirit and would constantly be disappointed by the modern world's banality. Instead of the fairy world conjured by her mother, she was forced to dwell in a world "too pedestrian, too filled with anxiety, with duty, with the necessity to be always right."

Clover's father, a strict Presbyterian with an Old Testament sense of right and wrong, made her feel that she never measured up. When she was eight and her sister, Lisa, was ten, he tried to teach them both Latin but gave up in frustrated rage. "We simply weren't ready for Latin yet, or at least I wasn't," she recalled. "We exasperated Father terribly. He was a scholar—very tense and high-strung—and he cared. As he was a professor, it was hard to have subnormal children."

Her mother, who was prone to debilitating migraines and would often take to bed for long "rest cures," was too involved with her own travails to provide her children with maternal love. There were nurse-maids for the children and housekeepers, and when Clover's mother was confined to bed under her pillowy white bedspread, an efficient domestic manager named Miss MacMillan would arrive and put the house in order. But Clover's mother would go into rapid decline as soon as Miss MacMillan departed, overwhelmed by the obligations of family life.

Clover's emotional touchstone in her family was her younger brother, Paul, a beautiful and sensitive boy the nursemaids enjoyed dressing like a girl. While still quite young, he began demonstrating precocious artistic skill, drawing "the most astonishing [pictures], queer animals always, each one different from the last and exhibiting the most extraordinary amount of skill and imagination." But their father thought Paul's nursemaids had turned him into a "sissy." He seemed too fragile for the rough-and-tumble of college life when he went away to Princeton in 1918, and at the end of his freshman year, he dropped out.

On the eve of Allen and Clover's wedding—which was held in October 1920 on the wooded estate of Todd family friends outside Baltimore—Paul sent word that he did not feel hearty enough to attend the festivities. "He said he didn't feel well enough and we thought it rather queer," Clover later noted in her diary, "but we were always all of us not being well and having all sorts of inhibitions and neurotic feelings."

Clover later tormented herself for not being more attuned to her brother's emotional condition as she prepared for her wedding. But she herself was in a state of great anxiety. "To me it was a terrible strain being engaged, trying all the time to act the way you suppose a normal person would act, instead of simply jumping out the window the way you naturally would. So I wasn't thinking very much about my brother." That December, when the newly wed couple arrived in Constantinople, Allen's next diplomatic port of call, Clover heard that Paul had suffered a nervous breakdown and been confined to a fashionable sanitarium in Greenwich, Connecticut. In November 1921, after being discharged, the twenty-one-year-old was found dead in bushes alongside a road not far from the sanitarium. He had shot himself between the eyes with a revolver.

Paul's death plagued Clover for many years. "In a certain sense I suppose I did kill [Paul], at least I let him die, yes, certainly I let him die without lifting a finger," she wrote nearly three decades later in a therapeutic journal she was keeping.

Clover quickly learned that the man she married was simply not suited to help someone with as much inner turmoil as she suffered. She was tortured by feelings of worthlessness, which Allen did little to allay. Throughout most of their early married life, Clover underwent Freudian analysis with various psychoanalysts in New York, and at one point she committed herself to a sanitarium for six weeks. "I started Freudian analysis," she wrote in a journal many years later, "because I was suffering so much that it was not possible to live unless I did."

Clover and Allen's oldest daughter, Martha ("Toddie"), also grappled with psychic demons throughout her life—bouts of manic depression that became so severe that she submitted to multiple rounds of electroshock therapy. In some ways, Toddie was the most like her father—energetically outgoing and self-confident. But his daughter's troubles failed to engage Dulles. Nor did he display much interest in his children's accomplishments, including those of his son and namesake, Allen Jr., even when the boy began to shine at Exeter, where the headmaster said he was the brightest student in the school.

Dulles seemed a guest in his own family home—amiable but detached. It was clear to his daughter Joan that "his life was somewhere else."

"My father was a benign figure at home," she remembered. "He was friendly, but he was clearly not interested in us. . . . I don't remember any anger. He never scolded us when we weren't doing well enough in school, or asked us how we were doing."

The one time Joan saw her father cry was after he heard on the radio about the fall of France to Hitler's troops. She watched this rare display of emotion with "astonishment" as her father wept in his library. But she had no idea why this dramatic bulletin—among everything else in his eventful life—had so profound an effect on him. He never discussed politics or world events at home, even though it was the fuel of his career. "At breakfast he would have the *New York Times* and I wouldn't be able to tell you anything about his attitude toward anything. He'd be buried in the newspaper."

There's a "price," Joan added, for this sort of emotional anesthesia in a family, for never "talking in the home about your life and your politics and what's going on"—about anything that truly matters. "I think it's devastating."

Dulles carefully insulated Clover from his life. He would fly off to distant locations at a moment's notice and not tell her where he was going or for how long. It had nothing to do with intelligence protocol, insisted Joan. "It was just the way he operated."

Mary felt that Dulles kept his professional life from Clover because he was afraid that she was too morally sensitive and would disapprove of his undercover work. But he seldom showed much of a protective instinct toward his wife. Dulles would fill his letters home to Clover with references to his many dalliances and infatuations with other women. The life he evoked in this correspondence was filled with beautiful countesses and expertly mixed cocktails, and was certain only to cruelly reinforce Clover's domestic confinement.

Eleanor Dulles once remarked on the difference between her two brothers. Foster, who was inseparable from his own wife, Janet, would go out of his way to help anyone in the family who was in distress. The pious older brother would even secure an abortionist—in his day, not an easy or legal task—if it came to that, she said. "As for Allen," added Eleanor, "when anyone was in trouble, Allen seemed always to be off somewhere, lying under a palm, getting himself fanned."

Clover tried to keep the distress of her marriage from her children. Despite her husband's frequent absences—and his constant social demands when he was home—she ran the family households in Manhattan and Long Island with calm efficiency. She took pains to compensate for his emotional shortcomings. In a letter she wrote Joan in February 1945, soon after reuniting with Allen in Bern, she tried to put his extreme self-absorption in the best possible light for their daughter. By then, Dulles had been away from home for over two years, during which time he had no contact with his children as they navigated their way through adolescence.

"Dad asked for news of you both very especially—[you] and Allen— and your coming of age," Clover wrote. "Otherwise it would not be possible for you to imagine how engrossed he is in his work, and how he neither thinks, speaks or asks of anything else. There is no doubt he is different from most but I do believe that he does everything that he does, not only because he likes it, but as a way of showing his affection for us, paying us the compliment of believing that what we want is for him to do something worthwhile in the world. Everyone here adores him and he has done incalculable good."

But many years later, Clover would write a more honest assessment of her husband in a diary that she left for her children. By then, she felt no obligation to window-dress their marriage. "My husband doesn't converse with me, not that he doesn't talk to me about his *business*, but that he doesn't talk about *anything*. . . . It took me a long time to realize that when he talks it is only for the purpose of obtaining something. . . . He talks easily with men who can give him some information, and puts himself out with women whom he doesn't know to tell all sorts of interesting things. He has either to be making someone admire him, or to be receiving some information worth his while; otherwise he gives one the impression that he doesn't talk because the person isn't worth talking to."

It was Clover's curse to spend her life with such a man, and it was Allen's to live with a woman who was finally able to understand him.

Near the end of the war, Clover went to great lengths to rejoin Allen in Switzerland, pulling every available string to acquire the visas and travel permits necessary for an American citizen to venture into war-torn Europe. At last, after hearing that the U.S. embassy in newly liberated Paris had ordered a shipment of official cars, she finagled an assignment as one of the drivers. After a rough ocean crossing, Clover disembarked in Lisbon and joined the convoy as it took an arduous course through Portugal and Spanish Basque country, crossing the Pyrenees into France, where she and the other dozen drivers came under the protection of French resistance fighters. It took a full week for the drivers to complete their painstaking journey to Paris. When the exhausted Clover delivered her vehicle to the American embassy, she was relieved to hear that her husband was also in Paris—but he installed her at a different hotel and kept her waiting for two full days before finally greeting her.

When he appeared in her hotel room, Dulles brusquely informed her that he could spare only ten minutes. He told her to meet him early the next morning at his own hotel to begin their automobile journey to Switzerland. Then, without making any effort to cushion the blow, he announced that her mother had died while Clover was crossing the Atlantic. And with that, he disappeared again, leaving her to mourn alone.

"My wife is an angel," Dulles told Mary soon after meeting her. "She's always doing things for other people." But that is not the way Allen generally made Clover feel. After Clover began treatment with Jolande Jacobi, the analyst encouraged her artistically inclined patient to begin expressing her inner turmoil in drawings. In one picture, Clover drew herself as a crying, forlorn donkey. That's the way she felt, she explained to Mary—like a weepy ass—whenever Allen was rushing around, "engaged in activities [Clover] didn't understand but suspected were not as important as his behavior implied."

When Dulles shifted his operations to Germany in the postwar period, Clover moved to Zurich so that she could work more closely with Jacobi. It was an intense, therapeutic relationship that Clover kept going long after she returned to the United States, returning to Switzerland on numerous occasions for prolonged visits. While visiting the United States, Jacobi would stay at the Dulles home in Washington. What Jacobi did for her suffering patient "was nothing short of a miracle," Clover later wrote. After each of her Swiss sessions, Clover would hurry to a Zurich café to jot down the insights she had unearthed with Jacobi. The treatment, she wrote at the time, filled her with a new self-confidence. Clover began to feel "liberated from the feeling that my husband's way of looking at things is the right way or has any particular glamour or reason attached to it."

The journals that Clover kept during her analysis are mercilessly introspective—wrenching cries from the darkest depths of her soul. Some of the journals were devoted to meticulous accounts of her dreams, which revealed the misery of her marriage as well as a vibrant but stifled erotic imagination. In one dream, which she recorded in her journal in November 1945, Clover was suffering from a terrible physical trauma, but Allen was completely oblivious to her pain. "My whole stomach had collapsed, or been cut open or cut in two. . . . [But] it was a great satisfaction, a sort of triumph even, a justification to myself that all the time there actually had been something seriously the matter with me, a proof that instead of making a big fuss about nothing, as my husband thought, I actually had made comparatively little out of a really big affliction."

In other dreams, Clover expressed shame about her husband's mysterious espionage exploits. She entered nameless towns where "men were taking part in dark and nefarious negotiations." In her dreams, as in life, she was excluded from these secret activities, which carried a tawdry air, but nonetheless sometimes held a powerful allure for her. Clover also gave vent to her sexual jealousy. In a dream fragment from September 1948, her husband complains that he has no fresh underwear. But when Clover peers into his dresser drawer, she finds it stuffed with undershorts. On closer inspection, however, each pair is stained with semen.

Other dreams overflow with her own libidinal energy and confusion. She finds herself in bed with young soldiers and naked women, an architect she knew, and in more than one reverie her disrobed sister. In a dream of October 1945, Clover was engaged to be married to a woman—who turned out to be Mary Bancroft. She was delighted to be marrying a woman but was horrified that "I didn't have the physical apparatus to play a masculine role. I felt very shaven and shorthand empty in front and very much concerned how I could marry. Then I realized that, after all, she knew I was a woman, she was a woman herself, it wasn't even my fault I was made that way. And as a matter of fact, what ever made me feel that I was supposed to be the man? Why wasn't she the man? Perhaps she didn't even expect me to be the man."

It was her severe, judgmental father—a man repelled by "the inferiority" of the female sex—who had bestowed on her "my disgust of women," Clover noted in another journal entry. "I want a penis," she stated in another.

In other journal entries, which she called her "hymns of hate," Clover expelled poisonous clouds of the rage and self-loathing that were billowing inside her. She fantasized about going on killing sprees with an ax or sledgehammer, and when those weapons proved too limited, she mused about poison gas. She unspooled long lists of potential victims, but she devoted one entire murder fantasy in March 1947 to her husband. "I hate my husband," it began. "I hate my husband, I hate my husband. Oh, how I hate my husband . . . I want to kill him . . . I will be like a fighting cock with knives on my talons, I will cut him in ribbons with sharp knives, I will cut him in the back, I will even perhaps cut his throat with a sharp sharp knife tied to my talons when I am a bloody murderous fighting cock."

Mary Bancroft sympathized with Clover, up to a point, as they compared notes about Dulles. By the time Clover arrived in Switzerland, Mary's own affair with Dulles was waning and she brought a more detached perspective to their discussions. Sometimes they could even share a laugh about the enigmatic man who occupied the center of both of their lives. Clover told Mary that she had once heard the Dulles brothers referred to as sharks. "And I do think they are," said the wife to the mistress. "I guess there's no solution but for you and me to be killer whales!" From then on, the two women referred to Allen as "The Shark" and to themselves as the "Killer Whales."

But Mary was more fascinated with the world of male power than Clover, and she prided herself on understanding men like Dulles in a way that his wife could not. In a later generation, Bancroft herself might have been a central player in that world. But she settled for taking an occasional place in the room, offering these men of action her insight and solace.

Mary, whose mother died hours after giving birth to her, was raised by her grandparents in a comfortable Cambridge, Massachusetts, household dominated by men whose ambitions always seemed just beyond their reach. Her grandfather was a former mayor of Cambridge and Harvard overseer who was once talked about as a candidate for governor but never made it beyond municipal politics. Her father had been a precocious young scholar, entering Harvard at the age of fourteen and graduating summa cum laude three years later. He became a lawyer and, like his father, a pillar of civic affairs, winning appointment as the director of the Port of Boston. But the top rung of power eluded Mary's father, too, and, overcome by the disappointments of his life, he committed suicide in middle age. The man who made the biggest impression on young Mary was a step or two away from her immediate family, Clarence W. Barron, the short, white-bearded, twinkly-eyed publisher of *The Wall Street Journal* and the stepfather of her stepmother. She spent as much time as she could in "CW's" lively vortex, watching him dictate memos from bed until noon and sending the male secretaries who were always at hand scurrying to and fro. At an early age, Mary became familiar with names like Rockefeller, Morgan, Carnegie, Harriman, Ford, and Du Pont. Their world always seemed to hover tantalizingly just beyond her fingertips.

Mary was disappointed in marriage. Her first husband—the father of her two children—turned out to be a dull company man. Her second—a French-Swiss banker who traveled frequently on business to the Balkans and the Far East—promised to be more exotic. But once she was installed in his Zurich home, they settled into a marriage of convenience that left Mary ready for more adventure.

When Mary was introduced to Dulles in December 1942, shortly after he arrived in Switzerland, they instantly took to each other. At thirty-nine, she was a decade younger than the OSS man, and by her own account she was "at the height of my sexual prowess and usually always on the prowl."

Mary was a big-boned woman with round cheeks and a ready smile that was all teeth. Nor was Allen the stuff of romantic dreams. Her first impression of him was of an aging man with "iron-gray hair" and the rumpled clothes of a distracted professor. But Mary not only possessed the right pedigree, she had a sharp intelligence and an accommodating warmth, and Dulles instantly knew he could put her to use. Mary, in turn, found herself immediately excited by the aura of power that seemed to surround Dulles. "He actually shimmered with it," she later wrote in a journal. "It seemed to cling to him as phosphorescence does to the oars when one is rowing a boat at night."

Here was the man who would finally take her into the world of action about which she had fantasized ever since she was a girl, when she watched Wild Bill Donovan parade down Fifth Avenue with his troops on Armistice Day. Ever since then, she wrote, "I longed for a life of adventure. I wanted to go everywhere, see everything." She even daydreamed about being a "glamorous spy" like Mata Hari. Now she had found the man to make her dreams come true.

Dulles never made Bancroft an official OSS agent, but he quickly found a role for her, phoning her at her Zurich apartment every morning at nine thirty and giving her the day's marching orders. She pumped information out of a variety of sources for him—from cleaning maids with German relatives to members of the intellectual and artistic elite in the German-Austrian exile community, a crowd with whom the well-read and over-analyzed Bancroft was more comfortable than Dulles.

Mary also proved that she was more tuned in to certain nuances of the spy craft than Dulles. She realized, for instance, that intelligence could be gathered from the enemy as well as Allied camps by tapping into the underground homosexual network that ran through Europe's diplomatic and espionage circles. "One of my [OSS] colleagues was frantic," Bancroft later recalled, "because he wanted to get a—how do the French say it, a *tuyaux*—you know, a line into this homosexual network. And he used to bang on the desk and say, 'I wish Washington would send me a reliable fairy! I want somebody with a pretty behind so I can get into that fairy network and find out what the British are doing in North Africa!'" Her colleague couldn't bring himself to discuss his delicate recruitment needs with the old-fashioned Dulles, who—as Mary repeatedly observed in her journals—had been born in the nineteenth century. So Mary broached the subject with Dulles, who did indeed prove clueless about the homosexual beau monde, including its sexual mechanics. "What do those people actually *do*?" he asked Mary.

Although Dulles and Jung met face-to-face in early 1943, Mary also continued to serve as the main link between the two commanding men in her life. Both men were excited by the idea of forging a pioneering marriage between espionage and psychology. Dulles's reports back to Washington were filled with Jung's insights into the Nazi leadership and the German people. Jung even correctly predicted that an increasingly desperate Hitler would likely commit suicide. Mary's appointments with Jung became dominated by Dulles's "ask Jung" questions, to the point that they more closely resembled espionage briefings than therapy sessions.

Dulles was so enamored with the flow of provocative psychopolitical perceptions from Jung that he gave the psychologist an OSS number—Agent 488. After the war, the spymaster hinted broadly to a Jung family friend that the sage of Zurich had even contributed to the Allied cause by leaking information he had gleaned from sessions with patients who were connected to the enemy side. But this might have been an exaggeration from a spy chief who liked to pride himself on all the influential personalities he had in his pocket.

While Dulles valued Mary as a go-between with men like Jung, he also found more personal uses for her. One morning he came rushing into her apartment when he knew that her husband was away on business. "Quick!" he barked, dispensing with any foreplay. "I've got a very tricky meeting coming up. I want to clear my head." When he had finished with her, Dulles quickly headed for the door. "Thanks," he said over his shoulder. "That's just what I needed!"

Afterward, Mary resolved to tell Dulles that she would no longer cooperate in "clearing his head," no matter how stressful his upcoming meetings were. But she continued to make herself available to him.

The spy chief was confident enough in his control over Mary that he felt he could loan her out to a German Abwehr agent with whom Dulles had established a relationship. Dulles arranged for Mary, who was fluent in German, to work with the tall, imperious Nazi double agent Hans Bernd Gisevius on his memoirs. Gisevius had secretly turned against Hitler after his once promising Gestapo career had stalled, and in frustration he began feeding Dulles important inside information on German military operations. One day, Gisevius, who had grown enamored of Mary as they toiled together over his manuscript, begged her to come with him to Lugano, where he would have use of a "beautiful apartment" and where he would be meeting with the first chief of the Gestapo, Rudolf Diels. The invitation appealed to Mary's appetite for danger, but she turned it down. When she told Dulles about it, he was upset, not because he had a rival for his mistress's affections, but because she had missed an opportunity to squeeze more information out of the amorous German. "Why the hell didn't you go?" he snapped at her. "It might have been very interesting."

Mary did, in fact, later become Gisevius's lover. But, as she confided to Jung, shuttling back and forth between the two men proved to be emotionally draining.

Gisevius became one of the principal conspirators in the July 20, 1944, bomb plot against Hitler, barely fleeing with his life to Switzerland after it failed. When she discussed her German lover's exploits with Jung, he was unimpressed with Gisevius's moral character. The Abwehr man was fighting for the same thing that Hitler possessed, Jung told Mary: "pure power." He added that Gisevius and his rival in the conspiracy ring, General Claus von Stauffenberg, "were like a pair of lions fighting over a hunk of raw meat." When she gave Jung some pages from Gisevius's book for his reaction, he pronounced them "saturated with Nazi ideology."

Jung told Mary that she would always attract "extremely ambitious men interested in gaining power for themselves." She would never be the type of woman who judged men like this, whatever their moral flaws. "Power was my natural element," she later reflected. "I felt as at home in situations of power as a fish did in water."

Dulles would gain notoriety for his promiscuity—at least among his biographers, some of whom expressed greater disdain for his sexual indiscretions than for his more egregious moral failings. But by Mary's standards, he was by no means sexually reckless. She took umbrage when British traitor Kim Philby described Dulles as a "womanizer" in his memoir. "Kim Philby of all people!" she harrumphed. "[Allen] was nothing of the kind."

One evening, while warming themselves by the fireplace at Herrengasse, Mary fell into conversation with Dulles about Napoleon's love life. She told him that she had read that the great conqueror had enjoyed nine women during his life. "Nine!" exclaimed Dulles. "I beat him by one!" Mary was amused by Allen's boast. "To anyone born in the 20th century as I was," she later noted in her journal, "that seemed a very modest score, particularly for a man who had traveled the world as Allen had. It certainly did not qualify him as a womanizer in my book."

Dulles was fortunate to find someone like Mary, a woman whose morals were conveniently flexible—or, as she herself put it, a woman with a "sophisticated point of view." She had a curious way of explaining her moral dexterity, but Dulles certainly would have endorsed her way of thinking. "In order to engage in intelligence work successfully," Mary observed, "it was essential to have a very clear-cut idea of your own moral values, so that if you were forced by necessity to break them, you were fully conscious of what you were doing and why."

But even the sophisticated Mary found herself unnerved by one of her conversations with Dulles. She had observed that despite his cunning reputation, Allen always seemed so "open and trusting," even with people about whom he clearly harbored suspicions or whom he "actually had the goods on." As he listened to Mary, Dulles grinned. "I like to watch the little mice sniffing at the cheese just before they venture into the little trap," he told her. "I like to see their expressions when it snaps shut, breaking their little necks."

Mary was taken aback by this outburst. She told him she found it repellent, but Dulles would have none of her outrage. "What's the matter with you?" he said. "Don't you realize that if I had not caught them, they were about to catch me?" It did not occur to Mary to ask why "little mice" could be so threatening, or how he could take such pleasure from their suffering.

Clover Dulles had great hopes for her second daughter, Joan, after she graduated from Radcliffe College in 1944, where many of her classes had been integrated with Harvard's due to the wartime shortage of professors. Clover wanted her daughter to escape the confinements of domestic life by pursuing a life of adventure. After graduating, Joan joined the Frontier Nursing Service, an organization that imported British midwives—because midwifery was outlawed in America—to help deliver babies in the back hills of Kentucky. Joan escorted the midwives on horseback through the remote hills and hollows of the Bluegrass State, sometimes riding for as long as five hours to reach their destinations. The young woman was enchanted by the beauty of the Kentucky backcountry and was thrilled by the rugged work.

In April of the following year, as the war was coming to an end, Joan sailed for Europe with her aunt Eleanor, who was on a diplomatic assignment to Austria, a country that was rapidly turning into a front line in the Cold War. Vienna, which was divided into Allied occupational zones, was suffused with the danger and intrigue later displayed in the 1949 film *The Third Man*. Joan was once threatened with arrest by Russian soldiers as she traveled by train through the Soviet zone. Government officials in the Western zones often disappeared off the streets, snatched by Soviet agents.

Not much more than a year out of college, Joan seemed well on her way to fulfilling her mother's hopes of creating a bold life for herself. She had studied international law and relations at Radcliffe, and she seemed well positioned to follow her aunt's pioneering path as a female diplomat, or even her father's as a legendary spy. She could speak French and German and was learning Russian, a language that she particularly loved, finding it "just like music."

But Allen Dulles had other plans for his daughter.

While Joan was living in Vienna, her father introduced her to one of his young agents from the war, a well-born and well-connected Austrian named Fritz Molden. The son of a prominent newspaper editor and a widely respected author and poet, Molden and his family had suffered cruelly at the hands of the Gestapo during the war. After escaping from a Wehrmacht punishment battalion on the eastern front that he had been forced to join, Molden took up with the Austrian resistance, where he was put in touch with Dulles. Molden grew attached to Dulles, though the spymaster kept asking the young man to "prove himself" by risking his life for him. After the war, the Communists accused Molden of continuing to work as a paid agent for Dulles, but he denied it.

When Joan and Fritz married in spring 1948, it was clearly a marriage of convenience—for Joan's father and her new husband. Molden, who became secretary to Austrian foreign minister Karl Gruber after the war and later an influential journalist and diplomat, was a vital intelligence connection for Dulles. The marriage was also a wise move for Molden. For the young, ambitious Austrian, having Allen Dulles as a father-in-law was obviously a big feather in his cap. But the match proved much less successful for Joan.

Just like her mother many years before, Joan had great difficulty explaining why she had married her husband. Joan suffered the same severe pre-wedding doubts that Clover had before marrying Allen. Joan found Fritz a "very erratic character, always given to creating dramatic situations," as she later wrote her mother. She worried about marrying "someone who wasn't ever satisfied with the simple everyday aspects of life." But, in the end, Joan gave in to the implacable intensity of her suitor and went through with the marriage, resigning herself to the fact that she would never have children or enjoy a stable family life with such a man.

Her marriage to Molden, who openly reveled in the company of other women, soon developed a striking resemblance to that of her parents. He often disappeared on mysterious rendezvous, leaving her to wonder when she would see him again.

"Fritz was a ladies' man, that's for sure," Joan recalled years later. "He was so extroverted that you just never knew where he was. He'd say,

'Let's rent a sailing ship in the Greek islands,' and I didn't know how many of his girlfriends would be on board or for how long we'd be at sea. Do I see similarities with my father? Probably, probably."

Joan divorced Molden in 1954, but, as if to not disappoint her father, she quickly replaced him with another high-ranking Austrian diplomat named Eugen Buresch. The son of a former Austrian chancellor, Buresch had succeeded Molden as director of the Austrian Information Service in New York. The following year, after being named Austria's ambassador to Iran, Buresch took Joan off to Tehran, another highly sensitive diplomatic posting. Joan suddenly found herself amid the imperial splendor of Shah Mohammad Reza Pahlavi's court, the emperor reinstalled on the Peacock Throne by her father, after the CIA overthrew Iran's democratically elected government in 1953.

Joan gave birth to two children with Buresch, a boy and girl. Like Fritz Molden, Joan's second choice for a husband seemed crafted primarily for her father's professional benefit. Iran was not only an oil-rich nation, it was a strategically located CIA surveillance platform bordering the Soviet Union. To have a son-in-law acting as his eyes and ears inside the shah's court was an espionage boon for Dulles, who by then was running the CIA.

But, again, the marriage turned out to be much less beneficial for Joan. In July 1959, Joan wrote her father a painful letter, made all the more poignant by its resolutely upbeat tone, informing him that she and Buresch had separated. Joan, who was living with her young children in Switzerland at the time, had recently visited her parents in Washington but found it easier to tell her father about the failure of her second marriage through the post. The separation had not been her idea, she assured her father—she "would have gone on trying endlessly for the sake of the children," she wrote. But, in any case, she was "very glad to be alone again."

Joan had good reason to welcome the breakup. Buresch, it turned out, had a violent streak. "Every six months, or every time I do something he doesn't approve of," she wrote her father, "he gets terrible fits of rage and tries to beat me up, etc. etc. Last summer, because I tried to come to Europe to see mother, he nearly kicked me out." When she said, "kicked me out," Joan added, she meant it "literally." Apparently Buresch vented his fury with his feet as well as his fists.

Joan did not dwell on the abuse that "Gino," as she called her husband, meted out. She was much more concerned that her father not worry about her, or worse, write her off as a hopeless case after the collapse of her second marriage. "Pa, you will think indeed that you have a black sheep in me, but I am glad to be free, I shall live alone and bring up my children, mind my own business and I am sure I will be happy."

Joan was clearly eager for her father's reassurance, even his forgiveness. "Pa," she continued, "I have never been scared of life and I am not now. I like being alive no matter what comes. I hope you know what I mean, and that you will not be either too angry or too upset."

Joan finally found sanctuary, not only from her husband but from her father, by moving with her children to the remote New Mexico high desert. It was about as far as possible from her father's world of power as she could venture. She made her home in Santa Fe, among artists and free spirits, returning to Zurich in the mid-1960s to study at the C. G. Jung Institute, where she became a certified psychoanalyst. After coming back home to Santa Fe, she married a prominent Jungian therapist named John Talley, with whom she lived and worked until his death in 2013.

Mary Bancroft believed that she had fallen in love with Allen Dulles. Among the many men in her life, she had only given her heart to two, and he was one. But Dulles himself was incapable of returning love. Jung told her this, in so many words. One day, while sitting in his study—a room stuffed with books, busts of Voltaire and Nietzsche, and primitive artifacts—Jung made an observation that stuck with Mary for many years. The opposite of love is not hate, he said. It's power. Relationships fueled by a drive for power, where one person seeks dominance over the other, are incapable of producing love.

Mary remained enthralled by the Dulles mystique all her life. But through years of agonizing self-exploration, Clover and Joan finally arrived at something close to the truth. As Jung observed, "One does not become enlightened by imagining figures of light, but by making the darkness conscious."

In the end, this is what Dulles's wife and daughter came to understand about the man who dominated so much of their lives. The drive for absolute control was the only passion that truly gripped Allen Dulles.

Little Mice

On a sweltering morning in August 1950, a slim, blond, attractive twenty-eight-year-old woman named Erica Glaser Wallach woke from a restless sleep in her West Berlin hotel room, locked her papers and most of her money in the cupboard, and walked east through the Brandenburg Gate to her doom. The young German-born woman left behind her husband, a former U.S. Army captain named Robert Wallach who was studying at the Sorbonne in Paris, and their two infant children. She was weak with fear as she entered the headquarters of the SED, the East German Communist Party. But she was determined to go through with her mission.

A year before, Erica Wallach's adoptive father, a hopelessly idealistic American Quaker relief worker named Noel Field, had disappeared after being lured to Prague with the promise of a university teaching position. When his equally wide-eyed wife, Herta, and younger brother, Hermann, went looking for Noel behind the Iron Curtain, they, too, vanished. Despite the obvious risk, Wallach was now determined to find out what had happened to the Fields, a family that had rescued her during the war when she was a seventeen-year-old refugee from Nazi Germany and Franco's Spain. Noel and Herta Field had whisked a sick and starving Erica and her ailing mother from a squalid French refugee camp, and later agreed to care for the teenage girl in Switzerland during the war when her parents fled to England. Wallach now felt honor-bound to track down the missing Fields, using her connections with German Communists whom she had met during the war.

When Wallach asked to see her old war comrades at the SED headquarters, she was told they were not available. She would later find out why: they were in prison, and Erica Wallach would soon join them. On her way out of the gloomy SED fortress, a hand suddenly gripped her shoulder. "Criminal police. Please come around the corner." She didn't even bother to turn around. "I knew that all was lost."

For the next five years, Wallach would suffer harsh imprisonment, first in Berlin's Schumannstrasse Prison, which she christened her "house of horrors," and then, for the longest stretch, in Vorkuta, the dread prison labor complex in Russia's Arctic wastelands a thousand miles northeast of Moscow. Wallach, the cultured daughter of a physician, learned to survive the gulag by giving up all hope that she would ever return to her family and the lost joys and comforts of her old life. She would rise early each morning in the dark with her labor gang and work as hard as she could to avoid freezing in the ferociously cold temperatures, shoveling gravel six days a week—and often seven—for new railroad embankments.

"This business of nothing to look at, the ugliness, the lack of color, the lack of good smell—that really is worse than the hunger," Wallach later recalled. "But you get used to it. I finally after three years got used to the fact that I was totally alone in this world."

Wallach learned to ingratiate herself with her fellow prisoners—Russian, Ukrainian, German, and Polish women, and even one American who had found small and less small ways of offending the Soviet state. She became a different person than the naïve woman who had walked through Brandenburg Gate that morning in August 1950. She even looked like someone else—muscled and thick and callused from her labors. The young woman made a grim new life for herself there "at the end of the earth" among the drunken, homesick Soviet guards and her fellow penal colony inmates. She found ways to break up the barren monotony of her days by listening to the Ukrainians' melancholy folk songs and attending the Sunday "salons" hosted by the educated women whose latrine-cleaning duties were the foulest of all prison jobs, but gave them enough leisure to indulge their intellectual curiosity.

In the end, the hardened Wallach decided that surviving a frozen hell like Vorkuta was a matter of mental adjustment. "Horror, fear, mental torture," she would later write, "are not physical facts but creations of one's own spirit. They were not forced upon me by outside acts or conditions, but lived within me, born of the weakness of my own heart. . . . I did not have to break if I did not want to."

While Wallach was enduring Vorkuta, the Fields were suffering their own nightmares behind the Iron Curtain. After Noel Field was arrested by Czech authorities in May 1949, he was drugged and driven to a secret location in Hungary. There he was dropped down a coal chute and subjected to a variety of tortures, including beatings, sleep deprivation, and round-the-clock interrogations.

Noel's brother Hermann Field, who was an architecture professor, suffered less vicious treatment after he was grabbed by Polish secret police three months later in Warsaw while searching for his brother. But he spent the first several months of his five-year incarceration in solitary confinement, which wore terribly on his spirit. When a field mouse suddenly appeared in his cell, Hermann was beside himself with joy. The mere brush of the mouse's fur against Hermann's leg was the source of enormous comfort. One night, while sleeping, he accidentally crushed the mouse, which had crawled under his mattress. Hermann was so grief-stricken that he feared he would lose his mind. "A person living a normal life simply cannot comprehend how sharply such apparently trivial happenings affect a human being deprived of all living contact and driven to the very edge of loneliness," he later observed.

During the harsh interrogations to which all four members of the Field family were subjected, including Erica Wallach, one name kept coming up. "How do you know Allen Dulles?" the inquisitors repeatedly asked. The spymaster was the one thread that seemed to connect all four of the deeply unfortunate prisoners as they languished in their cells.

By the time Noel Field was taken prisoner in Czechoslovakia in 1949, it had been nearly four years since Allen Dulles occupied an official position with U.S. intelligence. After the war, Dulles had returned to the fold at Sullivan and Cromwell, a business routine he now found quite dreary. "I must admit that these days I find it hard to concentrate on my profession of the law," Dulles confessed to a friend. "Most of my time is spent reliving those exciting days when the war was slowly dying."

A steady stream of former OSS colleagues came to pay their respects at Dulles's Wall Street office, chatting about the war while "the Old Man," as he was already affectionately known in spy circles, though he was only fifty-two, puffed genially on his pipe. But these conversations were not simply fond exercises in nostalgia. The men who called on Dulles—OSS veterans like Richard Helms, Frank Wisner, Tracy Barnes, and Kermit "Kim" Roosevelt—all shared the Old Man's view that the blissful reign of postwar peace would be short-lived and that the West must quickly gird itself to confront the growing threat from the East.

That threat was not simply a convenient creation of "Western imperialism." Stalin's military machine might have been no match for America's global reach and nuclear firepower. But it was quite capable of crushing democratic aspirations in Eastern Europe, which the Soviets, following the devastation of World War II, felt they were entitled to controlling as a buffer zone from Western aggression. American intelligence officials like Frank Wisner, who had been stationed in Romania near the end of the war and had witnessed the beginnings of the Soviet-dominated police state there, deeply empathized with the liberation struggles of the peoples in the Eastern bloc.

As they chatted in Dulles's law suite and gathered for drinks at William Donovan's town house on Sutton Place, this rarefied group of OSS veterans—who straddled the worlds of espionage, foreign affairs, and finance—were already plotting to create a powerful intelligence apparatus for the coming Cold War. Spurned by Harry Truman, Donovan began to feel that his own hopes for a return to postwar action would never be realized. "Our war is over, Allen," he told Dulles one day. But Dulles would have none of it. The man's irrepressible ego and ambition never ceased to amaze Donovan.

In truth, while Dulles punctually showed up for work at Sullivan and Cromwell each morning, he never retired from the intelligence game. No sooner had he resumed his life in New York than he began taking a leadership role in prestigious organizations and placing himself at the center of postwar political debates. At the end of 1945, Dulles was elected president of the Council on Foreign Relations, a group whose membership of prominent businessmen and policy makers played a key role in shaping the emerging Cold War consensus. Dulles would huddle with his colleagues in a soundproof room at the council's headquarters on the Upper East Side as if he were already running the robust new spy agency that he envisioned.

Dulles's stubborn insistence on staying in the middle of the postwar action paid off. In April 1947, he was asked by the Senate Armed Services Committee to present his ideas for a strong, centralized intelligence agency. His memo would help frame the legislation that gave birth to the CIA later that year.

Despite his controversial ties to Nazi Germany, John Foster Dulles had also managed to keep a foot in the political arena, putting himself forward as one of the Republican Party's leading wise men on foreign affairs. Both Dulles brothers pinned their political hopes on New York governor Thomas E. Dewey, the GOP front-runner for the 1948 presidential nomination. Dewey, a former Wall Street lawyer with an impressive political résumé, was the Eastern establishment's clear pick for the White House that year. Political prognosticators overwhelmingly predicted that Dewey would easily outclass President Harry S. Truman—a political hack from Missouri whom many New Deal loyalists considered unfit to carry on the Roosevelt mission and who, in fact, was facing a challenge on the left from independent candidate Henry Wallace, FDR's onetime vice president and secretary of agriculture. Dewey, already picking out his drapes for the White House, let it be known that

Foster would be his secretary of state and Allen would take charge of the new intelligence agency that he had helped create.

It was Allen who had the tougher views on foreign policy at this stage of the brothers' collaboration. As Foster started to flesh out his ideas for the Dewey campaign, he showed his brother a draft of his thoughts on the Soviet threat, in which he suggested that the United States and Russia might somehow find a mutual "accommodation." Allen promptly dismissed such soft thinking. "The difference between us," Allen told Foster, is that "you hold out the hope of some satisfactory accommodation being possible between the Soviet system . . . and the rest of the democratic world. I doubt this." Foster would eventually fall in step with his younger brother's hard Cold War line.

Harry Truman had inherited Franklin Roosevelt's antipathy toward the Dulles brothers and their circle. The Dulleses' close connections to the Dewey camp did nothing to soften Truman's sentiments. He would dismissively refer to Foster as "that Wall Street fella" or, more bluntly, as "that bastard." Truman was equally suspicious of Allen, who kept pushing the administration to take full advantage of the broad powers granted the newborn CIA under the National Security Act of 1947. The president, however, took a dim view of a powerful spy agency, fearing that it might turn into a rogue outfit, and he insisted that the CIA serve primarily as a coordinator of intelligence reports for the White House.

Allen Dulles believed that the shadow war between the West and the Soviet bloc would have few if any rules, and he was contemptuous of any attempts in Washington to put limits on the conflict. He assumed that the United States faced an utterly ruthless enemy in Moscow, and he was prepared to match or go beyond whatever measures were employed by Russia's KGB and the Eastern bloc's other security services. Dulles's aggressive Cold War stance found a key ally in President Truman's defense secretary, James V. Forrestal, a former Wall Street investment banker at Dillon, Read who moved in Dulles's circles and who shared Dulles's suspicions about the Soviet Union. In early 1948, Forrestal persuaded the politically vulnerable Truman, who knew he was facing a tough challenge from Dewey, to appoint Dulles to a blue-ribbon committee to study the year-old CIA and propose ways to make it more effective.

The so-called Dulles-Jackson-Correa Committee, over which Dulles quickly assumed control, allowed him to roam freely through the halls of the new intelligence agency and develop a plan for how to give it teeth. The committee's report was conveniently timed for January 1949, when Tom Dewey would presumably be inaugurated as president and Dulles would take over the CIA. The 193-page report would conclude its sharply critical assessment of the CIA by demanding that the agency take off its gloves in the growing confrontation with the Soviet Union. The CIA, it declared, "has the duty to act." The agency "has been given, by law, wide authority." It was time to take full advantage of these generous powers, the committee insisted.

Dulles and Forrestal didn't wait for the report to be finished before taking their own action. In March 1948, James Angleton flew back from Rome to meet with Dulles, warning his mentor that Italy's Communist Party was on the verge of taking power in the upcoming national elections in April. Seeing an opportunity for the kind of decisive counterattack that they had long envisioned against the Communist advance in Europe, Dulles and Forrestal flew into action, raising millions of dollars to tilt the election in favor of the U.S.-supported Christian Democrats. Within days, a satchel stuffed with American cash was being handed off to Italian agents at Rome's Hassler Hotel, the luxurious villa atop the Spanish Steps favored by Dulles during his stays in the Eternal City. More cash would soon come pouring in. The massive infusion of campaign money and U.S. aid ensured victory for the U.S. government's political clients. On the evening of April 17, the first day of Italian voting, Dulles scrutinized the election tallies from Rome at Forrestal's home in Washington. The two men raised a toast when it became clear that the Italian Communists had suffered a stunning defeat.

In November, Dulles suffered his own electoral defeat when Truman pulled off a shocking upset over Dewey. It was a humiliating reversal of fortune, not just for Dewey but for the Dulles brothers.

Soon afterward, Allen would lose his strongest ally in the Truman administration, Jim Forrestal, when the president ousted the Dulles ally from the Pentagon. By the time he was pushed out, Forrestal was showing signs of severe nervous exhaustion. Angry and despondent about his ouster, he began spiraling quickly downward, ranting about how the Soviets had infiltrated Washington and how they had marked him for liquidation. Early in the morning of May 22, 1949, after Forrestal was checked into the Bethesda Naval Hospital for psychiatric evaluation, he squeezed through the small bathroom window of his sixteenth-floor hospital suite and fell to his death. The tragic collapse of the defense secretary, a man who had controlled America's fearsome arsenal, was one of the stranger episodes of the Cold War.

With the Democrats maintaining control of the White House in the election of 1948, the Dulles brothers' dream of running U.S. foreign policy seemed dashed. But Allen would find ways to stay in the spy game, no matter who was president.

In June 1949, Dulles organized the National Committee for a Free Europe in conjunction with an illustrious board that included General Dwight D. Eisenhower, Hollywood director Cecil B. DeMille, and Time-Life publishing magnate (and close friend) Henry Luce. Ostensibly a private philanthropic group, the committee was actually a CIA front that channeled funds to anti-Communist European émigrés and financed major propaganda efforts like Radio Free Europe. At least $2 million of the money poured into the committee's clandestine projects came from the Nazi gold that Dulles had helped track down at the end of the war. In the early years of the Cold War, the Nazi treasure looted from Jewish families and German-occupied nations would become a key source of funding for Dulles's secret operations.

Private citizen Dulles further spread his influence by inserting close allies like Frank Wisner in key intelligence posts. Like Dulles, Wisner was a former Wall Street lawyer who had fallen for the glamour of espionage life. In 1949, Dulles helped create a new intelligence outpost and buried it in the State Department bureaucracy under a purposefully dull name—the Office of Policy Coordination. Despite its innocuous title, the OPC would evolve into the kind of combative agency that Dulles envisioned the CIA becoming in a Dewey administration. Wisner was maneuvered into position as OPC chief, and under his gung ho leadership, the obscure unit quickly threw itself into the black arts of espionage, including sabotage, subversion, and assassination. By 1952, the OPC was running forty-seven overseas stations, and its staff had ballooned to nearly three thousand employees, with another three thousand independent contractors in the field.

Dulles and Wisner were essentially operating their own private spy agency. The OPC was run with little government oversight and few moral restrictions. Many of the agency's recruits were ex-Nazis. While President Truman continued to regard the primary purpose of an intelligence agency as the gathering of information for the president and his national security advisers, Dulles and Wisner were engaged in their own no-holds-barred war with the Soviet bloc. They saw Eastern Europe as their primary battlefield in the great struggle to roll back the Soviet advance, but their field of combat often strayed into the sovereign territory of U.S. allies such as France, West Germany, and Italy.

During World War II, Dulles had resolutely pursued his own initiatives in Switzerland, often in conflict with the policies of President Roosevelt. Now, in the early years of the Cold War, he was doing the same, directly under the nose of another Democratic president. Although the OPC's tactics had been sanctioned by a National Security Council memo titled "NSC 10/2," which had been formulated in the heat of the 1948 presidential campaign—when Truman was fending off Dewey and the Republicans' charges that he was soft on Communism—it is uncertain how fully informed the president was about the exploits of the Office of Policy Coordination.

Whether or not Truman was fully briefed, Wisner pursued his job with a sense of daring abandon, dreaming up ever more inventive and dangerous ways to disrupt Soviet rule over its European dominion. Wisner would present his ideas to Dulles, as if the Sullivan and Cromwell attorney were still his boss. Dulles found one of Wisner's brainstorms particularly intriguing. The idea was sparked in May 1949 when British intelligence informed Wisner that one of Dulles's former wartime assets, a man named Noel Field, was planning to fly to Prague, where an attractive academic post was being dangled before him.

Why shouldn't U.S. intelligence take advantage of Field's ill-advised journey behind the Iron Curtain? Wisner had acquired a high-placed double agent inside the Polish security service, a man named Józef Światło. He could be told to spread the word, all the way from Warsaw to Moscow, that Field was actually coming to Prague on a secret mission, sent by his old spymaster, the infamous Allen Dulles. While in Prague, Field would be contacting his extensive network from the war years— the brave Communists, nationalists, and antifascists he had helped to survive when he was a refugee aid worker. These men and women were all part of the top secret Dulles-Field spy network.

None of this was true—but Wisner and Dulles knew that if they could successfully plant this seed in Stalin's mind, they might wreak havoc throughout the fragile Soviet empire.

Allen Dulles had a long history with the Field family. Most men with this sort of connection to a family would have found it impossible to use such old acquaintances as pawns in a game of geopolitical intrigue. But Dulles was not like most men. His plan was heartless but inspired. By turning the unsuspecting Field family into members of a far-reaching U.S. spy ring, Dulles would panic Stalin—already rattled by the 1948 defection of Yugoslavia's Marshal Tito—into launching witch hunts that would fracture the Communist governments throughout Eastern Europe. As with all the bold counterintelligence gambits he undertook during his career, Dulles threw himself into the Field affair with great relish, even personally giving it a code name: Operation Splinter Factor.

Dulles had first met the Fields in Switzerland during World War I, when he tried to recruit Noel's father as a spy. Herbert Haviland Field was a Harvard-educated, internationally renowned zoologist who ran a scientific institute in Zurich dedicated to the encyclopedic classification of the animal kingdom. The senior Field—a devout Quaker with a full, Darwinian beard—turned Dulles down, but he did feed him bits of information from time to time, and he invited the young diplomat to his home for dinners. It was here—in the Fields' four-story, hilltop villa overlooking Lake Zurich—that Dulles became acquainted with Noel and his three siblings. A shy, gangly adolescent at the time, with a long face and soft, searching, green eyes, Noel impressed Dulles, when he asked the boy what he wanted to be, by earnestly declaring, "I want to work for world peace." Noel became deeply committed to pacifism during the war, when he saw trainloads of horribly maimed soldiers in transit through neutral Switzerland. After Armistice, his Quaker father reinforced the boy's feelings by taking him on a tour of the war's blood-soaked battlefields.

When his father died suddenly of a heart attack after the war, a grief-stricken Noel vowed to dedicate his life to becoming a "saint" and helping lift the sorrows of mankind. He enrolled at Harvard, his father's alma mater, and after storming through his courses in two years and writing his dissertation on the League of Nations and disarmament, he graduated with honors in 1924. Shortly afterward, he married his Swiss-German sweetheart, Herta, whom he had known since they were both nine. Noel then applied for the U.S. Foreign Service, deciding with typical moral gravity that it was "by far the most practical field in which an individual can do his bit towards international understanding." In 1926, after passing the exams, Noel and Herta moved to Washington, D.C., where he began work as a junior foreign officer at the State Department.

From the very beginning, Noel was an odd man out in the insular world of the State Department, whose preppy officers liked to think of themselves as "a pretty good club." Noel was bookish and idealistic, and he betrayed a sentimental weakness for the left-wing causes of the day, from the trial of anarchists Sacco and Vanzetti to the Bonus March of impoverished war veterans on Washington in 1932 that turned violent when General Douglas MacArthur unleashed his troops on the protesters. While other young foreign service officers were dining with their own kind at Washington's exclusive clubs, Noel and Herta would frequent the capital's racially segregated theaters, where they sat with their black friends. The Fields also invited their racially mixed circle to their home in downtown Washington, a modest apartment overrun with cats.

Although he did not join the Communist Party, Noel was intrigued by the Soviet revolution, which he began to see as the hope for a world torn apart by war, greed, and poverty. He taught himself Russian by listening to phonograph records. He liked the sound of the language and wanted to read Lenin and Stalin in the original.

In a later era, Noel and Herta Field would have been just another young, free-spirited couple, given to utopian dreams, book clubs, nature hikes, and camping. But in the Washington of the late 1920s and early 1930s, as the growing misery of the Great Depression pushed the desperate and the idealistic in extreme directions, the Fields seemed marked for trouble.

In 1934, the couple fell in with a Viennese woman named Hede Massing, who turned out to be a Soviet intelligence agent. Noel began secretly passing information and copies of documents to Massing. But, increasingly tormented by his dual loyalties, he decided to quit the State Department, and in 1935 Noel and Herta moved to Geneva, where he took a job with the disarmament section of the League of Nations.

Field thought that by returning to Switzerland, he could maintain an honorable neutrality. For the rest of his overseas career—which took Noel from his League of Nations post to humanitarian work on behalf of Nazi refugees during World War II—he convinced himself that he could in good conscience serve his own country as well as the Soviet Union. But in the end, he would be crushed between these implacable forces. Both sides saw the dreamy Field as a useful victim. Earl Browder, leader of the U.S. Communist Party, would anoint him "a stupid child in the woods." As for Allen Dulles, the man who was so impressed by the teenage Field's sincerity, he came to see him as just another of those "little mice" whose necks would soon be snapped.

During the war, Field volunteered to work for Dulles, using his cover as a Unitarian Service Committee relief worker to transmit information back and forth across the Swiss border and to deliver packages of OSS cash to resistance fighters in France. Noel was particularly useful as a conduit to the German Communist underground. The Fields' foster daughter, Erica, also proved helpful for Dulles, bicycling guns and medicine across the border to France.

It was clear that Noel's antifascist work had a Communist tilt. In February 1945, he arrived at the OSS office in Paris with Dulles's written blessing. Field met with young OSS officer Arthur Schlesinger Jr., the future historian and Kennedy White House aide. Field proposed that the OSS subsidize the recruitment of left-wing German refugees in France, who would be dropped inside liberated areas of Germany, where they would begin to establish the country's new political foundations. Schlesinger, a man of the left, but an ardent anti-Communist, immediately sniffed out Field's proposal as a scheme to give the Soviet Union a head start in the occupation of Germany.

Schlesinger took a strong disliking to Field. Years later, he would describe him as a "Quaker Communist, filled with idealism, smugness and sacrifice." Or, as another observer put it, Field exuded "the arrogance of humility." In Schlesinger's estimation, he was less of a dangerous figure than a pathetic one. His pious dedication to the Soviet cause "did little damage to the interests of the United States." Nonetheless, after their Paris meeting, Schlesinger strongly advised his OSS superiors against buying into Field's scheme for postwar Germany.

Dulles ended up funding Field's project anyway, which later resulted in much ridicule from his counterparts in British intelligence. Some observers have suggested that this is why, later on, Dulles was able to betray Field with such ease, spreading the lie that he was a secret agent working behind the Iron Curtain for the Americans. But when Dulles decided to feed Noel Field to Stalin—and then, one at a time, three of his family members—there was probably very little spleen involved, just cold calculation.

After Noel dropped out of sight in Prague, his family implored Dulles to help. He had been a guest in the family's Zurich home. Both Field and his father had put themselves at his service. But Dulles did nothing to rescue Field. And he did nothing to prevent Noel's family members from walking headlong into the same trap.

Three months into his long ordeal as a captive of Poland's Stalinist regime, Noel's brother Hermann was taken from his cell for another round of grilling. This time Hermann's interrogator was someone like himself—a tweedy, academic type in his forties. He seemed eager to help Hermann out of his predicament, if only he would fully cooperate. There was no use in playing games any longer: Polish security knew that he and his brother were part of a conspiracy against the peace-loving peoples of the Communist world.

Hermann, a political innocent whose ideology amounted to nothing more than a kind of do-gooder Quakerism, was utterly confused. He had no clue about why he, or his brother, had fallen into this Kafkaesque nightmare. "But you're not talking sense," he told his inquisitor. "What conspiracy? Tell me what I have done to you. Give me just one example."

The tweedy man began pacing back and forth in front of the stool where Hermann sat. Suddenly he stopped and blurted out, "Who is Allen Dulles? Mr. Field, tell me precisely, what were your contacts with Allen Dulles, and what was the nature of your assignments from him?"

Hermann's interrogator clearly thought that by abruptly invoking Dulles's name, Field would finally crumble. But the question only served to deepen Hermann's confusion. Field had been too young to remember meeting Dulles as a child in Zurich. He had only a vague memory of the name.

"There's a John Foster Dulles," Hermann tried helpfully. "That's the only one I'm sure of. He's some sort of adviser on foreign affairs to the Republican Party."

But the interrogator would have none of this evasion. He kept on badgering Hermann, hour after hour. "I felt like I was in an insane asylum," Field later recalled.

In fact, the mysterious Allen Dulles *was* at the center of Hermann Field's ordeal. Field just didn't realize it.

Operation Splinter Factor succeeded beyond the OPC's wildest dreams. Stalin became convinced that the Fields were at the center of a wide-ranging operation to infiltrate anti-Soviet elements into leadership positions throughout the Eastern bloc. The Dulles-Wisner plot aggravated the Soviet premier's already rampant paranoia, resulting in an epic reign of terror that, before it finally ran its course, would destroy the lives of untold numbers of people. Hundreds of thousands throughout Eastern Europe were arrested; many were tortured and executed. In Czechoslovakia, where nearly 170,000 Communist Party members were seized as suspects in the make-believe Field plot, the political crisis grew so severe that the economy nearly collapsed.

Anyone whose life had been even remotely touched by Noel Field during his war relief work was subject to the sweeping purge. Many of the officials rounded up had been war heroes in their countries— antifascist fighters who survived the Nazi occupation only to be falsely accused as traitors by Stalin's secret police. Most victims were independent-minded nationalists, the sort of leaders who put their own people's interests ahead of blind obedience to Moscow. Jewish officials, whose "cosmopolitan" and "Zionist" sensibilities aroused suspicion, also bore the brunt of Stalin's crackdown.

Back in Washington, Wisner exulted over each wave of arrests and each new round of show trials, where the accused were made to publicly condemn themselves before they were executed. "The comrades are merrily sticking knives in each others' backs and doing our dirty work for us," Wisner gleefully reported.

The Office of Policy Coordination men knew that many of the Splinter Factor victims were patriots who were beloved by their own people. But, in the eyes of Dulles, this actually made them more dangerous. As one political observer of Splinter Factor remarked, "Dulles wished to leave Eastern Europe devoid of hope so that he could introduce a pro-American, anti-Soviet form of government. . . . Nationalist Communists were making communism acceptable to the people, and so, accordingly, they had to be removed."

As a result of the rapidly spreading inquisition, political dialogue in Eastern Europe was frozen, the screws of thought control were tightened, and cultural exchange and trade with the West were shut down. But Dulles saw all this as a positive development. Like the most rigid of Marxists, he believed that by increasing the suffering of Eastern Europe's enslaved populations, they would be pushed beyond their breaking point and forced to revolt against their Soviet masters. But, as was the case with the Communist true believers who advocated "heightening the contradictions" in order to bring about the glorious revolution, Operation Splinter Factor brought only more misery to the people of the Soviet bloc. Dulles would not live long enough to see their day of liberation.

Erica Wallach was freed from her arctic gulag in 1954, after Stalin died and the "Field conspiracy" was finally exposed behind the Iron Curtain for what it was—a devilishly clever Allen Dulles brainstorm. She was released into the custody of Soviet secret police officials, who apologized and offered her money, and then took her to East Berlin, where they put her in a taxi to the West. She walked to freedom through the Brandenburg Gate, exactly where she had started her harrowing journey five years and two months earlier.

The Fields, too, were released that year. Hermann returned to the United States, where he became an urban studies professor and a pioneering environmentalist at Tufts University and wrote novels. Noel and Herta shocked their family by staying in Hungary, where they quietly lived out the rest of their lives. For Noel, the personal betrayal by Dulles and his own country was, in the end, more unforgivable than the years of abuse at the hands of his Communist comrades. "He would never talk to me about his years in prison," Hermann said about his brother. "He dismissed the episode as a Stalinist aberration. He was a true believer . . . to the end of his life."

Wallach was eager to reunite with her husband and their two children, although so much time had gone by, she was unsure how she would begin again with her family. It would take two years before U.S.

authorities finally allowed her to enter the United States. "I was continuously interrogated—let's put it that way," she later said. "Not interviewed, interrogated. My visa was refused three times, even though I had an American husband and American children living here."

The irony was not lost on her. The official mind-set on both sides of the Cold War looking glass was remarkably the same. The American interrogators kept asking the same questions that their Soviet counterparts had.

After she was finally allowed into the United States, Wallach settled into a comfortable life with her family. Her husband had begun a successful career as a banker in Washington, and they lived in the lush Virginia horse country, not far from the new international airport that would be named for John Foster Dulles. Wallach taught French and Latin at the exclusive Highland School.

Wallach wrote a book about her years in captivity, but she didn't believe her ordeal bestowed any special distinction on her. "From a European point of view," she drily observed, "this is a rather common story."

Years later, Wallach came to realize that Dulles had played some significant role in her suffering. Wallach had worked briefly for Dulles immediately after the war, at the OSS base outside Wiesbaden, Germany, where the spy agency had taken over the gilded headquarters of the Henkell sparkling wine company. Wallach was one of the few OSS women on Dulles's payroll at the time, and she had undoubtedly caught his eye. She had also worked with Frank Wisner at the winery. But neither man ever expressed any regrets for what they had done to the young mother.

A few months before she died, in 1993, Wallach recalled her story for a journalist who found his way to her grand house in the northern Virginia countryside. In the final stages of the cancer that would claim her, she seemed to float above her own life in a way that gave her a lofty yet clear-eyed perspective on the past. She could even appreciate—in a detached sort of way—the spycraft behind the Dulles operation that had ambushed her life. "Allen Dulles's motives are easy to imagine," she remarked. "Anything that destabilized the situation in Eastern Europe was good for U.S. interests. Stalin was paranoid enough. The crackdown was real enough. By fanning the flames, you could turn the people against communism. The strategy is completely understandable."

She could even see how Noel Field made such a tempting mouse for someone like Dulles. "And then we have this fool Noel Field, a romantic, he had been everywhere, he was full of these enthusiasms, he went back and forth into these countries freely. I don't think Allen Dulles hated Noel Field, not at all. But the opportunity was too good to miss."

And yet, even in her enlightened state, Erica Wallach was not prepared to entirely forgive Allen Dulles. There was something disturbing about the man, at his core, that she wanted to put on record while she still had time. "Dulles had a certain arrogance in which he believed that he could work with the Devil—anybody's Devil—and still be Allen Dulles," she told her visitor. "He could work with Noel Field and betray him. He could work with the Nazis or with the Communists. He thought himself untouchable by these experiences and, of course, you cannot help be touched, be affected, no matter how noble your cause is."

Scoundrel Time

In late August 1947, Richard M. Nixon, a freshman congressman from Southern California, arrived in New York City to board the luxurious *Queen Mary* for a fact-finding tour of war-ravaged Europe that he would later call "one of the greatest thrills of my life." Nixon's parents came to see off their ambitious son, and before the ocean liner embarked, the family took in a performance of the long-running Broadway musical *Oklahoma!* The young congressman was part of a nineteen-member delegation chaired by Representative Christian Herter, a patrician Republican from Massachusetts tasked with investigating the devastation of the war. President Truman hoped the bipartisan delegation's well-publicized trip would help him win congressional approval for the Marshall Plan, his ambitious, multibillion-dollar aid package to reconstruct Europe. Truman's sweeping proposal was generating stiff opposition from GOP conservatives, who saw it as another example of Democratic extravagance.

Back home in Whittier, California, one of the conservative businessmen who had helped pave Dick Nixon's successful entry into politics the previous year warned the young congressman not to be taken in by the slick State Department types during the European junket. The country could only rid itself of "the hangover philosophies of the New Deal" if Republican congressmen like Nixon were "wise enough to refuse to be drawn into support of a dangerously unworkable and profoundly inflationary foreign policy."

Herter, a Boston Brahmin who was married to a Standard Oil heiress, was part of the bipartisan, internationalist political elite who rejected this type of thinking as narrow-minded and isolationist. Herter's circle saw the Marshall Plan not only as an essential antidote to the growing appeal of Communism in poverty-stricken Western Europe, but as a financial boon for America's export industries and international banks, which would profit enormously from the revival of European markets. Herter asked one of his oldest friends to accompany the delegation—Allen Dulles, a man who shared his views and was well known for his powers of persuasion. (Dulles had another motive for backing the Marshall Plan: he and Frank Wisner would later use funds skimmed from the program to finance their anti-Soviet operations in Europe.) As young diplomats in Bern during World War I, Dulles and Herter had shared the joys of bachelor life. Now, the Herter Committee's round-trip, transatlantic journey and lengthy tour of Europe—a political expedition that would stretch for longer than two months—would give Dulles and Herter ample opportunity to win over conservative skeptics like young Dick Nixon.

The opulent accommodations on board the *Queen Mary* were a far cry from the drab veterans' halls and school auditoriums where Nixon had been spending his days just a few months earlier on the campaign trail. On the eve of his trip, Nixon had earnestly declared, "This will be no junket. It will be no cross-Atlantic cocktail party." But in between delegation meetings, the luxury liner offered a wealth of diversions, from its grand, three-story-high dining salon, to its elegant, tiled swimming pool, to its Art Deco–style observation bar with dazzling ocean views. The storied cruise ship had hosted the likes of Clark Gable, Greta Garbo, Fred Astaire, Winston Churchill, and General Eisenhower. It was all heady stuff for the thirty-four-year-old Nixon, whose Quaker family's grocery store and gas station had always wobbled on the brink of bankruptcy.

Throughout his career, Nixon's all-consuming ambition was fueled by resentment and envy, by the sense that he would always be excluded from the top decks where men like Allen Dulles and Christian Herter belonged. When Nixon was finishing law school at Duke University in 1937, he spent a frigid Christmas week in New York searching for a starting position with a prestigious Wall Street firm. He managed to get on the appointments calendar at Sullivan and Cromwell, the firm of his dreams. As he waited in the lobby, he marveled at the "thick, luxurious carpets and the fine oak paneling," a picture of corporate power and comfort that stayed with him for many years. But he did not meet the Dulles brothers during his job interview, and Sullivan and Cromwell— which, like all the top New York firms of the day, drew their young talent almost exclusively from the Ivy League—showed no interest in this product of Whittier College and Duke Law. Nixon, who could only afford a room in the Sloane House YMCA on West Thirty-Fourth Street during his weeklong job hunt, felt a bitter sense of rejection by the time he returned to school. "He was not charmed by New York," remembered a Duke classmate of Nixon's. He felt the city had kicked him in the teeth.

Yet here he was, ten years later, being wined and dined on the *Queen Mary* in the same privileged company as Allen Dulles. The spymaster and Herter took the young congressman under their wing during the ocean crossing. They schooled him about the importance of foreign aid as a facilitator of U.S. economic and political interests. By the time the delegation returned to the United States in early October, Nixon was fully on board as a supporter of the Marshall Plan. The congressman's new enthusiasm for Truman's ambitious proposal did not go down well with his conservative supporters back home. But Nixon was shrewd enough to figure out that senior members of the GOP's East Coast elite like Dulles and Herter could be of more benefit to him than the Southern California citrus growers and businessmen who had launched his career.

The political relationship forged between the rising politician from California and Dulles's East Coast circle would become one of the most significant partnerships of the postwar era. Nixon grew into a potent political weapon for the Dulles group, a cunning operator who managed to accrue solidly conservative credentials with the Republican Party's popular base while dependably serving the interests of the GOP's priv-ileged leadership class. Together, the Dulles circle and Richard Nixon would bring about a sharp, rightward shift in the nation's politics, driv-ing out the surviving elements of the New Deal regime in Washington and establishing a new ruling order that was much more in tune with the Dulles circle's financial interests. The Dulles-Nixon alliance proved masterful at exploiting the Cold War panic that gripped the nation, using it to root out Rooseveltian true believers from government, along with a few genuine Communist infiltrators who posed a marginal threat to national security. When Washington's anti-Communist witch hunt raged out of control and threatened to consume even those who had lit the flame, Nixon again proved of great use to Dulles, working with him to keep the inferno within safe boundaries. In return for his services, Nixon won the patronage of the kingmakers in the Dulles circle, ensur-ing the politician's steady rise toward Washington's top throne.

Years later, after Nixon's climb to power was stalled by his loss to John F. Kennedy in the 1960 presidential election, Dulles sent Nixon a warm letter, reminiscing about their relationship and noting that "we have worked together since the days of the mission on the Marshall Plan." The Dulles-Nixon alliance actually preceded their voyage on the *Queen Mary*, but the spymaster was understandably loath to officially record its true origins. According to John Loftus, the former Justice Department Nazi hunter, the two men first came in contact in late 1945, when young naval officer Richard Nixon was shuttling up and down the East Coast, wrapping up war-related business for the Navy. While sifting through the military paperwork, Nixon came across eye-opening Nazi documents that had been shipped to an old torpedo factory on the Virginia side of the Potomac. Some of these documents revealed how the Dulles brothers had helped launder Nazi funds during the war. Loftus, citing confidential intelligence sources, alleged that Dulles and Nixon proceeded to cut a deal. "Allen Dulles," reported Loftus, "told him to keep quiet about what he had seen and, in return, [Dulles] arranged to finance the young man's first congressional campaign against Jerry Voorhis."

Dulles and his clients in the banking and oil industries had ample reason to target Voorhis, a five-term Democratic congressman and ardent New Dealer from Nixon's home district in Southern California. The crusading congressman was a particularly troublesome thorn in the sides of Wall Street and Big Oil. Voorhis shook the banking industry by pushing for the federal government to take over the nation's privately owned, regional Federal Reserve Banks—a radical proposal that briefly won President Roosevelt's support, but ultimately failed to overcome the banking lobby. Voorhis was more successful in his efforts to curb the power of the major oil companies. In 1943, after learning that the Navy was about to grant Standard Oil exclusive drilling rights in the sprawling Elk Hills naval reserve in central California, Voorhis exposed the sweetheart deal and succeeded in blocking it. The congressman earned yet more of the oil industry's wrath by taking aim at one of the industry's most cherished tax breaks, the oil depletion allowance, and by stopping offshore drilling plans along the California coast.

Voorhis also posed a direct legal threat to the Dulles brothers through his efforts to shine a light on the wartime collusion between Sullivan and Cromwell clients like Standard Oil and DuPont chemical company and Nazi cartels such as IG Farben. Voorhis further unnerved the Dulles circle by demanding a congressional investigation of the controversial Bank for International Settlements, charging that bank president Thomas McKittrick, a close associate of the Dulles brothers, was a Nazi collaborator.

Corporate America viewed Washington politicians like Voorhis as the personification of their New Deal nightmare. In his midforties, Voorhis had the granite-jawed good looks of a movie star. He also combined the same upper-class breeding and populist instincts that made Roosevelt such a formidable threat. The son of an automobile executive, Voorhis was educated at the Hotchkiss School and Yale. But as a young man, he rejected his privileged background, marrying a social worker, going to work on a Ford assembly line, and becoming a Socialist. He changed his registration to the Democratic Party in 1934 when he entered California politics, but his congressional voting record demonstrated he was a stalwart of the party's left wing.

In 1944, Voorhis published a book titled *Beyond Victory*, making clear that, as a leader of the progressive caucus in Congress, he was determined to keep pushing for ambitious reforms in postwar America. Voorhis sent alarms through the ranks of his corporate foes by calling for the nationalization of the transportation, energy, and utility industries as well as sweeping banking reforms. He wanted to create a national credit union to compete with private banks and to expand the Social Security system as a way to establish a nationwide minimum income.

Voorhis's business opponents began searching for a strong candidate to unseat their nemesis long before the 1946 congressional race. While still in uniform, Nixon was recruited to run against the popular progressive by Herman Perry, a family friend who managed the Bank of America's Whittier branch. Nixon later insisted that no powerful interests were behind his political debut, just "typical representatives of the Southern California middle class: an auto dealer, a bank manager, a printing salesman, a furniture dealer." But Voorhis knew the truth. He later wrote in an unpublished memoir that he had been targeted by powerful East Coast bankers and oilmen, who saw him as "one of the most dangerous men in Washington." In the fall of 1945, according to Voorhis, one major New York banker flew to Southern California, where he sat down with local bankers and "bawled them out" for allowing such a progressive firebrand to represent their district.

Nixon knew that it would take a large campaign war chest to defeat the five-term Voorhis—and he also made clear that he was not interested in running for office if it meant taking a pay cut. Republican business circles in New York and Los Angeles quickly rallied to make the campaign against Voorhis worth the effort of their candidate. An executive for Gladding, McBean, a major ceramics manufacturer whose chairman sat on Standard Oil's board, later recalled how the corporate message on behalf of Nixon was delivered. At a meeting of seventy-five executives held at an exclusive Ojai, California, resort, the president of Gladding, McBean touted the "young man fresh out of the Navy" who had been lined up for the congressional race. "Smart as all get out. Just what we need to get rid of Jerry Voorhis. . . . He says he can't live on a congressman's salary. Needs a lot more than that to match what he knows he could make in private law practice. The boys need cash to make up the difference. We're going to help."

Gladding, McBean became a key generator of cash for Nixon, shaking down its own executives for campaign contributions and spreading the word to other corporate donors. The company president demanded that his fellow executives deliver the money in cash to his office. "We just gotta get rid of that pinko Voorhis," he exhorted his team. The strong-arm appeal worked. Gladding, McBean alone raised at least $5,000 from its executive ranks, the equivalent of over $65,000 today. Together, Nixon's corporate backers amassed a campaign "pot big enough to engulf the world," as the Gladding, McBean financial officer later put it.

Gladding, McBean had a modest enough corporate profile to escape the scrutiny of election officials, but its board of directors boasted a variety of high-profile connections in the political and financial worlds. One director, Los Angeles corporate attorney Herman Phleger, had worked with Allen Dulles in postwar Germany and would later serve his brother as the State Department's legal adviser. The Nixon-Voorhis contest took place on the opposite side of the country from the East Coast power centers—in a remote suburban California district where orange groves still dominated the landscape—but its outcome would help shape national politics for years to come.

As the congressional race heated up in summer 1946, it became clear to Nixon's wealthy supporters that they had backed the right man to unseat Voorhis. The Republican challenger ran a ruthless campaign, cutting up the incumbent as an ineffectual left-wing dreamer, a Communist Party sympathizer, and a tool of Red-dominated labor unions—none of which was true. In fact, Voorhis had long battled against Communist Party encroachment in liberal organizations and had even spearheaded a 1940 bill requiring the registration of political groups that were affiliated with foreign powers—a law aimed as much at the Moscow-dominated CPUSA as it was against the pro-Hitler

166 · THE DEVIL'S CHESSBOARD

German-American Bund. But in Nixon's skilled hands, Voorhis's support for New Deal programs like school lunches became evidence of his obedience to the Communist Party line. In the final stretch of the campaign, Nixon released one last cloud of poison. Voters throughout the district began receiving anonymous phone calls, which turned out to emanate from Nixon campaign boiler rooms. "This is a friend of yours, but I can't tell you who I am," went a typical call. "Did you know that Jerry Voorhis is a Communist?"

The uniformly conservative Southern California press, including the mighty *Los Angeles Times*, echoed Nixon's baseless charges against Voorhis and enthusiastically endorsed the Republican candidate. On Election Day, Nixon rolled to an impressive victory, winning 56 percent of the vote. Voorhis was so dismayed by the experience that he abandoned the political arena for the rest of his life.

An outraged Voorhis aide later confronted Nixon. "Of course I knew Jerry Voorhis wasn't a Communist," Nixon told the man. "I had to win," he went on, as if enlightening a political innocent. "That's the thing you don't understand. The important thing is to win. You're just being naïve."

As promised, Nixon was well compensated for his efforts. When he and his family embarked for Washington, they took with them $10,000 (about $130,000 in today's dollars), a new Ford, and a generous life insurance policy. Nixon also arrived in the nation's capital with a game plan for Republican success that would embolden the likes of Senator Joseph McCarthy and change American history. Nixon's bare-knuckled race against the idealistic Voorhis was the political overture of a new era—a "scoundrel time" of patriotic bullying and rampant fear.

On August 11, 1948, a warm, sticky evening in New York, Rep. Dick Nixon walked into the lobby of the Roosevelt Hotel—the grand, midtown palace named after Teddy, not FDR—and took the elevator up to the fifteenth floor where Governor Tom Dewey, the Republican candidate for president, kept a suite. The freshman congressman was, once again, about to demonstrate his value to the Dulles brothers.

Nixon carried in his briefcase the congressional testimony of two men—Alger Hiss and Whittaker Chambers—whose epic duel would become one of the defining public spectacles of the Cold War. Chambers—a senior writer and editor at *Time* in Henry Luce's right-leaning publishing empire—had ignited a firestorm by alleging that he had worked as a courier for a Soviet spy ring in Washington during the 1930s, a ring that included Alger Hiss. The resounding denial by Hiss, a former high-ranking official in Roosevelt's State Department, was so persuasively delivered that the notorious House Un-American Activities Committee on which Nixon served seemed on the verge of terminating its investigation amid a chorus of catcalls from the press.

When the committee later reconvened in executive session after Hiss's "virtuoso" performance, Nixon recalled, his fellow congressmen were "in a virtual state of shock." Furious committee members turned on the staff, berating them for not thoroughly vetting Chambers before putting him on the stand. "We've been had! We're ruined," moaned one Republican. But Nixon stood firm. If HUAC shut down its probe of alleged Communists in federal government, he argued, "far from rescuing the committee's reputation, it would probably destroy it for good. It would be a public confession that we were incompetent and even reckless in our procedures." His impassioned plea succeeded in steadying the committee's nerves, and they agreed to carry on. But Nixon knew that before HUAC resumed its public hearings, he needed to get outside help if the committee was to prevail in the arena of popular opinion.

The Hiss case, Nixon later wrote in his soul-baring memoir *Six Crises*, was one of the defining crucibles in his career. Nixon was often wracked by self-doubt, and this was one of those contests that brought out his deepest anxieties. Nixon's antagonist boasted all the credentials that had eluded him in life. Hiss had been one of the most brilliant law students in his class at Harvard. After graduating, he was picked to serve as a law clerk to octogenarian Supreme Court justice Oliver Wendell Holmes, a living legend of American jurisprudence. Hiss quickly became one of the rising stars in the Roosevelt administration, capping his Washington career by accompanying FDR to his final summit at Yalta and playing a key role in the formation of the United Nations.

When he appeared before the House Un-American Activities Committee, Hiss made a striking impression—thin, handsome, smartly dressed, and self-assured. Even Nixon had to admit that his performance was a striking contrast to his accuser's "lackluster" appearance before the committee. Chambers was "short and pudgy," observed Nixon. "His clothes were unpressed. His shirt collar was curled up over his jacket. He spoke in a rather bored monotone." Hiss insisted that he had never met anyone named Whittaker Chambers—and he and the rumpled Chambers seemed to come from such different worlds that it was easy to believe him. But it was Chambers whom Nixon found convincing: he simply knew too many details about Hiss's personal life. And there was something about this sad sack—a troubled but intelligent man who seemed to exude a strange mix of admiration, envy, and resentment toward Hiss—that strongly resonated with Nixon.

Nixon quickly emerged as Hiss's most dangerous inquisitor, but Hiss held his ground under the young congressman's relentless questioning, slyly taking aim at the most vulnerable part of his psyche. "I am a graduate of Harvard Law School," Hiss coolly informed the committee. He let that sink in, and then fixed Nixon with a level gaze. "And I believe yours is Whittier?" It was an expertly aimed harpoon, certain to deeply wound the man who was so obviously afflicted by what sociologists would later term "the hidden injuries of class."

"It absolutely ripped Nixon apart," recalled Robert Stripling, HUAC's chief investigator. "I realized from that moment on that he could not stand Hiss."

Nixon knew that he was facing a formidable opponent. Hiss clearly had the Washington press on his side, as well as the White House. While the committee was interrogating him, President Truman told a press conference that the HUAC spy scare was nothing more than a "red herring" to divert Washington from more important business. Hiss's testimony was full of references to leading political personalities with whom he was on a familiar basis. And they weren't all Democrats. The biggest name he dropped—John Foster Dulles—produced a mighty echo in the cavernous caucus room of the Old House Office Building. Hiss reminded the committee that it was the Republican wise man who had offered him his current position as president of the prestigious Carnegie Endowment for International Peace, where Foster Dulles served as chairman of the board.

Nixon was well aware that Hiss, who accepted Foster Dulles's offer and took over the Carnegie Endowment in January 1947, belonged to a Washington aristocracy that transcended party lines. By accusing Alger Hiss of being a traitor to his country, Nixon was not only threatening the career of a well-connected and widely respected public citizen, he was jeopardizing the reputations of Hiss's prominent patrons— powerful men like the Dulles brothers, whom Nixon was counting on to advance his own career.

When he phoned Foster Dulles at his Wall Street office on the morning of August 11—the same office where he had been snubbed as a young law student—Nixon understood that it was another make-or-break moment for him. Foster agreed to meet that evening at Dewey's hotel suite to discuss the Hiss-Chambers case. The Wall Street attorney appreciated the delicacy of the situation. As Dewey's top foreign affairs adviser, Foster was poised to become the next secretary of state. The last thing he needed was a Washington tempest that tied him to a Soviet spy.

For Nixon, the anxiety hovering around the meeting was heightened by the fact that he harbored his own doubts about the case against Hiss. But men of action learn to conquer these disquieting voices inside, Nixon reminded himself. "One of the most trying experiences an individual can go through is the period of doubt, of soul-searching, to determine whether to fight the battle or fly from it," Nixon wrote in *Six Crises*. "It is in such a period that almost unbearable tensions build up, tensions that can be relieved only by taking action, one way or the other. And significantly, it is this period of crisis conduct that separates the leaders from the followers." A leader acted decisively. The failures are "those who are so overcome by doubts that they either crack under the strain or flee."

Published in 1962, *Six Crises* was Nixon's strangely belated answer to *Profiles in Courage*—the 1957, Pulitzer Prize–winning book by the charismatic man who had just beat him for president. Nixon intended his book to be a leadership manual, but it only highlighted his neuroses. Many observers thought Nixon's desperate self-puffery bordered on hysteria. Writing in his journal after the book's publication, Arthur Schlesinger Jr. called it "an orgy in unconscious self-revelation." President Kennedy told Schlesinger it showed that Nixon was a "sick" man.

But, as usual, Nixon's opponents underestimated him. Nixon may have suffered from a tortured psyche, but it made him acutely sensitive to the nuances of power. He had a Machiavellian brilliance for reading the chessboard and calculating the next series of moves to his advantage.

When Nixon walked into Suite 1527 at the Roosevelt Hotel that summer night in 1948, he faced a formidable array of power. With Foster were his brother Allen, Christian Herter, and Wall Street banker C. Douglas Dillon, who would later serve President Eisenhower in the State Department and presidents Kennedy and Johnson as Treasury secretary. These men made up a significant section of the Republican Party's ruling clique. If Nixon failed to convince them that he had a solid case against Hiss, HUAC would have to close its noisy show, and his political career would be wrecked just as it was gaining traction.

Foster felt that Nixon approached the group with the proper sense of humility, and no doubt trepidation. "It was clear he did not want to proceed [with the Hiss investigation] until people like myself had agreed that he really had a case to justify going ahead," Foster later remarked. Nixon knew that he was facing a skeptical audience. Herter, a mentor ever since their Marshall Plan junket, had already told Nixon he didn't think he had a case. Herter had checked with his friends at the State Department, who assured him Hiss was not a Communist.

But Nixon was also aware that he came into the room with his own unique leverage. As the leading inquisitor in the Hiss case—an affair whose tendrils laced their way as far as John Foster Dulles himself— Nixon had the power to upend the Republican presidential campaign.

Nixon sat quietly in the suite while the Dulles brothers carefully read through the Hiss and Chambers transcripts. When they were done, Foster got to his feet and began pacing the room with his hands clasped behind him. The brothers realized that Nixon was right—and they had a problem. "There's no question about it," Foster frowned. "It's almost impossible to believe, but Chambers knows Hiss."

The Republican wise men took Nixon into their confidence, and once again the ambitious young politician came to a mutually convenient arrangement with the Dulles circle. It was another significant step for Nixon through the portals of power. With the Republican brain trust's full support, Nixon would continue his aggressive pursuit of Hiss while keeping the spotlight carefully away from Foster and other GOP luminaries who were tied to the accused man. Meanwhile, Foster moved quickly to distance himself from Hiss, pressuring him behind the scenes to resign his Carnegie Endowment post, while Allen fed incriminating intelligence to Nixon to bolster his case. Some of this confidential information about Hiss likely came from the Venona project, the Army intelligence program that had been set up in 1943 to decrypt messages sent by Soviet spy agencies. The Venona project was so top secret that it was kept hidden from President Truman, but the deeply wired Dulles might have enjoyed access to it.

Nixon was impressed by the Dulles brothers' bold decision to politically exploit the Hiss affair rather than run from it. The HUAC investigation could have been "acutely embarrassing" to Foster, Nixon later noted. The Dulleses "could have suggested that I delay the proceedings until after the election." But instead, with Nixon's help, they turned the Hiss case to their advantage, with Dewey fulminating against the laxity of the Roosevelt and Truman administrations that had allowed Communists to penetrate the government. The meeting at the Roosevelt Hotel proved a turning point. For the next decade, Republicans would use Cold War hysteria not just to indict Communist Party members and sympathizers as traitors but to brand the entire New Deal legacy as un-American. Even former high-ranking New Dealers with impeccable credentials like Alger Hiss would be fair game in Washington's new inquisitorial climate.

The age of paranoia brought out Nixon's brilliance as a political performer. He had a deep, demagogic instinct for playing on the public's darkest fears. Robert Stripling, his right-hand man on HUAC, came to believe that there was no genuine ideological passion in Nixon's pursuit of the "traitor" Hiss, just the same cold-blooded calculation he had brought to his campaign against Jerry Voorhis. "He was no more concerned about whether Hiss was [a Communist] than a billy goat," the HUAC investigator later remarked.

This was not an entirely fair assessment of Nixon. The young politician clearly had developed deeply felt convictions about the brutality of the Communist system. When his Marshall Plan tour took him to Greece, Nixon was horrified to meet a young woman whose left breast had been hacked off by Communist guerrillas. He returned from the trip with a firm belief in the implacability of Communist regimes, and the conviction that they only understood force—a view that he would modify when he became president and engaged both the Soviet Union and China in strenuous diplomacy.

But at home, Nixon's anti-Communism reeked of political cynicism, earning him the nickname "Tricky Dick." He smeared his opponents with reckless abandon, labeling them as Reds or "dupes" or, in the case of his 1950 senatorial opponent, Helen Gahagan Douglas, a woman who was "pink down to her underwear." Nixon never proved that Hiss was a card-carrying Communist or a Soviet agent, but, with typical hyperbole, he treated him like he was a mortal threat to the American way of life.

The highlight of Nixon's obsessive, Javert-like pursuit of Hiss came when Chambers dramatically led HUAC investigators to a pumpkin patch on his Maryland farm, where he produced a hollowed-out pumpkin containing sixty-five pages of retyped State Department documents, four pages of copied government documents in Hiss's handwriting, and five rolls of classified film—all of which, Chambers claimed, had been slipped to him by Hiss in 1938. Nixon staged a dramatic return to Washington from a Caribbean vacation cruise, with the help of a Coast Guard rescue plane, in order to publicize the so-called pumpkin papers. The documents, which seemed to prove that Hiss did have an espionage connection to Chambers, sealed the diplomat's fate. He was indicted in December 1948 by a federal grand jury for lying to Congress.

Hiss continued to vigorously deny his guilt, insisting that the pumpkin papers had been forged by Chambers. Neither he nor his wife, Priscilla, could have retyped the State Department documents, said Hiss, because they had given away the Woodstock model typewriter that they allegedly used to copy the classified memos before 1938. Four jury members at his first deadlocked trial believed Hiss, agreeing that someone other than Hiss or his wife had retyped the State Department documents. Hiss's suspicion that he was framed was given further credence years later by John Dean, the former White House attorney who became a key witness in the Watergate scandal that ended the Nixon presidency. Writing in his memoir *Blind Ambition*, Dean alleged that Nixon told fellow White House aide Charles Colson, "We built [the typewriter] in the Hiss case," implying that with the help of FBI technicians, Nixon had used a replica of the Woodstock machine to trap his prey.

Hiss's second trial did not go in his favor. Among the witnesses who testified against him was John Foster Dulles, who disputed Hiss's recollection of the events leading to his resignation from the Carnegie Endowment. It was the final nail in Hiss's coffin by his former patron. In January 1950, Hiss was convicted of perjury and sentenced to federal prison, where he would serve three and a half years. Meanwhile, Chambers, a man who had launched his writing career by working for the Communist Party press, continued to enjoy his new life as a polemicist for the conservative media, first in Henry Luce's plush Time-Life tower and then in the more modest Manhattan offices of William F. Buckley Jr.'s *National Review*.

For Nixon, the Washington spy spectacle demonstrated not only the moral turpitude of Alger Hiss but the intellectual bankruptcy of the liberal elite. His successful pursuit of Hiss brought him national fame, Nixon later observed, but it also attracted the "unparalleled venom and irrational fury" of the liberal intelligentsia, which saw Hiss as a New Deal icon. He was convinced that he would never be forgiven by "substantial segments of the press and intellectual community" for exposing how the New Deal had been compromised by the Communist underground. Nixon brooded that it was this "hatred and hostility" that might have cost him the 1960 presidential election.

Chambers, too, saw his decision to incriminate Hiss as part of a broader assault on New Deal–style government and its "drift toward socialism." In his 1952 memoir *Witness*, Chambers conflated the Roosevelt presidency with the evils of Communist rule. The New Deal, he wrote, "was not a revolution by violence. It was a revolution by bookkeeping and lawmaking." Both types of revolution, he argued, led to a triumph of the state over the individual.

The Cold War furies that Nixon and the Dulles brothers helped to unleash scoured all nuance and charity from American politics. There were indeed a few committed Communist agents embedded here and there in Roosevelt's bureaucracy, such as Nathan Silvermaster, a Russian-born economist with the War Production Board during World War II who was dedicated to the dream of a Soviet America. But by far the more common "traitors" were men like Hiss: well-educated, progressive idealists. They were the type who had come of age after the stock market crash of 1929 and had grown sick of a hands-off government that allowed encampments of hungry and homeless people to spring up all over the country without taking action.

When Roosevelt was elected in 1932, and Hiss received a telegram from Felix Frankfurter, his former Harvard law professor and an adviser to FDR, urging him to come work for the new administration "on the basis of national emergency," Hiss knew that he had to sign up. For young New Dealers, "it was a call to arms, being told that the nation was in danger. I think many of us who went down [to Washington] in those first few weeks thought of ourselves as civilian militia going down for the duration of a real emergency, as if we were going to war. Roosevelt, in his first inaugural address, used the sacrifices of war as an analogy."

In despair over the enormous human suffering of the Depression, with some fifteen million jobless—a quarter of the U.S. labor force—some of these New Dealers found themselves drawn, at least for a time, to the discipline and militancy of the Communist Party. Some were intrigued by the Soviet economic experiment, which appeared at least comparatively functional, and thought their own ailing capitalist system might learn something from it. During World War II, when the Roosevelt administration urged Americans to regard the Russians as indispensable comrades-in-arms, some of these federal officials looked for ways to strengthen these bonds by sharing information with our allies. But while some of these men and women crossed the line, most saw themselves as patriots whose dreams for the future were deeply rooted in American traditions, not European ideologies. Roosevelt was their guiding light, not Stalin.

To this day, Alger Hiss—who was convicted of perjury, not treason—remains a conundrum, his guilt or innocence still hotly debated along ideological lines. When the Venona decrypts were declassified in the 1990s, some saw smoking-gun proof of his guilt, while others argued that the case had only entered an even murkier stage. In the end, Hiss will likely be seen as a perplexingly mixed bag: a fundamentally loyal American who had associated with left-wing circles in Washington and was not entirely forthcoming with Congress, but was never a serious threat to national security.

The least credible aspect of Hiss's testimony was his insistence that he had never known "an individual by the name of Whittaker Chambers." When Nixon later staged a face-to-face meeting between the two men, Hiss finally acknowledged that he had known Chambers, though under another name, and only briefly in 1935. But the evidence pointed to a more intricate relationship than that. The political complexity of the Hiss case was further entangled by its interpersonal complications. Although a married man with children, Chambers confessed to the FBI that he had led a secret homosexual life. He was clearly enamored of Hiss and his family. In *Witness*, he wrote that he came to regard Alger and Priscilla Hiss "as friends as close as a man ever makes in life." Under questioning from Nixon, Chambers warmly described Hiss—the man whose life he was in the process of ruining—as "a man of great simplicity and a great gentleness and sweetness of character." It was a far cry from how Nixon viewed the "cold and callous" Hiss.

Chambers recounted the final meeting he allegedly had with Hiss—when he went to Hiss's Washington home in 1938 to beg the diplomat to leave the Communist Party—with the wounded clarity of a man remembering a lovers' breakup: "We looked at each other steadily for a moment, believing that we were seeing each other for the last time and knowing that between us lay . . . a molten torrent. When we turned to walk in different directions from that torrent, it would be as men whom history left no choice but to be enemies. As we hesitated, tears came into Alger Hiss's eyes—the only time I ever saw him so moved. He has denied this publicly and derisively. . . . He should not regret those few tears, for as long as men are human, and remember our story, they will plead for his humanity."

Hiss came to believe that Chambers's accusations against him were those of a rejected suitor. Chambers had never made sexual advances, said Hiss, but "his attitude to me, and his relations, were strange . . . he had a hostility to the point of jealousy about my wife. . . . My guess is that he had some obscure kind of love attachment . . . about me."

Hiss's reluctance to acknowledge his relationship with his accuser might have been due to his uneasiness about the nature of his involvement with the man. Nixon concluded that Hiss had reciprocated Chambers's passion and that a homosexual drama lay at the heart of the political tempest. "The true story of the Hiss case," Nixon revealed to a congressional confidante on board his presidential yacht a quarter century later, was that Hiss and Chambers had been "queers."

But whatever human subtleties might have explained the Hiss affair were pounded to dust by the blunt instruments of Cold War discourse. The investigative apparatus that Nixon and his patrons built in Washington had no way to measure political nuances and peculiarities of the heart.

Alger Hiss had moved in political circles viewed as benign in Roosevelt's Washington but would take on a sinister cast in the panicky atmosphere of the Cold War. Even Allen Dulles had worked with Communists during the war. After the war, you could remain a Communist or Socialist in Western Europe and still be granted a place in the democratic arena. But not in Washington. There, even New Dealers were in danger.

On August 13, 1948, two days after Nixon met with the Dulles group at the Roosevelt Hotel, the HUAC "show trial"—as the hearings were being called in the liberal press—resumed in the Old House Office Building. Once again, the palatial caucus room, with its Greek revival décor and glittering chandeliers, was the scene of a media extravaganza. The day's leading witness was a man whom many considered the committee's top target, since he had held a considerably more important post in the Roosevelt administration than Hiss.

Harry Dexter White was a slight, bespectacled, fifty-five-year-old former government economist whose name meant little to the general public. But as the big thinker in Henry Morgenthau's Treasury Department, White had played a major role in shaping New Deal policy. Among his many accomplishments was the creation of the World Bank and the International Monetary Fund, two linchpins of the postwar global financial order that White was widely credited with spearheading. White joined forces with the esteemed British economist John Maynard Keynes to hammer out the plans for the world's new financial system, but while Keynes provided substantial intellectual input, it was the politically savvy White who was key to bringing the plans to fruition. White would later be hailed as "arguably the most important U.S. government economist of the 20th century."

There is little doubt that Harry Dexter White was one of the main topics for discussion, along with Alger Hiss, at the Roosevelt Hotel that night in August 1948. In fact, the Dulles group saw White as a bigger threat to their postwar plans than Hiss. The formidable White was intent on building a new financial order that would be a "New Deal for a new world," with the new global institutions channeling investment to needy countries in ways that produced the broadest public good rather than the greatest private gain. When the Roosevelt administration unveiled its plans for the World Bank and IMF, Secretary Morgenthau declared that the goal was "to drive . . . the usurious money lenders from the temple of international finance." Not surprisingly, Wall Street banks saw the new institutions, which were to be "instrumentalities of sovereign governments and not of private financial interests," as dangerous new competitors in the global capital markets.

For the Dulles group, there were a number of disquieting developments at the Bretton Woods Conference, held in the green foothills of New Hampshire in the summer of 1944, where 730 delegates from around the world thrashed out the final plans for the new financial system. Morgenthau and White led a movement at the conference to abolish the Bank for International Settlements, an institution they saw as an instrument of financial collaboration among New York, London, and Nazi Germany. It took a major, behind-the-scenes campaign at Bretton Woods—an effort mounted by representatives of Wall Street, the State Department, and the Bank of England—to head off the Morgenthau-White assault on BIS, which the New Dealers wanted to replace with the World Bank and the International Monetary Fund.

White further unnerved Wall Street and Republican circles by pushing for the Soviet Union to be integrated into the new international framework. The Treasury Department's financial wizard saw this postwar partnership with the Soviet Union—a nation with vast markets and resources—as a potentially enormous boon for the U.S. economy, which he feared could slip back into depression after the wartime stimulus disappeared. White also saw this East-West financial partnership as a way to continue the wartime alliance with Moscow and to ensure world peace, a goal that President Roosevelt had made clear was a priority.

By 1948, the visionary internationalism of the Roosevelt years was being rapidly replaced by the hardening nationalism of the Truman presidency. Men like Harry White had been driven from Washington, but he still served as a consultant to the IMF and he was still widely respected throughout the world. And White still had detailed, inside knowledge from his years as Morgenthau's top aide about the wartime activities of the Dulles group.

If the political winds had been blowing in a different direction in

1948, it might well have been men like Foster and Allen Dulles, Thomas McKittrick of BIS, and Walter Teagle and William Stamps Farish of Standard Oil instead of New Dealers like Hiss and White who were put under the investigative spotlight for treason. But by turning the table on New Deal officials such as White, who had long wanted to prosecute these high-level Nazi collaborators, the Dulles group ensured their own legal protection. By seizing the investigative momentum, Republicans like Dick Nixon, whom Loftus called "Allen Dulles's mouthpiece in Congress," made sure that the Dulles circle would never have to answer for their wartime actions.

By the time Harry Dexter White walked into the packed hearing room on the morning of August 13, he had been under FBI investigation for seven months. J. Edgar Hoover's agents had tapped his phones and conducted scores of interviews in a determined effort to find evidence that he was a Russian spy. White's two principal accusers were Chambers and an emotionally unstable alcoholic named Elizabeth Bentley, who had taken Chambers's place as a Soviet spy courier in wartime Washington after he fled the Communist Party in 1938. HUAC made Bentley, who appeared in front of the committee two weeks before White, one of its star witnesses. Earlier, she had told the FBI that White was not a "card-carrying Communist," but when she stepped in front of the dazzling newsreel lights, her story grew more dramatic. White was no longer simply a "misguided idealist" but a central player in the Nathan Silvermaster spy ring, feeding confidential information to the group and using his influence to place Communist "contacts" in key government positions.

Bentley, however, proved a highly problematic witness for HUAC. The former spy admitted she had never met White, and over time, as her alcoholism grew worse, she became an increasingly erratic "expert"—as the committee billed her—on Communist Party machinations. As her life spun out of control, Bentley blackmailed the FBI into putting her on its payroll. She would remain a deeply troubled ward of the bureau for the rest of her life, a witness-for-hire whom government investigators would drag into the spotlight in between blackouts, car wrecks, and tumultuous lovers' quarrels. Instead of the glamorous "red spy queen" of the tabloid media's dreams, the matronly, weak-chinned Bentley grew to become a pathetic symbol of Cold War exhibitionism.

When Chambers testified about White before HUAC, he was more circumspect than Bentley. He claimed that he had met with White from time to time as a Soviet courier, but he conceded that the Treasury economist was always cautious and never gave him government documents. "I cannot say he was a Communist," he testified. In fact, Chambers seemed not to know what to make of White. "His motives always baffled me," he wrote in his memoir.

Nixon and his fellow HUAC members knew that their case against White was weak. Earlier in the year, the former Treasury official had already made a successful appearance before a federal grand jury in New York that was investigating government subversion. The jury, which would later bring charges against Hiss, found insufficient evidence to indict White. And despite the FBI's obsessive surveillance of White, even Hoover's intimate colleague Clyde Tolson acknowledged that there was simply not enough proof to label him a "Soviet espionage agent" and warned that FBI officials were "making a great mistake in using this phraseology."

In his appearance before HUAC, White conducted himself with dignity and eloquence. The committee's badgering style often brought out the worst in witnesses, with many resorting to obfuscating tactics or outraged histrionics, and others cowering cravenly and surrendering all that was asked of them, including their self-respect. But White responded to the committee's questions head-on, and when he felt compelled to enlighten his inquisitors on constitutional principles and the fundamentals of the American legal system, he did so with a respectful, professorial calm. White began his testimony by firmly denying that he had ever been a Communist, explaining that he adhered instead to a set of beliefs that he called "the American creed."

I believe in freedom of religion, freedom of speech, freedom of thought, freedom of the press, freedom of criticism, and freedom of movement. I believe in the goal of equal opportunity, and the right of each individual to follow the calling of his or her own choice, and the right of every individual to an opportunity to develop his or her capacity to the fullest.

I believe in the right and duty of every citizen to work for, to expect, and to obtain an increasing measure of political, economic, and emotional security for all. I am opposed to discrimination in any form, whether on the grounds of race, color, religion, political belief or economic status.

I believe in the freedom of choice of one's representatives in government, untrammeled by machine guns, secret police, or a police state. I am opposed to arbitrary and unwarranted use of power or authority from whatever source or against any individual or group. I believe in the government of law, not of men. . . .

I consider these principles sacred. I regard them as the basic fabric of our American way of life, and I believe in them as living realities, and not as mere words on paper. . . .

"That is my creed. Those are the principles that I have worked for. Those are the principles that I have been prepared in the past to fight for," concluded White, who had enlisted in the Army during World War I, "and am prepared to defend at any time with my life, if need be."

White's statement, a ringing invocation of the embattled New Deal philosophy that was in full retreat in Washington, evoked a loud and sustained round of applause from the audience. The former FDR official's performance was so self-assured that committee members lunged at ways to rattle him. HUAC chairman J. Parnell Thomas, a New Jersey Republican who sought to ride the investigation to political glory but instead ended his career in prison for corruption, aimed a particularly low blow at White.

For a number of years, the economist had been grappling with a serious heart condition. The FBI had been forced to delay its interrogation of White the previous year, after he suffered a heart attack.

Before his HUAC appearance, he informed the committee of his medical history in a confidential letter. But when White began speaking about his connection with Nathan Silvermaster, explaining that it was a harmless relationship that consisted of such recreational activities as playing Ping-Pong in the accused spy's basement, Thomas shocked the room by interjecting a comment about White's illness. "For a person who had a severe heart condition, you certainly can play a lot of sports," sneered Thomas. It was a typically ugly moment for the HUAC chairman, and when White replied with gentlemanly restraint, pointing out that his athletic days were far behind him, the audience again burst into applause.

Nixon also got into a losing sparring match with White, clashing with the witness over whether or not the HUAC hearings were "star-chamber proceedings." The congressman insisted that they did not meet that definition because they were open to the public. But White pointed out that by denying alleged "subversives" the right to confront and cross-examine their accusers, HUAC veered dangerously close to operating as a royal tribunal. "Congressman," White patiently explained, "I am sure you appreciate that you need to balance the need for conducting a hearing of this kind against the dangers of doing irreparable harm to some innocent persons. That is a patient heritage which Americans have, that a man is presumed to be innocent until proven guilty . . . and certainly you would be the first to recognize that, in order for a man to have a fair trial, it requires all the rules and regulations of a court hearing."

Nixon, who had acknowledged that he was locking horns with a "rather noted scholar," a man who held degrees from Columbia, Stanford, and Harvard, could only bow in agreement. "You are absolutely correct," he told White.

The only committee member who found a weakness in White's story that morning was John McDowell, a Pennsylvania Republican, who suggested that the former Treasury official had kept some suspicious company when he served in the Roosevelt administration. Several of the men whom he called "good friends," including Silvermaster, were accused spies, McDowell pointed out. "In case we proved that these men are all part of an espionage ring, your place in history is going to be changed considerably, would you not think?" It proved to be a prophetic remark, since, after his death, White would indeed be widely condemned as a spy, a conclusion that was based largely on guilt by association.

White was certainly not entirely blameless. As the smartest man in Secretary Morgenthau's inner council, he had sometimes operated in the Washington arena with a reckless arrogance. He was dismissive of bureaucratic protocols and saw nothing wrong with pursuing his own diplomatic initiatives with the Soviets. As White's biographer, R. Bruce Craig, would conclude, he probably was guilty of "a species of espionage," but a fairly benign one. There is no evidence that White handed over classified documents or subverted U.S. policy to correspond with the Soviet line. But he was guilty of frequent indiscretion when discussing policy issues with Soviet officials or with his left-wing friends and colleagues.

To White this boldness was all in service to a higher good—his dream of a harmonious global financial order. White felt that his communications with the Soviet camp were not only in line with American interests but were in keeping with the sentiments of his bosses, Morgenthau and FDR. By pursuing this dialogue, he believed he could help rope the Soviets into Roosevelt's new world order. But White knew that he was taking a risk, and when the political mood in Washington shifted after FDR's death, he suddenly seemed not merely idealistic but dangerous.

White claimed not to know the political affiliations of the men he helped bring into the federal government, yet he certainly must have known that some were close to the Communist Party if not actual members. To White, what mattered was that they were talented economists who brought impressive skills to government. The fact that most of them were, like him, products of eastern European Jewish families, who had worked hard to climb the academic and professional ladders while maintaining a strong sense of public service, only reinforced the bonds that he felt with them.

Despite the committee's insistence that he disown former colleagues such as Silvermaster, White refused to do so. "You cannot erase seven or eight years of friendship with a man that way unless I see evidence, unless the court declares he is [guilty]—and until they prove he is guilty, I believe he is innocent." It was one final, heartfelt declaration of principle from White, and it brought forth yet another eruption from the crowd. White, at pains to avoid coming across as a grandstander, apologized to Thomas. "I am sorry, Mr. Chairman, this applause is not my fault."

After concluding his testimony, White left Capitol Hill for Union Station, where he boarded a train for New Hampshire. He and his wife had recently bought a farm there, known as Blueberry Hill, and he looked forward to some much-needed relaxation after the relentless stress of the FBI, grand jury, and HUAC investigations. On board the train, White felt chest pains, but when he arrived at the local station he insisted on continuing on to his remote farm, which lay at the end of a three-mile dirt road. The following day, August 14, he suffered a massive heart attack. Two physicians were summoned, but they declared the patient beyond their medical powers. Two days later, Harry Dexter White died at home, surrounded by his family.

For many, White seemed to be the victim of HUAC's "special sort of tyranny," in the words of one partisan reporter. An unusually passionate editorial in *The New York Times* condemned the committee for its coarse handling of White. HUAC could not be blamed for his heart disease, stated the editorial, but it could certainly be charged with having "aggravated" his condition by putting him through an investigative "ordeal" without "the due protection of laws. . . . This procedure is not the American way of doing things. It is the un-American way." But Nixon appeared unfazed by the press furor, moving quickly forward with his inquisition of Hiss—who, after White's passing, would serve as the next best emblem of Rooseveltian treachery.

Harry Dexter White's death signified the final collapse of Washington's New Deal order and the unique brand of utopian internationalism that he had championed. It was men like Nixon and Dulles who now moved into the vacuum.

By 1952, Richard Nixon's triumph as a Cold War inquisitor had won him the number-two spot on the Republican presidential ticket headed by war hero Dwight D. Eisenhower. But on September 29, Drew Pearson, Washington's leading muckraker, dropped a bombshell on Nixon—one of his favorite targets—that briefly threatened to end his political career. The story was part of a larger theme of corruption that reporters like Pearson believed hovered over Nixon's career. Nixon, the humble son of Whittier, always seemed hungry for ways to profit from his public service.

Earlier in the race, Pearson had discovered that Nixon's wealthy Southern California supporters had set up a slush fund for the politician's personal use—a revelation that had nearly forced the vice presidential candidate to resign as Eisenhower's running mate. It took Nixon's brilliantly homespun TV address to the nation—which would go down in history as the "Checkers speech" after the black-and-white cocker spaniel that had been given to Nixon's daughters by a supporter—to preempt the budding scandal and save his political career. "And you know, the kids love the dog," Nixon told the largest audience that had ever tuned in for a political speech. "And I just want to say this right now, that regardless of what they say about it, we're going to keep it." His shameless performance managed to transform a case of blatant political corruption into a domestic drama that touched the hearts of millions of Americans.

Nixon's enormous relief was shared by the GOP power brokers who had picked him for the race. It was the Dulles-Dewey group that had tapped Nixon for vice president. Their decision was conveyed to Eisenhower by Herbert Brownell Jr., a fellow Wall Street attorney who had taken a leave from his blue-chip firm to run the Republican campaign for the White House. The GOP brain trust convinced the aging general that the young senator from California not only brought regional balance to the ticket but the kind of slashing energy and anti-Communist fervor that the campaign needed.

But now, in the final weeks of the presidential contest, Pearson was again on the verge of blowing up Nixon's career. Reporting in his widely syndicated Washington Merry-Go-Round column, Pearson revealed that the vice presidential candidate had left out something very important from his Checkers speech: namely, his crooked relationship with a Romanian industrialist named Nicolae Malaxa. The wealthy Romanian émigré had collaborated with the Nazis during the war, and later with the Communist regime that took over his homeland. But Malaxa's reputation, Pearson reported, did not discredit him with Senator Nixon, who pulled strings on his behalf to allow him to continue living in the United States and to procure a major tax break for him.

Pearson knew that Nixon had performed these favors for Malaxa in return for an impressive bribe. But, lacking the documentary evidence, the columnist had to leave this crucial piece of evidence out of his story.

There was indeed a smoking gun: a $100,000 check from Malaxa deposited in Nixon's Whittier bank account. But Pearson was unable to get his hands on it. In a twist of bad luck for Nixon, one of the tellers at his bank branch turned out to be a Romanian refugee who loathed Malaxa. He sent a photostatic copy of the check to political rivals of the notorious industrialist in the exile community, who in turn forwarded the copied check to their contact in the CIA, Gordon Mason, chief of the agency's Balkans desk.

By fall 1952, Allen Dulles was the number two man at the CIA and was in line to take over the agency with an Eisenhower-Nixon victory in November. As deputy director, Dulles was already making the agency his own, working with loyal associates like Frank Wisner—who would soon take over the agency's action arm—on ways to escalate the covert war against the Eastern bloc. But the ambitious plans that Dulles and Wisner were hatching for a long-awaited Republican presidency suddenly seemed in peril when Gordon Mason walked into Wisner's office with a copy of the Malaxa check. "Jesus Christ!" Wisner burst out. "We'd better see Allen Dulles."

As he had long demonstrated, Frank Wisner was quite willing to recruit from among the ranks of ex-fascists for his espionage operations in Eastern Europe—many of whom he had slipped past immigration authorities into the United States despite their barbaric wartime records. But Wisner, somewhat mysteriously, had insisted on drawing the line with Nicolae Malaxa, whom he considered a particularly "unsavory" character. In a March 1951 CIA memo, Wisner had even urged that Malaxa—who had finagled his way into the United States after the war as part of a Romanian trade delegation—be deported. Wisner had served as the OSS station chief in Romania, and he considered the country his turf. He was acutely sensitive to the factions and feuds within the Romanian exile community, where Malaxa provoked feelings passionate enough to tear apart all hope of a united anti-Soviet front.

Despite Wisner's feelings about Malaxa, he realized that Allen Dulles was deeply implicated in the Romanian's "unsavory" story. Dulles had not only been Malaxa's lawyer, he had introduced him to Nixon. The Malaxa money trail, in fact, led in many compromising directions, including Nixon's bank account, Dulles's law firm, CIA front organizations like the National Committee for a Free Europe, and even some of Wisner's own secret combat groups. The Romanian industrialist, who reportedly stashed away as much as $500 million (worth over $6.5 billion today) in overseas accounts before he fled to the United States, had made himself extremely useful as a shadow financier for the underground Cold War.

Malaxa was the type of charming scoundrel with whom Dulles enjoyed doing business. The Romanian oligarch had no ideology; he believed only in opportunity. He had a witty sense of humor and the dark good looks of a dashing werewolf, with thick black hair and a pronounced widow's peak. He conducted himself with a cynical, Mittel-European confidence that everyone had a price, greasing his way through life by smoothly slipping cash to all the right people. Bribery came so naturally to Malaxa that he once tried to buy off the dedicated U.S. Immigration and Naturalization Service prosecutor who was handling his case—a man who, to Malaxa's great surprise, turned out to be incorruptible.

He began his career in modest fashion, as a locomotive repairman, but he had a talent for making connections and opening doors, and soon he amassed a small fortune as a manufacturer of railroad equipment. In the 1920s, he and his family moved into a mansion in Bucharest, where he entertained the capital's high society, and befriended the mistress of King Carol II, Madame Magda Lupescu. In a deft, *Game of Thrones*–like move, he cemented his royal connections by arranging for his own daughter to become the mistress of the king's son, Prince Michael. By forging a partnership with the king, who proved equally avaricious, Malaxa became a dominant player in the country's steel, munitions, and oil industries.

In the 1930s, as Hitler built his war machine in Germany, King Carol's rule came under increasing pressure from a homegrown fascist movement known as the Iron Guard. The virulently anti-Semitic organization blamed Jews for Romania's woes and targeted prominent Jewish figures such as Madame Lupescu. Despite the debt he owed the king's mistress for her patronage, the ever-opportunistic Malaxa began currying favor with the Iron Guard as the group grew more powerful, financing its activities and flying its flag from the roof of his stone mansion.

In September 1940, the Iron Guard forced King Carol to abdicate and a pro-German fascist government took power in Bucharest. With Hitler's influence expanding in Romania, Malaxa made another nimble move, merging his industrial empire with that of Herman Goering's brother Albert. "Your interests, my dear Mr. Malaxa, are the same as ours," the Nazi industrialist warmly assured him.

In January 1941, Malaxa's green-uniformed Iron Guard thugs, feeling betrayed by Romania's new fascist government, launched a coup attempt, using the industrialist's mansion as a base for their assault. During the coup, the Iron Guard fell upon the country's Jews in one of the most horrific spasms of violence in Romania's history. Thousands of Jews in Bucharest were rounded up and beaten and tortured, including one group of more than a hundred—among them children as young as five—who were marched into a municipal slaughterhouse and butchered. The Iron Guardsmen hung their victims, some still alive, on meat hooks and "mutilated them in a vicious parody of kosher slaughtering practices," according to one later account. The Iron Guard's Bucharest pogrom was so depraved that it shocked even the country's fascist regime, which appealed to Hitler to help put down the uprising.

After the coup was suppressed, Malaxa was jailed as a leader of the conspiracy and his industrial empire was confiscated by the Nazis and the Romanian government. But, in 1944, as the advancing Soviet army drove the Germans out of Romania, Malaxa again rose from the ashes, insinuating himself into the new Moscow-backed regime. He was the only Romanian capitalist to whom the Communist government returned his industrial property.

Nevertheless, Malaxa was savvy enough to realize that his future was not bright in a Communist Romania. He had already taken the precaution of salting away much of his huge fortune in U.S. accounts. After the war, by making a generous distribution of bribes—including jewels, Cadillacs, and cash—Malaxa persuaded Romanian officials to allow him to travel to the United States, ostensibly on trade business for the country. He arrived in 1946 and never returned home.

Malaxa wisely chose to apply for permanent residency, instead of American citizenship, knowing the process was not as demanding. But his résumé was so eyebrow raising that his battle to stay in the United States would drag on for years. Malaxa's OSS, CIA, FBI, and INS files bulged with condemnations of his morally dexterous, shape-shifting life. One government report labeled him "notorious." Another called him "the most perfidious man in Romania." He was a "master of the art of bribery" who had ushered in an "era of corruption" in Romania. He was a flagrant "opportunist" who "had been on all sides of the fence at various times." He had gone from playing "Hitler's game" to someone who "must be considered an agent of the Soviet government and of the Romanian Communists in the United States, even if he himself is not a Communist at heart."

According to a 1952 CIA memo, "perhaps the most concise appraisal of Malaxa" came from an American diplomat who found him "entirely unscrupulous, turning with the wind, and like a cat [he] has developed to a high art the knack of landing on his feet. He is considered to be essentially a dangerous type of man."

None of this mattered to Allen Dulles when Malaxa turned up at his office at Sullivan and Cromwell. The pertinent fact was that the Romanian had a huge fortune, and he was willing to spend millions of it where Dulles wanted him to. In return for financing Dulles's far-flung anti-Communist network—which stretched from Buenos Aires to Bucharest—Malaxa secured Dulles's influential help in his battle to stay in the United States. Some of Malaxa's treasure went to prominent Romanian exile leaders who hoped to take power after the Communist regime was toppled. Other funds went to Juan Perón's Argentina, where Malaxa was involved in a rising neofascist movement, and France, where he underwrote "scholarships" for exiled Romanian "students" who turned out to be veterans of the vicious Iron Guard.

By 1948, Malaxa was ensconced in a luxurious apartment on Manhattan's Fifth Avenue, but his wheeling and dealing had begun to attract unwanted press attention. In May, gossip columnist Walter Winchell exposed the notorious collaborator who was freely enjoying the city's pleasures—the "Balkanazi on Broadway," he called Malaxa. Winchell noted that the "distinguished" firm of Sullivan and Cromwell had recently dropped the Romanian as a client, presumably because he had grown too hot.

But Dulles did not abandon Malaxa; behind the scenes, he entrusted the Romanian's immigration battle to his political protégé Nixon. In return for Malaxa's substantial gift of $100,000, the California senator began vigorously lobbying INS officials on his behalf and pushing an immigration bill through Congress that was designed to win Malaxa U.S. residency. When those efforts stalled due to determined resistance from legislators who were repelled by the émigré's past, Malaxa and Nixon tried a different tack. With the help of Nixon cronies in Southern California, Malaxa announced that he was setting up a pipeline factory in Whittier that he called the Western Tube Corporation. Nixon wrote a letter to the Defense Production Administration, claiming that Malaxa's project was "strategically and economically important, for both California and the entire United States." The Western Tube factory was never built, but the phantom project succeeded in winning Malaxa a huge tax windfall. And it kept alive the Romanian's immigration campaign. California congressman John Shelley later denounced the Western Tube affair as "a complete fraud, a springboard for [Malaxa's] entry to the United States."

As the smoldering Malaxa scandal threatened to erupt into flames in the final days of the 1952 presidential race, Dulles moved quickly to douse it. After Wisner and Mason showed him Malaxa's $100,000 check, the deputy CIA director knew that he would have to send it up the chain of command to his boss, General Walter Bedell Smith. But Dulles also realized that, in this case, passing the buck was as good as destroying the evidence. CIA director "Beetle" Smith had served as Eisenhower's intensely dedicated chief of staff during the war, and he was just as devoted to Ike's presidential victory as Dulles.

It was Gordon Mason who was given the unpleasant task of showing the evidence of Nixon's corruption to General Smith, who predictably flew into a rage. "Smith was a man who could cuss in three languages and in almost every sentence," recalled Mason. "He also had a violent temper, and he acted as though I personally was trying to scuttle Eisenhower." Smith demanded that Mason immediately gather up every scrap of incriminating material against Nixon and bring it to his office. "The story was cleaned from the books," said Mason. Wisner, too, had no doubt what was done with the evidence. "Beetle just flushed it all down the toilet."

Without a copy of the Malaxa check, Drew Pearson could not keep the story going, and it soon petered out. On Election Day, Eisenhower and Nixon swept to a decisive victory, winning 55 percent of the vote and carrying thirty-nine of the forty-eight states.

After the Republican triumph, Dulles and Nixon were finally able to speed Malaxa's immigration case through the bureaucracy. In December 1953, officials in Eisenhower's Justice Department bypassed Congress and the INS and granted Malaxa permanent residence through an administrative decree. Justice Department officials explained that they had reached their decision due to the unique technical services provided by the Western Tube Corporation. The fact that Malaxa's company did not actually exist—and never would—was politely overlooked by the new administration.

Nicolae Malaxa lived out the rest of his days in the comfort of his Fifth Avenue apartment. He began to fancy himself a great benefactor. In January 1953, shortly before Eisenhower's inauguration, Malaxa reached out the hand of friendship to a prominent Jewish exile named Iancu Zissu. Malaxa sent word that he was eager to meet with Zissu, who was the cofounder of a Romanian exile group. The odd meeting took place in the New York apartment of a popular Romanian singer. According to one witness, "Malaxa told Zissu that he had wanted for some time to know him because he is a great friend of the Jews and a great admirer of the Jewish religion. Malaxa stated that if he could change his own religion, he would adopt the Jewish faith."

As he bid Zissu farewell, Malaxa "assured him that those who had been his friends had never had reasons to regret it." It was a surprising burst of goodwill—or, more likely, another attempt by the wily millionaire to buy political support.

From the financial patron of Iron Guard butchers to "great friend of the Jews"—it was just one more grotesque twist in a life filled with them.

The Power Elite

For the Dulles brothers, the Eisenhower-Nixon victory was the culmination of years of political strategizing dating back to the Roosevelt era. They had come achingly close to achieving their dreams in the 1948 election, only to see their longtime ally Tom Dewey lose in the most shocking upset in American history. But now they were headed for the very center of Washington power. As the new heads of the State Department and the CIA, they would direct the global operations of the most powerful nation in the world. The fraternal partnership gave the Dulles brothers a unique leverage over the incoming administration, and they were imbued with a deep sense of confidence that these were the roles they were destined to play.

The 1952 presidential election represented the triumph of "the power elite," in the phrase coined by sociologist C. Wright Mills, academia's most trenchant observer of Cold War America. Mills was a ruggedly independent, Texas-born scholar. He lived in a farmhouse forty miles outside of New York City and rode a motorcycle that he had built with his own hands to the classes he taught at Columbia University. He favored flannel shirts and work boots, and confided to friends that "way down deep and systematically I'm a goddamned anarchist." Mills rejected both the tired Marxist discourse that had dominated New York intellectual circles since the 1930s and the "romantic pluralism" that characterized conventional theories about American politics. According to Mills, power in America was not solely in the hands of Marx's "ruling class"—those who owned the means of production. Nor was it a balancing act of competing interests, such as big business, organized labor, farmers, and professional groups. This ebb-and-flow concept of power—which was clung to by liberal and conservative scholars alike—was a "fairy tale," in Mills's words, one that was "not adequate even as an approximate model of how the American system of power works."

Instead, Mills wrote in his 1956 masterpiece *The Power Elite*, America was ruled by those who control the "strategic command posts" of society—the big corporations, the machinery of the state, and the military establishment. These dominant cliques were drawn together by their deep mutual stake in the "permanent war economy" that had emerged during the Cold War. Though political tensions could flare within the power elite, Mills wrote, there was a remarkable unity of purpose among these ruling groups. The top corporate executives, government leaders, and high-ranking military officers moved fluidly in and out of one another's worlds, exchanging official roles, socializing in the same clubs, and educating their children at the same exclusive schools. Mills called this professional and social synchronicity "the fraternity of the successful."

Within this system of American power, Mills saw corporate chiefs as the first among equals. Long interlocked with the federal government, corporate leaders came to dominate the "political directorate" during World War II. The United States had largely become a democracy in form only. More than half of a century before the John Roberts–era Supreme Court that legally sanctioned corporate control of the electoral process, Mills recognized that the shift toward oligarchy was already well under way: "The long-time tendency of business and government to become more intricately and deeply involved with each other has [now] reached a new point of explicitness. The two cannot now be seen clearly as two distinct worlds."

The crucial task of unifying the power elite, according to Mills, fell to a special subset of the corporate hierarchy—top Wall Street lawyers and investment bankers. These men were the "in-between types" who shuttled smoothly between Manhattan corporate suites and Washington command posts. Little known to the general public, these skilled executors of power constituted in Mills's words America's "invisible elite." They were the men who forged the consensus on key decisions of national significance and who made certain that these decisions were properly implemented. Their work was largely unseen and vaguely understood, but it had enormous impact on the lives of ordinary men and women. It was men like John Foster Dulles and Allen Dulles whom Mills had in mind when he wrote of the power elite's inner core.

Born in Waco to an insurance salesman and a housewife and educated at the University of Texas and the University of Wisconsin, Mills was steeped in a native populism rather than the European ideologies of the New York intelligentsia. A big, broad man with an endless appetite for argument, he could debate for hours on end with the likes of Dwight Macdonald and Irving Howe. But he eschewed the hothouse sectarianism of the New York left, as well as the compulsory mood of "American celebration" that had been embraced by nearly all of his intellectual colleagues in the Eisenhower years, searching instead for a new language to explain the American colossus that had emerged in the postwar era. Mills took aim at the most important topics in American society: the soul-killing, "cheerfully robotic" regimentation of corporate life; the unique terrors of the nuclear age—an age, he argued, when war itself had become the enemy, not the Russians; and, of course, the overworld of American power, a realm that he believed few average citizens could grasp, even though it cast a long shadow over their daily existence.

"Take it big!" the intellectually ambitious Mills liked to exclaim. He wrote in a vigorous, clear style that rejected the academic caste's "bloated puffery of Grand Theory," in sociologist Todd Gitlin's words. Soon after *The Power Elite* was published, it began stirring wide debate, catapulting over the ivy-covered walls of academia onto the bestseller list.

Writing in *The New York Times Book Review*, corporate lawyer and presidential adviser Adolf Berle—a member in good standing of the power elite—found "an uncomfortable degree of truth" in Mills's book but fought off his discomfort by concluding that it was essentially "an angry cartoon, not a serious picture." Mills also struck a sensitive nerve with Cold War liberals like Arthur Schlesinger Jr., whom he accused of abandoning their intellectual independence by joining the era's American celebration. Schlesinger fired back, charging that Mills's book seemed more intent on stirring the masses than on stimulating serious academic debate. "I look forward to the time when Mr. Mills hands back his prophet's robes and settles down to being a sociologist again," he wrote in the *New York Post*.

Mills considered himself an intellectual loner—"I am a politician without a party," he wrote in a letter. But *The Power Elite* touched a deep chord with a rising new generation of revolutionaries and radicals that was soon to make its impact on history. Young Fidel Castro and Che Guevara pored over the book in the Sierra Maestra mountains. And, at home, Tom Hayden drew heavily on Mills's writing for the Port Huron Statement, the manifesto of the emerging New Left.

By the time the Port Huron Statement was presented to the Students for a Democratic Society convention in June 1962, C. Wright Mills was dead—felled by a heart attack in March of that year, at age forty-five. But his critique of the power elite—and his sense of its fundamental, undemocratic illegitimacy—would continue to heavily influence the 1960s generation. Six years after his death, in the wake of the global youth uprisings of 1968, the CIA continued to identify him as one of the leading intellectual threats to the established order.

Schlesinger was partly right about Mills. Though he was a rigorous researcher and a careful craftsman, *The Power Elite* did indeed resound here and there with a prophet's moral urgency. Mills, who was deeply concerned about the runaway nuclear arms race of the Eisenhower era, knew that America's rulers not only possessed terrifying instruments of violence, these men felt largely unrestrained by democratic checks and balances. The ability of American leaders to end life on the planet imbued them with a dark power in Mills's mind—one that inspired impassioned passages like the concluding paragraph of *The Power Elite*:

> The men of the higher circles are not representative men; their high position is not a result of moral virtue; their fabulous suc-

cess is not firmly connected with meritorious ability. . . . They are not men shaped by nationally responsible parties that debate openly and clearly the issues this nation now so unintelligently confronts. They are not men held in responsible check by a plurality of voluntary associations which connect debating publics with the pinnacles of decision. Commanders of power unequaled in human history, they have succeeded within the American system of organized irresponsibility.

Men like the Dulles brothers rejoiced in such "organized irresponsibility." Democracy, in their minds, was an impediment to the smooth functioning of the corporate state. John Foster Dulles had made this clear early in his Wall Street career as he jousted with FDR's New Deal bureaucracy. Complaining to Lord McGowan, chairman of Imperial Chemical Industries, about government efforts to control the spiraling power of global cartels, Foster once acidly remarked, "The fact of the matter is that most of these politicians are highly insular and nationalistic . . . [so] business people . . . have had to find ways for getting through and around stupid political barriers." Allen, for his part, had gone through his espionage career with similar disdain for presidential directives and "stupid political barriers." As Richard Helms put it, with typically droll understatement, "There can be no question that Dulles felt most comfortable running things on his own with a minimum of supervision from above."

When Franklin Roosevelt moved into the White House in 1933, he was well aware of the entrenched interests that he would be confronting as he attempted to reform the country's financial system and to create a social buffer against the havoc of the Depression. "The real truth," FDR wrote to Colonel Edward M. House, President Wilson's close adviser, "as you and I know, is that a financial element in the larger centers has owned the Government ever since the days of Andrew Jackson." For a brief period during the widespread devastation of the 1930s, the New Deal was able to challenge this "plutocracy," as Roosevelt called it. The Roosevelt presidency did not dismantle the power elite, Mills later wrote, "but it did create within the political arena, as well as in the corporate world itself, competing centers of power that challenged those of the corporate directors."

But the militarization of government during World War II began to return power to the corporate elite, as captains of industry and finance moved into key government posts. The Eisenhower presidency would complete this political counterreformation, as Washington was taken over by business executives, Wall Street lawyers, and investment bankers—and by a closely aligned warrior caste that had emerged into public prominence during World War II.

During the Eisenhower administration, the Dulles brothers would finally be given full license to exercise their power in the global arena. In the name of defending the free world from Communist tyranny, they would impose an American reign on the world enforced by nuclear terror and cloak-and-dagger brutality. Elevated to the pinnacle of Washington power, they continued to forcefully represent the interests of their corporate caste, conflating them with the national interest.

C. Wright Mills was among the first to take note of how "national security" could be invoked by the power elite to more deeply disguise its operations. The Dulles brothers would prove masters at exploiting the anxious state of permanent vigilance that accompanied the Cold War. "For the first time in American history, men in authority are talking about an 'emergency' without foreseeable end," Mills wrote. "Such men as these are crackpot realists: in the name of realism they have constructed a paranoid reality all their own."

This chilling observation, which still has disturbing echoes today, captured the gloomy zeitgeist of the Eisenhower-Dulles era. It was a time of American celebration—of unprecedented prosperity and unparalleled military prowess—as well as hair-trigger nuclear tensions. Only a few maverick voices—like that of the intellectual loner from Texas—grasped the frightening amorality that prevailed at the pinnacle of American power.

President Eisenhower enjoyed being in the company of wealthy and powerful men. He filled his administration with power players from the Dewey–Dulles–Rockefeller–Luce–dominated New York nexus, as well as from the higher rungs of industry and the Pentagon. Wall Street lawyer Herbert Brownell was named attorney general after running Ike's campaign, General Motors CEO Charles Wilson was tapped to run the Defense Department, and Chase Manhattan chairman and former diplomat John McCloy—the very personification of the power elite—was called upon as a national security adviser. Even the Eisenhower administration's second rung of power—the undersecretaries and deputies level—was weighted with men like Wall Street banker C. Douglas Dillon, another close associate of the Dulles brothers. The exclusive ranks of the Council on Foreign Relations, where the brothers had long held sway, was a particularly fertile ground for administration recruiters.

Ike also liked to spend his leisure time with the high and mighty. The avid "golfer-in-chief" often had prominent business executives and Army generals in tow during his twice-weekly trips to the verdant links at Burning Tree Country Club in Bethesda, including the CEOs of General Electric, Coca-Cola, Reynolds Tobacco, and Young & Rubicam.

Merriman Smith, the longtime White House wire service reporter, defended Ike's strong affinity for the power elite: "It would be unfair to say that he likes the company of kings of finance and industry purely because of their Dun and Bradstreet ratings. He believes that if a man has worked up to become president of the Ford Motor Company [or] head of the Scripps-Howard newspapers . . . then certainly the man has a lot on the ball, knows his field thoroughly and will be literate and interesting." To which one observer, quoted by Mills, mordantly responded: "This business of working your way up will come as quite a surprise to young Henry Ford or young Jack Howard [the scion who inherited the Scripps-Howard chain]."

Eisenhower was comfortable in the company of these men because he shared their conservative, business-oriented views. President Truman, who had helped pave the general's path to the White House by appointing him the first supreme commander of NATO forces in

1951, tried to persuade Eisenhower to run for president as a Democrat, promising that he would "guarantee" him his party's nomination. But Eisenhower replied, "What reason have you to think I have ever been a Democrat? You know I have been a Republican all my life and that my family have always been Republican." When Truman persisted, Ike made it even more plain, telling him that his differences with the Democrats, particularly when it came to the party's pro-labor positions, were simply too immense for him to consider such a course.

Meanwhile, the Dewey-Dulles group's courtship of Eisenhower to become the Republican standard-bearer, which had begun two years earlier, was coming to a successful conclusion. Dewey had first broached the subject of a White House run at a private meeting with Eisenhower in July 1949, following the governor's own traumatic presidential defeat. Dewey had beseeched the reluctant general to jump into the political arena, telling him that he was the only man who could "save this country from going to Hades in the handbasket of paternalism, socialism [and] dictatorship."

By early 1952, the Dulles brothers had come to agree that throwing their support behind the popular war hero was their best path to the White House. In May, Foster flew to France, meeting with the general twice at NATO headquarters in Fontainebleau and urging him to run. The two men did not immediately hit it off. Foster was uncharacteristically diffident and uncertain in the presence of the legendary warrior. Eisenhower, accustomed to crisp military briefings, found Foster's discursive and lawyerly monologues boring. Foster quickly wore out the general's patience, which he was in the habit of communicating by tapping out a restless drumbeat on his knee with a pencil and, when that failed to end the ordeal, by gazing blankly at the ceiling and "signaling the end of all mental contact," in the words of one aide. Foster later brought out the wicked wit in Churchill, who proclaimed him "Dull, Duller, Dulles."

But the foreign policy paper that Foster presented to Eisenhower in France was far from dull. The memo, which Foster appropriately titled "A Policy of Boldness," urged the next president to take a much sharper stand against the Soviet bloc than Truman, aiming to roll back Communism in Eastern Europe rather than simply containing it. Foster called for an escalation of the underground war against Moscow that his brother was already operating, including a redoubled commitment to psychological warfare. "We should be dynamic, we should use ideas as weapons, and these ideas should conform to moral principles. That we do this is right, for it is the inevitable expression of a faith—and I am confident that we still do have a faith." Foster's paper had the italicized cadences of a preacher's sermon; it was filled with the missionary fervor that had run for generations through his family.

Foster was at his most zealous in his discussion of nuclear arms policy. He proposed an unsettling shift in thinking about America's fearsome nuclear arsenal, moving away from the concept of doomsday weapons as an instrument of last resort to one of first resort. The United States must reserve the right to massively retaliate against any Soviet aggression in the world, wherever and whenever it chose, he wrote. By making it clear to the world that Washington was not afraid to wield its nuclear arms as if they were conventional weapons of war, the United States would gain a commanding strategic advantage. It was the type of leverage enjoyed by a heavily armed madman in a crowded room. But Foster had a more diplomatic way of expressing it. Weapons of mass destruction "in the hands of statesmen . . . could serve as effective political weapons in defense of peace."

Foster further sweetened his argument by pointing out that a nuclear-based military strategy would help contain the growing costs of America's "far-flung, extravagant" defense complex that was threatening to bankrupt the nation. Instead of maintaining an expensive troop presence at every global flashpoint, Foster wrote, all the United States had to do was keep a ready finger on its nuclear trigger.

Even master of war Eisenhower was initially taken aback by Foster's proposal for a "first-use" nuclear strategy. After making his presentation to the noncommittal general, Foster returned to his suite at the Ritz Hotel in Paris, where he frantically paced the room, telling a confidant that Eisenhower somehow failed to grasp that the world was facing a dire Soviet threat. But Eisenhower did share Foster's passionate anti-Communism. And the cost efficiencies of the massive retaliation strategy appealed to the budget-minded general, who was equally concerned about the growing burden of military spending on the economy. So began the reign of nuclear terror—or "brinksmanship"—that would hold the world in its grip for the next decade.

Foster's new "policy of boldness" became a centerpiece of Eisenhower's presidential campaign, and the Wall Street lawyer was widely touted as the next secretary of state. Henry Luce helped enshrine Foster by running his foreign policy paper in *Life* magazine in May 1952. "No one has a broader bipartisan understanding of U.S. foreign policy than John Foster Dulles," stated the respectful biography that accompanied the article.

After Foster was duly confirmed as secretary of state in January 1953—a position he had long coveted and felt he was destined to hold—he addressed several hundred foreign service employees gathered in front of the State Department building in Foggy Bottom. The weather was uncomfortably cold, but the sixty-five-year-old Foster stood on the steps overlooking the crowd with a sturdy self-confidence—a "solid tree trunk of a man," in the words of one biographer, "gnarled and weathered and durable." He carried himself like someone who owned the place. "I don't suppose there is any family in the United States," he told his assembled workforce, "which has been for so long identified with the Foreign Service and the State Department as my own family."

Once installed at Foggy Bottom, Foster quickly took command of Eisenhower's foreign policy, elbowing aside other experts in international affairs who sought the president's ear. Sherman Adams, President Eisenhower's chief of staff, found the new secretary of state a "tough-fibered individual . . . an aristocrat in his own domain" who insisted on maintaining his own direct line to the president. Foster was "a rather secretive person," Adams added, who assiduously deflected efforts by the White House staff to enter the tight loop he had built with the commander in chief. After their initial uneasiness with each other, Eisenhower ultimately decided that even though his secretary of state was "a bit sticky at first . . . he has a heart of gold when you know him." Foster soon had Eisenhower "in his palm," observed a State Department aide.

Allen Dulles felt as firmly entitled to run the CIA under Eisenhower as his brother did the State Department. The junior Dulles had worked uncomplainingly for two years as Walter Bedell Smith's deputy director at the agency, though he had considerably more intelligence experience than "Beetle." Dulles good-naturedly put up with the crusty general's foulmouthed explosions, with the expectation that Smith would anoint him his successor. "The general was in fine form this morning, wasn't he? Ha, ha, ha!" Dulles would chuckle, after returning to his office from what his CIA colleagues called one of Smith's "fanny-chewing sessions."

During the 1952 presidential race, Dulles proved his loyalty to the Eisenhower-Nixon campaign by channeling funds to the Republican ticket through CIA front groups and by leaking embarrassing intelligence reports to the media about the Truman administration's handling of the Korean War—flagrant violations of the CIA charter that forbids agency involvement in domestic politics.

But even though Smith recruited Dulles for the agency and made him his deputy, he never warmed up to his number two man. "Beetle"—who, as Eisenhower's former wartime aide, enjoyed unique access to the president-elect—became an impediment to Dulles's CIA ascension following the Republican victory. "After two years of close personal observation," wrote a CIA historian, "Smith lacked confidence in Dulles's self-restraint." The general felt that Dulles was too enamored of the dark arts of the spy trade. Smith would tell friends that running the CIA sometimes made it necessary to leave his moral values outside the door. But, he quickly added, clinging to his soldierly code of conduct, "You'd damned well better remember exactly where you left them."

Dulles struck Smith as a man who was all too blithe about abandoning his scruples. The deputy CIA director had no qualms about advocating the assassination of foreign leaders, even presenting a plan to Smith in early 1952 to kill Stalin at a Paris summit meeting. Smith firmly rejected the plan. He shuddered at the thought of Dulles taking over the top spot at the agency.

As Smith prepared to step down at the CIA, he lobbied against Dulles as his replacement, advising Eisenhower that it would be politically unwise to have the brother of the secretary of state serve as the administration's intelligence chief. Instead, Smith urged Eisenhower to select another one of his agency deputies, Lyman Kirkpatrick. Like Dulles, Kirkpatrick was a product of Princeton and had an impressive espionage résumé dating back to the war—but, as his career at the CIA would prove, he also had a well-tuned sense of proper conduct. (Years later, Kirkpatrick would be called upon to direct the internal investigation of the Bay of Pigs debacle that nearly ruined the agency, doing such an honest job that some CIA old boys, including Dulles himself, never forgave him.)

Despite Beetle Smith's close ties to Eisenhower, he found himself outmaneuvered by the Dulles brothers. Anticipating Smith's objections, Foster got to Eisenhower first and convinced him that having his brother in charge of the CIA would actually be an asset, ensuring smooth cooperation in the running of foreign policy. When Smith began making his case against Dulles, Eisenhower cut him off, telling his old friend that he had already talked to Foster, who saw no problem at all with a fraternal reign of power.

Smith had never really stood a chance of blocking Allen Dulles. Eisenhower was deeply beholden to the Wall Street Republican power brokers who had not only recruited him for the presidential race but had helped finance his electoral battle, loaned him one of their own—white-shoe lawyer Herbert Brownell Jr.—to run his campaign, and had even tapped Dick Nixon as his running mate. The Dewey-Dulles group was Ike's brain trust and bank. When these men spoke, the general listened.

Under Allen Dulles, the CIA would become a vast kingdom, the most powerful and least supervised agency in government. Dulles built his towering citadel with the strong support of President Eisenhower, who, despite occasional misgivings about the spymaster's unrestrained ways, consistently protected him from his Washington enemies. As America extended its postwar reach around the world, with hundreds of military bases in dozens of countries and U.S. oil, mining, agribusiness, and manufacturing corporations operating on every continent, Eisenhower saw the CIA (along with the Pentagon's nuclear firepower) as the most cost-effective way to enforce American interests overseas. Presidential historian Blanche Wiesen Cook, author of *The Declassified Eisenhower*, initially regarded Ike as "a presidential pacifist." But after examining the administration's documentary evidence for her 1981 book, Cook arrived at the conclusion that "America's most popular hero was America's most covert president. Eisenhower participated in his own cover-up. His presidency involved a thorough and ambitious crusade marked by covert operations that depended on secrecy for their success."

The rise of Dulles's spy complex in the 1950s would further undermine a U.S. democracy that, as Mills observed, was already seriously compromised by growing corporate power. The mechanisms of surveillance and control that Dulles put in motion were more in keeping with an expanding empire than they were with a vibrant democracy. As journalist David Halberstam later observed, "The national security complex became, in the Eisenhower years, a fast-growing apparatus to allow us to do in secret what we could not do in the open. This was not just an isolated phenomenon but part of something larger going on in Washington—the transition from an isolationist America to imperial colossus. A true democracy had no need for a vast, secret security apparatus, but an imperial country did. . . . What was evolving was a closed state within an open state."

On a bright afternoon in September 1953, forty-three-year-old Senator Joseph McCarthy married his office aide, a twenty-nine-year-old former college beauty queen named Jean Kerr, with great pomp and ceremony at St. Matthew's Cathedral in Washington. Pope Pius XII bestowed his apostolic blessing on the couple, and twelve hundred guests—including Vice President Nixon, CIA director Allen Dulles, and young senator John F. Kennedy, whose father was a strong McCarthy supporter—crowded into the cathedral for the nuptials. Afterward, McCarthy and his new wife were whisked away by limousine to a celebrity-studded party held amid the Beaux-Arts splendor of the Patterson Mansion on Dupont Circle, where the couple cut their towering wedding cake and prizefighter Jack Dempsey kissed the bride. Feted by the capital's political luminaries and Hollywood royalty, McCarthy stood at the pinnacle of his power on his wedding day. Packed into his monkey suit and slugging champagne, the thick-built Washington heavyweight with the dark-stubbled jaw had the champion swagger of Dempsey himself.

The Republican senator had come a long way from the Wisconsin dairy farm where he had grown up. He had financed his political rise by taking payoffs from Pepsi-Cola bottlers and prefab construction moguls. In truth, he never lost his taste for the glitzy swag of politics. One of his wedding gifts, it was reported, was a pink Cadillac Coupe de Ville presented to him by a Houston businessman who shared his militant anti-Communism.

By 1953, McCarthy's anti-Red witch hunt was in full blaze, torching the careers of distinguished senators and statesmen and even beginning to flicker ominously outside the White House itself. The FBI's Hoover, long a powerful supporter, was growing increasingly anxious about McCarthy's inflamed ambitions. That summer Hoover warned the new administration that he had learned there was a "conspiracy" to sabotage Eisenhower's presidency and replace Ike with the hard-charging Wisconsin senator.

The carnival of shame and humiliation that McCarthy brought to Washington held the capital in its grip from February 1950—when he delivered the infamous speech in Wheeling, West Virginia, that kicked off his inquisition ("I have in my hand a list of names . . .")—to December 1954, when the Senate finally voted to censure him, triggering his rapid political and physical collapse. No one—from the loftiest general or cabinet member to the lowliest government clerk—was immune from Joe McCarthy's suspicious gaze. When he ran out of alleged Communist sympathizers to drag before his Kafkaesque-sounding Senate Permanent Subcommittee on Investigations, he began prowling the halls of Washington in search of closeted homosexuals—or "powder puffs," as he liked to call them.

The florid McCarthy pageant is a fascinating case study in the dynamics of Washington power. The senator was a glaring outsider in the capital's elite salons—a crude, hard-drinking ex-marine. He seemed to defy the neat power categories of C. Wright Mills, fueled more by the sort of ideological fervor, demagoguery, and murky sponsorship that would characterize the later Tea Party era of American politics.

McCarthy was not educated at Ivy League schools, and he was never courted by Wall Street firms. He had worked his way through law school at Marquette University in Milwaukee by pumping gas and going door-to-door selling caulking compound for doors and windows. He liked to drink bourbon, and in 1952, when an operation for a herniated diaphragm cut him open from gut to shoulder and left him in chronic pain, he drank harder still. Even after he was elected to the august U.S. Senate, he carried around a barroom bully's sense of grievance. He once assaulted Drew Pearson in the cloakroom of the exclusive Sulgrave Club, pinning the muckraker's arms behind him and kneeing him in the balls—vicious payback for all the columns Pearson had written about McCarthy's career. And yet, backed in the beginning by Hoover's investigative apparatus, as well as by the Catholic Church and the right-wing Hearst and McCormick press, the thuggish senator was able to turn his chairmanship of the previously obscure subcommittee into one of the capital's most powerful perches. Washington's VIPs hated and feared him, but most paid homage to him.

McCarthy was a monster of the Republican leadership's own creation. By the time he claimed the national spotlight in 1950, the GOP had long been using the dark incantations of "treason" and "un-Americanism" for political advantage against the Democrats. It was only a matter of time before a specter like McCarthy began to rise up in this toxic atmosphere. Nixon had exploited these themes to great effect in his congressional and Senate races, as did Tom Dewey—though with less success—in his 1948 presidential campaign. Despite Truman's victory, he was constantly on the defensive against Republican charges that Communists were honeycombed throughout the federal bureaucracy. In response, Truman imposed a loyalty test on federal employees and created an extensive surveillance apparatus to go with it, which turned up few real security threats. He also shredded the Bill of Rights by unleashing a wave of prosecutions against Communist Party officials, thereby effectively outlawing the party and demolishing much of the organized left. Realizing that he had crossed a constitutional Rubicon, a troubled Truman wrote to Eleanor Roosevelt—the New Deal's aging but unbending icon—and insisted that he was not trying to set off a witch hunt. But that's indeed what he did.

As Eisenhower took over the White House in 1953, it was uncertain whether the most dynamic force in Washington would be the new president or the senator from Wisconsin. Eisenhower confided that he reviled McCarthy nearly as much as he had Hitler—but he kept pulling back from confronting him. When Ike had ventured into McCarthy's home state during the 1952 campaign, making a whistle stop in Green Bay, the senator shared the platform with him. Before speaking to the crowd, Eisenhower leaned over to McCarthy and told him, "I'm going to say that I disagree with you." McCarthy looked the general squarely in the face: "If you say that, you'll be booed." Eisenhower stood his ground. "I've been booed before." But when it came time to speak, Eisenhower buckled, carefully smoothing over their differences.

The GOP campaign in 1952 thoroughly embraced McCarthyism. Nixon took the leading Republican role as hatchet man so that Eisenhower could assume a more dignified posture; in September Nixon vowed to make the "Communist conspiracy" the "theme of every speech from now until election." McCarthy, in turn, performed loyally for the party, putting his gutter techniques to use at the service of the campaign. Democratic presidential candidate Adlai Stevenson, he declared in a widely broadcast speech in October, "would continue the suicidal Kremlin-shaped policies of this nation." At one point McCarthy pretended to confuse Stevenson with the accused traitor Hiss, calling him "Alger—I mean Adlai."

But after Eisenhower's victory, McCarthy quickly made clear that he considered the new Republican administration fair game. The monster was loose and nobody in Washington was safe. Before the

Dulles-dominated Eisenhower administration could get on with its ambitious plans for running the world, it first had to secure the capital, where the dangerous senator continued to make strong men cower. During the first year of Eisenhower's presidency, McCarthy would boldly target the three institutions at the very center of Washington's global power: the State Department, the CIA, and finally the Army.

The different ways these institutions grappled with the assaults from McCarthy shed a fascinating light on Washington's pyramid of power—as well as on the distinctive personalities of the Dulles brothers. It would become clear in the course of this labyrinthine power struggle just who wielded the biggest sword on the Potomac.

There was little doubt about who the big brother was in the Dulles family. Foster had carried himself with a grave sense of familial responsibility ever since he was a boy, while Allen felt free to pursue more mischievous pleasures well into adulthood. Family members inevitably brought their requests and troubles to Foster, not Allen—though the elder brother's advice, as Eleanor discovered, was not always sound. She once lost her savings on a bad investment that Foster advised her to make. Nonetheless, the Wall Street wise man projected a sober wisdom; titans of industry paid close heed to his counsel, which he dispensed in a deliberative manner, confident that his every word was money.

As the brothers assumed their positions in the Eisenhower government, they brought with them a unique working chemistry, one that had been forged from the time they shared tasks on their Lake Ontario fishing expeditions. Their relationship was not without its tensions and petty squabbles. Allen thought he actually should have been named secretary of state, since he had more experience with foreign affairs and had a more intricate network of overseas connections. He sometimes chafed under his older brother's imperial rule.

Foster seemed blithely unaware of Allen's frustrations. "The thing that has puzzled me a great deal is that I'm not sure how much Foster realized this situation," Eleanor observed years later, after the older brother was dead. "If he realized it, he didn't show it by any overcompensation or by any overconsideration. All his dealings with Allen were as if there was no psychological essence or problem that had to be dealt with. They dealt with the subject matter and not with each other as people with certain sensitivities and certain prejudices, and so on."

But Eleanor, the psychologically acute sister, could feel Allen's jealousy and competitiveness. "I felt it in Allen. I didn't feel it in Foster. I think you can imagine why. Foster did have more power and more experience, and," she added matter of factly, "I think [Foster had] the better brain."

Allen was well aware of the Washington chatter about the unusual brother act. "Every once in a while we were teased, of course, as brothers are likely to be when each of them has a position of a certain amount of importance and are working together," he remarked in later years. "But I was very conscious of the danger in that situation and I tried to avoid either appearances or actions which would justify any criticism on that score."

It was very important to Allen that people not think he got his CIA position because of his brother. "You see," he told an oral historian after his brother's death, "I was in there before my brother became secretary of state. I was deputy director [of the CIA]. . . . So then when Bedell Smith retired, it was more or less normal that I would be appointed. I mean, that was not considered a particular show of nepotism on the part of Eisenhower. Personally, Eisenhower and I were very close to each other. We'd gotten to know each other very well. Nobody, as far as I know—I'm sure Foster exercised no pressure at all—because it was quite normal that I would take over that place." But the truth is that Foster *did* exert his influence on his brother's behalf, and Eisenhower *never* felt close to the younger Dulles, regarding him as a necessary evil in his shadow war with world Communism.

Despite its underlying complexities, the Dulles brothers' partnership proved very effective. They conferred on a regular basis during their Washington reign. "Normally they saw each other once, twice, maybe three times a week. Allen used to go to [Foster's] house on Saturday and sit down and talk to him for two or three hours," recalled Eleanor, who—after Foster reluctantly agreed to give her the State Department's

Bonn desk—sometimes joined her brothers at the spacious stone house in a wooded neighborhood of Washington. "I know Foster valued these conversations."

Unlike the gregarious Allen, Foster was somewhat of a loner. "I'm not sure that there are more than a half dozen people in Washington that he felt really at home with. Maybe a dozen," said Eleanor. Allen was Foster's essential link to the Georgetown power circles where the spymaster easily circulated. He collected vital gossip and inside information from his social outings, bringing it back to his brother. Allen was the only frequent visitor that Eleanor ever saw in Foster's home.

It was Allen, the master of persuasion and seduction, who also expertly handled relations with the press. He counted among his friends not only press barons such as Luce and *New York Times* publisher Arthur Hays Sulzberger and TV network moguls like William Paley of CBS, but also leading Washington pundits such as Joseph and Stewart Alsop. Allen enjoyed wining and dining the nation's opinion makers, while Foster would "almost rather negotiate with the Russians than be bothered by that," in Eleanor's estimation.

The brothers sometimes clashed. David Atlee Phillips, a CIA counterintelligence official whose career flourished under Allen Dulles, later recalled the time Foster instructed his brother to arrange a secret CIA payment to a foreign political candidate. After consulting with his operatives in the field, Allen informed his brother that it was a bad idea. "The secretary of state, in crisp terms, said he had not asked whether the idea was good or bad," Phillips recounted, "but that he had instructed the CIA chief that it be done." The cash was duly delivered—and the candidate still lost (a fact noted by Phillips with evident satisfaction).

On other occasions, Allen expressed his opposition to his brother in more vehement terms. He once told Foster that a speech he planned to deliver on the Soviet Union was "rotten" and he should scrap it. "I am the secretary of state and it is my speech," Foster insisted. "And I damned well will say it if I want to." But Allen would not back down. "*My* Soviet expert here says it is wrong. And I won't let you make a damned fool of yourself, secretary of state or not!"

By and large, though, the Dulles fraternal partnership was a machine of humming efficiency. "We didn't realize in the early winter months of 1953 as the new administration took shape just how cozy the Dulles brothers' arrangement for handling all American business abroad would be," recalled veteran CIA officer Joseph Smith. "It came to mean very quickly that when a situation would not yield to normal diplomatic pressure, Allen's boys were expected to step in and take care of the matter."

Before business abroad could be addressed, however, there was some messiness at home that needed to be taken care of. Allen Dulles might have labored under the shadow of his more esteemed older brother through most of his career, but he was about to show Washington who was the tougher power player.

As the Eisenhower presidency got under way in January 1953, the State Department was the target of no less than ten separate, ongoing congressional probes by McCarthy and his Capitol Hill confederates, who saw Foggy Bottom as a hotbed of pansies, pointy-headed intellectuals, parlor room pinkos, and other soft types who were vulnerable to the siren song of Communism. In the beginning, Foster thought McCarthy's reign of terror could be useful. He was just as eager as the Republican right wing to purge the State Department of all New Deal remnants.

Foster, courting favor with party hard-liners, agreed to hire a security deputy to oversee the massive screening of all State Department employees. Scott McLeod, the man he hired, was an ex-FBI agent and former reporter for the influential right-wing New Hampshire newspaper, the *Manchester Union Leader*. McLeod, who proudly displayed an autographed photo of McCarthy on his desk inscribed "To a Great American," was the Wisconsin senator's man inside the State Department. Like McCarthy, McLeod brought a cynical Irish beat cop's attitude to the complex task of sorting out the beliefs and allegiances of the U.S. diplomatic corps. McLeod was "anti-intellectual, shrewd, conspiratorial, quick-tempered [and] vindictive," as John Foster Dulles biographer Townsend Hoopes later observed. A State Department colleague of McLeod put it more sympathetically: "Scotty lived in an essentially simple world."

As with the other paroxysms of paranoia that seized Washington during the Cold War, McLeod's witch hunt turned up very few genuinely worrisome suspects. Most of its victims were highly competent, experienced members of the foreign service whose policy differences with the new Dulles regime simply rendered them "incompatibles," in McLeod's Orwellian term. A number of these purge victims, such as John Carter Vincent and John Paton Davies Jr., were veterans of the China desk, where their only crime was infuriating the right-wing Taiwan lobby by honestly evaluating why Communist revolutionary Mao Tse-tung had been able to defeat corrupt warlord Chiang Kai-shek. The civil service apparatus was supposed to protect respected officials like this, many of whom had made valuable contributions to the U.S. government's understanding of the world. But ideology trumped ability in Foster's intensely politicized State Department.

Foster even forced out one of the brightest, most respected intellectual stars in the foreign service firmament, Soviet expert George F. Kennan, simply because he took exception to the secretary of state's "liberation" strategy aimed at Eastern Europe—a policy so dangerously unviable that even Eisenhower and the Dulles brothers themselves would soon make clear that they had no intention of following through on this campaign promise to "roll back" the Iron Curtain.

As McLeod's quickly assembled battalion of some 350 inexperienced but gung ho investigators began snooping through State Department employee records, a cloud of fear settled over Foggy Bottom. Those whose files were tagged and sent over to McCarthy's subcommittee knew their days in government were over—nobody who endured the snide and relentless grilling at the hands of McCarthy and his equally ruthless chief counsel, Roy Cohn, could expect their career to survive. By the time McCarthy's Washington bonfires were extinguished two years later, the careers of several hundred State Department officers and employees lay in ashes.

Early in the McCarthy-McLeod inquisition, Foster realized that it could burn out of control. While he was happy to see political opponents consumed in its flames, he soon grew worried that the State Department itself was at stake. By subjecting employees to humiliating loyalty tests and exposure of their private lives, the wide-reaching security program was emptying the State Department of its best and brightest.

Even Eleanor Dulles, who was reluctant to confront her impregnably self-confident brother, felt compelled to complain to him. After all, the State Department was the family business, it had been entrusted to Foster—and now he was allowing McCarthy to ruin it. Eleanor had seen the danger early on, when the Eisenhower-Nixon campaign made its unsavory alliance with McCarthy. She first confronted Foster then. "I went over to New York. I called up Foster and said I was coming. He said, 'Come to dinner.' You know, he was generous and friendly in that sort of thing, even if he was busy. He was very frank though, if he didn't want you, he would tell you. . . . But I went to dinner, and he made a very fine martini. I had one. Then he started to fill my glass again, and I said, 'No, I don't need another.'

"He looked at me sort of queerly and he said, 'You must have come over here for a serious purpose, if you won't have two martinis.'

"I said, 'I have.' So then I said to him, 'I want you to know that I think this is an evil business that's going on. If the Republicans don't repudiate McCarthy, I'm going to vote the Democratic ticket.'"

Eleanor's threat only had the effect of "amusing" Foster, who asked his sister a few questions about why she felt the way she did, and then simply dropped the subject.

In the end, Foster Dulles never confronted McCarthy—even when the senator repeatedly embarrassed both the president and the secretary of state. The administration had no sooner taken office than McCarthy began using his Senate power to hold up the nominations of key appointments, including close Eisenhower associates like Beetle Smith, who had been nominated to serve as Foster's undersecretary of state. Smith had annoyed McCarthy at some point by saying something positive about a State Department official whom the senator considered a card-carrying Communist.

Eisenhower was infuriated by McCarthy's antics. The senator was challenging the new president's authority to control his own government. Ike's Cold War propaganda adviser, C. D. Jackson—a fascinating and somewhat mysterious character who had a background in the OSS and served as a sort of intelligence link among the White House, the CIA, and Henry Luce's media empire—advised the president to launch an all-out attack on McCarthy. But Nixon, who thought of McCarthy as a friend and essential ally, urged that the administration try to make the troublesome senator a member of the team. Nixon was supported by others in the president's inner circle, including even the hot-tempered Beetle Smith himself, who warned that a direct assault on McCarthy would risk splitting the Republican Party.

Eisenhower and the Dulles brothers decided to use Nixon as their mediator with McCarthy. The two men were, in some ways, cut from the same rough cloth. Aggrieved outsiders in the Ivy League/Wall Street world of the power elite, they had both grabbed onto the club of anti-Communism as the blunt tool of their ferocious ambition. They had a working stiff's bitterness that they clearly enjoyed venting at Harvard types like Alger Hiss as much as they did at hard-core Communists. McCarthy went as far as challenging the nomination of Harvard University president James B. Conant as high commissioner to Germany, before Nixon talked him down.

But Nixon was more sophisticated and intelligent than McCarthy. McCarthy's ambition was a raw force that he wielded with little or no concern for where his blows might land—even if President Eisenhower or the mighty Dulles brothers stood in his way. Nixon, on the other hand, knew that men like these controlled his path to the top, and he was eager to please them. He was, in Adlai Stevenson's words, "McCarthy with a white collar." The vice president kept setting up private meetings with the headstrong senator, where he would try to talk sense into him, dangling political favors before his eyes.

The easily dazzled McCarthy would take Nixon's bait for a while, but a few days later he would come out swinging again, usurping Eisenhower's power by announcing his own anti-Communist measures or accusing another administration nominee of some shocking infamy. In the end, not even the wily Nixon could bring McCarthy under control as he thrashed about in the Washington arena.

Foster, deathly afraid of losing the job for which he had been groomed since boyhood, did everything he could to placate the reckless McCarthy. The elder Dulles, observed the veteran diplomat Charles "Chip" Bohlen, was a man "with one obsession: to remain secretary of state." To do that, Foster was willing to sacrifice nearly everything, including his dignity and the integrity of his department.

"My brother was never a witch hunter," Allen insisted years later, still defensive about the reputation his brother had developed during the McCarthy era. "I mean, he realized the subtleties of Communist penetration, and all that. But he didn't go along with the sort of blanket condemnation of people." The truth, however, is that Foster Dulles's groveling efforts to pacify McCarthy not only encouraged his aggression but institutionalized his witch hunt within the State Department.

When Eisenhower nominated Chip Bohlen, who had served in the U.S. embassy in Moscow before and during the war, to be his ambassador to the Soviet Union, McCarthy inevitably detected something amiss with the distinguished diplomat—a hint of homosexuality somewhere in his family (it turned out that the allegations involved his brother-in-law). Bohlen was as upstanding a member of the foreign service club as the American establishment had ever produced: grandson of a U.S. senator, graduate of Harvard, respected member of the diplomatic corps since 1929, adviser to three presidents. Eisenhower decided that this time he would take a stand, and he recruited his rival—Senator Robert Taft, leader of the GOP's right wing—to help push through Bohlen's nomination.

But Foster remained a bundle of nerves throughout the Bohlen confirmation process, terrified that if the nominee's head were lopped off, his would be next. The secretary of state was ready at any moment to urge Eisenhower to abandon Bohlen if things got too hot on Capitol Hill. When Foster and Bohlen were being driven to the nominee's Senate confirmation hearing, Foster awkwardly asked Bohlen not to be photographed with him. Later, after Bohlen was finally confirmed, Foster asked the new ambassador—who planned to fly to Moscow a week or two ahead of his family—to delay his trip, so his solo arrival in Russia would not set off another round of heated speculation about his sexuality.

During the early months of the Eisenhower presidency, Foster repeatedly surrendered to the McCarthy onslaught. When the senator shifted his target from Communists to homosexuals in the State Department, Foster allowed his employees' privacy to be blatantly violated. Ironically, it was McCarthy's aggressive chief counsel, Roy Cohn, who took the lead in questioning suspected homosexuals. Cohn, whose heavy-lidded eyes and leathery, perpetually tanned skin gave him a serpentine look, was not only gay but had installed his twenty-six-year-old playmate, a rich golden boy with no particular credentials named David Schine, on his staff. The son of a hotel and movie theater tycoon, Schine was known while a Harvard undergraduate for paying secretaries to take class notes for him. "Essentially," observed one Cold War historian, "Schine was Cohn's dumb blonde." Despite his own sexual leanings, Cohn took obvious pleasure in humiliating the gay witnesses who appeared before the subcommittee, demanding to know the locations of their illicit trysts and the names of their sexual partners.

McCarthy next went after the Voice of America, the State Department's Cold War propaganda arm, which Allen Dulles had helped create, absurdly declaring it another hotbed of Communist infestation. By April, 830 of the Voice of America's 1,400 employees had been purged, including its chief.

That same month, Cohn and Schine announced that they were setting off for Europe together to inspect the libraries maintained by U.S. embassies. These embassy libraries were supposed to be a "balanced collection of American thought"—showcases for U.S. tolerance and diversity. But Cohn and Schine were determined to cleanse the libraries of all books they suspected of a leftward tilt. The pair's investigative junket, which one subpoenaed author labeled "a book burning," turned into a public relations disaster for the United States, provoking widespread revulsion and ridicule in the European press.

While visiting Frankfurt, Cohn and Schine found other ways to embarrass their country, according to a local newspaper, engaging in flirtatious antics in a hotel lobby and leaving their hotel room in a shambles after a vigorous round of horseplay that the reporter left up to the reader's imagination. But instead of criticizing McCarthy's rowdy henchmen, Foster Dulles dutifully culled the embassy libraries of all ideologically impure books, including works by Jean-Paul Sartre and Langston Hughes. Cohn even wanted to ban the soaringly American music of Aaron Copland from the libraries, which also loaned records, because the composer had made the mistake of signing petitions defending the civil rights of labor leader Harry Bridges and other beleaguered left-wing heroes.

This was Washington at the dawn of the Eisenhower-Dulles era, when the most powerful men in the capital lived in fear of being served subpoenas by a drunken senator, when even John Foster Dulles trembled before McCarthy's brute force. It would take Foster's more iron-nerved brother to bring the beast to heel.

In July 1953, after having his way with Foster Dulles's State Department, McCarthy came after his brother's CIA, announcing in his usual imprecise way that he possessed "tons" of evidence that revealed widespread Communist infiltration of the spy agency. McCarthy's prime suspect was a bespectacled, Ivy League–educated CIA analyst named William Bundy, whose profile made him the perfect embodiment of the Dulles agency man. A member of Yale's secretive Skull and Bones society—breeding ground for future spooks—Bundy joined Army intelligence during the war, working at Bletchley Park in England as part of the Ultra operation that cracked Nazi codes. Dulles was close to Bundy's father, Harvey, a top diplomat who had helped oversee the Marshall Plan, as well as his younger brother, McGeorge, another product of Skull and Bones and Army intelligence who had worked with

Dulles at the Council on Foreign Relations and on the Dewey presidential campaign.

McCarthy hoped to make Bill Bundy his Alger Hiss, and, in fact, one of the main pieces of incriminating evidence he waved against him was that Bundy had contributed $400 to the Alger Hiss defense fund. But the Bundys were solid members of Allen Dulles's inner circle, and Dulles did not easily abandon men like Bundy. The spymaster finally decided to draw the line with McCarthy—and the ensuing, explosive confrontation led ultimately to the inquisitor's downfall.

Taking on McCarthy at the height of his power was a daunting task, even for the director of the CIA. Dulles knew that, despite J. Edgar Hoover's growing doubts about McCarthy, the FBI still fed him a stream of damaging information about his Washington enemies. Hoover, a sworn rival ever since Dulles outmaneuvered him to create the CIA in 1947, had amassed a thick file on Dulles and his busy adulterous life. Hoover even suspected Dulles of "secret communist leanings," a delusion as fantastic as any of McCarthy's wild claims. At least one high-ranking CIA official—Robert Amory, the agency's top intelligence analyst—was convinced that the FBI had tapped his office phone.

But Dulles, too, was a master at this sort of game, and he made sure his agency kept its own files on Hoover. Jim Angleton liked to say that any intelligence service that didn't keep a close eye on its own government wasn't worth its salt. "Penetration begins at home," he quipped. The CIA counterintelligence chief was rumored to occasionally show off photographic evidence of Hoover's intimate relationship with FBI deputy Clyde Tolson, including a photo of Hoover orally pleasuring his longtime aide and companion. Dulles's wisecracking mistress Mary Bancroft liked to call the FBI director "that Virgin Mary in pants," but there was nothing virginal about Hoover.

Dulles compiled even more scandalous files on Joe McCarthy's sex life. The senator who relentlessly hunted down homosexuals in government was widely rumored to haunt the "bird circuit" near Grand Central Station as well as gay hideaways in Milwaukee. Drew Pearson got wind of the stories but was never able to get enough proof to run with them. But the less discriminating Hank Greenspun, editor and publisher of the *Las Vegas Sun*, who was locked in an ugly war of words with McCarthy, let the allegations fly. Greenspun had been given access to the Pearson files, and he had picked up his own McCarthy stories involving young hotel bellboys and elevator operators during the senator's gambling trips to Vegas. "Joe McCarthy is a bachelor of 43 years," wrote Greenspun. "He seldom dates girls and if he does, he laughingly describes it as window dressing. . . . It is common talk among homosexuals who rendezvous at the White Horse Inn [in Milwaukee] that Senator Joe McCarthy has often engaged in homosexual activities."

McCarthy's wedding announcement triggered more wicked chatter in the capital, where many saw it as an obvious ploy to dispel the rumors. The senator was as surprised as many others to read the announcement of his pending nuptials—it was his mother-in-law-to-be who placed the notice in the newspapers. McCarthy's young bride was described in one gossip magazine as "a bright, shrewd and very ambitious young lady. 'Opportunist' was the word many people used."

One Hoover aide later denied the gay reports about McCarthy, insisting that the allegations were blowback against the senator because he had dared to take on the Dulles brothers. But Hoover kept his own secret files on McCarthy, one of which was filled with disturbing stories about McCarthy's habit of drunkenly groping young girls' breasts and buttocks. The stories were so widespread that they became "common knowledge" in the capital, according to one FBI chronicler. Walter Trohan, Washington bureau chief of the conservative *Chicago Tribune*, who witnessed McCarthy's molesting behavior, said, "He just couldn't keep his hands off young girls. Why the Communist opposition didn't plant a minor on him and raise the cry of statutory rape, I don't know."

"The Communist opposition" might have missed the opportunity, but the CIA was clearly prepared to leak stories about McCarthy's behavior—stories so sordid, they would have destroyed his career. This gave Dulles leverage in his battle with McCarthy that none of the senator's other political opponents enjoyed. There was an explosive sexual subtext to the CIA's power struggle with McCarthy, one that was largely hidden from the public but would eventually erupt in the Senate hearings that brought him down.

What the public witnessed was fascinating enough: a clash of titans that verged on a constitutional crisis. When McCarthy tried to subpoena Bill Bundy, Dulles simply stonewalled him. The agency had Bundy spirited away to an undisclosed location, and when Roy Cohn called to demand that he testify before the subcommittee—that very day—he was told that Bundy was on leave. Walter Pforzheimer, the CIA's legislative liaison, later remembered the phone call. "Roy was furious. . . . What a fight! Later that day, my secretary tracked me down to tell me Cohn wanted to talk to me [again]. And he wanted me to testify about Bundy's file." But Dulles simply "wouldn't allow it." When a subpoena arrived for Pforzheimer, the CIA director was unfazed. "Allen Dulles just took it and gave it to somebody. I wanted it for posterity, but no one's ever found it."

On July 9, 1953, an outraged McCarthy took to the floor of the Senate to denounce Dulles's "blatant attempt to thwart the authority of the Senate" and demanded that Dulles himself appear before his subcommittee. Dulles still refused to bend, but he did drop by McCarthy's office to explain his position. Because of the highly sensitive nature of the CIA's work, Dulles informed the senator, his agency must be granted immunity from congressional investigations. McCarthy just had to take his word that there were no Communists hidden in the agency. If he ever did find any Reds, Dulles later explained to the press, "I'd kick them out. I have the power to do it and don't have to have proof they work for the Kremlin. The fact that a man is a Communist would be enough."

Dulles's defiant position on congressional oversight astonished even the anti-McCarthy Democrats on the subcommittee, like Senator Stuart Symington. But the CIA director never wavered from his stand, and he soon won Eisenhower's support. Nixon was again dispatched to meet with McCarthy, to work out a face-saving way for the senator to back down. Soon after, McCarthy announced that he and Dulles had come to a mutual agreement to suspend the probe of the CIA. Dulles drove home his victory by making sure that his friends in the Washington press corps reported McCarthy's losing confrontation with the CIA as a major humiliation for the senator.

On July 17, syndicated columnist Joseph Alsop—a journalist so deeply entwined with the CIA that he once declared it was his patriotic duty to carry the agency's water—announced that "Senator Joseph R. McCarthy has just suffered his first total, unmitigated, unqualified defeat. . . . [Administration strategists] have allowed McCarthy to conceal his defeat behind a typical smoke screen of misleading statements. But the background story proves that the junior Senator from Wisconsin went down for the count of ten, all the same."

Dulles proudly collected newspaper coverage of his battle with McCarthy. He was no doubt particularly pleased by one of the clippings he gathered, an article by *The Buffalo Evening News*'s Washington correspondent, which reported that the CIA director is "known here as 'John Foster Dulles's tougher, younger brother.'"

Not all of the press reaction to Dulles's display of defiance was so enthusiastic. Two journalistic pillars whom the CIA director considered old friends—syndicated columnist Walter Lippmann and *New York Times* correspondent Hanson Baldwin—took strong issue with the way Dulles had flouted Senate authority. "The argument that the CIA is something apart, that it is so secret that it differs in kind from the State Department or, for that matter, the Department of Agriculture, in untenable," Lippmann opined. Baldwin struck an even more critical note, warning of "a philosophy of secrecy and power" taking hold in Washington under the banner of national security.

But Dulles's firm stand against McCarthy—a man Richard Helms compared to Goebbels—proved enormously popular within the CIA, particularly among the ranks of the liberal, intellectual types whom Dulles had recruited. While Dulles and his family were stalwart Republicans, he recognized that many of the most passionate Cold Warriors were ex-Communists and liberals who not only had firsthand knowledge of bare-knuckled Communist Party practices but were eager to prove their patriotism and join the American celebration. Dulles further cemented his position with this liberal crowd when he stood by CIA recruit Cord Meyer, another bright young product of Yale, who came under FBI suspicion in August 1953 for his postwar peace activities.

After enduring years of relentless harassment from Red hunters, many Washington liberals cheered Dulles as a savior. His CIA became known as a haven for the intelligentsia and for others looked on with suspicion by McCarthyites. "I emerged from [my FBI] ordeal with increased respect for Allen Dulles," Meyer later wrote. "Dulles proved to be a pillar of courageous strength inside the Eisenhower administration during the McCarthy era. Once he had determined the facts and satisfied himself as to the loyalty of a CIA official, he was prepared to defend him and he refused to give in to the pressures that McCarthy was able to bring to bear. As a result, morale within the agency was high during this period, in contrast to morale in the State Department where John Foster Dulles was less willing to defend the innocent victims of McCarthy's campaign."

Dulles's defiance of McCarthy won the widespread devotion of liberals, but it established a dangerous precedent. In his very first year as director, Dulles began molding an image of the CIA as a super agency, operating high above mere senators. The CIA would grow more powerful and less accountable with each passing year of Dulles's reign.

McCarthy never got over his rough treatment at the hands of the CIA, and he would threaten on more than one occasion to reopen his investigation of the agency. But if he had, he might have encountered an even more severe response. In March 1954, McCarthy's subcommittee convened a hearing on "alleged threats against the chairman." One witness—a military intelligence officer named William Morgan who had worked for C. D. Jackson in the White House—stunned the subcommittee by recounting a conversation that he had the previous year with a CIA employee named Horace Craig. As the two men were discussing how to solve the McCarthy problem, Craig flatly stated, "It may be necessary to liquidate Senator McCarthy as was [assassinated

Louisiana senator] Huey Long. There is always some madman who will do it for a price."

The Dulles slapdown of McCarthy proved to be a fateful turning point for the senator, inspiring a new boldness within the Eisenhower administration that would lead to his collapse. A month later, in August 1953, when McCarthy took aim at Reds in the Agriculture Department, of all places, Nixon advised Agriculture Secretary Ezra Taft Benson to "take a firm stand, like Allen Dulles, if McCarthy gets out of line." In September, after returning from his honeymoon, McCarthy made his final—and fatal—mistake, by taking on another central institution of U.S. national security, the Army.

Like Foster Dulles, the spineless Army Secretary, a former textile executive named Robert Ten Broeck Stevens, had done everything he could to appease McCarthy, but the senator had only grown more frothing in his attacks, accusing the Army of sloppy security measures that had led to the hiring of subversive civilians. At one point, McCarthy dragged a decorated D-day hero, General Ralph W. Zwicker, before his panel and dressed him down like he was a bumbling Beetle Bailey, barking at the dignified, ramrod-stiff officer that he was "not fit to wear that uniform."

Much of the anti-Army spleen in the McCarthy office was inspired by the adolescent frustrations of the senator's twenty-six-year-old chief counsel, Roy Cohn. When Cohn's boyfriend, David Schine, was drafted into the Army in October 1953, McCarthy's point man began frantically pulling strings on his behalf. Assigned to Fort Dix in New Jersey for basic training, Schine was showered with special privileges, including frequent exemptions from KP duty and weekend passes so he could be chauffeured to New York City for R&R with Cohn. (Their chauffeur would later testify that the two men also used his vehicle's backseat for their passionate reunions.) Schine, who found his Army issue boots uncomfortable, was even allowed to wear custom-made boots. When Cohn was told that his boyfriend might be transferred overseas, he flew into a rage. "We'll wreck the Army," he spluttered at the Army's liaison to the subcommittee. "The Army will be ruined . . . if you pull a dirty, lousy, stinking, filthy, shitty double cross like that."

After months of trying to manage McCarthy, Eisenhower finally reached his breaking point. In February 1954, Massachusetts Republican senator Henry Cabot Lodge, a close ally of the president, privately warned that the Army investigation was "an attempt to destroy the president politically. There is no doubt about it. He is picking on the Army because Eisenhower was in the Army." The following month, the president authorized Lodge to ask for the publication of a damning report that the Army had been secretly compiling on the numerous ways that McCarthy and Cohn had bullied and blackmailed military authorities on Schine's behalf. In response to the scorching Schine report, McCarthy's subcommittee removed him as chairman and called for hearings on the Army's allegations. The stage was set for the Army-McCarthy hearings, a televised spectacle that turned the inquisitional tables on the senator and finally ended his infamous reign.

McCarthy—who was allowed to participate in the proceedings—gave his usual crude performance, badgering witnesses and shouting "point of order" whenever he felt the urge to disrupt the drama. But captured in the glare of the TV lights, his coarse act had a repellent effect on the viewing public. By the time the Army's distinguished Boston attorney, Joseph Nye Welch, uttered his devastating and instantly memorable line—"Have you no sense of decency, sir? At long last, have you left no sense of decency?"—the American people knew the answer.

In December 1954, the Senate voted to censure McCarthy, and he continued his slide toward oblivion, drinking more and more heavily until he was polishing off a bottle of the hard stuff a day. By 1956, those who knew the senator were describing him as a "sick pigeon" suffering from a host of physical ailments and shuttling in and out of detox. During a visit home to Wisconsin in September, he was seized by delirium tremens and saw snakes flying at him. In May 1957, he was admitted to Bethesda Naval Hospital, where he died of acute liver failure at age forty-eight. Joe McCarthy had drunk himself to death.

McCarthy's confrontation with the Army would become famous for his undoing, but it was his earlier battle with Allen Dulles that had drawn first blood and made him vulnerable. As McCarthy's stature in Washington shrank, Dulles's grew. No politician during the Eisenhower era would ever again seriously challenge the CIA director's rule. With his Washington power base secure, Dulles was ready to take on the world.

The Dulles Imperium

On the afternoon of August 18, 1953, Mohammad Reza Pahlavi, the thirty-three-year-old shah of Iran, and his glamorous twenty-one-year-old wife, Queen Soraya, swept into the gilded lobby of the Hotel Excelsior on Rome's fashionable Via Veneto. The young royal couple cut a striking image, with the slim shah wearing a trimly tailored, light gray, double-breasted suit and dark glasses, and his petite, voluptuous queen calling to mind the exotic beauty of Sophia Loren. Soraya was half Persian and half German and had almond-shaped, green-blue eyes described as the most beautiful in the world by an Italian director who years later cast her as the leading lady in one of his movies. But on this day, the Iranian royals looked "worn, gloomy and anxious" in the words of a *Times* of London reporter—one of a flock of scribblers and paparazzi who had swarmed the couple when they disembarked from their BOAC plane at Ciampino Airport and pursued them to their hotel. Back home in Tehran, violent mobs controlled the streets of the capital, and after twenty-eight years on the Peacock Throne, the Pahlavi dynasty seemed on the verge of collapse. Fearing for their lives, the shah and his wife had fled his homeland carrying only a couple of suitcases, taking off in his private Beechcraft jet for Baghdad—the first leg of their journey—with such haste that they forgot to take the queen's beloved dog.

Accustomed to royal opulence and the slavish attentions of his court, the young shah seemed lost in exile. "We do not have much money," the shah warned his wife, who as the daughter of a prominent Iranian diplomat was also used to a luxurious lifestyle. He told Soraya they would have to be "very careful" with their spending. Before they fled, he had even asked her whether they could sell some of their wedding gifts, which included a mink coat and a desk set with black diamonds from Joseph Stalin and a Steuben glass bowl designed by Sidney Waugh that had been sent by President Truman.

During their first night at the Hotel Excelsior, the distraught shah paced the living room of their small suite, unable to sleep. He kept his personal pilot awake late into the night, fretting about the future that awaited him. The shah begged the pilot, one of only two retainers who accompanied the royal couple to Rome, to stay with him in exile. "Who is going to play tennis with me if you leave me?" asked the forlorn ruler.

But the shah was far from abandoned as he and Queen Soraya took up residence at the Excelsior. The CIA, which had prevailed upon the Persian industrialist who owned the fourth-floor suite to make it available to the royal couple, was keeping the shah under its watchful care. The Iranian monarchs found their accommodations to their liking. The luxury hotel's Belle Époque–era grandeur had been drawing royal guests since the turn of the twentieth century. In the 1950s, the hotel enjoyed a la dolce vita revival, attracting a new wave of kings and queens from Hollywood, including Humphrey Bogart and Lauren Bacall, and Audrey Hepburn and Gregory Peck. (John Wayne claimed that he scored his most memorable one-night stand at the Excelsior, with Marlene Dietrich. "I took her on the staircase," he boasted.)

The Excelsior had also become a favorite rendezvous spot for espionage agents from around the world, as well as Italian men of mystery. Licio Gelli—leader of Propaganda Due, the conspiratorial Masonic order whose intrigues undermined Italian democracy for many years— kept three adjoining rooms at the hotel. The discreet gentlemen who paid visits to Gelli—whose secret anti-Communist operations drew funding from the CIA—would enter Room 127, conduct business in Room 128, and then exit through Room 129.

More important from the shah's point of view, the Excelsior was also favored by Allen Dulles on his visits to Rome. That August, he and

Clover were vacationing in Switzerland when the spymaster suddenly informed his wife they were leaving for Italy, and on the afternoon of August 18 the Dulleses checked into the Excelsior at the same time as the shah and Queen Soraya. Frank Wisner insisted the simultaneous arrival of the two couples was a complete coincidence. "They both showed up at the reception desk at the Excelsior at the very same moment," Wisner told a CIA associate, with tongue undoubtedly firmly in cheek. "And Dulles had to say, 'After you, Your Majesty.'"

Dulles's arrival in Rome was conveniently timed. By the following morning, the mobs running riot through the streets of Tehran were led and financed by the CIA—the final act in a covert drama aimed at overthrowing the democratically elected government of Prime Minister Mohammad Mossadegh and restoring the shah's autocratic rule. Mossadegh, a dedicated patriot and wily survivor of Iran's treacherous politics, had antagonized the British government by nationalizing the powerful Anglo-Iranian Oil Company (later renamed British Petroleum) soon after taking office in 1951. The British behemoth—the third-largest producer of crude oil in the world—ruled Iran with imperial arrogance for much of the twentieth century, crushing labor strikes in the hellish oil fields and propping up and replacing local regimes at will. Mossadegh's defiant seizure of Iran's oil treasure set off a global thunderclap. "By the end of the 1980s, most countries in the Middle East and North Africa, as well as Asia and Latin America, had nationalized their oil, and thus gained influence over world prices," observed historian Ervand Abrahamian. "In the early 1950s, however, such a loss was seen as heralding the 'end of civilization'—not only for Britain but also for consumers throughout the industrial world."

After Mossadegh's bold move, the British spy agency MI6 began working strenuously to undermine his government. When the prime minister responded to the British plotting by shutting down the British embassy in Tehran and ejecting the ambassador, London turned to Washington for assistance.

The Dulleses were more than willing to help. Through their law firm, the brothers had long ties to major U.S. oil companies like Standard Oil, which strongly supported the tough British stand against Mossadegh, with hopes of securing their own stake in the Iranian oil fields. Allen had another former client with a big interest in the Iranian oil dispute: the London-based J. Henry Schroder Banking Corporation, on whose board he served, was the financial agent for Anglo-Iranian Oil.

The Dulles brothers had demonstrated their dedication to their former Sullivan and Cromwell petroleum clients soon after President Eisenhower took office by sabotaging a Justice Department antitrust case against the Seven Sisters oil giants. The price-fixing case against the oil cartel, a holdover from the Truman years, was reduced from a criminal to a civil charge and conveniently transferred to Foster Dulles's jurisdiction, the first time in U.S. history that an antitrust case was handed over to the State Department for prosecution. Foster argued that the case had national security implications, and it quietly disappeared, leaving Big Oil unscathed.

Furthermore, Allen Dulles had a business history with the shah. In 1949, while still employed as a Sullivan and Cromwell rainmaker, Dulles had flown to Tehran, where he met the shah and negotiated a stunningly lucrative deal on behalf of a new company called Overseas Consultants Inc., a consortium of eleven large U.S. engineering firms. Iran agreed to pay OCI a Croesus-like fortune of $650 million for which the consortium pledged to modernize the backward nation, building hydroelectric plants, importing industries, and transforming entire cities. "This would be the largest overseas development project in modern history," noted Dulles biographer Stephen Kinzer. "It was the greatest triumph of Allen's legal career. For Sullivan and Cromwell it opened a world of possibilities."

The shah realized that Allen Dulles could be an important ally. And indeed Dulles repaid the young ruler's generosity by opening doors for him in New York and Washington. In November 1949, Dulles hosted an exclusive dinner party for the visiting potentate in the dining room of the Council on Foreign Relations. The shah's remarks were music to the ears of the dinner guests. "My government and people are eager to welcome American capital, to give it all possible safeguards," he assured them. "Nationalization of industry is not planned."

But the rise of Mossadegh and his National Front political alliance disrupted the dream of prosperity that the shah had spun for his privileged audience. Mossadegh's coalition led the opposition to the OCI deal, which National Front leaders denounced as a massive giveaway that would "break the back of future generations." This patriotic rhetoric stirred the passions of the Iranian people, whose fate had long been determined by foreign powers. In December 1950, Iran's parliament voted not to fund the monumental development project, thereby killing the chances of Dulles and OCI for a huge payday and forever poisoning the spymaster's perceptions of Mossadegh.

Western observers found Mossadegh a perplexing character— strongly phobic to British colonial attitudes but touchingly hopeful about an alliance with the growing U.S. empire. The aging, balding leader was a mercurial personality, given to emotional outbursts and fainting spells. His long, mournful face gave him a funereal look, but he was capable of boyishly enthusiastic behavior. On a visit to Washington in October 1951, the new prime minister charmed Truman administration officials. Secretary of State Dean Acheson was tickled by his "delightfully childlike way of sitting in a chair with his legs tucked under him."

In the beginning, Eisenhower also seemed sympathetic to Mossadegh, who sent the president-elect a heartfelt note on the eve of his inauguration, bemoaning the economic blockade that Britain had imposed on Iran and asking for U.S. assistance. There was a beguilingly innocent tone to the Iranian leader's plea: "It is not my desire that the relations between the United States and the United Kingdom should be strained because of differences with regard to Iran. I doubt however whether in this day and age a great nation which has such an exalted moral standing in the world [as the U.S.] can afford to support the internationally immoral policy of a friend and ally. . . . The Iranian people merely desire to lead their own lives in their own way. They wish to maintain friendly relations with all other peoples. [But Anglo-

Iranian Oil Company], which for years was engaged in exploiting [our] oil resources, unfortunately has persisted in interfering in the internal life of [our] country."

Eisenhower's innate midwestern sense of decency initially made him recoil from backing Britain's colonial siege of Iran. He rebuffed the Dulles brothers' advice, suggesting that it might be a better idea to stabilize Mossadegh's government with a $100 million loan than to topple it. If Eisenhower had followed through on his original instincts, the bedeviled history of U.S.-Iran relations would undoubtedly have taken a far different course.

An air of tragic heroism clung to Mossadegh. When American envoys made a last-ditch effort to persuade him to appease the British oil giant, he proudly refused. The history of Iran's leadership was plagued by cowardice and corruption, said Mossadegh, and he would not continue this sorry legacy. Anglo-Iranian Oil had already been offered fair compensation for its losses; Mossadegh would not compromise the resource rights of his country any further. If he cut a deal with the British, the prime minister told U.S. mediators, his reputation would be forever stained with the Iranian people, who would immediately assume that their nation had been sold out once more. Mossadegh's adamant defense of Iranian sovereignty made him a beloved figure in his homeland, with a popular referendum at the height of the Iran crisis giving him nearly unanimous support.

Realizing that Eisenhower was not inclined to defend British imperial interests, the Dulles brothers reframed their argument for intervention in Cold War terms. On March 4, 1953, Allen appeared at a National Security Council meeting in the White House armed with seven pages of alarming talking points. Iran was confronted with "a maturing revolutionary set-up," he warned, and if the country fell into Communist hands, 60 percent of the free world's oil would be controlled by Moscow. Oil and gasoline would have to be rationed at home, and U.S. military operations would have to be curtailed.

In truth, the global crisis over Iran was not a Cold War conflict but a struggle "between imperialism and nationalism, between First and

Third Worlds, between North and South, between developed industrial economies and underdeveloped countries dependent on exporting raw materials," in the words of Ervand Abrahamian. Dulles made Mossadegh out to be a "stooge" of the Communists—but he was far from it. The scion of an aristocratic Persian family, the prime minister was educated in France and Switzerland, and tilted more toward the West than in the direction of Iran's feared Soviet neighbor to the north. Mossadegh was a fervent nationalist, not a secret Communist—another Gandhi, in the assessment of one British foreign official, not a Mao. The Tudeh, Iran's Communist Party, regarded Mossadegh with a decided wariness, viewing him as a "liberal bourgeois" with dangerous illusions about America. Mossadegh, in turn, relied on the Tudeh's support when it suited him but kept his distance, seeing the party as too subservient to Moscow. Meanwhile, Soviet leadership remained reluctant to get too deeply involved in Iranian politics for fear of threatening the West's interests there.

But after weeks of intensive lobbying by the Dulles brothers and the British government, Eisenhower became convinced that Iran was a Cold War battleground and that Mossadegh had to go. In June 1953, Allen presented the CIA plan to overthrow Mossadegh's government to his brother at a special meeting of national security policy makers held in Foster's office.

The coup plan had been drawn up by Kermit "Kim" Roosevelt Jr., Allen's handpicked man to run the operation on the ground in Iran. The well-bred grandson of Theodore Roosevelt did not seem like the sort of cutthroat character to carry out such a disreputable task. Roosevelt was well regarded even by ideological enemies like Kim Philby. "Oddly enough, I dubbed [Roosevelt] 'the quiet American' five years before Graham Greene wrote his book," Philby once noted. "He was a courteous, soft-spoken Easterner with impeccable social connections, well-educated rather than intellectual, pleasant and unassuming as host and guest. An equally nice wife. In fact, the last person you would expect to be up to the neck in dirty tricks."

Indeed, Roosevelt was taken aback by the blithe way that the fate of

Iran's democracy was discussed in Foster's office that day. "This was a grave decision to have made," he later observed. "In fact, I was morally certain that almost half of those present, if they had felt free or had the courage to speak, would have opposed the undertaking."

But the Dulles brothers had already made up their minds about Iran and they allowed no room for debate. And once the brothers fixed the administration on its fateful course, they were confident that they had the right man for the job. The Dulleses could see the ruthless streak beneath Kim Roosevelt's smooth Groton and Harvard polish. Three years earlier, they had recruited Roosevelt to work in Iran as a lobbyist for their ill-fated Overseas Consultants Inc. deal. And for the past two years, he had been spearheading a secret CIA operation to organize an underground resistance network inside Iran, burying crates of guns and cash in the desert to distribute to tribal warriors in case of a Soviet invasion. Roosevelt now turned this clandestine effort against Iran's elected government, hiring bands of mercenaries and paying military leaders to betray their country. When push came to shove, Kim Roosevelt revealed that he shared his grandfather's enthusiasm for imperial misadventures.

The U.S. and British intelligence operatives running the anti-Mossadegh operation were prepared to go to any lengths to accomplish their task. Key officials in the military and government who remained loyal to Mossadegh were kidnapped and murdered, such as General Mahmoud Afshartous, the officer in charge of purging the armed forces of traitorous elements. The general's mangled corpse was found dumped on a roadside outside Tehran as a message to all officials who chose to stand by the prime minister. Other prominent loyalists had their throats slit and their bodies buried far away in the Alborz Mountains.

In the end, as Tudeh Party leaders feared, Mossadegh was undone by his faith in the American government. The prime minister still controlled the streets of Tehran on August 18, with National Front and Tudeh militants roaming throughout the capital and toppling royal statues and other symbols of the shah's rule. But after conferring with Roosevelt, U.S. ambassador Loy Henderson—the Dulles brothers' other canny emissary in Iran—arranged a fateful meeting with Mossadegh.

During the hourlong meeting, Henderson vehemently protested the anti-Western "mob attacks"—which he claimed had even threatened the U.S. embassy and assaulted his chauffeur. Henderson warned that if the prime minister did not restore order, the United States would have to evacuate all Americans and withdraw recognition of Mossadegh's government. The gambit worked. Mossadegh "lost his nerve," according to Henderson, and immediately ordered his police chief to clear the streets. It was, the U.S. diplomat later observed, "the old man's fatal mistake."

With Mossadegh's supporters off the streets, the CIA's hired thugs were free to take their place, backed by rebellious elements of the military. On the morning of August 19, as Mossadegh huddled in his home at 109 Kakh Street with his advisers, tanks driven by pro-shah military officers and street gangs whose pockets were literally stuffed with CIA cash converged on the prime minister's residence.

For two hours, a firefight raged outside Mossadegh's home, which was protected by three tanks commanded by officers loyal to the prime minister. But the rebel forces had two dozen tanks at their disposal, including two powerful U.S.-built Shermans, and the outcome was predictable. As shells tore into his residence, Mossadegh ordered his tank commander to cease fire. The seventy-one-year-old prime minister and his top aides then scaled the wall to a neighboring house, barely escaping the wrath of the hired mob, which proceeded to smash down the green grill gate and ransack the official residence. One of the brave officers in charge of defending the prime minister was torn limb from limb by the rampaging mob. Soon after, Mossadegh and the other officials were arrested and imprisoned in a military barracks, thereby ending Iran's brief interlude of democracy.

Mohammad Mossadegh had been violently evicted from office, but the CIA coup could not be successfully completed until the shah returned home to reclaim his throne. As the coup got under way, Kim Roosevelt had worked frantically to prevent the shah from fleeing the country, telling him that it was his duty to stand with the rebel forces and assuring him of U.S. protection. But courage failed "the king of kings." He was "a wimp," in the candid estimation of Roosevelt, who had stuck it out in Iran even after the shah had taken flight and the CIA had told their intrepid agent that he should do the same.

As the tumultuous events unfolded in Tehran, the shah and Queen Soraya were photographed on a shopping excursion along Via Condotti, dipping in and out of the Gucci, Dior, and Hermès showcases that lined Rome's fashion avenue. Despite his budget worries, the shah mustered the nerve to buy himself four tennis rackets and a pair of black antelope shoes, as well as lingerie, two crocodile handbags, and a dozen summer frocks for his wife. The paparazzi later snapped Soraya in one of her stylish outfits, an eye-catching polka-dot dress that exposed her lovely bronzed shoulders.

As the coup reached its climax, Dulles was monitoring the operation from his bunker in the U.S. embassy, just down the block from the Excelsior. The spymaster's vigil was no doubt enlivened by the presence of the American ambassador to Rome, the seductive and witty Clare Booth Luce, wife of Henry Luce and a celebrated playwright. While Clover entertained herself at the Excelsior, Dulles, who was rumored to be sexually involved with the attractive ambassador, spent long nights at the embassy. Although Clare Luce was an ardent convert to Catholicism and was later known for a widely reprinted speech decrying the anything goes "new morality" toward sex, she and her husband seemed to have a sense of aristocratic license when it came to their own sex lives. While Dulles was dallying with Luce's wife, the magazine mogul was enjoying himself with Dulles's wartime mistress, Mary Bancroft.

But the strongest link between Dulles and the Luces was their shared conviction that they were driving forces behind what Henry had christened "the American Century." Luce coined the term in a 1941 *Life* magazine editorial, calling for the United States to take a dominant role in global affairs, "exert[ing] upon the world the full impact of our influence, for such purposes as we see fit and by such means as we see fit." In effect, Luce was calling for the United States, on the brink of entering World War II, to replace Britain as the new world empire—

not by holding overseas territories, as in the passing colonial era, but by flexing its military, commercial, and cultural strength. Luce's missionary vision of American power, which would find echoes in a later generation's embrace of "American exceptionalism," meshed neatly with that of the Dulles brothers. But while Luce could only preach about the historic imperative of American power, Allen Dulles was in a position to act on it.

Dulles's main mission in Rome was to stiffen the shah's spine and whisk him back to the Peacock Throne. The royal couple were taking their lunch in the Excelsior dining room when they heard that Mossadegh had been overthrown. The shah seemed shaken by the news instead of overjoyed. His "jaw dropped," according to one observer, and "his trembling fingers reached for a cigarette." He looked chastened. "I have to admit that I haven't had a very important part in the revolution," he murmured. But Soraya was upbeat. "How exciting," she trilled, placing a reassuring hand on her husband's arm. Dulles quickly arranged a special commercial flight to take the shah home.

Soraya, pronouncing herself not quite ready to face the clamor, stayed on in Rome a while longer. She was also consulting feverishly with a prominent American gynecologist flown in by the CIA to help her get pregnant. "Four times a night," she told the doctor, "and twice every afternoon. Still I don't have a baby." Soraya never overcame her infertility. Frustrated by the queen's inability to provide the Pahlavi dynasty with an heir, a weeping shah would announce their divorce in 1958. Aided by a generous royal settlement, Soraya returned to luxurious exile in Rome, where she became the lover of Italian director Franco Indovina and had a brief film career.

As the shah boarded his chartered KLM airliner home, he knew that he was returning to a roiling tempest in Iran, where he was widely reviled by his subjects as a puppet of Western powers. But, according to some accounts, Dulles himself helped brace the shaky ruler by accompanying him on the flight to Tehran. The CIA also spread around more cash to make sure his arrival would be greeted by cheering crowds. Two retainers flung themselves on the ground to kiss his feet as he made his way down the reception line at the airport. The shah warmly greeted Ambassador Henderson, one of the "heroes" of the coup. By the time he was carried back to the palace in the royal limousine, past the dutifully enthusiastic throngs on the streets, the shah had convinced himself that he was indeed a man of destiny—instead of just another creature of the CIA.

"The shah is living in a dream world," Henderson drily remarked. "He seems to think his restoration was due entirely to his popularity with his people."

Dulles would look back on the coup in Iran as one of the two greatest triumphs of his CIA career, along with the regime change he engineered in Guatemala the following year. This was the sort of daring high-wire act that gave him the biggest professional thrill, and it left him with a taste for more. Dulles imagined himself a character in a John Buchan spy novel, Kim Roosevelt told CIA Middle East hand Miles Copeland, and the spymaster "wouldn't be able to restrain himself—or us" if the opportunity arose anywhere else to repeat the agency's exploits in Iran. "Allen would give his left . . . well, let us say index finger," said Roosevelt, "if he could go somewhere in the field and engineer a coup d'état himself."

Dulles's handiwork could also be seen in the compliant U.S. press coverage of the regime change. News reports on the coup assiduously avoided looking into the CIA's deep involvement. *Newsweek* gave Dulles's appearance at the Excelsior a curious wink and a nod, but then quickly passed on. Amid "the hubbub" over Mossadegh's fall, noted the magazine, the CIA director suddenly was spotted in the hotel—but "no one paid any attention to him."

Dulles not only persuaded his high-placed friends in the press to throw a cloak over the CIA's operation, he convinced them to share his exuberance over its success. A *Washington Post* editorial saw the overturning of Iran's democratic government as a "cause to rejoice." *The New York Times* took a similar celebratory line, calling Mossadegh "a rabid, self-seeking nationalist" whose "unlamented" disappearance from the political stage "brings us hope." The U.S. press even avoided using awkward words like "coup," preferring to describe the CIA-engineered operation as a "popular uprising" or a "nation's revolt."

If Dulles carefully concealed the CIA's role from the American public, he made sure that the shah was made fully aware of the debt he owed the agency. U.S. national security forces would continue to prop up the shah's reign for the next quarter of a century, encouraging the ruler's "megalomania," as Jesse Leaf, who served for a time as the CIA's chief analyst on Iran, remarked. But the agency's contempt for the man on the Peacock Throne only grew with time. Leaf found him "basically a hollow man, a straw man, a pipsqueak."

But the hollow man proved very useful for Western interests, including those of some of the Dulles brothers' leading former clients. Under a new agreement with the major oil companies orchestrated by the shah a few months after the coup, Iran's oil industry was denationalized. Once again, the country's natural treasure was handed over to foreign corporations, with 40 percent of the spoils now going to American oil producers, including Gulf, Texaco, Mobil, Standard Oil of New Jersey, and Standard Oil of California.

Kim Roosevelt was among those who cashed in on the coup, leaving the CIA in 1958 to join the management of Gulf Oil, where he took charge of the company's relations with foreign governments, including the Iran regime. Later, he became an international consultant, representing the shah and serving as a middleman for weapons manufacturers doing business with Iran. The shah remained deeply loyal to his CIA friends, once toasting Roosevelt at a palace ceremony as one of the powerful forces, along with the Almighty, to whom he owed his throne.

The Iran coup had an intoxicating effect on the Eisenhower administration, coursing through the Oval Office, the CIA, and the State Department like a champagne glow. "It was a day that should never have ended," stated a rapturous internal CIA report on the coup. "For it carried with it such a sense of excitement, of satisfaction and of jubilation that it is doubtful whether any other can come up to it." The president summoned the now mythic Roosevelt to the White House to make a special presentation on his Persian escapade. A spellbound Eisenhower later said that it was more like listening to a rousing "dime novel" than a government briefing. When Roosevelt looked over at the secretary of state midway through his presentation, Foster was leaning back leisurely in his chair, and it appeared for a moment as if he might be dozing. But then Roosevelt realized that Foster's "eyes were gleaming. He seemed to be purring like a giant cat."

But what for Washington was a tale of derring-do right out of *The Scarlet Pimpernel* was for Iran a disaster without end. The country's fledgling democracy was dismantled, and members of oppositional parties and the press were rounded up or driven underground. With the CIA's strong encouragement, the shah unleashed his secret police organizations—first the Second Bureau, and in 1957 the infamous SAVAK—in a ruthless campaign to root out "subversion." The Tudeh bore the brunt of the crackdown. With CIA assistance, the shah's U.S.-trained security forces tracked down over four thousand party members between 1953 and 1957. Many were subjected to primitive torture methods, including whippings and beatings, the smashing of chairs on heads, and the breaking of fingers. A few were subjected to the gruesome *qapani*, in which they were hung from hooks. At least eleven people died under torture during this period, most from brain hemorrhages, and dozens more were executed.

The regime grew alarmed when reports began circulating about the condemned prisoners' heroism—how they had gone to their deaths singing defiant songs and denouncing the shah. It was reported that the firing squads' bullets often missed their targets, either "through nervousness or deliberate avoidance," and that officers had to dispatch the prisoners with pistol shots. The regime was forced to clamp a tighter lid on future rounds of executions, out of fear that the prisoners' show of "bravado" was "impressing large segments of the public."

All hope for change was ripped from the hearts of the Iranian people, replaced by poisonous seeds whose bitter fruit grew slowly over the next two decades. The shah ultimately reaped what he had sown, driven into his final exile in 1979 by a popular revolt led by the country's Islamic mandarins, the only oppositional sector of Iranian society not crushed by the Pahlavi regime. The Americans and Iranians are still paying for "the day that should never have ended."

After his arrest, Mossadegh was put on trial for treason. He responded by telling the court that his real crime was that he had "resisted imperialism." The U.S. embassy fretted that his trial was a "serious blunder," since it reinforced the popular leader's "demigod" status and his mystical "hold over the public." Fearing that executing him would only make him more of a martyr, the regime sentenced Mossadegh to three years of solitary confinement and then banished him to his rural village, sixty miles north of Tehran, where he lived out the rest of his days in a small, white-walled house. When he died nine years later, at age eighty-four, the shah blocked efforts to organize a public funeral ceremony. Even in death, Mossadegh was taunted by the U.S. press, with a wire story by the Associated Press portraying him as an "iron dictator" who had terrorized his enemies and "brought the country to economic chaos." The ambulance carrying his body from a hospital in Tehran to his home went "almost unnoticed," the news item gloated. "In the downtown bazaar, crowds went about their shopping for the Persian New Year."

The shah refused Mossadegh's final request—to be buried in the main Tehran cemetery, alongside the bodies of his supporters who had been shot down in the streets by the army. Instead, he was buried underneath his own sitting room, near a mantelpiece where a picture of Gandhi gazed serenely over him.

The Eisenhower-Dulles era was a Pax Americana enforced by terror. The administration ensured U.S. postwar global dominance by threatening enemies with nuclear annihilation or with coups and assassinations. It was empire on the cheap, a product of Ike's desire to avoid another large-scale shooting war as well as the imperial burdens that had bankrupted Great Britain. By leveraging the U.S. military's near monopoly on nuclear firepower, the president hoped to make war an unthinkable proposition for any and all American adversaries. And by utilizing the CIA's dark sleight of hand, the commander in chief aimed to render it unnecessary for the Marines to go crashing ashore in far-flung locales where unfriendly governments had taken office.

Dwight Eisenhower himself was a peace-loving warrior, the son of a pacifist mother who had cried when he was admitted into West Point. Though he never experienced combat firsthand—a gap in his military résumé that he sorely regretted through much of his career—Eisenhower saw more than his share of the effects of war, touring the blood-soaked battlefields after World War I and the still-smoking ruins of Europe and newly liberated Nazi death camps following World War II. As the Supreme Allied Commander, Eisenhower acutely felt the sacrifice that he was asking of the thousands of young men under his leadership. While the general and his staff prepared to dispatch waves of soldiers onto the beaches of Normandy in June 1944—over ten thousand of whom would be killed or wounded on D-day—he suffered wrenching stomach pains, soaring blood pressure, recurring headaches and throat infections, and chronic insomnia. "He was as nervous as I had ever seen him and extremely depressed," recalled Kay Summersby, the general's wartime secretary and intimate companion.

Eisenhower also felt the enormous responsibility of sitting in the Oval Office at the dawn of a new era in which science had given U.S. leaders the means to destroy virtually all life on the planet. But while privately grasping the unprecedented gravity of the moment, he publicly adopted a disturbingly nonchalant attitude toward the new weapons of mass destruction.

Eisenhower biographer Evan Thomas later called his nuclear brinksmanship "Ike's bluff," a bold strategy to keep the world at peace by threatening total war. There was a perverse logic to the Eisenhower-Dulles policy of massive retaliation. But by reserving the right to use nuclear weapons anytime and anyplace that U.S. interests were threatened, the administration kept the world in a state of perpetual anxiety. As the Soviet Union began narrowing the nuclear weapons gap in the 1950s, the planet was held hostage by the growing tensions between the two superpowers—the United States and the USSR were "two scorpions in a bottle" in the memorable phrase of nuclear physicist J. Robert Oppenheimer.

Did Eisenhower really believe that nuclear explosives were just another conventional military tool, as he indicated at a March 1955 press conference when asked if he might consider using them during a confrontation with China over two tiny, obscure islands in the Formosa Strait? "I see no reason why they shouldn't be used just exactly as you would use a bullet or anything else," Eisenhower announced. Or did he realize that nuclear arms had made war unthinkable, as he noted in his diary the following year, soon after declaring his candidacy for a second term? "The problem is not man against man, or nation against nation," Eisenhower wrote. "It is man against war."

Eisenhower seemed to revel in the terrible uncertainty that he created, seeing it as a way to intimidate enemies and keep them off balance. After the president's nuclear "bullet" statement, White House press secretary Jim Hagerty nervously asked his boss how he planned to handle follow-up questions about the atom bomb option. Ike smiled and said, "Don't worry, Jim, if that question comes up, I'll just confuse them."

The problem with Eisenhower's strategy was that by keeping Washington in a constant state of high alert, he empowered the most militant voices in his administration, including the Dulles brothers and Pentagon hard-liners like Admiral Arthur Radford and Air Force general Curtis LeMay—who, taking their commander in chief at his word, continually agitated for a cataclysmic confrontation with the Soviet Union. Eisenhower once said that he feared his own "boys" in the military more than he did a sneak attack from the Soviets, who, as he observed, had suffered so devastatingly during World War II that they would be deeply reluctant to risk World War III. The president did not think any of his nuclear commanders would go rogue, but he knew that the constant Pentagon pressure for bigger doomsday arsenals produced equally strong temptations to use the weapons—particularly while the United States still enjoyed a clear margin of nuclear superiority over the Soviet Union.

Eisenhower might have been certain of his ability to rein in the Strangelovian figures in his national security establishment, but his chronic health troubles made his control of the country's war apparatus seem questionable at times. Eisenhower, who wrestled with high blood pressure, suffered a heart attack in September 1955 that was more serious than the White House publicly admitted. He was not able to return to the Oval Office on a regular basis until January. As the sixty-five-year-old Eisenhower debated whether or not to seek reelection in 1956, his heart specialist advised that there was a fifty-fifty chance he would not live out a second term—an opinion that was also kept secret. Nine months after his heart attack, Eisenhower was operated on for a painful bowel obstruction and remained hospitalized for three weeks. And in November 1957, the president suffered a mild stroke in the Oval Office, which affected his speech and caused severe headaches for weeks. During Eisenhower's periods of incapacitation, it was Foster Dulles and Vice President Nixon, the Dulles brothers' acolyte, who moved into the presidential power vacuum. Neither man was known for his sense of moderation in dealing with Communist adversaries.

From the very beginning of the administration, Secretary of State Dulles argued that the United States must overcome the "taboo" against nuclear weapons. At a February 1953 National Security Council meeting, just three weeks into Eisenhower's presidency, Foster raised what he called "the moral problem" that hovered over all nuclear decision-making. He was not referring to the profound questions about mass slaughter and human survival. Foster meant the moral revulsion against doomsday weapons that prevented policy makers from seriously contemplating their use.

Foster pushed Eisenhower to consider using the ultimate weapons during one crisis after the next, including the climactic stage of the Korean War in 1953, the final French stand in Vietnam at Dien Bien Phu in 1954, the battle of nerves with China over the islands of Quemoy and Matsu that same year, and the 1958 confrontation with the Soviets over Berlin. At various, hair-raising moments of these crises, Eisenhower seemed poised to take Foster's advice, and was only dissuaded by the alarmed opposition of allied leaders or the cooler-headed responses of the Chinese and Soviet governments.

John Foster Dulles was the exemplar of Mills's "crackpot realism."

He was a "wise man" who, in sober and solemn tones, advocated positions that were the height of madness. "We are at a curious juncture in the history of human insanity," Mills wrote in *The Causes of World War III*, his 1958 jeremiad against the growing fever for the final conflict. "In the name of realism, men are quite mad, and precisely what they call utopian is now the condition of human survival."

"Utopian action"—by which Mills meant active diplomacy among the superpowers, a ban on nuclear arms testing, a moratorium on the production of "extermination" weapons, scientific and cultural exchanges, and free travel between the West and East—was actually "realistic, sound, common sense," he wrote. In contrast, "practical actions are now the actions of madmen and idiots. And yet these men decide; these men are honored, each in his closed-up nation, as the wise and responsible leaders of our time who are doing the best they can under trying circumstances."

Foster seemed to have a chillingly remote perspective on what it meant to drop a nuclear bomb. When the French garrison at Dien Bien Phu was on the verge of collapse, he offered to give two "A-bombs" to French foreign minister Georges Bidault. The French official was deeply shaken by Foster's blithe offer. Bidault responded "without having to do much thinking on the subject." He pointed out to Foster that "if those bombs are dropped near Dien Bien Phu, our side will suffer as much as the enemy." Likewise, during the Formosa Strait crisis, Foster was surprised to learn that the "precision" nuclear bombing of Chinese targets that he was advocating would kill more than ten million civilians. Still, he was not chastened enough to stop his campaign to "punish" the Chinese.

Mills noted that, like the Nazis before them, the national security leaders "rationally" planning for a nuclear holocaust were characterized by a "moral insensibility." Official violence had become so bureaucratized that "in official man there is no more human shock." Mills believed that humanity would continue to teeter on the brink of the eternal void until Eisenhower's secretary of state, whom he accused of a "doctrinaire and murderous rigidity," was replaced by a diplomat who was serious about the prospects for peaceful coexistence.

The death in March 1953 of Joseph Stalin, the Moloch of Soviet brutality and despair, offered the Eisenhower administration the opportunity to redefine the U.S. relationship with Moscow, as the Kremlin's new leaders began the process of de-Stalinization. But Foster continued to counsel a hard line against the Soviets, interpreting any signs of a Cold War thawing in Moscow as evidence that the tough U.S. line was working. The secretary of state even sternly cautioned Eisenhower not to smile at Soviet officials or shake hands with them at the July 1955 Geneva Summit. This proved difficult for Ike, observed Stewart Alsop, since "his whole instinct was to smile and be friendly. And then he'd kind of draw back, remembering what Foster had said."

Nikita Khrushchev, the canny and down-to-earth political survivor who was emerging from the Kremlin's scrum as the top Soviet leader, closely observed the personal dynamics between Eisenhower and his secretary of state in Geneva and concluded that Foster was in charge. "I watched Dulles making notes with a pencil, tearing them out of a pad, folding them up, and sliding them under Eisenhower's hand," Khrushchev later wrote in his memoir. "Eisenhower would pick up these sheets of paper, unfold them, and read them before making a decision on any matter that came up. He followed this routine conscientiously, like a dutiful schoolboy taking his lead from his teacher. It was difficult to imagine how a chief of state could allow himself to lose face like that in front of delegates from other countries. It certainly appeared that Eisenhower was letting Dulles do his thinking for him."

Before jumping on the Eisenhower bandwagon in 1952, the Dulles brothers calculated that he would not make a strong president. But Ike's malleability offered its own advantages, in their eyes. As secretary of state, Foster succeeded in undermining or deflecting every tentative step that the president made toward détente with the Soviet Union. In August 1955, following the Geneva Summit, Foster sent out a long cable to all U.S. diplomatic mission chiefs around the world, warning that the free world must not let down its guard despite the air of goodwill wafting out of the conference. "Geneva has certainly created problems for the free nations," he wrote. "For eight years they have been held together largely by a cement compounded of fear and a sense of moral superiority. Now the fear is diminished and the moral demarcation is somewhat blurred." The free world must not "relax its vigilance," he declared, dismissing the post-Stalin Soviet peace efforts as a "classic Communist maneuver." Hope was Foster's enemy, fear his righteous sword.

By 1958, five years into the process of de-Stalinization, Khrushchev was understandably deeply puzzled and frustrated by Washington's failure to diplomatically engage with his regime. The main obstacle to peace, he rightly concluded, was John Foster Dulles.

Foster's staunch resistance to making peace with the Soviets did not reflect a perverse contrariness or extreme anti-Communism. Nor did it suggest his true assessment of the Soviet threat. His belligerence was strategic. As his revealing cable stated, this militant sense of alert was the "cement" that held together the Western alliance. And as Mills pointed out, the "continual preparation for war" was also the main factor holding together America's power elite. Or, in the mordant observation of Randolph Bourne as the United States plunged into the epic madness of World War I, "War is the health of the state." Foster, who always acted in the interests of the American establishment, understood this. It was this permanent war fever that empowered the country's political and military hierarchies and enriched the increasingly militarized corporate sector. It was the very lifeblood of this ruling group's existence—even if, in the atomic age, it threatened the existence of humanity.

The Eisenhower-Dulles foreign policy operated on twin levels of psychic violence and actual violence. While the secretary of state threatened to evaporate entire populations with "tactical" nuclear strikes, the director of central intelligence actually eliminated individuals around the world whenever they were deemed to be a threat to national security. Determined to use the CIA more aggressively than President Truman, who had feared creating an "American Gestapo," Eisenhower unleashed the agency, giving Allen Dulles a license to kill that the spymaster utilized as he saw fit.

Years later, in the 1970s, when post-Watergate congressional committees forced the CIA to account for its lethal reign under Dulles, the agency tried to downplay its ruthlessness. CIA witnesses testifying before the Church and Pike Committees insisted that while the agency had targeted foreign leaders such as the Congo's Patrice Lumumba, South Vietnam's Ngo Dinh Diem, Rafael Trujillo of the Dominican Republic, and Fidel Castro, its assassins had proved inept or were beaten to the punch. Assassination, went the CIA line, was simply not the sort of business at which its people excelled. But the agency was being too modest.

In truth, the CIA became an effective killing machine under Dulles. Allen Dulles was an assassination enthusiast throughout his espionage career, from the days of his involvement in the Operation Valkyrie plot against Hitler onward. Later in his career, any nationalist leader who seemed a problem for U.S. interests was viewed as fair game. During the 1957 Suez crisis, as a group of foreign policy officials and commentators gathered for dinner at the Washington home of Walter Lippmann, the conversation turned to Egypt's defiant leader, Gamal Abdel Nasser. One of the guests jested, "Allen, can't you find an assassin?" To the group's amazement, Dulles took the comment in dead seriousness. "Well, first you would need a fanatic, a man who'd be willing to kill himself if he were caught," said the spymaster, puffing thoughtfully on his pipe. "And he couldn't be an outsider. He'd have to be an Arab. It would be very difficult to find just the right man."

The Dulles brothers assured multinational firms that Washington would stop at nothing to protect their overseas investments. In August 1956, during yet another period of upheaval in the Mideast, Foster addressed a private meeting of oil company officials in Washington. The secretary of state assured the oilmen that if any sultan or despot were to be as unwise as Mossadegh and try to nationalize his underground desert treasure, the country would soon find itself the target of an "international intervention." Fortunately for Eisenhower, who sought to avoid such costly military operations, his administration would only feel compelled to mount one such intervention, sending the Marines into Lebanon in 1958 to ensure that the Beirut government remained in friendly hands. The rest of America's imperial mission during the Eisenhower years remained firmly in the hands of Allen Dulles.

Whispers about Dulles's tactics began making themselves heard in the White House during Eisenhower's first term. Some of the anxious reports came from those Washington circles that took a permanent interest in the nation's affairs, no matter which party was in power. Some emanated from within the spy agency itself. In July 1954, Eisenhower asked a trusted military friend, retired Air Force general James H. Doolittle, a World War II hero, to look into the agency and give him a confidential report. After Doolittle finished his investigation in October, the president blocked out an afternoon to hear his briefing. The general told Eisenhower that the CIA was badly managed and that Dulles was overly zealous. Furthermore, the relationship between the Dulleses was "unfortunate"—an alliance based on blood that allowed the brothers to establish their own, largely unaccountable power center within the administration. Eisenhower responded defensively, insisting that he found the Dulles brother act to be "beneficial." As for Allen, he might have his peculiarities, conceded the president, but the CIA was "one of the most peculiar types of operations any government can have, and it probably takes a strange kind of genius to run it."

Ironically, the Doolittle Report gave Dulles even more justification for his remorseless shadow war by concluding, "It is now clear that we are facing an implacable enemy whose avowed objective is world domination by whatever means and at whatever cost. There are no rules in such a game. Hitherto acceptable norms of human conduct do not apply." Dulles could not have put it more zealously himself.

Dulles's CIA operated with virtually no congressional oversight. In the Senate, Dulles relied on Wall Street friends like Prescott Bush of Connecticut—the father and grandfather of two future presidents—to protect the CIA's interests. According to CIA veteran Robert Crowley, who rose to become second-in-command of the CIA's action arm, Bush "was the day-to-day contact man for the CIA. It was very bipartisan and friendly. Dulles felt that he had the Senate just where he wanted them."

The CIA director found the House side of Congress to be equally amenable. Each year, Dulles had to go through the formality of making the agency's budget pitch to the armed services panel of the House Appropriations Committee, which was chaired at that time by Rep. Clarence Cannon of Missouri. On one occasion, the CIA's congressional liaison Walter Pforzheimer had to track down the elusive Cannon to find out when that year's CIA budget hearing would be scheduled. Pforzheimer cornered Chairman Cannon in the Capitol's Statuary Hall, alerting the congressman to the fact that Dulles would be asking for a 10 percent increase in the CIA's budget. "All right, Walter, you tell Mr. Dulles that he had his hearing and that he got his 10 percent."

Eisenhower was perfectly happy to have Congress stay out of the CIA's business, fearing a repeat of the McCarthy circus if legislators were allowed to probe the agency's operations. The president—who didn't know everything about the agency's dark side, but knew enough —was also keenly aware of the dangers of such exposure. "The things we did were 'covert,'" the president wrote in a diary entry that was not declassified until 2009. "If knowledge of them became public, we would not only be embarrassed . . . but our chances to do anything of like nature in the future would almost totally disappear."

John Eisenhower, who served his father as a White House aide, later blamed the Dulles spy set for manipulating the president. Ike was no match, said the younger Eisenhower, for the slick Ivy League types at the CIA. "Dad could be fooled. He was better when the guy was in uniform and knew him. But all those guys from Princeton and Yale . . ." Yet, throughout most of his presidency, Eisenhower was all too willing to be fooled by the CIA. Ike knew that Dulles's "strange genius" had its uses.

In 1956, to appease critics who charged that the CIA was operating with extremely minimal supervision, Eisenhower again ordered a discreet investigation of the agency by national security insiders—this time, diplomat David Bruce and Wall Street banker-statesman Robert Lovett. Eisenhower and Dulles felt there was nothing to fear from this new inspection, since Bruce and Lovett were longtime friends of the spymaster. But the Bruce-Lovett report shocked Dulles, taking strong aim at the CIA's penchant for creating political mayhem around the globe. There was an airy arrogance to Dulles's "busy, monied and privileged" agency, with its obvious fondness for overseas "kingmaking," declared the report. The promiscuous freedom that had been granted to Dulles and his "extremely high-powered machine" to "go barging around into other countries . . . scared the hell out of us," Lovett later remarked.

But, once again, Eisenhower ignored the strong criticisms leveled at the spy agency. Dulles's operation was simply too essential a component of the president's Cold War strategy for him to rein it in.

Unmanaged by the White House and unsupervised by Congress, Dulles's CIA grew to become the most potent agency of the Eisenhower era. Dulles was a master at seeding Washington bureaucracies with agency men, placing his loyalists in top positions in the Pentagon, State Department, and even the White House. The CIA became increasingly intertwined with the armed services, as military officers were assigned to agency missions, and then sent back to their military posts as "ardent disciples of Allen Dulles," in the words of Air Force colonel L. Fletcher Prouty, who served as a liaison officer between the Pentagon and the CIA between 1955 and 1963. Prouty, who observed Dulles at close hand, marveled at his mastery of the Washington power game. "He simply worked like the Colorado River in the Grand Canyon; he eroded all opposition."

Late on September 9, 1954, as midnight approached, Jacobo Arbenz, the recently deposed president of Guatemala, was escorted into the Guatemala City airport with a small entourage, including his wife, Maria Vilanova, and two of their children. Arbenz was beloved among his dirt-poor country's peasants and workers for his land and labor reforms, but he was reviled by Guatemala's aristocracy. As he prepared to leave his homeland, Arbenz was showered with abuse by a smartly dressed crowd of several hundred ill-wishers. "Assassin! Thief! Piece of shit!"

they screamed at him as he hurried into the airport terminal with his family.

Arbenz was fortunate to make it past the venomous crowd unharmed. Shortly before he and his family were driven to the airport, a decoy car masquerading for security purposes as the vehicle actually transporting the Arbenz family was blown up by his enemies.

Howard Hunt, one of the principal CIA orchestrators of the Guatemala coup, later acknowledged that he had helped organize the hostile send-off party at the airport for the benefit of the press. But Hunt claimed that he had spread the word among his people to let Arbenz leave the country unscathed. He knew that if the deposed leader were assassinated, "we'd [the CIA and the United States] get blamed for it." Relatives of Arbenz later said they found Hunt's professed concern for their family's security "hard to believe," considering his role in the Guatemalan president's violent downfall.

Before he was allowed to board the chartered DC-4 waiting to take him to Mexico City—the first stop in what would turn out to be a permanent exile—Arbenz was subjected to a final humiliation. Authorities of the new military regime demanded that the ex-president strip to his underwear in full view of a mob of jostling reporters and cameramen, ostensibly so that they could make sure he was not smuggling out cash. After his traumatic overthrow, Arbenz's nerves were shot. He and his family had spent seventy-three days and nights in miserable asylum at the Mexican embassy in Guatemala City, which had become so packed with political refugees that typhus and other diseases had broken out. At the airport, Arbenz looked pale and drawn in the glare of the camera lights. Every time a flashbulb popped, he visibly flinched. And yet, even as he disrobed in full view of the press pack, he held on to a kind of dignity, his head erect, his eyes looking straight ahead. "It gave the impression that a cold statue was taking off his marble clothes," remarked one of the ogling reporters.

"They were trying to break him down psychologically," said Dr. Erick Arbenz, a New York anesthesiologist and grandson of Jacobo Arbenz, who has led the family's campaign to reclaim his legacy. "Can you think of another example like this, where the elected leader of a nation was forced to undergo this sort of humiliation—to be publicly undressed in front of news cameras? The CIA was afraid of him—an educated, articulate reformer who had stood up to the local elite and the U.S. government. He was a big threat to these powerful interests."

For the rest of the exiled Guatemalan leader's life, the CIA was determined to strip away whatever shred of respectability still clung to him. The agency's disinformation campaign began immediately after Arbenz's downfall, with a stream of stories planted in the press—particularly in Latin America—alleging that he was a pawn of Moscow, that he was guilty of the wholesale butchery of political foes, that he had raided his impoverished country's treasury, that he was sexually captivated by the man who was the leader of the Guatemalan Communist Party. None of it was true.

CIA operatives had swarmed the presidential palace after he was ousted, collecting official documents and personal correspondence. They knew everything about Arbenz's private life. They knew about the intricate dynamics of his marriage, as well as the gruesome details of his father's suicide, and that he had once sought treatment for a drinking problem. When their discoveries weren't sensational enough, they embroidered them and sent them fluttering around the world.

While the CIA did all that it could to ruin Arbenz's name, the State Department pressured foreign governments to give the deposed president and his former deputies a chilly reception wherever they turned up. When Mexico City grew too inhospitable for Arbenz and his family, they tried Switzerland, land of his father's birth. But the Swiss authorities demanded that Arbenz give up his Guatemalan citizenship, which he refused to do, so the next stop was Paris. They settled on the Right Bank; his beautiful daughter Arabella was enchanted by the city. But every time Arbenz went for a walk, he felt he was being tailed. When he tried to hold a press conference to present his case against the powerful men who had overthrown him, French authorities threatened to deport his family unless he canceled the event. Arbenz began drinking again, dwelling on his final days in Guatemala, and his fateful exit from the political stage to avoid a bloodbath. The tragedy was "trapped in his head," said one of his friends.

To escape the hostile environment in the West, Arbenz fled with his family behind the Iron Curtain, first to Czechoslovakia and then to the Soviet Union. The howling in the press grew louder: here, at last, was *proof* of Arbenz's true, Bolshevik heart. "Finally Arbenz has found asylum in a place that he must love," crowed the *New York World-Telegram and Sun*, when he first alighted in Prague, "a land from the Iron Curtain where they practice the same sort of democratic regime as his." Newspapers around the world sounded the same refrain, as if all following the same conductor.

In fact, Arbenz's misery continued unabated behind the Iron Curtain. He hated the cold and sunless days; he missed the lush colors and radiance of the tropics. And he soon discovered that he had replaced one system of surveillance with another. Arbenz had only ended up in Russia because no other country wanted him. He reached out to every leader in Latin America, but the State Department had made it clear that any nation that took in the top men from the Arbenz government would incur Washington's wrath. Finally, Uruguay agreed to host Arbenz, but he was informed that he could not speak out, teach, publish his writing, or even take a job. He was, during his Montevideo sojourn, the invisible man.

But Arbenz still loomed large in the eyes of the CIA. Howard Hunt, who by then had taken over as the agency's chief of station in Uruguay, continued to closely track the man he had driven into exile. A neighbor of the Arbenz family told them that their house seemed to be under constant watch from a black car parked on the corner. Making the surveillance even easier for the CIA, Arbenz and his family had been installed on the same street where Hunt himself lived. Some evenings, Hunt and his wife even showed up at the same restaurant where the Arbenzes dined.

In 1960, Arbenz was invited to Cuba, and at last he and Maria felt they had found a safe place to raise their children. He was energized by the revolutionary fervor on the island, which was still luxuriating in the glory of its historic accomplishment. Arbenz was allowed to be a public man again, invited to speak at political rallies and to the Cuban press. But everywhere Arbenz went, he heard the militant slogan: "Cuba is not Guatemala!" His downfall had become a cautionary tale.

"After the Bay of Pigs, Cuban officials would compare my grandfather's defeat to the heroic Cuban victory over the U.S.," said Erick Arbenz. "He was used for propaganda purposes, to build up the esteem of the Cuban people. It was humiliating for him."

The Arbenzes met with Fidel Castro, to see if they could find a place for themselves in the new Cuba. Arbenz suggested that he could teach at the University of Havana, but the Cuban authorities were as leery of the former Guatemalan leader's democratic politics as the CIA was. During his Cuban exile, Arbenz grew increasingly disenchanted with the island's Communist rule. The family was moved into a small house in Varadero, a resort town safely removed from the political action in Havana.

The charge of cowardice had haunted Arbenz from the moment he surrendered his office. A young Argentinian doctor named Che Guevara—who had come to Guatemala to help the bold Arbenz experiment in progressive democracy—was among those who implored the besieged president to arm the people, when Arbenz's army officers began to melt around him under pressure from the CIA. But the Guatemalan leader was no Che or Fidel—he had lacked the cold-blooded courage to plunge his country into civil war. "My grandfather knew that the peasants were not trained to fight—so arming them would have just resulted in a bloody mess," said Arbenz's grandson. "He loved Guatemala and its people too much to do that."

Arbenz's beloved daughter, Arabella, refused to stay with the rest of the family in Cuba. Tired of their endless search for sanctuary, she fled back to Paris and began to create her own life—and her own tragedy. Arabella's beauty launched her on a modeling career and even landed her a movie role. She fell in love with a famous matador, who was equally celebrated for his many romances. Their stormy love affair provided the international press with another sensational Arbenz story to pursue. One day in 1965, after arguing loudly in a café in Bogotá, Colombia, Arabella rushed outside, returning soon after with a gun. She pointed it first at the matador, and then she stuck it in her mouth and pulled the trigger.

"The family had been hounded all over the world—they were suffering from post-traumatic stress because of their ordeal," said Erick Arbenz. "On top of that, there was a history of depression on my grandfather's side."

Arbenz was never the same after the death of his twenty-five-year-old daughter. She had been his special one, the child with whom he had clashed the most and loved the most. The press was merciless, portraying him as a cold and remote father, a man who had sacrificed the well-being of his children on the altar of his ideals. When Arbenz and his family were forced to run the ugly gauntlet at the Guatemala airport, he had told his children, "Don't be afraid, keep your chins up. We'll get through this." But, in the end, he could not protect them.

Arabella was buried in Mexico, and the Mexican government allowed the family to relocate there. Arbenz still struggled to find a means of support, and Maria, forced to become the family's provider, had to fly frequently to El Salvador, where her father had business interests. In his later years, Arbenz was an increasingly forlorn figure. He frequently visited Arabella's grave; it seemed as if he, too, belonged more in the world of shadows. But he continued to hold on to the dream of one day returning to Guatemala.

All that ended in January 1971, when Jacobo Arbenz died a strange and lonely death at age fifty-seven in the bathtub of a Mexico City hotel room. Authorities said he had climbed into a tub filled with scalding hot water and had either burned to death or drowned. He reportedly had been drinking. But Maria Arbenz always believed that her husband had been assassinated. In later years, it was revealed that the CIA had compiled a list of assassination targets during the planning for the 1954 coup. Arbenz's family was convinced that the agency was still working its way through the list when the former president suffered his terrible end.

What had Jacobo Arbenz done to deserve such a heartbreaking journey through life—a tale of grief and lament out of a Gabriel García Márquez novel? Simply put, he had tried to uplift his people. In doing so, he defied the gods of his country, the almighty United Fruit Company and its powerful friends in Washington, as well as Guatemala's medieval land barons. In June 1952, Arbenz pushed a sweeping land reform bill through his nation's legislature aimed at redistributing the heavily rural country's farm acreage, 70 percent of which was in the hands of 2 percent of the landowners. Among the properties expropriated under the new law and handed over to poor farmers were some of the vast estates of United Fruit.

Until Arbenz's election in 1950, the giant company, whose operations sprawled throughout the Caribbean, ran Guatemala less like a banana republic than a banana colony. United Fruit not only owned huge plantations but almost every mile of railroad track in the country, the only major Atlantic port, and the telephone system. In the capital, rulers came and went at the whim of the company. One of Arbenz's more cold-blooded predecessors, Jorge Ubico, thought of peasants as nothing more than beasts of burden. Before the 1944 revolt that toppled his dictatorship—an uprising that Arbenz had helped lead—farm workers were roped together like animals by Ubico's army and delivered to plantations where they were forced to work in debt slavery to the landowners.

Jacobo and Maria Arbenz were the Kennedys of Guatemala's fledgling democracy—young, rich, good-looking, and dedicated to improving the lives of their people. Jacobo, the son of a Swiss immigrant father and a mixed-race *ladina* mother, had overcome a sad childhood, including the suicide of his father, to become a rising officer in the Guatemalan army. He met his striking, dark-eyed wife, the daughter of a wealthy Salvadoran coffee plantation owner, at a dance while she was visiting Guatemala in 1938. The twenty-three-year-old Maria—who had been educated at a Catholic women's college in California and who loved to read and paint—was more cultured than the young lieutenant. But at twenty-five, Jacobo Arbenz cut a dashing picture in his uniform, with a noble profile that called to mind F. Scott Fitzgerald. He had a solemn and thoughtful air about him that lent him a gravity beyond his years.

Maria had been born "between silk sheets," in her words, but she had never been comfortable with the way that her family's privileges were built on the backs of her father's campesinos. Jacobo, who had been raised by an indigenous nanny, was similarly sensitive to the suffering of Guatemala's native population. When Maria asked Jacobo what he would like to do with his life, he answered with great sincerity, "I would like to be a reformer."

They married a few months later, and their home became an oasis of enlightenment in backward Guatemala. The promising young officer and his rich, charming wife felt more comfortable in the company of reform-minded professors, artists, and even young Communists than they did with members of the local aristocracy, who did not invite the couple to their social functions. "But what did we care?" Maria later remarked. "They were parasites—like in El Salvador. I wanted to broaden my horizons. I hadn't come to Guatemala to be a socialite and play bridge or golf."

Jacobo and Maria Arbenz proved to be a dynamic match. She encouraged his bold entrance into Guatemalan politics in 1944, when he helped lead the plot to overthrow the tyrannical Ubico. She fed his hunger for more learning by giving him a feast of books, from Emerson to Marx. Their vision for Guatemala became more ambitious, and dangerously radical by the authoritarian standards of the banana colony.

As Guatemala made the transition to democracy following the 1944 revolt, Arbenz got increasingly involved in political affairs. In 1950, he decided to run for president, focusing his campaign on agrarian reform, which he knew was the key to his country's liberation. He consulted with Maria's brother, Tonio, who was an agricultural expert, with a progressive Mexican economist, and with young leaders of the Guatemalan Communist Party whom he had come to respect as some of the most dedicated and intelligent agents of change in the country. Together, they formulated a plan for sweeping land reform and social progress in Guatemala.

After her husband's presidential victory, Maria Arbenz came under fire from his enemies as an evil influence over the newly elected Guatemalan president—a beguiling, Communist-leaning sorceress. But Arbenz ignored the poisonous political chatter and allowed his well-informed wife to participate in cabinet meetings. She soon established herself as one of his top advisers.

The land reform bill that the new president hammered out and then ushered through the legislature two years later was relatively moderate—Arbenz's government only expropriated acreage from United Fruit's huge holdings that was not under cultivation, and it offered the multinational corporation fair compensation for the seized land. But by Guatemala's retrogressive standards, Arbenz's land redistribution measures were breathtakingly bold. Many of the political colleagues in Arbenz's reform faction feared that he had gone too far, and that he would trigger a terrible backlash from the superpower to the north. Their fears were well founded.

The powerful influence of the United Fruit Company could be felt throughout Washington, where the company had high-placed friends and stockholders in both parties. The company's advocates were scattered throughout Congress and the foreign policy establishment. One would have to go far back in time, to the seventeenth and eighteenth centuries—when the Dutch East India Company ruled a far-flung empire, with the power to make war, negotiate treaties, hang convicts, and mint its own money—to find another corporation that wielded such clout.

United Fruit was especially well connected to the Eisenhower administration. As the agribusiness giant began lobbying the White House to overthrow Arbenz, Walter Bedell "Beetle" Smith, the president's trusted friend and undersecretary of state, was seeking an executive position with the company. After the coup, he was named to United Fruit's board of directors. Henry Cabot Lodge, who argued the United Fruit case against Arbenz as Eisenhower's UN ambassador, belonged to one of the blue-blooded Boston families whose fortunes were long entwined with the banana company. John Moors Cabot, who was in charge of Latin American affairs at the State Department, was the brother of United Fruit's former chief executive. Even the president's personal secretary, Ann Whitman, was connected to United Fruit: her husband was the company's public relations director. But United Fruit had no more powerful friends in the administration than the Dulles brothers.

The Dulleses had served as United Fruit's lawyers from their earliest days at Sullivan and Cromwell. On the eve of World War I, young Foster made a discreet tour of Central America on behalf of United Fruit, which was growing concerned about labor unrest and creeping Bolshevism in its tropical empire. Upon returning from his corporate spy mission, Foster made a confidential report to his uncle, Robert Lansing, who was not only a former counsel for United Fruit but President Woodrow Wilson's secretary of state.

Allen became so frequent a visitor to Guatemala as a legal envoy for United Fruit that he began taking along Clover, who fell under the spell of the country's beauty and culture. The couple's Tudor-style home on Long Island's North Shore was adorned with colorful native fabrics and rugs they brought back from their trips to the banana colony, giving their otherwise ordinary residence a surprisingly exotic touch. But Dulles's interest in Guatemalan artifacts did not extend to the people who had produced them.

United Fruit's cries of alarm about Arbenz's land reform soon produced the same results that Anglo-Iranian Oil's protestations did in Iran. The Eisenhower-Dulles administration moved swiftly to isolate Guatemala, labeling it a Soviet "beachhead" in the hemisphere. The Arbenz government, Foster charged, was imposing a "Communist-type reign of terror" on the Guatemalan people. Ambassador John Peurifoy, the Dulles brothers' handpicked man in Guatemala, tried to bribe Arbenz to fall in line, offering him $2 million to abort his land reforms. When that tried-and-true tactic of winning over Latin dictators did not succeed, Arbenz was physically threatened. And when that, too, failed to persuade the resolute leader, the Dulles brothers began arranging for his removal.

The CIA found a disgruntled, exiled Guatemalan colonel named Carlos Castillo Armas, who was working as a furniture salesman in Honduras at the time, to lead the uprising against Arbenz. His revolutionary "army" turned out to be a ragtag band of mercenaries and other unsavory types. Castillo Armas led his motley force across the border into Guatemala, driving a battered station wagon. The real threats to Arbenz's presidency came from the sporadic bombing raids on the capital carried out by CIA pilots, which sowed panic among the population, and from the agency's successful campaign to subvert the Guatemalan military. One army commander reportedly was paid $60,000 to surrender his troops.

When Arbenz realized that his army officers could not be counted on to obey his orders to defend the capital, he knew the game was over. Unwilling to take to the mountains to lead a guerrilla resistance, like the one that would make history in Cuba's Sierra Maestre, Arbenz began the long and winding descent that would end in a Mexico City hotel bathroom.

On June 27, 1954, as he prepared to flee the presidential palace, he made a final radio broadcast, denouncing the "fire and death" that had been rained upon Guatemala by United Fruit and its allies in "U.S. ruling circles." Few of his fellow citizens heard Arbenz's farewell address: in a last act of sabotage aimed at his government, the CIA jammed the radio speech. As he signed off, Arbenz declared with certainty that— despite his personal downfall—the cause of progress in Guatemala would triumph. The social accomplishments of the past few years, he insisted, could not be undone. History would prove him terribly wrong.

After Arbenz was overthrown, Dulles assembled his Guatemala task force in the White House to brief the president on the victorious operation, which had been confidently code-named PBSUCCESS. Less than one year after the Iran coup, the CIA director and his team had won a second opportunity to puff out their chests. PBSUCCESS would forge deep, lifelong bonds among Dulles and his Guatemala crew, which included Richard Bissell, Tracy Barnes, Howard Hunt, David Phillips, and David Morales. Many of the team members would be reunited for the Bay of Pigs. In later years, some of the Guatemala veterans would again pop into the spotlight under even more notorious circumstances.

But when they filed into the East Wing theater for their Guatemala slideshow, the PBSUCCESS team was at the height of its glory. The room was filled with the administration's top dignitaries, including the president himself, his cabinet, and the vice president. Afterward, Eisenhower, ever the soldier, asked Dulles how many men he had lost. Just one, Dulles told him. "Incredible!" exclaimed the president.

But the real body count in Guatemala started after the invasion, when the CIA-backed regime of Castillo Armas began to "clean" the nation of political undesirables, labor organizers, and peasants who had too eagerly embraced Arbenz's land reforms. It was the beginning of a blood-soaked era that would transform Guatemala into one of the twentieth century's most infamous killing fields. The "stainless" coup, as some of its CIA engineers liked to call it, would actually result in a tide of gore, including assassinations, rampant torture and executions, death squad mayhem, and the massacres of entire villages. By the time that the bloodletting had run its course, four decades later, over 250,000 people had been killed in a nation whose total population was less than four million when the reign of terror began.

The U.S. press coverage of the Guatemala coup offered a sanitized account, one that smacked of CIA manipulation. The leading newspapers treated the overthrow of Arbenz's government as a tropical adventure, an "opéra bouffe," in the words of Hanson Baldwin, one of Dulles's trusted friends at *The New York Times*. Nonetheless, reported Baldwin, the operation had "global importance." This is precisely how Dulles liked his overseas exploits to be chronicled—as entertaining espionage capers, with serious consequences for the Cold War struggle. *New York Times* publisher Arthur Hays Sulzberger was extremely accommodating to Dulles throughout the covert operation, agreeing to keep foreign correspondent Sydney Gruson, whom Dulles considered insufficiently compliant, out of Guatemala and even assuring the CIA director that Gruson's future articles would be screened "with a great deal more care than usual."

The strangely lighthearted tone of U.S. news dispatches about Guatemala would seep into history books about the CIA and Dulles biographies for years. But, in truth, Guatemala was less opéra bouffe than *Le Théâtre du Grand-Guignol*.

The murderous intrigue began long before the actual coup. As early as January 1952, the CIA started plotting to eliminate the top officials of the Arbenz government. Howard Hunt might have wanted to avoid the embarrassment of an Arbenz assassination in full public view, but the CIA had no qualms about compiling a secret "disposal list" of at least fifty-eight key Guatemalan leaders during the planning for the coup. The assassination memo was among several hundred documents relating to the 1954 coup released by the CIA in 1997 during one of the agency's occasional exercises in carefully managed "openness," which one critic labeled "a brilliant public relations snow job." Still, the documents were revealing enough to send shock waves through the international press.

In one of the declassified documents, an unnamed CIA official expressed his confidence on the eve of the Guatemala coup that "the elimination of those in high positions of the [Arbenz] government would bring about its collapse." Another document—a chillingly detailed, nineteen-page CIA killing manual titled "A Study of Assassination"—offered the most efficient ways to butcher Guatemala's leadership. "The simplest tools are often the most efficient means of assassination," the manual helpfully suggested. "A hammer, axe, wrench, screw driver, fire poker, kitchen knife, lamp stand, or anything hard, heavy and handy will suffice." The manual also advised assassins which parts of the body to strike for the most lethal effect, noting that "puncture wounds of the body cavity may not be reliable unless the heart is reached. . . . Absolute reliability is obtained by severing the spinal cord in the cervical region." The authors of the manual did make a passing reference to the morality of killing elected leaders of a sovereign nation. "Murder is not morally justified," the manual briefly acknowledged. "Persons who are morally squeamish should not attempt it."

The CIA compiled its death list with bureaucratic diligence, circulating the names of those nominated to die within agency departments and among Guatemala's military plotters, and asking for comments (as well as suggestions for the names of additional targets) like an interoffice memo. Because the CIA deleted the names on the list when it declassified the document, there is no way to tell how many—or if any—of the fifty-eight or more prominent Guatemalans were eventually assassinated. But what is known is that by training and encouraging Guatemala's new military masters in the art of political murder, the CIA injected a death spore into the nation's bloodstream that would wreak havoc for decades.

As soon as the dictator Castillo Armas was installed in the presidential palace, the CIA began pressuring him to purge Guatemala of leftist elements. His army rounded up some four thousand suspected Communists. As they revealed under interrogation, few of the prisoners had ever heard of Karl Marx and none belonged to the Communist Party— but they *were* guilty of belonging to democratic political parties, labor unions, and farmworker associations. They all had been infected with dangerous ideas during the Arbenz era because, in the words of one observer, "they believed [that] in a democracy the people chose the government, Guatemala needed land reform, and workers deserved protection under the law."

For the rest of his regime, Castillo Armas would do everything in his power to purify Guatemala of these thoughts. The CIA, enamored of making ominous lists, helped the new regime assemble a *lista negra* of subversives that soon grew to seventy thousand names. Eventually the names on the blacklist amounted to a staggering 10 percent of the country's adult population. Many of the names came from the Arbenz government documents that the CIA had seized when it raided the presidential palace. In August 1954, Castillo Armas announced Decree 59—the beginning of Guatemala's fascist legal architecture—which gave his regime the right to arrest those on the blacklist and to hold them for up to six months without trial. Those unfortunate enough to be rounded up were put in the care of José Bernabé Linares, the notorious chief of the Guardia Judicial, who was known for extracting confessions from prisoners with electric-shock baths and steel skullcaps.

Guatemalan journalists who attempted to report on the regime's abuses were themselves thrown into prison and tortured. But as Castillo Armas consolidated his brutal reign, with the CIA's energetic support, the U.S. embassy in Guatemala City continued to cover for the regime, insisting that there was "little basis for apprehension that the country could become a harsh police state very soon."

Meanwhile, the barbarism spread to the countryside, where peasant leaders were summarily executed, setting the stage for Guatemala's future death squads. Exiles reported that the regime was encouraging the rise of vigilante groups, telling them, "You can go and rob and kill in such-and-such sector, at this address, and you can be sure there won't be any police around to bother you about it." The worst massacre at the time took place in Tiquisate, a center of farmworker activism, where as many as a thousand peasants were seized by soldiers from plantations owned by United Fruit and local despots, lined up, and machine-gunned into open trenches.

Castillo Armas's own bloody end came in July 1957, when he was assassinated by one of his own palace guards. But his death did nothing to abate the slaughter, which continued on and off for decades, reaching new heights of ferocity during the Reagan presidency. One of the military dictators who succeeded Castillo Armas vowed, "If it is necessary to turn the country into a cemetery in order to pacify it, I will not hesitate to do so."

The enormous suffering of the Guatemalan people weighed heavily on Jacobo and Maria Arbenz during their long exile. "It haunted my grandparents every day," said Erick Arbenz. "That was another reason there was so much depression in our family. They lived and felt the Guatemala holocaust every day. They had tried to bring about a Guatemala Spring—and then to suffer not only their own defeat, but to see everything that was done to their people . . . it was an overwhelming tragedy."

The anguish of the Arbenz family seemed to have no end. In 2004, the Arbenzes' other daughter, Maria Leonora, followed the path of her sister and killed herself. "She felt as if she were being pursued and persecuted her whole life," said Erick. "Those feelings never went away from her."

After the Eisenhower administration overthrew Jacobo Arbenz, U.S. officials boasted that they would turn Guatemala into "a showcase for democracy." It became, instead, a bottomless well of sorrow.

Strange Love

The 1951 World Series was an epic sports event. The "subway series" not only featured two exciting New York teams, the Yankees and the Giants, but it marked the climax of what became known as "The Season of Change." Joe DiMaggio, the legendary "Yankee Clipper," would bow out of baseball after the series. And two young future Hall of Famers—Yankees rookie Mickey Mantle and Giants rookie Willie Mays—would make their World Series debuts. The twenty-year-old Mays, who idolized DiMaggio, finally had a chance to exchange a few words with his hero when photographers urged the two sluggers to stand together for a picture. "It was a dream come true," said the rookie, who played the series in a daze.

Game 6, which was played on October 10 in front of nearly sixty-two thousand people in Yankee Stadium, would assume mythic proportions in baseball fans' memories. The Yankees withstood a thrilling ninth-inning comeback charge by the Giants, winning the game 4–3 and taking the series. As DiMaggio trotted off the field to the roar of the crowd, he was already fading into history. "I've played my last game," Joltin' Joe told his teammates, who gathered around him in the locker room, handing him baseballs, bats, and other mementoes for him to sign. At thirty-six, DiMaggio's body was failing him and he didn't want to let down his fans and fellow players. "He quit because he wasn't Joe DiMaggio anymore," his brother Tom later said.

Among those sitting in the stands on that bittersweet day at Yankee

Stadium were two well-dressed German gentlemen in their forties, accompanied by a younger man who was their CIA handler. Like DiMaggio, the older German, Reinhard Gehlen, was a legendary figure, but his achievements were of a completely different order. Gehlen did not look like an imposing figure. He was slightly built and had a receding hairline, brush mustache, and ears that were as sharply peaked as a bat's. His skin was so pale that it seemed "translucent" to his CIA companion. Only his striking blue eyes gave any indication of the intense ambition that had driven Gehlen throughout his career.

During the war, Gehlen had served as Hitler's intelligence chief on the eastern front. His Foreign Armies East (*Fremde Heere Ost*) apparatus relentlessly probed for weaknesses in the Soviet defenses as the Nazi juggernaut made its eastward thrust. Gehlen's FHO also pinpointed the location of Jews, Communists, and other enemies of the Reich in the "bloodlands" overrun by Hitler's forces, so they could be rounded up and executed by the *Einsatzgruppen* death squads. Most of the intelligence gathered by Gehlen's men was extracted from the enormous population of Soviet prisoners of war—which eventually totaled four million—that fell under Nazi control. Gehlen's exalted reputation as an intelligence wizard, which won him the Führer's admiration and his major general's rank, derived from his organization's widespread use of torture.

Though many in the Yankee Stadium crowd that day would have been deeply displeased to learn Gehlen's identity, the German spymaster, wearing his trademark dark glasses, sat undisturbed in the stands, enjoying the carnival exuberance of the afternoon. The game itself was of little interest to Gehlen—it was his German companion, Heinz Herre, who was the rabid baseball fan. Herre, who had served as Gehlen's indispensable deputy ever since their days together on the eastern front, became so enamored of America's favorite pastime after the war that he could spit out players' statistics like the most obsessive of baseball card collectors. During the war, Herre had studied the Soviet enemy with equal intensity, learning the Russian language and immersing himself in the country's politics and culture. Now his compulsive curiosity was focused on all things American.

Herre, a tall and lean man with an appealing smile, had a knack for ingratiating himself with his U.S. colleagues. Though the socially awkward Gehlen lacked his deputy's facility with Americans, he knew it was an essential skill. In the final days of the war, Gehlen astutely concluded that the U.S.-Soviet alliance would inevitably break apart, providing an opportunity for at least some elements of the Nazi hierarchy to survive by joining forces with the West against Moscow. He knew that his own fate depended on his ability to convince his new American masters of his strategic value in the emerging Cold War. Gehlen did this by trekking into the Bavarian mountains, as U.S. forces approached, and burying cases of microfilm containing Nazi intelligence on the Soviet Union. The German spymaster then leveraged his expertise and underground connections in Eastern Europe, convincing U.S. military officials of his indispensability as an authority on the Soviet threat.

Gehlen's canny maneuvers won him and his top staff a flight out of war-ravaged Germany on a DC-3 military transport to the United States, where they were moved into comfortable quarters at Fort Hunt in Virginia. Here Gehlen was introduced to his American intelligence counterparts, including Allen Dulles, who, after listening to the German spymaster's pitch, decided that the U.S. government should bring the former Nazi intelligence operation under its supervision.

Instead of being handed over to the Soviets as war criminals, as Moscow was demanding, Gehlen and his top deputies were put on a troop ship back to Germany.

Back home, Gehlen's spy team was installed by U.S. military authorities in a compound in the village of Pullach, near Munich, that had once served as the headquarters of Hitler confidante Martin Bormann. Gehlen's dream of reconstituting Hitler's military intelligence structure within the U.S. national security system was about to be realized. With the generous support of the American government, the Gehlen Organization—as it came to be known—thrived in Pullach, becoming West Germany's principal intelligence agency.

In 1948, after a heated internal debate, the CIA decided to take over supervision of the Gehlen Organization from the U.S. Army, which had growing concerns about the type of agents Gehlen was recruiting and the quality of their intelligence work. Gehlen had promised Army officials that he would not hire former SS or Gestapo officials. But as his organization grew, it absorbed some of the most notorious figures of the Nazi regime, such as Dr. Franz Six. A former professor at Berlin University, Six left the classroom to become an intellectual architect of the Final Solution as well as one of its most enthusiastic enforcers, personally leading an SS death squad on the eastern front. After the war, Six was hired by the Gehlen Organization but was later arrested by U.S. Army counterintelligence agents. Convicted of war crimes, Six served four years in prison. However, within weeks of his release, Six was back at work in Gehlen's Pullach headquarters.

Many in the CIA vehemently opposed any association with such a stigmatized organization, including Admiral Roscoe Hillenkoetter, the agency's first director, who in 1947 strongly urged President Truman to "liquidate" Gehlen's operation. The following year, the CIA station chief in Karlsruhe, Germany, expressed his own disgust at the prospect of a merger with Gehlen's group, calling it an old boy's network of ex-Nazi officers "who are in a position to provide safe haven for a good many undesirable elements from the standpoint of a future democratic Germany." But Gehlen had his influential supporters in Washington.

Gehlen's backing came primarily from the Dulles faction within the national security establishment—and once again, this faction would prevail. In October 1948, James Critchfield, the new chief of the CIA's Munich station, was given the task of evaluating Gehlen's operation and recommending for or against it. The thirty-one-year-old Critchfield was a Dulles man: he had been identified as a talented prospect by Eleanor Dulles while serving with Army intelligence in postwar Vienna, and he was later recruited into the CIA by her brothers. In his final report, Critchfield firmly concluded that the CIA should fold Gehlen's group under its wing. It was the beginning of a fateful relationship that would shape Cold War politics for decades to come.

The CIA officially assumed responsibility for the German spy organization in July 1949, with Jim Critchfield taking over as Gehlen's supervisor. Critchfield moved his base of operations to Pullach, setting up his office in Bormann's former bedroom. Gehlen had turned Pullach into its own separate world, with over two hundred of his top staff and their wives and children living and working in the compound. Before Critchfield moved in, the German spymaster himself had lived with his wife and four children in Bormann's two-story house. Known, ironically, as the "White House," its décor still retained touches of Nazi kitsch, including a stone German eagle looming over the front door, whose claws were now empty after U.S. soldiers chiseled away the swastika they once held.

As Critchfield's CIA deputies and their families moved into Gehlen's gated community, an intimate social fusion began to develop between the former enemies. The Germans and Americans worked and partied together, their children attended the same one-room school, and their families even went on ski trips together in the nearby Bavarian Alps. By 1953, the CIA and Gehlen Organization were so entwined in Germany that some Washington officials, including Deputy Secretary of Defense Roger Keyes, expressed strong concern.

Just a few years before, Gehlen and his top men—who included high-ranking officers of the German General Staff, FHO, and even SS—had been dedicated warriors of the Third Reich. And yet Critchfield convinced himself that, except for "some borderline cases [who] worked in peripheral areas of the organization . . . [Gehlen's] key people . . . had come out of the war and the Nuremberg Trials with reasonably clean slates."

Critchfield was the son of a small-town North Dakota doctor and schoolteacher, graduating from North Dakota State University and joining the Army on the eve of the war. He had the thick, wavy hair and dark good looks of a central casting military hero. Critchfield served in North Africa and Europe, rising through the ranks to become one of the Army's youngest colonels and winning the Bronze Star twice and the Silver Star for gallantry. Crossing the Rhine in the final weeks of the war as the commander of a mobile task force, the young colonel was one of the first American officers to witness firsthand the results of Hitler's Final Solution. In late April, his unit came across an annex of Dachau. The camp was nearly empty, but there was evidence all around of the horror that had taken place there. At one point, the young Army colonel and his soldiers watched in "shocked silence" as two skeletal camp survivors chased after an escaping SS guard, wrestled him to the ground, and choked him to death.

Despite his war experiences, Critchfield prided himself on keeping an open mind about the ex-Nazi commanders with whom he later worked. "Gehlen and his senior staff, and their wives (many of whom also worked in Pullach), all impressed us as being unusually intelligent and well educated," Critchfield observed. "In personal characteristics, apparent values, and thoughts about the future of Germany and Europe, these [ex-Nazi] officers did not seem to me significantly different from my contemporaries in the U.S. Army."

Critchfield knew from the beginning of his professional relationship with Gehlen that he was dealing with a "difficult personality." Gehlen once subjected his CIA supervisor to a three-hour "harangue" against U.S. interference in his spy organization's affairs. Despite Gehlen's occasional histrionics, Critchfield expressed admiration for his German colleague's pragmatic, businesslike style and his welcome habit of "getting right to the point." If Gehlen had not been rescued by U.S. intelligence authorities after the war, he almost certainly would have been convicted of war crimes at Nuremberg. But Critchfield graciously overlooked Gehlen's past. "He had a high standard of morality," Critchfield later observed, without a hint of irony, "with Christian beliefs that were evident and reinforced by his wife Herta and their family." This simple, trusting American attitude made Critchfield an easy mark for Gehlen and the other quick-witted Nazi veterans whom he supervised.

Reinhard Gehlen was a man of ratlike cunning. He had managed to work his way up through the Wehrmacht's intelligence hierarchy; to survive a falling-out with Hitler late in the war over his increasingly dire intelligence reports; and not only to avoid the hangman's noose at Nuremberg but to persuade the Americans to give him a leading role in their shadow war against the Soviet Union. His overriding goal was to rebuild the Nazi power network and return Germany to a dominant role on the European stage. Gehlen harbored deeply mixed feelings about Germany's American conquerors; he had a cringing respect for their power and money but was deeply resentful about being forced to answer to them. He often treated his handlers, including Critchfield, more as enemies than allies, keeping them in the dark about his operations and even putting them under surveillance.

Late in his life, Critchfield admitted to a *Washington Post* reporter, "There's no doubt that the CIA got carried away with recruiting some pretty bad people." In a secret 1954 memo, later declassified, the agency acknowledged that at least 13 percent of the Gehlen Organization was made up of former hard-core Nazis. But, to the end of his life, Critchfield insisted that Gehlen was not one of these "bad people."

"I've lived with this for [nearly] 50 years," Critchfield told the *Post* in 2001. "Almost everything negative that has been written about Gehlen, in which he has been described as an ardent ex-Nazi, one of Hitler's war criminals—this is all far from the fact."

Happily deluded about Gehlen's true character, Critchfield worked hard to develop a good rapport with the German spymaster throughout their six-year partnership at Pullach. It was Critchfield who arranged the trip to America for Gehlen and his alter ego Heinz Herre in the fall of 1951, highlighted by the final game of the World Series. Gehlen's CIA caretaker saw the American odyssey—which was scheduled to include high-level meetings in Washington, as well as a train trip west to California—as a way to cement the agency's relationship with the cagey German and strengthen his bond with America.

As Critchfield put together the itinerary for Gehlen and Herre, the CIA hierarchy realized that the Germans' trip was fraught with potential problems. Gehlen remained a controversial figure within U.S. national security circles, where some were still pushing to fire him. An October 1950 CIA report on Gehlen, remarking on his tendency to throw fits and make demands on his American overseers, dismissed the German as "a runt, and, even as runts go, a rather unimpressive one . . . he suffers from a 'runt complex.'" A flurry of interoffice CIA memos on the eve of Gehlen's U.S. junket fretted that "his trip can obviously produce a variety of political embarrassments" and predicted that "Gehlen will be somewhat difficult to control on this trip."

In the end, the trip was a triumph for Gehlen and his supporters in the CIA. After Gehlen and Herre arrived in New York on September 23, 1951, Critchfield escorted them on their railway tour of America. On their way to the West Coast, they stopped over in Chicago, dropping by a 1930s-era speakeasy one night where, "much to the surprise of all of us," recounted Critchfield, "we were greeted by a famous member of the Mafia." As they rolled westward on the rails, the three men shed their business skins and eased into the lazy pace of tourists. But the Germans could not drop all their espionage training. "We looked out on the Rockies from the top of Pike's Peak and walked among the great redwoods outside San Francisco," recalled Critchfield. "Gehlen was an insatiable photographer and Herre, like the General Staff officer that he was, equipped himself with maps and sought out the highest observation point for surveying each tourist objective."

Returning to Washington, D.C., on October 8, they checked into a suite at the Envoy, an ornate, old-world hotel in the leafy Adams Morgan neighborhood. Dulles arranged for Gehlen and Herre to meet with CIA director Beetle Smith. Dulles hosted a private dinner at the Metropolitan Club for the Germans and several CIA officers with whom they felt comfortable, including Richard Helms, who had run U.S. intelligence operations in Germany after the war.

The 1951 trip to America sealed the relationship between "UTILITY," as Gehlen was code-named by the Americans, and the CIA. Over the years, the agency would occasionally wrestle with its conscience over the alliance. But CIA officials invariably suppressed these doubts and moved on. In 1954, an unsigned CIA memo to the chief of the agency's Eastern Europe division acknowledged that a number of individuals employed by Gehlen "appear from a qualitative standpoint particularly heinous." By way of illustration, the author of the memo attached biographical summaries on several of Gehlen's most repellent recruits, including Konrad Fiebig, who was later charged with murdering eleven thousand Jews in Belarus during the war. Nonetheless, the memo concluded, "We feel it is a bit late in the game to do anything more than remind UTILITY that he might be smart politically to drop such types."

But the CIA's intimate relationship with Gehlen came with a price in the global arena. Soviet propagandists made much of the arrangement, and even British intelligence allies vented their outrage. In an August 1955 memo to Dulles, the chief of the CIA's Eastern European division reported on a diplomatic luncheon in Bonn, during which British officials freely aired their disgust to their American friends. "They were quite blunt in expressing their feelings that the Americans had sold their souls to the Germans because of their frantic and hysterical desire to thwart Soviet military strength," the CIA official informed Dulles.

Allen Dulles was unruffled by the controversy that swirled around his German colleague. He airily dismissed concerns about Gehlen's wartime record. "I don't know if he's a rascal," Dulles remarked. "There are few archbishops in espionage. . . . Besides, one needn't ask him to one's club." But, in fact, Dulles and Helms *did* invite Gehlen to their clubs—including the Metropolitan and the Chevy Chase Club—whenever the German spymaster visited Washington. Dulles had no reservations about working with such men, so why shouldn't he also drink and dine with them? Dulles even brought along Clover on those occasions when Gehlen's talkative wife, Herta, accompanied him to America.

Dulles went to generous lengths to maintain a congenial relationship with Gehlen, sending him gifts and warm greetings on Christmas and his birthday, and even on the anniversaries of their professional alliance. One of Gehlen's favorite gifts from Dulles was a small wooden statuette of a cloak-and-dagger figure that the German spymaster described as "sinister" looking, but nonetheless kept on his desk for the rest of his life. Gehlen, in turn, cabled his own chummy messages to the U.S. intelligence chief, and once sent him a gold medallion of St. George slaying the dragon—the Gehlen Organization's emblem—"as a symbol of our work against bolshevism."

Dulles knew that Gehlen was a devoted family man. The German intelligence chief closely managed the affairs of his extended family, installing a number of them in positions with "the firm," as his organization was known by its employees. In late 1954, when Dulles heard that Gehlen was seeking to get his oldest daughter, Katharina, into a good U.S. college, the CIA director immediately began making inquiries on her behalf. Radcliffe, where his own daughter Joan had gone, made it clear that it was not inclined to give the daughter of a former Nazi commander special treatment. But Katharina Gehlen did win admission to Hunter College in New York City.

She later followed family tradition and went to work for her father, acting as a junior spy on occasion and carrying confidential packages across borders. Gehlen proudly confided to American colleagues that on one such mission, Katharina had the foresight to hide her diplomatic pouch "below a layer of soiled feminine niceties" in her suitcase when crossing the border. In those more decorous times, the inquisitive customs official promptly terminated his inspection as soon as he came to the young woman's dirty underwear.

In 1955, as the CIA prepared to transfer the Gehlen Organization to the West German government, the agency generously continued to back Gehlen, giving him enough money to buy a lakeside estate near Pullach, where he enjoyed sailing his boat on weekends. Critchfield claimed that Gehlen bought the manor with a modest interest-free loan of 48,000 deutsche marks (about $12,000) from the CIA, which Gehlen himself insisted he repaid in full. But reports in the Soviet bloc press characterized the estate as a gift from Dulles that was worth as much as 250,000 DM.

Gehlen was deeply grateful to Dulles, whom he code-named "The Gentleman," for his unflagging support. "In all the years of my collaboration with the CIA, I had no personal disputes with Dulles," Gehlen wrote in his memoir. "He pleased me by his air of wisdom, born of years of experience; he was both fatherly and boisterous, and he became a close personal friend of mine."

Despite the deep affection he had for Dulles, Gehlen felt free to air his complaints about U.S. government policy whenever he suspected that America's Cold War vigilance was softening. The Gehlen Organization saw the Cold War as the final act of the Reich's interrupted offensive against the Soviet Union. In August 1955, after Eisenhower's tentative peace efforts at the Geneva summit, a CIA memo reported that "UTILITY was blunt in his criticism of the U.S. position at Geneva. He expressed the opinion that in the realm of international politics one should never tell a Russian that one will not shoot him, and should under no circumstances be as convincing in this position as President Eisenhower was at Geneva."

Western leaders negotiated with Moscow at their own peril, Gehlen firmly believed. The Soviet Union enticed you with this and that, but underneath its skirt, "one will see the cloven hoof of the devil," he said.

Gehlen kept up his martial drumbeat throughout his intelligence career. Thomas Hughes, who served as director of foreign intelligence in the Kennedy State Department, recalled an evening early in the Kennedy presidency when Dulles gave Gehlen a platform for his militarism. "Allen Dulles had a soft spot in his heart for the 'good Germans,' expansively defined," said Hughes. "One of my first social events in the Kennedy administration's intelligence community was a dinner given by Allen Dulles one night at the Chevy Chase Club in honor of Gehlen, who was visiting from his Munich headquarters. Gehlen led the discussion, advising us how to deal with 'the Bear,' his term for the Soviet menace. J. Edgar Hoover, sitting next to me, kept murmuring, 'The Bear, the Bear. That's it. The Bear.'"

Gehlen liked to say that his cold-steel view of the Soviet adversary came from his hard-won experience on the eastern front. But it was also calculated to please American hard-liners, particularly his masters, the Dulles brothers. Some critics in Western security circles attacked the ideological bias of the Gehlen Organization's intelligence reports, which exaggerated the Soviet bloc's military strength and nuclear capability. But the "cooked" intelligence served the Dulleses by giving them more ammunition for their militant Cold War stance.

The covert Cold War in the West was, to an unsettling extent, a joint operation between the Dulles regime and that of Reinhard Gehlen. The German spy chief's pathological fear and hatred of Russia, which had its roots in Hitler's Third Reich, meshed smoothly with the Dulles brothers' anti-Soviet absolutism. In fact, the Dulles policy of massive nuclear retaliation bore a disturbing resemblance to the Nazis' exterminationist philosophy—a link that would be darkly satirized in Stanley Kubrick's 1964 film *Dr. Strangelove,* with its Führer-saluting doomsday scientist. No other cultural artifact of the period captures so perfectly the absurd morbidity of the Cold War, and its Wagnerian lust for oblivion. We live "in an age in which war is a paramount activity of man," Gehlen announced in his memoir, "with the total annihilation of the enemy as its primary aim." There could be no more succinct a statement of the fascist ethos.

In the months leading up to the CIA's transfer of the Gehlen Organization to the government of West Germany, there was another flurry of debate about Gehlen in Washington and Bonn, which grew so heated that it spilled into the press. At the same time, the Federal Republic of Germany, under the rigid leadership of the elderly, conservative Catholic Konrad Adenauer, was also involved in delicate negotiations with the United States over West Germany's proposed entry into NATO. In October 1954, during a visit by Adenauer to Washington, General Arthur Trudeau, chief of U.S. Army intelligence, met privately with the chancellor to discuss the Gehlen problem, telling the German leader that he did not trust "that spooky Nazi outfit at Pullach." Trudeau advised Adenauer to clean house before Germany was admitted into NATO.

All hell broke loose in Washington when Dulles learned that Trudeau had trespassed on his turf. Although the Joint Chiefs of Staff continued to back their man, it soon became clear (if it wasn't already) who was running the intelligence show under Eisenhower. Trudeau found himself transferred out of military intelligence to a remote post in the Far East, and a few years later he quietly retired from his country's service.

During this turbulent, transitional period in West German affairs, Reinhard Gehlen was confronted with a strong domestic challenger for his espionage throne. In fact, Otto John—the head of BfV, West Germany's internal security organization (the equivalent of the FBI)—was the only serious rival Gehlen would face during his long reign at Pullach. British intelligence saw Otto John as a far superior alternative to Gehlen. As a survivor of the ill-fated Valkyrie plot against Hitler, John lacked Gehlen's unsavory baggage. After the coup failed, John narrowly escaped with his life to London, where he worked with British MI6 for the remainder of the war, returning to Germany after Hitler's defeat to assist with the prosecution of Nazi war criminals.

A self-described liberal, John worried about the "re-Nazification" of Germany, as he witnessed the growing power of Gehlen and the many other former Third Reich officials who were finding key positions in Bonn. High among these officials was Chancellor Adenauer's right-hand man, Hans Globke, who had helped draft the notorious Nuremberg Laws, the racial identification system that served as the basis for the extermination of German Jews.

A CIA comparative analysis of Gehlen and Otto John unsurprisingly found that "John is the more moral of the two." But, the report continued, John was "no match for UTILITY in the knock-about of German intelligence politics"—as was soon to be revealed.

In May 1954, John flew to the United States to meet with Eisenhower officials and discuss his democratic vision for postwar Germany. Dulles invited him to lunch at his Georgetown house, and afterward they walked and chatted in his garden. Dulles was eager to hear John's thoughts on the rearmament of West Germany, a hotly debated issue at the time that Cold Warriors like Dulles strongly supported. John assured the CIA director that he, too, favored rearmament, but only if it was done in a grassroots, democratic way by forming local defense units, instead of "from the top downwards," which would further empower the militaristic types from Germany's past. Dulles was not pleased with what he heard. "My whole impression of John," he wrote in a memo later that year, "was that he was not a very serious character."

Dulles was predisposed against John to begin with. Gehlen had filled the CIA director's ears with venomous reports about his German intelligence rival, calling him "unsteady and rootless," professionally inexperienced, and even prone to alcoholism. What Gehlen clearly found most disturbing about John, however, was his heroic past as an anti-Nazi resister. His moral stature, particularly among the British allies, made him a powerful threat to Gehlen.

John's meeting with Dulles probably sealed his fate. After he returned home, the BfV chief became the target of a covert campaign engineered by Gehlen to politically undermine him. Soon, Otto John's life would take a sensational turn. In July, while on a trip to West Berlin to commemorate the tenth anniversary of the failed putsch against Hitler, John disappeared. The news that West Germany's security chief had vanished sent shock waves around the world. But the story grew even stranger when John later surfaced in East Germany, denouncing Adenauer's rearmament policy and his administration's weakness for ex-Nazis. Gehlen gloated over his political enemy's exit from the Bonn stage. "Once a traitor, always a traitor," remarked the man who still considered opposition to Hitler as treason.

Then came the final twist in the bizarre spy drama. In December 1955, as the Bundestag (West Germany's parliament) launched an inquiry into the John affair, he suddenly reappeared in West Germany, claiming that he had been drugged and bundled off to East Berlin against his will. West German authorities did not buy John's story, and he was arrested and convicted of working on behalf of East Germany's Communist government, serving four years in prison. But for the rest of his life, John insisted that he was the victim of political treachery, and he strongly implied that it was Reinhard Gehlen, the man who benefited the most from his downfall, who was responsible.

The elimination of Otto John paved the way for Gehlen to consolidate his power. In February 1956, the West German government formally moved to create a foreign intelligence service, the BND (*Bundesnachrichtendienst*), and soon after, with Dulles's strong endorsement, Gehlen was officially named its first chief. Gehlen's triumph was complete: through ruthless determination he had transformed his Nazi intelligence apparatus into the Gehlen Organization and finally into the BND, giving him an official power base and legitimacy that made him the envy of his fellow Wehrmacht warriors.

In March 1956, Reinhard Gehlen's staff prepared to lower the Stars and Stripes, which had flown over the Pullach compound ever since Hitler's defeat, and replace it with the black-red-gold tricolors of the Federal Republic of Germany. But as Jim Critchfield and his wife packed their family belongings in preparation for his transfer to the Middle East, there was one more urgent piece of business for the departing CIA station chief to handle. On March 13, after returning from a week of secret government meetings in Bonn, Gehlen requested that Critchfield come alone to his office to discuss "a matter of some importance and considerable sensitivity." The German spymaster was suffering from a cold and he seemed worn down, but he was too anxious to speak with Critchfield to delay their meeting.

Gehlen quickly dispensed with the usual pleasantries and proceeded to present an urgent report on the state of European security. France and Italy, he said, seemed to be moving toward "the reestablishment of [left-center] Popular Front governments." Likewise, political trends in West Germany could lead to the fall of Adenauer's conservative government and its replacement by a coalition including the Social Democratic Party and "anti-Adenauer elements of the Right." Though not Communistic itself, such a government would inevitably take a softer, "neutralist" line toward the Soviet Union, Gehlen predicted, and he himself "would not survive" in this pro-détente atmosphere. If a government like this took over in Bonn, Gehlen warned, it would be "vulnerable to political penetration and eventual control by the East."

After painting this ominous portrait, Gehlen got to the heart of the matter. He was prepared to take drastic action to prevent such a political scenario from unfolding in Bonn—going as far as to overthrow democracy in West Germany if necessary. Critchfield immediately reported on his startling conversation with Gehlen in a cable sent directly to Dulles in Washington. In the event of a leftward shift in Bonn, Critchfield informed the CIA director, "UTILITY would feel morally justified in taking all possible action, including the establishment of an illegal apparatus in the Federal Republic, to oppose elements in Germany supporting a pro-Soviet policy." Gehlen, Critchfield added, would like to "discuss a plan for such an eventuality" with his friend Dulles, "in great privacy."

It is unlikely that Dulles was shocked by Gehlen's proposal to reinstitute fascism in Germany, since CIA officials had long been discussing such authoritarian contingency plans with the Gehlen Organization and other right-wing elements in Germany. In 1952, West German police discovered that the CIA was supporting a two-thousand-member fascist youth group led by ex-Nazi officers who had their own alarming plans for terminating democracy. Police investigators revealed that the CIA-backed group had compiled a blacklist of people to be "liquidated" as "unreliable" in case of a conflict with the Soviet Union. Included on the list were not just West German Communists but leaders of the Social Democratic Party serving in the Bundestag, as well as other left-leaning government officials. There were cries of outrage in the German parliament over the revelations, but the State Department worked strenuously behind the scenes to suppress the story, and similar alarming measures continued to be quietly contemplated throughout the Cold War.

These authoritarian plans were part of a sweeping covert strategy developed in the earliest days of the Cold War by U.S. intelligence officials, including Dulles, to counter a possible Soviet invasion of Western Europe by creating a "stay-behind network" of armed resisters to fight the Red Army. Code-named Operation Gladio, these secret CIA-funded networks attracted fascist and criminal elements, some of which later played subversive roles in West Germany, France, and Italy, disrupting democratic rule in those countries by staging terrorist acts and plotting coups and assassinations.

In the end, Gehlen didn't feel the need to overthrow democracy in Bonn, but his organization did undertake a variety of secret activities over the years that seriously undermined democratic institutions in Germany. Backed by U.S. intelligence, Hitler's former spymaster implemented wide-ranging surveillance of West German officials and citizens, including opening private mail and tapping phones. Gehlen defended the snooping as an internal security measure aimed at ferreting out Soviet and East German spies, but his net grew wider and wider until it was cast across an increasingly broad spectrum of the population, including opposition party leaders, labor union officials, journalists, and schoolteachers. Gehlen even used his spy apparatus to investigate survivors of the Valkyrie plot against Hitler, including Dulles's wartime comrade Hans Gisevius, all of whom he suspected of being Soviet agents.

One of Gehlen's more ethical deputies complained, "Gehlen is becoming a megalomaniac. He actually wants to play Gestapo for the Americans." Gehlen was acting not just on behalf of his U.S. patrons, but his clients in Bonn. Even some CIA officials worried that Gehlen was being improperly used by Hans Globke to gather information on political opponents and fortify the Adenauer administration's power. Gehlen, warned a CIA dispatch from Bonn, "has let himself be used most indiscriminately by Globke to further the latter's quest for power." On one occasion in the 1950s, the savvy Globke paid a visit to Gehlen's Pullach headquarters, poring over the dossiers of various German political figures—and taking the opportunity to remove his own file.

Ironically, while justifying his political snooping as a necessary countermeasure against enemy infiltration, Gehlen's own organization became notorious for its penetrability. The Heinz Felfe affair was the most notorious Soviet mole case during Gehlen's career—and, indeed, one of the biggest scandals in Cold War espionage history. Felfe, a former Nazi bully boy who had led rampaging gangs on Kristallnacht in 1938, was recruited into the Gehlen Organization in 1951. Not long after, the adaptable Felfe became a Soviet double agent. Fed a steady stream of inside tips by his Russian handlers, Felfe began to impress Gehlen as a master spy, and he rose quickly through the Pullach ranks. Finally, the bedazzled Gehlen named Heinz Felfe head of all anti-Soviet counterintelligence operations, a position that put the double agent in ongoing contact with the CIA and other Western spy agencies. Felfe's reign as a top-level Soviet mole in the Gehlen Organization stretched for over a decade. By the time he was finally caught, he had wreaked inestimable damage on the West German apparatus, resulting in the arrest of dozens of senior Gehlen agents behind the Iron Curtain, as well as the breaking of numerous codes and secret channels of communication. A significant swath of German and American intelligence fieldwork had to be uprooted and started all over again.

After the Felfe scandal exploded in the press in 1963, Gehlen tried to minimize the importance of the deep breach. But though he would hold on to power by the skin of his teeth for the next several years, the spymaster never fully recovered from the political fallout. Adenauer never forgave Gehlen. For the "runt" Gehlen, who craved the approval of Germany's father figure, the falling-out with the chancellor was a grievous blow. The spymaster was already in Adenauer's doghouse for another scandal that had broken the previous year, when Gehlen was accused of leaking classified information about West Germany's nuclear armament plans to the magazine *Der Spiegel*. The leak—which was calculated to damage Adenauer's defense minister, yet another rival of Gehlen—made the chancellor so furious that he had considered ordering Gehlen's arrest, finally deciding against it out of fear that it would only add to his administration's political embarrassment.

But Adenauer was still in a foul mood about Gehlen in June 1963, when Allen Dulles dropped by the chancellor's office in Bonn for a visit. By then, Dulles himself had been forced out of office by President Kennedy. But the former CIA director still traveled the world like he was running the show, and whatever capital he stopped in, Dulles found open doors. That day in Bonn, Adenauer asked Dulles point-blank what he thought of Gehlen. According to a CIA memo, Dulles "replied, as usual, that he had known [Gehlen] long and well and regarded him as a stout and honest fellow."

Adenauer was not satisfied by the answer. The aging leader, who felt Dulles had imposed Gehlen upon him, was in no mood to be manipulated again by the American spymaster. The chancellor responded "surprisingly," the agency memo continued, "by asking [Dulles] if any-body involved in his business could be really honest. [Dulles] asked if [Adenauer] did not regard him as an honest fellow." The chancellor offered an elusive reply.

The following month, Adenauer was still fuming about Gehlen. One afternoon in July, he ordered the U.S. ambassador to be dragged out of a Bonn luncheon so that the chancellor could give him an earful about Gehlen. In his opinion, said Adenauer, Gehlen "is and always was stupid," which the Felfe fiasco had underlined in red. There was only one reason, said the chancellor, that he had put up with the spymaster all these years: because of Dulles's "personal interest" in Gehlen.

After Dulles left the CIA, the relationship between the agency and Gehlen was never as congenial. The German stopped visiting America, and the old tensions began to resurface. By 1966, Gehlen was even airing his suspicions that the CIA had put his family residence un-der surveillance. He expressed these fears, according to one CIA official, "apparently more in sorrow than anger."

But by the time he retired, all this unpleasantness had been forgot-ten and the agency threw itself into planning an elaborate farewell for its longtime comrade. In September 1968, an illustrious crowd of CIA and U.S. military officials gathered for a Washington banquet to honor Gehlen. In the months leading up to the farewell ceremony, the CIA mulled over the proper medal to bestow on the German—the agency's Intelligence Medal of Merit, or the National Security Medal. Dulles was among those who attended the gala event. He later sent a warm note to his old colleague Dick Helms, who by then was running the CIA, thanking Helms for including him in the Gehlen dinner and ex-pressing how much he had enjoyed "the opportunity to see so many old and mutual friends of the General."

Reinhard Gehlen lived out the rest of his years at his lakeside re-treat, surrounded by his family—including his son, daughter-in-law, and grandchildren, who moved into one of two houses on the estate—and his German shepherds, who provided the only security he felt he needed. On windy days, he still enjoyed soaring back and forth across the lake in his sailboat, another gift from the CIA.

The occasional journalists who dropped by found him in good spirits, happy to relive his past and to share his thoughts about the state of world affairs. During his reign at Pullach, he had maintained an abstemious regimen, drinking only mineral water or soda at meals. But now he would indulge in a glass of sherry with his visitors. Gehlen had no qualms when the conversation turned to the war years; he seemed to enjoy talking about his exploits on the eastern front.

The journalists who came by for sandwiches and sherry tended to be a generous sort. They asked the kinds of questions usually directed at retired statesmen or business leaders.

"When you look back on your life, how do you see it?" asked a reporter from a Danish newspaper, as she and Gehlen strolled in the garden that sloped down to the lake.

"I can only be grateful to fate," he replied thoughtfully. "Everybody makes mistakes here in life. [But] I don't at the present moment know what fundamental mistakes I have made." What made him "especially" happy, said Gehlen, was that he had been able to give so much "human help" to the world.

Brain Warfare

On April 10, 1953, CIA director Allen Dulles delivered an alarming speech about Russia's latest secret weapon—an insidious mind control program that Dulles labeled "brain warfare." Dulles chose an idyllic setting for his remarks, speaking to a Princeton alumni conference sprinkled with old friends, held in Hot Springs, Virginia, a fashionable resort in a verdant bowl of the Allegheny Mountains where Thomas Jefferson once took the waters. "I wonder," Dulles told the gathering, "whether we realize how sinister the battle for men's minds has become in Soviet hands. . . . The human mind is the most delicate of all instruments. It is so finely adjusted, so susceptible to the impact of outside influences that it is proving a malleable tool in the hands of sinister men. The Soviets are now using brain-perversion techniques as one of their main weapons in prosecuting the Cold War. Some of these techniques are so subtle and so abhorrent to our way of life that we have recoiled from facing up to them."

Dulles reported that the Soviets were engaging in sick science, seeking to control human consciousness by "washing the brain clean of the thoughts and mental processes of the past" and creating automatons of the state who would speak and act against their own will.

Dulles's speech, which he made sure received wide media distribution, marked an ominous new phase in the Cold War, a militarization of science and psychology aimed not simply at changing popular opinion but at reengineering the human brain. What Dulles did not tell his audience in Hot Springs was that several days earlier, he had authorized a CIA mind control program code-named MKULTRA that would dwarf any similar efforts behind the Iron Curtain. In fact, at the same time that he was condemning Soviet "brainwashing," Dulles knew that U.S. military and intelligence agencies had been working for several years on their own brain warfare programs. This secret experimentation would balloon under the CIA's MKULTRA program. Launched by Dulles with a $300,000 budget, this "Manhattan Project of the Mind" would grow into a multimillion-dollar program, operating for a quarter of a century, and enlisting dozens of leading universities and hospitals as well as hundreds of prominent researchers in studies that often violated ethical standards and treated their human subjects as "expendables."

Dick Helms, who oversaw MKULTRA, advised Dulles that the scientific research underwritten by the program would have to be carried out in complete secrecy, explaining that most credible scientists would be very "reluctant to enter into signed agreements of any sort which connect them with this activity, since such a connection would jeopardize their professional reputations." Many of the MKULTRA projects involved the use of experimental drugs, particularly LSD, which Helms saw as a potential "A-bomb of the mind." The goal was to bend a subject's mind to the agency's will.

Most undercover recruits in the spy trade were sketchy, undependable characters who were motivated by greed, blackmail, revenge, lust, or other less than honorable impulses. But the CIA's spymasters dreamed of taking their craft to a new technological level, one that flirted with the imaginative extremes of science fiction. They wanted to create human machines who would act on command, even against their own conscience. Dulles was particularly keen on finding out if LSD could be used to program zombielike saboteurs or assassins. He kept grilling Sidney Gottlieb, the CIA's top drug expert, asking him if the psychedelic compound could be used to make "selected individuals commit acts of substantial sabotage or acts of violence, including murder," recalled the scientist.

The Manchurian Candidate, the 1959 bestselling thriller by Richard

Condon that was later adapted for the screen, dramatized this concept of a flesh-and-blood robot, a man so deeply programmed that he could be turned into a cold-blooded assassin. It was a paranoid fantasy that had its roots in the Korean War, that confusing debacle in a remote Asian land that would continue to haunt the American public until another Asian misadventure came along. During the war, three dozen captured American pilots confessed to dropping biological weapons containing anthrax, cholera, bubonic plague, and other toxins on North Korea and China. The charges were hotly denied by the U.S. government, and when the airmen returned home after the war, they retracted their charges—under the threat of being tried for treason—alleging that they had been subjected to brainwashing by their Communist captors.

The Korean War "brainwashing" story worked its way deeply into America's dream state, through the aggressive promotional efforts of CIA-sponsored experts like Edward Hunter, who claimed to have coined the term. Writing bestselling books on the alleged Communist technique and testifying dramatically before Congress, Hunter "essentially modernized the idea of demonic possession," in the words of one observer. The self-described "propaganda specialist" described how all-American boys fell victim to an insidious combination of Asian mesmerism and Soviet torture science, which turned each captured pilot into a "living puppet—a human robot . . . with new beliefs and new thought processes inserted into a captive body."

In the end, the Korean brainwashing story itself—the seedbed of so much creeping, Cold War fantasy—turned out to be largely fictitious. Dulles made much of it in his Hot Springs speech, invoking in outraged tones the image of "American boys" being forced to betray their own country and "make open confessions—fake from beginning to end" about how they had waged germ warfare on China and North Korea. But a study later commissioned by Dulles himself—conducted by two prominent Cornell Medical Center neurologists, including Harold Wolff, a friend of the CIA director—largely debunked the brainwash panic. They rejected reports that the Communists were using esoteric mind control techniques, insisting that there was no evidence of drugs or hypnosis or any involvement by psychiatrists and scientists in the Soviet or Chinese interrogation procedures.

Most of the abuse meted out to POWs and political prisoners in Communist countries, Wolff and his colleague observed, amounted to nothing more sophisticated than isolation regimens and stress positions, like being forced to stand in the same spot for hours, and the occasional application of brute force. "There is no reason to dignify these methods by surrounding them with an aura of scientific mystery, or to denote them by terms such as 'menticide' or 'brain washing' which imply that they are scientifically organized techniques of predictable effectiveness," concluded the Cornell scientists.

In response to the brainwashing bugaboo that the CIA itself had conjured, the agency constructed its own intricate mind control machinery that was part Orwell and part Philip K. Dick. In Hot Springs, Dulles bemoaned the fact that, unlike the ruthless Soviets, the United States had no easy access to "human guinea pigs" for its brain experimentation. But, in fact, the CIA was already subjecting helpless victims to its "brain perversion" techniques. Dulles began by feeding Soviet prisoners and captured double agents into this merciless psychological apparatus; then drug addicts, mental patients, prison inmates, and other "expendables." By the end, Allen Dulles would put his own family members in the hands of the CIA's mad scientists.

In June 1952, Frank Olson—a balding, forty-one-year-old CIA biochemist with a long face, mournful eyes, and a smile that revealed an upper deck of prominent incisors—flew to Frankfurt, where he was picked up at the airport and driven twelve miles north to Camp King, an extreme interrogation center of the sort that would later be known as a "black site." Olson helped oversee the Special Operations Division at Camp Detrick in Maryland, the biological weapons laboratory jointly operated by the U.S. Army and the CIA. The top secret work conducted by the SO Division included research on LSD-induced mind control, assassination toxins, and biological warfare agents like those allegedly being used in Korea.

Olson's division also was involved in research that was euphemistically labeled "information retrieval"—extreme methods of extracting intelligence from uncooperative captives. For the past two years, Olson had been traveling to secret centers in Europe where Soviet prisoners and other human guinea pigs were subjected to these experimental interrogation methods. Dulles began spearheading this CIA research even before he became director of the agency, under a secret program that preceded MKULTRA code-named Operation Artichoke, after the spymaster's favorite vegetable. CIA officials later purged their files of evidence of the program, but in one of the few surviving documents, dated February 12, 1951, Dulles wrote to his ever-accommodating deputy Frank Wisner about "the possibilities of augmenting the usual interrogation methods by the use of drugs, hypnosis, shock, etc. . . . The enclosed folder, 'Interrogation Techniques,' was prepared in my Medical Division to provide you with a suitable background."

It was in secret overseas detention centers like Camp King where the CIA found many of the subjects for its Artichoke interrogations: defectors, double agents, and other unfortunates from the East who had fallen into U.S. hands. Some of the captives had been delivered to the CIA by the Gehlen Organization, which for a time operated out of Camp King until relocating to Pullach. During the war, Camp King had been a Nazi interrogation center for captured U.S. and British fliers. Afterward, the U.S. military turned the camp into a stockade for notorious Nazi POWs like the propagandist "Axis Sally" and the swashbuckling commando Otto Skorzeny. But by 1948, the camp was operating as an extreme interrogation center for Soviet prisoners, a program jointly administered by an unscrupulous alliance of CIA scientists and ex-Nazi doctors who had presided over medical experiments on concentration camp inmates during the war. At Camp King, CIA scientists and their German colleagues subjected victims to dangerous combinations of drugs—including Benzedrine, Pentothal-Natrium, LSD, and mescaline—under a research protocol that stipulated, "Disposal of the body is not a problem." More than sixteen hundred of the Nazi scientists recruited for U.S. research projects like this would be comfortably resettled with their families in America under a CIA program known as Operation Paperclip.

One of the CIA-sponsored researchers who worked on the Artichoke interrogations in Germany, a Harvard-trained physician named Henry Knowles Beecher, was brought to Camp King by the agency to advise on the best way to induce amnesia in Soviet spies after they had been subjected to the agency's interrogation methods. Beecher, the chief of anesthesiology at Massachusetts General Hospital in Boston, was an outspoken proponent of the Nuremberg Code, which forbade medical experimentation on humans without their informed consent. But he was one of many prominent American doctors and scientists who lost their moral direction during the Cold War, enticed by the generous CIA patronage that featured virtually unlimited funding and unrestricted research parameters. Lured into a world where nearly everything was permitted in the name of national security, Beecher even began drawing on the work done by Nazi doctors at Dachau.

After reading a captured Gestapo report in 1947 that indicated that mescaline could be an effective interrogation tool, Beecher set off on a decadelong search for a magical "truth serum" that would compel prisoners to reveal all, a quest that later focused on LSD and would involve unwitting subjects in Germany as well as at his own Boston hospital. Urging the government to expand its research into LSD as an "offensive weapon," Beecher subjected his involuntary subjects to severe overdoses of the hallucinogen, despite knowing that it caused "acute panic," "paranoid reactions," and other trauma in his victims—a "psychosis in miniature," he coolly observed in one government report, that "offers interesting possibilities."

Ever since the Nuremberg trials, international legal authorities had moved to formally condemn the physical and psychological abuse of the powerless. In 1948, the United Nations General Assembly emphatically stated in its Universal Declaration of Human Rights, "No one shall be subjected to torture or to cruel, inhuman or degrading treatment or punishment." The following year, the third Geneva Convention reiterated this fundamental commandment: "No physical or mental torture, nor any other form of coercion, may be inflicted on prisoners of war to secure from them information of any kind whatever. Prisoners of war who refuse to answer may not be threatened, insulted, or exposed to unpleasant or disadvantageous treatment of any kind." But by defining the Cold War as a ruthless struggle outside the norms of military conduct and human decency, the national security regime shaped by men like Dulles was able to brazenly defy international law. Few of those involved in CIA brain warfare expressed any ethical concerns about their work. "I never gave a thought to legality or morality," one agency case officer readily acknowledged after he retired. "Frankly, I did what worked."

But Frank Olson did suffer profound moral anxieties about his work, and the result was a serious crisis within the CIA itself. Dr. Olson began having serious doubts after traveling to various CIA research centers in England, France, Norway, and West Germany, and observing the human experiments being conducted at these black sites. Olson's trip to Germany in summer 1952—during which he visited Haus Waldhof, a notorious CIA safe house on a country estate near Camp King—left him particularly shaken. Soviet prisoners were subjected to especially severe interrogation methods at Haus Waldhof, which sometimes resulted in their deaths. The cruelty he witnessed reminded Olson of Nazi concentration camps. After returning home to the United States, Olson began wrestling with his conscience, according to his wife and colleagues. "He had a tough time after Germany . . . drugs, torture, brainwashing," recalled Norman Cournoyer, a Camp Detrick researcher with whom Olson had worked on projects that had once made him proud, like designing protective clothing for the soldiers landing at Normandy on D-day.

Olson and Cournoyer had also collaborated on projects that made them less proud. After the war, they had traveled around the United States, supervising the spraying of biological agents from aircraft and crop dusters. Some of the tests, which were conducted in cities like San Francisco as well as rural areas in the Midwest, involved harmless chemicals, but others featured more dangerous toxins. In Alaska—where the two men sought to stage their experiments in an environment that resembled wintertime Russia—"we used a spore which is very similar [to] anthrax," Cournoyer recalled. "So to that extent we did something that was not kosher." One of their research colleagues, a bacteriologist named Dr. Harold Batchelor, learned aerial spray techniques from the infamous Dr. Kurt Blome, director of the Nazis' biological warfare program. Years later, a congressional investigation found these open-air experiments conducted by Camp Detrick scientists "appalling."

Olson began to worry about how his airborne spray research was being utilized by the military. His wife, Alice, said that, in addition to being deeply disturbed by the interrogation procedures he witnessed in Germany, her husband was also haunted by the suspicion that the United States was practicing biological warfare in Korea. By the time he returned from Germany, Olson was suffering a "moral crisis," according to his family, and was seriously considering abandoning his science career and becoming a dentist.

Olson's objections to the CIA's brain warfare research apparently began to raise alarms within the Camp Detrick bureaucracy. One document in Olson's personnel file, dated after his return from Germany, indicated that his behavior was causing "fear of a security violation."

In November 1953, before Frank Olson could change his life, he became one more unwitting victim of the CIA's mind control program. A week before Thanksgiving, Olson and several other SO Division scientists were invited to a weekend retreat at a secluded CIA facility near Deep Creek Lake, a lushly forested resort area in western Maryland. The scientists were greeted by Sidney Gottlieb, the chief wizard of the CIA's magic potion division, the Technical Services Staff. Gottlieb was one of the agency's more unique characters, a stuttering, clubfooted biochemist whom friends described as a kind of untethered genius. Despite his infirmity, Gottlieb threw himself into such passionate, if unlikely, recreations as folk dancing and goat herding. The son of Orthodox Hungarian Jews, he rejected Judaism and spent his lifetime searching for his own form of enlightenment, experimenting with Zen Buddhism and becoming an early celebrant in the cult of LSD. Gottlieb devoted himself enthusiastically to the CIA's mind-manipulation program, subjecting hundreds of unsuspecting Americans to experimental drugs. The CIA chemist preyed on "people who could not fight back," as one agency official put it, such as seven patients in a federal drug hospital in Kentucky who were dosed with acid for seventy-seven straight days by a Gottlieb-funded doctor who ran the hospital's addiction treatment program. Gottlieb also excelled at cooking up rare toxins and clever delivery mechanisms in his laboratory to eliminate people the CIA deemed political enemies. Gottlieb strongly adhered to the Dulles ethic that there were no rules in war. "We were in a World War II mode," said a CIA psychologist who was close to Gottlieb. "The war never really ended for us."

After dinner on the second night of the Deep Creek retreat, Gottlieb's deputy spiked a bottle of Cointreau and offered it to the unsuspecting Olson and his colleagues. It was the beginning of a nightmarish ordeal for Olson, which would end a week later when the scientist went crashing through the window of the tenth-floor hotel room in midtown Manhattan where he was being held by the CIA and plunged to his death. After being dosed at Deep Creek, Olson never seemed to recover; he remained anxious and confused throughout the week leading up to his fatal fall. The CIA officials who took charge of him that week later claimed they were planning to put him in psychiatric care. But instead they shuttled him around from place to place, taking him to a New York City allergist on the CIA payroll named Dr. Harold Abramson, who had conducted LSD tolerance experiments for the agency, and even to a magician named John Mulholland, who taught CIA agents how magic techniques could improve their spycraft. As the days went by, Olson became increasingly agitated, telling Dr. Abramson—not without reason—that the CIA was trying to poison him.

Shortly after Olson fell to his death from the Statler Hotel (now the Hotel Pennsylvania), someone placed a brief phone call from the scientist's hotel room to Dr. Abramson. "Well, he's gone," said the caller. "Well, that's too bad," Abramson responded, and then the caller hung up.

Agents from the CIA's Office of Security—the department made up of former FBI agents and cops that cleaned up the spy agency's messes—quickly descended on the hotel, nudging aside New York police investigators. James McCord, later known for his role in the Watergate break-in, was one of the security agents who took charge of the Olson "investigation" for the CIA. The agency termed Olson's death a suicide, the tragic end of an emotionally unstable man, and the case was buried for over two decades.

In 1975, the case resurfaced during the Rockefeller Commission investigation of CIA abuses ordered by President Gerald Ford. Olson's widow and grown children were invited to the White House by President Ford, who apologized to them on behalf of the government. The Olson case would become enshrined in history as one of the more outrageous examples of CIA hubris and mad science. But as the years went by, the Olson family became convinced that Frank Olson's death was more than simply a tragic suicide; it was murder.

"Frank Olson did not die as a consequence of a drug experiment gone awry," the family declared in a statement released in 2002. He died, they said, because he knew too much, and he had become a security risk.

In 1994, Frank's eldest son, Eric, decided to have his father's body exhumed and a second autopsy performed. The team of pathologists was led by James Starrs, professor of law and forensic science at George Washington University. The panel (with one dissenter) found evidence that Olson had suffered a blunt force trauma to the head and a chest injury before his fall—evidence that was called "rankly and starkly suggestive of homicide." While acknowledging that his team had not found "any smoking gun," Starrs told the press, "I am exceedingly skeptical of the view that Dr. Olson went through the window on his own."

But Olson's children failed in their efforts to reopen the case on the basis of the new evidence. In 2012, a federal judge dismissed the family's lawsuit against the CIA, in which they asked for compensatory damages as well as access to documents related to their father's death. In ruling against the family, primarily on technical grounds, the judge nonetheless noted "that the public record supports many of the allegations [against the CIA], farfetched as they may sound."

A llen Dulles was coldly efficient when it came to ridding his agency of security problems. On the night of March 31, 1953, several months before Frank Olson met his end, Dulles invited an old friend and protégé named James Kronthal to his Georgetown house for dinner. The CIA director said he had business to discuss. But it turned out that the evening's most pressing item of business was Kronthal's own fate.

The forty-two-year-old Kronthal was a rising star at the CIA, where his profile fit the mold for Dulles's "very best men." The son of a prominent New York banker, Kronthal was educated at Yale and Harvard, and served under Dulles in the Bern OSS station during the war. Before the war, he had rejected the banking career that his family had planned for him in favor of teaching art history at Harvard. But Kronthal brought a keen business instinct to the art trade, establishing himself in Germany during the 1930s as a broker for Goering, Himmler, and other Nazi leaders who were selling art treasures stolen from Jewish collectors. After the war, he sought to redeem himself by trying to track down the looted art pieces and return them to their rightful owners.

The slightly built, brilliant young man became a favorite of Dulles, who helped Kronthal take over the Bern station in 1947, after it became one of the CIA's first overseas outposts. When Dulles took charge of the agency in 1953, he brought Kronthal back to the Washington headquarters, with big plans for the younger man's intelligence career.

Kronthal wasn't a charming extrovert like Dulles, but his superiors recognized a rare intelligence behind his reticence. Helms was one of those who shared Dulles's admiration for the up-and-coming agent, writing that Kronthal was a "top flight intelligence officer who commands respect from his subordinates more through demonstrated knowledge and IQ than through personal warmth and affability. He is rather retiring as a person but this does not affect his leadership or firmness of purpose."

Kronthal, whom Dulles fondly referred to as "Jimmy," reminded the CIA director of his only son, Allen Jr., another sensitive, highly intelligent young man whose life once held so much promise. But in November 1952, young Dulles had suffered a serious head wound while fighting with the Marines in Korea, a brain injury from which he would never fully recover. For the rest of Dulles's life, his son would rotate in and out of hospitals, sanitariums, and private nursing care, growing increasingly remote from his father. And, on that night in March 1953, Dulles would also lose Kronthal, a man the spymaster had considered a member of the family and even a possible successor.

Kronthal's proclivity for the espionage game derived, in part, from a lifetime of hiding his own personal secrets. He was a gay man with a weakness for young boys. The Gestapo discovered his sexual tastes while he was working in the German art market before the war. Later, while Kronthal was running the CIA station in Bern, the NKVD, the Soviet secret police agency, got access to Kronthal's Gestapo files after penetrating the Gehlen Organization. The Soviets set up a "honey trap" for Kronthal in Switzerland, with Chinese boys as bait. He was secretly filmed and blackmailed, and by the time he returned to Washington in May 1952, Jim Kronthal was a double agent in the iron grip of the NKVD.

It was Colonel Sheffield Edwards, the former Army intelligence officer who ran the CIA's Office of Security, who informed Dulles that his protégé had been turned. Edwards's internal security department was tasked with protecting the CIA against enemy penetration. The security unit was also in charge of what was delicately called "enforcement," providing the muscle to eliminate any potential threats or embarrassments to the agency.

On the night of March 31, as Dulles confronted Kronthal with the Office of Security's revelations over dinner at his home, two agents from Edwards's department were quietly eavesdropping in an adjoining room. The sense of betrayal was certainly overwhelming for Dulles. But the CIA director, whose fits of rage were legendary, held his fury in check that evening. The spy chief sounded sadly contemplative as he spoke with the traitor in whom he had invested so much hope, remarking on the mystery of personal demons and how they could set flame to the most promising careers.

After the two men reviewed Kronthal's impossible position and his dismal options, the shattered agent walked back home—a white brick town house with a small garden of spring daffodils in front, just two blocks from Dulles's residence. He was followed by the two CIA security men. When Kronthal's housekeeper arrived the next morning, his bedroom door was still closed and he had left a note that he was not to be disturbed. Later that morning, two men who identified themselves as colleagues of Kronthal appeared at his house and told the housekeeper they needed to bring him to an urgent meeting. When they opened his bedroom door, they found a lifeless Kronthal splayed across his bed, fully clothed, with an empty vial near his body.

The investigation into Kronthal's death was quickly taken over by Lieutenant Lawrence Hartnett of the Washington, D.C., Metropolitan Police, a homicide detective with a history of helping tidy up CIA-related problems. Hartnett revealed that Kronthal had left a letter for Dick Helms, in which he revealed that he was "mentally upset because of pressure connected with work," as well as a letter for Dulles. An autopsy concluded that Kronthal had taken his own life, but the report left more questions lingering than it answered, failing to determine the cause of his death or the contents of the vial found in his bedroom. Sometime before his death, Kronthal had mailed a letter to his sister, revealing his homosexuality (which came as no surprise to her) and referring to the "tremendous difficulties" that his sexual identity posed for him. He then signed off in a perplexing way. Kronthal's final words to his sister were, "I can't wait till 1984. Love, Jim." Was it his mordant way of saying that for him, Big Brother's suffocating authoritarianism was already an unbearable reality?

The James Kronthal case was, like the Frank Olson matter later that year, another mess that Dulles's Office of Security had to clean up. If Kronthal's death was a suicide, it appeared to be assisted. This is what one high-ranking CIA official, Robert Crowley, later suggested. One way or another, said Crowley—who was interviewed after he retired by journalist Joseph Trento—Kronthal was induced to do the right thing for the good of the agency and of the men who had been his professional benefactors. "Allen probably had a special potion prepared that he gave Kronthal should the pressure become too much," Crowley speculated. "Dr. Sidney Gottlieb and the medical people produced all kinds of poisons that a normal postmortem could not detect."

Dulles never spoke in public about Kronthal after he was gone. Kronthal's sister's efforts to extract more information from the CIA about his death proved futile; the press made little effort to investigate the case. James Kronthal was dropped down the dark well where CIA complications disappeared.

Until he was wounded in Korea, Allen Macy Dulles Jr. was the brightest hope of his family. A brilliant student, he excelled at Exeter, sped through Princeton in three years, and then took himself off to Oxford, where he completed his degree in history, writing his thesis on the permanent undersecretary system of the British Foreign Office. "Sonny," as his father called him, intellectually outshone the elder Dulles, whose own academic performance had been indifferent.

If Dulles took pride in his son's educational achievements, he never showed it. At some point in their young lives, Dulles's two daughters, Toddie and Joan, gave up any expectation that their father would shine his attention on them. But they kept hoping that Dulles would finally acknowledge their brother's extraordinary mind. "Both my sister and I would have liked my father to recognize him and tell him that here was this next generation [of the family] producing special people," Joan remarked late in her life.

"I would imagine," she said on another occasion, "that my brother, especially my brother, would have felt badly about having no special attention from his father."

Allen Jr. was closer to his mother, sharing her sensitive and perceptive temperament. He was acutely aware of Clover's moods and the strains in his parents' marriage. To one family observer, it seemed as if Dulles felt judged by his son.

Sonny had thrived in the cloistered boys' world of Exeter. But unlike his father, young Dulles recoiled from the hearty, fraternity-centered social life at Princeton. He was not elected to any of Princeton's men's clubs, and he dismissed the university's intellectual atmosphere as insufficiently challenging.

One of Allen Jr.'s classmates at Exeter, a friend with whom he remained in touch even after his life-altering war wound, was gay. There were rumors that Sonny, too, was similarly inclined.

"Well, there could have been all kinds of experimentation at prep school," Joan observed. "I know nothing except [my brother] professed interest in girls and had a girlfriend. . . . I never saw him with girls, but there was somebody he liked—I can't think of her name right now. . . . Of course that was still an era when you didn't come out in any way."

Even before his brain injury, Allen Jr. seemed to inhabit his own world. "He was very introverted," said Joan. "He took after my mother in that respect. And he was someone who wasn't that aware of people. I mean . . . you'd go out in New York walking with him, and he'd be ten feet ahead."

In 1950, shortly after getting his degree at Oxford, Sonny stunned his family by announcing he was joining the Marines, as war broke out in Korea. His uncle Foster used his connections to line up a comfortable stateside desk job for him, far from harm's way. But the twenty-two-year-old enlistee volunteered instead for duty in Korea. It was as if he were still trying to win his father's admiration by outperforming the old man. The senior Dulles had fought both world wars in bars and hotels, surrounded by suave foreign agents and accommodating mistresses, and never firing a gun. Sonny would show him what real heroes were made of.

Sonny's letters to his father from the Marine Corps were filled with a new assertiveness. He lectured the senior Dulles about the deficiencies of the military, filling page after page with detailed critiques of the wasteful and corrupt supply system and the unfairness of the commendation process. He even made suggestions on how to improve the CIA's recruiting methods. Dulles's letters of reply, which he signed "Affectionately, Allen

W. Dulles," were not particularly warm, but they showed respect for his son's intricate line of thinking.

By summer 1952, Allen Jr. found himself on the front lines in Korea as a second lieutenant with the First Marine Division. He displayed a gung ho attitude in combat that was sometimes reckless. On the night of November 14, the young lieutenant took charge of a rifle platoon that was dug into an advanced position. Despite being nicked in the leg by a North Korean shell fragment, he charged an enemy sniper's nest by himself, braving intense fire. His gun was shot out of his hand and he was wounded in the wrist, but that day he was lucky. "He didn't have to do any of that, but I guess he felt he had something to live up to," said Robert Abboud, one of Sonny's commanding officers, who had known young Dulles ever since they were prep school debate opponents. "He never wanted to be treated differently from the rest of us."

The next morning, after he was patched up, Lieutenant Dulles returned to the embattled outpost. Once again defying heavy machine gun and mortar fire, Dulles crawled within thirty yards of the enemy position, armed with rifle grenades, and began to direct a Marine mortar attack on the North Koreans. Shortly before the enemy soldiers began to pull back, the lieutenant was hit in the head by fragments from an 81 mm mortar shell, which lodged in his brain. "I was there when they brought him back in," recalled Abboud. "He kept trying to get off the stretcher and go back. Some of his men were crying. I've never really known anyone quite like him."

Allen Jr. was evacuated to a U.S. naval hospital in Japan, where he underwent brain surgery. Clover, who was on one of her Jungian sojourns in Switzerland at the time, flew to her son's bedside. His surgeons told her that they were not able to remove all the deeply embedded shrapnel from Sonny's brain and that he would never fully recover.

By late February 1953, young Dulles was strong enough to be flown home. His father, who was to be confirmed the following day as CIA director, greeted Sonny at Andrews Air Force Base. Dulles was photographed hovering solicitously over his son, as he was unloaded from the plane on a stretcher, with his head swathed in bandages. "How do you feel, son?" he asked. "You're looking good." Sonny's soft reply was inaudible.

As the young man underwent further treatment at Bethesda Naval Hospital, he seemed to recover some of his old self. He recognized people, made jokes, and inquired about the latest world events. But other times, he stared off into the distance, began shaking with fear, or erupted in angry outbursts at those around him.

When Sonny was discharged to his parents' home in Georgetown, it soon became clear that Clover would need help to care for him. A young marine was recruited as a companion for Allen Jr., and the injured young man tried to resume something resembling a normal life. Dulles arranged an undemanding clerical job for his son in the State Department, and he even began taking road trips with friends. But these experiments in independence did not turn out well. In August 1953, Dulles wrote an apologetic letter to the American consul general in Montreal, explaining that his brain-damaged son had forgotten his car registration when he left on a driving trip to Canada, and asking the diplomat's help in relaying the document to Sonny, which he needed to reenter the United States. The following year, Dulles had to intervene to sort out a car insurance problem when Sonny was involved in a collision, the details of which could not be recalled by the young man. "My son was very severely wounded in the head and has only partially regained his memory and certain other mental faculties," Dulles explained in a letter to the United Services Automobile Association.

Allen Jr. still showed flashes of his brilliance. He continued to read voraciously, but he had trouble retaining information. Once familiar geography was now a mystery to him. He felt most comfortable in New York City, and his parents experimented with letting him stay there for brief periods. They rented a room for him in "a lovely, old brownstone that was lived in by an older lady," recalled Joan. But the young man had lost what doctors called his "executive function." He had a hard time organizing his thoughts and making his way through life. "He couldn't really think, and he couldn't really put two and two together," Joan said. "And he began to get really depressed, and crazy."

Sonny's debilitated mental condition placed an emotional and financial strain on the family. For the next two decades, he would go back and forth between expensive institutions and home care. Unlike his brother, Allen Dulles was not a wealthy man. His salary as CIA director, $14,800 [about $130,000 today], was healthy enough for him to maintain the family's comfortable home on Long Island, but he had long since burned through his partner's equity from Sullivan and Cromwell, and he could only afford to rent his second home in Washington because the owner, the relative of an old colleague, charged a token sum. The family's finances were soon stretched by the cost of private treatments and medical consultations for Sonny, which ate away at the family's savings, including Clover's modest inheritance.

Though Dulles himself rarely showed it, Sonny's gravely reduced abilities wore down the family's spirit too. Allen Jr. had been headed for a distinguished career in academia or public life, but now he had trouble finding his way home when he went out for lunch. Now and then, Sonny would stare at his father—and at Uncle Foster and Aunt Eleanor, too—with a look of such rage that it made Dulles shudder. He sometimes launched into angry denunciations of his father as a Hitler-lover and Nazi collaborator, outbursts that the family labeled "paranoid," but were close enough to the truth to unnerve the senior Dulles. "I don't know what we're going to do with him," Dulles began saying to Clover.

By 1954, Dulles turned in desperation to MKULTRA-sponsored doctors for help with Sonny. It is unclear whether Dulles paid for his son to be treated by these CIA-connected physicians, or whether their compensation came in the form of the generous agency research contracts that they received.

Among the first CIA-funded medical experts the spymaster enlisted to treat his son was the eminent Dr. Harold Wolff, chief of the neurology department at New York Hospital–Cornell Medical Center and former president of the American Neurology Association, who became one of the agency's leading experts on mind control. Wolff was a sophisticated and cultured medical scientist with an international reputation for his research on migraine headaches, which he himself sometimes suffered. His global roster of patients included both the shah of Iran and the shah's political nemesis, Prime Minister Mossadegh.

An intense and tightly wound man, Wolff set himself the goal of a new experiment every day. Dr. Donald Dalessio, who interned with the renowned neurologist and later worked with him as a research associate, remarked that Wolff's "relentless drive for accomplishment epitomized the migraine personality that he so vividly documented in hundreds of patients." He ordered his life around a "strict attention to the clock," said Dalessio, "so that he was always on time, always prepared." Trained by the renowned Russian father of behavior science, Ivan Pavlov, Wolff spent long hours in his sixth-floor laboratory at New York Hospital researching the mysteries of the brain. The lab was simple and "not cluttered with gear and impedimenta which characterize today's [scientific facilities]," observed Dalessio, "for it was made to study people, not animals or molecules or other subunits, but functioning human beings."

The wiry, balding neurologist brought an obsessive drive even to his recreational life, swimming every day at his athletic club, mountain climbing, and challenging his younger colleagues to slashing squash games on the rooftop court of his hospital—"an eerie place," recalled Dalessio, "where the wind would shriek about the stone battlements." The son of an artist, Wolff also married an artist, and he and his wife listened to classical music every day and visited a museum or art gallery every week.

Wolff was a supremely confident man. After his death, another migraine specialist commented that his career was marked by a "mixture of greatness and narrowness." The narrowness came from "a desire to be on top and to win, and from an intellectual point of view, his dogmatism" and overcertainty about his medical theories. When Wolff was asked by a colleague why he had never bothered to be board-certified in neurology, he looked puzzled for a moment, and then replied, "But who would test me?" When Wolff was asked by the CIA to take a leading role in its MKULTRA program, he had no moral qualms. He himself would set the ethical boundaries of his mind control experimentation.

Wolff was sufficiently aware of the professional, and perhaps legal,

pitfalls of the MKULTRA research to make sure that the CIA would assume responsibility for the most risky procedures. In a revealing passage
in Wolff's CIA grant proposal, he wrote that his Cornell research team
would test "potentially useful secret drugs (and various brain damaging
procedures)" on behalf of the agency, "to ascertain [their] fundamental
effect upon human brain function and upon the subject's mood." But
Wolff carefully stipulated that any dangerous experiments would have
to be conducted at CIA facilities, not in his hospital. "Where any of the
studies involve potential harm to the subject, we expect the Agency to
make available suitable subjects and a proper place for the performance
of necessary experiments."

In 1955, Wolff agreed to become president of the Society for the
Investigation of Human Ecology, the primary CIA front for channeling
research funds to a wide array of mind control researchers in medicine,
psychology, and sociology. Wolff's prestige became a major asset for the
CIA as the agency attempted to bend the science profession to its Cold
War aims. The neurologist also benefited greatly from the relationship,
garnering CIA grants of up to $300,000 for his own research projects,
and steering millions more to academic colleagues in various disciplines.

Wolff became a friend of Dulles and was an occasional dinner guest
at his Georgetown home. His dominating personality made him one of
the few men who could hold his own in Dulles's company. It was only
natural for the CIA director to ask the prominent neurologist if there
was anything he could do for his son. Wolff, of course, readily agreed
to treat Allen Jr.—it was the least he could do for such an important
benefactor. But, as a result, Sonny became another victim of his father's
MKULTRA program.

Joan has disturbing memories of visiting her brother at New York
Hospital, where he was subjected to excruciating insulin shock therapy,
one of the experimental procedures employed on the CIA's "human
guinea pigs." Used primarily for the treatment of schizophrenia, insulin overdoses were meant to jolt patients out of their madness. The
procedure resulted in coma, and sometimes violent convulsions. The
most severe risks included death and brain damage, though one study

at the time claimed that this mental impairment was actually beneficial because it reduced patients' "tension and hostility."

"They used insulin at New York Hospital," recalled Joan. "I think those initiatives—God knows if they were from my father. I don't know, but I've always wondered about that, because it didn't sound like a good idea.

"When I went to visit my brother, it was hard for me, because he kept saying, 'Can't you do something for me? I'm going mad.' At the time, I didn't know what he was getting at, or what I could do. I was just visiting him."

It was not until years later, when Joan read exposés about MKUL-TRA, that she realized how far her father had gone—even with his own son—in the name of brain research. "Once you go to the dark side, there seems to be no limit."

Sonny showed no signs of improvement after enduring the insulin treatments, although he did write his father a poignant letter from New York, indicating a new docility and a strong desire not to cause his family any more trouble. "Dear Father," he wrote, "I have just understood the nature of the psychological structure that was built around me, and will work to free myself. I realize that I have not been given correct information, but will try to learn the truth anyhow. Love to you and Mother and anyone else we know. I want to be united with you all soon and will do anything convenient for you."

Despite Wolff's lack of success, Dulles next reached out to Dr. Wilder Penfield, a prominent neurosurgeon at Montreal's McGill University, whose psychiatric facility, the Allan Memorial Institute, became a major center of CIA mind control research. To Dulles's great gratitude, Penfield agreed to consult on Allen Jr.'s case, which he continued to do until he retired in 1960.

Like Wolff's operation at New York Hospital–Cornell, Penfield's academic-medical complex also benefited from its relationship with the CIA. Penfield brought in a prominent, Scottish-born psychiatrist named Donald Ewen Cameron, who had known Dulles since the war, to run McGill's new Allan Institute for psychiatry. Cameron, who had met Dulles while consulting on the Rudolf Hess insanity case at the Nuremberg Trials, would become the most notorious scientist in the MKULTRA program. By 1957, Cameron was receiving a steady stream of CIA funding, through Dr. Wolff's Society for Human Ecology, to conduct brainwashing experiments at McGill that would later be widely condemned as barbaric.

Despite his impeccable credentials, Cameron saw himself as an icon-oclastic innovator, pushing psychiatry to embrace the latest pharmaceu-tical technology and the most cutting-edge developments in the newly influential behavioral sciences. Cameron's experiments in the Allan In-stitute's notorious "Sleep Room" involved putting subjects into "electric dream" states, as one victim put it, through insulin overdoses, massive infusions of hallucinogens like LSD and other experimental drugs, and alarming amounts of electroshock therapy—a process he called "de-patterning," to wipe the brain clean of "bad behavior patterns." After blasting away these negative thoughts, Cameron sought to replace them with "good ones," through what he called "psychic driving"—playing taped messages encouraging positive behavior to his nearly comatose victims for between sixteen and twenty hours a day, week after week, as they slipped in and out of consciousness. In one case, a patient under-went reprogramming in Cameron's Sleep Room for 101 days.

The people who came to Cameron were generally seeking relief from everyday psychological ailments like depression and anxiety, even for help dealing with marital problems. But as author Naomi Klein later wrote, Cameron's "shock and awe warfare on the mind" brought only much deeper misery to the patients—many of them women—in his care. "Though he was a genius at destroying people, he could not remake them," Klein observed. "A follow-up study conducted after Cameron left the Allan Memorial Institute found that 75 percent of his former patients were worse off after treatment than they were before they were admitted."

Cameron himself indicated that the true aim of his CIA-funded research was not to improve patients' lives but to contribute to the Cold War effort by perfecting the science of mind control. He compared his patients to prisoners of war who were undergoing interrogation, saying that they, "like prisoners of the Communists, tended to resist [treatment] and had to be broken down."

Gail Kastner, a promising young McGill nursing student, was one of the victims of Cameron's experimentation. She had come to Cameron for help with anxiety issues stemming from her relationship with her emotionally overbearing father. A tall man with pale blue eyes, Cameron exuded a paternal warmth, addressing female patients as "lassie" in his soft brogue. But in the end, Kastner would come to think of the doctor as "Eminent Monster"—he was the distinguished man in the white coat who loomed over her, as she was lit up with so much electrical voltage that she broke teeth and fractured her spine while convulsing on the table.

Years later, Kastner told Klein what it felt like to be held in the Sleep Room. "I hear people screaming, moaning, groaning, people saying no, no, no. I remember what it was like to wake up in that room, I was covered in sweat, nauseated, vomiting—and I had a very peculiar feeling in the head. Like I had a blob, not a head."

Patients' minds were made blank slates; they lost much of their memory, and thus, much of their lives. "They tried to erase and remake me," said Kastner. "But it didn't work."

Val Orlikow, a young mother suffering from postpartum depression, was another patient whose life was emptied out by Cameron. After she came home from the Allan Institute, Orlikow could not remember her husband, David, who was a member of Canada's parliament, or their children. Her mind had been reduced to that of a toddler. She could not use a toilet.

In the mid-1970s, after Cameron had died, the secrets of the Sleep Room and other inhumane MKULTRA research centers began to emerge, as journalists filed Freedom of Information requests and Congress opened investigations into the CIA horror chambers. Eventually, the CIA paid out $750,000 in damages to nine families whose lives were turned upside down by Cameron's experiments—the largest settlement against the agency at the time. The agency made it seem as if its mind control experiments were isolated relics of the past. Testifying before a Senate hearing in 1977, CIA psychologist John Gittinger called MKULTRA "a foolish mistake . . . a terrible mistake."

But the work of Cameron and other MKULTRA scientists lives on at the agency, incorporated into a 1963 CIA torture manual titled *Counterintelligence Interrogation* that would be used to extract information from prisoners during the wars in Vietnam and Central America, and at black sites operated by the agency after 9/11. U.S. agencies and their overseas allies have continued to run their own versions of Cameron's Sleep Room, where captives are subjected to similar types of sensory deprivation, electroshock, and drug overdoses, until their psychological resistance has been broken.

Allen Dulles was fully aware of the experiments being conducted at McGill when he sent his own son there. Joan doesn't think her brother fell into the hands of Dr. Cameron while he was a patient there. Yet, whatever was done to Sonny in Montreal was not a pleasant experience for him.

When Allen Jr. began treatment at McGill, Dr. Wilder Penfield insisted that the young man could improve. But Sonny knew his limitations by then, and the medical regimen imposed on him only made him feel worse. "He thought my brother could do better," recalled Joan. "But my brother was furious, because he realized he couldn't."

In the end, Penfield finally admitted that Sonny was beyond even the medical wizardry of McGill. In February 1959, the year before he retired, the neurosurgeon wrote Dulles a letter, conceding defeat. "I wish I could help him," Penfield told Dulles. "What a loss this mind de-railment is—to him, to his parents and indeed to the world, for he had a splendid brain."

After Penfield pronounced Allen Jr.'s condition hopeless, Clover continued to agonize over his care. She often confided her troubles to Mary Bancroft, who by then was living in New York. Caring for Allen Jr. was a never-ending job, Clover wrote Bancroft in November 1961. She felt "joy" at having her son "accessible," but when he was home with his parents in Georgetown, there was "such an unbelievable amount of planning, telephoning and hi-jinks of everything connected with [his] comings and goings—engaging Georgetown [University] students [to help] etc., etc. Will not burden you with a recital."

In another letter to Mary, Clover wrote, "Here everything is all right and all wrong, whichever way you wish to take it. Great Allen very tense and no wonder with everything he carries, young Allen none too well, great Allen all too busy to attend to all the things I have to try to get [Sonny] to do and too pulled to pieces by it all. You know it's always everything too much or nothing enough and me so full of fear all the time and nothing to do about it."

From time to time, Sonny would explode in frightening rages. After weathering one such outburst in February 1960, Clover wrote Joan, "It wasn't exactly terrifying but almost." She assured her daughter that there was "nothing broken," but confessed there was a "terrific uncertainty [to] how everything is going to turn out. One of our Georgetown med. students was here and one of Father's aides and another came up from the office. I telephoned the hospital but first they said they couldn't come over the District line and then they said the aide would have to have half an hour for dinner before starting!"

Allen Jr. was "endlessly patient in general," remembered Joan. But he violently rebelled when his family tried to return him to an institution. Sometimes "it would take three people to hold him down when he would get really angry—not wanting to go back to the hospital."

Her sensitive, wounded son reminded Clover of her lost brother, Paul, who had found life too daunting a challenge. They had the same artistic temperaments, the same physical awkwardness. Paul had "the hands of a person who thinks and does not do," she once wrote in her journal. "My son has them." In 1959, Reverend John Sutherland Bonnell, a prominent New York Presbyterian minister who for a time offered young Allen pastoral guidance, informed his parents that Sonny "believes that he has latent within himself the tendency that was 'active in Paul Todd and which led him to kill himself.'" It was one more emotional burden for Clover to bear, the fear that the family tragedy would repeat itself.

Allen Jr. wasn't the only family member Clover worried about. Her oldest daughter, Toddie, started to suffer from manic depression in early adulthood, a condition she thought Toddie inherited from her, and began undergoing shock treatments. It is unknown whether CIA doctors were involved in Toddie's electroshock therapy. But Dulles was quite willing to steer suffering relatives toward MKULTRA-connected physicians.

Lobotomies were among the more extreme mind control measures undertaken in the CIA program. At one point, Dulles arranged for his niece Edith—the daughter of his sister Margaret—to be lobotomized by a CIA brain surgeon. "She had cancer and was in great pain," recalled Joan. "They tried lobotomy on her—all that came from my father, he was the one who suggested the doctor. It didn't work at all, it didn't stop the pain. It just made her odd."

Sometimes Clover thought that all the sadness and anxiety in her life was about to crush her. She felt that she was "walking on the bottom of the sea," she wrote Mary in 1961. "It isn't funny to feel all the time so impossible," Clover told her confidante on another occasion. "I envy the manic depressives having their turn to be up." Her husband's secretive life—which, she suspected, continued to involve other women—and his emotional remoteness only made Clover feel more alone with her misery.

At one low point in Clover's life, a well-meaning CIA doctor recommended that she see Dr. Cameron. She knew Cameron from her husband's CIA dinner parties, and for some reason always felt uneasy in his presence. But out of desperation, she agreed to have lunch with the McGill psychiatrist at the Mayflower Hotel during his next visit to Washington. Over lunch, she related her life's many laments to Cameron—including her husband's affairs—while he stared intently at her. After she finished, Cameron explained to her that her husband's sexual transgressions were a natural outgrowth of his complex and driven personality, and that she must not take them personally. He suggested that she come to Montreal, where he could treat her in his clinic and help her develop a more positive outlook on her life. Clover spent days agonizing over the decision, but in the end she decided not to go. She did not know that by avoiding Cameron's Sleep Room, she was likely preserving her sanity.

By 1962, a newly determined Clover had taken full control of her son's well-being. On the advice of Jolande Jacobi, her longtime Jungian analyst, she arranged to have Allen Jr. admitted to the Bellevue Sanatorium, a venerable, family-run institution on the Swiss side of Lake Constance, whose directors had strong ties to the Jung Institute in nearby Zurich and to the great man himself. After all the frustrating and harrowing treatments that Allen Jr. had been put through for the past ten years, Clover was convinced that it was time to try a softer, Jungian approach, based on talk therapy, artistic expression, and dream analysis.

Sonny's mother and father accompanied him on the trip to Kreuzlingen, the quiet lakeside village where the sanitarium was located. Before they left for Switzerland, Dulles wrote to Dr. Heinrich Fierz, the facility's medical director, telling him that the family realized there was little hope for the young man. "It is a difficult case," Dulles wrote, "and with the extent of the wound and the brain damage, we can only hope for limited results." Dulles wasn't even sure that he could get his son to take the flight to Switzerland. "At the last minute, he might refuse to make the trip," he told Fierz. By that point, Sonny's faith in the psychiatry profession—and in his father's judgment—was extremely low.

But Allen Jr. did move into Bellevue, and he found the facility so soothing an environment that he stayed there for over ten years. Like Hans Castorp's "magic mountain" retreat in the novel by Thomas Mann, the Swiss sanitarium became Sonny's refuge from a hostile world. Bellevue was built on a "beautiful, great, old estate," recalled Joan, who often visited her brother there, and it had treated a wide range of patients over the years, including Freud's famous case study, "Anna O" (Bertha Pappenheim). There was, Joan said, "a leisurely sort of European grace about your situation"—as long as you went on paying, she added. American institutions had a different attitude, she observed. "America is 'You've got to be doing something, buddy,' whereas in Europe, you can just 'be.'"

Young Dulles worked with Jacobi and some of her most promising protégés, including William Willeford, an American who had graduated from the Jung Institute. Willeford later recalled that he made a "connection" with Sonny despite his severe brain impairment, taking time to write his parents each month about his daily routine and assure them that their son "had some kind of life." The young analyst met with Sonny's parents once in person at the Swiss clinic. He found Clover so insistent about communicating her views of young Allen that he asked her to leave his office so he could hear her husband's take on Sonny. But Allen Sr. had nothing of interest to say about his son, recalled Willeford. "He didn't have any insights." Later, Dulles passed word to Willeford that if he was interested in joining the CIA, he should let him know. Apparently Dulles had been impressed when the analyst had cut off Clover during their meeting in his office. "He liked it when I said, 'Let's hear what the father has to say.'"

The work that Willeford later published revealed a strong interest in the father-son dynamic, that primal and fateful relationship that had weighed so heavily on Allen Jr.'s life. "Whether the son comes to experience his father as Saturn eating his children, depends on the kind of father the son has and the kind of male society he is being asked to join," Willeford wrote in one book. "But it also depends very significantly on his mother's sense of the value of her own femininity, and on her way of mediating the values of the Father World."

After Sonny had been in Bellevue for some time, his father suggested that it might be time for him to return to the United States, but he recoiled violently at the idea. "Never!" he shouted. "I'm never coming home to you, ever!"

Bellevue was his mother's world—a humane, Jungian oasis far from the cruel science of New York Hospital and McGill University and the other institutions associated with his father's world.

Allen Jr. did not leave Bellevue until he heard that his father was dead. Joan eventually arranged to take him out of the sanitarium and move him to Santa Fe, where she had found her own sanctuary and was able to look out for her brother. Sonny never returned to an institution. Joan became his legal guardian. The two elderly siblings still live in Santa Fe, in the same house now, both trying to make sense of their past, in their own ways.

Dangerous Ideas

Shortly after 9:00 p.m. on March 12, 1956, Jesús de Galíndez, a lecturer in Spanish and government at Columbia University, finished leading a graduate seminar at Hamilton Hall and headed home. One of his students offered to drive him to the Columbus Circle subway station so he could take a downtown train to his Greenwich Village apartment. He was never seen again by friends or colleagues.

Galíndez was a charming, forty-year-old bachelor, popular with his students and attractive to women. Born to a prominent Basque family in Spain and educated as a lawyer, Galíndez was tall, slim, well dressed, and good-looking, with deep, dark eyes, and a receding hairline that added to his distinguished appearance. He emanated a warm, if somewhat melancholy, intelligence. He had the look of a man who had seen perhaps too much of the world but was determined not to be undone by it.

During the Spanish Civil War, Galíndez had fought in a Basque brigade against Franco's forces. After Franco's triumph, he fled for his life to France and booked passage on a ship to the Dominican Republic, where strongman Rafael Trujillo had promised sanctuary to Spanish exiles. Arriving in late 1939 in Santo Domingo, the capital city, which the dictator had renamed Ciudad Trujillo after himself, Galíndez found work as a professor of history and languages, and later as a government adviser. But he and most of his fellow Spanish refugees soon discovered that they had "left Franco's frying pan and landed in Trujillo's fire," in the words of a Dominican diplomat.

Rafael Trujillo had ruled the Dominican Republic since 1930, an operatic reign of terror that combined equally florid measures of violence and pageantry. His theater of blood included the horrific 1937 mass slaughter of thousands of Haitian immigrant workers, including women and children, many of whom were hacked to death with machetes. Trujillo's political enemies were rounded up and tortured in the notorious concentration camp at Nigua and in the La Cuarenta dungeon. Others were assassinated and their bodies displayed in macabre festivals, like the murdered rebel leader Enrique Blanco, whose corpse was tied to a chair and paraded throughout his home province, where his peasant followers were forced to dance with his remains.

Those who fell into disfavor with Trujillo's regime lived in mortal fear of being denounced in the notorious gossip column of the leading government newspaper, *El Caribe*. Denunciations could ruin careers or destroy lives. It was "a method of [execution] that was slower and more perverse than when he had his prey shot, beaten to death, or fed to the sharks," as the novelist Mario Vargas Llosa observed. "*El Jefe*," as the dictator was known, was a master of fear. During the later years of his regime, in the 1950s, all it took to spread panic in the capital was for one of his security cars to crawl through a neighborhood. The black VW Beetles, known as *cepillos*, created the suffocating "sensation that Trujillo was always watching," in the words of one historian.

Trujillo was also infamous for his official larceny, taking over all of his country's core industries, including oil, cement, meat, sugar, rice— and even the prostitution trade. Running the Dominican economy as a family business, he amassed a personal fortune that made him one of the wealthiest men in Latin America. Trujillo's sexual appetites were equally gluttonous, earning him the title of "The Goat" on the streets of the capital. He plowed his way through three wives, two mistresses, and countless young women whose physical charms briefly captivated him. Trujillo, whose mother was a Haitian mulatto, sought out plump white women—the beauty standard of the local aristocracy, which never fully accepted the coarse former army sergeant. At his 1929 wedding to socialite Bienvenida Ricardo, Trujillo horrified the guests and confirmed Dominican high society's worst suspicions when he used his military sword to cut the elegant wedding cake, sending the towering confection—adorned with frosty angels and delicately sculpted sugar flowers—crashing to the floor.

But Trujillo's common ways won the admiration of many in the poor, uneducated ranks of Dominican society. He was especially popular among men, who admired his naked ambition, sexual aggression, and dandified fashion style. He embodied a strutting style of masculinity known by locals as *tigueraje*, an earlier version of "gangsta" bravado that turned flashy bad boys, or "tigers," from the barrios into emblems of cool. Trujillo also provided thousands of young men from the lower orders—including *mestizos*, blacks, and other traditional social outcasts—a path upward, by expanding the Dominican civil service as well as the military, transforming his army into the second most powerful force in Latin America, after Venezuela's.

Trujillo further ensured his control of the presidential palace by assiduously courting the powerful giant to the north, pledging his nation's allegiance to the United States during World War II and the Cold War, and showering money on Washington politicians and lobbying firms. Trujillo's courtship of Washington paid off. By 1955, John Foster Dulles's State Department was celebrating the strongman as "one of the hemisphere's foremost spokesmen against the Communist movement." That same year, Vice President Nixon visited the Dominican Republic and made a public display of embracing Trujillo. The United States should overlook the notorious defects of the Dominican dictator, Nixon later advised Eisenhower's cabinet, because, after all, "Spaniards had many talents, but government was not among them."

Despite his enormous wealth, Trujillo himself was too thuggish a character to work his way into polite company, at home or abroad. But by the 1950s, his roguish social circle had produced several personalities smooth enough to be embraced by the international jet set, including his first daughter, the sexy bad girl, Flor de Oro, and the suave ladies' man she was once married to and never got over, playboy-diplomat Porfirio Rubirosa. The leading symbol of Dominican masculinity on the world stage, Rubirosa started his career as a lowly military aide to Trujillo, parlaying his connections, good looks, and sartorial elegance into becoming one of the most celebrated Latin lovers of his day—"the Dominican Don Juan," the "Caribbean Casanova," as the international press anointed him.

Rubirosa, affectionately known as "Rubi," was the son Trujillo always wanted—much more polished than his own crude, debauched offspring, Ramfis (named, in Trujillo style, for a character in the Verdi opera *Aida*). The dictator, like the rest of the Dominican male populace, reveled in the tales of Rubi's romantic exploits. The dapper playboy had passionate affairs with blond movie goddesses like Kim Novak and courted some of the world's richest women, including American heiresses Doris Duke and Barbara Hutton, both of whom he married. Some in high circles sneered that Rubirosa was unworthy of their company, a lounge-room charmer with a permanent tan and an oily sheen. But women sang his praises. Hutton was particularly graphic about Rubi's appeal, recalling her former husband with ripe fondness even after their divorce: "He is the ultimate sorcerer, capable of transforming the most ordinary evening into a night of magic . . . priapic, indefatigable, grotesquely proportioned."

This was the Dominican image—lusty and glamorous—that Trujillo wanted to project to the world, and particularly to the United States. Maintaining this positive image of robust vitality with his neighbors to the north was not simply a matter of ego gratification for the dictator. Trujillo reaped $25 million a year in foreign aid from Washington, much of which ended up in his personal overseas bank accounts, and he was eager to keep the American dollars flowing. The CIA further enriched the dictator with secret payments, delivering suitcases stuffed with cash to his hotel suite whenever he visited New York for UN meetings.

While Trujillo succeeded in crushing dissent at home, by 1956 there was one man—Jesús de Galíndez—who, in the dictator's mind, threatened his regime's world image. Galíndez, who lived in a book-stuffed apartment on lower Fifth Avenue and enjoyed going to Latin dance clubs at night, did not strike his academic colleagues at Columbia as an international man of danger. But to Trujillo, he was a treacherous serpent who was poisoning opinion against his regime. Not long before he vanished, Galíndez had completed a damning, 750-page dissertation on the dictator's odious rule, "The Era of Trujillo," and submitted it for a PhD degree at Columbia. Scholarly theses do not normally incite violent passions. But Trujillo knew that Galíndez, who had worked in the Dominican civil service, had inside information about his savage and corrupt regime. *El Jefe*, who saw the Galíndez monograph as a stab in the back, brooded about the betrayal. Trujillo agents tried to convince Galíndez to sell the manuscript to them, offering as much as $25,000, but the scholar refused. The dictator decided that left him with only one course of action.

Galíndez saw his scholarly exposé of the Trujillo tyranny as part of a broader campaign of popular liberation. In the mid-1950s, ironfisted regimes like Trujillo's dominated Latin America, with dictators ruling thirteen of the region's twenty nations. The Eisenhower administration found these despots to be useful Cold War allies; they allowed U.S. corporations to exploit their nations' people and resources, and they cracked down on labor agitation and social unrest as Communist-inspired. But Galíndez's scholarly activism—which included numerous magazine articles and pamphlets he published in Mexico and the United States, attacking the Trujillo regime and championing human rights in Latin America—was part of a new intellectual ferment that was challenging the old order.

It was his experience as an exiled Basque freedom fighter, said Galíndez, that made him deeply sympathetic to the region's social struggles. His own people's doomed crusade for self-determination made "the problems of Puerto Ricans in New York . . . or the drumbeat of a black Caribbean" reverberate inside him, he wrote.

Galíndez's life in New York, as a politically active refugee at the height of the Cold War, was a complex web. In addition to his activism against Trujillo, the scholar served as the U.S. representative of the Basque government-in-exile. Galíndez also maintained an ambiguous relationship with U.S. security officials. Galíndez's escape to the United States in 1946 was no doubt made smoother by the fact that he had been secretly working as an informant for the FBI during the war, passing along information about suspicious pro-Nazi activity in the Caribbean. After he arrived in New York, the bureau asked him to spy on Communist-affiliated members of the anti-Franco resistance in the United States. In May 1951, the special agent in charge of the bureau's New York office told FBI chief Hoover that Galíndez was "an invaluable informant," whose reports were "extremely detailed, accurate and thorough."

But FBI reports on Galíndez also noted that the Basque exile was strongly critical of U.S. foreign policy in the Eisenhower-Dulles era. He had been heard denouncing the administration for supporting the admission of Franco's Spain to the United Nations, and for backing Latin dictators like Trujillo and Nicaragua's Anastasio Somoza. In April 1955, Galíndez told an FBI informant in Miami that "since John Foster Dulles entered into the picture, the United States has started to write the blackest pages of its international relations. Never before in the history of the world has one single Government more effectively supported dictatorial powers in free nations."

Despite his scathing remarks about Eisenhower-Dulles policy, which made their way into Galíndez's FBI files, the bureau continued to have confidence in him, paying the university lecturer up to $125 a month plus expenses for his information. The FBI also helped Galíndez gain permanent residence status in the United States. The activist-intellectual placed limits on what he would do for the FBI—he refused, for instance, to publicly testify against suspected Communists in the anti-Franco movement, arguing that it would blow his cover. He was clearly playing a deeply intricate game of exile politics, perhaps believing that his relationship with the FBI provided him and his embattled causes some protection.

But the bureau knew that Galíndez was not safe. On March 6, 1956—five days before he disappeared—an FBI official noted in a memo that Galíndez's dissertation on Trujillo "may involve informant in personal difficulties . . . this matter will be watched closely and the Bureau kept advised."

Galíndez was well aware of his perilous situation. Trujillo maintained a network of agents in the United States, and they had already killed at least one opponent of his regime in New York. Strange notes were slipped into his books on campus and disturbing phone calls were made to his home. One day, two tough-looking Dominicans in bright tropical shirts sat in on a class he was teaching.

But it was not Trujillo thugs who were responsible for Galíndez's disappearance on that chilly March night after he taught his final class. His kidnapping was a sophisticated operation run by Robert A. Maheu and Associates, a private detective firm staffed by former CIA and FBI employees that the intelligence agency used as a "cut-out" to do dirty jobs on U.S. soil, where the CIA was forbidden by law to operate.

Grabbed by Maheu agents who were waiting for him in his apartment, Galíndez was drugged and carried into an ambulance, then driven to a small airport in Amityville, Long Island. There he was loaded into a twin-engine Beech airplane that was specially equipped to fly long distances and flown south, stopping for refueling after midnight in West Palm Beach, before continuing on to the Dominican Republic. After landing in Trujillo's kingdom, Galíndez—still half conscious—was transported to Casa de Caoba, the dictator's favorite hideaway. There, Trujillo, dressed in a riding outfit, confronted the traitor with the evidence of his betrayal—a copy of the dissertation, which his agents had stolen. "Eat it," he commanded. The dazed Galíndez took the pile of papers but could not keep hold of them, letting them fall to the floor as his head slumped to his chest. "*Pendejo!*" screamed the dictator in his high-pitched squeal as he flayed Galíndez's head with a riding crop.

Galíndez was taken to a torture chamber in the capital city, where he was stripped, handcuffed, and hoisted on a pulley. Then he was slowly lowered into a tub of boiling water. What remained of him was thrown to the sharks, a favorite disposal method of the dictator.

The abduction of the Columbia University academic from the

streets of Manhattan is the first flagrant example of what would become known during the War on Terror, with bureaucratic banality, as "extraordinary rendition"—the secret CIA practice of kidnapping enemies of Washington and turning them over to the merciless security machinery in undisclosed foreign locations.

During his final seminar, Galíndez mentioned several times that he was being "threatened by Trujillo people." Maria Joy, one of his students, thought that he was showing off. But later, after she read about his disappearance in the newspapers, Joy felt "horrified"—not only because Galíndez had vanished but because something like this "could happen in the United States."

"If this can happen here, what is left?" she wrote in a letter printed in *The New Republic*. "There is no hope. . . . Everybody who has some sense of responsibility and a feeling for democracy and freedom should be concerned."

There was a flurry of public concern over Galíndez's disappearance. On April 24, a group of Columbia University professors asked the Justice Department to investigate charges that Trujillo's regime had assassinated their colleague. The following day, the case worked its way into President Eisenhower's press conference when a reporter for the *Concord* (New Hampshire) *Monitor* asked if the administration planned to examine whether "the agents of a dictatorship which enjoys diplomatic immunity are assassinating persons under the protection of the United States flag?" Eisenhower replied that he knew nothing about the Galíndez affair but said he would look into it.

But, in truth, the CIA had already moved swiftly to shut down the case. New York Police Department officials, informed that the disappearance was a highly sensitive national security matter, put the case in the hands of the Bureau of Special Services (BOSS), the NYPD's intelligence section. The CIA, which had no jurisdiction to investigate domestic criminal cases, used secret police units like BOSS to take charge of delicate investigations within the borders of the United States. Dulles himself communicated the importance of the Galíndez case to the NYPD, asking police officials to send a detective to the scholar's

Greenwich Village apartment to retrieve the contents of his briefcase. Police commissioner Stephen Kennedy made sure the CIA director's request was promptly carried out, and the papers inside Galíndez's briefcase were delivered to Dulles. Kennedy made it clear to the detective that he was to keep his mouth shut about the errand.

John Frank, the Maheu operative who organized Galíndez's kidnapping, was closely connected to some of the principal BOSS inspectors working on the case. Frank was a shrewd, ambitious operator who, like Maheu himself, had begun his career as an FBI agent during World War II, before going to work for the CIA. The forty-two-year-old Frank lived in Washington, where Maheu's detective agency was based. But he kept an office in Trujillo's salmon-colored, Italian Renaissance–style palace, as the high-paying dictator became an increasingly important client of the Maheu firm. Frank won the trust of the volatile *El Jefe*, who made him his bodyguard during state visits to Europe and the United States. The Maheu agency was also given a lucrative contract to upgrade Trujillo's security in the Dominican Republic.

Although Frank liked to play tennis with friends in the spy set and boasted of reading Voltaire in French, he was not part of the CIA's Georgetown inner circle. Men like Frank and his boss, Maheu, were CIA contractors, entrusted with some of the agency's most risky and squalid tasks. They were not the sort of men who played tennis on Allen Dulles's backyard court. Maheu later claimed that the *Mission: Impossible* TV series was based on his firm's exploits—a secret team whose actions would be "disavowed" by the government should any of their agents be "caught or killed." Men like Maheu and Frank were expendable.

Bob Maheu fit the profile of an FBI gumshoe more than a CIA spook. A balding, rubbery-faced man, he had the bright-eyed, genial looks of a comedian who was overly eager to please his audience. But his eyes could go suddenly dead, and his jaw could become grimly set. He came from humble origins—the son of devout Catholic, French-Canadian immigrants who ran a small soda bottling company in a Maine mill town. Maheu worked his way up, graduating from Holy

Cross and then Georgetown Law, and getting hired as a field agent by the FBI, where he worked on sensitive national security cases during the war. But Maheu was not content to stay on J. Edgar Hoover's civil service payroll.

In 1954, he opened up his own security business, with the CIA—which put him on a $500 monthly retainer—as his leading client. The CIA used Maheu and Associates as a front, putting undercover agents on Maheu's staff. The agency also directed a stream of highly sensitive, and rewarding, contracts to Maheu, including a major job for Greek shipping tycoon Stavros Niarchos that established the company as a leading player in the private security field. Maheu's firm was hired to help sabotage an agreement between Niarchos's business rival Aristotle Onassis and the Saudi royal family that the international oil cartel and the Dulles brothers feared would corner the oil shipping business and harm Western interests. The oil caper involved a series of shady maneuvers aimed at smearing the reputation of Onassis—and perhaps even more ruthless actions to eliminate supporters of the Onassis deal in the Saudi royal court. After the successful resolution of the case, a grateful Niarchos gave Maheu a bonus big enough for him to buy a dark blue Cadillac and a split-level house in Sleepy Hollow, Virginia, to which he added a swimming pool. Maheu would become the top-paid security contractor in the country, taking on confidential missions for Vice President Nixon and eccentric billionaire Howard Hughes, who later hired him to run his Las Vegas empire.

Despite his success, Maheu liked to say that he never forgot where he came from. Among the multitude of celebrity photos and gold-plated plaques hanging in his office, he claimed to cherish most of all the wood sign that said "Elm City Bottling," his family's mom-and-pop business. "Call it my personal Rosebud," he wrote in his memoir.

Maheu did not socialize with the top CIA men like Helms, Angleton, and Wisner. He met Dulles only once. "It was an accident," Maheu recalled years later. There was something about the Dulles brothers' cozy power act that did not sit well with Maheu. "I always resented the fact that Allen Dulles's brother was secretary of state. You can't have respect for the diplomatic pouch and be in intelligence at the same time. The State Department should not have to know how you got the information."

It was his CIA handlers—Sheffield Edwards, who ran the agency's security office, and Edwards's deputy, the hulking Jim O'Connell—whom Maheu trusted and invited to his home. These were the cops of the CIA—tough men, many of them ex-FBI and Catholic, who, like Maheu, were not afraid to get their hands dirty. The CIA had an elite reputation, but within the organization there was a distinct class system: the Ivy League types on the top; the ex-FBI hard guys and former cops in the middle ranks of enforcement; and the even more ruthless, and disposable, hired guns at the bottom.

On Saturdays, Maheu would invite Edwards, O'Connell, and other Washington security types like Scott McLeod—the zealous anti-Communist watchdog who had been hired by Foster Dulles to clean house at the State Department during the McCarthy red scare and then conveniently ditched—to watch Notre Dame football games and enjoy barbecue banquets and clambakes in his backyard. Maheu, who prided himself on his cooking skills, carefully monitored the boiling pots filled with lobsters that he had shipped from Maine. Buoyed by the free-flowing booze at the clambakes, Maheu's regular crowd would find themselves in cheerful conversation with a curious range of special guests, from senators to gangsters. They were all part of Maheu's colorful world, where the powerful mingled with the infamous.

Working with Shef Edwards's team and their contacts in the NYPD's BOSS unit, Maheu and Frank initially succeeded in containing the Galíndez story. Columbia University president Grayson Kirk—a friend of Dulles and a trustee of several foundations that served as pipelines for CIA funding—did nothing to keep the missing lecturer's case alive, prompting charges of university "indifference." Meanwhile, the Trujillo regime spread the word that Galíndez was "suffering from a persecution complex" and had likely disappeared for personal reasons. Phony Galíndez sightings were reported throughout Latin America and as far away as the Philippines.

At the same time, the CIA disseminated other disinformation about Galíndez to its friendly press assets, claiming that the missing scholar had absconded with more than $1 million of CIA funds, which the agency allegedly had given him to set up an anti-Franco underground in Spain. Other CIA documents, which circulated as high as Dulles's office, tried to brand Galíndez as "a witting tool of the Communists." The agency's smear campaign succeeded in making Galíndez's character the story, rather than the shocking crime, and public interest in the case began to wane.

But in December, just as the story seemed to be flickering out, Trujillo threw gas on the smoldering fire when, in predictable fashion, he went too far and ordered the murder of the young American pilot who had flown Galíndez to the Dominican Republic. Twenty-three-year-old Gerald Murphy had dreamed of being a pilot his whole life, but, prevented by poor eyesight from joining the U.S. Air Force, he pursued a career as a mercenary pilot, winding up in the Dominican Republic, flying missions for Trujillo. "It beats the hell out of Oregon," the handsome Portland native—who affected a James Dean look, complete with Ray-Bans—told his friends about life in the tropics. But Murphy's life took a fateful turn when he was engaged by John Frank to fly the heavily sedated Galíndez to Ciudad Trujillo.

John Frank told Murphy that Galíndez was a wealthy invalid who wanted to visit Dominican relatives one last time before he died. But after photos of Galíndez began appearing in the press, the pilot figured out the true identity of his passenger. Given to reckless chatter when he was drinking, Murphy began boasting in Ciudad Trujillo watering holes about the big story that he was sitting on, and his chances of striking it rich by making a deal with the Dominican regime to stay quiet. Trujillo, however, preferred a more certain method of ensuring the pilot's silence. Frank brought Murphy to the National Palace, telling him he had been granted an audience with *El Jefe* himself. It was the last time the pilot was seen. On December 4, the young American's Ford was found on a cliff near a slaughterhouse, where the offal that was dumped into the sea attracted swarms of sharks. Known as the "swimming pool," the lagoon was a favorite disposal site for Trujillo's enemies.

Murphy's suspicious disappearance ignited a new uproar, with his Oregon congressman, Charles Porter, demanding that the Eisenhower administration get to the bottom of this latest Trujillo-related mystery. In March 1957, even Stuyvesant Wainright, the wealthy Republican congressman from Long Island's Gold Coast, waded into the growing controversy, writing directly to his neighbor Dulles and asking for more information about the Galíndez affair, which he called "an incredible invasion of a human being's personal protection in our country." Wainright told Dulles that he felt a personal connection to the case, since Murphy had flown Galíndez to his fate from a Long Island airport. Dulles blandly replied that the CIA had no jurisdiction on American soil, so the congressman's inquiry about the case was better directed to the FBI.

The Galíndez case, in fact, was turning into a major source of friction between the two federal agencies. Hoover, who informed Attorney General Herbert Brownell Jr. that Galíndez had been a valued informant for the FBI, took his probable murder personally. Hoover was further enraged by the suspicious disappearance of young Gerald Murphy and the new round of embarrassing political fallout from the case. To make matters worse, the FBI soon tied John Frank to the crimes, a man who was not only a former bureau agent, but, like his boss, Maheu, was now part of the shadowy CIA orbit that operated serenely above the law. As was common when Hoover sought revenge in Washington's political wars, he leaked much of the Galíndez story to the press. In late February, *Life* magazine ran a dramatic version of the affair under the headline "The Story of a Dark International Conspiracy."

The Eisenhower Justice Department knew that despite the sensitive national security ramifications, someone had to take the fall in the sensational case, and John Frank was the obvious choice. But, as federal prosecutors began to build a case for conspiracy, kidnapping, and homicide against Frank, the CIA's general counsel, Lawrence Houston, and Dulles himself huddled anxiously with the attorney general. Brownell assured the CIA that he would keep the case tightly held to avoid further press leaks because he realized that the affair involved "keen" national security interests. Brownell's deputies grew frustrated as they tried to peel away the layers surrounding the case. In March 1957, Assistant Deputy Attorney General Warren Olney III complained in a memo to Brownell, "In my opinion the information given to you by CIA is vague and uncertain and does not resolve the question as to whether [Frank] has in fact been used in any capacity by CIA." Olney recommended that the CIA "be requested directly and definitely" to state its exact relationship with the man at the center of the Galíndez mystery.

After intricate negotiations between the Justice Department and the CIA, John Frank was finally charged with an astonishingly light offense: failure to register as a foreign agent. "I fully appreciate that to indict a person involved in a possible murder and kidnapping for violation of the Registration Act is like hitting a man with a feather when he should be hit with a rock," acknowledged one chagrinned Justice Department official. But considering the highly charged political atmosphere surrounding the case, he observed, it was the only way to ensure that "the subject will [not] escape scot-free."

In December 1957, Frank was convicted of multiple counts of violating the Registration Act and sentenced to a maximum eight months to two years in federal prison. But the following year, his conviction was overturned by a federal appeals court in the District of Columbia that ruled that Frank had been denied a fair trial because of "the prosecutor's attempt to connect him in the jury's mind with the Galíndez-Murphy affair." As he entered the second round of his legal battle, Frank made it clear that he was not going to be the fall guy for the CIA on the Galíndez case. Before his new trial began, Frank played his trump card, making it known that his line of defense would be that he had been working for U.S. intelligence throughout the affair. When Frank's lawyer issued subpoenas for several CIA witnesses to appear in court, agency officials quickly moved to block them from testifying, thereby aborting the trial. The Justice Department was forced to strike a plea bargain with Frank, and in March 1959, he paid a modest fine, signed an agreement not to work as a foreign agent, and walked out of court a free man. Nobody was ever charged in the murders of Jesus de Galíndez or Gerald Murphy.

Allen Dulles's CIA believed in the power of ideas. It was easy for Dulles's Ivy League–educated executive team to understand why the Trujillo regime became so obsessed with a doctoral dissertation written by an obscure academic. They knew that ideas mattered: they floated like seeds on the wind, over mountains and seas, and took root in the most unexpected places. The Cold War was, in fact, a war of ideas, fought primarily in the realm of the symbolic, through propaganda campaigns and "proxy" conflicts, instead of on battlegrounds where the superpowers clashed head-to-head.

Joseph Stalin, too, understood the power of words, calling writers "the engineers of the human soul." The Soviet leader had a way of expressing himself with industrial bluntness. "The production of souls," he stated, "is more important than the production of tanks." Stalin engineered a conformity of Soviet thought by executing writers, intellectuals, and artists who did not toe the party line, or by exiling them to the gulag's frozen extremities.

The CIA's methods of cultural engineering were far more subtle but no less effective. The agency spent an inestimable fortune on the war of ideas, subsidizing the intellectual and creative labors of those who were deemed politically correct and seeking to marginalize those who challenged the "crackpot realism" of Cold War orthodoxy. The main front organization used by the CIA to spread its largesse and influence was the Congress for Cultural Freedom, "a kind of cultural NATO," in one critic's words, founded in 1950 to counter the propaganda efforts of the Soviet bloc. The Congress for Cultural Freedom grew to become one of the biggest arts patrons in world history, sponsoring an impressive array of book publishing start-ups and literary magazines—including the influential *Encounter* and *Paris Review*—as well as art exhibits, literary prizes, concert tours, and international conferences held in Paris, Berlin, and the Rockefeller Foundation's Bellagio retreat overlooking Lake Como.

There was a seductive appeal to the CIA's cultural patronage, for it offered not only the satisfaction of doing one's patriotic duty and resisting Stalinist tyranny, but also a comfortable reprieve from the financial anxieties of the freelance, creative life. "These stylish and expensive excursions must have been a great pleasure for the people who took them at government expense," remarked Jason Epstein, former Random House editorial director and cofounder of *The New York Review of Books*. "But it was more than pleasure, because they were tasting power. Who wouldn't like to be in a situation where you're politically correct and at the same time well compensated for the position you've taken?"

Many leading artists and intellectuals fell into the ranks of the CIA's generously funded culture war, including Arthur Schlesinger Jr., Mary McCarthy, Robert Lowell, Dwight Macdonald, Daniel Bell, Isaiah Berlin, George Plimpton, Peter Matthiessen, and Mark Rothko. But the recipients of CIA sponsorship paid a price: their intellectual independence. As historian Frances Stonor Saunders observed, "The individuals and institutions subsidized by the CIA were expected to perform as part . . . of a propaganda war." Those who took agency funds became "cheerful robots" of the Cold War, in C. Wright Mills's memorable phrase. Mills, one of the few prominent American scholars to actively resist the siren calls of the Cold War intelligentsia, was predictably attacked in these circles. While Mills was coming under fire in the pages of CIA-funded publications like *Encounter*, he was embraced by leftist intellectuals in Europe such as Ralph Miliband (father of British Labour Party leader Ed Miliband) and historian Edward Thompson, who declared, "Wright is fortunate in his enemies."

Mills was fortunate in other ways, too. His intellectual gifts and personal fortitude allowed him to carve out a prominent public position for himself, even at the height of Cold War conformity in America. But most of those who challenged the era's mandatory spirit of American triumphalism soon found themselves intellectually isolated and professionally invisible. Under the reign of CIA-approved thought, unpleasant realities about the U.S. imperium were considered out-of-bounds for scholarly or journalistic exploration, including the bloody regime changes in Iran and Guatemala and the boiling cauldron of racial injustice at home. The grants, literary prizes, journalism awards, and academic endowments went to those who saw America as the hope of the world, not to those who focused on its deep flaws.

Those CIA-approved intellectuals who dared to assert their independence soon found that once-welcoming doors were closed to them. In 1958, Dwight Macdonald—a frequent intellectual sparring partner of his friend Mills—broke out of the Cold War thought bubble with a cranky article for *Encounter* titled "America, America," in which he railed against the idiocy of the country's mass culture. There was nothing particularly surprising about Macdonald's highbrow lament about the spread of primitivism in pop culture. But the article was deemed unacceptable by the editors of *Encounter*, and though Macdonald was a former editor of *Encounter*, the magazine refused to publish it.

Like many of the CIA-sponsored literary projects, *Encounter* reflected the aesthetics of James Jesus Angleton, the CIA's unofficial cultural commissar. As a Yale undergraduate, Angleton had founded the avant-garde literary magazine *Furioso* and befriended Ezra Pound and e.e. cummings. The spy wizard was a devotee of the modernist school of poetry—particularly its high priest, T. S. Eliot—and the pages of *Encounter* were dominated by an Eliotic sensibility, though Eliot himself shunned the London-based publication as so "obviously published under American auspices."

A new generation of Beat poets led by Allen Ginsberg was beginning to challenge the reign of literary modernism, invoking the lush populism and unabashed deviancy of Walt Whitman. As the Beats laid siege to Eisenhower-era cultural banality, the CIA-funded poetry establishment struggled to keep these barbarians outside the gates. Years later, Ginsberg imagined a confrontation between himself and Angleton's favorite poet on the fantail of a boat in European waters. "What did you think of the dominance of poetics by the CIA?" Ginsberg asks Eliot. "After all, wasn't Angleton your friend?" The old master admits he knew of the infamous spook's "literary conspiracies" but insists they were "of no importance to Literature." But Ginsberg passionately disagrees. The

CIA, he tells Eliot, secretly funded a "whole field of Scholars of War" and "nourished the careers of too many square intellectuals," thereby undermining efforts to "create an alternative free vital decentralized culture." The result, as Ginsberg wrote in his 1956 masterpiece, *Howl,* was the unchallenged rise of the American Moloch, "vast stone of war . . . whose soul is electricity and banks," and a culture that devoured the souls of its own children.

Angleton carried an elaborate portfolio at the CIA, from the politics of art to the metaphysics of assassination. In December 1954, Dulles officially named him chief of counterintelligence, the department tasked with blocking enemy penetration of the agency. But, in reality, his manifold duties were as hard to get a hold on as the smoke curling up from the chain of cigarettes he inhaled throughout the day. "I remember Jim as one of the most complex men I have ever known," recalled Dick Helms, one of Angleton's vital defenders and patrons within the agency. "One did not always have to agree with him to know that he possessed a unique grasp of secret operations. As a friend remarked, Jim had the ability to raise an operational discussion not only to a higher level but to another dimension. It is easy to mock this, but there was no one within the agency with whom I would rather have discussed a complex operational problem than Angleton."

Angleton's activities ranged from purloining documents at foreign embassies to opening the mail of American citizens (he once jocularly referred to himself as "the postmaster") to wiretapping the bedrooms of CIA officials. It was his job to be suspicious of everybody, and he was, keeping a treasure trove of sensitive files and photos in the locked vault in his office. Each morning at CIA headquarters, Angleton would report to Dulles on the results of his "fishing expeditions," as they called his electronic eavesdropping missions, which picked up everything from gossip on the Georgetown party circuit to Washington pillow talk.

As Dulles was well aware, Angleton had even tucked away explosive secrets about the CIA director himself. That is why Dulles had rewarded him with the most sensitive job in the agency, Angleton confided to journalist Joseph Trento near the end of his life. "You know how I got to be in charge of counterintelligence? I agreed not to poly-graph or require detailed background checks on Allen Dulles and 60 of his closest friends. They were afraid that their own business dealings with Hitler's pals would come out."

Angleton's selection as the top hunter of Soviet moles struck many in the agency as peculiar. During and after the war, Angleton had been badly fooled by his close chum in British intelligence, the legendary double agent Kim Philby. The witty, bibulous, stammering Philby, who had betrayed his class and country by secretly going to work for So-viet intelligence as a young Cambridge graduate in the 1930s, forged a tight friendship with Angleton in London during the war. Philby and the Anglophilic Angleton, who had attended the upper-crust British boarding school Malvern, renewed their relationship when Philby was posted to Washington, D.C., in 1949, as the British Secret Intelligence Service liaison. The two men shared long, sodden lunches at Harvey's, a Washington power restaurant also favored by the likes of Hoover and his companion, Clyde Tolson.

Angleton's children remembered the drunken nursery games played by Philby and his friends Guy Burgess and Donald Maclean, who be-longed to the same secret ring of Cambridge-bred traitors, when they were invited to the Angleton home in Arlington for dinner. "They'd start chasing each other through the house in this little choo-choo train," according to Siri Hari Angleton, the spymaster's youngest daughter, "these men in their Eton ties, screaming and laughing!" At another raucous party, she recalled, "Philby's wife passed out, and was just lying on the floor. Mummy said, 'Oh, Kim, don't you want to see how Mrs. Philby is doing?' And he said, 'Ahhh . . .' and just stepped right over her to get another drink."

Angleton struck people as a wispy figure of a man. He was known as the "Gray Ghost" in agency circles—a tall, stooped, ashen-faced figure, with a bony, clothes-rack frame, draped in elegant, European-tailored suits, and wreathed in his customary rings of smoke. But around Philby, Angleton seemed to come alive, to glow. They were boarding school boys again.

After Philby was finally exposed, ultimately fleeing to Russia, Angleton's anti-Soviet sentiments hardened into a fundamentalism that clouded his judgment. "I have no doubt that the exposure of Kim Philby was lodged in the deepest recesses of Jim's being," Helms later commented. If he were the sort of chap who murdered people, Angleton told a friend in British intelligence, "I would kill Philby." The betrayal was painfully intimate, and it bred a paranoia that bloomed darkly within Angleton. When he was named counterintelligence chief, he saw traitors and signs of Soviet treachery everywhere. His compulsive mole hunting ruined the careers of dozens of CIA agents, doing more to damage agency security than to fortify it. "I couldn't find that we ever caught a spy under Jim," said William Colby, the CIA director who finally terminated Angleton's long tenure in 1975.

But under Dulles, Angleton enjoyed free rein to pursue his demons. He dreamed up Cold War phantasms and bogeymen, and then invented all-too-real methods of destroying these horrible apparitions. He operated a kind of virtual CIA within the CIA, reporting only to Dulles himself—and even the top spymaster was not fully aware of his murky activities. "My father once said, 'I'm not a genius, but in intelligence I am a genius,'" recalled Siri Hari Angleton, who changed her name from Lucy as a young woman, after following her mother and older sister into the Sikh religion.

Dulles and Angleton went way back together, to the dark maze of postwar Rome. Like Helms, Dulles admired Angleton's complex mind and the deep calculus of his spycraft. "Jim," Dulles once told Angleton's wife, Cicely, "is the apple of my eye." Angleton, in turn, grew deeply fond of Dulles, whom he looked up to as a father figure, and of Clover Dulles, too, with whom he shared a creative temperament.

"Angleton was fascinating," recalled Joan (Dulles) Talley. "My mother liked him a lot, he was very talkative, very intellectual. He was an odd one, he fussed over the orchids he grew—which I think was a wonderful obsession of his—and he drank too much. But he was lots of fun for anyone to talk to, you'd never know where the conversation was going to go. He'd jump from orchid colors to flyfishing to poetry and music. He was a real scholar, and he was an oddball. A totally unique creation."

Angleton expressed an appreciation for Clover's art, and he once begged her for a self-portrait that she had painted. Clover suspected that the aesthetic spy was "in his cups" when he made the request, but she agreed to give it to him, as she later told Joan, "because Jim labors day and night for CIA and Dad." The two couples enjoyed each other's company, and the Angletons were often invited for dinner at Q Street. Cicely Angleton came from a prosperous family that had made a fortune in Minnesota iron ore—and, educated at Vassar, she shared Clover's interests in spirituality and the arts. Cicely later published several volumes of poetry, taking the creative path that her husband otherwise might have gone down.

Dulles and Angleton shared a disdain for Washington bureaucracy and for the governmental oversight that comes with a functioning democratic system. Later, in the post-Watergate '70s, when the Church Committee opened its probe of CIA lawbreaking, Angleton was called to account for himself. As he completed his testimony, the Gray Ghost rose from his chair, and, thinking he was now off the record, muttered, "It is inconceivable that a secret intelligence arm of the government has to comply with all the overt orders of the government." It was a concise articulation of the Angleton philosophy; in his mind, CIA overseers were a priestly caste that, because the fate of the nation had been placed in its hands, must be allowed to operate unfettered and above the law.

"Allen wasn't red-tape and neither was daddy," said Siri Hari. "You know, back then, people were much more interesting. . . . I don't think it was a case of resenting bureaucracy, because the bureaucracy just never came that close to them anyway, so why would they resent it? They probably just felt, you know, a little beyond it, a little above it."

Dulles entrusted Angleton with the agency's most vital and sensitive missions. He was the principal CIA liaison with the key foreign intelligence services, including those in frontline Cold War nations like France, West Germany, Turkey, Taiwan, and Yugoslavia, as well as with Mossad, the Israeli spy agency. Angleton developed a special bond with

Allen and Clover Dulles, around the time of their 1920 wedding. A sensitive, artistic woman, Clover grew increasingly confounded by their secrecy-filled marriage. "My husband doesn't converse with me . . . about *anything*," she confided in her diary. (COURTESY OF JOAN TALLEY)

SS Colonel Eugen Dollmann (*center*) translates a conversation between Italian air marshal Italo Balbo and Adolf Hitler. The adaptable Dollmann smoothly shifted between the worlds of decadent Italian royalty and Nazi power—and later made himself useful to U.S. intelligence.
(BPK, Berlin/Bayerische Staatsbibliothek München Abtlg. Karten u. Bilder/ Heinrich Hoffmann/Art Resource, NY)

Among the devils whom Dulles quietly bargained with during World War II were SS leader Heinrich Himmler (shaking hands with Reichsmarschall Hermann Goering, *far right*) and SS general Karl Wolff (to the immediate rear of Himmler). (Ullstein Bild/Getty Images)

Goering, Hitler's second-in-command, enjoys himself at the Nuremberg war crimes tribunal in 1946. William Donovan, Dulles's OSS boss, even tried to cut a deal on Goering's behalf, outraging the top U.S. prosecutor. (KURT HUTTON/GETTY IMAGES)

Above left: Reinhard Gehlen, Hitler's spy chief on the eastern front, was among the "rats" rescued after the war by Dulles, who helped install Gehlen as the powerful director of West Germany's intelligence apparatus. (AP PHOTO)

Above right: William Gowen, a young U.S. Army intelligence agent, tried to track down war criminals fleeing justice through the Nazi "ratlines" in Italy. But he was no match for Dulles and his counterintelligence protégé in Rome, James Jesus Angleton. (COURTESY OF WILLIAM GOWEN)

Clover Dulles (*left*) and Mary Bancroft formed a lifelong bond when they met in Switzerland during the final days of the war. The women took to calling Dulles—the cold, relentless man who dominated their lives—"The Shark." (COURTESY OF JOAN TALLEY)

Quaker relief worker Noel Field was one of the innocent "little mice" who fell into Dulles's trap during the Cold War. (© CORBIS)

The young congressman Richard Nixon (*far right*), with fellow members of the House Un-American Activities Committee in 1948, rode the anti-Communist inquisitions to power with the help of the Dulles brothers. (© BETTMANN/CORBIS)

Above left: Harry Dexter White, the most celebrated New Deal economist, was one of Nixon's victims. (© BETTMANN/CORBIS)

Above right: Senator Joseph McCarthy, with his aide Roy Cohn in 1954, was such a powerful exploiter of the red scare that he became a threat to President Eisenhower and the Dulles brothers. (© BETTMANN/CORBIS)

Secretary of State John Foster Dulles (*left*) and President Dwight D. Eisenhower presided over a growing U.S. empire enforced by nuclear "brinksmanship" terror and CIA cloak-and-dagger intrigue.
(Courtesy of Joan Talley)

The maverick sociologist C. Wright Mills, who rode a motorcyle that he built himself, was America's most incisive analyst of the Cold War "power elite." His provocative scholarship won a wide following—and got him listed by the CIA as an intellectual threat even after his premature death in 1962.
(Photo by Yaroslava Mills. Courtesy of the estate of C. Wright Mills)

The shah of Iran, Mohammed Reza Pahlavi, and Queen Soraya arrive at the Rome airport in August 1953, in flight from their country's democratic uprising. A CIA-engineered coup would soon put the shah back on the Peacock Throne. (© BETTMANN/CORBIS)

Wealthy, young, attractive, and dedicated to uplifting their impoverished country, President Jacobo Arbenz and his wife, Maria, were the Kennedys of Guatemala. But Arbenz was overthrown by a CIA-sponsored military rebellion in 1954 after his land reforms antagonized United Fruit Company and the Dulles brothers. (CORNELL CAPA/GETTY IMAGES)

The programming of the assassin in the 1962 political thriller *The Manchurian Candidate*, starring Angela Lansbury and Laurence Harvey, eerily evoked the massive CIA mind control program—code-named MKULTRA—that was launched by Allen Dulles in 1953. (COURTESY OF MGM MEDIA LICENSING)

Cuba's new leader Fidel Castro was amused by reports of an assassination plot when he visited New York in April 1959. (© CORBIS) But the campaign to kill Castro became a more serious matter when the CIA hired security contractor Robert Maheu (*right*) to enlist the Mafia in its lethal plot.
(RALPH CRANE/GETTY IMAGES)

The Congo's brief moment of post-colonial euphoria ended in December 1960 when Patrice Lumumba, the country's first democratically elected leader, was arrested by rebel troops under the guidance of the CIA. (STRINGER/GETTY IMAGES)

President John F. Kennedy, a strong supporter of African independence, was stunned when he received a call from United Nations ambassador Adlai Stevenson in February 1961 informing him of Lumumba's brutal execution. The CIA had kept the news of Lumumba's murder from the newly inaugurated Kennedy for nearly a month. (© THE ESTATE OF JACQUE LOWE)

President-elect Kennedy greets adviser Arthur Schlesinger Jr. outside the Harvard historian's home in Cambridge, Massachusetts, in January 1961. Schlesinger's diaries would later provide a remarkable inside view of the Kennedy presidency as it was torn apart from within by national security conflicts. (© Bettmann/Corbis)

Allen Dulles, followed by Clover, trudges through the snow to Kennedy's inauguration. Though JFK decided to retain Dulles as CIA director, the two men would soon suffer a bitter break over the disastrous Bay of Pigs operation in April 1961.
(Alfred Eisenstaedt/Getty Images)

While President Kennedy was wrestling with CIA and Pentagon advisers over the Bay of Pigs, he suddenly found himself thrust into another CIA-connected tempest, when President Charles de Gaulle of France charged that U.S. intelligence officials were backing a military coup against him. During a visit to Paris in June 1961 with First Lady Jacqueline Kennedy, JFK tried to repair U.S. relations with France. (RDA/Getty Images)

Kennedy with his vice presidential running mate, Lyndon B. Johnson, at a 1960 campaign stop. "One out of every four presidents has died in office," LBJ told Clare Boothe Luce when she asked him why he settled for the number-two spot on the ticket. "I'm a gamblin' man, darlin'." (© Bettmann/Corbis)

The Rockefeller brothers—led by banker David (*far left*) and politician Nelson (*second from left*)—were central members of "the deep state," the discreet nexus of power whose chief "fixer" was Allen Dulles.
(BERNARD GOTFRYD/GETTY IMAGES)

Top CIA administrators like Richard Helms (*left*) and key operations officers like Howard Hunt remained loyal to Dulles even after President Kennedy forced him out of the agency. (BOTH PHOTOS © BETTMANN/CORBIS)

Lee Harvey Oswald was a born "patsy," as he called himself after his arrest for assassinating President Kennedy. His wife, Marina—shown with their baby June in 1962, the year he returned to the U.S. from Russia—thought Lee "did not know who he was really serving. . . . He tried to play with the big boys." Senator Richard Schweiker later saw "the fingerprints of intelligence" all over the doomed young man. (© CORBIS)

Above left: International businessman and CIA informant George de Mohrenschildt took Oswald under his wing in Dallas. He later deeply regretted how he helped frame him for the assassination. (© BETTMANN/CORBIS)

Above right: Quakers Ruth and Michael Paine also befriended the Oswalds. Filled with the arrogance of good intentions, the Paines firmly denied they played an intelligence role in Dallas. But the Paine family was well known to Dulles and his mistress, Mary Bancroft. (© BETTMANN/CORBIS)

Supreme Court chief justice Earl Warren hands his commission's report on the assassination of President Kennedy to President Johnson in September 1964. Dulles (*second from right*) lobbied aggressively to be named to the Warren Commission—a panel he so thoroughly dominated that some thought it should have been called the "Dulles Commission." (© BETTMANN/CORBIS)

David Lifton, pictured here around the time he confronted Dulles about the Warren Report's flaws at a UCLA gathering in 1965, was a graduate student in engineering and physics, and the only person who ever grilled Dulles in public about the assassination. He later recalled feeling that he was in the presence of "evil" that night.
(COURTESY OF DAVID LIFTON)

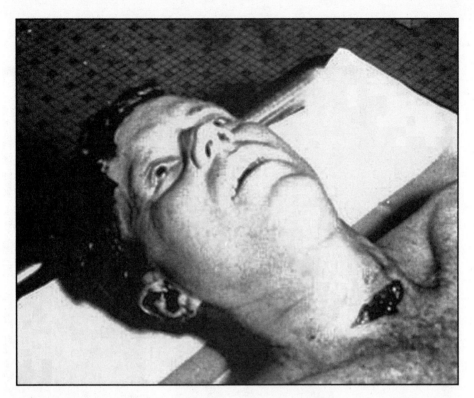

An autopsy photograph of President John F. Kennedy, following his assassination in Dallas on November 22, 1963. Two of the surgeons at Parkland Memorial Hospital who worked in vain to save the mortally wounded Kennedy saw clear evidence that he was struck by bullets from the front as well as the rear, demonstrating that he was the victim of a conspiracy. But afraid to reveal what they observed in the emergency room, they remained silent until years later. (APIC/GETTY IMAGES)

Senator Robert F. Kennedy tours a tenement building on Manhattan's Lower East Side in May 1967. Despite the fears of his family, RFK threw himself into the presidential race the following year, privately confiding to close aides that he planned to reopen the investigation into his brother's death. (FRED W. MCDARRAH/GETTY IMAGES)

James Jesus Angleton, the CIA's legendary counterintelligence wizard, photographed in 1976 after he was finally ousted from the agency. He served Dulles with a devout sense of mission, but by the end of his life he came to believe that the CIA's archangels were far from godly men.

(PHOTOGRAPH BY RICHARD AVEDON © THE RICHARD AVEDON FOUNDATION) the Israelis, forging a realpolitik relationship, with both parties conveniently overlooking Angleton's role in the Nazi ratlines after the war. The Israelis maintained close ties to the American espionage oracle until the end of his life. Several members of Mossad came to Angleton's home as he lay dying in the spring of 1987, to pay their last respects—and perhaps to make certain the vapory Gray Ghost was indeed finally leaving this mortal coil.

Dulles also put Angleton in charge of the CIA's relationship with the FBI—a delicate task considering the rivalry between the two agencies. At the same time he was working with the federal bureau in charge of fighting organized crime, Angleton was also pursuing a CIA partnership with the Mafia. Angleton possessed one of those rare intellects—and characters—that allowed him to lead a life filled with contradiction. He easily passed back and forth between Washington's overworld and the criminal underworld. He was the sort of man who could crossbreed a new orchid, cook a delicious pasta with slivered truffles imported from Ristorante Passetto in Rome, and then sit down with a criminal mastermind to discuss the fine points of murder. Though he dined and drank with Georgetown high society, Angleton's work also brought him into close contact with the agency's rougher characters, including Shef Edwards's security cops, who helped install Angleton's bugs, and Bill Harvey, the hard-drinking gun nut who figured prominently in a number of the agency's assassination jobs.

It was all of a piece, in the intricately wired mind of Jim Angleton: countering dangerous ideas by publishing CIA-vetted literature, or by eliminating the intellectuals and leaders who expounded these ideas. One day, shortly after Fidel Castro took power in Havana, Angleton had a brainstorm. He summoned two Jewish CIA officers, including Sam Halpern, who had recently been assigned to the agency's covert Cuba team. Angleton asked them to fly to Miami and meet with Meyer Lanksy, organized crime's chief financial officer, who had been forced to flee Havana ahead of Castro's revolutionaries, leaving behind the Mafia's highly lucrative casino empire. Lansky was part of the Jewish mob but had close business ties to the Italian Mafia. Angleton told Halpern and the other Jewish CIA agent to see if they could convince Lansky to arrange for the assassination of Castro.

Angleton's emissaries met with Lansky, but the crime mogul drove too hard a bargain for his services and the deal fell through. This was only the beginning of the CIA's endless, Ahab-like quest to kill the Caribbean leviathan, however. Castro would never stop haunting the dreams of the CIA high command. The Cuban revolutionary was not only intellectually formidable and politically fearless; his dream of national liberation was backed up with guns. Castro and his equally charismatic comrade, Che Guevara, made it clear from the start that they would not share the fate of Jacobo Arbenz in Guatemala: they would fight fire with fire. Che, a twenty-five-year-old doctor and adventurer in search of a grander meaning to his life, was living in Guatemala City when Arbenz was overthrown. He saw what happened when Arbenz's moderate reforms came up against the imperial force of United Fruit and the CIA.

"I am not Christ or a philanthropist, old lady," Che wrote to his mother, Celia, in the bantering style he had developed with her, as he and Fidel prepared to board the leaky yacht *Granma* in Mexico with their band of guerrillas to make history in Cuba. "I fight for the things I believe in, with all the weapons at my disposal and try to leave the other man *dead* so that I don't get nailed to a cross."

To avoid Arbenz's fate, Castro and Guevara would do everything he had not: put the hard-core thugs of the old regime up against a wall, run the CIA's agents out of the country, purge the armed forces, and mobilize the Cuban people. By militarizing their dream, Fidel and Che became an audacious threat to the American empire. They represented the most dangerous revolutionary idea of all—the one that refused to be crushed.

It was after midnight, on September 20, 1960, when Fidel Castro came uptown to Harlem. The white, terra-cotta facade of the Hotel Theresa on Seventh Avenue and West 125th Street—"the Waldorf of Harlem"—gleamed under a battery of police spotlights as brightly as a Hollywood movie premiere. Outside the hotel entrance, a boisterous crowd was steadily growing, in defiance of the pelting rain and the intimidating phalanx of policemen, awaiting the international political celebrity who was rumored to be checking in. Suddenly a lusty roar went up from the throng as an official-looking car suddenly glided to a stop outside the hotel and the familiar, tall, bearded figure emerged from the vehicle. "Cuba si, Yanqui no!" shouted the crowd as a beaming Castro swept his arms through the air, before being hustled into the hotel.

The Cuban leader and his fifty-member delegation, who were in New York for the annual United Nations General Assembly meeting, had not received such a warm welcome at their first choice of accommodations, the midtown Shelburne Hotel. When the Cuban delegation checked in two days earlier at the Shelburne, they were greeted by a militant group of anti-Castro exiles calling itself La Rosa Blanca (The White Rose), which threatened to blow up the hotel. The Shelburne management promptly informed Castro's party that they would need to put up a $20,000 security deposit, and an outraged Fidel, insisting that his government did not have ready access to that kind of cash, announced that they would leave the hotel and pitch tents outside the UN if necessary.

Castro's 1960 trip to New York marked a sharp turning point in U.S.-Cuba relations. The previous year, in April 1959, the Cuban leader had enjoyed a much more hospitable reception during his eleven-day visit to the United States. Fresh from his revolutionary victory on New Year's Eve, Fidel was still something of a political mystery to the Eisenhower administration, and the media embraced him as the silver-tongued conqueror who had liberated the Cuban people from Fulgencio Batista's gangster reign. During his earlier visit to New York—a city he loved—Fidel roamed the streets followed by packs of reporters and photographers, dropping by a Queens elementary school, where the children all wore cardboard cut-out beards in his honor, and the Bronx Zoo, where he gulped down a hot dog and an ice cream cone, and alarmed zoo guards by sticking his hand through the bars of a cage to pat the cheek of a Bengal tiger. "This is like prison—I have been in prison, too," said Fidel, who had survived Batista's cages. Even the CIA seemed charmed by Castro during his 1959 visit. After meeting with the Cuban leader in his New York hotel suite, an ecstatic CIA agent reported, "Castro is not only not a Communist, but he is a strong anticommunist fighter."

But there had been many changes over the following year, as Castro moved to deliver on the promise of the revolution, nationalizing the sugar and oil industries, and beginning to transform Cuba from a vassal state of the United States to a sovereign nation. By early 1960, Dulles had resolved the debate within his intelligence agency over Castro's true identity, deciding that he was a dedicated Communist and a serious threat to U.S. security. The CIA director's hardening line mirrored that of friends in the business world like William Pawley, the globetrotting entrepreneur whose major investments in Cuban sugar plantations and Havana's municipal transportation system were wiped out by Castro's revolution. One of a coterie of vigorously anti-Communist international businessmen who provided the CIA with foreign information and contacts, as well as guns and money, Pawley began lobbying the Eisenhower administration to take an aggressive stand against Castro when he was still fighting Batista's soldiers in the rugged peaks of the Sierra Maestra. After Fidel rode into Havana on a tank in January 1959, Pawley, who was gripped by what Eisenhower called a "pathological hatred for Castro," even volunteered to pay for his assassination. As the Eisenhower administration took an increasingly belligerent posture toward the Castro regime, Pawley found himself at the center of the action, boasting that he was "in daily touch with Allen Dulles."

The Eisenhower administration responded to Castro's expropriation of American-owned plantations, factories, and utilities by cutting imports of Cuban sugar—the country's economic lifeblood—and by launching a secret campaign aimed at sabotaging Castro's government. In February 1960, mercenary pilots hired by the CIA dropped bombs on Cuban sugar mills, and in March, a French freighter loaded with Belgian weapons was blown up in the Havana harbor, killing dozens of sailors and stevedores. A second explosion killed many more, including firefighters and emergency medical workers, as they rushed to the scene. The same month, President Eisenhower approved a plan to train a paramilitary force outside of Cuba for a future invasion of the island. The operation, which was spearheaded by Vice President Nixon and the CIA, would culminate the following year on the beaches of the Bay of Pigs.

The explosion in Havana's harbor was a milestone in the Cuban revolution. At a funeral ceremony the next day at Colon cemetery, an emotional Castro vowed that "Cuba will never become cowardly" in the face of U.S. aggression. He ended his oration with the declaration that became a ringing slogan of the Cuban revolution: *Patrio o Muerte, Venceremos!* (Motherland or Death, We Shall Win!) Determined that Cuba would not become another Guatemala, Castro turned to the Soviet Union for economic and military aid, and the tragic dance began, locking Cuba, the United States, and Russia in a fateful embrace for years to come, and nearly ending in a nuclear inferno.

When Castro and his retinue landed at New York's Idlewild Airport on September 18, 1960, he appeared to be in a "subdued mood," reported *The New York Times*, for reasons that were not yet known to the American people. The Cuban airliner that flew the delegation to the United States had to be immediately refueled and flown back to Havana, to avoid being impounded, as a result of legal claims against the revolutionary government by U.S. business interests. It was just one of the numerous ways that Castro's delegation was subjected to harassment during his weeklong visit to New York, as the Eisenhower administration maneuvered against the Cuban leader on multiple fronts. By the time his retinue was forced out of the Shelburne Hotel, Castro seemed persona non grata in New York. The State Department had ruled that the Cubans could not leave Manhattan, and no city hotel was willing to accommodate them. If New York was incapable of providing hospitality to world leaders, Castro fumed, perhaps the UN should be moved to another city, such as Havana.

But then Castro turned his humiliation into a propaganda triumph.

As the Cuban delegation was preparing to leave the Shelburne, a political sympathizer put them in touch with Black Muslim leader Malcolm X, who intervened on their behalf with the operators of Hotel Theresa. The tallest building in Harlem, the thirteen-story hotel was a lofty—if somewhat worn-down—landmark in the black community. In its heyday, the Theresa had accommodated a glittering array of African American celebrities when they were not welcome at New York's downtown hotels, including Josephine Baker, Louis Armstrong, Duke Ellington, Nat King Cole, and Lena Horne. In June 1938, Joe Louis celebrated his heavyweight championship victory over Max Schmeling, Nazi Germany's great white hope, at the Theresa, as thousands of fans cheered on the streets outside.

When word spread that the Cuban delegation was headed uptown, Love B. Woods, manager of the Theresa, immediately came under the same political pressures as other New York hotel operators. Even Harlem's outspoken congressman, Adam Clayton Powell Jr., opposed Castro's relocation to Harlem, calling it "a publicity stunt." Powell told reporters, "We Negro people have enough problems of our own without the additional burden of Dr. Castro's confusion." But Woods, an elderly and unruffled man who had grown up in Jim Crow South Carolina, knew what it was like to be denied a roof over your head. Woods stood his ground and opened the doors of Harlem's finest hotel to the Castro delegation. "We don't discriminate against anybody," he said.

Other prominent figures in Harlem also stuck out their necks for Castro. Knowing that Woods might have trouble cashing the Cubans' check because of the rising political tensions between the two countries, a Harlem attorney named Conrad Lynn arranged to have a local gambling kingpin put up $1,000 in cash to cover the delegation's hotel costs. The gangster was not "a communist or politically developed," Lynn recalled, "but something told me that this was a man, and that he wanted to help. And he did."

Young Harlem activists also rallied around Castro, like Preston Wilcox, who was among those cheering the Cuban leader outside the Theresa. Wilcox saw a "spiritual connection" between Fidel's decision to come to Harlem and the rising dynamism of the civil rights movement. He noted the color division between the opposing lines of Cubans in the crowd: the black Cubans were pro-Castro, while those loudly denouncing him were lighter-shaded. Whenever Juan Almeida, Castro's black military commander and a hero of the revolution, left the hotel during the delegation's stay and went strolling through the neighborhood, enthusiastic crowds swirled around him. The *New York Citizen-Call*, an African American newspaper, commented, "To Harlem's oppressed ghetto dwellers, Castro was that bearded revolutionary who . . . had told white America to go to hell."

Harlem's show of hospitality for Castro turned out to be a public relations disaster for the Eisenhower administration. By moving to Harlem, the Cuban leader not only shamed the U.S. government for its lack of manners but focused a sharp spotlight on the nation's seething racial tensions. Some of the city's finest hotels suddenly offered entire floors to the Cuban delegation, free of charge, but Castro refused to move. When world leaders—including Khrushchev, Nasser, and Nehru—began coming uptown to meet with Castro, with TV camera crews close behind, Washington's embarrassment only grew.

Castro's mastery of the media game was on full display during his Harlem sojourn. After Eisenhower snubbed him by not inviting him to an official reception for Latin leaders, the Cuban premier responded by inviting Theresa's all-black staff to a steak dinner in the hotel banquet room with him and the popular Almeida. When articles suddenly began appearing in New York newspapers, alleging that the Theresa was overrun with hookers, Fidel again parried the propaganda thrust, declaring in his speech at the UN, "They began spreading the news all over the world that the Cuban delegation had lodged in a brothel. For some, a humble hotel in Harlem, a hotel inhabited by Negroes of the United States, must obviously be a brothel."

By the time he delivered his speech before the UN General Assembly on September 26, Castro had seized the moral high ground in his growing war of words with Washington. His UN speech, a marathon performance that stretched for over four hours, was a passionate defense of Cuba's autonomy. For years, his colonized nation had no voice in world affairs, Castro told the international assembly. "Colonies do not speak. Colonies are not recognized in the world. That is why our [nation] and its problems were unknown to the rest of the world. . . . There was no independent republic; there was only a colony where orders were given by the ambassador of the United States." But now, at long last, Castro was giving Cuba a full-throated voice.

What had his small, impoverished nation done to so offend its powerful neighbor, asked Castro? "We instituted an agrarian reform that would solve the problems of the landless peasants, that would solve the problem of the lack of basic foodstuffs, that would solve the great unemployment problem on the land, that would end, once and for all, the ghastly misery which existed in the rural areas of our country.

"Was it radical?" asked Castro, with the rhetorical skill he had mastered as a young lawyer, when his own life was on the line in Batista's courtrooms. "It was not very radical. . . . We were not 150 percent communists at the time. We just appeared slightly pink. We were not confiscating lands. We simply proposed to pay for them in 20 years, and the only way we could afford to pay for them was by bonds—bonds which would mature in twenty years, at 4.5 percent interest, which would accumulate annually." See, Castro was telling the world, revolutionary Cuba had been willing to play by capitalist rules. But this was not enough for Washington. Cuba's new government "had been too bold. It had clashed with the international mining trusts, it had clashed with the interests of United Fruit Company, and it had clashed with the most powerful interests of the United States. So then the example shown by the Cuban revolution had to receive its punishment. Punitive actions of every type—even the destruction of Cuba's foolhardy people—had to be carried out against the audacity of the revolutionary government."

Journalist I. F. Stone pronounced Castro's oration—which he delivered, hour after hour, by consulting just a single page of notes—a "tour de force." It was unlike anything ever heard before in the United Nations: a scholarly, eloquent, and heartfelt broadside against the arrogance of imperial power, delivered in the capital of world finance, by a charismatic rebel leader who had risked his life to challenge that power. If Allen Dulles's imperial guard still had any doubts about how serious a threat Fidel Castro represented, his dramatic performance at the UN that day thoroughly dispelled them.

The CIA knew how seductive Fidel's appeal was—even in the West, particularly among college students, intellectuals, and artists. In April 1960, Robert Taber—the first African American reporter for CBS News, who had scored an exclusive interview with Castro when he was still fighting in the mountains—stirred liberal circles by purchasing a full-page ad in *The New York Times* that passionately endorsed the Cuban revolution. The appeal was signed by an impressive list of literary names—including Jean-Paul Sartre, Simone de Beauvoir, Norman Mailer, James Baldwin, and Truman Capote—and sparked a wave of popular interest in the Cuban cause that led to the formation of the Fair Play for Cuba Committee (FPCC). Within six months, the committee had enrolled seven thousand members in twenty-seven "adult chapters" across the country and had struck a chord on college campuses, where forty student councils were formed.

While Castro was staying at the Theresa, the FPCC organized a party in his honor in the hotel's shabby ballroom. Among the guests were Allen Ginsberg, Langston Hughes, and C. Wright Mills, whose own impassioned defense of the Cuban revolution, *Listen, Yankee*, had sold four hundred thousand copies within months. Mills's book was based on his brief tour of the island, including three eighteen-hour days in the indefatigable company of Fidel, a man who, in the words of his friend Gabriel García Márquez, was "addicted to the habit of conversation . . . he rests by talking."

These were the early, honeymoon days of the revolution, before Castro's *caudillo* tendencies had hardened, and before the Soviet "partnership" with Cuba had become its own kind of colonialism. The relentless U.S. pressure on the island would never succeed in toppling Castro, but it would help turn his nation into the tropical police state that CIA propagandists insisted it was from the very beginning, amounting to a victory of sorts for Washington hard-liners.

But there was still a glow around Castro as he and his retinue settled into the Hotel Theresa. It was the dawn of the 1960s, the gray Eisenhower-Dulles reign was coming to an end, and the world seemed to shimmer with new possibilities. The most electric moment of Castro's week in Harlem came one evening when Malcolm X—wearing a long, double-breasted, black leather coat and tie—swept past the press pack in the hotel lobby and was whisked to Fidel's suite on the ninth floor. Fidel invited Malcolm to sit next to him on the bed, the only comfortable oasis in a room thick with cigar smoke and crowded with aides, bodyguards, and a few specially selected members of the African American press. The two revolutionary icons seemed hesitant with each other at first, their communication made precarious by their language differences. But as Castro plunged ahead with his uncertain English, they slowly found common ground. Fidel told Malcolm that the Cubans appreciated the warm reception given them in Harlem. "I think you will find the people in Harlem are not so addicted to the propaganda they dish out downtown," Malcolm replied.

Castro's young foreign minister, Raúl Roa Kourí, later said that he thought the meeting between the two revolutionaries, though lasting only a half hour, turned out to be historically significant because it helped broaden the Black Muslim leader's narrow racial parameters. Malcolm began to understand that blacks were not the only poor and oppressed group, said Kourí, "and the struggle of all was a common struggle." Afterward, Malcolm maintained a strong interest in the Cuban revolution, saying, "The only white person that I have really liked was Fidel." He planned to visit Cuba but never had the chance.

The meeting between Fidel and Malcolm sent shudders through U.S. security circles, where a potential alliance between the Cuban revolutionary and the militant black nationalist was seen as the stuff of nightmares. Malcolm's broadening political outlook, which accelerated after his split with the Nation of Islam in 1964, made him an increasingly dangerous figure—and Kourí, among others, was convinced that it led to his assassination in 1965. By 1960, Malcolm was the target of intensive FBI surveillance. In fact, one of the people who had squeezed into Castro's hotel bedroom that evening was an undercover FBI agent, who later reported back to the bureau on the two men's conversation. According to a confidential FBI memo based on the source's report, Malcolm told Fidel that he was predisposed to like him, because "usually when one sees a man whom the United States is against, there is something good in that man."

By the time Castro came to Harlem, he, too, was the target of increasingly ominous U.S. intelligence scrutiny. Just days before the Cuban delegation checked into Hotel Theresa, Bob Maheu—on orders of the CIA—met at another Manhattan hotel with Johnny Rosselli, the handsome, silver-haired Mafia lord who presided over the underworld's Las Vegas empire, to develop a plan to assassinate Castro. Maheu and Rosselli were joined at the Plaza Hotel meeting by Jim O'Connell, Maheu's handler in the CIA security office. O'Connell posed as an American businessman who had been dispossessed by Castro's revolution and was willing to pay for his elimination. But the savvy Rosselli was not fooled: he quickly figured out that the Mafia was being recruited for a top secret government assignment.

Once again, Bob Maheu found himself at the center of a lethal CIA operation. Near the end of his life, he recalled what he went through when the CIA asked him to serve as the main emissary with the Mafia in the Castro assassination plot. Sitting with two visitors in his ranch house on the edge of a Las Vegas golf course, sipping vodka on the rocks as golf balls periodically clunked off the roof, Maheu recounted a long night of soul-searching as he wrestled with the CIA request. Shef Edwards and Jim O'Connell framed their pitch to Maheu in terms a good Catholic would understand—killing Castro was an act of "just war," they said; it would save thousands of lives. They made it clear that the execution order came from the top of the agency, from Old Man Dulles himself. Nonetheless, Maheu realized that he would "have blood on [his] hands."

To ponder the morally difficult question, Maheu went down to the recreation room in the basement of his Virginia home, where he made all of his big decisions, and listened all night long to classical music on the state-of-the-art sound system that the CIA had installed for him. In conversation with his visitors years later, Maheu tried to make it seem like his decision was a tortured process. But it actually sounded like a relative no-brainer for the security contractor. The CIA had made Bob Maheu's career—he owed everything to the agency, even the extravagant stereo system that made his Bach and Glenn Miller records sound like they were "coming out of everywhere, even the waste paper baskets." He wasn't about to give it all up to spare the life of a bearded, bombastic Cuban revolutionary. Maheu told the CIA yes. When it came down to it, he didn't mind having Castro's blood on his hands, or that of his brother Raúl Castro and Che Guevara, for that matter.

It was the beginning of a long U.S. intelligence campaign to kill the Cuban leader, stretching over several presidencies and involving untold numbers of accomplices—including mobsters, soldiers of fortune, disaffected members of the Havana regime, and security contractors like Maheu.

As Castro prepared to return home at the end of his tumultuous week in New York, he gave a spirited press conference at the airport. Why was the Cuban delegation departing on a Soviet jet, a reporter shouted? Because the United States had impounded all of Cuba's airliners as a result of claims against his government, he responded. "What do you want us to do?" Castro asked plaintively. "You leave us without petroleum—Khrushchev gives us petroleum. You [cut] our sugar [imports]—Khrushchev buys our sugar. . . . You take away our planes—Khrushchev gives us his plane."

The CIA knew what it wanted Castro to do. Shortly after the Cuban leader arrived home in Havana, as he addressed a teeming crowd from the balcony of the Presidential Palace, a bomb went off in the park behind the palace, followed by a second explosion within the hour. Later in the day, a third bomb—more powerful than the other two—rocked Havana. The CIA-sponsored terror campaign aimed at killing Castro and destroying his government was quickly escalating.

Two weeks after Fidel Castro checked out of the Hotel Theresa, another young dynamo made an appearance at the hotel. On the afternoon of October 12, 1960, Senator John F. Kennedy brought his presidential campaign to Harlem, speaking to a large crowd from a platform erected in front of the hotel. Kennedy was well aware that Castro had just put the Harlem hotel on the world map. JFK was fascinated by the charismatic Cuban, whose biography bore some resemblance to his own. Both men were the products of Catholic immigrant families who had worked their way up to wealth and success (Castro's father had immigrated from Spain); both were the second sons of shrewd, entrepreneurial fathers and devout mothers; both were educated at elite schools; and both had rejected their class privilege, dedicating themselves to improving the lives of those less fortunate and to making their countries beacons of change.

After Castro's triumph over Batista, Kennedy had warm words for the victorious revolutionary, declaring, "Fidel Castro is part of the legacy of Bolivar, who led his men over the Andes Mountains vowing 'war to the death' against Spanish rule." The young senator criticized the Eisenhower administration for not giving Castro a more friendly greeting "in his hour of triumph" when he visited Washington in April 1959.

But during the presidential campaign, Kennedy, determined not to be tarred by Nixon as soft on the global Communist threat, carved out a position on Cuba that was even more militant than the Republican candidate's, declaring that Castro had "betrayed the ideals of the Cuban revolution" and calling his regime "a Communist menace that has been permitted to arise under our very noses, only 90 miles from our shores." Kennedy went so far as to suggest that the United States should take decisive action to remove the threat. His militant campaign rhetoric evoked a heated response from Castro during his epic UN speech, who called JFK an "illiterate and ignorant millionaire" with no understanding of Cuba's plight.

In truth, Kennedy was keenly aware of Cuba's colonial history and was outspokenly critical of how U.S. business interests had despoiled the country. In the same campaign speech in which he attacked Castro as a "dangerous enemy on our very doorstep," JFK ripped into America's corporate plunder and political domination of the island in surprisingly unvarnished terms. He also denounced Washington's shameful practice of "propping up dictators throughout Latin America," including the "bloody and repressive" Batista.

Kennedy's campaign rhetoric on Cuba revealed a man who was painstakingly trying to work out the correct position for himself—and his country—on the revolutionary convulsions that were shaking the world. He did not want to appear naïve about Communist exploitation of these national liberation movements. But he was even more concerned that the United States be on the right side of history, by supporting the aspirations of the peoples of Latin America, Africa, and Asia as they threw off their colonial shackles.

On that brisk fall day outside the Hotel Theresa, where Kennedy was joined on the platform by a formidable supporting cast of Democratic dignitaries, including Eleanor Roosevelt and Congressman Powell, the presidential contender sounded more like a supporter of the bearded revolutionary in whose wake he was following than an enemy. "I am happy to come to this hotel, a little late, but I am happy to come here," he began, to loud applause from the crowd. "Behind the fact of Castro coming to this hotel, Khrushchev coming to Castro, there is another great traveler in the world, and that is the travel of a world revolution, a world in turmoil. I am delighted to come to Harlem and I think the whole world should come here and the whole world should recognize that we all live right next to each other, whether here in Harlem or on the other side of the globe. We should be glad [that Castro and Khrushchev] came to the United States. We should not fear the twentieth century, for the worldwide revolution which we see all around us is part of the original American revolution."

The man who was soon to become America's youngest elected president showed Harlem that day that he, too, could deliver a speech—perhaps with less fire than Castro, but with equal passion and vision, and a bit more wit. Declaring that America's revolutionary ideals continued to inspire people throughout the world, Kennedy said, "There are children in Africa called George Washington. There are children in Africa called Thomas Jefferson. There are none called Lenin or Trotsky or Stalin in the Congo . . . or Nixon. There may be a couple called Adam Powell," he added, to loud laughter from the audience, which was well aware of the congressman's reputation for womanizing.

America could not continue to inspire the world, Kennedy went on, unless it "practiced what it preaches" at home. "If a Negro baby is born here and a white baby is born next door, the Negro baby's chance of finishing high school is about 60 percent of the white baby. This baby's chance of getting through college is about a third of that baby's. His chance of being unemployed is four times that baby's." All that must change, JFK told the audience. "White people are a minority in the world," he said. They could no longer hold back the dreams of the rest of the world. Kennedy vowed that if he were elected, he would align America with the winds of change. "I believe it is important that the president of the United States personify the ideals of our society, speak out on this, associate ourselves with the great fight for equality."

In the next three years, as Cuba became the flaming focal point of U.S. foreign policy, Kennedy would continue to wrestle with his relationship to Castro and the revolutionary change that he represented. As president, JFK's posture on Cuba gradually softened, with the White House inching awkwardly toward a state of peaceful coexistence with the neighbor whom Kennedy once called "dangerous." The fitful process of rapprochement with Cuba would set off a turbulent reaction in Washington, particularly within the national security circles still dominated by Dulles hard-liners. In these men's minds, it was not just Havana that loomed as a hotbed of dangerous ideas, it was the Kennedy White House.

The Torch Is Passed

The cruel circus of American politics has a way of exposing a candidate's inner self, particularly the hurly-burly of congressional campaigns, where the battle is fought up close and on one's home turf. Allen Dulles briefly threw himself into the political arena in August 1938, when he declared himself a candidate in the Republican primary for the Sixteenth Congressional District, on Manhattan's Upper East Side, where he and Clover maintained a town house. Like Foster, who later ran a similarly ill-fated campaign for the U.S. Senate, Allen had a nuanced feel for power but not for politics. The brothers were imbued with a sense of public service, but in their minds, democracy was something to be saved from the demos. "Democracy works only if the so-called intelligent people make it work," Allen told the press on the eve of his campaign. "You can't sit back and let democracy run itself."

Dulles's patrician sensibility did not play well in the campaign, even with the posh Republican voters on the Upper East Side. During the race, he put together all of the right elements, like a corporate lawyer meticulously building his case. He lined up the support of prestigious Republicans, such as Elihu Root Jr., the son of Teddy Roosevelt's secretary of state, who served as his honorary campaign chairman. He secured the endorsements of the leading New York newspapers, including the *Times* and the *Herald Tribune*. And he opened up a campaign office at the Belmont Plaza Hotel, where Clover dutifully wrote several hundred letters soliciting support from women voters in the district, like a

Junior League doyenne volunteering for a favorite charity. But there was no passion in the Dulles campaign. His speeches were stilted and his debate performance was lawyerly and bloodless.

The monthlong primary campaign pitted Dulles against the incumbent, a conservative Democratic congressman named John J. O'Connor, who had cross-filed in the Republican primary after President Roosevelt announced his intention to purge O'Connor as a traitor to the New Deal. During the brief race, Dulles tried to carefully parse his attacks on the popular president, expressing sympathy with FDR's "broad social aims" while denouncing his "dictatorial attitude." But O'Connor—who had established himself as one of the more effective opponents of the New Deal in Congress—came across as a more muscular enemy of Roosevelt. And when the battle-scarred political warhorse turned his invective on Dulles, accusing him of "selling out" his country to "international interests" and Wall Street titans like J. Pierpont Morgan, Dulles could only muster a rational-sounding, but feeble, reply.

On Election Day, September 21, Dulles went down to a thumping defeat, losing the Republican nomination by a three-to-two margin to a man who did not even belong to the party. Dulles promptly returned to the world of discreet power that he knew best, never again subjecting himself to the slings and arrows of electoral combat.

On the surface, John F. Kennedy seemed similarly unsuited for the rough-and-tumble of democracy. Privileged, reserved, and physically frail, young Jack Kennedy was a far cry from his glad-handing political forebears, such as his maternal grandfather, John "Honey Fitz" Fitzgerald, the perennial Boston politician who wooed voters with his gift for song and blarney. Late into his career, JFK continued to worry that he was too introverted for politics. In January 1960, three days after declaring his presidential candidacy, Kennedy confided to friends over dinner, "I'm not a political type." In contrast to his grandfather, who "wanted to talk to everybody," added Kennedy, "I'd rather read a book on a plane than talk to the fellow next to me."

When he made his political debut in 1946, running for Congress from the Boston-Cambridge Eleventh District, the twenty-eight-year-old

Kennedy was far from a shoo-in, despite his father's wealth and connections. The sprawling district encompassed a slew of tough Irish and Italian working-class neighborhoods and slums, and the Choate- and Harvard-educated candidate seemed too aloof a character to outrun the crowded pack of experienced political pros that he faced in the Democratic primary. Joe Kennedy tried to outfit his son with the best campaign brain trust that money could buy, but JFK preferred to work with young war veterans like himself. Jack Kennedy sought out Dave Powers, an Air Force veteran who had grown up in scruffy, Irish-Catholic Charlestown and was a local political wise guy. The son of a dockworker who had died when Powers was two, leaving his widow with eight children to raise, the political operator knew the dreams and heartaches of the families crowded into the neighborhood's "three-decker" tenements. Powers ushered five masses every Sunday at St. Catherine's Church and played second base on the parish baseball team. "I knew just about everybody in Charlestown."

When Kennedy first approached him in a Charlestown tavern to ask him to join his campaign, Powers turned him down flat. A millionaire's son running for Congress in a shot-and-beer district? He didn't stand a chance. Kennedy didn't seem cut out for Boston's brawling politics. In fact, the young man—who would soon be diagnosed with Addison's disease and told that he would not live past forty-five—did not seem long for this world. As the 1946 campaign got under way, Kennedy was plagued by severe back and abdominal distress that he had suffered ever since he was a teenager and had been aggravated during his war service in the South Pacific, where he had also picked up a case of malaria. He was painfully thin and his skin had an unhealthy, yellow tinge—whether from the atabrine he took for his malaria or from his Addison's, it was unclear.

Kennedy's shy manner and boyish good looks made him seem more a poet than a politician to Powers, but he soon discovered that JFK was "aggressively shy." Even after Powers turned him down over drinks at the bar, Kennedy kept dogging him, showing up a few nights later at his family's three-decker flat and peppering him with questions. *Well, if YOU were running in the district, what would YOU do?* "He was very inquisitive. He could pick your mind."

A few days later, when Kennedy invited him to come to his first campaign appearance, Dave Powers gave in to his political destiny. JFK was addressing a group of Gold Star mothers—women who had lost sons during the war—at the Charlestown American Legion Hall. As Kennedy began to speak, a polite hush fell over the crowd. Powers stood listening in the back of the room, and at first the political operator—who was used to the stem-winding oratory of Boston legends like James Michael Curley—cringed at what he was hearing. The young candidate was painfully nervous, stuttering and visibly struggling for a way to connect with his audience. And then, it happened. Kennedy—whose own family had lost its firstborn son, Joseph Patrick Kennedy Jr., in the final days of the war—found his voice. "I was getting sort of nervous," recalled Powers years later, "and then [Jack] looked out at all these wonderful ladies and said, 'I think I know how you feel, because my mother is a Gold Star mother too.' And all the years I've been in politics, smoke-filled rooms and from Maine to Anchorage, Alaska, this reaction was unbelievable. He immediately was surrounded by all these Charlestown mothers and in the background I can hear them saying he reminds me of my own John or Joe or Pat, a loved one they had lost. Even I was overwhelmed."

After the event, as they walked back to Kennedy's hotel suite, in an old political hangout on Beacon Street, the young candidate asked Powers how he had done. "It was great," said Powers.

"And then he reached out his hand and said, 'Then will you be with me?' And I shook his hand and I was with him from that day to Dallas.'"

Kennedy went on to win the Democratic primary and the general election by landslides. He spent the rest of his life in politics, a profession he regarded as honorable and at which he displayed a unique talent, even if he never felt entirely comfortable with its showmanship. As he prepared to run for president, he expressed hope that the country was ready for a new style of politics. Perhaps you didn't have to be a back-slapping "happy warrior" like Hubert Humphrey, a leading rival for the

1960 Democratic nomination. "I just don't think you have to have that type of personality to be successful today in politics," JFK told friends, a bit wishfully, early in his campaign. "I think you have to be able to communicate a sense of conviction and intelligence and rather, some integrity. . . . Those three qualities are really it."

Every great life in politics has a theme: with John Kennedy, it was his horror of war and the endless suffering it brings. He felt it in a way that most politicians, blithely untouched by the savagery and idiocy of war, never feel it. "All war is stupid," Kennedy had written home as a naval lieutenant in the South Pacific, where he had nearly lost his own life when his PT boat was carved in two by a Japanese destroyer. The death of his older brother only confirmed his deep disgust with war. "He was very close to my brother Joe, and it was a devastating loss to him personally," recalled Senator Edward M. Kennedy, JFK's youngest brother, near the end of his life. "He was a very different person when he came back from the war. I think this burned inside of him."

Allen Dulles had also felt the personal impact of war, when his son and namesake returned from Korea irreparably damaged. But his own family tragedy provoked no deep agonizing within Dulles about war or his central role in Washington's machinery of violence. The spymaster liked to talk, in a way that sounded almost boastful, about his ability to dispatch men—including his own loyal agents—to their deaths. In contrast, during his years in the White House, Kennedy continually wrestled with ways to avoid bloodshed, again and again deflecting belligerent counsel from his national security advisers. Dulles came to see this as weakness, while Kennedy would conclude that his CIA director was a man of the past, recklessly provoking Cold War confrontations when the world was crying out for a new vision. Though it was largely hidden from the public, the duel between Kennedy and Dulles would define Washington's "deep politics" in the early 1960s.

Dulles first met Kennedy in winter 1954, while JFK was at his family's Palm Beach mansion recovering from another agonizing round of back surgery. The freshman senator from Massachusetts, who had not yet made much of a political mark, did not strike the graying Washington power fixture as the sort of man with whom he would one day cross swords. Kennedy was so enfeebled from his latest surgical ordeal—which had put him in a coma, prompting a priest to administer the last rites—that he could barely hobble a few steps. He lay in bed most days, with nurses helping to turn him, reading, and taking notes for an article that would grow into his bestselling book, *Profiles in Courage.*

From an early age, Kennedy's afflictions had given him an acute sense of his fragile mortality. "At least one half of the days that he spent on this earth," his brother Robert later observed, "were days of intense physical pain." As president, JFK came to represent the very picture of youthful vigor and political revitalization. But in private, particularly during periods of extreme physical distress, Kennedy seemed to belong as much to the afterlife as to the living. In October 1953, while relaxing on Cape Cod after their wedding, Kennedy recited his favorite poem to his new wife, Jacqueline, "I Have a Rendezvous with Death." Written by a young American poet named Alan Seeger—the uncle of folk singer Pete Seeger—before he died in battle in World War I, the poem spoke to the shadows in Kennedy's soul, even in the bloom of marriage to a beautiful and vivacious young woman:

> God knows 'twere better to be deep
> Pillowed in silk and scented down,
> Where love throbs out in blissful sleep,
> Pulse nigh to pulse, and breath to breath,
> Where hushed awakenings are dear . . .
> But I've a rendezvous with Death
> At midnight in some flaming town,
> When Spring trips north again this year,
> And I to my pledged word am true,
> I shall not fail that rendezvous.

Dulles was a frequent houseguest of the Kennedys' Palm Beach neighbors, Charles and Jayne Wrightsman. Charlie Wrightsman was a globe-trotting oil millionaire who had met his much younger wife when he was pushing fifty and she was a twenty-four-year-old department store swimsuit model. Under his bullying tutelage, Jayne Wrightsman grew into a world-renowned art collector and high society hostess who would mentor Jacqueline Kennedy during the First Lady's elaborate restoration of the White House.

Charlie Wrightsman was a blunt-spoken former oil wildcatter whose ruggedly Republican values were right out of the pages of Ayn Rand. Wrightsman and Dulles, who served as the oilman's attorney when he worked at Sullivan and Cromwell, forged a tight, mutually beneficial friendship. Wrightsman generously shared his lavish lifestyle with the less affluent Dulles, inviting the intelligence chief for frequent winter retreats at his Spanish-style estate in Palm Beach, with its Renoirs and Vermeers and its parquet floors acquired from the Palais Royal in Paris. The oil baron also sometimes enticed Dulles to join his wife and him on their yachting expeditions in the Mediterranean as well as their aviation adventures in their Learstar jet. "Jayne and I are leaving Paris on Thursday August 20 for Stavanger, Norway and points North," Wrightsman wrote Dulles in July 1953 from the Hotel du Cap d'Antibes. "If you will join us, I will promise not to mention during our entire cruise that Senator McCarthy might be the next President of the United States."

Dulles, in turn, opened doors for Wrightsman in far-flung oil capitals like Baghdad and Tripoli, providing him with introductions to ambassadors, government ministers, and sheikhs. The oilman made sure to keep the spy chief in the loop, reporting back to him on the political intrigues in Europe and the Middle East.

Clover resented the way that her husband slid so easily into the lap of luxury provided by millionaires like Wrightsman. Spending time in this gilded atmosphere brought out all of Clover's mixed feelings about the world of privilege, a world where Allen served but did not fully belong.

"The mere mention of the Wrightsmans," recalled Mary Bancroft near the end of her life, "was apt to set off one of those fights [between Dulles and his wife] when they went at each other like a pair of fighting eagles—with Clover always being defeated by Allen's stronger claws, until she retreated from the fray with feathers awry and deep wounds from those claws. It was terrible to witness how they fought."

Clover blamed the Wrightsmans for bringing out her husband's "more reprehensible characteristics," Bancroft observed, "namely . . . that he liked good food, good wine, and the chance to swim in a heated pool and afterwards to dry himself with a large, soft, expensive towel that had been warmed ahead of time 'so you won't get a shock.' Clover liked luxury herself, but she certainly fought this 'weakness' tooth and nail and was always forcing herself to do uncomfortable and unpleasant things that she thought 'good for the soul,' like the most rigid of the Puritan fathers."

It was the Wrightsmans who introduced the Dulleses to young Jack Kennedy. Charlie Wrightsman was no fan of the New Dealer Joe Kennedy, but he and his wife found themselves charmed by Jack and Jackie, who seemed to have the air of American royalty. Years later, after JFK was dead, Dulles recalled the day in early 1954 that he met the young senator. Invited by Joe Kennedy to drop by the family's Palm Beach home while he was staying with the Wrightsmans, Dulles first came upon JFK as he was flat on his back. "He was suffering a good deal of pain, and he was lying on the sofa there in the study in Joe Kennedy's house," Dulles remembered, "and that was the first time that I saw him." As the two men discussed various international hot spots, JFK would get up from time to time, wincing with pain, and gingerly walk a few paces before returning to the sofa. "He obviously wanted to learn," said Dulles.

On another occasion, JFK was invited to dinner at the Wrightsmans' when both Dulles brothers were in attendance. "Jack Kennedy was quite a modest man in those days," recalled the CIA chief. "I remember my brother was there [and] I don't say [Kennedy] was overawed, but he was very respectful."

Thus began a relationship that Dulles regarded as tutorial—the education of a promising young man who had the proper regard for his elders. "He was always trying to get information—I don't mean secrets or things of that kind, particularly, but to get himself informed. He wanted to get my views, and when my brother was there, his views on what we thought about things, and we had many, many talks together." This, in Dulles's mind, was the proper order of things—Kennedy as prince and acolyte and the Dulles brothers as court regents.

If Dulles's attitude toward young Kennedy was condescending, his wife was awed. Clover's first real opportunity to become acquainted with JFK came in August 1955, when she and Allen were vacationing with the Wrightsmans on the beaches of southern France. "At Antibes, we did the usual thing," Clover wrote to Allen Jr., "sitting in the cabana, swimming, eating good meals at good restaurants." But the most memorable occasion, she wrote, took place when they dined with the Kennedy clan, who were also on holiday in France. "Joe Kennedy's son, the Senator, was there. He is 36 [actually he was 38], but looks no older than a college boy, is nice looking and so straight forward, sincere, intelligent and attractive and likeable that I haven't been so enthusiastic about anybody for ages." The aging Dulles, who still regarded himself as something of a ladies' man, must have found his wife's schoolgirl crush on the young senator somewhat unnerving. But JFK also brought out tender, motherly feelings in Clover, calling to mind her own disabled son. "We talked of you," Clover wrote Allen Jr., "for he too was wounded and only last winter had some operation on his back so that he was on crutches." Talking with the bright, boyishly handsome, and attentive senator must have reminded Clover of what could have been if her own son had not been so badly hurt in Korea.

The Dulles brothers were slow to realize that if young Senator Kennedy was their pupil, he was an increasingly rebellious one. Kennedy began questioning the rigid Cold War paradigm that dominated Washington policy-making as early as 1951, when he undertook a fact-finding mission to Asia while still a congressman. His stopover in Vietnam, where the French colonial regime was struggling to put down a growing national rebellion led by Ho Chi Minh, made a particularly deep impression on Kennedy. When he landed in Saigon, the U.S. congressman with the prominent family name was immediately swarmed by French officials, but he slipped away and met with independent-thinking diplomats and journalists. Saigon was a city on the edge when JFK arrived in October 1951, with explosions rumbling in the distance, French agents whisking suspects off the streets at night, and headless bodies found floating in the Saigon River by morning. At the rooftop restaurant of the Hotel Majestic, overlooking the gaslit, Parisian-tinged streets below, Kennedy met with an astute American embassy officer named Edmund Gullion. The diplomat told the inquisitive congressman that the French would never win. He said that Ho Chi Minh—who had once worked as a baker at JFK's favorite Boston hotel, the Parker House, and who was inspired by the blazing ideals of the American Revolution—was seen as a national hero. Ho had awakened thousands of his fellow Vietnamese, who would rather die than continue to live under their French colonial masters.

By April 1954, when Kennedy stood up on the Senate floor to challenge the Eisenhower administration's support for the doomed French war in Vietnam, he had become an informed critic of Western imperialism. Even as France headed toward its Waterloo at Dien Bien Phu that spring, the Eisenhower administration insisted that massive U.S. military aid and firepower could help turn the tide for the embattled French forces. But, as Kennedy told the U.S. Senate, "to pour money, materiel and men into the jungle of Indochina . . . would be dangerously futile and self-destructive." The young senator had a much firmer grasp of the realities of national insurgencies than Eisenhower and his aging secretary of state. "I am frankly of the belief that no amount of American military assistance in Indochina can conquer an enemy which is everywhere and at the same time nowhere, 'an enemy of the people' which has the sympathy and covert support of the people." History would soon prove him right.

Kennedy had an instinctive sympathy for the downtrodden subjects of imperial powers, one that was rooted in his Irish heritage. His political rhetoric often reverberated with extra passion when he addressed the subject of popular uprisings against imperial rule.

In July 1957, Kennedy once more took a strong stand against French colonialism, this time France's bloody war against Algeria's independence movement, which again found the Eisenhower administration on the wrong side of history. Rising on the Senate floor, two days before America's Independence Day, Kennedy declared,

> The most powerful single force in the world today is neither communism nor capitalism, neither the H-bomb nor the guided missile—it is man's eternal desire to be free and independent. The great enemy of that tremendous force of freedom is called, for want of a more precise term, imperialism—and today that means Soviet imperialism and, whether we like it or not, and though they are not to be equated, Western imperialism. Thus, the single most important test of American foreign policy today is how we meet the challenge of imperialism, what we do to further man's desire to be free. On this test more than any other, this nation shall be critically judged by the uncommitted millions in Asia and Africa, and anxiously watched by the still hopeful lovers of freedom behind the Iron Curtain. If we fail to meet the challenge of either Soviet or Western imperialism, then no amount of foreign aid, no aggrandizement of armaments, no new pacts or doctrines or high-level conferences can prevent further setbacks to our course and to our security.

Kennedy's speech was a bold challenge to the Eisenhower-Dulles worldview, which interpreted all international events through the prism of the Cold War, and allowed no space for developing nations to pursue their own path to progress. Breaking from the Cold War orthodoxy that prevailed in the Democratic as well as Republican parties, JFK suggested that Soviet expansionism was not the only enemy of world freedom; so, too, were the forces of Western imperialism that crushed the legitimate aspirations of people throughout the Third World.

Kennedy's thinking about the historical imperative of Third World liberation was remarkably advanced. Even today, no nationally prominent leader in the United States would dare question the imperialistic policies that have led our country into one military nightmare after another. Kennedy understood that Washington's militant opposition to the world's revolutionary forces would only reap "a bitter harvest." If the United States stifled these legitimate forces of national self-determination, he said, then rising generations around the globe would be left with a grim choice "between radicalism and feudalism."

Kennedy's Algeria speech was a political bombshell. Ike sounded off about JFK's speech at a cabinet meeting, sourly commenting, "That's fine—everybody likes independence. We can all make brilliant speeches. But these things are rather difficult problems, and maybe somebody ought to make a speech to remind the senator that they're not so easy." Eisenhower began referring to Kennedy as "that little bastard." Meanwhile, Secretary Dulles icily told the press that if the senator from Massachusetts wanted to crusade against imperialism, maybe he should target the Soviet variety.

JFK brushed aside the Eisenhower and Dulles criticisms as predictable croaks from Washington's ancien régime. Kennedy had little respect for Eisenhower, seeing him as a disengaged leader who would rather play golf with his millionaire cronies than confront the world's emerging new realities. "I could understand if he played golf all the time with old Army friends," Kennedy once told Arthur Schlesinger, "but no man is less loyal to his old friends than Eisenhower. He is a terribly cold man. All his golfing pals are rich men he has met since 1945." As for Foster, Kennedy dismissed him as an aging pontificator who saw the world through slogans—simplistic axioms like "godless Communism" and "Soviet master plan" that seemed increasingly "false . . . or irrelevant to the new phase of competitive coexistence in which we live."

While Kennedy's denunciation of French colonialism in Algeria brought sharp rebukes at home—even from Democratic standard-bearers like Adlai Stevenson, who called it "terrible," and *The New York Times*, which found the speech insufficiently "delicate"—it stirred hopes overseas, particularly in Africa, a continent swept by the anticolonial tempest. Dignitaries from African countries began calling regularly on Kennedy at his Capitol Hill offices, praising him for his "courageous position" on Algeria (in the words of an Angolan revolutionary). One of the senator's aides had to spend much of her time trying to find housing in segregated Washington for the steady stream of African visitors.

If Room 362 of the Senate Office Building was becoming a center of African aspiration, the Eisenhower administration remained a reactionary bastion. The president and his top advisers were convinced that the African people were not ready to take responsibility for their own affairs, and that any revolutionary mischief on the continent would only play into Communist hands. At one National Security Council meeting, Vice President Nixon observed, "Some of the peoples of Africa have been out of trees for only about 50 years," to which Budget Director Maurice Stans (who would later serve as President Nixon's commerce secretary) replied that he "had the impression that many Africans still belonged in trees." The president did nothing to elevate the discussion, remarking with assurance that in Africa "man's emotions still have control over his intelligence." On other occasions, Eisenhower expressed resentment when he had to invite "those niggers"—by which he meant African dignitaries—to diplomatic receptions.

But by spring 1959, the Eisenhower-Dulles regime was coming to an end. Foster was rapidly declining, as the colon cancer he had been fighting since 1956 spread throughout his body. On April 11, Allen, who was vacationing at the Wrightsmans' in Palm Beach at the time, was summoned by his brother to the nearby Hobe Sound estate of State Department undersecretary C. Douglas Dillon, where Foster was resting between hospital visits. Allen found a gaunt-looking Foster in bed, writing a letter of resignation on one of the yellow legal pads that he always kept close at hand. "I could see that my brother was in great pain," Allen later remembered. "He told me that he felt the time had come for him to resign, and he wanted me to go to see the president and persuade the president to accept his resignation."

Allen chartered a plane and flew to Augusta, Georgia, where Eisenhower was staying in his "little White House" on the carpeted greenery of the famed golf course. At first, the president refused to accept Foster's resignation—a gesture of respect for the secretary of state's centrality in the administration that Allen would always appreciate. But Foster, whose resignation was effective April 22, was soon forced to return to Walter Reed Hospital in Washington, where he died just after dawn on May 24, 1959, at age seventy-one.

Foster's implacable Cold War philosophy remained stiffly intact to the very end, as he brushed aside narcotic painkillers and went stoically to his death. The one burst of passion in his businesslike resignation letter came when he reminded Eisenhower of their long struggle against the "formidable and ruthless challenge from international Communism," an evil force that had made it "manifestly difficult" for their administration to "avoid the awful catastrophe of war." In his deathbed conversations with his brother and other close administration officials, Foster urged them to continue steering a vigilant course, warning them not to be bewitched by the enemy's siren songs of peace. Nixon dutifully took notes while listening to his mentor's parting words of wisdom. So did Foster's younger brother.

"Foster had only days, maybe hours, to live, and he knew it," Allen wrote. "Speech came hard as the cancer gripped him. I saw there was something very special he wished to tell me. Every word of what he said was a struggle and cost pain. This was his last legacy to me."

Foster's final testament, as recorded by Allen, was a remarkable war cry, undimmed by pain or the creeping fog of death—it was a gift of forged steel from a dying knight to his loyal brother-in-arms. Remember, Foster told his younger brother, America was facing "no ordinary antagonist. . . . The Soviets sought not a place in the sun, but the sun itself. Their objective was the world." Somehow, the American people must "be brought to understand the issues, their responsibilities and the need for American leadership anywhere, maybe even everywhere, in the world. This is what my brother said to me on that May day. This was his last message to me."

To defeat relentless Communism and to project U.S. power "everywhere in the world"—Allen Dulles was determined to continue pursuing his brother's holy war. But with Foster buried at Arlington National Cemetery, the younger Dulles had lost his principal Washington ally.

Allen had never been as close to Eisenhower as Foster. The president had given his CIA director a long leash, but he never felt fully confident in his judgment. The relationship between the two men would sharply fracture in May 1960 when a high-flying U-2 spy plane operated by the CIA was shot down over the Soviet Union—sabotaging an upcoming summit meeting with Khrushchev and ruining Eisenhower's final chance for a Cold War breakthrough. Eisenhower was agonizingly aware of the political risks he was taking by authorizing the U-2 spy missions over Soviet territory, calling his on-again, off-again approval for the surveillance flights one of the most "soul-searching questions to come before a president." But Dulles had repeatedly assured Eisenhower that the high-altitude spy planes were safe from Russian antiaircraft missiles.

On May 1, the president found out his CIA director's assurances were hollow, when a Soviet missile slammed into a U-2 plane flying over Russia's Ural Mountains, resulting in the downing of the aircraft and the capture of CIA pilot Francis Gary Powers. The flight on the eve of the Paris Summit seemed so badly timed and planned that at least one close observer, Air Force colonel L. Fletcher Prouty, suspected that the CIA had intentionally provoked the incident in order to ruin the peace conference and ensure the continued reign of Dulles dogmatism. Prouty, a liaison officer between the Pentagon and the CIA who was summoned by Dulles whenever CIA spy flights ran into trouble, later wrote that the U-2 shootdown was "a most unusual event" that grew out of a "tremendous underground struggle [between] the peacemakers led by President Eisenhower" and the Dulles "inner elite."

John Eisenhower, who was generally reluctant to give his father advice, was so disturbed by the deceitful way that Dulles handled the U-2 affair that he urged Ike to fire him. The president erupted at his son, "yelling at the top of his voice for me to drop dead." But the younger Eisenhower sensed that his father's rage came from the realization that he should have fired Dulles long before. The president told White House aides Andrew Goodpaster and Gordon Gray that he never wanted to set eyes on Dulles again.

In the final days of his presidency, Eisenhower was presented with yet another set of recommendations for getting Allen Dulles's CIA under control, this time by the President's Board of Consultants on Foreign Intelligence Activities, which urged the spy agency to de-emphasize the cloak-and-dagger adventures of which Dulles was so fond in favor of intelligence gathering and analysis. But it was far too late for Eisenhower to do anything about his spymaster and the parallel government that he seemed to run. "I've tried," Ike told Gray. "I cannot change Allen Dulles."

At a meeting of national security advisers convened in the White House to consider the panel's reform proposals, Dulles brushed aside any suggestion that his management of the CIA was flawed. It would be folly for him to delegate any responsibility for running the agency, he insisted. Without his leadership, the country's intelligence apparatus would be "a body floating in thin air."

Dulles's display of arrogance at last triggered an explosive reaction from Eisenhower. He had delegated far too much of his presidency to the Dulles brothers, and he suspected that history would not be kind to him. In a scolding tone, the president told Dulles that the CIA was badly organized and badly run—and as commander in chief, he had been utterly powerless to do anything about it, despite one blue-ribbon presidential task force after the next. He would leave the next president a "legacy of ashes," Eisenhower bitterly remarked.

Dulles had little reason to take Eisenhower's words to heart. He had already ensured his continued reign in the incoming Kennedy administration.

As the 1960 presidential election approached its climax, JFK's criticisms of Eisenhower-Dulles foreign policy grew sharper, focusing on the Republican administration's irresponsible record of nuclear brinksmanship as well as its disquieting ignorance of international affairs. (Foster, who had little interest in the world beyond the central poles of power, once mixed up Tunisia and Indonesia, and his State Department staff had a difficult time distinguishing between Niger and Nigeria.) But Allen Dulles did not let Kennedy's often cutting campaign rhetoric disrupt their relationship. Dulles knew that the race between Kennedy and Nixon would be close. He was confident of his continued command of the CIA if the Republican candidate, a longtime disciple of the Dulles brothers, won the November election. But Dulles realized that if his job were to survive a Democratic presidential victory, Kennedy would require more charm and effort on his part.

During JFK's run for the White House, Dulles received inside reports on the Kennedy camp from a number of mutual friends, including Charlie Wrightsman and Mary Bancroft. Wrightsman, whose Kennedy ties seemed to trump his Republican values, reported to Dulles on the growing confidence within the Kennedy family circle as the election neared. Meanwhile, Dulles's former mistress, who met John and Robert Kennedy through her Democratic Party activism in New York City politics, became increasingly smitten with JFK. In July 1959, Bancroft wrote Kennedy a gushing letter after meeting him at a New York political gathering, vowing that she would support his ambitions "all of the way—and not just for '60—but forever."

Dulles and Kennedy engaged in a careful minuet during the 1960 campaign. Both men knew they belonged to different political worlds, but there was some social overlap between their circles, and neither man saw any reason to antagonize the other. Kennedy knew that Dulles ruled a powerful empire that could help or hurt his campaign, and he made an effort to stay in the spymaster's good graces, going as far as to add his late brother's name to the "honorable roster" of political heroes Kennedy wrote about in *Profiles in Courage*.

It was Jackie Kennedy who tipped off Dulles to the pleasures of James Bond, giving him a copy of *From Russia with Love*, which became one of his favorite spy novels. After he got hooked on Ian Fleming, the CIA director would send copies of new Bond novels to the senator and his wife as soon as he got his hands on them.

In typical fashion, Dulles played both sides of the 1960 presidential campaign, currying favor with Kennedy as well as Nixon. On July 23, the CIA director met with the Democratic candidate at the Kennedy family compound in Hyannis Port to give him an intelligence briefing. After the election, Nixon charged that Dulles had given his opponent an unfair advantage at this meeting by briefing JFK about the CIA's plans for a paramilitary invasion of Cuba. In his memoir, *Six Crises*, Nixon accused Kennedy of using this inside information to straitjacket him on the Cuba issue. When JFK demanded militant action on Cuba on the eve of the final presidential debate, Nixon—who could not reveal that the administration was indeed secretly planning such a course—was forced to take a cautionary posture, chiding Kennedy for his "dangerously irresponsible recommendations."

Dulles later strongly denied Nixon's accusation, insisting that he did not brief Kennedy about the Bay of Pigs operation until after the election. But his denial had a slippery feel to it. "Nixon indicated he thought he'd been double-crossed," Dulles told former CIA colleague Tom Braden in 1964. "I said this is all a misunderstanding because *as far as I know* President Kennedy did not know about the training—*from me anyway* [italics added]. . . . He didn't know anything about it from me, until after the election took place." Dulles did not spell out whether any other CIA official might have tipped off Kennedy on the CIA chief's authorization.

If Dulles used his Kennedy briefings to win points with the Democratic nominee, he also used these private sessions to gain inside information for the Nixon camp. On a Saturday evening in September 1960, Robert Kennedy—his brother's notoriously aggressive campaign manager—phoned Dulles at home, interrupting a dinner he was hosting, to inform the CIA director that Jack wanted another intelligence briefing on Monday morning at his Georgetown home. It was the kind of brusque request that CIA officials would grow used to receiving from Bobby, who was not known for his patience or ingratiating manners when his brother's pressing needs were at stake. Dulles was not used to being summoned in so peremptory a fashion, particularly by political operatives like Bobby Kennedy, who was more than three decades his junior. But, still eager to please the Kennedys, he showed up at JFK's town house at the appointed hour.

When the presidential candidate, who was meeting with Senator Albert Gore Sr. of Tennessee at the time, kept the CIA director waiting, Dulles did not complain—and he even graciously allowed another waiting guest, a minor Middle Eastern prince, to see Kennedy before him. But after Dulles's half-hour meeting with the Democratic nominee, the spymaster promptly sent a memo about their conversation to Andy Goodpaster in the White House, knowing that Eisenhower's staff would certainly relay it to the Nixon campaign.

The September 21 Dulles memo focused on the U-2 controversy, of which Kennedy had already made a campaign issue. The CIA director, who was acutely aware of his responsibility for the crisis and how it was being exploited by the Democrats, informed Goodpaster that JFK asked him for his reaction to *Countdown for Decision*, a new book by retired Army general J. B. Medaris that was sharply critical of the Eisenhower administration's handling of the U-2 affair. "As I mentioned to you," Dulles wrote the White House aide in a follow-up memo a few days later, "I have reason to believe that this book will be cited in the campaign in view of certain statements which were made to me by Senator Kennedy when I briefed him last Monday."

Despite Dulles's efforts to help the vice president by informing on the Kennedy campaign, Nixon continued to hold a grudge about the CIA chief's duplicity. Until the end of his Washington career, Nixon would harbor suspicions about the CIA and its political treachery. Nixon, who had carried water for the Dulles brothers ever since the Alger Hiss affair, had expected the spymaster's uncompromising support in his run for the White House. But Dulles was not concerned with personal or political loyalties. By playing both sides of the closely contested 1960 race, Dulles ensured that he would be the victor, no matter who won.

On Wednesday evening, November 9, the day after JFK's breathtakingly close victory, the president-elect and several members of his inner circle sipped cocktails in the living room at Hyannis Port, recovering from their all-night ordeal and savoring the hard-won moment. At one point, the group of insiders began discussing what

Kennedy should do first as president. The group was keenly aware of the historical turning point and of the unique opportunities open to JFK with his generational changing of the guard. The first thing he should do, suggested one insider, is fire J. Edgar Hoover. While he was at it, said another, Kennedy should get rid of Allen Dulles. Both men were symbols of a reactionary past—and there was something sinister about their interminable reigns. A relaxed Kennedy encouraged the free-flowing conversation, and the guests retired to their rooms at the compound that night under the impression that the new president was in step with their recommendations. But the next morning, they were unpleasantly surprised to read in the daily papers that Kennedy had already announced that he was retaining both Hoover and Dulles.

Kennedy later explained to Arthur Schlesinger that, considering his slim margin of victory, he didn't feel that he had sufficient political capital to uproot two Washington pillars like Hoover and Dulles. Jettisoning these "national icons," as Schlesinger described them, would have provoked a sharp backlash from the influential network of allies that they had accumulated in the Washington bureaucracy and among the Georgetown and Manhattan chattering classes.

Schlesinger, ever eager to put Kennedy's actions in the best possible light, later called JFK's decision to include prominent Republicans in his administration—such as Dulles and C. Douglas Dillon, who was appointed Treasury chief—part of the youthful president-elect's "strategy of reassurance." The Harvard historian played a unique role in Kennedy's life: special assistant to the president, political adviser, court chronicler, and liaison to the liberal and intellectual circles with which JFK had a complicated and often prickly relationship. "Here's Arthur," JFK wryly remarked one evening, as his adviser joined a casual staff gathering in the Oval Office. "He used to be a liberal. Maybe he can explain why they do these crazy things." The bow-tied, bespectacled scholar seemed an unlikely member of the New Frontier inner circle, where handsome men of action—the kind who could throw a long, tight spiral and skipper a sailboat—dominated. But Kennedy had a respectful if sometimes teasing relationship with Schlesinger, often using him as a sounding board for new ideas and appointments that he was considering, as well as a voice of conscience.

When Schlesinger communicated to Kennedy liberals' growing concerns about his political appointments, the president told him he understood, "but they shouldn't worry. What matters is the program." JFK assured his adviser that his policies would be solidly liberal, no matter who held positions in his administration. Besides, said Kennedy, he had given men like Dulles only a temporary reprieve—they would be gone soon enough. "We'll have to go with this for a year or so. Then I would like to bring in some new people." But Kennedy was not naïve about the workings of Washington power. After a thoughtful pause, he added, "I suppose it may be hard to get rid of these people once they are in."

Kennedy already knew the man he wanted to replace Dulles—tall, brainy Richard M. Bissell Jr., the Groton- and Yale-educated chief of clandestine operations for the CIA. Bissell, a popular member of the Georgetown set, had managed to survive the political fallout from the U-2 disaster, even though he was in charge of the spy-in-the-sky program. With his impressive academic credentials, which included a degree from the London School of Economics, and his grasp of the latest surveillance technology, Bissell struck JFK as a man of the future.

In February, soon after Kennedy's inauguration, Dulles organized a well-lubricated mixer for his top CIA men and Kennedy's White House team at the Alibi Club, his favorite Washington watering hole. The venerable gentlemen's club—located in an old brick town house that had changed little since the days of its founding, in the muttonchop era of President Chester A. Arthur—catered to an exclusive membership list, including Supreme Court justices, Joint Chiefs chairmen, and former presidents. After breaking the ice with "a pleasant three-cocktail dinner," as one guest described it, the CIA men got up, one at a time, to explain their mysterious roles to the White House aides. Dulles himself was used to dominating these occasions. But on this evening, it was Bissell who took the spotlight. Dulles's deputy introduced himself by saying, "I'm your basic man-eating shark," an opening "with just the right mix of bravado and self-mockery to charm the New Frontiersmen," as historian Evan Thomas observed.

The president made no secret of his plan to shake up the CIA and to replace Dulles with his number two man. Kennedy's father had served on the foreign intelligence advisory board that had urged Eisenhower to overhaul the management of the spy agency. Joseph P. Kennedy had made his son fully aware of Dulles's dangerously unsupervised management style. After the November election, a member of Kennedy's transition team, aware of his low opinion of the CIA's leadership, asked him, "There must be someone you really trust within the intelligence community. Who is that?" Kennedy could think of only one man. "Richard Bissell," he answered.

But Allen Dulles had no intention of relinquishing power anytime soon, not even to one of his right-hand men like Bissell. To Dulles, the Kennedy transition was just one more seasonal Washington cycle that had to be finessed. In the days leading up to Kennedy's inauguration, the press was filled with stories about all the fresh new faces in Washington. But many of the Kennedy appointments had closer ties to the Dulles old guard than they did to the new president.

Among them was McGeorge Bundy, the owlish Harvard dean whom Kennedy appointed national security adviser. The long ties between Dulles and the Boston Brahmin Bundy family had been fortified when the CIA director rescued Mac Bundy's brother, CIA officer Bill Bundy, from Joe McCarthy's pyre. Mac Bundy regarded Dulles as a benevolent uncle, maintaining a warm correspondence with him that lasted until the end of the elder man's life. When Bundy became dean of Harvard's Faculty of Arts and Sciences in 1953—at age thirty-four, the youngest in the school's history—he used his post to identify future prospects for the CIA among the student body's best and brightest. Dulles could be assured that with Mac Bundy in the White House— and with his brother Bill moving to Kennedy's Defense Department, where the press dubbed him "the Pentagon's secretary of state"—the CIA director had eyes and ears in two of the most important command posts in the Kennedy administration.

Kennedy's New Frontier was laced throughout with other Dulles loyalists, especially in the foreign service and national security agencies. General Lyman Lemnitzer, the chairman of the Joint Chiefs of Staff whom Kennedy inherited from Eisenhower, had a long partnership with Dulles, going back to their wartime intrigues in Operation Sunrise. Kennedy's choice for secretary of state, Dean Rusk, was well known to the Dulles brothers from their membership in the Council on Foreign Relations and the Rockefeller Foundation, where Rusk served as president and Foster as a trustee. Rusk's State Department continued to be filled with Dulles men and women, including Eleanor Dulles herself, who remained at the German affairs desk. Even Jackie Kennedy's social secretary, Letitia Baldrige, had worked for the CIA in the early 1950s, specializing in psychological warfare. The "doyenne of decorum" had also served as an assistant to Dulles's close ally, Ambassador Clare Booth Luce, in the U.S. embassy in Rome.

Dulles was confident enough that the Dulles era would continue under JFK that he made boasts to that effect on the Washington dinner party circuit, within full earshot of Kennedy loyalists. Shortly after Kennedy took office, the painter William Walton, a close friend of JFK and Jackie, found himself at a gathering at Walter Lippmann's house where Dulles was a fellow guest. "After dinner, the men sat around awhile in an old-fashioned way, and [Dulles] started boasting that he was still carrying out his brother Foster's foreign policy. He said, you know, that's a much better policy. I've chosen to follow that one." Walton, who loathed the CIA boss, couldn't believe Dulles's audacity. The spymaster knew that Walton was one of Kennedy's inner circle, but he felt no need to hold his tongue. Dulles was clearly sending the new president a message—and Kennedy's close friend duly delivered it. Early the next morning, Walton phoned JFK at the White House and reported what Dulles had told Lippmann and his guests. "God damn it!" swore Kennedy. "Did he really say that?"

"The torch has been passed to a new generation of Americans," Kennedy declared in his inaugural address. But, in fact, the Dulles old guard was deeply reluctant to give up power to the New Frontier team. In fact, the power struggle between the new president and his CIA director started before Kennedy was even sworn in, when Dulles took advantage of the transition period to carry out a brazen act of insubordination.

Patrice Lumumba was fleeing for his life. Sworn in less than six months earlier as the Congo's first democratically elected leader, following the end of Belgium's brutal colonial rule, Lumumba was now on the run from the CIA-backed Congolese military forces that had deposed him. Lumumba had broken free from house arrest in the capital, Leopoldville, on the evening of November 27, 1960. He was now making his way through a tropical downpour across the countryside to Stanleyville, a bastion of loyal nationalism some 750 miles to the east, where he hoped to raise an army and reclaim his office. Lumumba was driven in a new blue Peugeot, with his wife, Pauline Opango, and their two-year-old son, Roland, part of a three-car convoy that included other high officials from his toppled government.

The election of Lumumba in June 1960 had electrified the Congo, a nation that had been enslaved and plundered by its Belgian rulers for over three-quarters of a century. In the late nineteenth century, King Leopold II had carved an empire out of this benighted African territory through a system of forced labor so vicious that Joseph Conrad modeled the colonial nightmare in his novel *Heart of Darkness* on it, calling Leopold's rape of the Congo "the vilest scramble for loot that ever disfigured the history of human conscience." The hands chopped from the arms of Congolese men who refused to work under their colonial masters' yoke became a world symbol of Belgium's vile rule. After Leopold, the looting of Congo continued, with rubber and ivory being replaced by gold, diamonds, copper, and tin as the objects of Western desire. Global mining companies turned the mineral-rich African nation into their private jewelry box, with huge fortunes amassed in Brussels, London, and New York.

But Patrice Lumumba's election threatened this long reign of greed. Lumumba, a slender, graceful man with glasses and a trim mustache and goatee, looked more like the postal clerk he had once been (one of the few civil service jobs open to Africans under Belgian rule) than a fiery nationalist leader. But he spoke with a heartfelt eloquence that dazzled his followers and alarmed his enemies.

On June 30, the Congo's independence was formally celebrated in the flag-draped National Palace in Leopoldville. King Baudouin of Belgium, a young monarch who never fully took to his role, and would become known as "the sad king," delivered a fatuous speech, praising his royal predecessors for bestowing the "fabric of civilization" on the primitive nation. The handsome king, who wore a white colonial uniform and round spectacles that gave him the wide-eyed look of silent screen comedian Harold Lloyd, seemed oblivious to the country's shameful past. It fell to Lumumba, who followed the king to the microphone, to set him straight. The Congo's colonial history, said the new prime minister, was "much too painful to be forgotten." Lumumba spoke passionately about his people's struggle against "the humiliating bondage forced upon us"—years that were "filled with tears, fire and blood." But he ended on a hopeful note, vowing, "We shall show the world what the black man can do when working in liberty, and we shall make the Congo the pride of Africa."

Lumumba's ardent remarks lifted up the Congolese people, who danced in the streets of the capital to celebrate their freedom. But King Baudouin and the other Western representatives who attended the independence ceremony were insulted by the prime minister's frank remarks. Lumumba had "marred the ceremonies," sniffed the *New York Times* correspondent.

After Lumumba's Independence Day speech, national security officials in Washington and Brussels—who were already monitoring the rise of the charismatic Congolese leader—began regarding him as a serious threat to Western interests in the region. More than his defiant rhetoric, it was Lumumba's refusal to be bought off by the multinational corporations controlling the Congo's wealth that undoubtedly sealed his fate. In speeches to his followers, Lumumba opened a door on the corrupt backroom dealings that continued to dominate African capitals in the neocolonial era. The United States, he declared, was rubbing its hands over the Congo's uranium deposits—the same deposits that supplied the uranium for the bombs dropped on Hiroshima and Nagasaki. Speaking to dinner guests at a political event in October 1960, Lumumba said that he could have made millions of dollars if he had been willing to "mortgage the national sovereignty."

Dulles, Doug Dillon (then serving as a State Department undersecretary), and William Burden, the U.S. ambassador to Belgium, led the charge within the Eisenhower administration to first demonize and then dispose of Lumumba. All three men had financial interests in the Congo. The Dillon family's investment bank handled the Congo's bond issues. Dulles's old law firm represented the American Metal Company (later AMAX), a mining giant with holdings in the Congo, and Dulles was friendly with the company's chairman, Harold Hochschild, and his brother and successor, Walter, who served in the OSS during the war. Ambassador Burden was a company director, and Frank Taylor Ostrander Jr., a former U.S. intelligence official, served the Hochschild brothers as a political adviser.

Corporate executives with major stakes in Africa were able to mingle and confer with U.S. national security officials at prestigious organizations like the Manhattan-based Africa-America Institute. The institute, which Harold Hochschild helped launch in 1953, sponsored the American education of future generations of African leaders, a goal the CIA found strategically valuable enough to help fund the group. Years later, after the Africa-America Institute was exposed as a CIA front, Hochschild appeared chagrinned when the subject came up with his son, Adam. The younger Hochschild cofounded *Mother Jones* magazine and later authored *King Leopold's Ghost,* a powerful indictment of the Belgian reign of terror in the Congo. After the CIA ties to the institute were exposed, Hochschild fils later recalled, "[Father] seemed uncomfortable. He defended the link, saying that in its early years there was nowhere else the institute could have gotten enough money for its work. But he was clearly embarrassed that the whole thing had to be kept secret."

The Eisenhower administration's increasingly militant policy toward

Lumumba took shape over cocktails in clublike environments such as the Africa-America Institute and the Council on Foreign Relations. The men driving the policy had little feel for the suffering or longing of the Congolese people. Ambassador Burden was a Vanderbilt heir—a big, paunchy, high-society boozer who was stuffed full of the imbecilities and prejudices of his caste; he was not fond of Jews, and he treated his legions of nameless servants as if they were indentured. Not particularly bright, he represented what his granddaughter, Wendy, would later call the "dead end gene pool." Everything was "marvelous," in Burden's world. He said it "the way a character in a Fitzgerald novel would," Wendy Burden recalled in a family memoir. "*Mah-velous.* He said it about a hundred times a day, as if it were the only adjective that could aptly describes the talents of a chef, or the plate of Belon oysters before him, or the Chateau Petrus he was drinking, or how he felt about the overthrow of the Libyan government."

Burden, who had acquired his ambassadorship by contributing heavily to the 1956 Eisenhower campaign, spent his days in Brussels attending diplomatic receptions, where he soaked up the finest Champagnes along with the racial prejudices of Belgium's shriveling empire. It was the ambassador who first raised alarms about the rising Patrice Lumumba, whom the Belgians only yesterday were calling "a dirty monkey" but now were labeling "Satan." Burden began sending agitated cables to Dulles in Washington well before Lumumba's election, suggesting that the growing aspirations of the Congolese people were Soviet-inspired and urging that strong measures be used to put down African unrest. "Dear Allan [*sic*]," Burden wrote in a November 1959 cable, misspelling his chum's name, "Have your organization and [the Department of] Defense done much work recently in studying the type of rioting which is occurring and might occur in the various countries of Africa [and] the degree to which new weapons, such as some of the newer gases, might enable such difficulties to be controlled?" By the following summer, Burden was cabling Washington "to destroy Lumumba government" as a threat to "our vital interests in Congo."

Dulles quickly embraced the idea that Lumumba was a diabolical agent of Communist subversion. In truth, Lumumba had less of a connection to Moscow than any other emerging African leader. He explicitly tried to keep his struggling nation out of the superpower vortex, vowing that the Congo would "never be a satellite of Russia or of the United States."

"We want no part of the Cold War," Lumumba declared. "We want Africa to remain African with a policy of neutralism." But in the Dulles worldview, there was no such thing as neutrality. And anyone who professed such notions belonged to the enemy camp. At a July 22, 1960, National Security Council meeting in the Eisenhower White House— just three weeks after Lumumba's independence day speech—Dulles denounced the Congolese leader as "a Castro or worse. . . . It is safe to go on the assumption that Lumumba has been bought by the Communists."

Doug Dillon strongly backed Dulles's distraught view of Lumumba as a Soviet accomplice. It was an alarmist view calculated to convince Eisenhower that the African leader had to be terminated. As it turned out, the president required little persuasion. By the summer of 1960, Ike was sick, tired, and cranky—and he had little patience or understanding for Third World freedom struggles. Conferring with the British foreign minister Lord Home, Eisenhower quipped that he hoped "Lumumba would fall into a river full of crocodiles." At an NSC meeting in August 1960, Eisenhower gave Dulles direct approval to "eliminate" Lumumba. Robert Johnson, the minutes taker at the NSC meeting, later recalled the shock felt in the room: "There was a stunned silence for about 15 seconds and the meeting continued." Johnson said there was nothing ambiguous about Eisenhower's lethal order. "I was surprised that I would ever hear a president say anything like this in my presence or the presence of a group of people. I was startled."

Over the next several months, the CIA, working with its allies in Belgian intelligence, engineered a military coup led by a cocky, ruthless, twenty-nine-year-old colonel named Joseph Mobutu that forced Lumumba out of office and placed him under house arrest. But that was not enough for the CIA. Lumumba "would remain a grave danger,"

Dulles told an NSC meeting on September 21, 1960, "as long as he was not yet disposed of." Three days later, Dulles made it clear that he wanted Lumumba permanently removed, cabling the CIA's Leopoldville station, "We wish give [sic] every possible support in eliminating Lumumba from any possibility resuming governmental position."

Washington ascribed a kind of witchcraft-like power to Lumumba. Dulles marveled at the man's political survival skills, and Dillon was amazed at his powers of persuasion. "He had this tremendous ability to stir up a crowd or a group," said Dillon. "And if he could have gotten out and started to talk to a battalion of the Congolese Army, he probably would have had them in the palm of his hand in five minutes."

To prevent that from happening, the CIA recruited two cutthroats from the European criminal underworld, whom they code-named QJ-WIN and WI-ROGUE. These Tweedledum and Tweedledee assassins were such loathsome mercenaries that even their CIA handlers found them "unsavory." ROGUE was the kind of morally unhinged man "who would try anything once, at least," said his agency supervisors, untroubled by the "pangs of conscience." While ROGUE went about trying to organize an "execution squad" to kill Lumumba, WIN focused on penetrating the protective ring of UN troops that encircled the house where the Congolese leader was in custody. QJ-WIN had been supplied with a tube of poison toothpaste, which had been delivered to the CIA station in Leopoldville by Sidney Gottlieb, the agency's wizard of toxins. Dr. Ewen Cameron, of the notorious Allan Institute, had analyzed Lumumba at the CIA's request and determined that he must brush his teeth regularly, since they looked gleaming white in photos. Therefore, Ewen assured Dulles, chemically altered dental products were the key to getting rid of Lumumba.

In the end, the CIA did not go through with the toothpaste plot, apparently deciding that poisoning a popular leader while he was under UN protective custody in his own house would be too flagrant a deed—one that, if traced back to the agency, would lead to unpleasant international repercussions. It would be wiser, the agency decided, to deliver Lumumba to his murderous political rivals in the Congo and let them do the job. And so Lumumba fled house arrest—or was allowed to escape—miraculously slipping past not only the UN troops that were guarding him but Mobutu's hostile forces, and making his dash for Stanleyville.

As Lumumba's convoy made its way along muddy and bumpy roads, he was pursued by Congolese troops, led by Captain Gilbert Pongo, Mobutu's notorious security chief. Pongo buzzed after Lumumba's party in a helicopter that had been provided courtesy of Clare Timberlake, the dapper, mustachioed U.S. ambassador who worked closely with the CIA delegation in the Congo. Lumumba's flight was slowed whenever his convoy drove through villages, where he was thronged by the local people and urged to deliver speeches. When he spoke, he gave voice to their dreams. "Our program is clear: complete independence, Congo for the Congolese," he told a group huddled around a fire one night. "Fourteen million Congolese want work, a better future for their children. They want to be citizens with full political rights, they want a new life."

When Lumumba's military pursuers drew too near, villagers delayed their advance by putting up roadblocks and tearing down bridges. On the evening of December 1, Lumumba's group reached the small village of Lodi, on the west bank of the Sankuru River. This wide, muddy stretch of the river was the last serious obstacle that lay between the group and sanctuary in Stanleyville. The other side of the river was a bastion of pro-Lumumba nationalism. There was only one canoe on the riverbank. Lumumba and a few of his top aides crossed first. As they disembarked from the dugout, they heard a commotion on the other side of the river. Mobutu's soldiers had caught up with the group left behind, including Lumumba's wife and toddler.

Lumumba's compatriots begged him not to return across the river, telling him "the life of the whole nation is at stake." But he could not stand to hear the cries of his wife. "When one struggles for one's country," he said as he got back into the canoe, "one has to expect a tragic end." As Lumumba's canoe glided back to the other side of the river, the soldiers waded into the water and grabbed him. Lumumba tried winning over

382 · THE DEVIL'S CHESSBOARD

Mobutu's men. For a while, his words seemed to work their magic—the soldiers were ready to join the cause of freedom and march with him to Stanleyville. But then Captain Pongo intervened, reminding his soldiers of the dire consequences that would befall them and their families if they did not do their duty. They turned in an instant and began beating Lumumba and even his little son.

Lumumba was hustled onto Pongo's helicopter and flown back to Leopoldville, where he emerged in the glare of TV news cameras, only to be subjected to another vicious round of beating by Mobutu's thugs, while the cameras rolled. Throughout it all, Lumumba maintained the serene dignity of the martyr that he soon would become. "On Lumumba's dazed face was the look of a man who did not yet believe that fate could be against justice for his people," remarked Andrée Blouin, the beautiful "Black Pasionaria" of the Congolese independence struggle and chief of protocol in Lumumba's government. "His white shirt was now spotted with blood, but his head was still erect. He personified the best of the race that would never again be slaves."

Over the next several weeks, Lumumba's fate became the focus of a tumultuous international drama, as the symbol of African freedom languished in a military prison south of Leopoldville. World leaders—including Khrushchev, Nasser, and Ghana's Kwame Nkrumah—issued fervent pleas for his release, with the Soviet leader promising that the "colonialists will be thrown out of the Congo once and for all." Lumumba's followers prayed that he could survive until the inauguration of Kennedy, whose election the Congolese leader had praised.

But in Leopoldville, U.S. and Belgian agents were feverishly maneuvering to ensure that no such release took place. The man at the center of this intrigue was Lawrence R. Devlin, the CIA station chief in the Congo, a Harvard man who had been handpicked for the spy service by his dean, Mac Bundy. Larry Devlin's aggressive campaign against Lumumba had won him the admiration of the agency's top command, including Dulles himself. At the end of November, when Mobutu's troops were in pursuit of Lumumba, Devlin had flown to Rome to meet with Dick Bissell, whom Dulles had put in charge of the Lumumba assassination. The CIA was still determined to carry out Eisenhower's termination order. But Devlin and his CIA superiors knew that time was running short.

U.S. intelligence officials continued to fret about the Congo situation, even after Lumumba's capture. With Mobutu's rule still shaky and Congolese politics in chaos, Devlin realized that Lumumba's imprisonment could not be ensured indefinitely. In fact, by the second week of January 1961, when Lumumba's jailers briefly mutinied and threatened to free him, his captivity seemed less secure than ever.

Meanwhile, Dulles and his Congo team were acutely aware that the presidential transition under way in Washington also put their Lumumba operation in jeopardy. Kennedy, whose inauguration was scheduled for January 20, had already signaled that he would shift U.S. policy in favor of African nationalists like Lumumba. In late December, after returning from a five-week tour of the Congo and other African countries, a Democratic fact-finding delegation that included JFK's brother Edward M. Kennedy predicted that the new administration would align itself with the continent's "movement for freedom and self-determination" and expressed strong sympathy for Lumumba's plight. Ted Kennedy later went further, calling for the release of Lumumba and suggesting his brother agreed with this position.

The raging battle over Lumumba's future broke into the U.S. press, with the CIA's media assets predicting drastic consequences if the Congolese leader returned to power. As the Congo crisis reached its climax, a new correspondent for *The New York Times* showed up in Leopoldville with a distinctly anti-Lumumba bias. Paul Hofmann was a diminutive, sophisticated Austrian with a colorful past. During the war, he served in Rome as a top aide to the notorious Nazi general Kurt Malzer, who was later convicted of the mass murder of Italian partisans. At some point, Hofmann became an informer for the Allies, and after the war he became closely associated with Jim Angleton. The Angleton family helped place Hofmann in the Rome bureau of *The New York Times*, where he continued to be of use to his friends in U.S. intelligence, translating reports from confidential sources inside the Vatican and passing them along to Angleton. Hofmann became one of the *Times*'s leading foreign correspondents, eventually taking over the newspaper's Rome bureau and parachuting from time to time into international hot spots like the Congo.

The *New York Times* coverage of the Congo crisis had always been slanted against Lumumba, with columns and commentaries labeling him "inexperienced and irresponsible" and a "virtual dictator." But Hofmann's Congo coverage was so virulent in its bias that it seemed as if he were acting as a "psywar" conduit for U.S. intelligence. In article after article, during the critical Congo end game, Hofmann portrayed Lumumba as a dangerous bogeyman, a "wily" conspirator in some pieces and a mentally unbalanced buffoon in others ("the weirdest character in a sort of *Alice in Tropical Wonderland*," as the *Times* man wrote). Even behind bars, Lumumba continued to work his dark mischief, Hofmann told his readers, plotting the murders of whites and bringing a flow of Soviet arms into the country, all while living the life of luxury in military prison "with three houseboys at his service." The message behind Hofmann's relentless barrage was clear: despite the "crocodile tears" cried by the Soviet Union over Lumumba's plight, no man as treacherous as this deserved mercy.

In its explosive 1975 report on CIA assassination plots against foreign leaders, the Church Committee absolved the agency of responsibility for Lumumba's murder. "It does not appear from the evidence that the United States was in any way involved in the killing," concluded the Senate panel. This became a convenient myth, one that is still routinely repeated in the press. But the truth is far less comforting.

As a new wave of historical research has determined, the CIA ensured Lumumba's violent end by making certain that he was delivered into the hands of his mortal enemies. Among his tormentors in the final hours of his life were CIA-funded goons. Devlin, the CIA's man in the Congo, later tried to portray himself as a blissfully ignorant player in the Lumumba affair, and indeed as a man who found assassination morally repugnant. But as former congressional aide and scholar Stephen Weissman has observed, "The CIA was not the innocent bystander, and its Congo operatives not the paragons of morally sensitive professionalism they claimed to be. In particular, Devlin was a key *participant* in the Congo government's decision to approve Lumumba's fatal rendition."

In fact, Devlin appears to have been more a driver of the action leading to Lumumba's death than a participant. On January 17, 1961—three days before Kennedy's inauguration—Lumumba was taken from his jail cell and hustled onto a Belgian chartered plane. Congolese authorities took this action under strong pressure from Devlin, who was the kingmaker behind the Mobutu regime. With Devlin's full knowledge, Lumumba was then flown to Katanga, a mineral-rich province that had broken away from the Congo and was run by violent enemies of Lumumba. The CIA station chief later acknowledged that Lumumba's transfer to Katanga amounted to a death sentence. "I think there was a general assumption, once we learned that he had been sent to Katanga, that his goose was cooked," Devlin told the Church Committee years later.

Devlin knew of Lumumba's imminent transfer by January 14, three days ahead of time. But he did nothing to inform Washington until January 17, when Lumumba was already well on the way to his doom. Devlin knew that cabling Washington risked tipping off Africa policy makers in the incoming Kennedy administration, who likely would have intervened to save Lumumba. By keeping quiet, Devlin sealed Lumumba's fate.

Larry Devlin was no rogue agent—he was an up-and-coming intelligence officer whose Congo exploits had won glowing marks back at CIA headquarters. The Congo station chief's decision to keep Lumumba's fate quiet until it was too late to do anything about it was clearly made in consultation with his supervisors. Devlin suffered no agency reprimands for his actions in the Congo, and, in fact, his intelligence career continued to thrive after Lumumba's demise. Before retiring from the CIA in 1974, to pursue a new career in the Congo's lucrative diamond industry, Devlin rose to become chief of the CIA's Africa Division.

Patrice Lumumba suffered a terrible martyrdom during his final hours on earth. He was beaten bloody during the flight to Katanga, and clumps of hair were torn from his head. When the plane landed, he was seized by armed guards sent by Moise Tshombe, Katanga's ruler, and subjected to another round of abuse. As he suffered the rain of blows, Lumumba maintained a resigned silence. He was then dragged to a jeep and driven to a remote farmhouse, where a group of men connected to U.S. and Belgian intelligence beat him to death, an orgy of sadism that stretched over several hours. According to one account, even Tshombe and his ministers appeared at one point to contribute to Lumumba's suffering, kicking and hitting what remained of his nearly lifeless body.

Despite the agency's evasions, CIA officer John Stockwell, who was stationed in the Congo in the tumultuous aftermath of the Lumumba assassination, had no doubt who was responsible for the African leader's death. "Eventually he was killed, not by our poisons, but beaten to death, apparently by men who had agency cryptonyms and received agency salaries," Stockwell concluded. Years after Lumumba's death, Stockwell fell into conversation with one of his more peculiar CIA colleagues, a "glisteningly bald" man whom Stockwell anointed "Goldfinger." The man regaled Stockwell with a story of the evening when he had driven around the capital of Katanga, with Lumumba's battered corpse in the trunk, "trying to decide what to do with it."

After Kennedy's inauguration, the CIA continued to keep Lumumba's death under wraps. On January 26, Dulles briefed the new president on the Congo. The CIA director said nothing about Lumumba's assassination, though his fate was well known by then within the agency. In early February, Devlin and Ambassador Timberlake were called back to Washington to participate in discussions about Congo policy with the new Kennedy team. The old Congo hands were alarmed by the administration's new position paper, which envisioned disarming Mobutu and freeing Lumumba. Devlin considered JFK's admiration for rising African nationalism naïve. Timberlake, meeting with Kennedy in the White House, argued that the Congolese people were too primitive for a functioning democracy. Neither Timberlake nor Devlin took the opportunity to inform Kennedy or his staff that any discussion about Lumumba's future was a moot point.

The Kennedy White House remained in the dark about Lumumba for a full month after his murder. When JFK finally heard of the leader's death, the news came not from Dulles but from UN ambassador Adlai Stevenson.

Jacques Lowe, the young photographer who had been unobtrusively documenting the Kennedy story from the earliest days of his presidential run, was in the Oval Office when JFK received the phone call from Stevenson. Lowe, a German Jew who had survived the war as a child by making himself unseen, deftly inserted himself into the ongoing Kennedy family drama, taking black-and-white pictures of John and Robert and their clan that would become iconic in their simple intimacy. After JFK's victory, the president-elect asked Lowe to "stick around and record my administration. Don't worry," he added, "I'll make it worth your while."

Kennedy made good on his promise. The photos Lowe was allowed to take during the intense rush of JFK's brief presidency were windows into its troubled soul. None was more powerful than the picture that the young photographer snapped at the moment when Kennedy was told of Lumumba's fate. The photo is one of the most searing documents of the Kennedy presidency. In the close-up shot, JFK looks physically stricken as he absorbs the news on the phone, with his eyes squeezed shut and his hand clasped to his face. It was an image of such anguish that it seemed to come from some harrowing time deep in his presidency instead of in its earliest bloom. The picture contains all of the sorrows that were to come.

Lowe later recalled the moment: "I was alone with the president; his hand went to his head in utter despair. 'Oh, no,' I heard him groan . . . [Lumumba] was considered a trouble-maker and a leftist by many Americans. But Kennedy's attitude toward black Africa was that many who were considered leftists were in fact nationalists and patriots. . . . He felt that Africa presented an opportunity for the West, and speaking as an American, unhindered by a colonial heritage, he had made friends in Africa. . . . The call therefore left him heartbroken, for he knew that the murder would be a prelude to chaos . . . it was a poignant moment."

When the killing of Lumumba was finally announced, furious street protests swept the world, from New Delhi to Warsaw to Tokyo. Lumumba's fellow leaders in the Third World—including Egypt's Nasser and Nkrumah of Ghana, who had been a mentor—were particularly outraged by his murder, lashing out at the West and at the UN for failing to protect him. Brazilian delegates to the UN expressed "horror and repulsion" over Lumumba's slaying. But, as much of the world mourned, the Western press continued its snide coverage of Lumumba, exhuming the martyred leader only to subject him to more abuse. *Time* magazine snickered at the traditional way his widow, Pauline, chose to mourn her husband, marching bare-breasted through the streets of Leopoldville in a funeral procession. Meanwhile, *The New York Times* continued to demean Lumumba, sometimes resorting to the most shopworn neocolonial stereotypes of the era. "Lumumba . . . combined the skills of the late Senator McCarthy with the brashness of a ward heeler and the magic touch of an African witch doctor," wrote Henry Tanner in *The New York Times Magazine*. "Then there was [his] name—musical, easily pronounced in all languages and yet exotic, African-sounding like the drums in the jungle."

After her husband's funeral procession, Pauline Lumumba crumpled to the floor in the dark corner of a friend's house, too spent to cry anymore. She raised her arms in the air and let them hang there, as if in surrender. Her husband's murderers did not even have the decency to give her his body, Pauline's brother told reporters. As little Roland Lumumba hovered anxiously over his mother, the room was filled with the wails of women: "Our strong leader is gone—our great father is no more."

In his final letter to his wife, Patrice Lumumba vowed, "Neither brutality, nor cruelty nor torture will ever bring me to ask for mercy, for I prefer to die with my head unbowed." It was an oath that Lumumba had kept throughout his ordeal. Lumumba also told his wife, "History will one day have its say, but it will not be the history that is taught in

Brussels, Paris, Washington or in the United Nations. . . . Africa will write its own history, and to the north and south of the Sahara, it will be a glorious and dignified history."

This promise did not come true for the Congo. The mourners at Lumumba's wake knew how profound a loss it was, and what it meant for their nation. "There is nothing for us to do now," muttered Lumumba's brother-in-law. "He is gone. There is no one to take his place."

With one of Africa's brightest lights extinguished, the Congo slid into an endless nightmare of tyranny and corruption. Propped up by the United States, Mobutu began a thirty-two-year dictatorship that looted the country of its wealth and left the nation in ruins. In his rampant thievery, Mobutu modeled himself on King Leopold. So smug was the dictator in his ironfisted rule that he declared Lumumba a national hero, a sick joke that only he could afford to enjoy.

The CIA officials responsible for Lumumba's murder also had a change of heart about the man who had once haunted their days. In 1962, shortly after Dulles's departure from the CIA, he remarked, "I think we overrated the Soviet danger, let's say, in the Congo." And Devlin, for his part, insisted he had never thought Lumumba's assassination was essential to U.S. security: "I didn't regard Lumumba as the kind of person who was going to bring on World War III," he later told the Church Committee. These expressions of remorse—if they can be called that—came far too late for the man who was the hope of the Congo.

Part III

Contempt

On Monday April 17, 1961, as over fourteen hundred CIA-trained anti-Castro exiles waded ashore at Cuba's Bay of Pigs—an operation that would quickly become the biggest debacle of Allen Dulles's career—the CIA director was sunning himself about a thousand miles away at a Puerto Rico resort. Dulles, who had flown down to San Juan that weekend, was the featured speaker at a Young Presidents' Organization conference, a global network of chief executives under age forty that had CIA affiliations. The gathering was held at La Concha, a new oceanfront luxury hotel that epitomized the Caribbean cool of the tropical modernism movement. The hotel's signature restaurant was shaped like a giant seashell, with wavy gaps to let in the sunshine and ocean breeze. Dulles spent the weekend swimming and playing golf with the young executives.

On Monday morning, when Dulles strode onstage to deliver his remarks, he looked like a man without a worry in the world. The CIA director's speech—which followed a panel discussion featuring Margaret Mead and Dr. Benjamin Spock on the subject of "Are We Letting Our Children Down?"—was a plea for globe-trotting American businessmen, like those gathered in the conference hall, to join the clandestine war against Communism. Afterward, there was more time to relax by the pool. The spymaster had brought Clover with him on the trip, completing the carefree picture. They seemed to all the world to be just another well-to-do American couple enjoying a long weekend in the

394 · THE DEVIL'S CHESSBOARD

Caribbean sun. But by that evening, as Dulles and his wife flew home, the Bay of Pigs operation was on the verge of collapse, and with it, the spymaster's long, storied career.

Dick Bissell, whom Dulles had put in charge of the invasion, sent one of the top men in the Cuba task force to pick him up at the airport, thinking that the CIA director would want to be briefed immediately on the growing calamity. Richard Drain, chief of operations for the Bay of Pigs expedition, rolled onto the runway at Baltimore's Friendship Airport in his well-traveled, CIA-issued Chevrolet as Dulles's small plane taxied to a stop. The CIA chief emerged from the plane with his wife and a young aide, wearing a dinner jacket and the relaxed smile of a man of leisure. Drain stepped forward and offered his hand.

"I'm Dick Drain. I was sent to brief you, sir."

"Oh yes, Dick, how are you?"

Drain drew Dulles away from the others.

"Well, how is it going?" asked Dulles.

"Not very well, sir."

"Oh, is that so?" Dulles wore an oddly bemused look, as if the unfolding tragedy was too remote to affect him.

Back at Quarters Eye, the CIA headquarters in downtown Washington, battle-hardened men were on the verge of hysteria. Bissell, who prided himself on his cool performance under pressure, seemed frozen. On the brink of failure, the Cuba operation lacked the kind of muscular leadership that could rescue the men pinned down by Castro's forces. Drain was hoping that Dulles would save the day. But he found the Old Man's unflappability disturbing.

Clover and the young aide were bundled into the Chevrolet, and Dulles and Drain drove back to Washington in the director's Cadillac. "It's a fast-breaking situation," Drain told him. "We're hanging on by our fingernails."

Dulles puffed quietly on his pipe as his deputy steered the car onto the highway heading to the capital.

"Today's air strike was killed," Drain told him—a stunning piece of news, since Dulles knew that the operation was damned unless President Kennedy agreed to escalate the action and provide the embattled anti-Castro brigade with U.S. air cover.

"Why did they do that?" Dulles asked softly. There was no anger or outrage in his voice.

The emotion all belonged to Drain. "If you're asking my guess, my guess is this thing is all going to hell."

By the disastrous end of the operation, when Castro's forces had killed more than a hundred of the invaders and taken the rest prisoner, Drain would be so wrung out that he vomited. Like the rest of the CIA planning team, Drain had worked closely with the exile leaders who were trapped on the desolate stretch of sand and shrubbery, and they took the men's fate personally. But Dulles's mind seemed elsewhere as he and Drain drove to the director's Georgetown residence. They rode in silence for a long time, until Drain let out a final burst of emotion.

"If it isn't presumptuous of me, sir, I wish your brother was still alive." Drain had served as the CIA liaison to Foster in the final months of his life. If he thought that invoking the memory of Dulles's late brother would light a fire under the spymaster, Drain was wrong. Dulles simply nodded and stared ahead at the road. By the time they reached the house on Q Street, Drain was deeply uncomfortable in his boss's presence and eager to flee back to his CIA command post. But Dulles insisted that he come inside for a drink.

When the two men settled into armchairs in Dulles's library with tumblers of Scotch in hand, Drain thought the chief would finally grill him on the details of the failing operation. Instead, the evening only became more surreal.

"Dick, you served in Greece, didn't you?" Dulles inquired. "I have to go to the White House tomorrow to a reception for [Greek Prime Minister Constantine] Karamanlis. Can you refresh my memory about him?"

The stunned CIA officer strung together some kind of reply and made his exit shortly after.

For years after the Bay of Pigs, Washington insiders and scholars tried to unravel the mystery of Dulles's AWOL behavior during the critical CIA operation. Some explained that his absence was part of his modus operandi—he was in the habit of leaving Washington on the eve of critical missions to make it seem as if nothing significant was about to occur. Dulles himself airily dismissed his strangely timed Puerto Rico trip. He had planned the Young Presidents speaking engagement months before, he explained, and if he had canceled at the last minute, it would have created suspicions. Besides, he added, "I knew I could get back with the speed of aircraft; it was only a question of six or eight hours." But the CIA's own official history of the Cuba fiasco, prepared in the late 1970s and early '80s, concluded that Dulles's absence was "inexcusable." Dulles, the report added, "was the one man who might have persuaded the president to permit the D-Day [air] strike."

Some of the sharpest criticisms of the Bay of Pigs operation, in fact, came from within the CIA itself. Dick Drain was among those who later aimed fire at Dulles, when he spoke with Jack Pfeiffer, the CIA historian who prepared the voluminous report on the Bay of Pigs. Drain was a gung ho officer who fit the agency profile, right down to membership in Yale's secretive Skull and Bones society (Class of '43). But years after he picked up Dulles at the Baltimore airport, Drain vented about the agency's handling of the doomed Cuba enterprise. He was astounded by the poor quality of the staff assigned to the high-stakes Bay of Pigs operation, Drain told Pfeiffer, despite Dulles's insistence that it would be run by the agency's best and brightest. "Allen Dulles, always meaning what he said, would say repeatedly, 'Now I want the very best people assigned to this project. There is nothing more important that we are doing than this. . . . I want people pulled out of tours overseas if necessary, this thing must be manned.'"

But in truth, said Drain, the Bay of Pigs operation drew agency castoffs. "We would tend to get the people that the [CIA] division chiefs found 'excess'—which normally meant found insufficient. With many notable exceptions, we did not get the very best people available."

Even he himself, Drain admitted, was not qualified to play a leading role in the operation. "I don't mean to be unduly immodest [sic], but really I didn't have any qualifications for this [job] except I was there and unemployed—had no Spanish language whatsoever, and my entire exposure had been punching cows in Arizona in 1940. That doesn't really bring you up much on Latin America and Latinos, and any of that. I had never been on amphibious operations, and if that was characteristic of my qualifications, it really characterized the whole damn operation—about which, it seemed to me, there was a good deal of well-meaning hypocrisy."

Drain's criticisms of the enterprise echoed those in an earlier CIA report, the damning internal investigation carried out by the agency's inspector general, Lyman Kirkpatrick, in the months immediately following the disaster. The Kirkpatrick Report, one of the most surprisingly honest self-evaluations ever produced within the CIA, found that despite Dulles's insistence on "high-quality personnel," the Bay of Pigs operation was staffed largely by the agency's losers. According to CIA files, seventeen of the forty-two officers assigned to the operation were ranked in the lowest third of the agency, and nine were ranked in the lowest tenth. The IG's report concluded that Dulles had allowed his division chiefs to dump "their disposal cases" on the Cuba project.

Robert Amory Jr., the CIA's highly respected chief of analysis, was one of those who was inexplicably kept away from the Bay of Pigs operation, despite his extensive experience with beach landings as an Army Corps of Engineers officer in the South Pacific during World War II. Amory—who had literally written the book on the subject, *Surf and Sand*, a regimental history of his twenty-six amphibious operations—was stunned by Dulles and Bissell's decision to keep him on the sidelines. The CIA men sent to Miami to work with the exile leaders and to Guatemala to help train the *brigadistas* were "a bunch of guys who were otherwise not needed," Amory later recalled. "They were a strange bunch of people with German experience, Arabic experience, and other things like that. And most of them had no knowledge of Spanish . . . and absolutely no sense or feel about the political sensitivities of these [Cuban exiles]. . . . I think we could have had an A team, instead of being a C-minus team."

The Kirkpatrick Report detailed a number of other glaring errors made by Dulles, Bissell, and their Bay of Pigs team. When plans for the Cuba invasion grew more ambitious and began leaking to the press as early as November 1960, the report stated, the CIA should have terminated its role in the mission since it had outgrown the agency's covert capability. "When the project became blown to every newspaper reader," the report noted acerbically, "the agency should have informed higher authority that it was no longer operating in its charter." The criticisms went on and on, each one more devastating than the last. "As the project grew, the agency reduced the exiled leaders to the status of puppets. . . . The project was badly organized. . . . The agency became so wrapped up in the military operation that it failed to appraise the chances of success realistically. Furthermore, it failed to keep [the president and his] policymakers adequately and realistically informed of the conditions essential for success."

Kirkpatrick, who prepared his devastating report with the help of three investigators, flatly rejected the main CIA alibi for the failed mission—that Kennedy was to blame by blocking the agency's last-minute requests for air strikes. The invasion was "doomed" from the start by the CIA's poor planning, the inspector general concluded. Even if the air strikes had allowed the invaders to move inland from the shore, his report stated, the "men would eventually have been crushed by Castro's combined military resources strengthened by Soviet Bloc–supplied military materiel."

Perhaps the most devastating revelation about the CIA operation emerged years later, in 2005, when the agency was compelled to release the minutes of a meeting held by its Cuba task force on November 15, 1960, one week after Kennedy's election. The group, which was deliberating on how to brief the president-elect on the pending invasion, came to an eye-opening conclusion. In the face of strong security measures that Castro had implemented, the CIA task force admitted, their invasion plan was "now seen to be unachievable, except as a joint [CIA/Department of Defense] action." In other words, the CIA realized that its Bay of Pigs expedition was doomed to fail unless its exile brigade was reinforced by the power of the U.S. military. But the CIA never shared this sobering assessment with the president.

Nor did Dulles and Bissell share with Kennedy their other "magic bullet" for success in Cuba—the agency's ongoing plot with the Mafia to assassinate Castro, which had been authorized by Eisenhower. With Cuba's revolutionary government decapitated, CIA officials were certain that the regime would soon topple. But the Cuban leader had learned from the annals of imperial history and had wisely taken precautions against such plots. He would thwart his enemies for decades to come, as he grew from a young firebrand to a gray-bearded legend.

Dulles and Bissell knew that Kennedy was deeply torn over the Cuba invasion plan. His denunciations of Western imperialism had raised high hopes throughout the hemisphere that the days of heavy-handed Yanqui interference were coming to an end. "Kennedy's election has given rise to an enormous expectancy throughout Latin America," Schlesinger noted in his journal in early February 1961. "They see him as another FDR; they expect great things from him." But Kennedy had also campaigned for a strong, though undefined, response to Castro. Eisenhower's final words of advice to him were to take out the Cuban leader—and he left behind an invasion plan and assassination plot to do just that. As William Bundy observed, the old general had handed Kennedy "a grenade with the pin pulled"—if he didn't use it, it could blow up in his face, with serious political consequences.

Kennedy agonized over giving final authorization for the Bay of Pigs plan to the very end. He kept downsizing the operation, to make it as little "noisy" as possible. "What the president really wanted, it seems, was for the CIA to pull off the neat trick of invading Cuba without actually invading it; an immaculate invasion, as it were . . . without all the messy business along the way," observed historian Jim Rasenberger.

Dulles kept accommodating the anxious Kennedy, convinced that once the *brigadistas* hit the beaches, JFK would be forced to do anything necessary for success—even if that meant getting very noisy and messy. The wily CIA chief set a trap for Kennedy, allowing the president to believe that his "immaculate invasion" could succeed, even though Dulles knew that only U.S. soldiers and planes could ensure that.

Years after the Bay of Pigs, historians—including the CIA's own

Jack Pfeiffer—painted a portrait of Dulles as a spymaster in decline, bumbling and disengaged and maybe too advanced in years, at age sixty-eight, for the rigors of his job. Only a spy chief with a shaky grasp on the tiller could have overlooked the deep flaws embedded in the Bay of Pigs strategy, it was stated.

But, as usual, there was method to Dulles's seeming carelessness. It is now clear that the CIA's Bay of Pigs expedition was not simply doomed to fail, it was *meant* to fail. And its failure was designed to trigger the real action—an all-out, U.S. military invasion of the island. Dulles plunged ahead with his hopeless, paramilitary mission—an expedition that he had staffed with "C-minus" officers and expendable Cuban "puppets"—because he was serenely confident that, in the heat of battle, Kennedy would be forced to send the Marines crashing ashore. Dulles was banking on the young, untested commander in chief to cave in to pressure from the Washington war machine, just as other presidents had bent to the spymaster's will.

It was Dick Bissell, the man in charge of the high-stakes operation, who stood to lose the most when the motley brigade of Cuban patriots and cutthroats inevitably bogged down on the beaches. That was perfectly fine with Dulles, who had been content all along for Bissell to take the lead on the Bay of Pigs—and also the heat. Bissell supported Dulles's decision to fly off to Puerto Rico on the eve of the mission. The ambitious deputy director was eager to run his own show. JFK had put out the word that Bissell was going to replace Dulles by July, and the supremely confident Bissell thought it was time to show what he could do. "I was prepared to run it as a single-handed operation," he later said. "I was impatient if Dulles raised too many questions."

Dulles was only too pleased to accommodate his rising deputy. As the mission went to hell, the CIA chief would be far from the Washington inferno. By the time Dulles returned home from his Puerto Rico retreat, he would look like one of the grown-ups riding to the rescue. The spymaster and the Pentagon brass would make the new president see that he had no choice: he had to escalate the fighting in Cuba and march all the way to Havana. Afterward, as the dust settled, if Bissell suffered an unfortunate career reversal because his ill-conceived escapade had to be salvaged by the big boys, well, so be it. After all, he was the face of the Cuba mission, just as Dulles had made him the front man for the risky U-2 enterprise and the assassination operations against foreign leaders.

Years later, Bob Amory would acknowledge that JFK was indeed "a little bit trapped" by the CIA on the Bay of Pigs, though Amory himself had nothing to do with it. But if Dulles thought he could force Kennedy to carry out his Cuba plan, he had seriously underestimated the young man in the White House.

Around midnight on Tuesday, April 18, in the midst of the unfolding fiasco, some of the principal advocates for a bigger war in Cuba made one final assault on Kennedy, gathering with him in the Oval Office after the annual congressional party in the East Room. Among those pressing the case for escalation were Bissell and two longtime Pentagon allies of Dulles, Joint Chiefs chairman Lyman Lemnitzer and Navy chief Arleigh Burke. Dulles was absent, still keeping his distance from the mess and hoping that Bissell would take the fall for it. The CIA director was placing his confidence in Lemnitzer and Burke, hoping that the two blunt-spoken, highly decorated warriors could strong-arm Kennedy into unleashing the U.S. military. The president was still in formal white-tie-and-black-tails attire from the East Room party, and the military men were in their full dress uniforms. But there was nothing polite or decorative about the intense discussion in the president's office.

Admiral Burke was especially gruff with Kennedy, treating him as if he were a weak-kneed ensign. Without informing the president, Burke had already taken the liberty of positioning two battalions of Marines on Navy destroyers off the coast of Cuba, "anticipating that U.S. forces might be ordered into Cuba to salvage a botched invasion." It was one of many extraordinary acts of Pentagon and CIA insubordination that plagued the Kennedy presidency from the very beginning. Now the Navy chief was browbeating Kennedy into taking the first steps toward a full-scale war with Castro.

"Let me take two jets and shoot down the enemy aircraft," growled "31-Knot" Burke, who had become legendary for his speed and daring as a destroyer squadron commander in the South Pacific during the war, while JFK was a mere PT boat captain. But by this point in the unfolding disaster, Kennedy was not inclined to take any more advice from his national security wise men, even if they were World War II idols. "What if Castro's forces return fire and hit the destroyer?" Kennedy sensibly asked.

"Then we'll knock the hell out of them!" Burke bellowed.

Now Kennedy began to show some of his own icy, if more restrained, temper. He had made it clear all along that he did not want the Bay of Pigs to blow up into an international crisis with the United States in the middle—and here was his Navy chief urging just such a course of action. "Burke, I don't want the United States involved in this," he firmly repeated one more time.

"Hell, Mr. President," the admiral shot back, "but we *are* involved!"

But Kennedy stood his ground. As he had repeatedly warned them, there would be no air strikes, no Marine landings—and the fate of the Bay of Pigs operation was sealed.

"They were sure I'd give in to them," Kennedy later told Dave Powers. "They couldn't believe that a new president like me wouldn't panic and try to save his own face. Well they had me figured all wrong."

JFK was even more vehement when he spoke with another old friend, Paul "Red" Fay Jr., whom Kennedy installed as undersecretary of the Navy. "Nobody is going to force me to do anything I don't think is in the best interests of the country," he vented. "We're not going to plunge into irresponsible action just because a fanatical fringe in the country puts so-called national pride above national reason."

As the last of the *brigadistas* were rounded up by Castro's troops in the swamps surrounding the Bay of Pigs, Dulles seemed shell-shocked. He had never suffered a humiliation like this in his career. Seeking consolation, Dulles made a Thursday night dinner date with his old protégé, Dick Nixon. The spymaster was acutely aware that if Nixon had been the one sitting in the White House, the events in Cuba would have taken a much different course. When he finally arrived at the Washington residence that Nixon still maintained, over an hour late, Dulles did not seem himself. It looked to Nixon like he was under "great emotional stress." The CIA chief shuffled in wearing slippers—a sign that he was in the midst of another agonizing gout attack, the recurring affliction that seemed to strike whenever Dulles was entangled in a high-stress operation. After asking for a drink, the Old Man collapsed into a chair and exhaled, "This has been the worst day of my life."

If Dulles thought he could escape Kennedy's wrath by making Bissell the scapegoat, he was deeply mistaken. Both CIA officials would eventually be ousted, but JFK placed most of the blame squarely on the top man. The CIA chief later swore that he never "sold" the president on the Bay of Pigs scheme. "One ought never to sell anybody a bill of goods," he told an interviewer for the JFK Presidential Library. But Kennedy knew the truth. Dulles had lied to his face in the Oval Office about the chances for the operation's success. "I stood right here at Ike's desk," Dulles told JFK on the eve of the invasion, "and I told him I was certain our Guatemalan operation would succeed—and, Mr. President, the prospects for this plan are even better than they were for that one."

Kennedy and Dulles had not gotten off to a good start with each other during the first months of the new presidency. The minor rifts and strains began accumulating from the very beginning. Still wedded to the ancien régime, Dulles never hung an official portrait of President Kennedy in the CIA headquarters. The CIA director immediately created an atmosphere of distrust between his agency and the White House, telling his deputies to make sure that they retrieved any sensitive documents they showed to Kennedy's staff, so they didn't wind up in White House files. Dulles "didn't really feel comfortable with" Kennedy, observed Bob Amory.

The spymaster regarded the young New Frontiersmen Kennedy brought into his administration as if they were an alien force. In February 1961, Adam Yarmolinksy, one of the young Ivy League–educated "whiz kids" assembled by Defense Secretary Robert McNamara to modernize the management of the Pentagon, scheduled an appointment with Dulles. Before the meeting, the spymaster requested a report on Yarmolinsky from CIA general counsel Lawrence Houston, as if he were meeting a foreign official. Dulles was briefed about Yarmolinsky's liberal inclinations by Houston, who then phoned the director's office with additional observations about the young Kennedy official. "Mr. Houston says [Yarmolinksy] is an extremely bright fellow," reported the Dulles aide who took the phone call, "although not particularly personally attractive. He is of Russian-Jewish background."

Dulles insisted on personally handling all of the agency's briefings at the White House, but JFK—who was more widely traveled and sophisticated about global affairs than his age would indicate—did not think much of the CIA chief's presentations. He found Dulles patronizing and uninformative. According to White House aide Theodore Sorensen, Kennedy "was not very impressed with Dulles's briefings. He did not think they were in much depth or told him anything he couldn't read in the newspapers."

But if relations between Kennedy and Dulles were strained before the Bay of Pigs, afterward they were all but nonexistent. Kennedy made it clear that he no longer wanted to be briefed by Dulles, so the agency began sending him briefing booklets called the President's Intelligence Checklist, filled with short summaries of world developments. Kennedy clearly preferred this method, firing off follow-up questions to the agency, along with requests to see source materials, such as the complete text of speeches by foreign leaders and the unabridged versions of CIA reports.

In public, the president took full blame for the Cuba fiasco. And Kennedy remained personally courteous in his face-to-face dealings with Dulles. "There was never any recrimination on the president's part," Dulles later recalled. "I might well have lost to some extent in the measure of confidence he placed on me—that's inevitable in things of this kind, I think, but I may say in his personal attitude toward me, in the many meetings we had, he never let that appear."

But behind the scenes, Dulles waged a vigorous battle with Kennedy to control the media spin on the Bay of Pigs and to hold on to his command of the CIA. The intelligence chief took immediate steps to rally his corporate base of support. On May 1, Dulles convened a private meeting of CEOs to discuss "current problems confronting business enterprise in Latin America and specific ways of meeting them." The gathering at New York's Metropolitan Club—which Dulles emphasized was "strictly off the record"—gave the spymaster and his corporate clientele an opportunity to reevaluate their strategy in the post–Bay of Pigs climate.

Dulles's corporate circle encouraged his aggressive political tactics by sending him supportive messages. Charles Hilles Jr., executive vice president of ITT, was among those who wrote Dulles to buck him up after the Cuban catastrophe. "I have the greatest admiration for your calmness and fortitude, and for your devotion to the country's good," wrote Hilles on May 4, "and I sense that I am one of an overwhelming majority." The following month, a conservative New York corporate attorney named Watson "Watty" Washburn, known as a tennis wizard in his youth and later as the attorney who defended P. G. Wodehouse against the IRS, offered Dulles more militant encouragement. Washburn urged Dulles to slough off his earlier failure and organize a new invasion of Cuba to liberate the Bay of Pigs captives from Castro's prison on the Isle of Pines. "This would be mere child's play as a military operation," assured Washburn, "and would qualify as an humanitarian enterprise rather than 'imperialism.'"

If Dulles had lost the battle at the Bay of Pigs, he was determined to win the war of ideas over the failed operation. He began his psywar campaign by sending an all-station cable to CIA personnel with his version of the Cuba disaster. According to Ralph McGehee, a twenty-five-year CIA veteran serving in Vietnam at the time, Dulles's cable to his troops "implied that had events taken their planned course, we would have been victorious in [the] invasion of Cuba." The Dulles message, which the Old Man continued to promote for the rest of his life, was emphatically clear: the mission had been doomed by Kennedy's failure of nerve, or, as he put it more diplomatically in his unpublished article for *Harper's*, by the president's lack of "determination to succeed."

Years after the Bay of Pigs, Dulles was still spinning reporters, scholars, and anyone else who showed an interest in the fading story. In April 1965, when a Harvard Business School student named L. Paul Bremer III—who would find his own place in the annals of American disasters as President George W. Bush's proconsul in Iraq—sent Dulles his dissertation on the Bay of Pigs, the spymaster sought to correct the young man's impression that it was a CIA failure. It was Kennedy's "final decision to eliminate the air action" that had killed the expedition, Dulles wrote Bremer. "I can assure you that it would never have been mounted . . . if it had been even suspected that this vital element of the plan would be eliminated."

Dulles's spin on the Bay of Pigs began appearing in the press as soon as the smoke cleared from the invasion. His version received prominent play in a September 1961 *Fortune* magazine article titled "Cuba: The Record Set Straight." The article was written by *Fortune* staff writer Charles Murphy, a journalist so close to Dulles that the spymaster used him as a ghostwriter. The previous year, Murphy had fawningly agreed to write a Dulles memoir, telling the CIA chief "you have honored me with your invitation to me to lend a hand with your book, and I am looking forward to the association." Much of Murphy's article in *Fortune* sounded like it was dictated directly by Dulles, shifting blame from the CIA to the White House. Murphy later claimed that Admiral Burke had been his source, but the Kennedy brothers suspected that Dulles's deputy, General Charles Cabell, was also involved.

Kennedy was furious about the *Fortune* article, and he had the White House prepare a point-by-point rebuttal for publisher Henry Luce. The media-savvy president knew that he was confronting a formidable opponent in the war of ideas over Cuba. At his first press conference following the Bay of Pigs, JFK put the Washington press corps on alert, telling reporters, "I wouldn't be surprised if information wasn't poured into you" from "interested agencies."

If the president could not match Dulles's wide network of media assets, he brought his own impressive skills to the public relations war with the CIA. Kennedy was adept at massaging influential journalists like *New York Times* Washington columnist James "Scotty" Reston. While the Bay of Pigs disaster was still unfolding, JFK invited Reston to lunch at the White House, confiding to him, "I probably made a mistake in keeping Allen Dulles on. . . . I have never worked with him and therefore I can't estimate his meaning when he tells me things. . . . Dulles is a legendary figure, and it's hard to operate with legendary figures. . . . It's a hell of a way to learn things, but I have learned one thing from this business—that is, that we will have to deal with the CIA."

Word quickly got back to CIA headquarters that if Kennedy was taking the blame in public for the Bay of Pigs, he was privately stabbing Dulles and the agency with his sharp invective, vowing to "splinter the CIA into a thousand pieces and scatter it to the winds."

Kennedy deployed two of his most passionately loyal White House aides, Sorensen and Schlesinger, in the war of words with Dulles's empire. Both men brought a cutting eloquence to the political duel. The week after the Bay of Pigs, Schlesinger, who had adamantly opposed the operation, observed, "We not only look like imperialists . . . we look like stupid, ineffectual imperialists. . . . Allen Dulles and Dick Bissell brought down in a day what Kennedy had been laboring patiently and successfully to build up in three months."

Dulles knew that JFK was maneuvering to dump him, but he made it clear that he would not go without a fight. On May 23, Schlesinger discussed the CIA director's fate with Dulles's mole in the White House, Mac Bundy. Bundy, no doubt channeling his headstrong patron, told Schlesinger that "there would be serious difficulties about procuring the resignation of Allen Dulles." According to Bundy, Dulles believed that "his only mistake was in not having persuaded the president that he must send in the Marines."

As JFK's national security adviser, Bundy was in a delicate position, trying to earn the confidence of the president whom he had just begun serving, while at the same time subtly advocating for Dulles. In the midst of the Bay of Pigs crisis, Bundy had tried to turn Bissell into the scapegoat. He told Schlesinger that Dulles "actually had more misgivings about the project than he had ever expressed to the president, and that he had not done so out of loyalty to Bissell." Bundy added that "he personally would not be able to accept Dick's estimates of a situation like this again." Bundy, who had endorsed the Bay of Pigs plan, was clearly acting on Dulles's behalf when he threw Bissell under the bus. But he failed to halt the White House momentum that was building for Dulles's termination.

The battle over Dulles's future as CIA director came to a head during the presidential investigation of the Bay of Pigs debacle. A few days after the failed invasion, Kennedy appointed General Maxwell Taylor to chair the official inquiry. Taylor, who would later become JFK's military adviser, was closely aligned with Dulles. Fletcher Prouty, an astute observer of Dulles's far-flung Washington network, later called Taylor another key "CIA man at the White House." Dulles, who was appointed to the Taylor Committee along with his ally Admiral Burke, must have thought he had the Bay of Pigs panel tightly wired—just the way he had controlled the blue-ribbon CIA oversight committees during the Eisenhower era.

But Max Taylor also felt a sense of loyalty to Kennedy, who had championed the handsome, ramrod-straight general when Taylor broke with the Eisenhower-Dulles policy of massive retaliation in favor of a more nuanced strategy he called "flexible response." JFK, who was influenced by Taylor's 1959 book, *The Uncertain Trumpet*, called the scholarly Taylor "my kind of general." As chair of the investigation, Taylor maintained a delicate balance, striving diplomatically to avoid putting too much blame on the CIA or the Pentagon. But Taylor's "strongest tilts," in the estimation of CIA historian Jack Pfeiffer, "were toward deflecting criticism of the White House."

Meanwhile, Bobby Kennedy, whom Pfeiffer archly observed "crossed all lines as the president's alter ego," used his position on the Taylor Committee to make sure his brother would be protected. The young, sharp-elbowed attorney general proved to be a tougher advocate for the White House than Dulles and Arleigh Burke were for their respective institutions. RFK deftly blocked the two Kennedy antagonists from focusing blame on the president. As the committee completed its report, Dulles and Burke were reduced to lobbying Taylor to at least insert a footnote stating that if Kennedy had approved air coverage of the landing, "it could well have caused a chain reaction of success throughout Cuba, with resultant defection of some of [Castro's] Militia, the uprising of the populace and eventual success of the operation." But this hypothetical scenario was a pipe dream that only Dulles and Burke were smoking.

Nearly two decades later, Pfeiffer's Bay of Pigs history still reflected agency resentment at how JFK's brother outmaneuvered the CIA and Pentagon during the Taylor investigation. "At the conclusion of the testimony of the witnesses," Pfeiffer wrote, "it was clear that Burke and Dulles . . . were headed for the elephants' burial ground—thanks to Robert Kennedy's denigration of them and their Agencies and, in no small part in the case of Dulles to his abysmal performance as a witness." By the end of the investigation, wrote Pfeiffer, the outplayed Dulles and Burke "were nattering at each other" over how much of the responsibility for the disaster the Navy should share with the CIA.

If the Taylor Committee, which presented its findings to Kennedy on May 16, badly damaged Dulles, the Kirkpatrick Report sealed his fate. Tall, handsome, athletic, and charming, Lyman Kirkpatrick had been one of the agency's rising stars. A graduate of Deerfield and Princeton, he served with the OSS and as an intelligence adviser to General Omar Bradley during the war. A streak of daring ran through the Kirkpatrick family. His sister, Helen, was an intrepid war correspondent, riding with the tanks of the Free French Forces to liberate Paris. Photos of the attractive reporter in a combat helmet and tailored uniform gave her dispatches for the *Chicago Daily News* a glamorous flair. After the war, Lyman Kirkpatrick joined the CIA in its infancy and made his way quickly up the ranks, becoming CIA chief Beetle Smith's right-hand man. Kirkpatrick appeared to be on a fast track to the top of the agency, as covert action chief and then perhaps director.

But in 1952, he was stricken by polio while on assignment in Asia. After a long hospitalization—including a nightmarish ordeal at Walter Reed Hospital, where Dulles had pulled strings to get him admitted—

Kirkpatrick returned to the CIA. He was paralyzed from the waist down and confined to a wheelchair, but he was determined to resume his career. Dulles, who had just taken over the CIA, appointed Kirkpatrick inspector general—an unpopular post since it involved monitoring the agency's internal affairs. By accepting the job, Kirkpatrick was acknowledging that his hopes for the top office were gone. But he demonstrated integrity as IG, recommending that the CIA employees who were responsible for the 1953 death of MKULTRA victim Frank Olson be punished, although they never were. Kirkpatrick also went on record within the agency as opposing the assassination of Lumumba.

Kirkpatrick, who had worked with Joe Kennedy on Eisenhower's intelligence advisory board, belonged to the pro-Kennedy faction inside the CIA. Kirkpatrick and JFK were on friendly terms. The president, who knew how important swimming exercises had been for the polio-afflicted Franklin Roosevelt, invited Kirkpatrick to use the White House pool, where Kennedy swam to ease his own back ailments. It was Kirkpatrick who noticed that there was no official portrait of President Kennedy on display at CIA headquarters, and after Dulles had left the agency, the inspector general arranged for one finally to be hung.

Still, Kirkpatrick was a lifelong CIA man, and he owed his resurrected career to Dulles. So the Old Man felt deeply betrayed when Kirkpatrick handed him and his deputy, Charles Cabell, copies of the highly critical Bay of Pigs autopsy. A furious Dulles denounced the report as a "hatchet job." Dulles and Cabell "were both exceedingly shocked and upset, irritated and annoyed and mad and everything else," Kirkpatrick recalled.

Agency loyalists like Sam Halpern began spreading the word that Kirkpatrick was acting out of acrimony. The report was "basically Kirk's vendetta against Bissell," said Halpern years later, still promoting the agency line. "He had been a real rising star. Once he had polio, he got sidetracked and became a bitter man." But, in truth, Kirkpatrick was a man of conscience. "When you speak honestly about what people did wrong, you're going to step on toes," said Kirkpatrick's son, Lyman Jr., a retired Army intelligence colonel. "But that was his job."

Dulles succeeded in suppressing the Kirkpatrick Report; it would remain locked away until the CIA was finally compelled to release it in 1998. But as word spread in Washington circles about the harsh report, it added to the anti-Kennedy passions flaring within the CIA.

The Bay of Pigs debacle produced a "stuttering rage" among CIA officers aligned with Dulles, according to CIA veteran Joseph B. Smith—especially among those on the Cuba task force. "I had the feeling all those [agents] there felt almost that the world had ended," Smith remembered. In August, months after the failed venture, when longtime veteran Ralph McGehee returned from Vietnam to agency headquarters, he, too, found the CIA in turmoil. Rumors spread that Kennedy was going to exact his revenge by slashing the CIA workforce through a massive "reduction in force," code-named the "701 program" by the agency.

"It seemed [to us] that the RIF program was aimed more at the CIA than other agencies," McGehee observed. "This was a tension-filled, dismal time. . . . The halls seemed filled with the strained, anxious looks of the soon-to-be unemployed."

When Kennedy's ax did fall, McGehee was stunned by the carnage. "About one of every five was fired. The tension became too much for some. On several occasions, one of my former office mates came to the office howling drunk and worked his way onto the 701 list."

The anti-Kennedy rage inside CIA headquarters also reverberated at the Pentagon. "Pulling out the rug [on the Bay of Pigs invaders]," fumed Joint Chiefs chairman Lemnitzer, was "unbelievable . . . absolutely reprehensible, almost criminal." Years later, the name Kennedy still made "31-Knot" Burke boil over. "Mr. Kennedy," the admiral told an oral historian from the U.S. Naval Institute, "was a very bad president. . . . He permitted himself to jeopardize the nation." The Kennedy team, he added, "didn't realize the power of the United States or how to use the power of the United States. It was a game to them. . . . They were inexperienced people."

If Kennedy's national security mandarins were filled with contempt for him, the feeling was clearly mutual. On the heels of the Bay of Pigs, when Lemnitzer urged militant action in other hot spots such as Laos, the president brushed him off. He disliked even being in the same room with the men who had led him astray on Cuba. JFK "dismissed [Lemnitzer and the others] as a bunch of old men," Schlesinger recalled years later. "He thought Lemnitzer was a dope."

Kennedy's vice president, Lyndon Johnson, was disturbed by JFK's growing estrangement from the military and the CIA. "Of course, Johnson was a great admirer of the military," recalled Jack Bell, a White House reporter for the Associated Press. "He didn't believe that Kennedy was paying enough attention to the military leaders."

Chatting with Bell one day, LBJ told the reporter, "You don't hardly ever see the chiefs of staff around [the White House] anymore." As Johnson was painfully aware, he was not part of JFK's inner circle either—"he just sat around with his thumb in his mouth," as Bell put it.

It was Bobby, the tough kid brother reviled by Johnson, who was the president's indispensable partner. "Every time they have a conference down there [at the White House], don't kid anybody about who was the top adviser," Johnson bitterly told Bell. "It isn't McNamara, the chiefs of staff, or anybody else like that. Bobby is first in and last out. And Bobby is the boy he listens to."

It was Cuba that created the first fracture between Kennedy and his national security chain of command. But while the Bay of Pigs was still dominating the front pages, the CIA mucked its way into another international crisis that required the president's urgent attention. The Cuba invasion has all but erased this second crisis from history. But the strange events that occurred in Paris in April 1961 reinforced the disturbing feeling that President Kennedy was not in control of his own government.

Paris was in turmoil. At dawn on Saturday morning, April 22, a group of retired French generals had seized power in Algiers to block President Charles de Gaulle from settling the long, bloody war for Algerian independence. Rumors quickly spread that the coup plotters were coming next for de Gaulle himself, and that the skies over Paris would soon be filled with battle-hardened paratroopers and French Foreign Legionnaires from Algeria. Gripped by the dying convulsions of its colonial reign, France braced for a calamitous showdown.

The threat to French democracy was actually even more immediate than feared. On Saturday evening, two units of paratroopers totaling over two thousand men huddled in the Forest of Orleans and the Forest of Rambouillet, not much more than an hour outside Paris. The rebellious paratroopers were poised for the final command to join up with tank units from Rambouillet and converge on the capital, with the aim of seizing the Élysée Palace and other key government posts. By Sunday, panic was sweeping through Paris. All air traffic was halted over the area, the Metro was shut down, and cinemas were dark. Only the cafés remained open, where Parisians crowded anxiously to swap the latest gossip.

News that the coup was being led by the widely admired Maurice Challe, a former air force chief and commander of French forces in Algeria, stunned the government in Paris, from de Gaulle down. Challe, a squat, quiet man, was a World War II hero and, so it had seemed, a loyal Gaullist. But the savage passions of the war in Algeria had deeply affected Challe and left him vulnerable to the persuasions of more zealous French officers. He had promised Algeria's French settlers and pro-French Muslims that they would not be abandoned, and he felt a soldierly responsibility to stand by his oath, as well as by the memory of the French servicemen who had lost their lives in the war. In his radio broadcast to the people of France, the coup leader explained that he was taking his stand against de Gaulle's "government of capitulation . . . so that our dead shall not have died for nothing."

De Gaulle quickly concluded that Challe must be acting with the support of U.S. intelligence, and Élysée officials began spreading this word to the press. Shortly before his resignation from the French military, Challe had served as NATO commander in chief, and he had developed close relations with a number of high-ranking U.S. officers stationed in the military alliance's Fontainebleau headquarters. Challe and American security officials shared a deep disaffection with de Gaulle.

The stubborn, seventy-year-old pillar of French nationalism was viewed as a growing obstacle to U.S. ambitions for NATO because he refused to incorporate French troops under allied command and insisted on building a separate nuclear force beyond Washington's control. De Gaulle's enemies in Paris and Washington were also convinced that the French president's awkward steps toward granting Algerian independence threatened to create a "Soviet base" in strategic, oil-rich North Africa.

In panic-gripped Paris, reports of U.S. involvement in the coup filled newspapers across the political spectrum. Geneviève Tabouis, a columnist for *Paris-Jour*, zeroed in directly on Dulles as the main culprit in an article headlined "The Strategy of Allen Dulles." Other news reports revealed that Jacques Soustelle—a former governor-general of Algeria who joined the Secret Army Organization (Organisation de l'Armée Secrète, or OAS), a notorious anti–de Gaulle terrorist group—had a luncheon meeting with Richard Bissell in Washington the previous December.

De Gaulle's foreign ministry was the source of some of the most provocative charges in the press, including the allegation that CIA agents sought funding for the Challe coup from multinational corporations, such as Belgian mining companies operating in the Congo. Ministry officials also alleged that Americans with ties to extremist groups had surfaced in Paris during the coup drama, including one identified as a "political counselor for the Luce [media] group," who was heard to say, "An operation is being prepared in Algiers to put a stop to communism, and we will not fail as we did in Cuba."

Stories about the CIA's French intrigues soon began spreading to the American press. A Paris correspondent for *The Washington Post* reported that Challe had launched his revolt "because he was convinced he had unqualified American support"—assurances, Challe was led to believe, "emanating from President Kennedy himself." Who gave these assurances, the *Post* reporter asked his French sources? The Pentagon, the CIA? "It's the same thing," he was told.

Dulles was forced to issue a strong denial of CIA involvement in the putsch. "Any reports or allegations that the Central Intelligence Agency or any of its personnel had anything to do with the generals' revolt were completely false," the spymaster declared, blaming Moscow for spreading the charges.

C. L. Sulzberger, the CIA-friendly *New York Times* columnist, took up the agency's defense, echoing Dulles's indignant denial. "To set the record straight," Sulzberger wrote, sounding like an agency official, "our Government behaved with discretion, wisdom and propriety during the [French] insurrection. This applies to all branches, [including] the CIA." Years later, investigative reporter Carl Bernstein exposed the ties between Sulzberger and the CIA. "Young Cy Sulzberger had some uses," a CIA official told Bernstein. "He was very eager, he loved to cooperate." (Bernstein conveniently left unexamined the long history of cooperation between the CIA and his own former employer, *The Washington Post*.)

But *The New York Times*'s Scotty Reston was more aligned with the sentiments of the Kennedy White House. Echoing the charges circulating in the French press, Reston reported that the CIA was indeed "involved in an embarrassing liaison with the anti-Gaullist officers." Reston communicated the rising fury in JFK's inner circle over the CIA's rogue behavior, in the wake of the Bay of Pigs fiasco and the French escapade: "All this has increased the feeling in the White House that the CIA has gone beyond the bounds of an objective intelligence-gathering agency and has become the advocate of men and policies that have embarrassed the Administration."

Allen Dulles was once again making his own policy, this time in France. There was a long history of acrimony between Dulles and de Gaulle, dating back to World War II and the complex internal politics of the French Resistance. As OSS chief in Switzerland, Dulles favored a far right faction of the Resistance that was opposed to de Gaulle. In his war memoirs, de Gaulle accused Dulles of being part of "a scheme" that was determined to "silence or set aside" the French general. Pierre de Bénouville, a right-wing Resistance leader on Dulles's OSS payroll, was later accused of betraying Jean Moulin, de Gaulle's dashing representative in the French underground, to the Gestapo. After he was captured, Moulin was subjected to brutal torture before being beaten to death—by the notorious war criminal Klaus Barbie, according to some accounts.

After de Gaulle was elected president in 1958, he sought to purge the French government of its CIA-connected elements. Dulles had made heavy inroads into France's political, cultural, and intelligence circles in the postwar years. According to some French reports, during his visits to Paris the spymaster would set himself up at a suite in the Ritz Hotel, where he would dispense bags full of cash to friendly politicians, journalists, and other influential figures. Some were wined and dined and enticed with beautiful Parisian call girls.

De Gaulle was particularly determined to shut down the secret "stay-behind army" that Dulles had organized in France—a network of anti-Communist militants with access to buried arms caches who were originally recruited to resist a potential Soviet invasion but were now aligned with the rebellious generals and other groups plotting to overthrow French democracy. De Gaulle ordered his young security adviser, Constantin Melnik, to shut down the murky, stay-behind network of fascists, spooks, and criminals, which Melnik agreed was "very dangerous for the security of France." But Melnik, who was trained at the RAND Corporation, a leading think tank for the U.S. national security complex, was another admirer of Dulles, and the stay-behind underground continued to operate in France. Melnik—who was the son of a White Russian general and the grandson of Czar Nicolas II's personal physician, who was executed along with the imperial family—was as passionately anti-Soviet as his U.S. security colleagues.

In May 1958, when de Gaulle returned to power in Paris after a twelve-year absence, Dulles flew to Paris for a face-to-face meeting with the legendary Frenchman to see if their differences could be resolved. Dulles had great confidence in his personal powers of persuasion. But the proud de Gaulle refused to see the spymaster, handing him off to one of his close associates, Michel Debré. A formal dinner was organized for Dulles and Jim Hunt, the CIA station chief in Paris, which was also attended by Melnik. Dulles seemed unfazed by de Gaulle's slight. But, as French journalist Frédéric Charpier later commented, "Upon returning to the Ritz Hotel, Dulles drew some lessons from the evening, which confirmed his fears. De Gaulle promised to be a tough and hostile partner who was sure to put an end to the laissez-faire attitude which up until then had characterized the [French government]."

World leaders defied Allen Dulles at their peril—even leaders like Charles de Gaulle, whose nation's warm, fraternal relations with the United States dated back to the American Revolution. After Dulles flew home to Washington, the CIA's reports on de Gaulle took a sharper edge. At a National Security Council meeting convened by Eisenhower in September 1958, gloomy prognostications were made about the French leader's ability to settle the Algerian crisis to America's satisfaction. The possibility of overthrowing de Gaulle and replacing him with someone more in tune with U.S. interests was openly discussed, but the idea was discarded at that point as too risky.

However, by the time Kennedy took office in January 1961, the CIA was primed for a power switch in Paris. On January 26, Dulles sent a report to the new president on the French situation that seemed to be preparing Kennedy for de Gaulle's imminent elimination, without giving any hint of the CIA's own involvement in the plot. "A pre-revolutionary atmosphere reigns in France," Dulles informed JFK. "The Army and the Air Force are staunchly opposed to de Gaulle," the spymaster continued, exaggerating the extent of the military opposition, as if to present the demise of the French president as a fait accompli. "At least 80 percent of the officers are violently against him. They haven't forgotten that in 1958, he had given his word of honor that he would never abandon Algeria. He is now reneging on his promise, and they hate him for that. De Gaulle surely won't last if he tries to let go of Algeria. Everything will probably be over for him by the end of the year—he will be either deposed or assassinated." Dulles clearly knew much more, but he wasn't sharing it with Kennedy.

When the coup against de Gaulle began three months later, Kennedy was still in the dark. It was a tumultuous time for the young administration. As he continued to wrestle with fallout from the Bay of Pigs crisis, JFK was suddenly besieged with howls of outrage from a major ally, accusing his own security services of seditious activity. It was a stinging embarrassment for the new American president, who was scheduled to fly to Paris for a state visit the following month. To add to the insult, the coup had been triggered by de Gaulle's efforts to bring French colonial rule in Algeria to an end—a goal that JFK himself had ardently championed. The CIA's support for the coup was one more defiant display of contempt—a back of the hand aimed not only at de Gaulle but at Kennedy.

JFK took pains to assure Paris that he strongly supported de Gaulle's presidency, phoning Hervé Alphand, the French ambassador in Washington, to directly communicate these assurances. But, according to Alphand, Kennedy's disavowal of official U.S. involvement in the coup came with a disturbing addendum—the American president could not vouch for his own intelligence agency. Kennedy told Alphand that "the CIA is such a vast and poorly controlled machine that the most unlikely maneuvers might be true."

This admission of presidential impotence, which Alphand reported to Paris, was a startling moment in U.S. foreign relations, though it remains largely unknown today. Kennedy then underlined how deeply estranged he was from his own security machinery by taking the extraordinary step of asking Alphand for the French government's help to track down the U.S. officials behind the coup, promising to fully punish them. "[Kennedy] would be quite ready to take all necessary measures in the interest of good Franco-American relations, whatever the rank or functions of [the] incriminated people," Alphand cabled French foreign minister Maurice Couve de Murville.

To solidify his support for de Gaulle, Kennedy ordered U.S. ambassador James Gavin to offer the French leader "any help" he might need—clearly indicating that U.S. troops would even fire on rebel forces from Algeria if they tried to land at American military bases in France. De Gaulle proudly declined the offer as "well-intentioned, but inappropriate"—perhaps horrified at the prospect of American GIs killing French soldiers on his nation's soil. But Kennedy did arrange for U.S. base commanders to take steps to camouflage landing sites, in case rebel planes attempted to use them.

In the wake of the crises in Cuba and France provoked by his own security officials, Kennedy began to display a new boldness. JFK's assertiveness surprised CIA officials, who had apparently counted on Kennedy to be sidelined during the French coup. Agency officials assured coup leaders that the president would be too "absorbed in the Cuban affair" to act decisively against the plot. But JFK did react quickly to the French crisis, putting on high alert Ambassador Gavin, a decorated paratrooper commander in World War II who could be counted on to keep NATO forces in line. The president also dispatched his French-speaking press spokesman, Pierre Salinger, to Paris to communicate directly with Élysée Palace officials.

As Paris officials knew, the new American president already had something of a prickly relationship with de Gaulle, but he had strong feelings for France—and they made sure to absolve JFK of personal responsibility for the coup in their leaks to the press. French press accounts referred to the CIA as a "reactionary state-within-a-state" that operated outside of Kennedy's control.

After JFK's death, Alphand spoke fondly of the bonds between Kennedy and France. "He thought that harmonious relations between the U.S. and France were a fundamental element of world equilibrium. He knew France as a boy. He came to France for his holidays—the south of France—and he knew France also through his wife. Jacqueline made many, many trips to Paris. I know that Jacqueline helped him very much to understand France. She loves France—she has French blood—she speaks our language very well and she asked him to read the memoirs of General de Gaulle."

Kennedy's strong show of support for de Gaulle undoubtedly helped fortify French resolve against the rebellious generals. In the midst of the crisis, the American president issued a public message to de Gaulle, telling him, "In this grave hour for France, I want you to know of my continuing friendship and support as well as that of the American people."

But it was de Gaulle himself, and the French people, who turned the tide against the coup.

By Sunday, the second day of the coup, a dark foreboding had settled over Paris. "I am surprised that you are still alive," the president of France's National Assembly bluntly told de Gaulle that morning. "If I were Challe, I would have already swooped down on Paris; the army here will move out of the way rather than shoot. . . . If I were in the position Challe put himself in, as soon as I burst in, I would have you executed with a bullet in the back, here in the stairwell, and say you were trying to flee." De Gaulle himself realized that if Challe did airlift his troops from Algiers to France, "there was not much to stop them."

But at eight o'clock that evening, a defiant de Gaulle went on the air, as nearly all of France gathered around the TV, and rallied his nation with the most inspiring address of his long public career. He looked exhausted, with dark circles under his eyes. But he had put on his soldier's uniform for the occasion, and his voice was full of passion. De Gaulle began by denouncing the rebellious generals. The nation had been betrayed "by men whose duty, honor and raison d'être it was to serve and to obey." Now it was the duty of every French citizen to protect the nation from these military traitors. "In the name of France," de Gaulle shouted, thumping the table in front of him, "I order that all means—I repeat *all means*—be employed to block the road everywhere to those men!"

De Gaulle's final words were a battle cry. "*Françaises, Français! Aidez-moi!*" And all over France, millions of people did rush to the aid of their nation. The following day, a general strike was organized to protest the putsch. Led primarily by the left, including labor unions and the Communist Party, the mass protest won broad political support. Over ten million people joined the nationwide demonstrations, with hundreds of thousands marching in the streets of Paris, carrying banners proclaiming "Peace in Algeria" and shouting, "Fascism will not pass!" Even police officers associations expressed "complete solidarity" with the protests, as did the Roman Catholic Confederation, which denounced the "criminal acts" of the coup leaders, warning that they "threaten to plunge the country into civil war."

Hundreds of people rushed to the nation's airfields and prepared to block the runways with their vehicles if Challe's planes tried to land. Others gathered outside government ministries in Paris to guard them against attack. André Malraux, the great novelist turned minister of culture, threaded his way through one such crowd, handing out helmets and uniforms. Meanwhile, at the huge Renault factory on the outskirts of Paris, workers took control of the sprawling complex and formed militias, demanding weapons from the government so that they could fend off rebel assaults.

"In many ways, France, and particularly Paris, relived its great revolutionary past Sunday night and Monday—the past of the revolutionary barricades, of vigilance committees and of workers' councils," reported *The New York Times*.

De Gaulle's ringing address to the nation and the massive public response had a sobering effect on the French military. Challe's support quickly began melting away, even—humiliatingly—within the ranks of his own military branch, the air force. Pilots flew their planes out of Algeria, and others feigned mechanical troubles, depriving Challe's troops of the air transport they needed to descend on Paris.

Meanwhile, de Gaulle moved quickly to arrest military officers in France who were involved in the coup. Police swooped down on the Paris apartment of an army captain who was plotting pro-putsch street riots, and de Gaulle's minister of the interior seized the general in charge of the rebel forces that were gathered in the forests outside Paris. Deprived of their leader, the insurrectionary units sheepishly began to disperse.

By Tuesday night, Challe knew that the coup had failed. The next day, he surrendered and was flown to Paris. Challe emerged from the plane "carrying his own suitcase, looking crumpled and insignificant in civilian clothes," according to *Time*. "He stumbled at the foot of the landing steps, [falling] heavily on his hands and knees." It was an ignominious homecoming for the man who had fully believed that, with U.S. support, he was to replace the great de Gaulle. Challe expected to face a firing squad, but de Gaulle's military tribunal proved surprisingly merciful, sentencing the fifty-five-year-old general to fifteen years in prison.

After the failed coup, de Gaulle launched a new purge of his security forces. He ousted General Paul Grossin, the powerful chief of SDECE, the French secret service, and he shut down its armed unit, the *11th Choc* (Shock Battalion), which he suspected of being a breeding ground for the coup. Grossin, who was closely aligned with the CIA, had told Frank Wisner over lunch that the return of de Gaulle to power was equivalent to the Communists taking over in Paris.

The 11th Choc had grown into a dangerously unhinged killing unit, targeting representatives of the Algerian independence movement and their European supporters, even on the streets of France. Those branded enemies of the French empire were gunned down, blown up, or poisoned by SDECE's action arm. Aided by ex-Nazi agents of Reinhard Gehlen's organization, the 11th Choc's assassination campaign reached the point where "liquidations [were] an almost daily routine," according to Philippe Thyraud de Vosjoli, a veteran SDECE agent who served as the liaison to the CIA.

Shortly after pushing out Grossin, de Gaulle also jettisoned his security adviser, Constantin Melnik, Dulles's close ally. Late into his life, Melnik continued to insist that the CIA was always a friend to de Gaulle—which would have come as a surprise to the French president. Writing in his 1999 memoir, *Politically Incorrect*, Melnik flatly declared, "I can testify that . . . despite suspicious yelping by Gaullist camp followers . . . the CIA always was a faithful ally of General de Gaulle, even of his often torturous Algerian policies." After de Gaulle dumped Melnik, Dulles—who by then had also been fired—immediately offered to hire him for a new private intelligence agency he was planning in the Third World. But Melnik declined, instead pursuing a career in French publishing and politics.

For the rest of his ten-year presidency, which ended with his retirement from politics in 1969, de Gaulle continued to take strong countermeasures against forces he regarded as seditious threats. In 1962, he expelled CIA station chief Alfred Ulmer, a gung ho veteran of Dulles's

Cold War battlegrounds. In 1967, de Gaulle evicted NATO from France to regain "full sovereignty [over] French territory" after discovering that the military alliance was encouraging Western European secret services to interfere in France's domestic politics.

Following the Algiers putsch, de Gaulle remained an assassination target—particularly during the explosive months before and after he finally recognized Algerian independence in July 1962. The most dramatic attempt on his life was staged the next month by the OAS—an ambush made famous in the Frederick Forsyth novel and movie *The Day of the Jackal.* As de Gaulle's black Citroën sped along the Avenue de la Libération in Paris, with the president and his wife in the rear seat, a dozen OAS snipers opened fire on the vehicle. Two of the president's motorcycle bodyguards were killed—and the bullet-riddled Citroën skidded sharply. But de Gaulle was fortunate to have a skilled and loyal security team, and his chauffeur was able to pull the car out of its spin and speed to safety, despite all four tires' being shot out. The president and his wife, who kept their heads down throughout the fusillade, escaped unharmed.

The French president demonstrated that he was willing to fight fire with fire. According to de Vosjoli, de Gaulle loyalists in SDECE even recruited their own secret assassins—including a particularly violent group of Vietnamese exiles—who blew up cafés in Algeria frequented by enemies of de Gaulle and kidnapped, tortured, and murdered other OAS combatants deemed a threat to the president. Democracy in France in the early 1960s was sustained as the result of a vicious underground war that the old French general was willing to fight with equal ferocity.

Because of the severe security measures he took, Charles de Gaulle survived his tumultuous presidency. He died of a heart attack the year after he left office, just short of his eightieth birthday, slumping over quietly in his armchair after watching the evening news.

President Kennedy met only once with de Gaulle, on his state visit to Paris at the end of May 1961, a month after the failed coup. The president and First Lady were feted at a banquet in Élysée Palace, where the old general—dazzled by Jackie—leaned down closely to hear every breathy word she spoke to him, in fluent French. During the three-day visit, the two heads of state discussed many pressing issues, from Laos to Berlin to Cuba. But Kennedy and de Gaulle never broached the touchy subject of the coup, much less the CIA's involvement in it. As French journalist Vincent Jauvert later observed, "Why wake up old demons who had barely fallen asleep?"

Kennedy knew that he would have to resume wrestling with those demons as soon as he returned home. He would have to decide how deeply to purge his own security agencies, as de Gaulle had already begun to do in France. Kennedy knew there would be steep political costs involved in taking on the CIA and Pentagon. But, as Walter Lippmann had told Schlesinger, "Kennedy will not begin to be President until he starts to break with Eisenhower." Continuity in Washington was no longer the new president's concern. Shaken by the traumatic events in Cuba and France, JFK was ready to remake his government.

A few weeks after the Bay of Pigs and the foiled French coup, JFK asked Jackie to invite Dulles for drinks or tea at the White House. Charlie Wrightsman and his wife were also dropping by, and Kennedy wanted to make a point. The Florida tycoon had self-righteously told Kennedy that he was *not* going to be seeing his old friend Dulles during his trip to Washington—his way of snubbing the spymaster for bungling the job in Cuba. The president was "disgusted" by Wrightsman's disloyalty to Dulles, according to Jackie, so he went out of his way to include the disgraced CIA leader in the White House's get-together. By now, enough time had elapsed since the disasters of April, and with Dulles on his way out, Kennedy was feeling magnanimous toward the Old Man.

"[Jack] was so loyal always to people in, you know, trouble," the First Lady later recalled. "And he made a special effort to come back from [the Oval Office] and sit around with Jayne and Charlie Wrightsman, just to show Charlie what he thought of Allen Dulles. And, I mean, it made all the difference to Allen Dulles. I was with him about five [or ten] minutes before Jack got there. He just looked like, I don't know, Cardinal Mindszenty on trial," she said, referring to the Hungarian prelate who was sentenced to life in prison after being found guilty of treason by a Soviet-run show trial. "You know, just a shell of what he was. And Jack came and talked—put his arm around him. . . . Well, wasn't that nice? It was just to show Charlie Wrightsman. But it shows something about Jack. I mean, he knew [that] Dulles had obviously botched everything up. [But], you know, he had a tenderness for the man."

But "poor Allen Dulles," as Jackie took to referring to him, was likely untouched by the president's gesture. The CIA director's resentment of Kennedy was growing by the day, as his fingers slowly lost their grip on power. Feeling the young man's arm wrapped paternally around his shoulder would have chilled Dulles, not warmed him. The spymaster had served every president since Woodrow Wilson. And now, here he was, being comforted by this weak pretty boy who did not belong in the same company as the great men who preceded him. It was appalling that he, *Allen Dulles*, should be consoled by such a man.

Though Dulles himself kept his fury carefully concealed, his most loyal aides and political allies freely vented their feelings against the Kennedy White House on the Old Man's behalf. Howard Hunt, who worked as the CIA's political liaison with the volatile Cuban exile community on the Bay of Pigs, called Dulles and Bissell "scapegoats to expiate administration guilt." Hunt, whose anti-Communist passions equaled those of his militant Cuban compadres, was deeply moved by the way his boss comported himself during his slow fadeout at the CIA. "As a member of Dulles's staff," Hunt remembered, "I lunched in the Director's mess, seeing him return from each [Taylor] Committee session more drawn and gray. But on taking his place at the head of the table, Mr. Dulles's demeanor changed into hearty cheerfulness—a joke here, a baseball bet there, came from this remarkable man whose long career of government service had been destroyed unjustly by men who were laboring unceasingly to preserve their own public images."

The summer following the Bay of Pigs, Prescott Bush—the CIA's man in the Senate—and his wife, Dorothy, invited Dulles to dinner at their Washington home. The spymaster showed up with John McCone in tow—the Republican businessman and former Atomic Energy Commission chairman Kennedy had just privately tapped as Dulles's replacement. Bush, who was still unaware that Dulles had been officially deposed, was surprised to see McCone, "whom," he later recalled in a letter to Clover, "we had not thought of as a particular friend of Allen's. But Allen broke the ice promptly, and said that he wanted us to meet his successor. The announcement came the next day." The dinner conversation around the Bush family table that night was awkward. "We tried to make a pleasant evening of it," Bush wrote, "but I was rather sick at heart, and angry too, for it was the Kennedy's [sic] that brot [sic] about the fiasco. And here they were making Allen seem to be the goat, which he wasn't and did not deserve. I have never forgiven them."

On November 28, 1961, Dulles was given his formal send-off at the CIA, in a ceremony held at the agency's brand-new headquarters, a vast, modernist complex carved out of the woods in Langley, Virginia. It was a day of clashing emotions for Dulles. The gleaming new puzzle palace, which Dulles had commissioned, was seen by many as a monument to his long reign—but he would never occupy the director's suite. Now some agency wits were snidely christening the Langley edifice "The Allen Dulles Memorial Mausoleum."

President Kennedy was gracious in his farewell remarks, as he bestowed the agency's highest honor—the National Security Medal—on Dulles. "I regard Allen Dulles as an almost unique figure in our country," he told the crowd gathered in a sterile, fluorescent-lit theater, including a somber-faced Clover and Eleanor Dulles, and an equally stern-looking General Lemnitzer and J. Edgar Hoover, who almost certainly were wondering when they would be next to go. "I know of no man," the president continued, "who brings a greater sense of personal commitment to his work—who has less pride in office—than he has."

This last piece of flattery was particularly overblown, as Kennedy well knew, because there were few men in his administration brimming with as much self-admiration as Allen Dulles. The departing CIA director had made sure that invitations to his medal ceremony were sent out to a who's who list of Fortune 500 executives, including the chiefs of General Electric, General Motors, Ford, DuPont, Coca-Cola, Chase Manhattan, U.S. Steel, Standard Oil, IBM, CBS, and Time-Life. He kept copies of all the flowery farewells that poured in from the corporate world, including letters from 20th Century Fox movie mogul Spyros Skouras, and conglomerate tycoon J. Peter Grace, who wrote, "It is almost unbelievable that one family could produce two men of the caliber of yours and your late, sorely missed, brother."

But, after the ceremony, Dulles looked a bit lost and forlorn as he waved to Kennedy's departing helicopter from the front steps of the headquarters he would never occupy. The following day was even more melancholy for Dulles as JFK swore in McCone at the old CIA building on E Street. Clover dropped him off at the ceremony in the family car, since Dulles was no longer entitled to a CIA limousine and driver. "Clover, I'll be home later in a taxi," the Old Man told his wife as he climbed out of the car. He was overheard by Lawrence "Red" White, the agency's efficient, nuts-and-bolts administrator, who insisted that Dulles be driven home in an official car. Dulles made a show of protesting but accepted the kind gesture—one of the few bright spots in what colleagues described as a very dark day for the espionage legend. "His morale," White recalled, "was pretty low on his last day as DCI [Director of Central Intelligence]."

Retired at home in Georgetown, the old spymaster's funereal mood did not lift as Kennedy proceeded to rid his administration of remnants of the fallen Dulles dynasty. First to go were the Dulles deputies most closely associated with the Bay of Pigs, Dick Bissell and Charles Cabell. Then Attorney General Bobby Kennedy, his brother's vigilant watchman, tracked down Eleanor Dulles, who was still working quietly on German affairs in Foggy Bottom, and had Secretary of State Rusk fire her. "I don't want any more of the Dulles family around," the attorney general was heard to say. Eleanor took it hard. "It was silly, I suppose," she later remarked. "I was 66 years old, and a lot of my friends asked why I should want to go on working. Well, I had psychological and financial reasons. My job at State was a valuable thing to cling to. Besides, I had debts. I had put two children through college, and I needed a salary."

Over at the Pentagon, JFK had already begun to purge Dulles Cold Warriors like Arleigh Burke, who was drummed out of the Navy in August. Next to go was Lemnitzer, who was replaced as Joint Chiefs chairman by Maxwell Taylor in November, the same month Dulles himself was shown the door.

Kennedy took further steps to signal that the Dulles era was over and that the CIA would no longer be allowed to run wild; he placed overseas agents under the control of U.S. ambassadors and shifted responsibility for future paramilitary operations like the Bay of Pigs to the Pentagon. It was the Kennedy brothers, not the Dulles brothers, who now ran Washington.

Dulles found it hard to adjust to life on the political sidelines. "He had a very difficult time to decompress," said Jim Angleton, his long-time acolyte. But it soon became clear that the Dulles dynasty was not entirely dismantled.

In truth, the Kennedy purge had left the ranks of Dulles loyalists at the CIA largely untouched. Top Dulles men like Angleton and Helms remained on the job. And the Old Man's shadow knights never abandoned their king. They continued to call on him in Georgetown, with Angleton visiting two or three times a week. They consulted with him on agency affairs, as if he were still DCI, and not John McCone. They collaborated with him on plans for books and film projects. They continued to kneel before Allen Dulles, their banished commander, and kiss his ring. And soon, Dulles began to emerge from his gloomy refuge, ready for action. By mid-January 1962, the "retired" spymaster was writing an old comrade, "As you know, I am not much of a believer in either retirement or long vacations." The house on Q Street was already on its way to becoming the seat of a government in exile. Dulles had been deposed, but his reign continued.

Rome on the Potomac

By the evening of June 16, 1962, when bow-tied Arthur Schlesinger Jr. went tumbling fully clothed into the swimming pool at Hickory Hill, Robert and Ethel Kennedy's estate in suburban Virginia, the dunking of party guests had become a New Frontier ritual. Dinner parties at Hickory Hill, where dogs and children ran wild through the house and across the rolling lawns, were already a colorful part of Washington society lore. Invitations to Bobby and Ethel's backyard fests signaled insider status in the youthful Kennedy court. Judy Garland sang; Harry Belafonte did the twist; national heroes like astronaut John Glenn faced bold, new challenges. On this particular evening, Glenn, who had recently become the first American to orbit the earth, was dared by the rambunctious Ethel to sit with her at dinner—on a plank that had been laid precariously across the pool. The astronaut succeeded in staying dry, but Ethel ended up in the pool when Schlesinger and another guest began mischievously bouncing up and down on the wobbly board. Later, as Schlesinger chivalrously leaned down to help Ethel out of the water, a prankster bumped him and the respected Harvard historian went headlong into the pool, taking the attorney general's wife down with him.

The raucous antics of the Kennedy crowd were greeted by much of the Washington establishment as a welcome relief from the fusty Eisenhower regime. The Kennedy brothers and their team brought such relentless vigor to their jobs, they were allowed to blow off steam in their off-hours. There had been no scolding in the press, for instance, the year before when Senator Edward M. Kennedy, the president's fun-loving baby brother, had emerged from his own swimming pool baptism at Hickory Hill, "a huge, dripping mass in a now hopelessly rumpled dinner jacket," as Schlesinger recalled.

But by June 1962, the Kennedy administration was deeply embattled, from within and without. And the Kennedy circle's unrestrained merrymaking now was regarded as unseemly in some quarters. Drew Pearson noted in his column that "Southern congressmen were especially interested in the fact that Ethel Kennedy, sister-in-law of the president, twisted with Harry Belafonte, well-known Negro singer." Meanwhile, Schlesinger's swimming pool high jinks were splashed across the front page of the anti-Kennedy *New York Herald Tribune.* As JFK's main link to the liberal intelligentsia and left wing of the Democratic Party, the White House adviser had become an especially tempting political target.

Henry J. Taylor, a syndicated newspaper columnist, led the press campaign against Schlesinger, taking advantage of the embarrassing publicity over his Hickory Hill water sports to level other charges against Kennedy's court philosopher. Taylor accused Schlesinger of violating the White House code of ethics by moonlighting as a freelance writer, churning out political essays for publications like *The New York Times* and *The Saturday Evening Post,* and doing movie reviews for a chic new glossy magazine called *Show.*

It turned out that the White House had no such ban against outside freelancing and that Kennedy, an ardent movie lover, thoroughly enjoyed Schlesinger's reviews. One night, when Roger Vadim's arty vampire movie *Blood and Roses* was being screened in the White House projection room, a bored Kennedy got up halfway through the feature and told Schlesinger he would be content to read his review. Before he left, the president shared some of his own rather sophisticated movie opinions with Schlesinger, urging him to do a comparative review of the Italian film *Girl with a Suitcase* and *A Cold Wind in August,* an obscure independent feature. He then declared his disappointment with *Break-*

fast at Tiffany's and expressed his regret "that Hollywood had no guts any longer and could not do a sharp or interesting film."

Taylor's attack on Schlesinger—in which he warned of the liberal historian's pernicious influence on Kennedy policy—spread to other media outlets, including *Time* magazine, which poked fun at Schlesinger's Hickory Hill frivolity and, taking the opposite tack from Taylor, questioned whether he really did much of anything as "special assistant" to President Kennedy. Thomas "Tommy the Cork" Corcoran, FDR's legendary adviser and a longtime Washington power broker, didn't like the beating that Schlesinger was getting in the press and he phoned his young friend at the White House. "I scent a manhunt," Corcoran told Schlesinger. "The play they gave to the swimming pool story was the tip-off. They are out to get you." The Cork warned Schlesinger that he had heard Republicans were spreading a vicious story that they had found someone claiming to be an old Harvard classmate of Schlesinger, and "he will swear that he knew you then as a member of the Communist Party."

In the midst of the media furor, Schlesinger felt tempted to offer Kennedy his resignation. Late one afternoon, when Schlesinger went to see the president in the Oval Office on another matter, JFK asked him how he was holding up. "It's been a bad couple of days," he told Kennedy. The president responded in a "kindly way," Schlesinger noted in his journal. "Don't worry about it," JFK told his downcast adviser. "Everyone knows that Henry Taylor is a jerk. All they are doing is shooting at me through you."

The media attack on Schlesinger bore the fingerprints of the Dulles group. Though he'd been out of office for half a year, Dulles's influence remained strong in the press—particularly with Luce publications like *Time*. Henry Taylor, too, had ties to the Dulles brothers, having served in Foster's diplomatic corps as ambassador to Switzerland before becoming a syndicated columnist for United Features.

On first glance, Schlesinger seemed like an unlikely target for the Dulles network, since he, too, had enjoyed a friendly relationship with the intelligence chief, dating back to World War II, when the young historian was one of many intellectuals recruited by the OSS. As an OSS analyst stationed in London and Paris during the war, Schlesinger held strongly anti-Communist views; after the war, Schlesinger became a leading architect of Cold War liberalism, joining the anti-Soviet propaganda campaign that was secretly funded by the CIA and endorsing efforts to root out Communist Party influence in the labor movement, cultural arena, and academic circles.

Schlesinger was a passionate believer in New Deal liberalism, which he saw as the only way to civilize capitalism. And he was an equally ardent anti-Communist, viewing the anti-Red crusade as a way to protect the American left, by ridding it of the Stalinist contamination that had seeped into Democratic Party circles during FDR's necessary wartime alliance with Moscow. Schlesinger believed that it was vital to purge these Communist Party influences, even though the CP's well-organized shock troops were behind many of the political and labor victories of the New Deal period, in order to fend off attacks from the right that sought to label liberalism as a paler version of Marxist-Leninism.

In 1949, Schlesinger endorsed a crude effort by Luce's *Life* magazine—which the young, Pulitzer Prize–winning historian sometimes wrote for—to develop a blacklist of celebrities that the magazine described as "Dupes and Fellow Travelers" of the Communist Party. Along with the predictable stalwarts of the Far Left, *Life* listed such liberal luminaries as Albert Einstein, Arthur Miller, Norman Mailer, Aaron Copland, and Leonard Bernstein. Schlesinger gave the *Life* magazine blacklist his stamp of approval, calling it "a convenient way of checking the more obvious Communist-controlled groups."

Though Schlesinger was an avid New Dealer, he was also a pampered product of the American elite—the son of esteemed Harvard historian Arthur M. Schlesinger Sr., a graduate of exclusive Phillips Exeter Academy at fifteen, a summa cum laude graduate of Harvard at twenty, and, at twenty-seven, winner of the Pulitzer Prize for his masterful work *The Age of Jackson*. Raised in the rarefied intellectual atmosphere of Cambridge, where the likes of James Thurber, John Dos Passos, H. L. Mencken, and Samuel Eliot Morison circulated through his family home, young Schlesinger "never stopped seeming like the brightest student in the class," as *The New York Times* observed.

Critics like C. Wright Mills and revisionist historian William Appleman Williams charged that Schlesinger—coddled by the East Coast establishment and subsidized by CIA front groups—clung to a one-sided view of the Cold War, placing sole responsibility for the tense, global standoff on Moscow. Russia was not merely seeking a protective buffer when it took control of Eastern Europe following the epic destruction of World War II, Schlesinger insisted; in his view, the Soviet Union was a "messianic state" whose "ideology compelled a steady expansion of Communist power." Even after the collapse of Stalin's regime, Schlesinger saw no significant modification in this implacable Soviet expansionism.

Not surprisingly, Schlesinger maintained friendly, if somewhat remote, relations with Allen Dulles throughout the 1950s. The Cold War consensus that dominated Democratic as well as Republican circles made for unlikely alliances; Schlesinger counted a number of top CIA officials among his friends, including Helms, Wisner, and Bissell, and he often joined them on the Georgetown cocktail circuit. *Washington Post* publisher Philip Graham and columnist Joe Alsop hosted the parties where the disparate Dulles and Kennedy entourages all intermingled.

Schlesinger had his differences with the CIA crowd, going back to his OSS days. He had been offended by "the notion of American spooks" like Dulles and Wisner "cheerfully consorting with people like General Reinhard Gehlen. . . . There was something aesthetically displeasing about Americans plotting with Nazis, who had recently been killing us, against Russians, whose sacrifices had made the allied victory possible." During the Eisenhower-Dulles years, Schlesinger found much more that was "aesthetically displeasing" about the Republican reign. "The Dulles brothers," sniffed Schlesinger's first wife, Marian, years later, "were self-righteous and egomaniacal." By the time Kennedy took office, Marian Schlesinger, a product of the same Cambridge background as her husband, regarded Allen Dulles as "passé."

But in the name of Cold War fraternity, Schlesinger was willing to make his own political compromises—even with men like Allen Dulles, whose Wall Street Republicanism and bullying foreign interventionism represented everything the historian opposed. Schlesinger made an effort to maintain cordial relations with the CIA chief, keeping up a friendly correspondence with Dulles that lasted late into the Old Man's life. Schlesinger wrote a favorable review of *Germany's Underground*, Dulles's 1947 book on anti-Hitler wartime intrigues, which elicited a warm thank-you note from the spook. Over dinner at Phil Graham's house in March 1958, they discussed *Doctor Zhivago*, Boris Pasternak's epic lament about the fragility of love and the human spirit in the grinding machinery of twentieth-century Russian history. CIA officials believed that the novel, which had been banned in the USSR, had "great propaganda value," and they were planning to sneak copies into Pasternak's homeland, though the author himself came to regret the political exploitation of his book.

On November 29, 1961, as Dulles was ushered out the door at the CIA, Schlesinger wrote to him again, telling the spy chief that it had been a "privilege" to work with him and urging him to write his memoirs: "You have had a fascinating life, and you owe it to your fellow countrymen to put it down on paper." Dulles responded warmly two weeks later, telling the historian that he was mulling over a couple of book ideas "and may seek your wise counsel."

Nobody in Washington was better positioned than Arthur Schlesinger Jr. to observe the growing split in Kennedy's government. He had played a leading role in the formation of the Cold War consensus that had held together Washington's opposing political camps. But that consensus began to shatter early in the Kennedy presidency, and Schlesinger found himself maintaining a delicate balancing act, with one foot on each side of the divide. In the months following the Bay of Pigs crisis, the cracks continued to lace their way through the administration, as JFK resisted the belligerent advice from his national security advisers and tried to maneuver his way around the minefields of Cuba, Laos, Berlin, and Vietnam. Kennedy drew more ire from his warlords—including men like Lemnitzer and Air Force chief Curtis LeMay, whom JFK considered mentally unbalanced—when he brusquely dismissed their persistent pleading for a nuclear confrontation with the Soviet Union and instead pursued a test ban treaty aimed at slowing down the race toward doomsday.

Following the Bay of Pigs, Schlesinger found his relations with the CIA crowd strained, but he still was invited to their dinner parties, and his Langley friends—like Helms, Ray Cline, and Cord Meyer—continued to keep him apprised of the agency's mood. Meanwhile, Kennedy, despite his occasional bemusement at Schlesinger's ivory-tower liberalism, increasingly drew the historian into his inner sanctum. Schlesinger earned points with JFK, not only by giving him the correct advice on the Bay of Pigs—"a great mistake"—but by resisting the temptation to crow about his wisdom to the press following the disaster, as some administration officials had done.

Kennedy soon began seeking the historian's advice on everything from nuclear policy to the handling of prickly liberal critics like Alfred Kazin, whom Kennedy sought to charm, on Schlesinger's advice, by inviting him for lunch at the White House in August 1961. Kennedy was nervous about meeting the formidable New York intellectual, suggesting that Jackie be invited too—"she knows all those obscure French writers." When Kazin arrived at the White House, JFK was at his dazzling best, offering fascinating insights into everyone from Malraux to Khrushchev, but he still fell short with the scholar, who later described the president as "slick, cool and devoid of vision." When Schlesinger reminded him that left-wing intellectuals said the same thing about FDR, Kazin replied that he was one of those who did. "And I still believe today that I was absolutely right!" Kazin declared.

Schlesinger, however, was the type of intellectual who saw nothing wrong about entering the inner circle of power to serve a Roosevelt or a Kennedy. He derided those cloistered academics who remained on the sidelines, speculating about the twists and turns of history but never actually participating in their times. In the beginning of his presidency,

Kennedy was a bit nervous about having a bestselling historian on his White House staff. Coming across Schlesinger pounding away at his typewriter one day in his remote East Wing office, JFK smiled, "Now Arthur, cut it out. When the time comes, I'll write *The Age of Kennedy.*" But after the Bay of Pigs, feeling increasingly besieged within his own administration, Kennedy embraced Schlesinger's role as court chronicler. The president encouraged Schlesinger to begin taking notes at White House meetings. "You can be damn sure that the CIA has its records and the Joint Chiefs theirs," JFK told him. "We'd better make sure we have a record over here."

Schlesinger's journal entries, letters, and memos provide a fascinating and invaluable inside look at the increasingly acrimonious civil war that would tear apart Kennedy's government. Critics often denounced Schlesinger as a toady to power, and there is no doubt that he fell under the spell of Camelot, sharing intimate weekends with the first couple at Hyannis Port and drinking champagne with the Kennedys on board their sailboats off Cape Cod and on the Potomac. During the Bay of Pigs debacle, Schlesinger took a particularly strong blast from the left, with C. Wright Mills denouncing "Kennedy and company" for "return[ing] us to barbarism," and singling out JFK's in-house historian, whom Mills charged had "disgraced us intellectually and morally."

But critics like Mills were not privy to the internal battles that raged within the Kennedy administration. In reality, Kennedy and trusted advisers like Schlesinger were determined to check the forces of "barbarism," not to succumb to them—and their efforts set off a powerful backlash within the president's own bureaucracy. The struggle fought between JFK and the national security elite, as Kennedy attempted to lead the country out of the Cold War, was largely invisible to the American people. Nor was it fully understood by observers like Mills, who died of a heart attack at forty-five in March 1962, before the Kennedy court drama reached its violent climax. Schlesinger himself did not entirely grasp the forces at play as he recorded the daily turmoil of the Kennedy presidency. But the picture that clearly emerges from reading his insightful journals and memos decades later is one of a government at war with itself.

The relationship between Kennedy and Schlesinger took a back-and-forth course, as the two men began to reevaluate America's Cold War policies. Sometimes it was the president whose thinking was boldest, other times it was his adviser who pushed Kennedy to be more courageous. The president's subtle grasp of U.S.-Soviet dynamics had the effect of making Schlesinger's own Cold War philosophy less rigid and more sophisticated. By 1963, Kennedy would come to the conclusion that "the hardliners in the Soviet Union and the United States feed on one another"—an observation that struck Schlesinger as wise. Kennedy liked to surround himself with intelligent men, but he was usually the most perceptive man in the room. He had a way of raising the thinking of his "best and brightest" to a higher level.

When it came to domestic politics, JFK was a shrewd strategist, and he thrashed out decisions by reviewing them with longtime political confidants and war horses, like his brother Bobby and special assistant Kenny O'Donnell. But Kennedy also realized that his political pragmatism could sometimes compromise his vision. So he often relied on New Frontier true believers like Schlesinger to be his voices of conscience and liberal touchstones. At other times, JFK used Schlesinger almost as a comic foil.

One day, Schlesinger urged Kennedy to replace Dean Rusk, a bland mouthpiece of Council on Foreign Relations conventional wisdom, with a more stimulating secretary of state. Kennedy glanced up at his adviser from a paper on his desk that he was perusing. "That's a great idea, Arthur," he said. After Schlesinger left his office, JFK turned to O'Donnell, who had been quietly taking in the bold pitch for revitalizing the State Department, and laughed. "Arthur has a lot of good ideas," the president told O'Donnell.

Schlesinger himself sometimes questioned his relevance within the Kennedy administration. "I have the feeling that the president somewhat discounts my views," the White House aide wrote in his journal in September 1962, "primarily because he regards me as a claimant agency for standardized liberalism, partly also because he considers me to be, after all, an intellectual and insufficiently practical and realistic."

But by 1963, the president himself was telling his brother and Phil Graham that he was seriously considering replacing Rusk with Robert McNamara, who had proven a smart and reliable ally in Kennedy's battles with the Pentagon's warlords.

Arthur had a lot of good ideas, and though he was careful not to overstep his bounds, he was unfailingly articulate and often persistent in the way he espoused them. His insights and suggestions had a way of working themselves into the recesses of Kennedy's mind. The president had been an avid reader of history since he was a boy, and here on his staff was someone who could raise the big historical questions at the very moment that the administration was making history. No wonder academic colleagues like Richard Rovere got somewhat carried away and compared Schlesinger's role in the Kennedy White House to that of Voltaire and Aristotle in the courts of Frederick and Alexander the Great. No prominent intellectual had held such a post of freewheeling influence in U.S. presidential history.

Schlesinger's most intrepid moment in the Kennedy presidency would come after the Bay of Pigs, when he boldly schemed to bring the CIA under presidential control, which neither Truman nor Eisenhower had been able to do. It took courage for Schlesinger to confront his old friends at the spy agency, some of whom denounced him as a traitor. The battle to take charge of the CIA would become the most fateful drama of the Kennedy presidency.

Schlesinger began lobbying Kennedy to play a big role in reorganizing the CIA even before the smoke had cleared from the Cuba debacle. He wanted to make sure that the current tempest over the agency did not simply fade away, resulting once again in a blue-ribbon oversight committee controlled by "Dulles stooges," as he put it. In an April 21, 1961, memo to the president Schlesinger wrote, "It is important, in my judgment, to take CIA away from the Club." Schlesinger was not enthusiastic about Kennedy's choice of General Taylor to oversee the White House's Bay of Pigs postmortem, regarding the general as "very pleasant [but] a man of limited interests and imagination." Nor

was Taylor the sort of crusading official who would follow through on
Kennedy's angry impulse to "splinter the CIA into a thousand pieces."
The general, Schlesinger noted, "is quite cautious and does not seem
disposed toward drastic reorganization of the intelligence services."

But it was Schlesinger whom Kennedy tapped to develop an ambitious CIA reorganization plan, while Taylor was limited to the Bay of
Pigs inquest. The historian was able to convince JFK of his qualifications for the job, reminding him, "I served in the OSS during the war,
and I have been a CIA consultant for a good deal of the period since;
so that, while I am far from a professional in this field, I am a relatively
experienced amateur."

Schlesinger threw himself into the CIA study with scholarly dedication, amassing a thick file that contained detailed critiques of the
organization by Washington liberals like George McGovern and agency
whistle-blowers, one of whom wrote, "The Central Intelligence Agency
is sick." Schlesinger also compiled disparaging essays and investigative
features about the Dulles reign from the liberal press, including *The
Nation* and *The New Republic*. These were not the sources typically
used when the CIA was subjected to reviews by handpicked friends of
Dulles.

The White House adviser completed his memo for revamping the
CIA on June 30. He acknowledged that his proposal "implies a fairly
drastic rearrangement of our present intelligence set-up." The basic
problem with the CIA, as Schlesinger saw it, was that it was out of
control. Under his plan, all future covert operations would be closely
supervised by a Joint Intelligence Board composed of representatives
from the White House and State Department. In addition, the CIA
would be divided into two separate organizations: one for clandestine
action, and one for the collection and analysis of intelligence. Furthermore, the agency's name—a tainted reminder of the Dulles era—would
be replaced by "some blameless title," Schlesinger suggested, like the
National Information Service. Kennedy had already made it clear that
he was in strong favor of this last recommendation. If he couldn't raze
Dulles's mausoleum to the ground, he would at least give it a new name.

No stranger to Washington politicking, Schlesinger attempted to rally support for his plan before submitting it to the president, sending copies to Washington power attorney Clark Clifford, veteran diplomat Chip Bohlen, and JFK's trusted aide and speechwriter Ted Sorensen. By the time the final draft was sent to Kennedy, it was a more complicated and unwieldy document than Schlesinger originally intended. When the Dulles forces, including Taylor himself and the CIA's congressional allies, immediately mounted a stubborn resistance to the new plan, Kennedy realized that overhauling the U.S. intelligence complex was going to be a much trickier political process than he had hoped. Taylor argued forcefully against the Schlesinger plan, telling JFK "this is not the time for surgery, so far as the CIA is concerned, that it would damage the morale of the employees too much." Taylor also opposed changing the agency's name, for the same reason.

On the morning of July 15, Bobby took Schlesinger aside at the White House and told him that the CIA reorganization was on hold until a replacement for Dulles was found. Undismayed, Schlesinger leaped immediately into the hunt for a new director. The president had briefly considered Bobby for the job but realized that his abrasive younger brother would be too politically charged a selection. Besides, RFK was already beginning each morning by dropping by CIA headquarters in Langley on his way to work in Washington so that he could keep an eye on the agency for the president. JFK even raised the possibility of putting Schlesinger in Dulles's chair. "I imagine that the president was joking," Schlesinger noted simply in his journal.

Fowler Hamilton soon emerged as the leading candidate for the CIA post. Hamilton had solid credentials as a successful Wall Street lawyer, former prosecutor in FDR's Justice Department, and a bombing analyst with the Army Air Force during World War II. Schlesinger gave the choice his blessing, telling JFK that Hamilton was a "sober, intelligent, hard-headed lawyer" who "would do the job well." But there was something about Hamilton that set off the Dulles crowd— perhaps it was simply because he was not one of them. Or it might have been connected to the fact that Hamilton had run the war frauds unit for President Roosevelt and knew too much about the Dulles brothers.

In any case, CIA opposition to Hamilton was so strong that Kennedy decided to abandon him, selecting instead an Eisenhower administration fixture—former AEC chairman, Republican counselor, and military industrialist John McCone.

Now it was Schlesinger's turn to erupt. Putting an Eisenhower retread in charge of the CIA would be a disastrous move, he warned Kennedy. It would send the wrong signal at the exact moment when the agency needed to be turned upside down. "McCone, for all his administrative qualities, is a man of crude and undiscriminating political views (or to put it more precisely, political emotions)," Schlesinger told the president in a memo. "He sees the world in terms of a set of emotion-charged stereotypes." But Schlesinger failed to block the announcement of McCone's appointment in September. Afterward, writing in his journal, Schlesinger tried to cheer himself up, but without much success. "The possibly consoling thought is that the President has a habit of designating 'liberals' to do 'conservative' things, and vice versa. . . . I am sure JFK knows what he is doing, and possibly my concern here will turn out to be as unwarranted as my concern last December over the appointment of Doug Dillon [as Treasury secretary], but I doubt it."

In October, still puzzling over McCone's selection, Schlesinger brought up the subject again with Kennedy in the Oval Office. He asked the president if he knew McCone well. Kennedy admitted that he was not very familiar with his new appointee, but he seemed undisturbed by the prospect of working with him. Kennedy then began to vent about his outgoing CIA chief. "He was very critical of Dulles," Schlesinger later noted, "and implied that, after Dulles, anyone would do."

If Kennedy thought that he was getting, in McCone, a respectable Republican front man who would readily do his bidding at the CIA, he was sorely disappointed. In May 1962, Schlesinger fell into conversation at a French embassy party with his friend, banker-diplomat W. Averell Harriman, the old Democratic Party wise man who had served as FDR's ambassador to Moscow and was now serving JFK as a globe-trotting ambassador at large. Harriman gave Schlesinger an astringent evaluation of the new McCone regime, which he saw as little changed from the Dulles days. This was clear, Harriman confided, from looking at the policy maneuvers around Laos, the Southeast Asia sideshow in which Kennedy was determined not to get embroiled. JFK's policy of neutrality was being "systematically sabotaged by the military and the CIA," Harriman warned. "McCone and the people in the CIA want the president to have a setback. They want to justify the [intervention] position CIA took five years ago. They want to prove that a neutral solution is impossible and that the only course is to turn Laos into an American bastion."

Harriman, a veteran of Washington infighting, then advised Schlesinger how the White House should handle the CIA and military seditionists in its midst. "General [George] Marshall once told me that, when you change a policy, you must change the men too. [The] CIA has the same men—on the desk and in the field—who were responsible for the disasters of the past, and naturally they do things to prove they were right. Every big thing the CIA has tried in the Far East has been catastrophic . . . and the men responsible for these catastrophes are still there." Kennedy's purge of the CIA, Harriman made clear, had not been sweeping enough.

The president had lopped off the heads of the top three men at the CIA, but Dulles's loyal deputies—like Helms and Angleton—were still running the show at Langley. And McCone, a CIA outsider who largely shared the former regime's views, was more or less content to go along with the old Dulles policies. "McCone has no business in the New Frontier," Harriman told Schlesinger in March 1963. Dulles's successor "doesn't believe in the administration," said Harriman, and "was full of mischievous ideas and projects."

Two years into McCone's tenure as CIA director, syndicated newspaper columnist Henry Taylor published a surprisingly critical piece about the intelligence agency, calling it a "sick elephant" and urging it to "quit stalking through foreign political backrooms and . . . building its own empire." A few days later, Dulles wrote his old colleague a letter, letting Taylor know that he viewed his column as a personal betrayal and as "a direct attack on me [since] most of what you say [about the agency] happened while I was Director." Taylor quickly replied with a long, groveling telegram, pleading that nothing he had written—or ever would write—was critical of the spy agency under Dulles's leadership. "Certainly you must know that any attack on you by me is inconceivable. . . . No one has served this country with greater distinction, selflessness and success than you." But Dulles made it clear to Taylor that he was still running the show at the CIA, so any distinction the columnist tried to draw between his tenure and McCone's was false. "Since my retirement," Dulles told Taylor, "there have been few important policy changes, and I am wholly in support of its new chief and of its recent work."

This is precisely what Schlesinger was afraid of when McCone took over the CIA in November 1961: that the Dulles era would continue undisturbed. That month, as Kennedy's special assistant contemplated the new administration's progress, he could not help falling into a glum mood. Recent conversations with liberal friends and colleagues, he wrote in his journal, "made me face up to the fact that there is no such thing as the New Frontier. We came in last January after a campaign which promised the American people a new beginning [but] we have really done damn little in the way of bold, new initiatives. JFK has given marvelous speeches, but they are almost too marvelous. The words kindle splendid hopes; but the reality remains as dismal as ever."

Schlesinger grew anxious whenever he began to sense that the old "Eisenhower-Dulles continuities" were "beginning to reassert themselves." He yearned for Kennedy to break free from the political past, to "ignore the wisdom of the Establishment and accept the implications of his own campaign and his own instincts." The liberal counselor's wishes were soon to become true.

By 1962, President Kennedy was challenging the bastions of American power on several fronts, including the corporate elite's control of the economy. The steel industry crisis that erupted that spring laid bare the growing tensions between JFK and the Fortune 500 circle. On April 6, after yearlong negotiations between steel companies and unions—which involved the personal participation of the president himself—a deal was announced that prevented the rise of steel prices. The steel agreement—which was based on labor concessions that Kennedy administration officials had helped wring from the unions—was a major victory for JFK. The three-way pact hammered out by industry, labor, and government ensured stability throughout the economy, since rising prices in the core industry had been the biggest inflationary factor in the postwar period. "Every time steel prices jump, your pocketbook jumps—with pain," Estes Kefauver, chairman of the Senate antitrust and monopoly subcommittee, told American consumers in 1959.

But just four days after the Kennedy-engineered steel pact was signed, U.S. Steel chairman Roger Blough scheduled a meeting at the White House and stunned the president by informing him that he was going to announce a 3.5 percent price increase, effective at midnight—a move that would trigger price jumps at other steel companies and send inflationary ripples throughout the economy.

Kennedy was furious at Blough's double cross, which he correctly saw as a direct challenge to his ability to manage the economy. "My father always told me that all businessmen were sons of bitches," said JFK at the height of the steel industry crisis, "but I never believed it until now"—a remark that he was happy to have leaked to *Newsweek*.

While the president saw Blough as a backstabber, Luce's *Fortune* magazine regarded the steel mogul as a capitalist hero, declaring him a "business statesman" who was fighting not just for his own company but on behalf of the entire corporate sector by defying the president's authority. Blough's company occupied a central position in the country's corporate pantheon, which was reflected in the U.S. Steel board of directors. Blough himself was well connected within the power elite—including to Dulles, with whom he served in organizations like the Council on Foreign Relations and the Lafayette Fellowship Foundation (part of the Ford Foundation).

Kennedy understood that if Blough and the other colluding steel executives prevailed, his leadership would be severely undermined, not only at home but abroad. He had staked his reputation with organized labor and American consumers on the deal—and now he was faced with "the most painfully embarrassing predicament of his career," in the view of his White House advisers. A steel industry victory would make it clear to the entire world who ran America.

Determined to protect his presidency, over the next three days JFK unleashed the full powers of the federal government in an all-out effort to crush the steel industry rebellion. Attorney General Bobby Kennedy announced a grand jury probe of steel price-fixing, which he followed by issuing subpoenas for the personal and corporate records of steel executives and by sending FBI agents to raid their offices. "We were going to go for broke: their expense accounts and where they'd been and what they were doing," JFK's brother and political enforcer later recalled. "I picked up all their records and I told the FBI to interview them all—march into their offices the next day. We weren't going to go slowly. . . . All of [the steel executives] were hit with meetings the next morning by agents." Meanwhile, Robert McNamara's Defense Department announced that it was reviewing its steel purchasing practices, making it clear that it would favor companies that did not follow U.S. Steel's price hike.

Kennedy's strong-arm tactics produced quick results. On April 12, Inland Steel—a smaller but still significant company—caved under the pressure, announcing that it would not raise prices. Bethlehem Steel soon followed, and by the next day U.S. Steel itself waved the white flag.

In victory, JFK adopted a genial and magnanimous posture. Over dinner at the White House on May 3, Schlesinger asked Kennedy what he had said to Blough when the U.S. Steel chairman surrendered. "I told him that his men could keep their horses for the summer plowing," smiled JFK.

But the resentment from the steel showdown never faded away. Corporate executives continued to snipe at the president, spreading the word that his administration had destroyed "business confidence" by bringing the steel industry to heel. Senator Barry Goldwater, the voice of the rising Republican right, escalated the rhetoric, calling Kennedy's bare-knuckled tactics against the steel barons "a display of naked political power never seen before in this nation. . . . We have passed within the shadow of police-state methods."

Chatting with Schlesinger in the Oval Office on June 4, Kennedy said, "I understand better every day why Roosevelt, who started out such a mild fellow, ended up so ferociously anti-business." JFK vowed that he was not going to appease his big business critics by taking what O'Donnell described as "an ass-kissing posture." To counter the corporate assault on his presidency, said Kennedy, "[w]e have to put out the picture of a small group of men turning against the government and the economy because the government would not surrender to them. That is the real issue."

Schlesinger discovered that some of the corporate sniping against the president came from within his own administration. While dining at Joe Alsop's in late July, the watering hole where Schlesinger kept in touch with the CIA crowd, the White House adviser was disgusted to hear McCone fulminate against Kennedy's economic policy, which the former industrialist regarded as too pro-labor. "I have rarely seen a man more completely out of sympathy" with the administration's economic direction, Schlesinger observed in his journal. The CIA director's "formula for economic stimulus," wrote Schlesinger, "is to kick labor in the teeth."

As he continued to wrestle with the disgruntled corporate community into the fall, Kennedy longed to make the battle over the economy the centerpiece of his presidency, telling Schlesinger that he "only wished there were no Cold War so he could debate the future of America with the businessmen." This is a remarkable and all but overlooked statement, indicating—once again—Kennedy's visionary thinking.

A year after the April 1962 steel blowup, Kennedy tried to make light of the controversy as he addressed a Democratic fund-raising dinner at the Waldorf Astoria hotel. Told that the steel industry was presenting former president Eisenhower with its annual public service award in another banquet hall at the same hotel, JFK grinned mischievously. "I was their man of the year last year," he told the Democratic crowd. "They wanted to come down to the White House to give me their award, but the Secret Service wouldn't let them do it."

Beset by the rising tensions in his government, Kennedy would bring up the awkward subject of assassination from time to time. In public, as on this occasion, he used it as a comedic device. But in private, with old friends like Red Fay, he mused about it in a more somber vein.

The climate of conflict surrounding the Kennedy presidency had a way of evoking the grim topic. Outraged by the president's strong stand against the steel industry, Henry Luce invoked the fate of Julius Caesar in a harsh editorial in *Fortune*, warning JFK that he should "beware the ides of April." But Kennedy never backed down from his ongoing duel with the steel industry. In October 1963, just weeks before his assassination, JFK's Justice Department filed price-fixing charges against U.S. Steel and other steel companies, based on Bobby's earlier grand jury probe of the industry. To the end of his life, Kennedy made it clear that there would be no "ass-kissing" for those corporate powers that tried to undermine his presidency.

After Dulles was ousted by JFK in late 1961, the Old Man's crowd had quickly closed ranks around him. The Luces immediately offered Dulles succor, inviting Clover and him to spend the New Year holiday at their winter home in Phoenix. Clare Boothe Luce often used the Arizona estate, with its cactus garden and mesmerizing view of Camelback Mountain, to recover from her own bouts of melancholy, dropping LSD with eccentric friends like Gerald Heard, a gay Anglo-Irish writer, devotee of Eastern mysticism, and psychedelic pioneer. Clover found the Luces' desert refuge a soothing respite from the Washington vortex, but, as she wrote Mary Bancroft from Phoenix, she knew that Allen didn't share her sentiments: "I do feel an immense relief of burden by Shark's being out, which he himself doesn't feel."

Dulles's growing sense of resentment toward Kennedy was shared by the Luces, who had known JFK since he was a young Navy ensign. Joe Kennedy had courted Henry Luce's support for his son during the 1960 presidential race, dropping by the magazine mogul's Fifth Avenue apartment for a lobster dinner on the final night of the Democratic Convention, and afterward watching TV together as JFK accepted his party's nomination. "It was a memorable moment in my life," Luce recalled. "It's quite a thing to sit with an old friend and watch his son accept the nomination for the president of the United States."

Luce was not the type to let sentiment cloud his political judgment, however, and he remained loyal to the Republican ticket. But *Life* magazine, his influential flagship publication, gave Nixon a tepid endorsement, leaving the door open for Kennedy. Luce admired JFK's intellect and cultural sophistication. But he questioned whether he would be a sufficiently aggressive foe of Communism. After finishing their lobster dinner that night, in fact, Luce had warned Joe Kennedy that he would not stand for it if JFK proved too much of a compromiser in the White House. "If he shows any signs of weakness in general toward the anti-Communist cause, or to put it more positively, any weakness in defending and advancing the cause of the free world, why then we'll certainly be against him," Luce told the Kennedy paterfamilias.

The Luce honeymoon with the Kennedy administration had been short-lived. After the Bay of Pigs, Luce's coverage of the presidency turned increasingly negative. By the spring of 1963, JFK was so exasperated with the relentless drumbeat of criticism from the Time-Life headquarters in New York that he invited the Luces to lunch at the White House to see if he could somehow sweeten the power couple's disposition. When the press lord launched into a lengthy diatribe on Cuba, demanding that Kennedy invade the island, the president suggested that Luce was a "warmonger" and the afternoon came to an unpleasant conclusion, with the Luces marching out of the White House before dessert was served. Shortly afterward, Luce convened a remarkable war council of his top editors at Time-Life, where he declared that if the Kennedy administration was not bold enough to overthrow Castro, his corporation would take on the task. Luce and his wife were already funding raids on Cuba, with the quiet support of the CIA. Now Luce would escalate his crusade against the Castro regime, in direct defiance of Kennedy.

Like the Time-Life building in Manhattan, Dulles's brick house on Q Street was a boiling center of anti-Kennedy opposition. The actively "retired" spymaster maintained a busy appointments calendar, meeting not only with retired CIA old boys like Frank Wisner and Charles Cabell, but with a steady stream of top-rank, active-duty agency officials such as Angleton, Helms, Cord Meyer, and Desmond Fitzgerald. More surprisingly, Dulles also conferred with midlevel officials and operational officers such as Howard Hunt, James Hunt (a key deputy of Angleton, and no relation to Howard), and Thomas Karamessines (Helms's right-hand man). McCone, too, routinely checked in with his predecessor, dining with him and sending him cordial notes.

Though Howard Hunt did not occupy the same social strata as Dulles, the two men were bonded in bitterness: they both felt they had been made scapegoats for Kennedy's failure of nerve at the Bay of Pigs. The retired spymaster sent Hunt his photograph, and Hunt gave him a copy of his angry Cuba memoir. "I wrote this book as an antidote to the despondency that seized me in the wake of the Cuba project," Hunt explained in an August 1962 letter, "and I hope it may give you some diversion now." Serving Dulles, Hunt wrote in an earlier letter, was "an honor I shall always cherish."

Fearing that his role in the Bay of Pigs fiasco would stall his CIA career under Kennedy, Hunt sought Dulles's help in starting a new career in the private security field. "It occurs to me that one of your many business contacts might have use for me abroad, particularly if something of my background were known," Hunt wrote Dulles in August.

Dulles, who told Helms, "I have always thought well of Hunt," and that he was "disposed" to help him, agreed to get together with Hunt in September. Afterward, Hunt decided to stay in the CIA, while moonlighting as a ghostwriter for Dulles. Hunt was a prolific author and had been churning out spy novels under various noms de plume since World War II. Dulles—who produced four books in retirement, including a war memoir, an intelligence handbook, and two volumes of espionage adventures—also worked on his literary projects with a young former CIA employee named Howard Roman, whose wife, Jane, was employed in Angleton's deeply submerged counterintelligence unit.

The CIA continued to provide a variety of services large and small for the former director, in addition to supplying him with ghostwriters and research materials. Shef Edwards, the agency's internal security chief, even stepped in to help Dulles renew his District of Columbia driver's license in early 1963 so that he could keep cruising the streets of Washington in his aging 1955 Pontiac sedan. Amassing wealth and luxuries had never been important to Dulles, but he did expect to be served and pampered, and the CIA continued to oblige him.

Dulles also stayed in touch with his extensive network of friends and supporters in the U.S. military, who continued to invite him to speak at defense seminars and to play golf on military bases. He lunched with his fellow Bay of Pigs casualty, Arleigh Burke, at the Metropolitan Club. After Kennedy forced him out of the Navy, Burke quickly found another perch in Washington's far-flung national security complex, becoming chairman of the newly created Center for Strategic Studies at Georgetown University (now the Center for Strategic and International Studies) that he cofounded with David Abshire, a platform he used to publicly air his grievances with the Kennedy administration. Burke made dark allegations about the White House's "dictatorial" tendencies, charging that his Georgetown offices were the target of a suspicious 1963 break-in.

Rising Republican politicians also sought out the retired spy chief, including a young Illinois congressman named Donald Rumsfeld, who, decades later, would achieve notoriety for his own national security reign. Rumsfeld arranged for Dulles to speak about the CIA and Cuba to the 88th Congressional Club in March 1963, an event the ambitious congressman declared a "tremendous success."

Cuba remained the source of greatest friction within the Kennedy government. In October 1962, these tensions came close to exploding during the Cuban Missile Crisis, when virtually the entire national security circle around the president urged him to take aggressive actions that would have triggered a nuclear conflagration. JFK's lonely stand—which was supported only by his brother and McNamara within his inner council—was a virtuoso act of leadership. As the world held its breath, the president painstakingly worked out a face-saving deal with Khrushchev that convinced the Soviet premier to withdraw his nuclear missiles from the island.

Kennedy achieved the compromise by agreeing to remove U.S. missiles from Turkey, which the Soviet Union found equally menacing. In fact, the president had been trying to get the obsolete Jupiter missiles demobilized for over a year but had been stymied by State Department foot-dragging—just one more example of the intransigence and insubordination that bedeviled his administration. JFK was furious when he learned that his original order to remove the Jupiter rockets from Turkey had been ignored. "The President believed he was President, and that, his wishes having been made clear, they would be followed and the missiles removed," Bobby Kennedy later wrote in *Thirteen Days*, his memoir about the missile crisis. *The President believed he was President . . .* it was a striking turn of phrase, one that captured JFK's uncertain grasp on the wheel of power.

The searing experience of teetering on the nuclear edge had the effect of creating a survivors' bond between Kennedy and Khrushchev. JFK came to respect the Soviet leader's earthy wisdom and his surprising eloquence on behalf of peace. "At the climax of events around Cuba, there began to be a smell of burning in the air," Khrushchev evocatively began a speech he gave a few weeks after the missile crisis, in which he denounced the "militarists" who had sought a nuclear confrontation. Kennedy read aloud part of the speech to Schlesinger, adding, "Khrushchev certainly has some good writers!"

The feelings of respect were mutual. The Soviet leader later said he came to greatly admire JFK during the missile crisis. "He didn't let himself become frightened, nor did he become reckless," Khrushchev commented. "He showed real wisdom and statesmanship when he turned his back on right-wing forces in the United States who were trying to goad him into taking military action in Cuba."

Kennedy's sincerity in the quest for peace continued to impress Khrushchev the following June, when the U.S. leader gave an electrifying oration at American University, in which he soundly rejected the bellicose assumptions of the Cold War. The address, which would go down in history as the Peace Speech, carried echoes of Khrushchev's own heartfelt pleas to Kennedy at the height of the Cuban crisis, when he had told JFK that the Russian people were neither "barbarians" nor "lunatics" and they loved life as much as the American people. At American University, Kennedy invoked the same sentiments, in the poetic cadence of speechwriter Sorensen. "We all inhabit this small planet. We all breathe the same air. We all cherish our children's future. And we are all mortal."

JFK reinforced his pathbreaking speech by dispatching Averell Harriman to Moscow the following month to hammer out a limited nuclear test ban treaty with Khrushchev—the first diplomatic breakthrough in the struggle to control the weapons race. When the triumphant Harriman returned home, his Georgetown neighbors poured into the street outside his brick town house on P Street to celebrate his achievement. One young woman, who was carrying a baby in her arms, told the old diplomat, "I brought him because what you did in Moscow will make it possible for him to look ahead to a full and happy life." The crusty millionaire was touched by the effusive neighborhood welcome. Harriman told Schlesinger that by picking him for the mission—instead of one of the usual Cold War envoys—Kennedy had "persuaded Khrushchev that we really wanted an agreement" and were not simply "going through the motions." Khrushchev had a fondness for Harriman, whom he called "my friend, the imperialist."

JFK once confided to his friend Bill Walton, "I am almost a 'peace-at-any-price' president." It was a wry reference to the insult that Barry Goldwater, positioning himself for the 1964 presidential race, had begun flinging at political opponents he deemed insufficiently hawkish. By 1963, the military and espionage officials in Kennedy's government were all too aware of their commander in chief's dedication to peace—a growing commitment to détente with the Communist world that, in the minds of the national security high command, demonstrated JFK's naïveté and weakness and put the country at risk. The leadership ranks in the Pentagon and the CIA were convinced that the Cuban Missile Crisis had been the ideal opportunity for Kennedy to finally knock out the Castro regime by launching a full-scale military invasion or even a nuclear broadside. The peaceful resolution of the crisis left Kennedy's warriors in an ugly mood. Daniel Ellsberg, who later became famous for leaking the Pentagon Papers, observed the seething fury among uniformed officers when he was serving as a young defense analyst: "There was virtually a coup atmosphere in Pentagon circles. Not that I had the fear there was about to be a coup—I just thought it was a mood of hatred and rage. The atmosphere was poisonous, poisonous."

The anti-Kennedy feelings were particularly virulent in the Air Force, which was under the command of cigar-chomping General Curtis LeMay, who had made his savage mark on history with the firebombing of Tokyo during World War II. The president and the general regarded each other with barely concealed disgust. Twenty-five years after JFK's death, LeMay and his top Air Force generals were still brooding about Kennedy when they sat down to be interviewed for an official Air Force oral history project. "The Kennedy administration," LeMay growled, "thought that being as strong as we were was provocative to the Russians and likely to start a war. We in the Air Force, and I personally, believed the exact opposite."

LeMay and his generals continued to angrily replay the "lost opportunity" of the Cuban Missile Crisis: it was the moment "we could have gotten the Communists out of Cuba," LeMay declared. "We walked Khrushchev up to the brink of nuclear war, he looked over the edge, and had no stomach for it," said General David Burchinal, who served as LeMay's deputy during the crisis. "We would have written our own book at that time, but our politicians did not understand what happens when you have such a degree of superiority as we had, or they simply didn't know how to use it. They were busily engaged in saving face for the Soviets and making concessions, giving up the . . . Jupiters deployed overseas—when all we had to do was write our own ticket."

By spring 1963, after two years of turbulence, it was clear that Kennedy was searching for a way to defuse Cuba as an international flashpoint. Abiding by his missile crisis agreement with Khrushchev, the president began to crack down on the anti-Castro raids operating out of Florida and to withdraw funding from the militant exile groups. In April, the leader of the Miami-based Cuban Revolutionary Council, the umbrella organization that tied together the anti-Castro movement, announced his resignation, accusing the administration of cutting a deal with Moscow to "coexist" with Castro. It was now clear that—despite his pronouncements of solidarity with Cuban "freedom fighters"— Kennedy was not serious about overthrowing the Havana regime. This marked the fateful turning point when the rabid, CIA-sponsored activity that had been aimed at Castro shifted its focus to Kennedy.

As Kennedy de-escalated the U.S. campaign against Havana, the violent anti-Castro network of spooks, political extremists, paramilitary adventurers, and assassins went underground. The scheming in hotbeds of exile activity like Miami, New Orleans, and Dallas grew more vicious in the spring and early summer of 1963. Mysterious characters with blood in their eyes began to make their appearance on history's stage.

One day, Dulles called his former lover, Clare Luce, to warn her about the Kennedy administration's crackdown on the maritime raids she was helping to finance. "He said to get out of that boat business—he was well aware of it, by the way—because the neutrality act has now been reasserted and it was against the law to aid or abet the Cubans in any attempts to free their country."

Dulles's old friend, Bill Pawley, the right-wing Miami entrepreneur who had long collaborated on secret CIA missions, was also warned about his involvement in the exile raids. But he remained defiant, hatching a plot so ambitious that he claimed it would bring down Kennedy himself. In April, Pawley wrote a long letter to his political comrade, Dick Nixon, declaring, "All of the Cubans and most Americans in this part of the country believe that to remove Castro, you must first remove Kennedy, and that is not going to be easy." Pawley's plan was to assemble a rogue's crew of Mafia hit men and Cuban desperadoes and to set sail on his sixty-five-foot yacht, the *Flying Tiger II*, for the waters off Cuba, accompanied by a reporter and photographer from *Life* magazine to document the daring mission. Once ashore in Cuba, the raiders were to rendezvous with two Soviet military officers based on the island who wanted to defect, bringing them back to the United States with explosive evidence that Khrushchev had double-crossed Kennedy and had never withdrawn his missiles. The mission went nowhere: there were no missiles or Soviet defectors, and the raiders themselves disappeared, presumably into the jaws of Castro's security forces.

Years later, two of the mercenaries who had slithered through Miami's anti-Castro underworld in the early 1960s claimed that the Pawley raid had really been a cover for yet another CIA-Mafia assassination attempt on Castro. The plotting against the Cuban leader continued to flourish, even after the CIA assured the Kennedy administration that it had terminated its alliance with the Mafia. Two emissaries from the CIA informed Bobby Kennedy of the assassination plots at a meeting in his Justice Department office in May 1962. The attorney general, who had built his law enforcement reputation as an aggressive mob hunter, listened to the CIA men with barely contained fury. "I trust that if you ever do business with organized crime again—with gangsters—you will let the attorney general know," he said with icy sarcasm. The CIA officials assured Bobby that the Eisenhower-approved plots had been shut down—but, in truth, they would continue, without the Kennedys' knowledge, throughout their administration and for many years after.

The displays of disrespect for President Kennedy's authority grew more glaring in the clubs and suites of Washington's permanent government. By the spring of 1963, JFK was painfully aware of the profound miscalculation he had made by appointing Eisenhower-Dulles holdovers and "designating conservatives to do liberal things"—particularly in the case of John McCone. In March, the president's secret White House recording system picked up a heated conversation between the Kennedy brothers about their increasingly disloyal CIA director. McCone, Bobby informed his brother, was going around Washington feeding anti-Kennedy information to the press. "He's a real bastard, that John McCone," responded JFK. "Well, he was useful at a time," observed Bobby. "Yeah," replied the president ruefully, "but, boy, it's really evaporated."

Meanwhile, Dulles—who had made a show of harmony with the White House early in his retirement, telling friends he would continue to consult with the president—no longer felt a need to keep up the pretense. He became increasingly outspoken in his remarks about Kennedy, despite the earlier reticence he had displayed "for the good of the country." In June, after delivering a lecture in Cold Spring Harbor, near his Long Island home, Dulles told reporters that he "doubted" he would ever be willing to work again for the Kennedy administration. He also made clear that the president was not serious about ousting Castro. "I don't know of anything that can be done about Cuba—short of intervention," he said. "Once a Communist regime gets fastened in a country and the military regime is built up, it's hard to get that [regime] changed."

In October 1963, Dulles went public with his most direct criticism of the Kennedy administration in a militant address that he titled "The Art of Persuasion: America's Role in the Ideological Struggle." In it, Dulles ridiculed the administration's "yearning to be 'loved' by the rest of the world. . . . No country that wishes to be really popular should aspire to or accept the role of leadership." The United States was "too rich and too powerful" to be loved, Dulles declared—and that's the way it must remain.

"I should much prefer to have people respect us than to try to make them love us," he continued. "They should realize that we propose to remain strong economically and militarily, that we have firm principles and a steady foreign policy and will not compromise with communism or appease it." Here it was, at last, Dulles's critique of the Kennedy presidency, in stark relief. JFK was an appeaser, a weak leader who wanted to be loved by our friends and enemies, when the man in the White House should be feared and respected.

Dulles maintained a busy schedule throughout 1963—speaking,

traveling, and meeting with an intriguing mix of intelligence colleagues, high-powered friends, and, at least on one occasion, a member
of the anti-Castro demimonde. The pages from Dulles's crowded 1963
calendar that were later released by the CIA contain numerous gaps
and blackouts. But, even with the curious blanks, his appointments
book has the look of belonging to an active espionage professional who
was still fully engaged in a subterranean life. Dulles's calendar pages
and other declassified documents give provocative hints about the retired spy chief's life, including the identities of some of the obscure
characters with whom he was associating. Here was a man, say these
pages, to whom people still looked to get things done.

In the summer of 1963, Peter Dale Scott, a young English literature professor at the University of California's Berkeley campus, found
himself in the thick of anti-Kennedy ferment. Scott, the son of distinguished Canadian poet F. R. Scott, a mentor of Leonard Cohen, had
served as a Canadian diplomat to Poland, and much of his social life
when he arrived in Berkeley revolved around passionately anti-Soviet
Polish émigrés. One day, a former Polish army colonel who had befriended Scott invited him to a dinner party at the Palo Alto home of
W. Glenn Campbell, the intellectual entrepreneur who built Stanford's
Hoover Institution into a leading center of the conservative resurgence
in America. At Campbell's home that evening, the conversation among
the sixteen or so guests soon grew heated as it turned to the man in
the White House. "In those days, I was not very active politically, but
I was amazed, even shocked, at how reactionary the conversation became around the dinner table," Scott later recalled. "Most of the talk
focused on the danger presented to the nation by its aberrant president,
John F. Kennedy. His failure to dispose of Castro, especially during the
missile crisis, may have been one of the chief complaints, but it was by
no means the only one. The complaints threatened to drag on forever,
until one man spoke up with authority. I'm not sure, but he may even
have stood up to do so."

The striking figure who commanded the group's attention was a
Russian Orthodox priest in a dark cassock with a crucifix around his

neck. He spoke quietly, but with confidence, assuring the group that they had no need to worry. "The Old Man will take care of it," he said simply.

At the time, Scott assumed the priest was referring to old Joe Kennedy, who presumably could be counted on to set his son straight. But by 1963, the Kennedy patriarch was confined to a wheelchair after suffering a massive stroke in December 1961 that left him severely debilitated. It was not until years later that Scott realized the Russian priest was more likely referring to someone else. By then, the Berkeley professor was a respected dean of the JFK assassination research community and had devoted years to studying the political forces surrounding the president's murder. In conversation with a fellow Kennedy researcher one day, Scott was reminded of the nickname by which Allen Dulles was affectionately known in intelligence circles: the Old Man.

On that summer evening in 1963, the Russian émigré priest spoke with the calm assurance of a man who knew something the other dinner guests did not. *The Old Man will take care of it.* That was enough to calm the heated discussion around the table. The Old Man will take care of the Kennedy problem.

Among the peculiar figures with whom Dulles met in the spring and summer of 1963 was a militant anti-Castro exile named Paulino Sierra Martinez, whose background and affiliations were so murky that even the CIA labeled him "a mystery man" in a memo dated November 20. According to an internal CIA document, Sierra arranged to meet with Dulles and retired Army general Lucius D. Clay in Washington on April 15, 1963. Dulles and Clay were unusual company for a man who, not long before, had been working as a judo instructor in Miami while studying for his law examinations.

Like Dulles, General Clay occupied positions in the top ranks of the American establishment. After serving as the U.S. military governor in postwar Germany, Clay had worked with Dulles in Cold War propaganda projects like the Crusade for Freedom, returning to Germany in 1961 as an adviser to President Kennedy during the Berlin Wall crisis.

Clay dangerously escalated the crisis without the president's authorization by threatening to knock down the recently erected wall with U.S. Army tanks. It took all of the Kennedy brothers' back-channel diplomatic skills to defuse the confrontation at Checkpoint Charlie. A disgusted Clay later accused Kennedy of losing his "nerve." By 1963, Clay had given up military service for a corporate career, taking a senior partner position with Lehman Brothers, the Wall Street investment firm, as well as board seats at General Motors and other major companies.

Paulino Sierra Martinez was not the type of man with whom Dulles or Clay normally dined at the Army and Navy Club or the Metropolitan Club. The son of a Cuban police sergeant, Sierra had worked his way up in Havana society, landing a job in dictator Fulgencio Batista's foreign ministry. But some of his intimates suspected that Sierra's government post was a cover for his true profession, as a Batista assassin. Fleeing Castro's Cuba, Sierra settled first in Miami, but after passing his U.S. bar exams, he went to work in the legal department of the Chicago-based Union Tank Car Company, a railroad freight company that had been built by the Rockefeller family. It was in Chicago that Sierra suddenly emerged as a mysterious player in the confusing and conflict-ridden Cuban exile movement.

In May 1963, following his Washington meeting with Dulles and Clay, Sierra—who was virtually unknown in anti-Castro circles—convened a meeting of Cuban exile leaders at the Royalton Hotel in Miami. The leaders were skeptical about the tall, well-dressed man from Chicago, with the long, homely face that put some people in mind of Lincoln. But the anti-Castro movement was in disarray following Kennedy's withdrawal of support, and Sierra arrived in Miami with an enticing proposal—and the promise of big money to go along with it.

Sierra told the group that he represented an alliance of major U.S. corporations that wanted to regain their lost investments in Cuba. He did not name the companies, but on other occasions he dropped such Fortune 500 brand names as United Fruit, U.S. Steel, DuPont, and Standard Oil. Sierra claimed that these corporations were willing to put up as much as $30 million if the fractured anti-Castro movement could reassemble itself and mount an invasion of the island. He explained that such an operation would not have Washington's official approval but would be supported by officers within the U.S. military, who would help provide weapons and training bases.

Freely spreading money around, Sierra attracted enough support from within the anti-Castro network to form a coalition he ambitiously titled the Junta of the Government of Cuba in Exile. He crisscrossed the country, drumming up support for the new organization and going on a weapons-buying spree. The sources of Sierra's funds, which were passed to him through Union Tank Car, remained something of a mystery, although an article in *The Miami News* indicated that at least some of his money was coming from organized crime lords who were intent on winning back their Havana gambling casinos and prostitution franchises, which before Castro had been a source of enormous underworld profits.

Law enforcement agencies began tracking Sierra as he pursued his shady agenda, but in June the FBI terminated its investigation after concluding that he was involved in nothing more than a "con job." The Chicago office of the Secret Service, however, suspected that Sierra was a more sinister figure. By November 1963, Chicago—like Miami, New Orleans, and Dallas—had become a nest of anti-Kennedy intrigue. On November 2, local Secret Service officials foiled a well-organized assassination plot against President Kennedy. After landing at Chicago's O'Hare Airport that day, Kennedy was scheduled to ride in a motorcade to Soldier Field for the annual Army-Navy football game. But the motorcade was canceled after the Secret Service exposed a plot to ambush the president from a tall warehouse building as his limousine slowed for a hairpin turn. The plot, which involved a sniper team composed of a disgruntled ex-marine who worked in the building and at least two Cuban marksmen, bore a disturbing resemblance to the series of events that would claim Kennedy's life twenty days later in Dallas.

The Secret Service could not connect Sierra to the Chicago assassination plot, but his name did come up in relation to another troubling report. On November 21, the day before JFK's assassination, a serious threat against the president was made by an outspoken anti-Kennedy

Cuban exile leader named Homer Echevarria. While negotiating an illegal arms purchase, Echevarria reportedly said that he had "plenty of money" and would conclude the deal "as soon as we take care of Kennedy." Sources told the Secret Service that the Echevarria weapons purchase was being financed by Sierra with mob money. After the president's assassination, the Secret Service planned to pursue an investigation into Echevarria's threat and the Sierra arms deal, but the agency's probe was shut down by the FBI after President Johnson gave the bureau responsibility for the case.

Following Kennedy's death, Paulino Sierra Martinez faded from the front lines of the anti-Castro campaign. Accused by Union Tank Car's legal counsel of wasting the Junta's funds, he was eventually replaced as head of the organization. But according to relatives of Sierra, he continued to pursue his underground war against Castro and other left-wing leaders in Latin America. Tough-looking men carrying concealed rifles showed up from time to time at Sierra's Chicago apartment—men whom one of his children described as "father's banditos." Sierra, who frequently packed his own gun, even when taking his young granddaughter to the zoo one day, continued to travel widely well into the 1970s, including to Chile, where he briefly relocated during the CIA-orchestrated unrest that led to the violent overthrow of President Salvador Allende in 1973.

Although Sierra never discussed his hidden life with his son, Paul Sierra became convinced that his father was involved with U.S. intelligence. "I think that personally, Father's patriotism and hatred for the Communists made him go a little overboard," the younger man concluded.

More than a dozen years after the Secret Service's abortive effort to find out more about Paulino Sierra Martinez, the House Select Committee on Assassinations—which reopened the JFK case in the 1970s—again raised questions about Sierra. The sprawling congressional investigation ultimately concluded that Kennedy was the victim of a conspiracy, but it was unable to pin down the identities of those involved or the source of their funds. Committee investigators were intrigued by Sierra's unsavory connections, including to three sketchy characters who showed up with Lee Harvey Oswald at the Dallas home of Silvia Odio, the daughter of a prominent anti-Castro activist, in September 1963. But, in the end, lacking the time and resources to fully pursue its leads, the congressional panel was forced to acknowledge that the "relevance to the assassination" of Sierra's activities "remained undetermined."

At least the House Select Committee on Assassinations tried to shed some light on Sierra and his auspices. The first official inquest into President Kennedy's assassination—conducted by the Warren Commission in 1964—made no serious effort to examine anti-Castro militants like Sierra and their connections to the CIA and organized crime. Despite the Secret Service's suspicions about Sierra, his name appears nowhere in the Warren Report's twenty-six volumes. Allen Dulles, a prominent member of the Warren Commission, could have revealed what he knew about Sierra. But Dulles never brought up Sierra's name—nor did he ever inform fellow commission members that he had met with someone whom the Secret Service regarded as a person of interest in the Kennedy assassination.

It remains one of the many enduring mysteries of the Kennedy case. Why did Dulles meet with Paulino Sierra Martinez in April 1963? What brought together the former CIA director and an obscure, Mafia-connected, anti-Castro conspirator with a penchant for violent action? As Dulles was keenly aware, organizing a paramilitary operation against the Cuban government was, by the spring of 1963, a violation of Kennedy administration policy and of federal law. By meeting with a character like Sierra, Dulles made it abundantly clear how little regard he had for the president's authority—and perhaps for his life.

The Parting Glass

In the summer of 1963, President Kennedy flew to Europe for what would be the final overseas trip of his life. Although he had left Washington, the forces of political tumult set loose by his presidency followed him abroad. These forces came swirling together in Rome during JFK's official visit to the ancient imperial capital, where tour guides still pointed out the stone steps on which Julius Caesar's blood was spilled.

On the sultry evening of July 1, Kennedy was feted by Italian president Antonio Segni at the Quirinale Palace, the official residence of popes, kings, and chiefs of state since the sixteenth century. At the formal banquet—watched over by the extravagantly uniformed Corazzieri honor guard, in their torso-hugging white tunics and gold helmets with flowing horsetails—Segni paid tribute during his toast to Kennedy's recent Peace Speech at American University. Kennedy's "dynamic" quest for peace, declared Segni, was a welcome break from the "static" era of nuclear deadlock. After Segni concluded his welcoming remarks, JFK stood up and reiterated his peace message, telling the assembled dignitaries that "war is not inevitable, and that an effective end to the arms race would offer greater security than its indefinite continuation." Invoking Italy's volatile political history, Kennedy then warned of "the siren temptation of those with seemingly swift and easy answers on the far right and the far left." It was up to those who advocated "social justice and progress and human rights," said Kennedy, to make the more difficult ideals of democracy a reality for people all over the world.

Kennedy's Italian itinerary, which included an audience with the new pope, Paul VI, at the Vatican and a side trip to Naples, was the finale to a triumphant European tour that was highlighted by a sentimental stopover in Ireland and his resounding challenge to Soviet tyranny at the Berlin Wall (*"Ich bin ein Berliner . . ."*). The crowds in Rome that greeted Kennedy's motorcade were comparatively sparse, as the presidential limousine and its police motorcycle squadron made the long and winding trip to the Quirinale along the boulevards and narrow streets of the capital. The Eternal City could be blasé about visiting dignitaries, and the summer heat was sweltering. Yet underneath the city's unruffled exterior ran a shiver of excitement about the visiting American president who cut such a *bella figura*—particularly in contrast to Italy's aging, white-haired leaders. Even *L'Unità*, the Italian Communist Party newspaper, appreciatively noted JFK's tall, tan good looks and his stylish blue-gray suit and purple tie.

But as the young American president was taking the spotlight at the Quirinale, the forces aligned against him were converging in Rome. Behind the elaborate festivities at the palace that night was an intense Italian political drama, one with international ramifications. Since the mid-1950s, Italy had been hotly debating *l'apertura a sinistra*—"the opening to the left"—a political deal that would peel away the Socialist Party from its traditional Communist Party allies and result in a left-center coalition with the ruling Christian Democrats. Pietro Nenni, the wily, seventy-two-year-old political survivor who headed the Socialist Party, had been diligently trying to maneuver his party away from its alliance with the Italian Communists ever since the Soviet invasion of Hungary in 1956. Nenni hoped that with a forward-looking new president in the White House, the United States—which had quietly dominated Italian politics since World War II—would finally give its blessing to the *apertura*.

The Eisenhower administration had flatly opposed the opening to the left, seeing a Socialist partnership with the Christian Democrats as a slippery slope that would lead to a Communist-dominated government in Rome. Eisenhower officials worried that if the Socialists were allowed into Italy's government, they would try to steer Rome on a neutral course between Washington and Moscow. The CIA—which had a proprietary sensibility about Italy, dating back to its well-funded, covert campaign to thwart a Communist Party victory in the country's 1948 elections—engaged in its usual schemes, along with its allies in the Italian intelligence services, to block the *apertura*. The agency's anti-left strategy in Italy was spearheaded by Jim Angleton who, with his deep personal roots in the country, had turned Rome into a key Cold War battleground. The Eisenhower administration's resistance to the *apertura* was further enforced by Clare Booth Luce, Ike's ambassador to Rome.

It was Arthur Schlesinger who convinced President Kennedy to break with Eisenhower policy and support Italy's opening to the left. "My impression is that [Nenni] has honestly broken with the Communists," the White House aide informed Kennedy in a March 1962 memo. Schlesinger had his own sentimental attachment to Italy, dating back to his boyhood when his father offered sanctuary in Harvard's history department to anti-Mussolini exile Gaetano Salvemini, an Italian Socialist politician and historian.

Angleton was so furious about the new tilt in favor of Nenni's Socialists that he began telling people that Schlesinger was a Soviet agent. Meanwhile, former ambassador Luce lobbied frantically against the *apertura*, dashing off a long, somewhat incoherent letter to JFK in February 1963, filled with random observations about the growing threat from the left in Rome. "Italy's pro-West government has had one foot on the Moscow banana peel for seventeen years," she observed. If the "pro-Communist Socialists" were brought into power, "the Italian Communist Party will negotiate Italy's future with the U.S.S.R." Luce concluded by warning the president not to fall into a left-wing trap during his visit to Rome. "In the present climate, there is a real possibility you may be very embarrassed by the enthusiastic reception you will get from the Communists! I can see the banners now: 'Vivo [*sic*] Kennedy e Khrushchev!'"

Frustrated by the stubborn bureaucratic resistance that Kennedy was receiving from within his own government to his shifting policy on Italy, Schlesinger sent the president an angry memo in January 1963. "Lest you think you run the U.S. government, the [Italy] matter is still under debate," the White House aide acidly remarked.

But President Kennedy eventually ignored the political pushback and embraced Italy's *apertura*. He became so enamored of the idea of building a strong center-left coalition to anchor Italy's turbulent politics that he arranged for United Auto Workers leaders Walter and Victor Reuther, to whom he had strong political ties, to help fund Nenni's party. JFK's trip to Rome gave him the opportunity to officially anoint the opening to the left.

After dinner at the Quirinale, Kennedy used the rest of the evening to quietly communicate his views to the leading Italian political figures gathered at the event. As the president strolled along the gravel paths of the lush palace garden, he was approached by various politicians and officials, including Palmiro Togliatti, the head of Italy's potent Communist Party, with whom he exchanged a few words. When an Italian news photographer snapped a shot of the two men in conversation, Kennedy later asked him for the film, concerned about the impact that the photo might have in Italy's fraught political climate. Amazingly, the photographer obliged the American president.

In a far corner of the garden, a low wooden platform bathed in spotlights had been set up for the president to hold private audiences with Italy's dignitaries. The longest conversation that Kennedy held that evening was with the old Socialist warrior, Pietro Nenni. As the two men huddled together on the little stage, their faces nearly touching, they were a study in contrasts: Kennedy tall, youthful, and glamorous; Nenni, diminutive, bespectacled, and balding. But Nenni clearly felt he had found a political soul mate in Kennedy. The previous year, Nenni had tweaked the U.S. foreign policy establishment with an essay in *Foreign Affairs*, in which he defended his party's neutralist stand in the Cold War and attacked Western imperialism, charging U.S. and European governments with backing "Fascist-type dictatorships" in the Third World. "They have spent hundreds of millions of dollars in shoring up rotten situations doomed in any case to crumble," wrote the Italian. "They have opened doors to Communists instead of supporting democratic and socialist forces that would be capable of directing the impulse to freedom of the colonial peoples." Now, as a long line of other Italian politicians waited impatiently to speak with Kennedy, Nenni was engaged in rapt conversation with an American president who had voiced the same sentiments.

When his audience with Kennedy finally came to an end, Nenni was "absolutely enraptured and happy as he could be," according to a U.S. embassy official who was there. Stepping off the platform, the old man wrapped his arms around his wife and murmured something into her ear. As they walked away, Nenni wiped tears from his eyes. Later, Nenni's wife told a group of American diplomats attending the Quirinale event that her husband had been "enchanted" by JFK. The Socialist leader was convinced that his political dream was about to come true: after years of determined U.S. resistance, Italy's democratic left was at last to become part of the government.

The president, too, thought his trip to Rome was a "considerable success," telling Schlesinger on his return to Washington that he had a "good talk" with Nenni and adding, "So far as I could see, everyone in Italy is for an opening to the left."

But Allen Dulles and his old cohorts in the CIA's Rome station did not share the president's enthusiasm for the Italian political developments, and they boldly communicated their dissent to Christian Democratic officials. This is a remarkable and, until now, unreported story, one that sheds new light on the growing fissures in the Kennedy administration. Shortly after JFK flew home from Italy, Dino John Pionzio, the CIA's leading operator in Italy at the time, huddled with Sereno Freato, the administrative secretary of Aldo Moro—a rising star in the Christian Democratic Party who would soon become Italy's prime minister. Pionzio, a Skull and Bones member at Yale (Class of 1950) and zealous Cold Warrior, was adamantly opposed to the opening to the left. The CIA man wanted to know what Moro had discussed with Kennedy a few days earlier during an afternoon stroll that JFK and the

Italian politician had taken through the Quirinale garden. To his great dismay, Pionzio was told that Moro and Kennedy had agreed the *apertura* should go forward.

Dulles and the CIA felt they had a proprietary relationship with the Christian Democrats, ever since those early Cold War days when the agency began funneling money to the Italian party. Dulles himself had confirmed this arrangement when he was CIA director, during a secret meeting with Moro that was held in Freato's Rome office. Following this meeting, the Christian Democratic Party became the beneficiary of CIA funds that arrived promptly on a monthly schedule. By the early 1960s, the party was receiving 60 million lire a month (about $100,000) from the spy agency. In the beginning, it was Freato who collected the cash in a large suitcase, a duty that later fell to other administrative secretaries of the party. These monthly CIA payoffs to the party were in addition to the under-the-table contributions made to the Christian Democrats during various political campaigns.

Pionzio's meeting with Freato put the Christian Democrats on notice: their budding alliance with the Socialists did not enjoy full support in Washington, particularly in national security circles. Afterward, Moro, who had received conflicting messages from Kennedy and the CIA within a matter of days, could be forgiven if he was confused about who was actually running the U.S. government. The CIA's attempt to subvert the *apertura* was one more flagrant example of how the agency sought to undermine the Kennedy presidency, as well as Italian democracy.

In November 1963, Aldo Moro finally formed a coalition government with the Socialists, despite the less-than-enthusiastic reaction from the Christian Democrats' patrons in the CIA. Socialist leaders hoped that the historic center-left partnership would lead to a new golden age of social progress for Italy. But their dreams were not fulfilled. Even before JFK's assassination on November 22, the die-hard opponents of the *apertura* in the CIA and Italian intelligence services were actively conspiring to sabotage the deal. When William K. Harvey arrived in Italy in summer 1963 to take over the Rome CIA station, the offensive against democracy, in Italy and the United States, took a dark turn.

Bill Harvey was an odd choice for Rome station chief. He spoke no Italian and he had no affinity for the Italian people or interest in their history and culture. A gruff, bulbous man with a frog-like voice, he was born and raised in a small Indiana town and had none of the cosmopolitan polish of his Ivy League–bred CIA colleagues. Harvey began his intelligence career as an FBI gumshoe, but his hard-drinking habits did not go down well in J. Edgar Hoover's stern nanny culture, and he jumped ship for the newly formed CIA in 1947. The blunt-spoken, pistol-packing Harvey was not a good fit with the CIA either, but the agency would find ways to put him to use. Dulles and Helms thought he had a "cop" mentality. Harvey, in turn, dismissed the CIA's upper echelons as "Fifth Avenue cowboys" and "fucking namby-pambies." He was no hayseed, he felt obliged to remind colleagues—he had been raised by a single mother who became a full professor at Indiana State University, and he had a law degree. He liked to rattle the agency's Ivy League types during meetings by pulling out one of the many guns he owned, spinning the cylinder and checking the load, as if he were about to use it.

From his days as an FBI Red-hunter, when he tracked down Communists and fellow travelers in Washington, Harvey became convinced that high society was riddled with traitors. Harvey's class resentments no doubt played a role when he became the first CIA official to sniff out Kim Philby, the witty, urbane, Cambridge-educated double agent who was stationed in Washington from 1949 to 1951. At one of Philby's liquor-soaked parties, Guy Burgess—the most flamboyant member of the Cambridge spy ring—drew a lewd, crotch-baring caricature of Harvey's wife, Libby, a boozy Indiana gal who never fit into the CIA social set. A drunken Harvey threw himself at Burgess and had to be pulled away by Angleton. It was the Indiana "cop" who saw through Philby, not Angleton, who remained forever beguiled by his British friend. Angleton and Harvey were the odd couple of CIA counterintelligence—"the poet and the cop," as one observer called them. They would alternately clash and connive together throughout their careers.

Harvey's star rose at the agency after he exposed Philby, and he was dispatched to the Cold War front lines in Germany, where he ran the CIA's Berlin station during the 1950s. His reputation continued to grow as he constantly searched for new ways to take the battle to the Soviet enemy. While in Germany, Harvey worked closely with Reinhard Gehlen's notorious organization, and Gehlen came to consider him a "very esteemed [and] really reliable friend."

The Berlin spy tunnel—an underground surveillance project that wormed its way into the city's Russian sector, permitting the CIA to eavesdrop on enemy communications—was Harvey's most dramatic coup. Dulles, who always had a soft spot for espionage theatrics, called Harvey's tunnel "one of the most daring and valuable operations ever," even though the Soviets quickly discovered the subterranean project and began using it to feed disinformation to the Americans. Despite Harvey's crude ways and his penchant for intemperate action, Dulles, who needed action heroes to boost the agency's image, helped turn him into a CIA legend, awarding him the Distinguished Intelligence Medal, the agency's highest accolade.

Dulles brought Harvey back to Washington in 1959. By then he had a second wife, Clara Grace ("CG") Harvey, a big, vivacious woman who had enjoyed her own successful career in the U.S. military and CIA. One of CG Harvey's secret assignments involved accompanying former Nazi rocket scientists, including Werner von Braun, and their families on flights to the United States, where they were put to work on U.S. missile and space projects. When Bill and CG—whom he called "Mommy"—returned home, they brought with them their adopted daughter, Sally, whom they had found as an infant when she was left in a cardboard shoe box on the doorstep of their West Berlin home. Back in Washington, Harvey had high ambitions: he wanted to run the agency's Soviet division, a top post that he thought he had earned by his aggressive performance in Germany. But the CIA elite, who continued to think of him as a cop, steered him into rougher assignments.

Dulles named Harvey chief of the agency's Division D, the unit in charge of signals intelligence—gathering information through various means of electronic eavesdropping, which the CIA shared with the National Security Agency. But Division D also seemed to have more mysterious functions. In October 1960, according to one agency document, Harvey made a trip to Europe that was largely intended for him to recruit criminal underworld figures for secret CIA missions. Among those he sought out were safecrackers and break-in specialists. Harvey would soon be dealing with men whose skills were of a more violent nature.

In November 1961, Harvey was put in charge of the top secret CIA operation to kill Castro, code-named ZR/RIFLE. He quickly nudged aside Bob Maheu, the independent contractor the CIA had originally hired to run its murder racket in the Caribbean, and began working directly with Mafia ambassador at large, Johnny Rosselli.

The dumpy, baggy-panted cop and the dapper, silver-haired gangster with the tailored suits formed a tight, if unlikely, bond. Harvey invited Rosselli to dinner at his family's spacious Chevy Chase home, where little Sally took to calling him "Uncle Johnny." The two men had secret, martini-fueled rendezvous in the Miami area, where the CIA maintained its largest station, JM/WAVE, and operated a bustling network of paramilitary training bases as well as safe houses in the posh Coral Gables and Key Biscayne neighborhoods. Harvey provided Rosselli with vials of poison and stockpiles of guns to pass along to the Mafia's hired killers in Cuba. Nothing ever came of the two men's Cuba schemes, and Castro continued to thrive. But Harvey never lost faith in his Mafia partner. Regardless of his criminal background, Rosselli was a man of "integrity as far as I was concerned," Harvey would tell Senate investigators years later, a man who was always loyal and dependable "in his dealings with me."

"I loved Rosselli," CG Harvey said during an interview at her Indianapolis retirement home in 1999, the year before she died. "My husband always used to say that if I had to ride shotgun, that's the guy I would take with me. Much better than any of the law enforcement people. Rosselli was the kind of guy that if he gave you his desires and friendship, well he was going to stick by you. And he definitely was Mafia, and he definitely was a crook, and he definitely had pulled off all kinds of stunts with the Mafia. But he was a patriot, he believed in the United States. And he knew my husband was a patriot, and that's what drew him to Bill."

In 1962, Helms—who, along with Angleton, had replaced the "retired" Dulles as Harvey's main patrons at the agency—promoted the agency tough guy, naming him head of the CIA's entire Cuba operation, Task Force W. Helms and Harvey kept much of the operation, including their assassination efforts against Castro, a secret from President Kennedy as well as from CIA director McCone. Harvey grew deeply contemptuous of the Kennedy brothers, whom he regarded as rich boys who were playing with the nation's security. He concluded that their subversion program aimed at overthrowing Castro's regime, code-named Operation Mongoose, was all for show. Harvey thought so little of the man JFK put in charge of Mongoose, Air Force officer Edward Lansdale, that he would lift his ass in the middle of their meetings and let loose a fart or pull out a knife and begin to trim his nails.

Harvey came to hate Bobby Kennedy—the CIA overseer who was constantly nipping at his heels—most of all. RFK browbeat Harvey so severely during one White House meeting on Cuba that Max Taylor later told the attorney general, "You could sack a town and enjoy it." Harvey took to calling RFK "that fucker" and began suggesting that some of the attorney general's actions bordered on treason.

"Bobby Kennedy and my husband were absolute enemies, just pure enemies," recalled CG Harvey in her retirement home, channeling Bill Harvey's deep resentments years later. "[Bobby] was an idiot . . . and he had no confidence in himself, because his brother put him in a job that he really wasn't capable of handling. It made for a lot of stress for the people who were working in law enforcement."

The tension between the two men finally exploded in October 1962, when Harvey schemed with the Pentagon to send a series of raiding parties into Cuba at the height of the missile crisis to pave the way for the U.S. military invasion that administration hard-liners hoped was imminent. RFK was outraged by Harvey's reckless behavior in the midst of the hair-trigger nuclear crisis. "You were dealing with people's lives," the younger Kennedy brother later exclaimed, "and then you're going to go off with a half-assed operation such as this?"

Harvey's protectors acted quickly before Bobby Kennedy could ax him. Helms realized that he would have to relieve Harvey of the Cuba command and hustle him out of Washington. Giving him Rome was Angleton's idea. Angleton thought the CIA station there had gone soft and was not doing enough to snoop on Soviet skullduggery in the Eternal City and not working hard enough to block the opening to the left. Harvey's ruthlessness had not played well with the Kennedys in Washington, but it was just what Angleton wanted in Rome.

Helms and Angleton did not tell McCone about Harvey's new assignment until it was a fait accompli. They knew that McCone was "something of a snob and a puritan," in the words of an aide—the kind of executive who liked to keep his hands clean—and the down-and-dirty Harvey "just wasn't his cup of tea."

Many imperial agents of America would have regarded Rome as a dream assignment. But Harvey and his wife never took to Italy; they "were very fond of Germany, and they didn't like anything about Rome," according to one CIA officer. Bill despised the Italian people, whom he called "goddam wops." CG complained about being constantly cheated by the locals whenever she went to the market, and she couldn't get used to navigating through the narrow cobblestone streets in the family's hulking Ford station wagon. Once, when CG was driving Sally and the daughter of another CIA officer along the ancient Appian Way on their way to the beach, she snarled, "I just don't understand why they don't bulldoze all this and make it a freeway." Like her husband, who would sit with his back to the wall whenever he dined out in Rome, his .38 revolver within easy reach, CG also felt besieged by enemies. She claimed that people in a "Communist compound" near the Harveys' villa would throw rats over the wall into their garden, forcing CG to chase the scurrying vermin out of the family dining room.

According to CG, one of her husband's less savory tasks was procuring prostitutes for President Kennedy while he was in Rome. "When Jack was in Rome visiting the Embassy, my husband had to assign two men, along with the [Secret] Service men who were protecting him. And these two men were required to get Italian prostitutes into Jack's bed, two at a time. . . . I mean [the Kennedys] were a lousy group of people, I mean they were really scum." Despite JFK's reputation for sexual adventurism, it is highly unlikely that the president would have relied on a notoriously anti-Kennedy CIA officer whom his brother loathed and distrusted to act as his pimp. Nor had Harvey even taken command of the Rome operation by the time of Kennedy's visit. It was, in fact, Harvey who seemed to indulge in a reckless sex life in Rome. Rumors about his sexual indiscretions circulated throughout the Rome station, including a story that Harvey had impregnated his young secretary.

While stationed in Rome, the Harveys were quartered in a lovely, fawn-colored villa on Janiculum Hill owned by the American Academy. Galileo once stargazed in the villa's gardens. But Bill and CG had little interest in ancient history. They spent a lot of time and money redecorating the house—"in poor taste," observed Harvey's deputy, F. Mark Wyatt. If the Harveys were the stereotypical Ugly Americans, Wyatt and his wife, Ann, were ideal representatives of the United States. The Wyatts, who had fallen in love in Rome after the war when they were both young CIA agents, were enchanted by the city and spoke Italian fluently. Ann Wyatt took her three young children on rambling tours of Rome, tracking down works by Caravaggio and other masters in galleries and churches and stumbling upon one of the sets where *Cleopatra* was being filmed at the time. One night, the Wyatts bumped into Marcello Mastroianni in a restaurant and brought home his autograph.

Mark Wyatt, who enjoyed good relations with local officials, was supposed to act as a buffer between the brusque Harvey and the CIA's counterparts in Italian intelligence. But Harvey soon bulled his way into the china shop and began throwing his bulk around. Italy's military intelligence unit, SIFAR (Servizio Informazioni Forze Armate, or Defense Information Service), had a long, subservient relationship with the CIA, providing the Americans with the results of their spying on Italian political figures and partnering with the United States on Operation Gladio, the secret "stay-behind army" program to resist left-wing advances in Europe.

But now Harvey pushed SIFAR officials to take even more aggressive actions. The CIA station chief urged Colonel Renzo Rocca, a top SIFAR counterespionage chief, to sabotage the center-left partnership that had gained decisive momentum with Kennedy's visit. Harvey pushed Rocca to use his "action squads" to carry out bombings of Christian Democratic Party offices and newspapers—terrorist acts that were to be blamed on the left.

Wyatt was no shrinking violet when it came to covert action. He had served as a CIA bagman during the 1948 elections in Italy, handing over suitcases filled with cash to Italian officials in the luxurious Hotel Hassler overlooking the Spanish Steps. Later, Wyatt was one of the main liaison agents between the CIA and Operation Gladio, frequently visiting the secret Gladio headquarters on the island of Sardinia. Nor was Wyatt one of those delicate desk heroes who had never risked his life. He had grown up in the farm country around Sacramento, picking fruit after school for his father's cannery. During the war, while serving as a young Navy officer in the South Pacific, Wyatt's ship was attacked by Japanese submarines and kamikaze planes, and he had seen men blown to bloody mist before his eyes.

But Wyatt had his limits when it came to carrying out Harvey's orders. Not only did Bill Harvey see nothing wrong with violating Italian sovereignty, but he saw murder as a legitimate political tool. One day, Wyatt was stunned to hear his boss propose recruiting Mafia hit men to kill Italian Communist officials. When Wyatt objected to his extreme suggestions, Harvey would fly into a rage. During one angry showdown between the two men, Harvey pulled a gun on Wyatt.

Harvey's secret efforts to subvert Italy's center-left government reached a climax in 1964, when General Giovanni de Lorenzo—former SIFAR director and chief of the carabinieri, Italy's paramilitary police—threatened to overthrow the government and arrest hundreds of leftist politicians unless Socialist officials agreed to abandon their reform proposals and accept a weaker role in the coalition government. The elderly Nenni, who had suffered exile and imprisonment under Mussolini's regime, harbored deep anxieties about a fascist revival in Italy, and he quickly gave in to General de Lorenzo's demands. Wyatt later insisted that he had no involvement in the coup plot. But de Lorenzo was widely considered a stooge of the CIA, and there is little doubt that Harvey played a role in the brusque and successful effort to intimidate Italian democracy. By then, Kennedy was dead and could not protect Italy's fragile political experiment as he had intervened against the French military putsch in 1961. When Nenni anxiously asked Schlesinger, who visited Rome in the spring of 1964, whether the new American president, Lyndon Johnson, could be counted on to continue JFK's Italy policies, Schlesinger had to give the old man the "chilling" truth.

Mark Wyatt was attending a meeting at the Gladio base in Sardinia with Bill Harvey when he heard that President Kennedy had been shot at high noon in Dallas. When the telex arrived, in the early evening local time, Wyatt found Harvey collapsed in bed, following a late-afternoon round of martinis. After Wyatt managed to rouse him, the CIA station chief blurted out some provocative remarks about the events in Dallas that deeply disturbed Wyatt for the rest of his life. According to his three children, Wyatt, who died in 2006, at eighty-six, would always suspect that Harvey had some prior knowledge of the Kennedy assassination or was in some way involved.

"My dad would sometimes talk about Harvey in the context of the Kennedy assassination," said Wyatt's son Tom. "He talked about the connection between Harvey and the Mafia—not just his involvement with Johnny Rosselli, but with the Mafia in Italy. Those connections in Italy worried my father a lot." Wyatt's suspicions about his Rome boss were so strong that his daughter, Susan, encouraged him to testify before the House Select Committee on Assassinations in 1978, but he couldn't bring himself to do it. "My father really believed in CIA—he really wanted to believe in it, and he was loyal to it, despite all its flaws," Susan recalled. "And he really didn't want to do things that would hurt it."

But Wyatt continued to be haunted by Harvey and the Kennedy assassination late into his life. In 1998, when a French investigative journalist named Fabrizio Calvi came to interview Wyatt about Operation Gladio at his retirement home on California's Lake Tahoe, the former CIA official felt compelled to raise the subject, out of the blue, as Calvi was leaving. "As he was walking me out to my car, Wyatt suddenly said, 'You know, I always wondered what Bill Harvey was doing in Dallas in November 1963,'" Calvi recently recalled. "Excuse me?" said the stunned French journalist, who realized that Harvey's presence in Dallas that month was extremely noteworthy.

Wyatt explained that he had bumped into Harvey on a plane to Dallas sometime before the assassination, and when he asked his boss why he was going there, Harvey answered vaguely, saying something like, "I'm here to see what's happening."

When Calvi tried to pursue the conversation, Wyatt cut it off as abruptly as he had started it and said good-bye. Calvi himself forgot about Wyatt's remarks until years later.

"I wouldn't be surprised to learn that Harvey was in Dallas in November 1963," House Assassinations Committee investigator Dan Hardway, who was assigned by the panel to probe possible CIA connections to JFK's murder, observed years later. "We considered Harvey to be one of our prime suspects from the very start. He had all the key connections—to organized crime, to the CIA station in Miami where the plots against Castro were run, to other prime CIA suspects like David Phillips. We tried to get Harvey's travel vouchers and security file from the CIA, but they always blocked us. But we did come across a lot of memos that suggested he was traveling a lot in the months leading up to the assassination." (More recent legal efforts by the author to obtain Harvey's travel records from the CIA also proved fruitless, despite the 1992 JFK Records Act, which required all federal agencies to release documents related to the Kennedy assassination.)

CIA officials later talked about Harvey's stint in Rome as a sad exile for a once-illustrious agent—a drunken last stand before his shameful exit from the agency. But that's not how Harvey himself—or his deputy—regarded his Rome interlude. Harvey still saw himself at the center of action, crawling through the criminal underworld, stockpiling weapons, conspiring with Italian security officials—in short, doing whatever was necessary for the cause of freedom. As for Wyatt, he saw his boss as a dangerous character, rather than a figure of pathos—a man who he would always suspect played a deeply sinister role in American history.

If Rome was filled with the greatest amount of political intrigue during JFK's final tour of Europe, then his four-day stopover in Ireland in late June 1963 brimmed over with the greatest emotion for Kennedy. There was no compelling political reason for the president to visit the Emerald Isle, as Kenny O'Donnell, his fellow Boston Irishman but tough-minded adviser, told him. "It would be a waste of time," O'Donnell said. "You've got all the Irish votes in this country you'll ever get. If you go to Ireland, people will say it's just a pleasure trip."

But to Kennedy—exhausted from the constant barrage of Cold War crises abroad and the turmoil within his own administration—that sounded exactly like what he wanted: a pleasure trip to Ireland.

For Kennedy—whose eight great-grandparents had all left Ireland for Boston, part of the heartbreaking depopulation of the island under British colonial rule—returning to Ireland was both a homecoming and a farewell. The first U.S. president to visit Ireland—and an Irish American one at that—JFK was embraced by the Irish people as one of their own as he traveled throughout the island, visiting his ancestral homes and drinking tea and eating cold salmon sandwiches with his few remaining Irish relatives. The young and old poured into the streets in Dublin and Galway and Cork and Limerick, cheering and frantically waving little American flags. Women with tears in their eyes held up rosary beads and shouted, "God bless you," as his open presidential limousine crept slowly along the weathered stone streets, with a beaming JFK standing tall in the back of the vehicle. Schoolchildren sang "Danny Boy" and "The Boys of Wexford," his favorite Irish songs. On jam-packed O'Connell Street in downtown Dublin, a group of nuns broke into a jig for Kennedy.

The Secret Service had warned local officials that Kennedy should be kept at a safe distance from the exuberant crowds because the jostling could injure his fragile back. But Kennedy himself ignored his guards, wading into packs of people, who grabbed at him and embraced him and clapped him on the back. Instead of exhausting him, the trip clearly rejuvenated Kennedy. When the president first arrived at the U.S. embassy in Dublin, where he and his entourage were staying, he looked "very tired . . . and he seemed in a very thoughtful mood," according to Dorothy Tubridy, a longtime Irish friend of the Kennedy family. "But as each day went on, he became happier and more relaxed."

"From the time he stepped off that plane [at Shannon Airport], it was love at first sight," Dave Powers, Kennedy's other indispensable Boston Irishman, later recalled. "He fell in love with Ireland, more and more after four days. And the Irish people fell in love with him . . . because he was one of theirs. He knew it, and they knew it. . . . He was president of the United States, and he was one of their own."

Ireland was still poor, still divided by religion and British rule, still exporting its sons and daughters across the ocean as laborers and hired help. But here was John Fitzgerald Kennedy, a shining symbol of Irish resilience and success, returned to them at last. "Here he was, a good-looking man, marvelous teeth, lots of hair, beautiful wife and children, quick intellect—an Irishman *and* a Catholic," recalled a Dublin journalist who covered JFK's majestic visit. "He could have been any of our cousins."

The trip brought out Kennedy's fine, dry wit. He seemed to get looser at each public event. "When my great-grandfather left here to become a cooper in East Boston, he carried nothing with him except two things—a strong religious faith and a strong desire for liberty," JFK told a crowd in the port town of New Ross, from where Patrick Kennedy had shipped out one hundred years before, only to die after ten years of backbreaking labor in his new homeland, leaving four young children behind. But JFK had the Irish gift for turning sorrow into laughter. "If he hadn't left, I'd be working over there at the Albatross Company," he said, pointing in the direction of a local fertilizer business, as the crowd broke into uproarious laughter. "Or," Kennedy continued, after a practiced pause, "perhaps for John V. Kelley"—a local pub owner, which brought new howls from the audience.

In Wexford, Kennedy told the crowd, "There is an impression in Washington that there are no Kennedys left in Ireland, that they are all in Washington, so I wonder if there are any Kennedys in this audience." A few hands fluttered in the air. "Well," smiled JFK, "I am glad to see a few cousins who didn't catch the boat."

But Kennedy was also deeply aware of Ireland's sense of loss and the sweet tragedy of life, and he beguiled crowds with verses of Irish poetry, snippets of Gaelic—the unconquered language—and quotations from the island's literary heroes. JFK had done his homework before the trip, reading and memorizing and dipping deeply into Ireland's cultural heritage. He knew that words were the key to the nation's heart. In February, as he was preparing for his Ireland trip, Kennedy had even invited the Clancy Brothers, the popular Irish singers, to perform for him at the White House. The folk group ended all of their concerts with a traditional drinking song called "The Parting Glass"—an achingly beautiful tune that captured all of the Irish farewells down through the years.

As Kennedy toured the green island, he carried within him that unique Irish sensibility, that deep knowingness of the inevitability, and the nobility, of defeat—and the implacable will to carry on, in defiance of one's fate. "He never would have been President had he not been Irish," Jackie Kennedy later wrote to Éamon de Valera, the eighty-year-old Irish president and legendary rebel leader who had hosted JFK during his visit. "All the history of your people is a long one of overcoming obstacles. He felt that burden on him as a young Irishman in Boston—and he had so many obstacles in his life—his religion, his health, his youth. He fought against each one from the time he was a boy, and by always striving, he ended as President. He was so conscious of his heritage—and so proud of it."

Reminiscing about his Ireland trip later with O'Donnell and Powers, JFK said that the emotional highlight for him had been his visit to Arbour Hill, hallowed ground for the Irish people. It was here where the leaders of the 1916 Easter Rising, who had been executed by the British at Kilmainham Jail, were laid to rest. Kennedy, who placed a wreath on their graves, was the first foreign head of state to honor the martyrs of Irish nationalism. It was a poignant moment, as the Irish Army Band played Chopin's "Funeral March" and a sad folk song called "Flowers of the Forest," with the young Irish American president standing silently next to frail, half-blind de Valera, who as a young rebel leader had also faced the hangman's noose at Kilmainham Jail.

Kennedy was fascinated by the story of little Ireland's rising against the mighty British Empire, and he grilled de Valera during the trip about his role in the rebellion. How did de Valera escape the fate of his fellow rebel leaders, JFK wanted to know? Only because he was born in New York, explained the Irish president, and the British—eager to cajole America into World War I—were reluctant to offend their essential allies. "But there were many times when the key in my jail cell was turned and I thought my turn had come," the old man told Kennedy.

After laying the wreath at Arbour Hill, JFK delivered a nationally televised speech before the Irish parliament. The speech made clear where Kennedy's sympathies lay in Ireland's long struggle for independence—a struggle that continued in Northern Ireland, where the British still held sway. The indomitable people of Ireland had inspired the world, Kennedy told the assembly. "For every nation knows that Ireland was the first of the small countries in the twentieth century to win its struggle for independence." By standing up to "foreign domination, Ireland is the example and the inspiration to those enduring endless years of oppression." JFK, fresh from his stirring speech at the Berlin Wall, certainly had the peoples of Soviet-ruled Eastern Europe in mind. But there were also echoes in Kennedy's liberationist rhetoric of his earlier speeches about the anticolonial struggles of Vietnam and Algeria.

As Schlesinger noted, Kennedy's speeches stirred the forces of freedom around the world. In Ireland, his visit electrified a new generation struggling to free itself from the medieval domination of the Catholic Church and centuries of colonial backwardness. Later, working on his 1965 White House memoir, *A Thousand Days*, Schlesinger banged out a random observation on his typewriter that captured the unique global power of the Kennedy aura: "JFK accomplished an Americanization of the world far deeper & subtler than anything JFD [John Foster Dulles] ever dreamed of—not a world Americanized in the sense of adopting the platitudes & pomposities of free enterprise—but a world American-ized in the perceptions & rhythms of life. JFK conquered the drm of yth [*sic*]; he penetrated the world as jazz penetrated it, as Bogart and Salinger [JD] and Faulkner penetrated it; not the world of the chancel-leries but the underground world of fantasy & hope."

But if Kennedy's presidency gave rise to dreams, it also triggered fear and reaction. To the Cold War establishment and other bastions of the old guard, JFK was not a charismatic symbol of change, he was a stark threat. It was clear by this point in his embattled presidency why Kennedy was so enthralled by legends of the Irish martyrs. Their deaths were his own death foretold. As he prepared for his trip to Ireland, Ken-nedy had come under the spell of an Irish poem about a fallen leader from days of old named Eoghan Ruadh O'Neill, reciting its verses so of-ten in the White House that they stuck in his staff members' heads. The poem, by the early nineteenth-century Irish patriot and poet Thomas Davis, who himself died young, at age thirty, was a lament for a be-loved, assassinated leader, poisoned by the treacherous agents of British villainy.

> Soft as woman's was your voice, O'Neill! Bright your eye,
> O! why did you leave us, Eoghan? Why did you die?
> Your troubles are all over, you're at rest with God on high,
> But we're slaves, and we're orphans, Eoghan!—why did you
>   die?

Kennedy's trip to his ancestral homeland was a celebration, but also a mourning. A melancholy note hovered over the ceremonial events, a sense of past and future loss, even as Kennedy tried to keep spirits high. On his final day in Ireland, while bidding farewell to a crowd in Limer-ick, Kennedy promised that he would return "in the springtime"—the same promise made by millions of other young Irish men and women as they left their dearest ones for distant shores.

Kennedy's days in Ireland were the happiest of his presidency. "The trip meant more to him than any other in his life," Jackie wrote to President de Valera after her husband's death. "I will bring up my children to be as proud of being Irish as he was. . . . Whenever they see anything beautiful or good, they say, 'That must be Irish.'"

Jackie, who was pregnant at the time, had not been able to accompany JFK on the trip. But she wrote to de Valera as if they were connected by blood, as if she had known the old Irish leader for years. "I know we were all so blessed to have him as long as we did," she ended the letter, "but I will never understand why God had to take him now."

The Big Event

Early in October 1963, Dulles sent Arthur Schlesinger a signed copy of his new book, *The Craft of Intelligence*, to give to President Kennedy. Schlesinger found the inscription that Dulles had scrawled in the book "a little tepid." By now, the White House historian clearly saw through what he later described as Dulles's "faux bonhomie." But still committed to maintaining civil relations with the CIA crowd, for his own good and that of the president, Schlesinger typed up an "agreeable" thank-you letter for Kennedy to send Dulles, ending with the vaguely cheery words, "I hope you will stop by and see me before too long." Looking over the letter before he signed it, JFK told Schlesinger, "That's a good Rooseveltian line." It had not occurred to Schlesinger before, but he immediately realized Kennedy was right. The letter he had written to Dulles, for the president's signature, did indeed recall FDR, a master of the polite brush-off.

Dulles's book was published by his friend, Cass Canfield, the legendary publisher of Harper & Row. Dulles spiced the book with a few colorful espionage tales, but it was essentially an argument for the kind of aggressive intelligence establishment that he had built. He drew a dire picture of the espionage battlefield in the Cold War, where Soviet agents employed the darkest tools available to achieve victory, while their Western adversaries—hampered by operating in open, democratic societies—were forced to play by more civilized rules. The Soviet spy "has been fully indoctrinated" in the Communist principle "that the ends alone count and any means which achieve them are justified," wrote Dulles. Meanwhile, he observed—taking another swing at the Kennedy philosophy of peaceful coexistence—U.S. leaders shy from Soviet-style ruthlessness, "because of our desire to be 'loved.'"

There was a strange, looking-glass quality to *The Craft of Intelligence*. Many of the extreme measures he accused the Soviet espionage network of employing were, in fact, standard operating procedure at the CIA, including "secret assassination" as a political weapon. According to Dulles, the KGB (the Soviet spy agency) had built an "executive action" section to murder enemies of the state. But this is precisely what Dulles himself had done within the CIA.

Dulles also denounced another flagrant example of Soviet "cold-blooded pragmatism": the "massive recruitment" of Nazi war criminals "for intelligence work." Coming from the man who salvaged Reinhard Gehlen and untold numbers of other Hitler henchmen—and, in fact, helped build the West German intelligence system out of the poisoned remains of the Third Reich—the utter gall of this statement surely provoked howls of derision inside the Kremlin.

Dulles was such a master of the "craft of intelligence" that he sometimes appeared to believe his own lies. In 1965, he sat for a remarkable interview with John Chancellor of NBC News for a TV special that was titled *The Science of Spying* but was actually more concerned with the morality of the CIA. Chancellor spoke with Dulles in his Georgetown study, where the retired spymaster usually dished out the artful hooey that was sopped up by the journalists who periodically sought him out. But Chancellor brought a more skeptical edge to his conversation with Dulles than other reporters, and the Old Man was compelled to justify himself more than usual. Did the CIA operate on a higher moral level than the KGB, Chancellor asked him? Certainly, Dulles replied. The Soviet spy agency was "one of the most sinister organizations ever organized. . . . As far as I know, we don't engage in assassinations or kidnappings or things of that kind. As far as I know, we never have."

So, Chancellor continued, did Dulles himself adhere to "moral standards" when he was director of the CIA? Dulles paused briefly, and a calculating look came over his face. Then he leaned confidently into the camera. "Yes, I did—and why? Because I don't think—given the caliber of the men and women I had working for me—I didn't want to ask them to do a thing that *I* wouldn't do." As if reading Chancellor's mind, Dulles felt compelled to further defend his personal sense of morality. "All I can say," he went on, "is . . . that . . . ah . . . I was a parson's son, and I was brought up as a Presbyterian. Maybe as a Calvinist—maybe that made me a fatalist, I don't know. But I *hope* I had a reasonable moral standard."

On occasion, Dulles did give journalists glimpses of the darker truth about the CIA, only to quickly pull the wool over their eyes. When Washington columnist Andrew Tully interviewed Dulles for his 1962 book, which promised the "inside story" on the CIA, he asked the espionage legend what his organization would do if a foreign agent threatened the security of the United States. "We'd kill him," Dulles replied matter-of-factly. But then his face resumed its genial expression, and he assured Tully that his question was hypothetical and that he "could not possibly conceive" of such an unpleasant scenario actually occurring.

When Cass Canfield asked Dulles to write a book drawing on his long career as a spook, Dulles was initially noncommittal, telling the publisher, "First of all, I shall have to persuade myself that I have the aptitude and the skills to do effective writing, as I am not much of a believer in 'ghosts.'" It was another less than truthful statement, for Dulles always relied on others, including CIA employees and media assets, to write his books, magazine articles, and speeches. Despite Dulles's retirement status, *The Craft of Intelligence* was an agency enterprise, drawing on the writing skills of Howard Hunt, Howard Roman, and friendly *Fortune* magazine reporter Charles Murphy, as well as the research and editing skills of top CIA analyst Sherman Kent and Dulles's former right-hand man Frank Wisner, whose career came to an end in 1962 because of deepening mental problems. Dulles also drew on his extensive academic contacts for help, including W. Glenn Campbell at Stanford's Hoover Institution, who provided ready access to his extensive files on the Communist threat. Kent also suggested that Dulles "use your potent association with Princeton to good effect" and "con" Joseph Strayer, the longtime chair of Princeton's history department, into drafting the section of Dulles's book dealing with the medieval roots of espionage.

Dulles was so deeply connected in the media world that the critical response to *The Craft of Intelligence* was all but assured when it was published in the fall of 1963. *The Washington Post* heralded what amounted to little more than a predictable Cold War screed as "one of the most fascinating books of our time." *The New York Times*'s critic found a clever way to celebrate a book that revealed very little of Dulles's actual spy craft, praising his "brilliantly selective candor." The *Times* review provided other blurb-worthy quotes for the book, declaring, "There is material enough here on breathlessly high-level sleuthery to keep Helen MacInnes and Ian Fleming busy writing all kinds of thrillers"—an absurdly exaggerated comment, considering the book's calculatedly tame contents.

Dulles had enjoyed a warm relationship with *New York Times* executives and editors for many years. When Dulles was named CIA director, *Times* general manager Julius Ochs Adler—"Julie," as Dulles affectionately called him—warmly congratulated his friend "Allie." The *Times* executive told Dulles that his appointment was "the best news I have read in a long time."

If Dulles needed any assurance that he continued to be a power player after he left the CIA, the publication of *The Craft of Intelligence* delivered it. Hailed by the leading publications, the book became an immediate bestseller and won him speaking invitations before influential audiences up and down the Eastern Seaboard, as well as in California. Dulles was also invited to appear in Texas, where, between October 25 and 29, he met with old friends in Houston and Dallas and spoke before the Dallas Council on World Affairs.

Dulles often used speaking engagements and vacations as covers for serious business, and his detour through Texas bears the markings of such a stratagem. His stopover in Texas stood out as an anomaly in a book tour otherwise dominated by appearances on the two coasts. The spymaster's date book during his Texas trip typically left out as much as it revealed, with big gaps in his schedule throughout his stay there. But Dulles was wired into the Texas oil industry—for which his law firm, Sullivan and Cromwell, had provided legal counsel for many years—as well as into the local political hierarchy, including Dallas mayor Earle Cabell, the younger brother of his former CIA deputy, Charles, a fellow victim of JFK's post–Bay of Pigs housecleaning. With Kennedy's trip to Texas just weeks away, the president was a hot topic in these local circles.

Dulles's strongly critical views of the Kennedy presidency were ardently shared by the men in his Texas milieu, where JFK was widely viewed as a dangerously weak leader. E. M. (Ted) Dealey, the reactionary publisher of *The Dallas Morning News*, thought so little of Kennedy that he once berated him at a White House luncheon, in front of a group of visiting Texas publishers. "We can annihilate Russia and should make that clear to the Soviet government," Dealey lectured Kennedy. "The general opinion of the grassroots thinking in this country is that you and your administration are weak sisters. We need a man on a horseback to lead this nation, and many people in Texas and the Southwest think that you are riding [your daughter] Caroline's tricycle."

The cool-tempered Kennedy did not let his anger flash in public gatherings. But he fixed Dealey—the man whose family name was on the plaza where he would die—with a hard look. "The difference between you and me, Mr. Dealey," replied Kennedy in his chilliest Boston staccato, "is that I was elected president of this country and you were not. I have the responsibility for the lives of 180 million Americans, which you have not. . . . Wars are easier to talk about than they are to fight. I'm just as tough as you are—and I didn't get elected president by arriving at soft judgments."

The Texas oil crowd was also furious at Kennedy for moving to close their tax loopholes, particularly the oil depletion allowance, which threatened to cost the oilmen millions—perhaps billions—of dollars a year. This kind of government mischief would have been unthinkable during the Eisenhower-Dulles years. As vice president, Lyndon

Johnson—Texas's native son—was supposed to make sure that the man in the White House didn't mess with their wealth. But by the fall of 1963, the once-powerful LBJ—former Senate majority leader and master of the backroom deal—was a fading figure in Washington, unable to take care of the oil tycoons who had paved his way to power. "He had promised to protect them," said petroleum industry lawyer Ed Clark, "and he couldn't deliver. He couldn't *deliver!*"

JFK had put Johnson on his 1960 ticket to win votes in the South. But, as the 1964 campaign approached, LBJ had lost so much clout below the Mason-Dixon Line—largely because of his subservient role in Kennedy's liberal, pro–civil rights presidency—that he couldn't even be counted on to deliver his home state. With the South looming like a lost cause for Kennedy, it was becoming more and more important to lock up states in the North and the West that he had lost to Nixon in 1960. Johnson began to seem like less of an attractive running mate than someone like Governor Pat Brown of California. On November 13, 1963, when Kennedy convened his first important strategy meeting for the '64 race at the White House, neither Johnson nor any of his staff were invited. The increasingly panicked vice president took it as one more sign that the Kennedys were maneuvering to dump him from the upcoming Democratic ticket.

If the Kennedys were indeed looking to get rid of Johnson, they were given the perfect opportunity by a growing Washington scandal that fall involving Bobby Baker, the Senate majority secretary who had long served as LBJ's influence peddler, shakedown artist, errand boy, and pimp. In September, lurid stories about Baker's wide network of corruption began appearing in the press—including the campaign slush fund and Capitol Hill "party houses," stocked with buxom young call girls who catered to every sexual whim, with which Baker bought the loyalty of Washington politicians. The titillating exposés soon led to Johnson, whom every capital insider knew was Baker's puppeteer. Baker, who was referred to as Johnson's "protégé" and "little Lyndon" in the press, resigned from his Senate office as the scandal intensified, hoping to protect the man he slavishly admired as "The Leader." But the heat under Johnson only grew, and the vice president was convinced that it was his longtime tormentor, Bobby Kennedy, who was stoking the flames by quietly feeding damaging information to the press.

Lyndon Johnson had entered the 1960 Democratic presidential sweepstakes with cocky self-assurance. He had run the U.S. Senate like it was his personal fiefdom from the moment he took over as majority leader in 1955. He was his party's mover and shaker, the biggest wolf in the 1960 Democratic pack, and he felt confident that the nomination was his for the taking. Even as the Kennedy campaign—under Bobby's wily management—outmaneuvered him at the Democratic Convention in Los Angeles that July, LBJ vowed not to give in and accept the vice presidential position. "Hand on heart," Johnson told his friends in Los Angeles, the omnipresent Henry and Clare Boothe Luce, "I wouldn't be on [JFK's] team if he got down on his knees."

Months later, on the VIP bus to Kennedy's Inaugural Ball, Clare found herself seated next to Johnson, and she teased him about taking the number two spot. "Come clean, Lyndon," she smiled wickedly. What did it feel like for the swaggering Texan to be in the rear position? The big man leaned close and whispered, "Clare, I looked it up. One out of every four presidents has died in office. I'm a gamblin' man, darlin', and this is the only one chance I got." It was another example of LBJ's coarse humor. But it also revealed something darker in the man. He undoubtedly *was* keenly aware of the presidential mortality rate.

By 1963, however, it was Johnson who was the ghost, a once commanding figure whose future grew dimmer by the day—and he knew it. In March, Susan Mary Alsop, Joe's convenient wife, told Schlesinger that LBJ had unburdened himself to her husband, while the columnist was dining "*a trois* with Lyndon and Ladybird." According to Alsop's wife, "Lyndon had been very dark and bitter about his frustrations and his prospects." After recounting the confessional dinner in his journal, Schlesinger added his own observation about Johnson: "He really has faded astonishingly into the background and wanders unhappily around, a spectral and premature elder statesman." Johnson began to even physically fade as the months went by, losing so much weight that his suits hung loosely off his shoulders and his eyes seemed to sink inside their sockets.

In January 1963, after listening to Bobby Kennedy deliver an inspiring speech at the National Archives celebrating the centennial of the Emancipation Proclamation, civil rights lawyer Joe Rauh passed Schlesinger a note. "Poor Lyndon," it said. When Schlesinger asked him what he meant, Rauh, a stalwart of the Democratic Party's left wing, said, "Lyndon must know he is through. Bobby is going to be the next president."

The Kennedys had turned the swaggering Johnson into a useless figure. LBJ used one of his memorable barnyard metaphors to describe his plight. "Being vice president is like being a cut dog," he told his old mentor, former Speaker of the House Sam Rayburn. He knew that he was the odd man out in the glamorous, Ivy League–groomed world of the New Frontier. "They're trying to make a hick out of me," he complained to *The New York Times*'s Scotty Reston. And, as usual, he focused his resentment on Bobby Kennedy, whom he blamed—not without reason—for isolating and diminishing him. "Bobby symbolized everything Johnson hated," observed Kennedy aide Richard Goodwin, who later worked in the Johnson White House. "He became the symbol of all the things Johnson wasn't . . . with these characteristics of wealth and power and ease and Eastern elegance; with Johnson always looking at himself as the guy they thought was illiterate, rude, crude. They laughed at him behind his back. I think he felt all that."

It was a mortifying position for Lyndon Johnson—a pathologically ambitious man, with an ego that was as mountainous as it was fragile—to find himself in. And yet, it was only to get worse for the vice president as Kennedy prepared to visit Johnson's home state in November. On November 14, the day after the White House strategy session on the 1964 campaign, the president privately confirmed that Johnson would not be on the ticket, while conversing with his secretary, Evelyn Lincoln. JFK told her that he was planning major government reforms during his second term, and to accomplish this ambitious agenda he needed a vice president "who believes as I do." Kennedy told Lincoln that he was leaning toward Terry Sanford, the young, moderate governor of swing state North Carolina. "But it will not be Lyndon," he said.

Dick Nixon, who had weathered his own "dump Nixon" movement as Eisenhower's 1956 reelection campaign drew near, was keenly attuned to Johnson's growing humiliation. Nixon was the first major national figure to voice Johnson's agonizing fear—and with typical cunning, he chose to do it in LBJ's backyard. Nixon showed up in Dallas on November 21, 1963, the day before JFK's presidential party was due to arrive in the city. Nixon was there on business—to attend a meeting of the Pepsi-Cola Company, a client of his New York law firm—but he was happy to roil the political waters by sharing his prognostications with the local press. Lyndon Johnson had become a "political liability," Nixon told Texas reporters, and if the upcoming presidential race looked close, he predicted that Kennedy would not hesitate to drop him.

Nixon's prediction, which was prominently displayed in *The Dallas Morning News* on November 22, was another blow to LBJ's ego. But he had even bigger concerns. Later that morning, a *Life* investigative team was scheduled to convene in the magazine's New York offices, to begin work on a deeper probe of Johnson's involvement in the Bobby Baker corruption scandal. William Lambert, the investigative unit's leader, was certain they were sitting on an explosive story that could bring down the vice president. "This guy looks like a bandit to me," he told his boss, *Life* managing editor George Hunt. LBJ, he told Hunt, had used public office to amass a fortune, shaking down political favor-seekers for cash and consumer goods, even putting the squeeze on an insurance executive for an expensive Magnavox stereo console that Lady Bird coveted. As Bobby Baker later commented, Johnson was "always on the lookout for the odd nickel or dime." In fact, that insurance executive—Don Reynolds—was scheduled to testify about Johnson's tawdry influence-peddling practices at another meeting on November 22, in a closed session of the Senate Rules Committee. The two meetings—one in New York, one in Washington—would have likely determined the political fate of Lyndon Baines Johnson, had they not been overshadowed by events in Dallas that day.

Lyndon Johnson's days might have been numbered as vice president, but he was not entirely abandoned in Washington. If LBJ was rapidly losing favor within the Kennedy administration, he had managed to retain the support of many key figures in the national security arena. Johnson had long been the dominant political figure in a state with a booming defense and aerospace industry, and he had long cultivated ties to generals and espionage officials.

At the very beginning of Kennedy's presidency, Johnson made a strange power grab, trying to get JFK to grant him extraordinary supervisory powers over the country's entire national security apparatus, including the Defense Department, CIA, State Department, and the Office of Civil and Defense Mobilization. Kennedy did not even bother responding to Johnson's maneuver, simply ignoring the executive order and accompanying letter that LBJ sent over to the Oval Office for his signature. But Johnson's "executive order" power play was never forgotten in the White House. Even a friend of LBJ—longtime Democratic presidential adviser Jim Rowe—was "flabbergasted" after Johnson showed him the proposed order, calling it, "frankly, the most presumptuous document any Vice President had ever sent to his President." Despite the White House rebuff, LBJ continued to enjoy a special bond with national security hard-liners during Kennedy's reign, often embracing their aggressive positions on Cuba and other hot spots, as well as leaking inside information about White House policy developments to his contacts at the Pentagon and CIA.

Dulles was among those who maintained warm relations with the vice president, even as both men's stars fell within the Kennedy court. In retirement, the spymaster continued to invite Johnson to Washington functions. And, in the summer of 1963, Johnson hosted Dulles at his ranch in the Texas Hill Country, sixty miles west of Austin. Dulles's visit to the LBJ Ranch did not appear in his calendar, but it was briefly noted in a syndicated news photo, which appeared in the *Chicago Tribune* on August 15, that showed the vice president astride a horse, while a beaming Lady Bird and Dulles looked on. Considering how estranged both men were from Kennedy—and how notoriously conniving they were—the picture could only have produced a sense of puzzlement in the White House.

Those resolute voices in American public life that continue to deny the existence of a conspiracy to kill President Kennedy argue that "someone would have talked." This line of reasoning is often used by journalists who have made no effort themselves to closely inspect the growing body of evidence and have not undertaken any of their own investigative reporting. The argument betrays a touchingly naïve media bias—a belief that the American press establishment itself, that great slumbering watchdog, could be counted on to solve such a monumental crime, one that sprung from the very system of governance of which corporate media is an essential part. The official version of the Kennedy assassination—despite its myriad improbabilities, which have only grown more inconceivable with time—remains firmly embedded in the media consciousness, as unquestioned as the law of gravity.

In fact, many people *have* talked during the past half of a century—including some directly connected to the plot against Kennedy. But the media simply refused to listen. One of the most intriguing examples of someone talking occurred in 2003, when an old and ailing Howard Hunt began unburdening himself to his eldest son, Saint John.

"Saint," as his father called him, was a loyal and loving son, who had suffered through the upheavals of the spy's life, along with the rest of his family. Late one night in June 1972, at the family's Witches Island home in suburban Maryland, Hunt had frantically woken up his eighteen-year-old son. "I need you to do exactly as I say, and not ask any questions!" said Hunt, who was in a sweaty and disheveled state that his son had never before witnessed. He ordered Saint John to fetch window cleaner, rags, and rubber gloves from the kitchen and to help him rub away fingerprints from a pile of espionage equipment, including cameras, microphones, and walkie-talkies. Later, Saint helped his father stuff the equipment into two suitcases, which they loaded into the trunk of his father's Pontiac Firebird. Hunt and his son drove through the darkness to the Chesapeake and Ohio Canal, where the spook got out and tossed the suitcases into the murky water. On the way back home, Hunt told Saint that he had been doing some special work for the White House, and things had gone south.

It was the beginning of the Watergate drama, in which Howard Hunt played a starring role as the leader of the "White House plumbers," the five burglars who were arrested while breaking into the Democratic Party's national headquarters. All five of the men had a long history with Hunt, dating back to the earliest days of the underground war against Castro, and at least two—Frank Sturgis and Virgilio Gonzalez—were rumored to have played roles in the Kennedy assassination.

As the Watergate scandal unfolded, Hunt drew Saint and the rest of his family deeper into his disintegrating life. Saint's beloved mother, Dorothy—an exotic beauty with her own espionage background— would die in a plane crash in the midst of the Watergate crisis, while serving as a mysterious courier for her husband. When her United Airlines flight from Washington's Dulles Airport crashed while landing at Chicago's Midway Airport in December 1972, Dorothy Hunt was carrying over $2 million in cash and money orders, some of which was later traced to President Nixon's reelection campaign.

As Nixon frantically tried to cover his tracks in the widening scandal, sketchy money began flowing back and forth. The president was desperate to keep Hunt quiet and during one White House meeting, Nixon— caught on his secret taping system—figured it would cost "a million in cash. We could get our hands on that kind of money." Hunt felt that Nixon owed him and his team. "I had five men whose families needed to be supported," Hunt later said. "And I had a big house, stalls for six horses, kids in private school—I had needs for contributions that were greater than the average person's. . . . There's a long tradition that when a warrior is captured, the commanding officer takes care of his family."

Nixon knew that Howard Hunt had played key roles in some of America's darkest mysteries. On June 23, 1972—while discussing the Watergate break-in with H. R. Haldeman, his devoted political deputy and White House chief of staff—Nixon was taped saying, "Hunt . . .

will uncover a lot of things. You open that scab, there's a hell of a lot of things. . . . This involves these Cubans, Hunt and a lot of hanky-panky that we have nothing to do with ourselves."

Nixon wanted Haldeman to lean on Dick Helms, who was then CIA director, by warning him that if the spy agency did not help shut down the growing Watergate scandal, "[t]he President's belief is that this is going to open up that whole Bay of Pigs thing . . . and it's going to make the CIA look bad, it's going to make Hunt look bad, and is likely to blow the whole Bay of Pigs thing . . . and we think it would be very unfortunate for the CIA and for the country at this time."

Nixon's ploy did not work. When Haldeman sat Helms down in his office and delivered the president's thinly veiled threat about "the Bay of Pigs thing," the normally icy-cool Helms exploded. "The Bay of Pigs had nothing to do with this!" he shouted. Nixon only succeeded in further antagonizing a very powerful Washington institution, one capable of far more deviousness than even he was.

What did Nixon mean by "the whole Bay of Pigs thing"? According to Haldeman, it was Nixon's way of referring to the unspeakable— the Kennedy assassination. Other historians have speculated that it was shorthand for the CIA-Mafia plots against Castro. In any case, "the Bay of Pigs thing" was an apt code name—it conjured all the swampy intrigue that began leaching through the Kennedy administration after Allen Dulles and his agency suffered their humiliation in Cuba, everything the CIA wanted to keep deeply hidden. And Howard Hunt was knee-deep in much of this muck.

Hunt's adventures in the spy trade eventually tore apart his family and sent him to federal prison for nearly three years. By 2003, the retired spy was living in a modest ranch house in north Miami with his second wife, Laura, who was twenty-seven years younger. She had fallen for him while watching him give a prison interview on Watergate. "I liked all those men—that must seem strange to you," Laura Hunt told a *Miami Herald* reporter. "Not for what he'd done—I don't admire that—but I admired him for serving the government, and I admired his intellect."

At eighty-four, Hunt seemed to be fading out, suffering from a variety of maladies, including hardening of the arteries, which had resulted in the amputation of his left leg and confined him to a wheelchair. He had a new family, including the two children he had with Laura. But Saint John Hunt felt it was time for his father to finally come clean for the sake of his first family. Following years of estrangement, Saint began to spend time with his father, watching his favorite Fox News shows with him at his Miami house and, when the old man felt up to it, dredging up the past. Laura did not want Saint John to reopen this history, but he felt strongly that his father owed him this honesty.

After his family fell apart, Saint John had gone on the road as a rock musician and drug peddler, a trip that eventually deposited him in the coastal redwoods of northern California. But by the time he reunited with his father, Saint was a sober, middle-aged, law-abiding citizen who was eager to make sense of his earlier life. He was particularly interested in talking with his father about the Kennedy assassination—which he knew his father had long been linked to in conspiracy literature.

Saint's father had always insisted that he had nothing to do with Kennedy's death, that he was at home in Washington the day of the assassination, not in Dallas, as many JFK researchers alleged. Hunt claimed that he was shopping for ingredients at a Chinese grocery store in Washington, to cook dinner that night with his wife, when the news bulletin about Kennedy came over the car radio. But Saint, who was in the fifth grade at the time, had no memory of his father being home that day when he was let out early from school, or later that evening. And he found his father's cover story about cooking the Chinese meal, which Hunt told under oath at a trial related to the Kennedy assassination, absurd. "I can tell you that's the biggest load of crap in the world," Saint John told *Rolling Stone* in 2007. "My dad in the kitchen? Chopping vegetables with his wife? I'm so sorry, but that would never happen. Ever."

His mother told Saint John, around the time of the assassination, that his father had indeed been in Dallas. The mystery of his father's whereabouts that day would prey on Saint for years. He was determined to engage his father on the subject before it was too late.

By 2003, Howard Hunt was ready to finally talk. He feared that his life was coming to an end, and he was deeply regretful that he had so little to leave his family after all they had endured. For a time, he flirted with the idea of telling all to actor Kevin Costner, who had starred in Oliver Stone's film *JFK*. Costner dangled a big financial reward in front of Hunt if he revealed everything he knew about Dallas, but when the money never appeared, Hunt finally dismissed the actor as a "numbskull." Saint John nonetheless urged his father to continue down the path of full disclosure while he was still of sound mind. He made his plea in a long letter to his father, telling him that it was time to finally reveal what he knew—he "owed it," wrote Saint, "to himself, the Nation, and his family to leave a legacy of truth instead of doubt."

Soon afterward, Hunt phoned his son in California and summoned him to Miami. On December 7, 2003, Saint John Hunt flew to Florida—where so much of his father's secret life had unfolded—to hear his final testament.

When he arrived at his father's house, at the end of a cul-de-sac in the Biscayne Bay neighborhood, Saint found Hunt in bed, looking frail and washed out. But the old man perked up when he saw his son. He asked Saint to wheel him into the TV room, where they shared some soup for lunch and watched an agitated round of Fox News at the high volume required by the hard-of-hearing Hunt. Finally, Saint broached the subject that he had come to discuss. "Papa, can we talk about my letter?"

Hunt suggested that Saint wheel him back to his bedroom, in case his wife returned. "We don't want her getting upset by this," Hunt told his son. "She believes what I told her: that I don't know anything about JFK's murder."

"I think Laura's very naïve about the darker side of politics," said Saint John.

"Well, that's one of the reasons I love her so much," his father replied.

Then, after making Saint John promise he would never reveal what he was about to tell him without his permission, Hunt launched into a remarkable story of the plot to kill John F. Kennedy. It was—even at this late date in Hunt's life—still a carefully parsed tale. He clearly was not telling everything he knew—and he seemed to be downplaying his own role in the crime as well as the complicity of former CIA superiors to whom he remained loyal. He also couched much of his narrative in an oddly speculative manner, as if he were not fully certain of the exact configuration of the plot. Nonetheless, what Hunt did tell Saint John that day was stunning enough. Over the following months, the spy elaborated on his story as his health occasionally improved. At one point, Saint brought in an expert on the Kennedy assassination and Watergate—Eric Hamburg, a Los Angeles writer-producer and a former aide to Senator John Kerry—to help videotape interviews with his father.

Laura Hunt ultimately cut short her husband's extraordinary journey of truth telling with his son. But before Hunt died in 2007, he left behind video interviews, audiotapes, and notes in his own hand—as well as a somewhat revealing memoir called *American Spy*. Hunt's confessional trove amounts to a tortured effort to reveal what he knew, while still guarding his family's sensitivities, old professional loyalties, and whatever was left of his good name. After his father died, Saint John would make a valiant effort to get Hunt's confessions—which should have been headline news—into the hands of the major media gatekeepers. A *60 Minutes* producer spent days poring over Saint John's rich material, but he was finally forced to apologize that the story had been spiked from above. In the end, only *Rolling Stone*—along with a scattering of alternative media outlets—covered the story of Howard Hunt's astonishing final statements about the crime of the century. Saint John's own memoir of his father's escapades and his family's ordeal, *Bond of Secrecy*, was released by a small Oregon publisher and received little promotion or attention.

This was the story that Howard Hunt left behind. Sometime in 1963, Hunt said, he was invited to a meeting at one of the CIA safe houses in Miami by Frank Sturgis, a soldier of fortune who had worked under Hunt in the anti-Castro underground—a man with whom Hunt would be forever linked when they were later arrested for the Watergate break-in. Also in attendance at the Miami meeting was David Morales, another CIA veteran of the anti-Castro campaign who was well known to Hunt. Morales—a big, intimidating man who had grown up in a poor Mexican American family in Phoenix—did not fit the polished CIA profile. But the agency found a use for "El Indio"—as Morales, with his strong indigenous features, was known by his colleagues.

"Dave Morales did dirty work for the agency," according to Wayne Smith, a diplomat who worked alongside Morales in the U.S. embassy in Havana before Castro took power. "If he were in the mob, he'd be called a hit man."

Thomas Clines, a colleague of Morales's in the CIA's Miami station, was more complimentary in his description, but it amounted to the same thing: "We all admired the hell out of the guy. He drank like crazy, but he was bright as hell. He could fool people into thinking he was stupid by acting stupid, but he knew about cultural things all over the world. People were afraid of him. He was big and aggressive, and he had this mystique. Stories about him permeated the agency. If the agency needed someone action-oriented, he was at the top of the list. If the U.S. government as a matter of policy needed someone or something neutralized, Dave would do it, including things that were repugnant to a lot of people."

Ruben Carbajal, Morales's lifelong friend from their boyhood days on the streets of Phoenix, was even more blunt about "Didi"—the man who was like a brother to him: "When some asshole needed to be killed, Didi was the man to do it. . . . That was his job."

According to Morales's daughter, he was the CIA's "peon." Her father was utterly devoted to the agency. "He did whatever he was told. They gave him a lifestyle that he would never have had under any circumstances. . . . He did everything for the Company. His family wasn't his life—the Company was his life."

At the secret Miami meeting, Morales told Hunt that he had been recruited for an "off-the-board" operation by Bill Harvey, with whom

El Indio had worked closely on the ZR/Rifle project to kill Castro. The aim of this "off-the-board" operation, it soon became clear, was to assassinate President Kennedy. Morales and Sturgis referred to the president's planned demise as "the big event."

In his account of the meeting, Hunt presented Harvey and Morales as the key operational figures in the plot; Harvey did not attend the meeting but seemed to loom over it. Hunt suggested that Harvey was in charge of hiring the sharpshooters to kill Kennedy and transporting the weapons to Dallas. According to Hunt, the gunmen were likely recruited from the Corsican underworld. As Harvey once indicated, when it came to highly delicate assignments, working with Corsican gangsters was preferable because they were harder to trace back to the CIA than Italian or American Mafia hit men.

Hunt found Harvey and Morales to be disturbing characters. The two men "could have been manufactured from the same cloth," Hunt wrote in his memoir. "Both were hard-drinking, tough guys, possibly completely amoral. Morales was rumored to be a cold-blooded killer, the go-to guy in black ops situations where the government needed to have someone neutralized. I tried to cut short any contact with him, as he wore thin very quickly."

To Morales, Kennedy was "that no good son of a bitch motherfucker" who was responsible for the deaths of the men he had trained for the Bay of Pigs mission. "We took care of that son of a bitch, didn't we?" Morales told his attorney, Robert Walton, in 1973, after an evening of drinking loosened the CIA hit man's tongue. It was one more confession that the media ignored, even after it was reported by one of their own, Gaeton Fonzi, a Philadelphia investigative journalist who, after going to work for the House Select Committee on Assassinations, unearthed some of the most important information related to the Kennedy case.

Hunt might have been wary of men like Harvey and Morales, but he shared their venomous attitudes toward President Kennedy. Toward the end of the Miami meeting, Sturgis made the group's pitch to Hunt: "You're somebody we all look up to. . . . We know how you feel about the man [Kennedy]. Are you with us?"

Hunt told the group his main reservation about joining them. It was a tactical concern, not a moral one. "Look," he told Sturgis, "if Bill Harvey has anything to do with this, you can count me out. The man is an alcoholic and a psycho." Sturgis laughed. "You're right—but that SOB has the balls to do it."

As Hunt related his story to his son, he remained fuzzy about his own involvement in the plot. In the end, he said, he played only a peripheral "benchwarmer" role in the killing of Kennedy. It was Bill Harvey who was the quarterback, according to Hunt. Despite Harvey's reputation for hard drinking, the agency's assassination chief had the experience and connections to pull off something like "the big event." While assembling his Castro assassination team, Harvey had reached out to a variety of underworld professionals, including (with Helms's permission) the infamous European assassin code-named QJ-WIN, whom the CIA had recruited to kill Patrice Lumumba. And Harvey was well positioned as Rome station chief to once again plumb the European underworld for a Dallas killing team.

In fact, among the strange and murderous characters who converged on Dallas in November 1963 was a notorious French OAS commando named Jean Souetre, who was connected to the plots against President de Gaulle. Souetre was arrested in Dallas after the Kennedy assassination and expelled to Mexico. Souetre's expulsion brought an urgent inquiry from French intelligence officials to the CIA about the dangerous outlaw's likely whereabouts, since de Gaulle was about to travel to Mexico for a state visit.

Hunt's speculations about the Kennedy conspiracy were in line with the suspicions of the House Assassinations Committee. When the congressional inquiry got under way in 1976, the panel's most energetic investigators zeroed in on the CIA's anti-Castro operation as the nest from which the JFK plot had sprung—and Bill Harvey soon emerged as a prime suspect.

"We tried to get Harvey's travel vouchers and security file from the CIA, but we were never able to," recalled Dan Hardway. Hardway was the bright Cornell Law School student to whom the congressional committee gave the weighty task of investigating the CIA's possible links to the assassination. "One CIA official told me, 'So you're from Congress—what the hell is that to us? You'll be packed up and gone in a couple years, and we'll still be here.'

"But we did come across documents that suggested Harvey was traveling a lot in the weeks leading up to the assassination, while he was supposed to be running the Rome station. . . . Near the end of our investigation, I typed up a memo, making my case against Harvey as a leading figure in the crime. I typed it up in the committee's secure room, on the yellow security paper with a purple border marked 'Top Secret.' That memo has since disappeared."

While the Miami conspirators made it clear that Bill Harvey was playing a central role in "the big event," they assured Hunt that the chain of command went much higher than Harvey. Vice President Johnson himself had signed off on the plot, Morales insisted. Hunt found this plausible. As he observed in his memoir, "Lyndon Johnson was an opportunist who would not hesitate to get rid of any obstacles in his way."

Hunt was mindful of Washington's strict "caste system," but he was convinced that "Harvey's rank and position was such that a vice president could talk to him."

This is where Hunt began to obfuscate. There is no evidence that Lyndon Johnson and Bill Harvey were ever in close contact, and, in fact, the two men's "rank and position" were disparate enough to make such communication unlikely. It is simply not credible that a man in Johnson's position would have discussed something as extraordinarily sensitive as the removal of the president with a man who occupied Harvey's place in the national security hierarchy.

The man Johnson did know best in the intelligence world was Allen Dulles. Unlike Harvey, Dulles had the stature and the clout to assure a man like LBJ that the plot had the high-level support it needed to be successful.

Howard Hunt was fully aware of the seating arrangements at the Washington power table. He knew, in fact, that Dulles outranked

Johnson in this rarefied circle. Hunt undoubtedly realized that the vice president might be a passive accessory, or even an active accomplice, in what would be the crime of the century. But Johnson was certainly not the mastermind. And yet, loyal to the end, even on his deathbed Hunt could not bring himself to name Dulles—that "remarkable man," as Hunt once gushed, whom it had been his "honor" to serve.

In his memoir, Hunt engaged in a kind of sleight of hand, hypothesizing about the likely identities of the conspirators, as if he didn't know for certain. But in his communications with Saint John, Hunt was more emphatic about the plotters. In addition to Harvey and Morales, the names David Atlee Phillips and Cord Meyer figured prominently in Hunt's "speculations."

Phillips was the CIA counterintelligence specialist who had worked closely with Hunt on the Guatemala coup and the Bay of Pigs invasion. Like Harvey and Morales, Phillips did not belong to the Ivy League elite. The Texas-born, roughly handsome, chain-smoking Phillips had been a nose gunner during World War II, not an OSS gentleman spy. After the war, he rambled around Latin America, trying his hand at acting and publishing before being recruited into the CIA. His covert work won the admiration of Helms, who made him chief of the agency's Cuba operations after Harvey was whisked off to Rome to escape Bobby Kennedy's wrath. In that position, Phillips was free to roam within the "yeasty" world of anti-Castro and anti-Kennedy ferment, as Senator Gary Hart later described it.

Meyer belonged to the agency's Georgetown set. At Yale, he had dreamed of a writing career and—after returning from the war in the South Pacific, partly blinded by a Japanese grenade—he devoted himself for a time to the cause of world peace. But after he was initiated into the spy fraternity—where he fell under the spell of Jim Angleton—he became chief of the CIA's culture war, secretly dispersing cash to the literary types whose ranks he once imagined joining. After his beautiful, artistic wife, Mary, left him, Meyer became an increasingly embittered Cold Warrior—and his disposition grew only gloomier when she became a mistress of JFK.

Hunt carefully refrained from naming Dulles in his confessions, but nearly every CIA official whom he implicated led directly to the Old Man. Dulles had recruited them or promoted them or given them the agency's most delicate assignments. Meyer was particularly beholden to Dulles, who had saved his career in 1953, when Joe McCarthy tried to purge the agency of those agents who had once been youthful idealists. In the fall of 1963, during the weeks leading up to the Kennedy assassination, Meyer was a guest at Dulles's home on more than one occasion—along with another important member of Angleton's shop, Jim Hunt (no relation to Howard), and Angleton himself.

Howard Hunt might have been wary about joining a JFK plot managed by Bill Harvey. But if he knew that Allen Dulles was at the top of the chain of command, that would have instilled in him all the confidence he needed. Despite his coyness about his own role, some felt that Hunt had been much more than a "benchwarmer." At one point, the CIA itself seemed poised to make Hunt the fall guy in the crime. In the 1970s, as congressional investigators inched uncomfortably close to some of the CIA's most disturbing secrets, Hunt's own colleagues seriously considered throwing him to the wolves.

In August 1978, as the House Select Committee on Assassinations entered the final stage of its probe, a former CIA official named Victor Marchetti published an eye-opening article in *The Spotlight*, a magazine put out by the right-wing Liberty Lobby whose pages often reflected the noxious views of the group's eccentric founder, Willis Carto. Marchetti wrote that CIA officials had decided that if the assassinations committee crept too close to the truth, the agency was prepared to scapegoat Hunt and some of his sidekicks, such as Sturgis. "[Hunt's] luck has run out, and the CIA has decided to sacrifice him to protect its clandestine services," Marchetti wrote. "The agency is furious with Hunt for having dragged it publicly into the Nixon mess and for having blackmailed it after he was arrested. Besides, Hunt is vulnerable—an easy target as they say in the spy business. His reputation and integrity have been destroyed. . . . In the public hearings, the CIA will 'admit' that Hunt was involved in the conspiracy to kill Kennedy. The CIA may go so far as to 'admit' that there were three gunmen shooting at Kennedy."

Marchetti described this CIA plan as a classic "limited hangout" strategy—spy jargon for releasing some of the hidden facts, in order to distract the public from bigger, more explosive information. While *The Spotlight* was a sketchy publication, Marchetti himself had credibility. A former Soviet military specialist for the CIA, he had risen to become a special assistant to Helms before resigning in 1969 over disagreements with agency policy. In 1973, Marchetti wrote a critique of the agency, *The CIA and the Cult of Intelligence*, which the agency forced his publisher, Alfred A. Knopf, to heavily censor. But Marchetti remained a CIA loyalist at heart, and he retained strong ties to the agency.

In the ensuing uproar over the *Spotlight* article, Hunt sued for defamation of character, insisting that he had nothing to do with the Kennedy assassination, but he ultimately lost his court case. The Liberty Lobby's attorney, famed JFK researcher Mark Lane, succeeded in convincing the jury that Hunt might indeed have been in Dallas, as his own son came to believe.

During the trial, Lane uncovered the surprising identities of Marchetti's sources: Jim Angleton and William Corson, a former Marine officer who had served with Dulles's son in Korea and later worked for the spymaster. Marchetti was clearly a conduit for the deep rumblings from within Langley. His article was a fascinating window into the CIA's organizational psychology during a period of the agency's greatest distress.

Marchetti himself was troubled by the unanswered questions swirling around the Kennedy assassination. "This is a thing in my mind that is not 100 percent certain—there is that two to three percent that remains open," he said. And much of Marchetti's suspicion focused on Hunt. "He might have been down there [in Dallas] for some other reason, but . . . who knows?" Some of the evidence about Hunt that came out during the Liberty Lobby trial, added Marchetti, "was just very, very strange."

As the CIA prepared its "limited hangout" strategy on the Kennedy assassination, Hunt was not the only officer considered "expendable" by the agency. Bill Harvey, too, felt that he was being hung out to dry when he was subpoenaed by the Church Committee to testify about the CIA's assassination plots against foreign leaders. Word circulated in Washington that Harvey had gone "rogue." Like Kurtz in *Heart of Darkness*, it was whispered, he had gone off the rails during his exploits in the espionage wilderness—his thinking had become unsound. Harvey was very familiar with the CIA's character assassination machinery, and he now found himself a target of it: he had never been one of the Fifth Avenue cowboys, and now they were turning on him. Long after he was gone, Harvey's family still resented the CIA high command for how they had treated him. They "threw him under the bus," in the words of his daughter, Sally.

Harvey's widow, CG, was bitterly aware of the CIA class system. "Bill always had very good opportunities for travel and learning," she said, still defending her late husband against the agency prejudices. "And for these people to turn up their noses and say that Bill was from nothing, just because he graduated in law school at Indiana University, always made me feel that they were jealous and that they really couldn't carry his briefcase when it came to intelligence. . . . Bill gave his life to his country."

All the stories that came spilling out of the agency about Harvey's wild ways—his love of guns, his fondness for birdbath-size martinis, his eruptions of black fury at the Kennedys—they were all meant to show that he was the type who could blow his top and do anything. But Harvey's consistently glowing CIA fitness reports tell a different story. There was nothing rogue about Bill Harvey in these pages—he was portrayed as a dedicated and highly valued professional. Even after Harvey had enraged Bobby Kennedy with his Cuban antics, he continued to win enthusiastic reviews from his superiors. "It is difficult to prepare a fitness report on this outstanding officer, largely because forms do not lend themselves to measuring his many unique characteristics," began Harvey's October 1962 report, which cited his "professional knowledge . . . toughness of mind and firmness of attitude."

Harvey, the report concluded, "is one of the few distinctly outstanding officers" in the CIA's action arm.

Likewise, after the violently inclined Harvey alarmed F. Mark Wyatt, his Rome deputy, so severely that Wyatt asked to be transferred home, Harvey's performance continued to be rated "outstanding" by agency officials. Harvey's March 1965 report commended "his determination to accomplish his basic objectives regardless of the obstacles which he encounters." The Rome station "must be guided with a strong hand," the report continued, "which Mr. Harvey is well able to supply." Dick Helms had sent Wyatt to Rome to help keep an eye on Harvey. But when Wyatt was recalled to Langley and told Helms about the extreme methods that Harvey was employing in Rome, the CIA did nothing to discipline Harvey. Instead, it was Wyatt who found his career stalled.

Harvey always vehemently denied that he was a reckless maverick. Testifying before the Church Committee, he insisted that he had never done anything that was "unauthorized, freewheeling or in any way outside the framework of my responsibilities and duties as an officer of the agency." The truly alarming thing is that Harvey was probably telling the truth. But the men who had authorized his extreme actions were quite willing for him to take the blame. Like Hunt, he was "an easy target" for the spymasters.

Bill Harvey and Howard Hunt both prided themselves on being part of the CIA's upper tier. But that's not how these men were viewed at the top of the agency. Hunt liked to brag that he had family connections to Wild Bill Donovan himself, who had admitted him into the OSS, the original roundtable of American intelligence. But it turned out that Hunt's father was a lobbyist in upstate New York to whom Donovan owed a favor, not a fellow Wall Street lawyer. Everyone knew Hunt was a writer, but they also knew he was no Ian Fleming.

Hunt didn't figure out how these men really saw him until it was much too late. "I thought—mistakenly—that I was dealing with honorable men," he said near the end of his life.

To the Georgetown set, there would always be something low-rent about men like Hunt—as well as Harvey and Morales. The CIA was a cold hierarchy. Men like this would never be invited for lunch with Dulles at the Alibi Club or to play tennis with Dick Helms at the Chevy Chase Club. These men were indispensable—until they became expendable.

Hunt, Harvey, and Morales were among the expendable men sent to Dallas in November 1963. But the most expendable of all was a young ex-marine with a perplexing past named Lee Harvey Oswald.

The Fingerprints of Intelligence

Lee Harvey Oswald was one of those bright, lost, fatherless boys whom society finds inventive ways of abusing. He never knew his father, Robert, who died of a heart attack before he was born. His mother, Marguerite, suffered from a high-strung disposition and was ill equipped to take care of her three sons. When Lee was three years old, his mother placed him in a New Orleans orphanage known as the Bethlehem Children's Home, where his two older brothers already resided. Some of the children there fell prey to predatory members of the staff, and Lee was said to have witnessed scenes of sexual exploitation at a tender age. Marguerite withdrew Lee from Bethlehem after a year, and his two brothers came home several months later. But life in the Oswald family continued on a turbulent course, as Marguerite married for a third time and divorced, put her older sons in a Mississippi military school, and moved with Lee to Forth Worth. When Lee's older brothers fled the domestic chaos and enlisted in the military, he was left adrift with his permanently unsettled mother.

In the summer of 1952, when Lee was nearly thirteen, Marguerite packed up the two of them and headed to New York, where they moved in with her oldest son, John, who was now married and living in an apartment on the Upper East Side. Life was no more stable for Lee in New York, and he often cut class, riding the subways and roaming the streets. Arrested for chronic truancy, Oswald was confined for three weeks in the city's Youth House for psychiatric evaluation.

Dr. Renatus Hartogs, a German-trained physician who was chief psychiatrist at Youth House, found the intelligent and free-floating Oswald to be such an interesting case that he made the thirteen-year-old the subject of one of his seminars. Hartogs's psychiatric profile of Oswald—which he would reprise for the Warren Commission a decade later—created the pathological framework by which the alleged assassin would be known for many years to come. Oswald, according to Hartogs, was an "emotionally disturbed, mentally constricted youngster" who was "suspicious and defiant in his attitude toward authority." While a probation officer had found Lee to be a "small, bright and likable boy" with a reasonable explanation for his truancy—he thought school was "a waste of time" and "the other children made fun of him because of his Texas drawl and his blue jeans"—Hartogs saw Oswald as a walking time bomb. The only reason he had not "acted upon his hostility in an aggressive or destructive fashion" was that he had not yet "developed the courage."

Hartogs himself was a curious case, one of those intrepid explorers of the human mind who—with government encouragement and funding—had been willing to go to the scientific fringes. His résumé included a stint at Montreal's Allan Memorial Institute, where Dr. Ewen Cameron conducted his diabolical "Sleep Room" experiments. Hartogs went on to work with Dr. Sidney Malitz of the New York State Psychiatric Institute, which received funding from the Army Chemical Corps and the CIA to conduct drug experiments on unsuspecting patients involving LSD and mescaline. Later, after Hartogs was drummed out of psychiatry by a sensational sex scandal, he turned himself into a hypnosis expert.

Young Oswald had a searching mind. After the teenager was handed a pamphlet on a New York street corner about Julius and Ethel Rosenberg—the spies condemned to death for passing atomic secrets to the Russians—he was moved to learn about Communism, forcing himself to read the heavy Germanic prose of Karl Marx. Oswald dreamed of an exciting world beyond the cramped hysteria of life with Marguerite—where he could make himself into whomever he wanted to be. *I Led Three Lives* was his favorite TV show—the serial based on the true story of Herbert Philbrick, the mild-mannered Boston advertising executive who had turned himself into an undercover agent for the FBI. The multilayered secrecy of Philbrick's life resonated with the boy who yearned to escape the drab one-dimensionality of his own. But ignored at home, and left to fend for himself, Lee's dreams only made him a soft target. As the teenaged Oswald ventured into the world, he was a mooncalf waiting to be exploited.

After returning to New Orleans with his mother in 1954, the fifteen-year-old Oswald hooked up with the Civil Air Patrol, a group of young men interested in learning how to fly. The military auxiliary group, which was founded during World War II to help defend America's coastlines against German and Japanese attack, not only trained future pilots, it inculcated the patriotic Cold War values of the time. Among its founders was David Harold Byrd, a right-wing Texas oilman and defense contractor. Byrd also owned the Texas School Book Depository, the Dallas warehouse where Oswald would be hired in the fall of 1963 and allegedly establish a sniper's lair on the sixth floor of the building. It was just one of the many curiosities that marked the life of Lee Harvey Oswald.

In New Orleans, young Oswald's life began to intersect with older men who saw how he could be of use, including characters who would later have flamboyant walk-on roles in District Attorney Jim Garrison's valiant but doomed investigation of the Kennedy assassination. David Ferrie—the Eastern Airlines pilot who supervised the local Civil Air Patrol chapter—was a particularly eccentric personality. Suffering from alopecia, Ferrie took to wearing an ill-fitting, reddish wig and filling in his missing eyebrows with theatrical slashes of greasepaint. Catholic-educated and homosexual, he led a secretive and tortured life. He liked to practice hypnosis techniques on the young cadets under his command and tried to lure them into a drug research program at Tulane University with which he was connected. A passionate anti-Communist, Ferrie threw himself into New Orleans's steamy anti-Castro politics. After the Bay of Pigs debacle, he denounced Kennedy with such vicious abandon during a speech to a veterans group that he was asked to step down from the podium. The president "ought to be shot," Ferrie began telling people.

In October 1956, Oswald—barely seventeen and less than a month into his tenth grade year—followed the same path as his older brothers, throwing off Marguerite's "yoke of oppression," as they put it, and joining the Marines. The following year, he was sent to Atsugi, a naval air base outside of Tokyo, which served as a takeoff point for the CIA's top secret U-2 spy flights over the Soviet Union. The Atsugi base was also one of the centers for the CIA's LSD experimentation. A CIA memo titled "'Truth Drugs' in Interrogation" revealed the agency practice of dosing agents who were marked for dangerous overseas missions. An operative who had tripped on acid before, the memo noted, would be less likely to crack up if subjected to hallucinogenic treatments by his captors. Some chroniclers of Oswald's life have suggested that he was one of the young marines on whom the CIA performed its acid tests.

Oswald's overseas tour of duty was a troubled one. He shot himself in the arm with a derringer, apparently by accident. He was court-martialed twice, once for the illegal possession of a firearm, the second time for pouring a drink over a sergeant in a bar brawl. He suffered a nervous breakdown. But he also continued to be defined by his intelligence and inquisitiveness. He began expressing an interest in traveling to Russia, to see for himself what it was like. In short, he was the sort of boy-man—unfinished, angry, defiant, and hungry to experience life—who stands out from the ranks and gets attention.

At some point, Oswald's growing curiosity about the Soviet Union—the forbidding land beyond the Iron Curtain that an entire generation of Americans had been taught to fear and hate—began to receive support and guidance. Transferred to El Toro Air Station in Southern California in December 1958, he applied himself to learning Russian, a challenging language difficult to master on one's own. J. Lee Rankin, the chief counsel for the Warren Commission, would later suggest that Oswald had received training at the Army Language School in Monterey, California, which was known for giving military and intelligence personnel crash courses in a wide range of languages and dialects.

Oswald was now launched on a grand adventure not entirely of his own making. He quit the Marines, claiming—falsely—that his mother was injured and required his help. On September 20, 1959, nine days after receiving his discharge, he set off for Russia, sailing first to England—where he disembarked at Southampton on October 9—and flying to Helsinki shortly thereafter. Oswald later told his wife, Marina, that he had taken a "hop"—a U.S. military transport flight—to get to Finland, which was the easiest point of entry to the Soviet Union.

There was a magical element to Oswald's journey. Despite the fact that he was a broke ex-serviceman who had only $203 in his bank account when he left America, Oswald enjoyed the best accommodations. In Helsinki, he stayed in two of the city's finest hotels, the Torni and the Klaus Kurki. After checking out, he still had enough money to buy a ticket on the overnight train to Moscow.

If Oswald was being moved by an unseen hand, his performance at the U.S. embassy in Moscow—where he arrived on a Saturday morning in October to theatrically announce his defection—seemed a particularly awkward piece of staging. There was a scripted quality to the way he renounced his citizenship and declared his intention to turn over military secrets to the Soviets. Listening to the slightly built young man, American consul Richard Snyder had the distinct feeling that "this was part of a scene he had rehearsed before coming into the embassy. It was a preplanned speech."

But Oswald never seemed certain of the role he was playing during his two and a half years in the Soviet Union. He clearly was not a genuine defector, since the CIA and other U.S. intelligence agencies reacted to his provocative performance at the U.S. embassy with a studied nonchalance, even though he threatened to hand over classified information from his tour of duty at the top secret U-2 base. It took a full year before Angleton's counterintelligence department finally bothered opening up a standard 201 file on the defector. Oswald did not seem particularly threatening to the Soviets either. While KGB officers found him puzzling, they did not regard him as a master CIA spy. He did not snoop around secure areas. And despite his military service, the Russians learned that he was a bad shot. When Oswald went on expeditions with his factory hunting club in Minsk, he never could hit anything. A co-worker took pity on him once and shot a rabbit for him.

A KGB official described Oswald in one document as "an empty person." He was the type who could be used as a "dangle" by a sophisticated puppet master like Angleton, someone to flush out moles, to find out what the Soviets knew about the U-2 program. In the Kabuki theater of Angleton's mind, people played parts whose significance only he understood. It was the paper record—the "legend"—that mattered most to Angleton. Under the covert wizard's direction, a person's file sometimes took on a life of its own, full of actions and dialogue that bore no relation to the subject's real life. To Jim Angleton, the young, pliable American playing the role of defector was a performer who had not yet reached his full potential. He was someone to watch over time.

If there was a real Oswald, the picture emerged in flickering light, only to be seen by the very few people he allowed to get close to him. Nobody was in a better position to observe Lee as he went about his new life in Minsk—where Soviet authorities had given him a sparsely furnished but comfortable apartment and a job in a radio factory—than Ernst Titovets, the medical student who would become Oswald's best friend in Russia. The two young men spent much of their free time together, pursuing women, playing records in their apartments, going to the opera, and debating the positive and negative aspects of life under capitalism and Communism. Titovets would become Oswald's Boswell, chronicling the young American's quotidian life in a revealing memoir that would be published in Russia a half century later, but remain largely unknown in the United States.

Titovets was better educated and more culturally sophisticated than his American friend. The Russian had to explain to Oswald who George Gershwin was. But in spite of the high school dropout's education gaps, Titovets recognized that Oswald was an innately smart young man. "I had ample opportunity to observe during our debates how quick he was to grasp the essence of an abstract philosophical idea," Titovets later wrote in his memoir. "I carried away an impression of him as a very intelligent, quick-witted person."

Oswald, whose childhood hardships had made him sensitive to the exploitation of the poor and weak, was drawn to Marxism's egalitarian promise and seemed genuinely intrigued by the Soviet system. But, American to the core, he soon began to chafe under the regimentation of life in Minsk, making fun of the omnipresent Lenin posters that loomed over his radio factory and grumbling about the compulsory exercise sessions and propaganda meetings in which workers had to participate. He once staged a one-man strike to protest what he said were the factory's outdated work practices. Work life in the United States was no paradise, Oswald acknowledged to Titovets, and racism was a national disgrace. But all in all, American workers enjoyed a higher standard of living and more freedom, he said. "You live like slaves!" Oswald once yelled during a particularly heated discussion with his Russian friend.

On the whole, Oswald did not strike Titovets as being the political extremist that he was widely portrayed to be after the Kennedy assassination. "Oswald did not produce the impression of a narrow-minded political zealot . . . nor would he push his ideas on others. A good listener, he was ready to learn new things and kept his mind open to new ideas." Titovets saw his American companion as a work in progress, someone trying to bridge the chasm between East and West, and develop his own political philosophy. As he prepared to return to America, Oswald began drafting his vision of the ideal society, one that combined the best features of capitalism and socialism, which he called the "Athenian system." One biographer would later describe Oswald as a "pioneer . . . a lonely American anti-hero a few years ahead of his time," working out his social theories thousands of miles away from home— ideas that mirrored the grassroots, participatory democracy that would soon be advocated by the New Left.

Nothing about the Oswald that Titovets knew conformed to the profile of the angry loner in the Warren Report. He was popular with women and he had an easy way with children. When tense confrontations arose with other men—like the time he got into an argument with a fellow worker named Max over a shop machine—Oswald seemed to go limp. Even after Max grabbed a fistful of his shirt and shoved him against a steel pillar, Oswald simply stood quietly contemplating his antagonist until the man's rage spent itself. "Judging by what I learned about Oswald," concluded Titovets, who studied psychiatry in medical school, "it would have been a psychological impossibility for him to kill a man."

While living in Minsk, Oswald displayed a sharp awareness of Soviet surveillance that seemed to indicate some prior training. Oswald kept his apartment in spartan condition, as if carefully refraining from giving his living quarters any identifying characteristics. He would painstakingly examine his room for KGB bugs, and play his record player loud during some conversations to frustrate any eavesdroppers. Visiting his apartment always gave Titovets a vaguely uneasy feeling. "I wondered what particular feature about the room generated that uncanny feeling of loneliness mixed with an unreasonable, animal-like feeling of being constantly watched. Nice to discover a sort of creeping paranoia coming over you!"

As when he was a boy, Oswald continued to be interested in the make-believe world of spies. Perusing Titovets's collection of English-language books one day, he chose to borrow *The Quiet American*, Graham Greene's mordant tale of a U.S. agent in French colonial Vietnam who wreaks havoc through his shiny idealism. Nonetheless, Titovets doubted that Oswald was an American spy. He seemed to show no interest in intelligence gathering during his years in Russia. And there was no evidence that he was turned by the KGB. "Oswald maintained his allegiance to his native country throughout his Russian period," Titovets later wrote. "His loyalty was evident in small gestures he made rather than in flashy bombastic pronouncements. He was proud of his service with the U.S. Marines. Whenever we compared Russia with the United States, he invariably defended the American side. . . . He would defend the American Army, American English, American girls, American food and American ways—you name it."

But if Oswald was not acting as a paid operative, he was being acted upon. By early 1961, when Oswald notified the U.S. embassy in Moscow that he wanted to return to America, he was the subject of an enormous amount of secret paperwork in the deep recesses of the CIA, FBI, State Department, and Office of Naval Intelligence.

Years later, Richard Schweiker—the Republican senator from Pennsylvania who was one of the first legislators to try to unravel the mystery of Lee Harvey Oswald, while serving with the Church Committee— eloquently summed up the strange malleability of Oswald's life. "Everywhere you look with him," said Schweiker, "there are the fingerprints of intelligence."

Oswald's reentry into the United States was absurdly easy, considering his treasonous track record. He had tried to renounce his citizenship; he had declared his intention to betray his country by handing over some of its most zealously guarded military secrets; he had lived as if he were a Soviet citizen for well over two years. And to top it off, he was bringing back with him a Russian wife, Marina, who had been raised by an uncle who was a KGB officer.

Titovets had taken an immediate disliking to Marina, whom he regarded as a chain-smoking, foulmouthed woman with none of Oswald's intellectual complexity. But Oswald immediately fell under the spell of the sad-eyed beauty with sensuous lips. "The girl emanated raw sexuality about her, repellent to me, but perhaps precisely the feature that attracted Lee," observed Titovets. Lee and Marina were introduced at a dance at the Trade Union House, one of Minsk's popular entertainment centers. "The low cut of her dress stressed the size of her breasts," Titovets recalled. He immediately suspected she was KGB bait for Oswald. When he later asked around about Marina, Titovets was told that she had been run out of Leningrad by local authorities. "Taking into account her past history and her legal problems," he concluded, "she certainly had given the KGB a sure hold over her." A month after he met Marina, Oswald proposed to her.

It was one more curious episode in Oswald's life. And yet none of his suspicious past, or that of his bride, caused U.S. authorities to block his return, place him under detention, or subject him to rigorous interrogation. At the height of the Cold War—when paranoia about spies, subversives, and "brainwashed" GIs ran rampant throughout America—Oswald and his Soviet wife were allowed to pass smoothly into the country. The State Department even provided a $435 loan to help pay for the couple's travel expenses. When the SS *Maasdam*, the cruise liner from Rotterdam carrying the Oswalds and their infant daughter, docked at a Hoboken pier on the rainy afternoon of June 13, 1962, there were no federal agents awaiting the defector.

The Oswalds were greeted only by a Travelers Aid Society caseworker named Spas Raikin. Despite persistent rumors, Raikin has always vehemently denied that he was working for the CIA. But Raikin—a Bulgarian refugee who was active in anti-Communist politics—was politically sophisticated enough to realize that there was something strange about Oswald's uneventful return to the United States. It was one more instance, in Oswald's endlessly mystifying life, when the dog did not bark. "I wondered why there weren't any government officials to meet him," Raikin recalled late in his life. "In my mind, there was the idea he could be a spy. . . . I had suspicion, but I did not want to get further involved into this thing."

The day after arriving in the United States, the Oswalds flew to Fort Worth, where they moved in temporarily with Lee's brother, Robert. It would take nearly two weeks before the FBI got around to interviewing Lee.

Oswald was now entering the final act of his abbreviated life. Over the next year and a half, the young man seemed to lead an aimless existence, drifting to New Orleans, returning to Texas, taking a side trip to Mexico City, as he jumped from one job to the next, before finally ending up in the Texas School Book Depository. But on closer examination, there was a method to his movements. While in Texas, Oswald and his family came under the watchful care of people who in turn were being closely watched. He met quietly with a prominent CIA officer in Dallas. He staged public scenes in New Orleans and Mexico City that called attention to himself as a hotheaded militant, as he had done at the embassy in Moscow. There were invisible wires attached to Oswald—and some of the more intriguing ones led to Allen Dulles.

Lee Harvey Oswald was given to grand daydreams. He had big ideas about how to change the world; he wanted to be part of a larger mission than his petty circumstances allowed. But there were others who had their own plans for him. "[Lee] did not know who he was really serving," Marina said years later. "He was manipulated and he got caught. He tried to play with the big boys."

George de Mohrenschildt dropped into the Oswalds' threadbare lives in Fort Worth like a beneficent fairy-tale prince. Tall, well groomed, cosmopolitan, with a network of high-placed friends that stretched from Dallas oil society to the European aristocracy, "Baron" de Mohrenschildt—as he enjoyed being called—was everything Oswald was not. He showed up one afternoon on the doorstep of the Oswalds' humble home—which he later described as "a shack near Sears Roebuck, as far as I remember . . . very poorly furnished, decrepit, on a dusty road." He was there, he said, on a mission of mercy—a White Russian émigré of noble birth who had done well for himself in America, lending a hand to an impoverished young couple recently arrived from his native land. De Mohrenschildt, a decadent old-world roué when it came to women, did not think much of Marina when he met her that day, finding her "not particularly pretty" and "a lost soul." But he immediately took a liking to Oswald, whom he found "charming."

Over the following months, de Mohrenschildt and his equally sophisticated wife, Jeanne—a fellow high-born Russian whose father had run the Far Eastern Railroad in China—hovered over the Oswalds, finding Lee jobs, installing the family in new living quarters, making sure that Marina's rotting teeth were fixed and their baby got her inoculations, taking the young couple to parties, and intervening in their quarrels when they became violent. Later, when people remarked on how unlikely the friendship between the sophisticated baron and the high school dropout was, de Mohrenschildt simply shrugged it off. "I believe it is a privilege of an older age not to give a damn what others think of you. I choose my friends just because they appeal to me. And Lee did."

De Mohrenschildt explained that he admired his young friend's rejection of the segregationist values of his native South, as well as Oswald's complete disinterest in the rampant materialism of American life—unlike Marina, whom the baron found crude and money-grubbing. "I am not a turkey which lives only to become fat," Oswald announced with a smile one day, lifting his shirt to show de Mohrenschildt his minimal belly. "Lee, your way of life is so un-American, it scares me to think what may become of you," the older man responded.

There was another reason he was drawn to Oswald, de Mohrenschildt later said. The scrawny young man with the big ideas about life reminded him of his only son, Sergei, who had died of cystic fibrosis a year earlier. Sweeping into Oswald's life when he was still grieving the loss of Sergei, de Mohrenschildt came to think of Lee as "almost a son."

But there were less sentimental reasons why the baron befriended the wayward young American. De Mohrenschildt was minding the Oswalds for the CIA.

George de Mohrenschildt came from that lost world of Russian cavalry officers and palace balls that had been vaporized by war and revolution. His father, Sergius, had been a czarist official and a director of Nobel Oil, the petroleum giant that struck fortune in the abundant Baku fields. When the Bolsheviks took power, Sergius was arrested and sentenced to a Siberian work camp, but the family fled to Poland. The de Mohrenschildts lost most of their old lives in exodus—including their land and their position, as well as George's mother, who succumbed to typhoid fever. The surviving members of the family—especially Sergius and George's older brother, Dimitri—developed a burning anti-Communist rage. His father "hated communism," George later said. "That was his life's hatred."

During World War II, as Poland became a "blood land" in the fighting between Hitler's Wehrmacht and Stalin's Red Army, Sergius fled west again, to Nazi Germany, where he was welcomed as a comrade in the war to the finish with Asiatic Bolshevism. Sergius was not a devoted

Nazi, but he soon acclimated himself to his new fatherland, doing work for the Abwehr, the German military intelligence agency. "George," he told his son, "the Nazis are no good, and Germany is going to lose the war, but I prefer to be in Germany than in Soviet Russia. At least I am free and nobody is bothering me." But history finally caught up with Sergius—he was killed near the end of the war during an Allied bombing raid.

Meanwhile, Dimitri von Mohrenschildt (George's brother preferred the German version of the family name) emigrated to America, where he would prosper—one of the cultured White Russians who managed to work their way into East Coast high society. Dimitri married Winifred "Betty" Hooker, a divorced Park Avenue socialite, and became a prominent scholar, winning appointment in 1950 as the first chairman of Dartmouth's Russian Civilization Department and launching the *Russian Review*, an anti-Communist journal. Dimitri moved in those circles where millionaires, academics, and spies commingled. He and his wife counted the Bouviers—the parents of future First Lady Jackie Kennedy—as well as the dynastic Bush family among their friends. Dimitri's coeditor at the *Russian Review*—the conservative author William Henry Chamberlin—was a friend of Allen Dulles's, with whom he worked on the Radio Liberty Committee, one of the Cold War propaganda projects launched by Dulles and his associates in the postwar period. Dimitri himself became a CIA asset in April 1950, when, according to an agency memo, he was approved as a contact for foreign intelligence purposes.

Dimitri had brought his younger brother to America in 1938. George—who stayed for a time with Dimitri and his wife in their Park Avenue apartment and Long Island estate—envied their good life, but seemed uncertain how to achieve it for himself. George lacked his brother's strong political convictions—veering between Nazi and Communist sympathies early in his life, and later between an aristocratic paternalism and a sentimental New Leftism. George was also missing Dimitri's professional discipline and sense of direction. After arriving in America, George tried his hand at selling sports clothes with his girlfriend at the time, and when that venture flopped, he briefly became a perfume salesman. Later, he gave the insurance business a shot but failed to sell a single policy.

Finally, George de Mohrenschildt settled on the oil business, figuring that he would follow in his father's footsteps. He eventually wound up in Texas, where he got a petroleum geology degree from the University of Texas, after cheating his way through the final exams. In typical de Mohrenschildt style, he charmed his way out of trouble when he got caught, explaining with an aristocratic wink that everyone in life cheats.

De Mohrenschildt—who sported the year-round tan of a yachtsman or skier—continued to rely on his good looks and old-world charm as he pursued his career in the oil business. He had a gift for bedding and wedding wealthy women—including an eighteen-year-old Palm Beach debutante—and then tapping their families for funds to launch his various oil ventures. The second of his four wives, Phyllis, was "a little bit wild—but very attractive and adventurous," the baron told the Warren Commission. She was in the habit of walking around the rugged oil field in the Colorado Rockies where de Mohrenschildt was working at the time, wearing only a bikini—a new fashion item in those days that the roughnecks working their drills undoubtedly found intriguing.

Albert Jenner Jr., the Warren Commission co-counsel in charge of questioning de Mohrenschildt, displayed a keen interest in his active love life. The baron conceded that he was something of a ladies' man. "I am not a queer, you know," he testified. "Although some people accuse me of that even." While he knew how to seduce women, de Mohrenschildt could also be cruel to them. Dorothy, his teenaged bride, later said that he manhandled her, once kicking her in the stomach and striking her on the head with a hammer. He also enjoyed "kissing and pawing other women" right in front of her. The baron's sexual habits were "abnormal," declared Dorothy as she fled the marriage.

None of de Mohrenschildt's oil ventures paid off particularly well, and he would soon drift away to try one more roll of the dice with the help of another rich relative or friend. His true skill was cultivating the wealthy and well connected. One of his first jobs in the oil business was working for Pantepec Oil—the petroleum company founded by the father of William F. Buckley Jr., the CIA-connected conservative publisher and pundit.

Later, de Mohrenschildt proved adept at working his connections at the Dallas Petroleum Club, a hotbed of anti-Kennedy ferment, whose leading members—including oilmen Clint Murchison Sr., H. L. Hunt, and Sid Richardson—were tied to Dulles, Lyndon Johnson, and J. Edgar Hoover. The Petroleum Club also counted D. H. Byrd, the Texas School Book Depository owner, and Mayor Earle Cabell, brother of Dulles's former CIA deputy, among its regulars. De Mohrenschildt put Byrd's wife on the board of the charity that he had set up to fund cystic fibrosis research. It all came together at the Petroleum Club—the deals, the good works, and the darker stuff—over drinks in the club's wood-paneled rooms, located downtown in the elegant Baker Hotel.

The international oil business and the U.S. intelligence establishment were overlapping worlds, and de Mohrenschildt soon found himself with a foot in each one. He alluded cryptically to this early in his Warren Commission testimony, when he mentioned that he was involved in "a controversial business . . . international business." But commission attorney Jenner quickly steered the conversation away from these dangerous shoals. "Also, I gather that you are a pretty lively character," Jenner interjected inanely.

De Mohrenschildt was indeed a colorful character, as Jenner observed more than once during the hearing. But this was a less relevant aspect of the baron's life than his involvement with American espionage. In the late 1950s, de Mohrenschildt stopped drilling dry wells in Texas and Colorado and started spending more time overseas, as a consultant on petroleum projects in Latin America, Europe, and Africa. His work sometimes took him to Cold War hot spots such as Yugoslavia (which ejected him as a suspected spy) and Cuba. When he returned from his trips abroad, de Mohrenschildt was routinely debriefed by the CIA's Dallas field agent, J. Walton Moore.

The baron always insisted that he was not a CIA agent, though his denials could sometimes be convoluted. "I cannot say that I never was a CIA agent, I cannot prove it," he wrote near the end of his life, in an unpublished memoir. "I cannot prove either that I ever was. Nobody can." While it was probably true that de Mohrenschildt was not an official agent, he was most certainly an agency asset, gathering confidential information on his foreign business trips under what the CIA called "commercial cover."

De Mohrenschildt was not motivated by ideology or patriotism. He was not like his brother, whom he described almost bemusedly as "really a ferocious anti-communist." The baron did "not believe in anything, either religious or political," said his Dallas neighbor, a fellow White Russian named Igor Voshinin. De Mohrenschildt believed only in himself. He had learned from his rootless, stateless existence to ingratiate himself with whomever had power or money. He was at your service, if he could also serve himself. He wasn't much of an oilman, but having friends in the spy world opened doors for him when doing business overseas.

So it was not surprising when de Mohrenschildt showed up at the Oswalds' front door that summer afternoon in the company of a man named Colonel Lawrence Orlov, a CIA informant who was a friend and frequent handball partner of J. Walton Moore, the agency's man in Dallas. De Mohrenschildt himself had also become friendly with Moore, when the CIA "domestic contacts" agent began debriefing him after his overseas trips. The baron thought of his CIA handler as a "very nice fellow . . . and we got along well." Moore, the son of missionary parents, had been born and raised in China, like de Mohrenschildt's wife, Jeanne. "So I invited him and his wife to the house and he got along fabulously well with Jeanne," the baron later recalled. "I used to see Mr. Moore occasionally for lunch. A cosmopolitan character, most attractive."

After the Oswalds arrived in Texas from Russia, it was Moore's turn to invite de Mohrenschildt to lunch. The CIA man had a request for his Russian-born friend. De Mohrenschildt was apparently tasked with keeping an eye on the young couple—a job he assiduously performed until the following spring, when he and his wife left on business for Haiti.

Lee was in thrall to de Mohrenschildt, the big, suave man of the world—the father figure he never had. They swapped political jokes from either side of the Iron Curtain. The baron grilled him about his life in Minsk, as if he were conducting an agency debriefing. But Lee didn't seem to mind—he glowed under the older man's attention. "Oswald would do anything that de Mohrenschildt told him to do," observed the baron's son-in-law, Gary Taylor, who lived in Dallas with de Mohrenschildt's daughter, Alexandra.

Marina Oswald later agreed that de Mohrenschildt and her husband had been "fairly good friends" and that the baron was "a good humanitarian who was interested in other people." But in an interview with FBI agents after the assassination, Marina added a provocative remark about the two men's relationship. Oswald "was somewhat afraid of de Mohrenschildt, who was big in stature and talked loudly," she reported. Her husband clearly knew who, between the two of them, had the power.

In the end, no Warren Commission witness betrayed Oswald more deeply than George de Mohrenschildt. His testimony before the commission—the lengthiest of the hearings—did more to convict Oswald in the eyes of the press and the public than anyone else. He tied Oswald to the alleged murder weapon, telling the commission about the day when an agitated Marina showed him and his wife the rifle that Lee had stashed in a closet. And most important, de Mohrenschildt gave the Warren Commission the motive for killing Kennedy that the panel had sorely lacked. Oswald, the baron speculated with devastating effect, "was insanely jealous of an extraordinarily successful man, who was young, attractive, had a beautiful wife, had all the money in the world, and was a world figure. And poor Oswald was just the opposite. He had nothing. He had a bitchy wife, had no money, was a miserable failure in everything he did." Shooting Kennedy, he concluded in one of the more memorable phrases produced by the official investigation, made Oswald "a hero in his own mind."

De Mohrenschildt had enough of a conscience to feel uneasy about his Judas-like performance before the commission, and—as if to make amends—he offered contradictory testimony about Oswald. "But what I wanted to underline, that was always amazing to me, that as far as I am concerned [Oswald] was an admirer of President Kennedy," he told the panel. During a conversation they had about JFK, acknowledged de Mohrenschildt, Oswald described him as "an excellent president, young, full of energy, full of good ideas." Oswald's own words about Kennedy completely erased the motive that de Mohrenschildt proposed to the panel. But the Warren Commission simply glided over the glaring inconsistencies in de Mohrenschildt's testimony. It was the baron's unfounded and irresponsible remarks about the "crazy lunatic" Oswald—a man supposedly driven to kill by the resentments born of his pathetic life—that stuck with the commission. De Mohrenschildt took the young man with whom he had spent hours discussing politics and offering advice about love and marriage—the man who hung on his every word, whom he thought of as a son—and threw him under the wheels of infamy.

On the morning of April 22, 1964, when he appeared at the Veterans Administration building in Washington—where the Warren Commission had set up shop—George de Mohrenschildt was not in possession of his customary smooth, self-composed demeanor. The months after the assassination had been extremely difficult ones for the baron and his wife. He had been summoned to the U.S. embassy in Port-au-Prince and treated like he was a suspect in the case. His business affairs in Haiti began to suffer as rumors spread about the mysterious Russian who had been Oswald's closest confidant. It is highly unlikely that de Mohrenschildt knew in advance about how Oswald was to be used on November 22, 1963. This sort of messy business was not part of the baron's portfolio. But he was sharp enough to quickly begin connecting the dots.

De Mohrenschildt was not certain how he would come out of the Warren Commission hearings. Would his career be ruined? Would he be put on trial? Or did he face even more dire consequences? America was not Soviet Russia, but the baron had learned from his worldwide wanderings that power was capable of anything, no matter where it operated.

De Mohrenschildt was quite anxious when he entered the hearing room that morning. His eyes fixed immediately on Allen Dulles. The spymaster "did not interfere in the proceedings" that day, observed de Mohrenschildt, letting Jenner handle the interrogation. But the baron found Dulles's silent presence to be unnerving. "[He] was there as a distant threat," de Mohrenschildt later wrote in his memoir—a provocative remark that he did not explain further. Was the mere presence of Dulles, looming over the proceedings, a reminder that de Mohrenschildt must carefully mind his words?

The baron found his entire experience as a star witness for the Warren Commission—which dragged on for two days—to be a grueling exercise in "intimidation." As he prepared to begin his testimony, de Mohrenschildt later claimed, Jenner put him on stern notice. "We know more about your life than you yourself, so answer all my questions truthful[ly] and sincerely," Jenner warned him. Over the next two days, Jenner switched between chilly aggressiveness and ingratiating flattery as he worked over de Mohrenschildt. Afterward, Jeanne de Mohrenschildt followed her husband to the witness table, bringing along their two Manchester terriers, Nero and Poppaea, for emotional support. When the de Mohrenschildts' interrogation was all over, the baron told his wife, "It was an unpleasant experience, but in Russia we would have been sent to Siberia for life."

Jenner raked over the most embarrassing details of de Mohrenschildt's private life, but he stayed resolutely clear of his espionage connections. The baron realized just how thoroughly the commission had penetrated his personal life when Dulles got his hands on private correspondence that de Mohrenschildt had exchanged with the First Lady's mother, Janet, following the Kennedy assassination. After divorcing Jackie's rakish father, "Black Jack" Bouvier, Janet had married Washington stockbroker Hugh Auchincloss, whose family fortune derived from his grandfather's Standard Oil partnership with John D. Rockefeller. De Mohrenschildt was forced by the Warren Commission to read out loud from his own letters to Janet Auchincloss, whom he had known from the time that her daughter Jackie was a girl, romping on the sands of Long Island's Gold Coast. Jenner put the baron on the spot, asking him to explain why he had questioned Oswald's guilt in one letter he sent Jackie Kennedy's mother. "Somehow," he wrote Mrs. Auchincloss three weeks after the assassination, "I still have a lingering doubt, notwithstanding all the evidence, of Oswald's guilt." Since his letter obviously undermined his own testimony about Oswald as the "crazy lunatic" who killed the president, de Mohrenschildt was put in the awkward position of trying to clarify his contradictory remarks.

After the de Mohrenschildts concluded their Warren Commission "ordeal," they were invited by Janet Auchincloss and her husband to their home on O Street in Georgetown. Relaxing with his old friend in the comfortable splendor of her home, the baron and his wife felt confident enough to voice their true feelings about the assassination. By now, it was dawning on the couple that the Warren Commission was not interested in the real story of the president's murder. They suspected that the true purpose of the investigation was "to waste the taxpayers' money and to distract [the] attention of the American people from the [real culprits] involved in the assassination."

Jeanne de Mohrenschildt risked upsetting the civility of the gathering by directly challenging Mrs. Auchincloss. "Why don't you—the relatives of our beloved president, you who are so wealthy—why don't you conduct a real investigation as to who was the rat who killed him?"

Mrs. Auchincloss regarded Jeanne coldly. "But the rat was your friend Lee Harvey Oswald." She was in no mood to be lectured by friends of Oswald. Upstairs in her attic, Mrs. Auchincloss was still keeping the blood-spattered pink Chanel suit that her daughter had worn in Dallas.

Jackie Kennedy's mother had no doubt arrived at her conviction about Oswald's guilt with the help of her neighbor and family friend, Allen Dulles. Her husband, Hugh—who had served in Navy intelligence before pursuing his investment banking career—and Dulles were from the same world. The Auchinclosses, in fact, had more in common politically with Dulles than they did with the late president. When de Mohrenschildt had bumped into JFK's mother-in-law on a plane trip during the 1960 campaign, he was surprised to hear Mrs. Auchincloss tell him that she was a staunch Nixon supporter and that Jack did not stand a chance.

It was a remarkable scene at the Auchincloss mansion that spring evening in 1964. Fresh from their cowardly performance before the Warren Commission, the de Mohrenschildts were now urging JFK's in-laws, who had never supported him politically, to show some moral courage and use their wealth to solve the crime. Despite how his wife had been rebuffed, de Mohrenschildt continued to argue the point with Mrs. Auchincloss. "Janet, you were Jack Kennedy's mother-in-law, and I am a complete stranger. But I would spend my own money and lots of time to find out who were the real assassins or the conspirators. Don't you want any further investigation? You have infinite resources."

But Mrs. Auchincloss was unmoved. "Jack is dead and nothing will bring him back." Finally, as the discussion reached an emotional crescendo, the two women—Janet and Jeanne—fell into each other's arms and began weeping.

As if the evening were not unsettling enough, at some point Dulles himself showed up. The spymaster circled in on de Mohrenschildt and began asking him pointed questions about Oswald, as if they were still in the hearing room. Did the accused assassin have any reason to hate Kennedy? The "astute" Dulles, as the baron described him, knew that this was the most mixed-up part of de Mohrenschildt's testimony and it was imperative to "fix" it, if the commission were to succeed in portraying Oswald as a lone nut. But de Mohrenschildt again frustrated Dulles, giving him the answer Dulles did not want to hear. No, he said, Oswald did not hate Kennedy—in fact, he was "an admirer" of the president. At this point, Dulles would have certainly noted that—despite his accommodating performance before the Warren inquiry—George de Mohrenschildt might pose a problem further down the line.

Later that evening, as the de Mohrenschildts took their leave, Janet Auchincloss took the baron aside. "Incidentally," she said in a voice now tinged with frost, "my daughter Jacqueline never wants to see you again because you were close to her husband's assassin."

"It's her privilege," was the baron's courtly reply.

It was the beginning of another kind of exile for the rootless cosmopolite, who would find himself increasingly banished from the high society world that he depended on for contacts and contracts. It all seemed grossly unfair to the baron. His only sin had been to believe his CIA friend Moore when Moore told him that Oswald was merely a "harmless" eccentric who needed some friendly supervision. De Mohrenschildt prided himself on his worldliness. But in the end, he realized, he had been used—just like Oswald, who, after being taken into police custody, had shouted out frantically that he was "a patsy." De Mohrenschildt, too, had been set up to play a role—to incriminate Oswald. And, like Oswald, he didn't realize it until it was too late.

In the last years of his life, de Mohrenschildt sought atonement for his sins, to make it right with the ghost of Lee Harvey Oswald. In his memoir, *I Am a Patsy!*—an outpouring from the heart whose raw, Russian-accented syntax de Mohrenschildt did not bother to polish—he apologized for the "damage" he had caused "to the memory of Lee, my dear friend." He proclaimed Oswald's innocence and took back the damning things he had told the Warren Commission. In truth, "Lee was not jealous of [the] Kennedys' wealth," he wrote, "and did not envy their social positions, of that I was sure. To him wealth and society were big jokes, but he did not resent them."

De Mohrenschildt had described Oswald to the Warren Commission as a "semi-educated hillbilly"—someone "you can't take seriously . . . you just laugh at." But now, he wrote of his late friend's "original mind" and his "nonconformist" thinking. Along with the Titovets chronicle, *I Am a Patsy!* stands out as the most convincing portrait we have of the true Oswald. De Mohrenschildt's manuscript, which his wife gave to the House Select Committee on Assassinations after his death, remains unpublished but is available online.

Oswald comes across in the baron's memoir as a budding '60s

radical—a man sensitive enough to identify with the plight of black Americans and Native Americans in a white-dominated society, and hardheaded enough to recognize the fundamental flaws of American democracy. "Under dictatorship, people are enslaved but they know it," he told de Mohrenschildt, recalling his days in the Soviet Union. "Here, the politicians constantly lie to people and they become immune to these lies because they have the privilege of voting. But voting is rigged and democracy here is a gigantic profusion of lies and clever brainwashing." Oswald worried about the FBI's police-state surveillance tactics. And he believed that America was turning more "militaristic" as it increasingly interfered in the internal affairs of other countries. Someday, he predicted, there would be a coup d'état.

As de Mohrenschildt contemplated America in the mid-1970s, when he wrote his manuscript, he began to regard Oswald as a prophetic figure. By then, the United States was a country debased by war, assassination, government corruption, and constitutional subversion. "My wife and I spent many an agonizing moment thinking of Lee, ashamed that we did not stand up more decisively in his defense," he wrote. "But who would have listened to us at the time and would have published anything true and favorable [about] him?"

De Mohrenschildt's life took on a frantic quality near the end, as he began working on his memoir and trying to make sense of his entangled relationship with Oswald. In September 1976, he mailed a distraught, handwritten letter to his old family friend, George Bush, who was then serving as CIA director in the Gerald Ford administration. De Mohrenschildt knew Bush from his prep school days at Phillips Academy, when Bush was the roommate of Dimitri von Mohrenschildt's stepson. Now the baron was appealing to the CIA director's sense of family and class loyalty to help him. De Mohrenschildt claimed that he and his wife were the targets of some sort of harassment. "Our phone [is] bugged, and we are being followed everywhere. . . . We are being driven to insanity by the situation." De Mohrenschildt thought the surveillance campaign began after he suffered the death of a second child from cystic fibrosis—his daughter Nadya—a traumatic event that had made him start "behaving like a damn fool" and delving into his painful past. He began "to write, stupidly and unsuccessfully, about Lee H. Oswald," de Mohrenschildt told Bush, "and [I] must have angered a lot of people I do not know. But to punish an elderly man like myself and my highly nervous and sick wife is really too much."

The baron ended with a forlorn plea, for old time's sake. "Could you do something to remove the net around us? This will be my last request for help and I will not annoy you any more."

Bush sent back a sympathetic reply, assuring de Mohrenschildt that he was not the target of federal authorities and blaming his troubles on renewed media interest in the Kennedy assassination and overly inquisitive journalists.

By the following March, the sixty-five-year-old de Mohrenschildt was separated from his wife, struggling with depression, and living with family friends in a wooden bungalow tucked between the more luxurious mansions that stretched south of Palm Beach. His testimony was once again in demand—this time from the House Select Committee on Assassinations, whose investigators were showing a keener interest in the truth than the Warren panel had. On the morning of March 29, 1977, committee investigator Gaeton Fonzi rolled up outside the dark-shingled beach house, and when told that de Mohrenschildt was not at home, the congressional staffer left his card with the baron's daughter, Alexandra. Early that evening, after returning to his Miami home, Fonzi got a call from Bill O'Reilly, who was working in those days as a Dallas TV reporter. O'Reilly had some stunning news. George de Mohrenschildt had been found dead at home, his head blown apart by the blast from a 20-gauge shotgun. Fonzi's card was found in the dead man's pocket. (In his 2012 book, *Killing Kennedy*, O'Reilly exaggerated his personal involvement in the drama, placing himself on de Mohrenschildt's doorstep as the shotgun blast rang out. As subsequent news reports pointed out, O'Reilly was actually in Dallas at the time.)

The Palm Beach County coroner ruled de Mohrenschildt's death a suicide, but his violent demise incited heated public speculation for a time. His death came amid a flurry of other sudden exits during that season of renewed congressional inquiry into the Kennedy case. Witnesses succumbed to heart attacks and suicides, or were dispatched in more dramatic ways—as in the case of Mafia-CIA go-between Johnny Rosselli, who was garroted, chopped up, stuffed into an oil drum, and dumped in Biscayne Bay. Some investigators felt the rising mortality rate of Kennedy witnesses was connected to the creeping dread in Washington that justice was finally to be done.

Was de Mohrenschildt murdered before he could begin talking to the House Assassinations Committee? Or did he take his own life, in atonement for what he had done with it? Either way, he was one more victim of the past.

If a "legend" was being woven around Lee Harvey Oswald, there was nobody who did more to move Oswald's story along during his days in Dallas, besides George de Mohrenschildt, than a young housewife named Ruth Paine. It was Ruth Paine who took in Marina and her young children as the Oswalds' marriage started coming apart. It was she who most closely observed the intimate details of Lee's life. Oswald would plant clues for Ruth—like the draft of a puzzling letter to the Soviet embassy in Washington that he left on her typing desk—that made her suspect he was some sort of spy. Did he do this sort of thing on purpose? she later wondered. Was it part of the profile he was supposed to leave behind?

Ruth was the curious type—you could say even a busybody, the sort of woman who felt she could set the world straight, and it was her obligation to do so. After her husband, Michael, took an engineering job at Bell Helicopter in Fort Worth, Ruth found herself marooned in Texas—a lonely, liberal arts–educated Quaker from up north who was stuck in a cowboy culture. Her isolation only grew when she and Michael began drifting apart and he moved out of the family house into his own apartment in September 1962.

So when a friend invited her to a party at his house the following February, Ruth eagerly agreed to come. Among the other guests who would be there, she was told, was a young couple recently arrived from

Russia. Ruth had taken up Russian several years before, and here was an opportunity to polish her skills with people more fluent than she.

It was the de Mohrenschildts who brought the Oswalds to the party and who introduced them to Ruth. Later, JFK conspiracy researchers made much of this, suggesting that it was not just an introduction but a "hand-off" as the de Mohrenschildts prepared to leave Dallas for Haiti. But if Ruth Paine was assuming de Mohrenschildt's role as Oswald's monitor, she was not doing so as a witting agent. Paine would later tell the Warren Commission that she had never met Baron de Mohrenschildt before and had not seen him since that fateful evening.

Ruth's motives for getting tangled up in Lee and Marina's messy lives had nothing to do with Cold War stratagems—her reasons were far more human than that. While she found Lee somewhat tedious and full of himself, she was immediately taken by Marina. "In spite of my faulty Russian, I found Marina easy to talk to and very personable," she later recalled. Ruth got Marina's address and wrote her soon after, asking if she could come visit her sometime. It was the beginning of a friendship that would change both women's lives forever.

Decades later, Paine collaborated with author Thomas Mallon on a bestselling book intended to prove that there was nothing conspiratorial about the events in Dallas, only a kind of terrible serendipity. A generous young mother takes in the family of the future assassin of President Kennedy, and her life is never the same. End of story. Except that it wasn't—Ruth's story was far more interesting than that.

Paine is a woman of stubborn conviction, even in quiet retirement at a pleasant Quaker-run home in Northern California. She continues to dismiss all evidence of a conspiracy in Dallas as "nonsense" and—in contrast to de Mohrenschildt's late-life conversion—she still insists on Oswald's guilt as the sole assassin. She still wears the same sensible, bobbed haircut that she sported as a Dallas housewife, though now it's snowy white. And, despite her advanced age, she holds herself erect, with the fierce determination of a woman who refuses to bend to time or to new information about her storied past.

During a recent visit to her home, some fifty years after the assassination, there was only a fleeting moment when Ruth acknowledged that Oswald might have been a pawn in a historical drama much larger than himself. When her visitor suggested that dreamy-eyed adventurers like Oswald can become easy prey for those with cynical intentions, she quickly nodded. "My parents had a name for that: 'shut-eyed liberals,'" she said.

It's a term that applies equally to Ruth Paine. In April 1963, she was thirty years old, and—like Marina—the mother of two small children and estranged from her husband, when she invited the Russian woman and her little girls to move into her modest, two-bedroom clapboard house in Irving, outside of Dallas. Paine was filled with the generosity of her faith when she took in Marina. She would grow to love Marina, she said later, "as if she were a sister." (To some, it seemed that Ruth was also romantically infatuated with her exotic houseguest, who exuded a kind of seductive distress.) But despite Ruth's best intentions, she helped lay waste to the Oswalds' lives. In the end, Marina would wish she had never met her rescuer.

Ruth Paine has always scoffed at the idea that she played an intelligence role in the Oswald story. A visitor asked her point-blank if she had any contact with the CIA. "Not that I'm aware of," she laughed. This is true, as far as it goes. Ruth and her husband, Michael, were not the cloak-and-dagger type—they were too starry-eyed and idealistic for that. But they *were* the sort of people who would come to the attention of security agencies. In fact, Allen Dulles himself knew all about the unusual family backgrounds of the Paines.

Ruth Paine's parents, William and Carol Hyde—who met as Stanford University students in the 1920s—were dedicated foot soldiers in Norman Thomas's Socialist Party crusade. Ruth remembered passing out Norman Thomas presidential campaign buttons at the Socialist Party convention in Washington, D.C., in 1940, when she was just eight years old. Her parents were also active members of the cooperative movement, and William went to work as an executive for Nationwide Insurance, a company that originated as a co-op. The Hydes' involvement in the Socialist Party and co-op movement brought them into bare-knuckled conflicts with the Communist Party, which was in the habit of trying to muscle in on left-wing enterprises that had energy and promise.

The CIA, which took a strong interest in the anti-Communist left, eventually took an interest in Ruth's father. According to a CIA document, Hyde was considered "for a covert use" in Vietnam in 1957, but for unexplained reasons the agency decided not to utilize him. Hyde did work for a year in Peru, setting up co-op credit unions for the U.S. Agency for International Development (AID), an organization whose work was often entwined with that of the CIA. Government documents suggest that Ruth's sister, Sylvia, later went to work for the CIA, and Sylvia's husband, John Hoke, was employed by AID.

In short, the young Dallas housewife who took the Oswald family into her care was not simply a Quaker do-gooder but a woman with a politically complex family history. She grew up in that strongly anti-Communist wing of the American left that overlapped with the espionage world. Ruth Paine was not an operative herself, but there was a constellation of dark stars hovering all around her, even if she chose not to pay attention.

But it was the family background of Ruth's husband, Michael, that most directly overlapped with Allen Dulles's world. Mary Bancroft, Dulles's mistress, was one of the oldest friends of Michael Paine's mother—also named Ruth. Michael's parents, George Lyman Paine Jr. and Ruth Forbes Paine, were the kind of odd ducks that Mary liked collecting—quirky offspring of prominent New England heritage with minds as restless as hers. Lyman was an architect and a gentleman Trotskyite whose political activities earned him a place on the FBI's watch list. Ruth Forbes Paine hailed from a Boston blue-blood family that had made its fortune from the China tea and opium trade, and counted Ralph Waldo Emerson among its progenitors. She would give herself over to the pursuit of world peace and the exploration of human consciousness. In the 1920s, Mary was a regular at the salons presided over by Lyman and Ruth in their spacious studio apartment on the

Upper East Side—gatherings that drew a colorful menagerie, including artists, trust-fund revolutionaries, truth seekers, and other devotees of the esoteric.

Ruth Forbes Paine came from such established Yankee wealth that her family owned its own island, Naushon Island, off Cape Cod. After she and Lyman divorced, Ruth would take her sons, Michael and Cameron, to summer on the island. The Forbes family often extended invitations to their circle of friends to join them in the cottages on their private paradise. Among those invited to Naushon Island by Ruth Forbes Paine were Mary Bancroft and Allen Dulles.

As the Warren Commission went about its business, Mary wrote Dulles chatty letters about the Forbes and Paine families, and their horrified reaction to the events in Dallas, as if she were back in wartime Switzerland and still filing espionage reports. Bancroft reminded Dulles that she had known Michael Paine's mother "extremely well" for over forty years and had spent summers with her on Naushon Island. She enumerated the families' many lovable oddities and their sense of grand entitlement. "I was always fascinated by those proper Boston homes—and by the Forbes family at Naushon where I spent a lot of time," wrote Mary in a March 1964 letter to Dulles. "In those homes, anyone could say absolutely anything—everything was accepted and examined. One met labor leaders, pacifists, Negroes—everything but Catholics! Lyman Paine, Ruth's first husband and Michael Paine's father, came from a similar background—authentic, proper Bostonians, the kind of people who still believe today that the U.S. is their invention on lease to all the rest of us."

In another letter to Dulles, Mary summed up the privileged and politically eccentric world of the Paines by making a devastating comparison—one that had certainly already occurred to Dulles. "I would only like to point out that this is the same kind of 'background' that one runs into with both Noel Field and Alger Hiss—this Quaker–early American family thing." Dulles knew this type well—he had a history of putting such people to good use. They were the blissful do-gooders who later wondered how they had stumbled into history's grinder.

It was another striking "coincidence" in the endlessly enigmatic Oswald story. The housewife who took the Oswalds under her wing had married into a family whose foibles and weaknesses were well known to Dulles and his mistress. Ruth Paine was aware of her mother-in-law's connection to Bancroft and Dulles. Her mother-in-law, in fact, had told her that she invited the couple to enjoy a get-away on the family island. But with typical obstinacy, Ruth refused to see any particular significance in this Dulles link to her family.

Dulles himself acknowledged the flat-out weirdness of these curious facts and, in his own characteristic fashion, simply laughed it off. The conspiracy-minded would have a field day, he chuckled, if they knew that he had visited Dallas three weeks before the assassination and that he had a personal connection to the woman whom he identified as Marina Oswald's "landlady."

But Ruth Paine was more than that. She was also the woman who— the month before JFK's arrival in Dallas—informed Lee about the job opening in the Texas School Book Depository, the warehouse building that loomed over the final stretch of President Kennedy's motorcade route. Ruth had been told about the warehouse job by a neighbor. The building was owned by yet another intriguing character in the Oswald drama, right-wing Texas millionaire, David Harold Byrd.

D. H. Byrd received scant attention after the Kennedy assassination, despite his building's role in the crime. The Warren Commission never questioned him, and reporters did not profile him—even after the millionaire took the odd step of removing the eight-pane window from which Oswald allegedly fired his shots at Kennedy's limousine and hanging it in his Dallas mansion. Byrd said he feared that souvenir hunters might steal Oswald's so-called sniper's perch from the book warehouse, but he displayed the infamous window in his own home like a trophy.

Byrd's name was woven through the turbulent politics of the Kennedy era. He was a crony of Lyndon Johnson and a cousin of Senator Harry Byrd of Virginia, a white supremacist and a leader of the rising conservative movement. He also belonged to the Suite 8F Group, an association of right-wing Texas tycoons that took its name from the Lamar Hotel room in Houston where they held their meetings. The group included George Brown and Herman Brown of Brown & Root—a construction giant built on government contracts—and other military industrialists and oil moguls who had financed the rise of LBJ.

The owner of the Texas Book Depository was closely associated with a number of passionate Kennedy adversaries, including Curtis LeMay, the Air Force chief whose relentless quest for a nuclear showdown with the Soviet Union caused the president to question the general's sanity. LeMay bestowed a glowing Air Force commendation on Byrd in May 1963 for his role in founding the Civil Air Patrol, the military auxiliary group that counted a teenaged Oswald among its cadets.

Did Byrd and his associates in the national security field use Ruth Paine to maneuver Oswald into the Texas Book Depository by passing word of the job opening to her through her neighbor? Always looking for ways to help the distressed couple in her care, Ruth quickly tipped off Lee about the job. The earnest Quaker might have played a pivotal role in unknowingly sealing his fate. But one way or the other, Oswald seemed doomed to end up in the building and to meet his date with infamy. By October 1963, when he went to work in the building, there were too many unseen forces at work on the young man—who turned twenty-four that month—for him to call his life his own.

In the months leading up to the Kennedy assassination, Oswald was moved here and there with the calculation of a master chess player. In April, he returned to his hometown, New Orleans, with Marina and the girls, where he called attention to himself by jumping into the combustible world of Cuban politics. He reached out to the Fair Play for Cuba Committee, the leading pro-Castro group in the United States, which was the target of such heavy FBI and CIA pressure that its two founders later succumbed and offered their services as government informers. At the same time he was dallying with the Fair Play for Cuba Committee, Oswald also made contact with the Directorio Revolucionario Estudiantil (DRE)—a group of young, militant, anti-Castro Cuban exiles overseen by the CIA's point man on Cuba, David Phillips. Playing both sides of the Cuba fence, Oswald began passing out Fair Play leaflets in the streets while working out of the same building where Guy Banister, a former FBI agent who was involved in anti-Communist operations, maintained his office.

Oswald's double-dealing was bound to lead to a blowup, and in August it did, when he was angrily confronted by DRE activists while passing out his pro-Castro flyers. A New Orleans police lieutenant who later investigated the tussle reported that Oswald seemed to have staged the whole thing "to create an incident—but when the incident occurred, he remained absolutely peaceful and gentle." The New Orleans fracas recalled Oswald's theatrics in the U.S. embassy in Moscow, where he had announced his defection.

In early September, Oswald popped up again in Dallas, where he and his family would move back later that month. This Oswald sighting is an extremely suggestive one, since he was spotted in the company of none other than David Atlee Phillips—one of the more glaring indications that the ex-marine was the focus of an intelligence operation. Oswald and Phillips were observed talking together in the lobby of a downtown Dallas office building by Antonio Veciana, a prominent Cuban exile leader whose violent group, Alpha 66, had come close to killing Castro with a bazooka attack. Veciana—who arrived at the Dallas building for his own meeting with Phillips, his CIA supervisor—would later recognize the slight, pale man he had seen with Phillips that afternoon, when Oswald's face was splashed across front pages and TV screens. Phillips had trained him well, Veciana later said. "He taught me how to remember faces, how to remember characteristics. I am sure it was Oswald."

Veciana told his story to House Assassinations Committee investigator Gaeton Fonzi in the late 1970s and later repeated it to journalists. But even when the aging exile leader climbed onstage at a Washington conference of JFK assassination researchers in September 2014 to retell his remarkable story, the mainstream press still did nothing to spotlight it. "I was trained by the CIA, as was Oswald," said Veciana, who was the accounting manager for a Havana bank before he joined the anti-Castro movement. "Oswald and Fidel Castro were ideal scapegoats for the murder of the president. . . . It really was a coup d'etat."

In late September, Oswald took a bus trip to Mexico City and again made a spectacle of himself while trying in vain to obtain travel visas for Cuba at the Cuban and Soviet embassies. While Oswald visited Mexico City, someone impersonating him made phone calls to the Cuban and Soviet embassies—calls that were intercepted on CIA surveillance tapes. The agency later claimed that these tapes were routinely destroyed. But J. Edgar Hoover himself listened to them immediately after the assassination and the FBI chief informed Lyndon Johnson, the new president, that the voice on the tapes was not Oswald's. Both men knew the stunning significance of this audio fakery by the CIA—it showed that Kennedy's alleged killer was somehow entangled in espionage business. He was not simply a deranged loner.

In the final weeks of his life, Oswald was the subject of particularly intense CIA coverage. Much of this scrutiny emanated from the offices of Jim Angleton and David Phillips. After sifting through declassified government documents from this period, John Newman—a University of Maryland history professor and former U.S. military intelligence officer—concluded that the agency had demonstrated "a keen operational interest in Oswald." Newman's skilled decryption of the intelligent design behind Oswald's activities—which he first outlined in his 1995 book, *Oswald and the CIA*—was a historical breakthrough in understanding the alleged assassin's mysterious life.

Oswald was ostensibly being closely tracked by the CIA as well as by the FBI because he was a recent defector and a self-proclaimed revolutionary. But, as President Kennedy prepared to visit Dallas, something curious occurred within this surveillance labyrinth. On October 9, Oswald was suddenly removed from the FBI "FLASHLIST"—the bureau's index of suspicious individuals to be kept under close watch. FBI officials took this surprising step despite Oswald's suspicious behavior in Mexico City. The day after the FBI took Oswald off its watch list, the CIA also downgraded him as a security risk. On October 10, four senior counterintelligence officials who reported to Angleton and Helms signed off on a curious cable to the CIA station chief in Mexico City, assuring him there was no reason to be concerned about Oswald because his stay in the Soviet Union had a "maturing effect" on him.

These signals about Oswald circulating in the intelligence community had a fateful effect. By being downplayed as a security risk, Oswald became an unchecked pawn, free to be moved wherever he was useful.

Appearing before the Warren Commission, Ruth and Michael Paine seemed confused and tentative when it came to assigning guilt to Oswald. They both agreed that while he was a man of headstrong convictions, he did not impress them as a dangerous sort, and, like George de Mohrenschildt, they said Oswald rather liked Kennedy. "I had never thought of him as a violent man," Ruth testified. "He had never said anything against President Kennedy. . . . There was nothing that I had seen about him that indicated a man with that kind of grudge or hostility."

Michael—a lean man with sensitive eyes and a soft, watery demeanor—seemed particularly at sea when he tried to make sense of Oswald. When Dulles asked him if he was convinced that Oswald was the assassin, Michael launched upon a rambling, only somewhat coherent reply, winding up with this less-than-decisive conclusion: "I never did discover—and it didn't quite make sense, but for the most part, I accept it, the common view that he did it."

In truth, Michael never knew Oswald very well. They only talked at length on about four occasions, he told the Warren Commission. They would run into each other some weekends when they visited their wives and kids at the Paine family house in Irving. One evening, Michael took Oswald to a meeting of the local chapter of the ACLU, which the Paines belonged to. Afterward, Lee told Michael that he could never join a civil libertarian group like that because it wasn't sufficiently militant.

Neither of the Paines was fond of Oswald. To Ruth, he was an opaque, self-involved, and ill-tempered man who could be cruel to

Marina. He was just part of the equation that she had to put up with in order to have Marina in her life. "I would have been happy had he never come out, indeed happier had he not come out on the weekends," she would testify.

Michael and Lee seemed to have more in common—two men who had grown up, for the most part, without fathers, and were now struggling to hold on to their own families. There was something lost about both young men, a searching quality that left them too open to new experience. But they never really hit it off with each other. Lee was too "dogmatic" for Michael, too set in his Marxist ways. He reminded him of his distant Trotskyite father, too wrapped up in his adamant political theories to connect with other people.

Apart from providing a few suspicious, circumstantial details, this was the Paines' main contribution to establishing Oswald's guilt. Guided primarily by Warren Commission lawyers Albert Jenner and Wesley Liebeler—as well as by Dulles—the couple painted a portrait of Oswald as a grim subversive.

But the Paines also confirmed Oswald's guilt by just being themselves. Here were two left-wing oddballs—their appearance before the panel seemed to signify—a man and woman with peculiar and vaguely seditious family pedigrees. They were just the type whom you would expect to unwittingly harbor a dangerous man like Oswald. In their immaculate innocence, the Paines played right into the hands of those who were manipulating Oswald.

The Paines reunited for a time after the assassination but later divorced. In old age, they now live in the same Quaker retirement compound north of San Francisco, connected by the bonds of time. Not long ago, Michael sat down for an interview at the nearby commune where their middle-aged son, Christopher, and two dozen or so others live—a ramshackle collection of cottages in a green gulch near the Russian River that Ruth calls "a latter-day hippie ranch." Sitting on a lumpy couch in one of the cottages, the retired engineer came across as boyishly charming and given to whimsical ideas—an "innocent," as Ruth described him.

While serving with the Army in the Korean War, Michael mentioned at one point during the afternoon, "I thought of going over to the other side and saying to the Chinese, 'We don't have to fight like this.' But I thought I'd be blown up if I did. I also thought it would be unlikely I could find someone I could talk to, and they'd put me in a concentration camp. I prefer democracy, but I thought communism for China was an appropriate thing—they needed to all go in the same direction." This is the sort of idiosyncratic thinking that might well have made Michael Paine stand out to someone like Dulles.

The Paines seemed to grow more convinced of Oswald's guilt over time. But nowadays Michael is not as cocksure as Ruth. As he talked about those ancient, catastrophic days, he seemed bewildered, like someone trying to explain a collision he had survived long ago. He still wavered back and forth, just as he did with the Warren Commission. "Oswald wanted to overthrow something, the enemies, capitalists, the oppressors . . . he wanted action, and you had to be tough, brutal." But then again . . . he *liked* Kennedy. "Oh, he did! He said, 'JFK is my favorite president.'"

Michael Paine still does not know what to think. But perhaps, like the rest of the country, he has found a kind of comfort in his confusion.

As November 22, 1963, dawned—the day John F. Kennedy would die—Allen Dulles was away from Washington, as he typically was at the outset of major operations. In September and October, Dulles had maintained the busy schedule of a man still in the thick of clandestine affairs, meeting with key officials from the CIA's covert action side such as Desmond Fitzgerald, who—along with David Phillips—oversaw the violent intrigue swirling around Cuba; Angleton and his deputy, Cord Meyer; and a top Helms aide, Thomas Karamessines. All of these men would later be connected by investigators, in one way or another, to the Kennedy assassination.

But as Friday, November 22, drew near, Dulles spent much of his time away from his Georgetown home base. His book tour for *The Craft of Intelligence* provided the spymaster with a good excuse to get away from home. In the days leading up to the assassination, he made bookstore and media appearances in Boston and New York. Early on the morning of November 22, Dulles caught a Piedmont Airlines flight back to Washington, landing at National Airport around 8:30 a.m. He was then driven to a hotel in Williamsburg, Virginia, where he addressed a Brookings Institution breakfast meeting. After receiving the news from Dallas, around 1:30 that afternoon, Dulles took a car back to Washington with John Warner, a CIA attorney.

But, according to Dulles's date book, he did not spend the evening at home in Washington. He headed back to the northern Virginia countryside, where he would spend the entire weekend at a top secret CIA facility known officially as Camp Peary, but within the agency as "the Farm."

At the time of the Kennedy assassination, Dulles had no formal role in government. As far as the public knew, he was a figure of the legendary past, a graying gentleman who supplemented his civil service pension by recycling colorful espionage tales of yesteryear and by delivering sobering Cold War speeches. But the Farm was not a club for CIA retirees. It was a bustling clandestine center that Dulles himself had inaugurated soon after taking over as CIA chief, and it served a variety of tightly guarded functions.

Before the CIA took over Camp Peary—a sprawling compound in the densely wooded tidelands near Williamsburg—it was used as a Navy Seabees base and then as a stockade for captured German sailors. Dulles turned it into a spy training base for recruits who were headed overseas. According to former CIA agents Philip Agee and Victor Marchetti, among the well-trained professionals turned out by the Farm were skilled assassins. The facility was also what would later be termed a "black site"—a secure location where enemy captives and suspicious defectors were subjected to extreme interrogation methods.

As CIA director, Dulles had built himself a comfortable home at the Farm. Years later, consultants like Chalmers Johnson—an Asian affairs expert who became a scorching critic of U.S. empire—would

be housed there during agency conferences. Johnson recalled the retired spymaster's well-stocked library, which—as late as 1967—still
contained the latest CIA reports, intelligence estimates, and classified
journals.

"The Farm was basically an alternative CIA headquarters, from
where Dulles could direct ops," said former congressional investigator
Dan Hardway.

This is the CIA command post where the "retired" Dulles situated
himself from Friday, November 22, through Sunday, November 24—a
highly eventful weekend during which Oswald was arrested and questioned by Dallas police, Kennedy's body was flown back to Washington
and subjected to an autopsy riddled with irregularities, and Oswald was
gunned down in the basement of the Dallas police station by a shady
nightclub owner.

A year after the assassination, Dulles was interviewed by an old CIA
colleague, Tom Braden, for the oral history project at the JFK Library
in Boston. Braden asked Dulles what he had thought of Kennedy "as a
man." Dulles put on his mask of mourning and sympathy, as he could
do in an instant. "Oh, I rated him high. . . . I shall never forget when I
first heard the news of the Dallas tragedy. I felt that here is a man who
hadn't had the chance really to show his full capabilities, that he was
just reaching a point where his grasp of all the intricacies of the presidency were such that now he could move forward."

While serving on the Warren Commission, Dulles told Braden, he
had the opportunity to examine the assassination in exquisite detail.
He talked about the events of that day as if he were inspecting the
inner mechanism of a fine watch. He seemed in awe of the intricate
meshing of synchronicities that had to occur in order for Kennedy
to die that day. His description made it sound like the operation of a
lifetime.

"If the employees of the Book Depository had eaten their lunch in a
little different place," said Dulles, "if somebody had been at one place
where he might easily have been instead of another at one particular
time—the 'ifs' just stand out all over it. And if any one of these 'ifs' had

been changed, it might have been prevented. . . . It was so tantalizing to go over that record [of events], as we did, trying to find out every fact connected with the assassination, and then to say if any one of the chess pieces that were entered into the game had been moved differently, at any one time, the whole thing might have been different."

For the Good of the Country

In his calendar for October 2, 1963, Dulles penciled in an interesting appointment. "Dillon," he wrote—by which he meant C. Douglas Dillon, the Treasury secretary and former Wall Street financier. After Dillon's name, Dulles scrawled "Bank Reps." There was no further explanation for the scheduled appointment. But the proximity of the meeting to the Kennedy assassination raises compelling questions, particularly since Dillon, as Treasury chief, was in charge of President Kennedy's Secret Service protection. And the banking industry was locked in a long-running battle with the president over his economic policies.

When it came to undertaking secret missions, Allen Dulles was a bold and decisive actor. But he acted only after he felt that a consensus had been reached within his influential network. One of the principal arenas where this consensus took shape was the Council on Foreign Relations. The Dulles brothers and their Wall Street circle had dominated this private bastion for shaping public policy ever since the 1920s. Over the years, CFR meetings, study groups, and publications provided forums in which the organization's leading members—including Wall Street bankers and lawyers, prominent politicians, media executives, and academic dignitaries—hammered out major U.S. policy directions, including the decision to drop atomic bombs on Japan and the Cold War strategy of "containment" aimed at the Soviet Union. The CIA-engineered coup that overthrew Guatemala's democratic government was put in motion by Dulles after a CFR study group urged tough action against Arbenz's left-wing administration. If CFR was the power elite's brain, the CIA was its black-gloved fist.

As the global reach of American industry and finance grew during the postwar era, so did the U.S. national security complex. America's vast system of military and covert power was aimed not just at checking the Soviet threat but at protecting U.S. corporate interests abroad. Behind the rapid international growth of multinational giants like Chase Manhattan, Coca-Cola, Standard Oil, and GM lay a global network of U.S. military bases, spy stations, and alliances with despotic regimes. The twin exigencies of the Cold War and U.S. empire gave the national security establishment unprecedented free rein to operate. The CIA was empowered not only to engage in the deadly "spy versus spy" antics against the KGB that became the stuff of Cold War legend but to subvert democratic governments that were deemed insufficiently pro-American and to terminate these governments' elected leaders.

Dedicated to the dark necessities of expanding American power, this security complex began to take on a hidden life of its own, untethered from the checks and balances of democracy. Sometimes CIA officials kept the White House and Congress informed; often they did not. When John Chancellor of NBC News asked Dulles if the CIA made its own policy, the spymaster insisted that during his tenure he had regularly briefed congressional committees about the agency's budget and operations. But, he added, Congress generally preferred to remain blissfully ignorant of the distasteful things done in the government's name. "When I appeared before them," said Dulles, "again and again I've been stopped by members of the Congress, who said, 'We don't want to hear about that, we might talk in our sleep. Don't tell us this!'"

This head-in-the-sand attitude gave men like Dulles enormous leverage to take drastic action when they felt so inclined. But Dulles was not some out-of-control freebooter within the system of American power. Though his actions often revealed the knife-cold psyche of a murderer, in many ways he remained a sober-minded corporate lawyer. When he took extreme action—or "executive action" in the CIA's euphemistic parlance for political murder—he did so with the confidence that he was implementing the will of his circle—not the will of *the* people, but of *his* people.

Doug Dillon was the kind of affluent Washington power player Allen Dulles listened to. Over the years, the Dulles brothers and Dillon grew quite close. It was in Dillon's comfortable Florida retreat, at Hobe Sound, where the dying Foster spent some of his final days. And Allen was invited to enjoy himself at the palatial château overlooking the legendary vineyards that the Dillon family owned in southern France. The week he once spent at the Dillons' Château Haut-Brion "renewing my acquaintance with my favorite wines from the Bordeaux country" was among the most "delightful" memories of his life, Dulles later wrote Dillon's wife, Phyllis.

When it came to taking executive action, Dulles might have been chairman of the board, but he answered to a group of men with far more wealth and, in some ways, more power than he had—men like Doug Dillon. Dulles controlled the country's secret machinery of violence throughout much of the Cold War, but the spy chief's power came from the fact that—even after his departure from the CIA—his wealthy sponsors continued to invest him with it. In retirement, Dulles was still asked to take prestigious positions with the Princeton Board of Trustees, the Council on Foreign Relations, and various defense advisory and blue-ribbon committees.

Dulles was invited to play leadership roles in these organizations because the men who funded them knew that he shared their aggressive views about maintaining America's wealth and prestige in the world. The men who sat on Dulles's board of directors, as it were—the men with whom he discussed major decisions, exchanged correspondence, and shared sunny getaways—occupied the very center of American power. Threats to these men's wealth and stature brought out their lethal impulses. This is when they turned to Dulles, the gentlemanly enforcer with the ice-blue eyes.

Nobody occupied a more central position in the Dulles brothers' power circle than the Rockefeller brothers. Nelson and David were the most public of the five grandsons of John D. Rockefeller—the founder of the Standard Oil behemoth, an unprecedented empire of wealth that would grow to include global banks, mining companies, sprawling ranches, and even supermarkets. The glad-handing, irrepressible Nelson would become the cheery face of centrist Republican politics in mid-century America, working as an adviser to President Eisenhower on Cold War strategy and later becoming a popular governor of New York and perennial factor in Republican presidential equations. His less gregarious and more analytical younger brother, David, would rise to become chief executive of the family's bank, Chase Manhattan, as well as a leading spokesman for international finance. Less well known, both brothers were militant advocates of U.S. imperial interests, particularly in Latin America, where the Rockefeller family had extensive holdings. And they both had backgrounds in U.S. intelligence.

During World War II, Nelson did not follow other sons of East Coast high society into the OSS. Instead the elder Rockefeller brother, who had a strained relationship with top spy Wild Bill Donovan, ran his own private intelligence network in Latin America, as FDR's south-of-the-border point man. Nelson resumed his espionage duties under President Eisenhower, who put him in charge of a special advisory group that oversaw the CIA. In the press, Rockefeller was described as Ike's "Cold War general"—a title that probably said more about the sway that the Rockefeller name had with the media than about Nelson's actual clout within the administration.

Meanwhile, David Rockefeller served with a special Army intelligence unit in Algeria during World War II, where he was assigned to spy not on Nazis but on the country's nascent anticolonial movement. After being transferred to Paris, he was asked to snoop on the Communist Party elements that had played a key role in the French resistance and were emerging as a strong political force in postwar France. Rockefeller also set up a spy ring inside the provisional government of General de Gaulle and soon came to dislike the "arrogance, inflexibility and single-mindedness" of the French war hero.

The Dulleses identified the Rockefeller brothers, who were a generation younger, as up-and-coming players, and they sought to bring them into the inner circle of the Cold War establishment. Over the years, the two sets of brothers became close partners in the country's game of thrones, helping advance one another's ambitions. The Dulleses ushered David Rockefeller into the Council on Foreign Relations, where he soon became a major force, and Foster would become chairman of the family-controlled Rockefeller Foundation. The Rockefellers contributed campaign funds to Dulles-favored Republican candidates, including Foster himself when he ran unsuccessfully for the Senate from New York in 1950. In January 1953, while Allen nervously waited to see whether newly inaugurated president Eisenhower would appoint him CIA director, David took him to lunch in Manhattan and assured him that if things didn't work out in Washington, he could return to New York and take over the Ford Foundation, which—like the Rockefeller Foundation—Dulles had already used to secretly finance CIA activities. After Allen did win control of the spy agency, he again turned to the Rockefellers to help finance CIA projects like MKULTRA mind control research.

The Rockefeller brothers served as private bankers for Dulles's intelligence empire. David, who oversaw the donations committee of the Chase Manhattan Bank Foundation, was a particularly important source of off-the-books cash for the CIA. Tom Braden, one of Dulles's top propaganda men, later recalled David's largesse. "I often briefed David, semi-officially and with Allen's permission," Braden said. "[David] was of the same mind as us, and very approving of everything we were doing. He had the same sense as I did that the way to win the Cold War was our way. Sometimes David would give me money to do things which weren't in our budget. He gave me a lot of money for causes in France. I remember he gave me $50,000 for someone who was active in promoting an [anti-Communist] united Europe [campaign] amongst European youth groups. This guy came to me with his project, and I told David, and David just gave me the check for $50,000."

When the ambitious Nelson overreached as Eisenhower's Cold War adviser and began to infringe on the Dulles brothers' territory, Foster became exasperated with him and succeeded in having him jettisoned from the administration. But Allen managed to stay on genial terms with Nelson, and with David, too. As he left the Eisenhower White House in December 1955, Nelson sent the CIA chief a gushing letter. "I can't begin to tell you how much my association with you over this past year has meant to me," Nelson told Allen. "I have admired tremendously your strength and courage, your understanding, and your penetrating insight into the many problems which confront us. You give yourself quietly and unselfishly, but your qualities of human understanding have shone forth to give courage to us all. Only a few will ever know how great your contributions have been to the security of our country."

Even Dulles, who had a robust self-regard, seemed stunned by Rockefeller's effusive praise. "Dear Nelson," he replied. "To say that I appreciate your kind remarks is an understatement—overwhelmed would be a little more accurate."

Dulles and the Rockefellers continued their mutual courtship over the years, with both sides keenly recognizing the value in the relationship. After his 1958 election in New York, Nelson invited Allen to speak at the 1959 conference of state governors, which was held in Puerto Rico that year. While there, Dulles stayed at the exclusive Dorado Beach Club, a palm-shaded luxury resort created by Nelson's brother, Laurance, on prime coastal real estate owned by the Rockefeller family. When he got home, the CIA director wrote Laurance, asking him to pull strings so that a friend and his wife could become club members, "as they are both devotees of golf and swimming." Meanwhile, Dulles supplied the Rockefellers with CIA information about global hot zones like Iran, Cuba, and Venezuela, where the family had petroleum interests.

Although Jack Kennedy, as a young congressman and senator, often used the language of the Cold War that was the lingua franca of American politics, he was never fully accepted within this inner sanctum of power. Members of the American elite were uneasy about Kennedy's presidential bid from the very beginning. Their skepticism started with old Joe Kennedy, the candidate's father, who was remembered as an ardent New Dealer—despite his prickly relationship with FDR—and as a banking maverick (or some would say traitor) who had agreed to serve as Roosevelt's Wall Street watchdog. Nor did the young senator's provocative criticisms of Western imperialism inspire confidence in corporate circles, where aggressive overseas expansion was viewed as American capital's next great frontier. John McCloy, the diplomat and banker known as "the chairman of the establishment," could not bring himself to support JFK in 1960, despite the two men's shared Irish ancestry. Kennedy's standoffish attitude toward the Council on Foreign Relations crowd put off McCloy, who was the organization's chairman at the time. While McCloy found Nixon hard to warm up to, he dismissed Kennedy as a lightweight who had not been properly indoctrinated in the ways of the American establishment.

If the establishment harbored suspicions about the Kennedy family, the feelings were mutual. Despite his privileged upbringing, JFK had imbibed his father's bitter feelings as an Irish Catholic outsider. After he narrowly won the presidency, Kennedy told his aide Theodore Sorensen that he suspected that Wall Street bankers had tried to sabotage his election by spreading word that his election would set off a financial panic.

In public, President Kennedy tried to defuse Wall Street hostility against him with his dry wit. During a June 1962 press conference, Kennedy was asked about a news report that big business was using the current stock market slump "as a means of forcing you to come to terms with business. . . . [Their] attitude is now they have you where they want you." After a well-timed pause, Kennedy replied, "I can't believe I'm where business—big business—wants me," to gales of laughter from the press auditorium. But, as usual, there was a point—an *edge*—to JFK's humor. After the laughter died down, he drove home his message, making it clear that he would regard any such corporate sabotage of the economy as beyond the pale of acceptable politics.

The growing gulf between Kennedy and the corporate class was epitomized by the increasingly fractious relationship between JFK and the Rockefeller brothers. Kennedy's domestic and foreign policies posed a direct threat to the Rockefeller dynasty on multiple fronts, and, considering the central role in U.S. finance and industry played by the network of Rockefeller interests, any such threats were viewed by the business community as challenges to American capitalism itself.

Kennedy's tax reform policies, which sought to place a heavier burden on the superrich, were a primary source of friction. When the president—who was concerned about the flight of capital in the emerging era of the global market—tried to crack down on overseas tax shelters, international bankers like David Rockefeller cried foul. Wall Street financiers saw the Kennedy move as an assault on their ability to transfer wealth to any corner of the globe as they saw fit.

Walter Wriston—the rising young leader of First National City Bank, and David Rockefeller's chief competitor in the global finance arena—frankly expressed Wall Street's frustration with Kennedy. "Who is this upstart president interfering with the free flow of capital?" he demanded to know. "You can't dam capital."

While many Wall Street executives complained bitterly about JFK in private, David Rockefeller took it upon himself to challenge the president's economic policies in public. Henry Luce helped elevate Rockefeller as a Kennedy antagonist by giving the two men a debate forum in *Life*, the picture magazine of the American masses. The magazine's introduction to the piece touted the young banker as "an eloquent and logical articulator for the sophisticated business community." In the open "businessman's letter" to Kennedy that followed, Rockefeller took issue with the president's tax policies, which he insisted put too much burden on the investor class, and demanded "a material reduction in the corporate income tax rate." The banker also took the president to task for his social spending, urging him to cut expenditures and make a "vigorous effort to balance the budget."

The Rockefellers were perhaps even more alarmed by Kennedy's foreign policies—particularly in Latin America, which was not only home to the family's oil and real estate holdings but also the primary target for Chase Manhattan's overseas expansion. It seemed like an affront to the Rockefellers' southern dominion when Kennedy announced the

Alliance for Progress in March 1961, a massive foreign aid program for Latin America designed to stimulate economic growth, redistribute wealth, and promote democratic governments in the region. The alliance was spearheaded by Richard Goodwin, one of JFK's youngest and most ardent New Frontiersmen. And White House officials made no secret that the program was designed not only to counter Castro's revolutionary appeal in the area but also to sideline the corporate interests that had long been exploiting the impoverished hemisphere.

Goodwin began pushing a variety of measures, which, by the standards of the pro-business Eisenhower era, were decidedly radical, including providing equipment for nationalized mines in Bolivia and offering U.S. government financing to state-run oil companies—"even if Standard Oil and David Rockefeller objected," added Kennedy's young Turk. Soon enough, the corporate pushback—along with the inevitable Republican Party and media fireworks—did come. "Neither U.S. nor Latin American businessmen took kindly to indications by Richard Goodwin, the president's chief Latin American adviser, that he thought private enterprise had a bad connotation in Latin America because it is associated with U.S. imperialism," harrumphed a business newsletter specializing in coverage of south-of-the-border investments.

Under increasing political pressure, JFK finally caved on Goodwin, transferring him from the Alliance for Progress to the Peace Corps. But Kennedy continued to resist efforts to privatize the alliance led by David Rockefeller. America's reputation in Latin America as an imperial bully mortified Kennedy. He was sick of the U.S. government being seen "as the representative of private business," he told Goodwin. He was tired of Washington propping up "tinhorn dictators" and corrupt regimes in countries like Chile where "American copper companies control about 80 percent of all the foreign exchange. We wouldn't stand for that here. And there's no reason they should stand for it. . . . There's a revolution going on down there, and I want to be on the right side of it."

Kennedy's Latin American policies continued to be a point of contention between the Rockefeller brothers and him for the rest of his presidency. Even after JFK's death, his brother continued to fight the battle. During a 1965 tour of Latin America, Robert Kennedy—by then a senator from New York—found himself in a heated discussion about Rockefeller influence in Latin America, during an evening at the home of a Peruvian artist that had been arranged by Goodwin. When Bobby brashly suggested to the gathering that Peru should "assert [its] nationhood" and nationalize its oil industry, the group was stunned. "Why, David Rockefeller has just been down here," one guest said. "And he told us there wouldn't be any aid if anyone acted against International Petroleum [a local Standard Oil subsidiary]."

"Oh come on, David Rockefeller isn't the government," Bobby shot back, still playing the role of Kennedy family tough guy. "We Kennedys eat Rockefellers for breakfast."

The Kennedys were indeed more successful at the rough-and-tumble of politics than the Rockefellers. But, as JFK had understood, that was not the full story when it came to evaluating a family's power. He fully appreciated that the Rockefellers held a unique place in the pantheon of American power, one rooted not so much within the democratic system as within what scholars would later refer to as "the deep state"—that subterranean network of financial, intelligence, and military interests that guided national policy no matter who occupied the White House. The Kennedys had risen from saloonkeepers and ward heelers to the top of American politics. But they were still overshadowed by the imperial power of the Rockefellers.

JFK always displayed a sharp curiosity about the much wealthier family, pumping mutual friends—like presidential adviser Adolf Berle—for inside information about the Rockefellers. Jack and David had been contemporaries at Harvard, but as David was quick to point out, "we moved in very different circles." As Kennedy pursued his own career, he always kept one wary eye on the politically ambitious Nelson, who had openly proclaimed his desire to occupy the White House. It was an ambition he nursed "ever since I was a kid," he once said. "After all, when you think of what I had, what else was there to aspire to?"

Nelson let slip his cheery facade only when contemplating looming threats to his family's wealth. He had long fretted about "losing

FOR THE GOOD OF THE COUNTRY · 559

our property" to nationalist movements overseas. When Castro gave a bearded face to these fears, expropriating the Standard Oil refinery and other Rockefeller properties in Cuba, Nelson was outraged. He grew increasingly frustrated with Kennedy as he sidestepped opportunities to invade Cuba, becoming convinced that the president had cut a deal with the Russians to leave Castro alone.

It was Nelson's growing sense of Kennedy as a Cold War "appeaser" that drove him to begin mounting a presidential challenge for 1964. In his final political speeches before the Kennedy assassination, Rockefeller lashed into the president for his "indecision, vacillation and weakness" in foreign policy. The Kennedy administration's dynamic image was a public relations myth, Rockefeller insisted. In truth, he charged, JFK's unassertive leadership had encouraged our enemies and demoralized our allies, and had made the world more dangerous.

These views of Kennedy were widely echoed in the pages of the business press, where JFK was portrayed as a soft-spined commander in chief who was putting the country at risk and, in the estimation of *The Wall Street Journal*, an incompetent economic manager with a pronounced hostility to "the philosophy of freedom." Like the Luce press, the *Journal* became increasingly vitriolic in its descriptions of the president, describing him as an enemy of big business and as a hopeless left-wing romantic "living in a dream world" and laboring under the spell of "deep and damaging delusion." In short, Kennedy was seen as an aberrant president in elite circles—an unqualified man who, it was broadly hinted, had barely squeezed into office thanks to the underhanded dealings of his Mafia-connected father.

The attitudes toward Kennedy were even more rabid in national security chambers, where men like Angleton and LeMay regarded the president as a degenerate, and very likely a traitor. If the Soviets launched a sneak nuclear attack on America, Angleton brooded, the Kennedys would be safely cocooned "in their luxury bunker, presumably watching World War III on television, [while] the rest of us . . . burned in hell."

Angleton seemed obsessed with Kennedy's sex life. He reportedly bugged JFK's White House trysts with Mary Meyer, the ex-wife of his deputy, Cord Meyer—an artistic blond beauty with whom Angleton himself was enamored. He told friends and family that Kennedy's rule was marked by sexual decadence, as well as criminality—a particularly ironic twist, since Angleton himself was later revealed to have been connected to the Mafia ever since his wartime days in Rome.

Over the final months of JFK's presidency, a clear consensus took shape within America's deep state: Kennedy was a national security threat. For the good of the country, he must be removed. And Dulles was the only man with the stature, connections, and decisive will to make something of this enormity happen. He had already assembled a killing machine to operate overseas. Now he prepared to bring it home to Dallas. All that his establishment colleagues had to do was to look the other way—as they always did when Dulles took executive action.

In the case of Doug Dillon—who oversaw Kennedy's Secret Service apparatus—it simply meant making sure that he was out of town. At the end of October, Dillon notified the president that he planned to take a "deferred summer vacation" in November, abandoning his Washington post for Hobe Sound until the eighteenth of the month. After that, Dillon informed Kennedy, he planned to fly to Tokyo with other cabinet members on an official visit that would keep him out of the country from November 21 to November 27. If he was later asked to account for himself, Dillon would have a ready explanation. The tragic events in Dallas had not occurred on his watch; he was airborne over the Pacific at the time.

There is no evidence that reigning corporate figures like David Rockefeller were part of the plot against President Kennedy or had foreknowledge of the crime. But there is ample evidence of the overwhelming hostility to Kennedy in these corporate circles—a surging antagonism that certainly emboldened Dulles and other national security enemies of the president. And if the assassination of President Kennedy was indeed an "establishment crime," as University of Pittsburgh sociology professor Donald Gibson has suggested, there is even more reason to see the official investigation as an establishment cover-up.

Oswald was still alive, and that was a problem. He was supposed to be killed as he left the Texas School Book Depository. That's what G. Robert Blakey, the former Kennedy Justice Department attorney who served as chief counsel for the House Select Committee on Assassinations, later concluded about the man authorities rushed to designate the lone assassin. But Oswald escaped, and after being taken alive by Dallas police in a movie theater, he became a major conundrum for those trying to pin the crime on him.

To begin with, Oswald did not act like most assassins. Those who decapitated heads of state generally crowed about their history-making deeds (*Sic semper tyrannis!*). In contrast, Oswald repeatedly denied his guilt while in custody, emphatically telling reporters as he was hustled from one room to the next in the Dallas police station, "I don't know what this is all about. . . . I'm just a patsy!" And the accused assassin seemed strangely cool and collected, according to the police detectives who questioned him. "He was real calm," recalled one detective. "He was extra calm. He wasn't a bit excited or nervous or anything." In fact, Dallas police chief Jesse Curry and district attorney William Alexander thought Oswald was so composed that he seemed trained to handle a stressful interrogation. "I was amazed that a person so young would have had the self-control he had," Alexander later told Irish investigative journalist Anthony Summers. "It was almost as if he had been rehearsed or programmed to meet the situation he found himself in."

Oswald further signaled that he was part of an intelligence operation by trying to make an intriguing phone call shortly before midnight East Coast time on Saturday, November 23. The police switchboard operator, who was being closely monitored by two unidentified officials, told Oswald there was no answer, though she actually did not put through the call. It was not until years later that independent researchers traced the phone number that Oswald tried to call to a former U.S. Army intelligence officer in Raleigh, North Carolina. CIA veteran Victor Marchetti, who analyzed the Raleigh call in his book, *The CIA and the Cult of Intelligence*, surmised that Oswald was likely following his training guidelines and reaching out to his intelligence handler. "[He] was probably calling his cut-out. He was calling somebody who could put him in touch with his case officer."

The Raleigh call probably sealed Oswald's fate, according to Marchetti. By refusing to play the role of the "patsy" and instead following his intelligence protocol, Oswald made clear that he was trouble. What would be the CIA procedure at this point, Marchetti was asked by North Carolina historian Grover Proctor, who has closely studied this episode near the end of Oswald's life? "I'd kill him," Marchetti replied. "Was this his death warrant?" Proctor continued. "You betcha," Marchetti said. "This time, [Oswald] went over the dam, whether he knew it or not. . . . He was over the dam. At this point it was executive action."

Oswald was not just alive on the afternoon of November 22, 1963; he was likely innocent. This was another major problem for the organizers of the assassination. Even close legal observers of the case who continue to believe in Oswald's guilt—such as Bob Blakey who, after serving on the House Assassinations Committee, became a law professor at Notre Dame University—acknowledge that a "credible" case could have been made for Oswald's innocence based on the evidence. (The 1979 congressional report found that Kennedy was the victim of a conspiracy involving Oswald and other unknown parties.) Other legal experts, like San Francisco attorney and Kennedy researcher Bill Simpich, have gone further, arguing that the case against Oswald was riddled with such glaring inconsistencies that it would have quickly unraveled in court.

As Simpich has detailed, the ballistics evidence alone was a mess. The bullets and shells from the crime scene did not match the murder weapon and were poorly marked by law enforcement officers. The so-called magic bullet that supposedly struck Kennedy in the back of his neck before proceeding on its improbable course later turned up just as magically, in nearly pristine condition, on a stretcher at Parkland Memorial Hospital where the fatally wounded president was rushed. Then there was the alleged murder weapon—a $19.95 Italian military surplus rifle from World War II with a faulty sight. Using such a clumsy tool to pull off the crime of the century with rapid-fire precision—especially in the hands of a marksman who had a hard time shooting rabbits—simply defied the imagination. There was also the fact that FBI technicians who tested the Mannlicher-Carcano rifle could find none of Oswald's prints on the weapon, and the Dallas police failed to detect any trace of gunpowder on the arrested man's cheek, which indicated that he had not fired a rifle that day.

In addition, Buell Wesley Frazier, the young Texas School Book Depository employee who drove Oswald to work that morning, insisted that the package the alleged assassin carried into the building that day was not big enough to contain a rifle. The nineteen-year-old Frazier refused to change his story, despite being arrested and subjected to a withering interrogation by Dallas police, including threats to charge him as a co-conspirator. "I was interrogated for many, many hours—interrogators would rotate," Frazier recalled years later. "The way they treated me that day, I have a hard time understanding that. I was just a rural boy; I had never been in trouble with the law. I was doing my best to answer their questions." He could never figure out in his own mind whether Oswald was guilty or not. But there was one thing he knew for certain, he told a newspaper reporter fifty years later: the brown paper package that Oswald put on the backseat of his car on the morning of November 22, 1963, did not hold a rifle. "There is no way it would fit in that package."

And then there was the inconvenient home movie taken by dress manufacturer Abraham Zapruder, as Kennedy's limousine passed by him in Dealey Plaza. The film captured the moments JFK was struck by gunfire in gruesome detail and—along with the testimony of dozens of eyewitnesses—graphically demonstrated that bullets were fired from the front, as well as the rear, of the presidential motorcade. As many as twenty-one law enforcement officers stationed in the plaza—men trained in the use of firearms—said their immediate reaction to the sound of the gunfire was to go search the area looming in front of Kennedy's advancing limousine, the tree-topped rise that would become famously known as "the grassy knoll." Even if Oswald did shoot at the president, this meant that there was at least one other gunman and Kennedy was the victim of a conspiracy. The CIA's own state-of-the-art photography analysis unit came to this conclusion after analyzing the Zapruder film. (FBI analysts would later concur.) But the CIA technicians' report was quickly suppressed.

The surgeons who labored futilely over the mortally wounded president at Parkland Hospital also saw clear evidence that Kennedy had been struck by gunfire from the front as well as the rear. But the doctors came under severe pressure to remain silent and it would take nearly three decades before two of them mustered the courage to speak out.

Fortunately for the conspirators, the deeply flawed case against Lee Harvey Oswald never made it to court. The Oswald problem was abruptly eliminated on the morning of Sunday, November 24, when the accused assassin was shot in the stomach in the basement of the Dallas police station while in the process of being transferred to the county jail. He died two hours later in the same emergency room where President Kennedy was pronounced dead.

Oswald's shocking murder—broadcast live into America's homes—solved one dilemma for Dulles, as he monitored the Dallas events that weekend from the Farm, his secure CIA facility in Virginia. But it soon became apparent that Oswald's murder created another problem—a wave of public suspicion that swept over the nation and beyond. Jack Ruby, Oswald's killer—a stocky, fedora-wearing nightclub operator—looked like a triggerman right out of a B-movie. Ruby even sounded like a Hollywood gangster as he gunned down Oswald, snarling, "You killed my president, you rat!" To many people who watched the horrifying spectacle on TV, the shooting smacked of a gangland hit aimed at silencing Oswald before he could talk.

In fact, this is precisely what Attorney General Robert Kennedy concluded after his investigators began digging into Ruby's background. Bobby, who had made his political reputation as a Senate investigator of organized crime, pored over Ruby's phone records from the days leading up to the Dallas violence. "The list [of names] was almost a duplicate of the people I called before the Rackets Committee," RFK later remarked. The attorney general's suspicions about the death of his brother immediately fell not just on the Mafia, but on the CIA—the agency that, as Bobby knew, had been using the mob to do some of its dirtiest work.

Robert Kennedy was not the only one in Washington who immediately sensed a conspiracy behind the killing of his brother. The nation's capital was filled with edgy chatter about the assassination. Talking on the phone with Kennedy family confidant Bill Walton, Agnes Meyer, the outspoken mother of *Washington Post* publisher Katharine Graham, snapped, "What is this—some kind of goddam banana republic?" Eisenhower, retired on his Gettysburg farm, had the same reaction. He remarked that the bloodshed in Dallas reminded him of his tour of duty in Haiti as a young Army major; when he visited the national palace in Port-au-Prince, he was shocked to realize that two-thirds of the former heads of state whose marble busts were on display had been slain in office.

Meanwhile, down in Independence, Missouri, another retired president, Harry Truman, was fuming about the CIA. On December 22, 1963, while the country was still reeling from the gunfire in Dallas, Truman published a highly provocative op-ed article in *The Washington Post*, charging that the CIA had grown alarmingly out of control since he established it. His original purpose, wrote Truman, was to create an agency that simply coordinated the various streams of sensitive information flowing into the White House. "I have never had any thought that when I set up the CIA that it would be injected into peacetime cloak and dagger operations," he continued. But "for some time, I have been disturbed by the way CIA has been diverted from its original assignment. It has become an operational and at times a policy-making arm of Government." The CIA had grown "so removed from its intended role that it is being interpreted as a symbol of sinister and mysterious foreign intrigue." But the increasingly powerful agency did not just menace foreign governments, Truman warned—it now threatened democracy at home. "There is something about the way the CIA has been functioning that is casting a shadow over our historic position [as a] free and open society," he concluded ominously, "and I feel that we need to correct it."

The timing of Truman's opinion piece was striking. Appearing in the capital's leading newspaper exactly one month after the assassination, the article caused shock waves in political circles. There was a disturbing undertone to the straight-talking midwesterner's warning about the CIA. Was Truman implying that there was "sinister and mysterious intrigue" behind Kennedy's death? Could that have been what he meant when he suggested that the agency represented a growing danger to our own democracy?

Overseas, the speculation about Kennedy's murder—and the suspicious shooting of his alleged assassin—was even more rampant. The foreign press was filled with commentary suggesting that there were powerful forces involved in the assassination and naming Cold War militarists, big business, and Texas oilmen as possible culprits. Some of this coverage, unsurprisingly, came from Soviet bloc newspapers, eager to dispel the rumors that Oswald was part of a Communist plot— rumors that were often traceable to CIA propaganda shops. But much of the conjecture about Dallas came from publications in the Western European alliance. In Hamburg, the daily *Die Welt* editorialized that the official handling of the Kennedy and Oswald cases left a "forest of question marks." In London, the *Daily Mail* spoke of "whispers" that Oswald was a fall guy who was rubbed out, and the *Daily Telegraph* derided Police Chief Curry's announcement that Oswald's death put a close to the Kennedy case as a "monumental absurdity." And in Italy, where the limitations of the Mannlicher-Carcano rifle were well known to a generation of World War II veterans, the newspaper *Corriere Lombardo* observed that there was no way Oswald could have used the bolt-action weapon to squeeze off three shots in six seconds, as official reports from Dallas were claiming.

Suspicions of a conspiracy were particularly strong in France, where President de Gaulle himself had been the target of CIA machinations and had survived a barrage of gunfire on his own limousine. After returning from Kennedy's November 24 funeral in Washington, de Gaulle gave a remarkably candid assessment of the assassination to his information minister, Alain Peyrefitte. "What happened to Kennedy is what nearly happened to me," confided the French president. "His story is the same as mine. . . . It looks like a cowboy story, but it's only an OAS [Secret Army Organization] story. The security forces were in cahoots with the extremists."

As a matter of survival, de Gaulle and his loyal deputies had been compelled to investigate the underworld where intelligence forces, political zealots, and gangsters all converged. More than any other Western leader, he was well aware of how security services—in the name of combating Communism—joined hands with some of the most extreme and vicious allies to win their goals. De Gaulle was convinced that Kennedy had fallen victim to the same forces that had tried repeatedly to kill him.

"Do you think Oswald was a front?" Peyrefitte asked de Gaulle.

"Everything leads me to believe it," he replied. "They got their hands on this communist who wasn't one, while still being one. He had a sub par intellect and was an exalted fanatic—just the man they needed, the perfect one to be accused. . . . The guy ran away, because he probably became suspicious. They wanted to kill him on the spot before he could be grabbed by the judicial system. Unfortunately, it didn't happen exactly the way they had probably planned it would. . . . But a trial, you realize, is just terrible. People would have talked. They would have dug up so much! They would have unearthed everything. Then the security forces went looking for [a clean-up man] they totally controlled, and who couldn't refuse their offer, and that guy sacrificed himself to kill the fake assassin—supposedly in defense of Kennedy's memory!

"Baloney! Security forces all over the world are the same when they do this kind of dirty work. As soon as they succeed in wiping out the false assassin, they declare that the justice system no longer need be concerned, that no further public action was needed now that the guilty perpetrator was dead. Better to assassinate an innocent man than to let a civil war break out. Better an injustice than disorder.

"America is in danger of upheavals. But you'll see. All of them to-gether will observe the law of silence. They will close ranks. They'll do everything to stifle any scandal. They will throw Noah's cloak over these shameful deeds. In order to not lose face in front of the whole world. In order to not risk unleashing riots in the United States. In order to preserve the union and to avoid a new civil war. In order to not ask themselves questions. They don't want to know. They don't want to find out. They won't allow themselves to find out."

These astonishing observations about Dallas were captured in Pey-refitte's memoir, *C'était de Gaulle* (*It Was de Gaulle*), which was pub-lished in France in 2002, three years after the author's death. Snippets of the conversation appeared in the U.S. press, but the book was not translated and published in America, and de Gaulle's remarks about the Kennedy assassination were never fully reported outside of France.

A half century later, this extraordinary commentary by the French leader—a political colossus of the twentieth century—remains one of the most disturbing and insightful perspectives on this traumatic American event. *They don't want to find out. They won't allow themselves to find out.*

Allen Dulles knew the danger of words, the wrong kind of words. As CIA director, he had spent an untold fortune each year on countering the Soviet propaganda machine and controlling the world's conversation, including the political and media dialogue in his own country. Within minutes of the Kennedy assassination, the CIA tried to steer news reporting and commentary about Dallas, planting sto-ries that suggested—falsely—that Oswald was a Soviet agent or that Castro was behind JFK's murder. In actuality, both Khrushchev—who broke down weeping in the Kremlin when he heard the news—and Castro were deeply distressed by Kennedy's death. Both men had been greatly encouraged by Kennedy's peace initiatives in the final year of his presidency, and they feared that his assassination meant that mili-tary hard-liners would take control in Washington. "This is bad news," Castro muttered to a visiting French journalist, who was carrying an olive branch from Kennedy when the Cuban leader was informed of the gunfire in Texas. "Everything is changed."

Castro immediately predicted that the agency would try to pin the murder on him. And sure enough, as the Cuban leader and French journalist listened to U.S. radio, a broadcaster suddenly connected Oswald to the Fair Play for Cuba Committee.

But despite the CIA's strenuous efforts, press coverage of the Kennedy assassination began spinning out of its control. Dulles knew that immediate steps must be taken to contain the conversation. One of his first concerns was the Washington echo chamber itself. He quickly realized the danger posed by Truman's explosive piece in *The Washington Post*, which instantly caught fire and inspired similar anti-CIA editorials in newspapers from Charlotte, North Carolina, to Sacramento, California. Syndicated columnist Richard Starnes, a bête noire of the spy agency, used the Truman op-ed to launch a broadside against the CIA, calling it "a cloudy organism of uncertain purpose and appalling power." Meanwhile, Senator Eugene McCarthy, another agency critic, weighed in with an essay for *The Saturday Evening Post*—the popular middle-American magazine that featured the homespun art of Norman Rockwell—bluntly titled, "The CIA Is Getting Out of Hand."

There was no telling how far the media whirlwind would go and what it would stir up. The frenzy of criticism that was suddenly directed at the CIA's cloak-and-dagger operations seemed to be connected, if only subliminally, to the billowing anxiety that the public felt about the unsolved mysteries in Dallas. If Harry Truman—the man who created the CIA—was worried that it had become a Frankenstein, it might be only a matter of time before prominent European figures, and even some stray voices in America, began to question whether the agency was behind JFK's murder.

It was Dulles himself who jumped in to put out the Truman fire. Soon after the *Post* published Truman's diatribe, Dulles began a campaign to get the retired president to disavow his opinion piece. The spymaster began by enlisting the help of Washington power attorney Clark Clifford, the former Truman counselor who chaired President

Johnson's intelligence advisory board. The CIA "was really HST's baby or at least his adopted child," Dulles pointed out in a letter to Clifford. Perhaps the attorney could talk some sense into the tough old bird and get him to retract his harsh criticisms of the agency.

Dulles also appealed directly to Truman in a strongly worded letter, telling the former president that he was "deeply disturbed" by his article. In the eight-page letter that he mailed on January 7, 1964, Dulles tried to implicate Truman himself. Calling Truman the "father of our modern intelligence system," Dulles reminded him that it was "*you*, through National Security Council action, [who] approved the organization in CIA of a new office to carry out covert operations." So, Dulles continued, Truman's ill-advised rant in the *Post* amounted to "a repudiation of a policy" that the former president himself "had the great courage and wisdom to initiate."

To an extent, Dulles had a point. As the spymaster pointed out, the Truman Doctrine had indeed authorized an aggressive strategy aimed at thwarting Communist advances in Western Europe, including CIA intervention in the 1948 Italian elections. But Truman was correct in charging that, under Eisenhower, Dulles had led the CIA much deeper into skulduggery than he ever envisioned.

Unmoved by Dulles's letter, Truman stood by his article. Realizing the threat that Truman posed, Dulles continued his crusade to discredit the *Post* essay well into the following year. Confident of his powers of persuasion, the spymaster made a personal trek to Independence, Missouri, in April, arranging to meet face-to-face with Truman at his presidential library. After exchanging a few minutes of small talk about the old days, Dulles mounted his assault on Truman, employing his usual mix of sweet talk and arm-twisting. But Truman—even on the brink of turning eighty—was no pushover, and Dulles's efforts proved fruitless.

Still, Dulles would not accept defeat. Unable to alter reality, he simply altered the record, like any good spy. On April 21, 1964, upon returning to Washington, Dulles wrote a letter about his half-hour meeting with Truman to CIA general counsel Lawrence Houston. During their conversation at the Truman Library, Dulles claimed in his letter, the elderly ex-president seemed "quite astounded" by his own attack on the CIA when the spymaster showed him a copy of the *Post* article. As he looked it over, Truman reacted as if he were reading it for the first time, according to Dulles. "He said that [the article] was all wrong. He then said that he felt it had made a very unfortunate impression."

The Truman portrayed in Dulles's letter seemed to be suffering from senility and either could not remember what he had written or had been taken advantage of by an aide, who perhaps wrote the piece under the former president's name. In fact, CIA officials later did try to blame a Truman assistant for writing the provocative opinion piece. Truman "obviously was highly disturbed at the *Washington Post* article," concluded Dulles in his letter, " . . . and several times said he would see what he could do about it."

The Dulles letter to Houston—which was clearly intended for the CIA files, to be retrieved whenever expedient—was an outrageous piece of disinformation. Truman, who would live for eight more years, was still of sound mind in April 1964. And he could not have been shocked by the contents of his own article, since he had been expressing the same views about the CIA—even more strongly—to friends and journalists for some time.

After the Bay of Pigs, Truman had confided in writer Merle Miller that he regretted ever establishing the CIA. "I think it was a mistake," he said. "And if I'd known what was going to happen, I never would have done it. . . . [Eisenhower] never paid any attention to it, and it got out of hand. . . . It's become a government all of its own and all secret. . . . That's a very dangerous thing in a democratic society." Likewise, after the *Washington Post* essay ran, Truman's original CIA director, Admiral Sidney Souers—who shared his former boss's limited concept of the agency—congratulated him for writing the piece. "I am happy as I can be that my article on the Central Intelligence Agency rang a bell with you because you know why the organization was set up," Truman wrote back to Souers.

In a letter that Truman wrote to *Look* magazine managing editor William Arthur in June 1964—two months after his meeting with

Dulles—the ex-president again articulated his concerns about the direction taken by the CIA after he left the White House. "The CIA was set up by me for the sole purpose of getting all the available information to the President," wrote Truman. "It was not intended to operate as an international agency engaged in strange activities."

Dulles's relentless effort to manipulate Truman—and failing that, the Truman record—is yet one more example of the spymaster's "strange activities." But Dulles's greatest success at reconstructing reality was still to come. With the Warren Report, Dulles would literally rewrite history. The inquest into the death of John F. Kennedy was another astounding sleight of hand on Dulles's part. The man who should have been in the witness chair wound up instead in control of the inquiry.

How did Allen Dulles—a man fired by President Kennedy under bitter circumstances—come to oversee the investigation into his murder? This crucial historical question has been the subject of misguided speculation for many years. The story apparently began with Lyndon Johnson, a man not known for his devotion to the truth. It has been repeated over time by various historians, including Johnson biographer Robert Caro, who one would think would be more skeptical, considering the exhaustive detail with which he documented LBJ's habitual deceit in his multivolume work.

In his 1971 memoir, Johnson wrote that he appointed Dulles and John McCloy to the Warren Commission because they were "the two men Bobby Kennedy asked me to put on it." With Bobby safely dead by 1971, LBJ clearly felt that he could get away with this one. But the idea that LBJ would huddle with the man he considered his rival and tormentor, in order to discuss the politically sensitive composition of the commission, is ludicrous.

The Warren Commission's inquiry had the ability to shake the new Johnson presidency—and the U.S. government itself—to their very core. In making his choices for the commission, Johnson later wrote, he sought "men who were known to be beyond pressure and above suspicion." What LBJ really wanted was men who could be trusted to close the case and put the public's suspicions to rest. The Warren Commission was not established to find the truth but to "lay the dust" that had been stirred up in Dallas, as McCloy stated—"dust not only in the United States, but all over the world."

Equally preposterous is the notion that Bobby Kennedy would nominate Dulles and McCloy—two men who had fallen out with President Kennedy while serving on his national security team—to investigate his brother's murder. Like Dulles, whose former agency Bobby immediately suspected of a role in the assassination, McCloy was a Cold War hard-liner. McCloy had resigned as JFK's chief arms negotiator at the end of 1962, in frustration with what he felt was Soviet intransigence. But it was McCloy himself who was the obstacle. Several months after Kennedy replaced him with Averell Harriman—a man the Russians trusted—the two superpowers reached a historic agreement to limit nuclear arms testing.

McCloy, who had served as chairman of Chase Manhattan before David Rockefeller moved into the bank's leadership role, was closely aligned with Rockefeller interests. After leaving the Kennedy administration, McCloy joined a Wall Street law firm where he represented anti-Kennedy oilmen Clint Murchison and Sid Richardson, with whom he had done business since his days at Chase Manhattan.

It was the national security establishment, not Bobby Kennedy, that advised the new president to put Dulles and McCloy on the Warren Commission. And Johnson—finely tuned to the desires of the men who had put him in the Oval Office—wisely obliged them.

The Dulles camp itself made no bones about the fact that the Old Man aggressively lobbied to get appointed to the commission. Dick Helms later told historian Michael Kurtz that he "personally persuaded" Johnson to appoint Dulles. According to Kurtz, Dulles and Helms "wanted to make sure no agency secrets came out during the investigation. . . . And, of course, if Dulles was on the commission, that would ensure the agency would be safe. Johnson felt the same way—he didn't want the investigation to dig up anything strange."

William Corson, a former Marine Corps officer and Navy intelligence agent who was close to Dulles, confirmed that the spymaster pulled strings to get on the Warren Commission. He "lobbied hard for the job," recalled Corson, who had commanded young Allen Jr. in the Korean War. After he took his place on the commission, Dulles recruited Corson to explore the Jack Ruby angle. After spending months pursuing various leads, Corson eventually concluded that he had been sent on a wild-goose chase. "It is entirely possible I was sent on an assignment which would go nowhere. . . . Allen Dulles had a lot to hide."

Among those urging Johnson to give Dulles the Warren Commission job were establishment allies like Secretary of State Dean Rusk, former president of the Rockefeller Foundation. These same voices were raised on behalf of McCloy. In fact, the commission was, from the very beginning, an establishment creation. It was sold to an initially reluctant LBJ by the most influential voices of the Washington power structure, including Joe Alsop—the CIA's ever-dependable mouthpiece—and the editorial czars of *The Washington Post* and *The New York Times*. Johnson wanted the investigation handled by officials in Texas, where he felt more in control, instead of by a "bunch of carpetbaggers." But in a phone call to the White House on the morning of November 25, Alsop deftly maneuvered Johnson into accepting the idea of a presidential commission made up of nationally renowned figures "beyond any possible suspicion."

When Johnson clung to his idea of a Texas investigation, the sophisticated Alsop set him straight, as if lecturing a country simpleton. "My lawyers, though, Joe, tell me that the White House—the president— must not inject himself into local killings," LBJ said, almost pleadingly. "I agree with that," Alsop said as he smoothly cut him off, "but in this case it does happen to be the killing of the president."

Dulles immediately accepted Johnson's request to join the commission when the president phoned him on the evening of November 29. "I would like to be of any help," Dulles told Johnson, though he did feel compelled to at least raise the propriety of appointing a former CIA director who was known to have a troubled relationship with the deceased president: "And you've considered the work of my previous work and my previous job?" Dulles asked inelegantly.

"I sure have," LBJ replied, "and we want you to do it. That's that. . . . You always do what is best for your country. I found that out about you a long time ago."

In the end, it all worked out just as the Washington establishment wanted—and as de Gaulle had predicted. The commission to investigate Kennedy's murder was made up of pliable senators and congressmen who were close to the CIA, FBI, and Johnson—and it was dominated by the two craftiest men in the hearing room, Dulles and McCloy. After months of investigative wheel spinning, the panel would reach its foregone conclusion. Lee Harvey Oswald had acted alone in the killing of the president. Case closed.

When President Kwame Nkrumah of Ghana—one of the new African leaders who had considered Kennedy a vital ally—was handed a copy of the Warren Report by U.S. ambassador William Mahoney, he opened it up, pointed at the name Allen Dulles in the list of commissioners, and handed it back to Mahoney.

"Whitewash," Nkrumah said simply. It summed up the entire charade.

The Warren Commission was named after Supreme Court chief justice Earl Warren, the distinguished jurist President Johnson strongarmed into chairing the JFK inquest. But as attorney Mark Lane—one of the first critics of the lone-gunman theory—later observed, it should have been called the "Dulles Commission," considering the spymaster's dominant role in the investigation. In fact, Dulles was Johnson's first choice to chair the commission, but LBJ decided that he needed Warren at the helm to deflect liberal criticism of the official inquiry. Although the chief justice was a former Republican governor of California and an Eisenhower appointee to the bench, he had a sterling reputation among liberals for his court's strong record on civil rights.

"I don't think Allen Dulles ever missed a meeting," Warren remembered years later. Behind the scenes, Dulles was even more active than the commission chairman. Warren was forced to juggle his commission duties with his ongoing responsibilities on the high court. But Dulles was the only member of the panel without a day job. He was free to devote himself to commission work, and he promptly began assembling his own informal staff, drawing on the services of his former CIA colleagues and his wide network of political and media contacts.

The other two principal players in the inquest were Dulles's long-time friend and fellow Cold War heavyweight, McCloy, and future president Gerald Ford, who was then an ambitious Republican congressman from Michigan with close ties to the FBI. While the rest of the commission—Congressman Hale Boggs of Louisiana and Senators Richard Russell of Georgia and John Sherman Cooper of Kentucky—shuttled back and forth between the Capitol building and the National Archives, where the panel's legal team had set up shop, the Dulles-McCloy-Ford triumvirate took control of the investigation.

The three men demonstrated their dominance at the commission's first executive session, held on December 5, 1963, when they joined forces to block Warren's strong personal favorite for the chief counsel position, Warren Olney, a longtime political disciple of the chief justice. As an assistant attorney general in the Eisenhower Justice Department, Olney had earned the wrath of the FBI's Hoover for his aggressive prosecution of civil rights cases and was suspected of being "hostile" to the bureau. Instead of Earl Warren's man, the trio installed their own veteran of the Eisenhower Justice Department—a Republican Party stalwart named J. Lee Rankin. In 1958, Dulles had "heartily" recommended Rankin for membership in the Century Association, the exclusive midtown Manhattan social club. As the Warren Commission's lead counsel, Rankin worked closely with the Dulles trio to set the parameters of the investigation, keeping the focus tightly on Oswald and assiduously avoiding any areas that carried the faintest tinge of conspiracy.

Dulles tried to establish the framework for the inquiry early on by handing the other commission members copies of a book titled *The Assassins* by Robert J. Donovan, a Washington journalist. Donovan's history of presidential assassins argued that these dramatic acts of violence were the work of solitary fanatics, not "organized attempts to shift political power from one group to another." It was quickly pointed out to

Dulles that John Wilkes Booth, who shot Lincoln as part of a broader Confederate plot to decapitate the federal government, rather famously contradicted Donovan's theory. But, undeterred, Dulles continued to push the commission to keep a tight frame on Oswald.

Dulles was a whirlwind of activity, especially outside the hearing room, where he deftly maneuvered to keep the investigation on what he considered the proper track. He showered Rankin with memos, passing along investigative tips and offering guidance on commission strategy. There was no detail too small for Dulles to bring to the chief counsel's attention. "A great deal of the description of the motorcade and the shooting will be unclear unless we have a street map and, if possible, a photo taken from the sixth floor window," Dulles wrote Rankin in a July 1964 memo. "Is this possible?" Dulles was particularly eager to explore any leads suggesting Oswald might be a Soviet spy—a soon discredited idea that Angleton would nonetheless keep promoting for the rest of his life.

Despite Dulles's efforts to keep the commission away from any hints of a domestic conspiracy, from time to time uncomfortable questions along these lines cropped up. During an executive session convened by the panel on December 16, 1963, Warren raised an especially sensitive matter—the mysterious failure of the country's security agencies to keep close watch on someone with Oswald's background. How, for instance, did a defector simply stroll into the U.S. immigration office in New Orleans—as he did the previous summer—and obtain a passport to return to Russia? "That seems strange to me," Warren remarked.

Actually, passports were rather easy to obtain, Dulles observed. When the discussion turned to the puzzling ease with which Oswald got permission to return to the United States with his Russian wife, Dulles offered that he would like to get these aspects of the inquiry "into the hands of the CIA as soon as possible to explain the Russian parts."

Senator Russell, long used to dealing with the intelligence community, reacted skeptically. "I think you've got more faith in them than I have. I think they'll doctor anything they hand to us."

Russell was edging painfully close to the fundamental problem at the core of the Warren panel's impossible mission. How could the board run a credible inquest when it had limited investigative capability of its own and was largely dependent on the FBI and the other security agencies for its evidence—agencies that were clearly implicated in the failure to protect the president?

The Warren Commission was, in fact, so thoroughly infiltrated and guided by the security services that there was no possibility of the panel pursuing an independent course. Dulles was at the center of this subversion. During the commission's ten-month-long investigation, he acted as a double agent, huddling regularly with his former CIA associates to discuss the panel's internal operations.

Despite the chronic tensions between the CIA and FBI, Hoover proved a useful partner of the spy agency during the JFK inquiry. The FBI chief knew that his organization had its own secrets to hide related to the assassination, including its contacts with Oswald. Furthermore, taking its cues from the CIA, the bureau had dropped Oswald from its watch list just weeks before the assassination. An angry Hoover would later mete out punishment for errors such as this, quietly disciplining seventeen of his agents. But the FBI director was desperate to avoid public censure, and he fully supported the commission's lone-gunman story line. Angleton, who had a good back-channel relationship with the FBI, made sure that the two agencies stayed on the same page throughout the Warren inquest, meeting regularly with bureau contacts such as William Sullivan and Sam Papich.

Angleton and his team also provided ongoing support and advice to Dulles. On a Saturday afternoon in March 1964, Ray Rocca— Angleton's right-hand man ever since their days together in Rome— met with Dulles at his home to mull over a particularly dicey issue with which the commission was grappling. How could the panel dispel persistent rumors that the CIA was somehow a "sponsor" of Oswald's actions? The story had broken in the press the previous month, when Marguerite Oswald declared that her son was a secret agent for the CIA who was "set up to take the blame" for the Kennedy assassination.

Rankin had obligingly suggested that Dulles be given the job of clearing the CIA by reviewing all of the relevant agency documents that were provided to the commission. But even Dulles thought this smacked too much of an inside job. Instead, after conferring with Rocca, Dulles proposed that he simply provide a statement to the commission swearing—as Rocca put it in his report back to Dick Helms—"that as far as he could remember he had never had any knowledge of Oswald at any time prior to the date of the assassination."

But Senator Cooper thought the allegations that Oswald was some kind of government agent were too serious to simply be dispelled by written statements. During a Warren Commission executive session in April, he proposed that the heads of the CIA and FBI be put under oath and questioned by the panel. It was a highly awkward suggestion, as Dulles pointed out. "I might have a little problem on that—having been [CIA] director until November 1961." There was a simple solution, however: put his successor, John McCone, on the witness stand. That was fine with Dulles, because—as he knew—McCone remained an agency outsider, despite his title, and was not privy to its deepest secrets.

When McCone appeared before the Warren Commission, he brought along Helms, his chief of clandestine operations. As McCone was well aware, Helms was the man who knew where all the bodies were buried, and he deferred to his number two man more than once during his testimony. Conveniently ignorant of the CIA's involvement with Oswald, McCone was able to emphatically deny any agency connection to the accused assassin. "The agency never contacted him, interviewed him, talked with him, or received or solicited any reports or information from him," McCone assured the commission.

It was trickier when Helms was asked the same questions. He knew about the extensive documentary record that Angleton's department had amassed on Oswald. He was aware of how the agency had monitored the defector during his exploits in Dallas, New Orleans, and Mexico City. David Phillips—a man whose career was nurtured by Helms—had been spotted meeting with Oswald in Dallas. But when Helms was sworn in, he simply lied. There was no evidence of agency contact with Oswald, he testified. Had the agency provided the commission with all the information it had on Oswald, Rankin asked him. "We have—all," Helms replied, though he knew the files that he had handed over were thoroughly purged.

Helms was "the man who kept the secrets," in the words of his biographer, Thomas Powers. Commission staff attorney Howard Willens politely called him "one of the most fluent and self-confident government officials I ever met." Helms was the sort of man who could tell lies with consummate ease. It would eventually win him a felony conviction, and he wore it like a badge of courage. When one was defending the nation, Helms would lecture the senators who pestered him late in his career, one must be granted a certain latitude.

It was David Slawson, a thirty-two-year-old attorney on leave from a Denver corporate law firm, who was given the unenviable job of dealing with the CIA as part of the Warren Commission's conspiracy research team. Rankin had told Slawson to rule out no one—"not even the CIA." If he did discover evidence of agency involvement, the young lawyer nervously joked, he would be found dead of a premature heart attack. But Rocca, the veteran counterintelligence agent assigned to babysit the commission, made sure nothing turned up. "I came to like and trust [Rocca]," said the young staff attorney, who found himself dazzled by his first exposure to a spy world he had only seen in movies. "He was very intelligent and tried in every way to be honest and helpful." Slawson was equally gullible when evaluating Dulles, whom he dismissed as old and feeble—precisely the aging schoolmaster act that the spymaster liked to put over on people.

Years later, as the Church Committee began to reveal the darker side of the CIA, Slawson came to suspect that Rocca had not been so "honest" with him after all. In a frank interview with *The New York Times* in February 1975, Slawson suggested that the CIA had withheld important information from the Warren Commission, and he endorsed the growing campaign to reopen the Kennedy investigation. Slawson was the first Warren Commission attorney to publicly question whether the panel had been misled by the CIA and FBI (he would later be joined by Rankin himself)—and the news story caused a stir in Washington. Several days after the article ran, Slawson—who by then was teaching law at the University of Southern California—got a disturbing phone call from James Angleton. After some initial pleasantries, the spook got around to business. He wanted Slawson to know that he was friendly with the president of USC, and he wanted to make sure that Slawson was going to "remain a friend" of the CIA.

Far from shuffling through the Warren Commission proceedings, the septuagenarian Dulles seemed to spring back to life for the inquiry. In fact, the entire denouement to the Kennedy presidency gave new meaning to his career. While Earl Warren, who turned seventy-three during the investigation, seemed exhausted and demoralized by the experience, Dulles was energized. When a friend congratulated Dulles on his seventy-first birthday in April 1964, he responded, "There have been many, too many, of them. At least I can say that I don't feel any older, despite the passage of time; and with the work of the President's Commission, I find myself busier than ever."

Dulles went about the grave business of probing Kennedy's death with an oddly sprightly attitude. When it came time for the commission to examine JFK's gore-soaked clothing, Dulles stunned his fellow investigators with an inappropriate quip. "By George," he exclaimed, as he inspected Kennedy's tie, which had been clipped off with surgical scissors by the Parkland doctors, "the president wore a clip-on tie." By contrast, when Warren had to view Kennedy's autopsy photos, he later remarked, "[They] were so horrible that I could not sleep well for nights."

His new job on the commission gave Dulles an opportunity to connect with old friends, such as Mary Bancroft and actor Douglas Fairbanks Jr.—who passed along tips and bits of gossip related to the case—as well as British novelist Rebecca West. In March, Dulles wrote West, beseeching her to draw on her fertile imagination to come up with possible motives for Oswald's crime. The commission was so baffled by the question that Warren even suggested leaving that part of the report blank. "I wish sometime you would sit down and write me a line as to why you think Lee Oswald did the dastardly deed," Dulles wrote the novelist in March, as if discussing the plot of a whodunit. "All I can tell you is that there is not one iota of evidence that he had any personal vindictiveness against the man Kennedy."

Meanwhile, the following month, Mary relayed a news report about Mark Lane to Dulles, informing her old lover in high dudgeon that Lane had apparently told a conference of lawyers in Budapest "that the killers—plural—of JFK were still at large . . . even I am amazed that Lane has the temerity to go to Budapest and shoot off his mouth in that fashion. I regard him as insane—but nevertheless I do hope the FBI has its eye on him."

Dulles and McCloy, in fact, were very concerned about European public opinion regarding the Kennedy assassination, and they urged the commission to closely monitor both Lane and Thomas G. Buchanan, a Paris-based American journalist who had written the first JFK conspiracy book, *Who Killed Kennedy?*—an advance copy of which was airmailed to Dulles from the CIA station in London, where it was published. During an executive session in April, Dulles even proposed that Buchanan be subpoenaed to appear before the commission.

Earl Warren was obsessed with press coverage of the inquiry and agonized over press leaks, including a May report by Anthony Lewis in *The New York Times*—midway through the panel's work—that the inquiry was set to "unequivocally reject theories that the assassination was the work of some kind of conspiracy." Warren was very upset by the premature news report, which suggested that the commission had rushed to judgment before hearing all the evidence. The leak was clearly intended to counter the publicity being generated by authors like Lane and Buchanan.

While the commission frantically attempted to determine the source of such leaks, the answer was sitting in their midst. The two most active leakers were Ford and Dulles. It was Ford who kept the FBI constantly informed, enabling Hoover to feed the press with bureau-friendly stories about the inquest. And Dulles used the CIA's own network of media assets to spin Warren Commission coverage.

The New York Times was a favorite Dulles receptacle. In February, the *Times* had run another leaked story—also bylined by Lewis—that clearly led back to Dulles. Lewis reported that Robert Oswald, the accused assassin's brother, had testified that he suspected Lee was a Soviet agent. As the commission hunted the source of the leak, a staff attorney suggested that the *Times* reporter might have overheard a dinner table conversation that he and Dulles had with Robert Oswald at a Washington restaurant—a highly unlikely scenario that nonetheless provided Dulles with the fig leaf of a cover story.

There was a smug coziness to the entire Warren investigation. It was a clubby affair. When Treasury secretary Dillon finally appeared before the commission in early September—less than three weeks before its final report was delivered to the president—he was warmly greeted by Dulles as "Doug." Dillon was treated to a kid-gloves examination by the commission, even though there were troubling questions left unanswered about the Secret Service's behavior in Dallas, where Kennedy's protection had mysteriously melted away.

Led by Willens, the commission staff had tried for months before Dillon's appearance to obtain Secret Service records related to the assassination. Willens believed that "the Secret Service appeared to be neither alert nor careful in protecting the president." This was a delicate way of characterizing what was a criminally negligent performance by the service entrusted with the president's safety. The buildings surrounding Dealey Plaza and its shadowy corners were not swept and secured by the Secret Service in advance of Kennedy's motorcade. There were no agents riding on the flanks of his limousine. And when sniper fire erupted, only one agent—Clint Hill—performed his duty by sprinting toward the president's vehicle and leaping onto the rear. It was an outrageous display of professional incompetence, one that made Robert Kennedy immediately suspect that the presidential guard was involved in the plot against his brother.

But Dillon stonewalled Willens's efforts to pry loose Secret Service records, and when the commission staff persisted, the Treasury secretary huddled with his old friend, Jack McCloy, and then appealed to President Johnson himself. "Dillon was a very shrewd guy," Willens marveled late in his life. "I still can't believe he involved President Johnson in this."

Instead of being grilled by the commission about why he had withheld records and why his agency was missing in action in Dallas, Dillon was allowed to make a case for why his budget should be beefed up. If the Secret Service was given more money, staff, and authority, Senator Cooper helpfully asked, would it be possible to offer the president better protection in the future? "Yes, I think [we] could," Dillon replied brightly.

If any blame was assigned in the death of the president during Dillon's gentle interrogation, it was placed on the victim himself. Soon after the assassination, Dillon and others began circulating the false story that Kennedy preferred his Secret Service guards to ride behind him in motorcades, instead of on the side rails of his limousine, and that Kennedy had also requested the Dallas police motorcycle squadron to hang back—so the crowds in Dallas could enjoy an unobstructed view of the glamorous first couple. This clever piece of disinformation had the insidious effect of absolving the Secret Service and indicting Kennedy, implying that his vanity was his downfall. And with Dulles's help, Dillon was able to slip this spurious story into the commission record.

When the Warren Commission delivered its 912-page report and twenty-six volumes of appendices to President Johnson in the White House on September 24, 1964, the towering stack seemed designed to crush all dissenting opinions with its sheer weight. But the bulk of the Warren Report was filler. Only about 10 percent of the report dealt with the facts of the case. On Dulles's insistence, most of it was taken up with a biography of Oswald that, despite its exhaustive detail, managed to avoid any mention of his contacts with U.S. intelligence. The CIA, in fact, was given a clean bill of health by the report, which reserved its modest criticisms for other arms of government.

Predictably, *The New York Times* and *The Washington Post* set the euphoric tone of the press coverage, with Robert Donovan—the same journalist whose book on assassinations had already proved so useful for Dulles—trumpeting the official report in the *Post* as a "masterpiece of its kind." *Newsweek* national affairs editor, John Jay Iselin, sent Dulles a complimentary copy of the issue with the Warren Report on its cover, along with a fawning note. "Without exception, every one of our editors who was involved in our too-hasty assimilation exercise found himself deeply impressed with the judiciousness and thoroughness of the Commission's findings. I think we can all be proud of your labor." Iselin thanked Dulles for helping to guide the magazine's coverage of the report, telling him that the editorial staff's efforts to absorb the massive report on a tight deadline "was made easier through your kindness in giving us some idea of what to be on the watch for." Meanwhile, just as he had put Dulles in charge of investigating himself, LBJ put Dillon in charge of implementing the Warren Report's recommendations.

This pattern continued into the next decade when now president Ford appointed Dillon to another panel that examined a possible CIA connection to the Kennedy assassination. The 1975 commission was chaired by a lifelong friend of Dillon—none other than Vice President Nelson Rockefeller. After pondering the matter, the Rockefeller Commission—which also included another old Kennedy antagonist and Dulles ally, retired general Lyman Lemnitzer—surprised no one by concluding that any allegations of a CIA conspiracy in the JFK case were "far-fetched speculation."

Following the release of the Warren Report, there were still a few murmurs of doubt, including some within the commission itself. Senator Russell, who strongly suspected that Oswald had been backed by others, seemed eager to distance himself from the report as soon as it was released. He fled home to Georgia, refusing to make himself available to sign ceremonial copies of the report or to autograph the official group photo of the commission.

Some tendrils of suspicion even fluttered here and there in Dulles's own social circle. Bill Bundy over in Foggy Bottom was among those who did not find the Warren Report completely convincing. "I think he accepted the Warren Report, but did he believe it? That's another matter," recalled Bundy's daughter, Carol, after his death. "I think he thought it was for the good of the country—this is what we put together and now we need to move forward."

Even those establishment personalities who were nagged by doubts about the official story convinced themselves that the national shame had to be laid to rest. But the nightmare of Dallas kept afflicting the nation's slumber. Its telltale heart kept beating beneath the floorboards where it had been buried. And it would not leave Dulles alone.

"I Can't Look and Won't Look"

In December 1965, a year after the Warren Commission wrapped up its business, Allen Dulles agreed to spend a few days on the Los Angeles campus of the University of California, as a well-paid Regents Scholar lecturer. All he had to do, for what was described as "a princely sum," was to give a few talks and rub elbows with students in casual settings. Dulles—looking forward to a relaxing winter respite in the California sun—brought Clover with him.

By this point, however, a wide network of Warren Report critics had begun to flourish—men and women from all walks of life, none of them famous (except for Mark Lane, whose CIA-inspired bad press and bullish personality had rendered him notorious). Among these critics of the official story were a poultry farmer, sign salesman, small-town newspaper editor, philosophy professor, legal secretary, civil liberties lawyer, United Nations research analyst, and forensic pathologist. They spent untold hours poring over the most arcane details of the Warren Report, analyzing photos taken during the fateful moments in Dealey Plaza, and tracking down eyewitnesses. Their zeal for the truth would make them the target of unrelenting media mockery, but they were doing the work that the American press had shamefully failed to do—and in many cases, they went about their unsung labors with great skill and discipline.

Among this band of loosely connected independent researchers was a twenty-six-year-old UCLA graduate student in engineering and physics named David Lifton. Lifton had not given the Kennedy investigation much thought—assuming, like most Americans, that the distinguished Warren Commission would get it right—until he happened to attend a Mark Lane lecture one evening in September 1964, around the time the report was released. The grad student went to the lecture on a lark. "For similar reasons I might have listened to an eccentric lecturer that the earth was flat," he later recalled. But as he took in Lane's lawyerly presentation that night at the Jan Hus Theater—inside a hulking, old, red-brick church on New York's Upper East Side—Lifton found it so disturbing that it changed his life forever. Soon afterward, he threw himself into the Kennedy case with an engineer's passion for detail and precision.

Back in Los Angeles, Lifton plunked down $76 at a local bookstore to buy the entire, twenty-six-volume set of the Warren Report and spent a full year methodically working his way through its contents. He added another dimension to his understanding of the case by reading the best of the conspiracy literature that was starting to emerge, primarily in left-wing publications like *The Nation* and *Liberation*, and in more obscure sources like *The Minority of One*, a cerebral monthly published by a brilliant Auschwitz survivor named Menachem [M.S.] Arnoni that boasted such luminaries as Albert Schweitzer, Bertrand Russell, and Linus Pauling on its editorial board. Lifton further honed his analysis of the assassination by intellectually sparring with Wesley Liebeler—one of the few members of the Warren Commission legal staff to at least consider the possibility that their report was flawed—whom he found teaching law at UCLA.

By the time Allen Dulles arrived at UCLA, David Lifton was ready to do battle. Contacting the student who was acting as Dulles's host, Lifton passed word that he would like to sit down with the spymaster for a private fifteen-minute interview to discuss the Warren Report. Dulles refused to meet with Lifton alone but did agree to answer his questions in public at a student chat session scheduled for that evening in a dormitory lounge. The student host warned Lifton not to "badger" Dulles. Another Warren Report critic had tried to get the best of Dulles the previous night, the host told Lifton, and the wily old spook had made "mincemeat" of him.

That evening, when Lifton showed up at the Sierra Lounge in Hedrick Hall, he was wracked with anxiety. "I have never been more frightened in my life, in connection with speaking to anyone," he later wrote Vincent Salandria, a Philadelphia lawyer who had established himself as one of the foremost critics of the Warren Report. Dulles entered the lounge with Clover and the evening's moderator. He lit up his trademark pipe and leaned back in his chair. Still alert at seventy-two, Dulles scanned the group of forty or so students sitting in chairs arranged in semicircles in front of him, quickly picking out the young man positioned front-row center who had obviously come to duel with him. Lifton had brought along an arsenal of evidence, including two hefty volumes of the Warren Report, a file box filled with documents, and photo exhibits of Dealey Plaza, including copies of the "kill-shot" frames from the Zapruder film. The engineering student had made a point of wearing his best suit, and his friends who accompanied him for moral support were similarly attired. "It was obvious," he told Salandria, "we were not beatniks of any kind."

After Dulles wittily deflected a question from a student about the CIA budget, the spymaster suddenly found himself confronted by the earnest, bespectacled student sitting directly in front of him. Lifton, not knowing how long he would be given the floor, leaped right to the heart of the matter, directly challenging the foundation of the Warren Report. "Mr. Dulles," he began, "one of the most important conclusions of the Warren Commission goes something like this: 'There was no evidence of a conspiracy—'"

"Wasn't it, 'We have found no evidence of conspiracy?'" interrupted Dulles. There was a twinkling charm to his manner, but he made clear that he was prepared to counter Lifton every step of the way.

Undeterred, Lifton plunged forward. Contrary to the commission's conclusion, he asserted, there was ample evidence to suggest a conspiracy, not least of which was the Zapruder film, which graphically demonstrated that Kennedy's head was "thrust violently back and to the left by [the fatal] shot." Lifton knew his law of physics, and the conclusion was unavoidable to him. "This must imply someone was firing from the front."

Dulles would have none of it. He calmly informed the gathering that he had "examined the film a thousand times" and that what Lifton was saying was simply not true.

At this point Lifton walked over to the evening's honored guest and began showing him grisly blowups from the Zapruder film. "I know these are not the best reproductions," said Lifton, but the images were clear enough. Nobody had ever directly confronted Dulles like this before, and the Old Man grew agitated as he glanced at the photos that Lifton had thrust onto his lap.

"Now what are you saying . . . just what are you saying?" Dulles sputtered.

"I'm saying there must be someone up front firing at Kennedy," Lifton responded.

"Look," Dulles said, in lecture mode, "there isn't a single iota of evidence indicating conspiracy. No one says anything like that. . . ."

But now it was Lifton's turn to school Dulles. Actually, the engineering student informed Dulles, of the 121 witnesses in Dealey Plaza, dozens of them reported hearing or seeing evidence of gunfire from the grassy knoll. "People even saw and smelled smoke."

"Look, *what are* you talking about?" fumed the now visibly angry Dulles. "*Who saw smoke?*"

Lifton began giving the names of witnesses, citing the research done by Harold Feldman, a freelance writer for scientific journals.

"Just who is Harold Feldman?" Dulles scornfully demanded. Lifton informed him that he frequently wrote for *The Nation*.

This elicited an explosion of derision from Dulles. "*The Nation!* Ha, ha, ha, ha, ha." If Dulles assumed the group of students would join in his mocking laughter, he quickly discovered that he was alone. "It is to the everlasting credit of the students," Lifton later remarked, "that even if they did not understand the full meaning of the dialogue that was taking place, they did sense the obscenity of that laugh, that it was an attempt to intellectually smear, in disguise, and *not one student* laughed. Allen Dulles laughed all alone."

Dulles tried to retrieve the upper hand by making his antagonist look like an obsessive "time hog," as Lifton put it. "Look," the distinguished guest said to the group, "I don't know if you're really all interested in this, and if you're not, we'd just as well . . ." But the students emphatically assured him that they were *very* interested. "No, no," they insisted, "keep going."

So with a shrug, Dulles was forced back into the ring. But having failed to knock out Lifton with his display of contempt, he seemed at a loss how to continue the battle. "I can't see a blasted thing here," the old spy angrily muttered, taking another look at the hideous photos in his lap. "You can't say the head goes back. . . . I can't see it going back . . . it does not go back . . . you can't say that . . . you haven't shown it."

But—after passing the photos around the room—Lifton had the final word. "Each student can look and see for himself," he told Dulles.

After the heated exchange between Lifton and Dulles, the evening began to wind down. Dulles was given the opportunity to restore some of his dignity when a starstruck student asked a question that allowed him to discourse at length on Cold War spycraft. Then Dulles bade good night to the students, and he and Clover retired to their campus quarters. As Dulles withdrew, dozens of students gathered around Lifton, peppering him with questions about the assassination, and for the next two hours he gave a presentation based on the pile of evidence that he had brought with him. "It was really a neat night," he reported to Salandria. "I really felt tonight as if I'd won."

But talking about that evening nearly fifty years later, Lifton conveyed a darker feeling about his encounter with Dulles. He had the sense he was in the presence of "evil" that night, recalled Lifton—who by then was a man in his seventies, like Dulles at the time of their UCLA duel. "It was the way he looked, his eyes. He just emoted guile, and it was very, very scary."

David Lifton was the only person who ever gave Allen Dulles a taste of what it would have been like for him to be put on the witness stand. No doubt Dulles would have reacted the same way if he had ever been cross-examined. First, he would have tried charm to disarm his prosecutor, then scorn, and finally an eruption of fury—perhaps accompanied by vague threats, as he did with Lifton, when he suggested that the grad student should submit to an FBI interrogation, if he had anything new to report.

Dulles's performance at UCLA offered a glimpse of how vulnerable the spymaster was underneath all his bluster, and how quickly he might have cracked if he had been subjected to a rigorous examination. But with the failure of Congress and the legal system, as well as the media, to investigate the assassination more closely, it was up to freelance crusaders like Lifton to hold Dulles and his accomplices accountable.

Dulles would be forced to spend the rest of his life grappling with the charges leveled by these headstrong men and women, trying to discredit their books, sabotage their public appearances, and—in some cases—to destroy their reputations. He had written Jerry Ford in February 1965, telling him he was "happy to note" that attacks on the Warren Report "have dwindled to a whimper." But it was wishful thinking. The whimper of criticism was about to become a roar.

Sometime in the winter of 1965–66, after Dulles's showdown at UCLA, he suffered a mild stroke. But he soon rebounded and Clover despaired that she would ever persuade him to slow down. In February 1966, she wrote Mary Bancroft, asking her advice for how to convince "Allen to take some care." He insisted on keeping up his busy social schedule, Clover complained, even when he wasn't feeling well. "He quite often gets a chill and as I give him electric pads, hot water bottles, etc., he says he will be getting up in a minute. This morning he said he didn't feel well, he had done too much (two dinners in the same evening, one from 5:30 to 7:30 where he spoke, the other purely social) and that he wouldn't go out to lunch at the Club. But of course he went and the chill came next. I try to wash my hands of it all when I see I do no good, but when I think of how awful for him and for everybody if his next stroke was worse, then I start once again, thinking of how to present the prospect of taking some care of himself."

The two women knew that Dulles would not scale back until his health failed him. He was "The Shark," propelling himself relentlessly forward. If he slowed down, it would mean the end of him. He dined with old CIA friends like the Angletons and hosted overseas guests like Dame Rebecca West and her husband, Henry Andrews, when they visited Washington. He hopped up to New York for meetings at the Council on Foreign Relations with longtime associates like Bill Bundy and Hamilton Armstrong. And in November 1966, he even sat for Heinz Warneke, a German-born sculptor best known for his depictions of animals, who produced a bas-relief of Dulles for the lobby of CIA headquarters.

That same year, Dulles published a rose-colored memoir of his World War II spy days, *The Secret Surrender*, and with the help of former CIA comrade Tracy Barnes, he tried to turn the book into a Hollywood movie. But the project never went beyond the Tinseltown wheel-spinning stage, demonstrating that when it came to dealing with the movie industry labyrinth, even espionage wizards were sometimes at a loss. Or perhaps trying to turn SS General Wolff into a screen hero proved too much even for Hollywood's imagination.

Much of Dulles's time during his golden years was absorbed by the growing controversy surrounding the Warren Report. He knew that his legacy was tied to the credibility of the investigation and he took the lead in defending the report, while encouraging other commission pillars to also engage in the propaganda battle. By 1966, Dulles and his commission colleagues found themselves besieged by skeptical reporters and filmmakers, as bestselling books like Mark Lane's *Rush to Judgment*, Edward Jay Epstein's *Inquest*, and Harold Weisberg's *Whitewash* ripped holes in the Warren Report, soon to be followed by Josiah Thompson's *Six Seconds in Dallas*, which was excerpted in the deeply middle-American *Saturday Evening Post*. Thompson's book would even land the Haverford philosophy professor-turned-private-eye an editorial consultancy with Luce's *Life* magazine, which had earlier played a key role in the assassination cover-up by buying the Zapruder film and locking it away in the company vault.

Dulles was particularly disturbed by *Inquest*, a methodical dissection of the report's weaknesses that had begun as Epstein's master's thesis at Cornell. To their later regret, some commission staff members had cooperated with Epstein's research, which gave the book more credibility than other attacks on the Warren Report. In July 1966, Dick Goodwin lauded the book in *The Washington Post* and used his review to call for a reopening of the investigation—a bombshell that marked the first time a member of Kennedy's inner circle had issued such a call. Alarmed by the steady erosion of support for the Warren Report, Dulles anxiously conferred with Lee Rankin and Arlen Specter, the future senator from Pennsylvania who had been one of the commission's more ambitious young attorneys, concocting the infamous "magic bullet" theory to reinforce the lone-gunman story line. As the groundswell for a new investigation grew, Dulles realized that a major counteroffensive needed to be mounted. Once again, he rallied his media allies, like *U.S. News & World Report* founder David Lawrence—whom Dulles described to Rankin as "an old and close friend of mine"—who published a ringing defense of the Warren Report by Specter in October.

The propaganda campaign on behalf of the Warren Report was primarily run out of the CIA by Dulles stalwarts like Angleton and Ray Rocca. A 1967 CIA document, later released under the Freedom of Information Act, stated that growing criticism of the report was "a matter of concern to the U.S. government, including our organization." In response, the agency sought to provide friendly journalists with "material for countering and discrediting the claims of the conspiracy theorists." One way that its media assets could impugn conspiracy theorists, the CIA suggested, was to portray them as Soviet dupes. "Communists and other extremists always attempt to prove a political conspiracy behind violence," declared another agency document.

As part of the campaign to smear Warren Report critics, Dulles compiled dirt on Mark Lane, whom he considered a particularly "terrible nuisance" because of his growing media visibility and his influence overseas, where he was often invited to speak. Dulles received one report from an unidentified source that amounted to a sludge pile of salacious unsubstantiated rumors about Lane. "I have been told that his wife was—even is—a member of the Communist Party and I have also been told that Lane is not divorced from his wife as some people claim." A district attorney in Queens "has in his possession pictures," the report continued, "showing Lane engaged in 'obscene acts' with minors (girls— not boys—groups of girls). I have not seen these pictures personally but know those who have. Lane has the most unsavoury possible reputation."

Dulles's informer also offered some crude observations about the lawyer's race, ethnicity, and mental status. "He is supposedly Jewish— but there are those who claim he is half Negro or at least has Negro blood. He is very dark complexioned, wears horn-rimmed glasses and he's always in a hurry. My own personal opinion is that he is deranged."

According to Lane, the CIA went beyond spreading ugly gossip about him, subjecting him to relentless surveillance and harassment. As his public profile started to grow, the agency pressured TV and radio programs to cancel interviews with him. When he traveled to foreign countries to speak about the Kennedy assassination, the agency sent bulletins to the U.S. embassies there announcing that Lane's local appearances had been canceled.

Dulles assiduously avoided direct confrontations with his articulate nemesis. In August 1966, when he was asked to debate Lane by the producer of a TV public affairs program in New York City called *The Open Mind*, Dulles declined. Perhaps the Old Man figured that if a UCLA student could rattle him in a casual campus forum, he would be seriously outmatched in a televised duel with an aggressive legal warrior like Lane. Dulles also rejected an invitation to be interviewed for a British documentary in which Lane was involved. The spymaster preferred more nimble surrogates like the Warren Commission staff attorneys to do his fighting for him.

As time went by, even friends of Dulles began to air their doubts to him about the Warren Report. His European friends grew particularly skeptical, but some of his intimates closer to home—including Mary Bancroft—also started challenging Dulles's explanation of the assassination. After feeding Dulles with tattletale reports about "the quite fiendish" Lane throughout the Warren Commission inquiry, Bancroft—a weather vane of shifting opinion in her Upper East Side circle—started to consider whether the outspoken critic might be right after all. "After listening to him, even I begin to wonder!" Mary wrote Dulles in July 1964. By 1966, Dulles's longtime confidante had gone over to the other side, much to his chagrin. That November, after Mary sent Clover a letter about the commission's many failings, Allen wrote back, telling her, "I imagine that we will have to agree to disagree about the Warren Report. . . . I respect your views and I doubt whether I can have any great influence on them, but I may make a try when we next get together."

By 1967, polls showed that two-thirds of the American public did not accept the Warren Report's conclusion that Lee Harvey Oswald was the lone assassin. That same year, against the backdrop of growing public skepticism, New Orleans district attorney Jim Garrison launched the first (and what will likely be the only) criminal investigation related to the Kennedy assassination. "At the beginning of the investigation," Garrison later wrote, "I had only a hunch that the federal intelligence community had somehow been involved in the assassination, but I did not know which branch or branches. As time passed and more leads turned up, however, the evidence began pointing more and more to the CIA."

In February 1968, Garrison subpoenaed Dulles to testify before an Orleans Parish grand jury—which undoubtedly came as a cold slap for a man long accustomed to being invited to speak before gatherings of the Brookings Institution, Princeton alumni association, Council on Foreign Relations, Carnegie Endowment, and other august forums. As Garrison and his investigators examined the work of the Warren Commission, they discovered that "leads pointing to the CIA had been covered up neatly by [the panel's] point man for intelligence issues, former CIA director Allen Dulles. Everything kept coming back to Cuba and the Bay of Pigs and the CIA." The New Orleans district attorney wanted to question Dulles under oath about the CIA's connections to Oswald and to local figures in the Kennedy case, like David Ferrie and

Guy Banister, whose paths had crisscrossed intriguingly with that of the accused assassin.

The Garrison investigation set off alarm bells in CIA headquarters. It soon became clear, however, that the authority of a crusading district attorney was no match for the U.S. intelligence establishment. Days after Garrison sent off the Dulles subpoena to the nation's capital, he received a letter from the United States attorney in Washington, D.C., who tersely informed the DA that he "declined" to serve the subpoena on Dulles. Meanwhile, the CIA—which, by then, was led by Helms— mounted an aggressive counterattack on the district attorney. Subpoenas like the one sent to Dulles were simply ignored, government records were destroyed, Garrison's office was infiltrated by spies, and agency assets in the media worked to turn the DA into a crackpot in the public eye. Even the private investigator Garrison hired to sweep his office for electronic bugs turned out to be a CIA operative. After Dulles was subpoenaed by Garrison, the security specialist—Gordon Novel—phoned the spymaster to slip him inside information about the DA's strategy.

In the end, Garrison's powerful enemies managed to turn the tables on him, and the New Orleans prosecutor himself became the target of an investigation, on trumped-up federal corruption charges. "This is what happens to you," he observed years later, "when you do not go along with the new government's ratification of the coup."

Despite the public's overwhelming rejection of the Warren Report, Dulles could count on the unwavering support of the Washington establishment and the corporate media. An exchange of letters between CBS news director William Small and Dulles in July 1967 summed up the media's lockstep allegiance to the official story, no matter how many holes were punched in it by new research. "I hope you had a chance to view the four-part series on the Warren Commission," wrote Small, referring to his TV network's massive apologia for the Warren Report. "We are very proud of them and I hope you found them a proper display of what television journalism can do." Dulles commended Small for a job well done, although he noted that he had missed the third installment. After reviewing transcripts of the entire series that Small had obligingly provided him, Dulles assured the CBS news executive, "If I have any nitpicking to pass on to you, I shall do so as soon as I have read them." The spymaster was always happy to offer guidance to his media friends, down to the smallest details.

Even the prominent group of men who had served President Kennedy were loath to break ranks with the establishment on the Warren Report. Dark talk of conspiracy had begun circulating within the Kennedy ranks immediately after Dallas, but with the exception of Dick Goodwin, no one dared to voice these suspicions in public.

Arthur Schlesinger was cast adrift by Kennedy's murder. The scholar had thrived in Kennedy's court, where his intellectual and political aspirations intersected. Working in the Kennedy White House not only gave Schlesinger a voice in global affairs, it offered the decidedly unglamorous intellectual a chance to rub elbows with everyone from French novelist and cultural minister André Malraux to Hollywood siren Angie Dickinson. He gossiped over lunch with the sultry actress about Frank Sinatra, who had been deeply wounded when he was jettisoned from the Kennedy circle because of his association with the mob. Schlesinger was sipping midday cocktails with publishing queen Kay Graham and her *Newsweek* editors, who had flown him to New York to advise them on a magazine makeover, when the devastating news from Dallas was announced.

Schlesinger soon realized that he was odd man out in the anti-intellectual Johnson administration. More than a month after the assassination, Schlesinger confided woefully in his journal, he still had not received "a single communication from the [new] president—not a request to do anything, or an invitation to a meeting, or an instruction, or a suggestion, not even the photographs or swimming or cocktail invitations which have gone to other members of the Kennedy staff."

The entire mood of the White House suddenly shifted under Schlesinger's feet. "LBJ differs from JFK in a number of ways—most notably, perhaps, in his absence of intellectual curiosity," Schlesinger observed. "He has the senatorial habit of knowing only what is necessary to know for the moment and then forgetting it as soon as the moment has passed. . . . LBJ lacks the supreme FDR-JFK gift of keeping a great many things in his mind at the same time, remembering them all, and demanding always to know new things." On January 27, 1964, two months into Johnson's presidency, Schlesinger submitted his resignation. "It was accepted with alacrity," he drily noted.

Schlesinger's early resignation from the Johnson administration—which came seven months before Bobby Kennedy's own departure, to run for the Senate—solidified his position of trust within the Kennedy enclave. The historian was the recipient of murmured confidences, from Bobby, Jackie, and members of their entourage. Schlesinger heard disturbing reports about the events in Dallas. RFK told him that he was wracked with suspicions about what had happened to his brother. Even CIA director McCone thought "there were two people involved in the shooting," Kennedy confided to Schlesinger. Meanwhile, Air Force general Godfrey McHugh, who had served as JFK's military aide in Dallas, gave Schlesinger a harrowing account of "that ghastly afternoon" when they bumped into each other at a French embassy party in June. McHugh had found LBJ huddled in the bathroom of his private quarters on Air Force One before the plane took off from Dallas. The panic-stricken Johnson was "convinced that there was a conspiracy and that he would be the next to go."

Schlesinger took an interest in the first wave of Kennedy conspiracy articles that began appearing in the press, sending RFK a piece titled "Seeds of Doubt" from the December 21, 1963, issue of *The New Republic*. Nobody was more aware than Schlesinger of the explosive tensions that had surged within the Kennedy presidency. "Certainly we did not control the Joint Chiefs of Staff," the historian would acknowledge late in his life. And, as he knew from his futile efforts to reform the CIA, the Kennedy White House perhaps had even less control over the spy agency. But despite Schlesinger's inside knowledge of the Washington power struggle during the Kennedy years—and his ability to see through such shoddy work as the Warren Report—the historian did nothing to explore the truth about Dallas.

In the years after the assassination, Schlesinger secured his reputation as the official historian of Kennedy's Camelot with his epic, Pulitzer Prize–winning book on the abbreviated presidency, *A Thousand Days*. The 1965 bestseller—which carefully avoided the dark, unanswered questions about Kennedy's murder—burnished the historian's intellectual celebrity and opened new doors for him on the cocktail party circuit. His bold-faced name popped up in New York gossip columns, including a sighting at a raucous Norman Mailer party in January 1967, highlighted by a trapeze apparatus that the more daring guests used to go flying through the air. "Any party with Arthur Schlesinger, Jr. and me in it can't be a failure," chirped Monique van Vooren, a Belgian-born actress who was once the va-va-voom girl of the moment.

Schlesinger was frequently invited to appear on talk shows, and that year he found himself at a Los Angeles TV station where he was the guest of local news personality Stan Bohrman. After the show, Bohrman asked Schlesinger whether he would be willing to meet backstage with Ray Marcus, a respected Warren Report critic. Marcus, who had concluded that the official report was "the most massively fraudulent document ever foisted on a free society," thought it was urgent that former Kennedy officials like Schlesinger examine his photographic evidence. He was certain that it would convince the New Frontiersmen that there had been a conspiracy. But when Schlesinger set eyes on Marcus's display—which included the Zapruder film's infamous Frame 313 kill shot—he visibly paled. "I can't look and won't look," Schlesinger said, turning his head and walking briskly away from Marcus. This was a perfect summation of the prevalent attitude among the Kennedy crowd. It was best not to linger on the horrors of Dallas.

Despite the bad blood between Kennedy and the CIA, Schlesinger managed to maintain affable relations with the spy set after Dallas. As he had throughout his career, Schlesinger kept up a friendly, chatty correspondence with Dulles. In December 1964, Schlesinger even commiserated with the spymaster over Hugh Trevor-Roper's "disgraceful piece" in the *London Sunday Times*, in which the eminent Oxford historian denounced the Warren Report as "suspect" and "slovenly." After

Dulles thanked him for the letter, Schlesinger wrote again in January, informing Dulles that British political scientist (and dependable Cold War pundit) Denis Brogan was working on a "detailed dissection of Trevor-Roper" for the CIA-funded *Encounter* magazine. "Perhaps if you are feeling up to it," Schlesinger warmly signed off, "I could come by and see you one of these afternoons." Schlesinger's courtship of Dulles in the midst of the Trevor-Roper controversy was oddly sycophantic, especially considering the fact that Schlesinger himself shared some of the British historian's doubts about the Warren Report.

The cordial relationship between Schlesinger and Dulles suffered a bit of strain in the summer of 1965 when *Life* magazine ran an account of the Bay of Pigs that was excerpted from *A Thousand Days*. In his book, Schlesinger put the onus for the disaster on the CIA, which—he accurately wrote—had maneuvered Kennedy into the sand trap. Dulles found the *Life* article—along with a similar one that *Look* magazine excerpted from Ted Sorensen's memoir, *Kennedy*—"deeply disturbing and highly misleading." The Schlesinger and Sorensen broadsides on the Bay of Pigs spurred Dulles into action, but after wrestling with a long, belabored—and unbecomingly bitter—response for *Harper's*, he decided it was best to take the high road. President Kennedy had done the honorable thing and taken responsibility for the fiasco, he told journalists calling for comment, and he would leave it at that. By November, Dulles had resumed amiable relations with Schlesinger, sending him condolences on the death of his father.

In October 1966, Schlesinger again rushed to Dulles's defense when *The Secret Surrender* was harshly reviewed in *The New York Review of Books* by revisionist historian Gar Alperovitz, who suggested that the spymaster had helped kick off the Cold War by going around Stalin's back to cut a deal with Nazi commanders in Italy. "I was so irritated by the wild Alperovitz review that I sent [the magazine] a letter," Schlesinger wrote Dulles. In his letter to the *Review*, Schlesinger ridiculed the attempt to blame the Cold War "on poor old Allen Dulles. . . . Nothing the United States could have done in 1945 would have dispelled Stalin's mistrust— short of the conversion of the United States into a Stalinist despotism."

When it came to fighting the cultural Cold War, Schlesinger and Dulles were still brothers in arms.

It was not until many years later, long after Dulles was dead, that Schlesinger began to question his cozy relations with the Georgetown CIA crowd. By then, some of the skeletons in the CIA closet had come rattling out the door, when it was opened just a crack by post-Watergate congressional investigations. In 1978, seated at an awards banquet next to Jimmy Carter's CIA director, Admiral Stansfield Turner—who was trying to at least straighten up the closet—Schlesinger listened wide-eyed as Turner regaled him with CIA horror stories. Many of the CIA director's astonishing tales related to Jim Angleton, who—though deposed three years earlier—still cast a shadow over the agency. "Turner obviously regards Angleton as a madman and cannot understand a system under which he gained so much power," Schlesinger later wrote in his journal.

In September 1991, Schlesinger found himself at the Sun Valley estate of Pamela Harriman—Averell's widow—with fellow guest Dick Helms, with whom he had been friends ever since their days together in the OSS. Schlesinger characterized their relationship as a "rather wary friendship, since we both know that there are matters on which we deeply disagree but about which, for the sake of our friendship, we do not speak." Still, he had socialized regularly with Helms over the years, sipping cocktails with him at the Wisners, swapping information with him over lunch during the Kennedy years, and later, during the 1970s, playing tennis and enjoying barbecues in the backyard of Dick and Cynthia Helms's comfortable home near Washington's Battery Kemble Park. One evening, Schlesinger's son Andrew accompanied him to a Helms barbecue. "I remember feeling kind of weird about [being there] . . . but my father thought he was the most honorable of the CIA people."

By 1991, however, Schlesinger had begun to question his assessment of Helms. He had recently read a series of articles about the CIA's brainwashing experiments on Canadian medical patients, in which Helms had played a central role. "It is a terrible story of CIA recklessness and arrogance, compounded by an unwillingness to assume responsibility that went to the point of destroying incriminating documents," Schlesinger wrote in his journal. "Helms was a central figure both in recommending the experiments and in getting rid of the evidence."

Now Schlesinger found himself relaxing in Idaho's alpine splendor with the man who had been convicted of one felony—lying to Congress—and undeniably should have been prosecuted for more. But the historian held his tongue. "In view of my long truce with Dick Helms and my liking for him, I certainly did not bring up the [CIA medical experiments]. But I did wonder a bit at one's capacity to continue liking people who have been involved in wicked things. Bill Casey [Reagan's CIA director and another old OSS comrade] is another example, though my friendship with Helms is considerably closer; [Henry] Kissinger, I guess, still another. Is this deplorable weakness? Or commendable tolerance?"

It's a measure of Schlesinger's decency that he could raise these painful, introspective questions. And it's a sign of his weakness that he could never break with these "wicked" men.

In the 1990s, Schlesinger found himself dragged back into the Kennedy assassination swamp, with the release of Oliver Stone's explosive 1991 movie, *JFK*, a fictional retelling of Garrison's ill-fated investigation that proposed Kennedy was the victim of reactionary forces in his own government. On Halloween evening that year, Stone himself showed up at the door of Schlesinger's New York apartment. The filmmaker had ignited a media uproar (stoked, in part, by the CIA's reliable press allies), and Stone—looking for support in the Kennedy camp—was reaching out for Schlesinger's support. The historian found the director "a charming, earnest man, but, I surmise, scarred into paranoia by his experience [as a soldier] in Vietnam and dangerously susceptible to conspiracy theories."

In truth, Schlesinger had long been racked by his own doubts about the Warren Report. His second wife, Alexandra, firmly believed that JFK was the victim of a conspiracy, but to her endless frustration, Schlesinger evaded the tough question by declaring himself an "agnostic" on the subject. As his son Andrew later observed, the historian simply didn't have the "emotional resources" to confront the sordid facts surrounding the assassination.

Near the end of his life, when Schlesinger was weakened by Parkinson's disease and withering away, Andrew asked him if there was one book he never wrote but wished that he had. His father got "a little agitated," recalled Andrew. "He said he wished he'd written a book about the CIA. He felt the CIA was terribly corrupting our democracy. He emotionally was saying [this]. He believed until the end that the CIA was undermining our democracy."

End Game

It was always difficult for Angelina Cabrera, the woman who managed Senator Robert F. Kennedy's New York office, to grab a few minutes of his time. As the freshman senator from New York during the volcanic '60s and the inheritor of his brother's heavy legacy, Bobby was always in demand, always on the move, always in the middle of the growing debate over the Vietnam War and the fight for social justice. Cabrera was respectful of the time that the senator needed to himself behind his closed office door. And she was keenly aware of the shadow that always seemed to loom over him. "He was sad most of the time," she recalled years later. "He was preoccupied most of the time about something—probably his brother. I had the thought that he would not make it. I was praying for him."

The grief that clung to Bobby did not make him a remote figure in his New York office. He had a gentler aura after his brother's death, and he created a sense of warm camaraderie among his staff. Aides felt they could challenge him, joke with him, and he responded in kind, with his dry and lightly teasing sense of humor. "The senator dearly loved Angie Cabrera and [his New York staff]," remembered RFK aide Peter Edelman. "He loved them very dearly; he just enjoyed being around them. . . . It was kind of a one big happy family thing."

Cabrera would accompany Bobby to political rallies in Spanish Harlem and Bedford-Stuyvesant, where Kennedy's commitment to community development and empowerment made him an increasingly popular figure. Cabrera, whose parents had emigrated from Puerto Rico to Brooklyn Heights and who had worked as an executive secretary for the governor of Puerto Rico, helped connect RFK to his Hispanic constituents. In 1967, Bobby and Ethel invited her to fly with them to the island, where he was scheduled to speak in the old Spanish colonial city of San Germán. Kennedy was stunned by the size and exuberance of the crowds that greeted him in Puerto Rico. Everywhere he went, people celebrated him as if he were their best and brightest hope. He was the second coming of his brother.

One day, that same year, while working in the New York office, Cabrera barged through Bobby's door with a timely item of business. She caught him as he was finishing what seemed like an intense phone call. "As I walked in, he thought I might have heard," Cabrera later recounted. "Actually I didn't hear what he said and I had no idea who he was talking to. But he thought that I did, and he trusted me. After he hung up the phone, he turned to me and said, 'There's something more to this. I've got to pursue who really killed my brother.'"

In the hours and days immediately following his brother's assassination, Bobby had frenetically chased every lead he could think of, quickly concluding that JFK was the victim of a plot that had spun out of the CIA's anti-Castro operation. But after this initial burst of clarity, Bobby soon sank into a fog of despair, unable to develop a clear plan of action. His depression came, of course, from the devastating loss of his beloved brother—the northern star on whom he had fixed his life's course. But Bobby was also filled with despair because there was no clear way to respond to his brother's murder. His mortal enemy Lyndon Johnson was in charge of the government and his own power as attorney general was dwindling so quickly that J. Edgar Hoover—another bitter opponent—no longer bothered responding to his phone calls. Meanwhile, Kennedy antagonists such as Hoover and Dulles were in control of the official murder investigation. If RFK tried to circumvent the system and take his suspicions directly to the American people, he risked sparking an explosive civil crisis.

The astute writer and political activist M. S. Arnoni, in fact, drew such a chilling scenario in a December 1963 article he published in *The Minority of One*, a publication to which Kennedy's Senate office subscribed: "To move against such formidable conspirators might start a disastrous chain of events. It could lead to American troops shooting at other American troops. It could lead to a direct take-over by a military clique. To avert such catastrophes, it might well be considered prudent to pretend utter ignorance, in the hope that the conspirators might be removed from power discreetly, at a later date, one by one."

And so, for the most part, Bobby Kennedy maintained a pained silence on the subject of his brother's assassination. In private, he dismissed the Warren Report as a public relations exercise. But he knew that if he attacked the report in public, it would set off a political uproar that he was in no position to exploit. When the report was released in late September 1964, Bobby was on the Senate campaign trail in New York. He tried to avoid commenting at length on the report by canceling his campaign appearances that morning. He was obliged to issue a brief statement, giving the inquiry his perfunctory blessing, but adding, "I have not read the report, nor do I intend to." It was an impossible balancing act that Bobby would strain to make work for the rest of his life.

The CIA used Kennedy's silence to bolster the Warren Report. "Note that Robert Kennedy . . . would be the last man to overlook or conceal any conspiracy," the CIA instructed friendly journalists in its 1967 memo on how to rebut critics of the report.

But by 1967, emboldened by the growing campaign to reopen the JFK case and Jim Garrison's investigation, Bobby began to refocus on Dallas. Before, he had deflected friends' efforts to discuss their suspicions about the case, but now he tentatively began probing the agonizing wound. After seeing Garrison's face on a magazine cover at an airport newsstand, the senator turned to his press aide, Frank Mankiewicz, and asked him to begin reading all of the assassination literature he could find—"so if it gets to a point where I can do something about this, you can tell me what I need to know." Meanwhile, Kennedy sent his trusted friend and longtime investigator, former FBI agent Walter Sheridan, to New Orleans to size up Garrison's operation. The buttoned-down ex-G-man took an immediate disliking to the flamboyant DA and reported back to Bobby that Garrison was a fraud. Sheridan's take on Garrison—which was reflected in the harsh NBC News special that Sheridan helped produce in June—foiled Garrison's efforts to build an investigative alliance with RFK.

The Garrison camp implored Kennedy to speak out about the conspiracy, arguing that such a public stand might even protect his own life by putting the conspirators on notice. But RFK preferred to play such deeply crucial matters close to the chest. He would reopen the case on his own terms, Kennedy confided to his closest aides—suggesting that day would come only if he won the executive powers of the White House.

"One of the things you learned when you were around Kennedy, you learned what it was to be serious," said RFK's Senate aide, Adam Walinsky. "Serious people, when faced with something like that—you don't speculate out loud about it. . . . He had an acute understanding of how difficult that kind of investigation is, even if you had all the power of the presidency."

On March 16, 1968, Robert F. Kennedy announced his candidacy for the presidency of the United States. He was motivated, he said, by his desire to "end the bloodshed in Vietnam and in our cities" and to "close the gaps that now exist between black and white, between rich and poor, between young and old, in this country." Kennedy left unstated another reason for his White House run—to finally close the case that still tormented his family and the nation.

RFK launched his presidential campaign in the same chandeliered room in the Old Senate Office Building where his brother had declared his bid for the White House eight years earlier. But a more somber mood hung over Bobby's announcement. Not only was the country—and RFK's own party—more torn by war and racial divisions than in 1960, but there was an acute sense that his own life might be at stake. After Richard Nixon and several aides sat watching Kennedy announce his presidential run on a hotel room television, the TV was turned off, and Nixon sat silently looking at the blank screen for a long time. Finally he shook his head and said, "Something bad is going to come of this." He pointed at the dark screen. "God knows where this is going to lead." A few days after RFK's announcement, Jackie Kennedy—who had begged him not to run—fell into a bleak conversation with Schlesinger at a New York party. "Do you know what I think will happen to Bobby?" she said. "The same thing that happened to Jack."

Robert Kennedy—the father of ten children, with an eleventh on the way—was terribly aware of the risk he was taking. But, notwithstanding the youthful euphoria around Senator Eugene McCarthy's "children's crusade" for president, there was no political figure in America besides Bobby who had the ability to win the White House and heal the country. Kennedy spent many days—and long, anguished nights—wrestling with his decision. At one point, he sought the advice of Walter Lippmann, one of the last of his breed of Washington wise men. "Well, if you believe that Johnson's reelection would be a catastrophe for the country—and I entirely agree with you on this," said the sage, "then, if this comes about, the question you must live with is whether you did everything you could do to avert this catastrophe."

Kennedy's mere entry into the race was enough to panic LBJ into abandoning his reelection bid. But there still was Johnson's surrogate—Vice President Hubert Humphrey—to contend with, as well as the specter of Nixon, rising from the ashes. Entering the campaign late, Kennedy threw himself into the primary race with raw determination, knowing that he was fighting an uphill battle against the Democratic Party establishment as well as competing with McCarthy for the antiwar vote. Bobby waded, virtually unprotected, into frenzied crowds on every stop of his campaign; his presidential race was perhaps the bravest, and most reckless, in American history. "Living every day is like Russian roulette," he told political reporter Jack Newfield. RFK was so moved by something Ralph Waldo Emerson had written that he copied it down and carried it with him: "Always do what you are afraid to do."

Bobby's courage gave strength to those around him, to those ambitious, idealistic men who had served his brother and were now following RFK on his perilous path. His heroism inspired their own. Men like Schlesinger, who could not bring himself to break from the establishment without a Kennedy leading the way; and Kenny O'Donnell, who had begun drinking himself to death, instead of telling the world what he had seen that day in Dealey Plaza with his own eyes; and even Robert McNamara, who had allowed himself to be debased by his allegiance to Johnson and the folly of his war. They now rallied around this new Kennedy crusade, and they were better men for doing so. They joined the battle for America's soul, as if it were their own.

JFK's assassins knew that Robert Kennedy was the only man who could bring them to justice. They had sought to keep him close after Dallas, with Dulles showering his condolences on the Kennedy family. "You have been much in my thoughts and Jackie, Ethel and you have my deep respect and admiration," the spymaster wrote RFK in January 1964. He made sure that Bobby—as well as his parents and siblings—received complete, bound sets of the Warren Report. He fell all over himself, with unctuous eagerness, to respond to queries from RFK, including Bobby's request that he sit for an interview with the Kennedy Library. In his oral history for the library, Dulles further disgraced himself and the memory of John F. Kennedy by singing false praises of the slain president.

But when Robert Kennedy announced his run for the presidency, he became a wild card, an uncontrollable threat. The danger grew as Kennedy got closer to his goal of winning the Democratic nomination. The June 4 California primary would be the make-or-break moment of his campaign. If he won the Golden State, the pundits declared, his momentum would be unstoppable.

Oh, God, not again." That was the collective moan that erupted from deep within the crowd at Los Angeles's Ambassador Hotel on the night of Kennedy's victory, as he lay mortally wounded on the grimy floor of the hotel pantry. As in Dallas, official reports immediately pinned sole responsibility for the shooting on a troubled loner, a twenty-four-year-old Palestinian immigrant named Sirhan Sirhan. The accused assassin was undeniably involved in the assault on Kennedy as the senator and his entourage made their way through the crowded, dimly lit hotel pantry on the way to a press briefing room. But numerous eyewitnesses—including one of the men who subdued Sirhan—insisted that the alleged assassin could not have fired the shot that killed Kennedy. Sirhan was several feet in front of Kennedy when he began firing with his revolver. But the fatal shot—which struck RFK at point-blank range behind the right ear, penetrating his brain—was fired from behind. Furthermore, evidence indicated that thirteen shots were fired in the pantry that night—five more than the number of bullets that Sirhan's gun could hold. Dr. Thomas Noguchi, the Los Angeles coroner who conducted the autopsy on Kennedy, thought that all of the evidence pointed to a second gunman. "Thus I have never said that Sirhan Sirhan killed Robert Kennedy," Noguchi would flatly state in his 1983 memoir.

Then there was Sirhan himself. Like Oswald, he did not claim credit for the assassination. In fact, from the moment he was taken into custody, he seemed utterly perplexed by the tragedy in which he found himself playing the starring role. The dazed Sirhan had no memory of attacking Kennedy. He struck many observers, including hypnosis experts who interviewed him, as a "Manchurian candidate"—an individual highly susceptible to mind control programming.

A security guard named Thane Eugene Cesar who guided Kennedy into the pantry later fell under suspicion. He was seen pulling his gun as the chaos erupted that night in the cramped passageway. But investigators quickly cleared Cesar, and his gun was never tested. Over the years, Cesar's possible role in the assassination of Robert Kennedy has been debated by researchers and lawyers associated with the case. Some—like Sirhan's current legal team—declare that Cesar, if not the actual assassin, played a role in the plot, perhaps helping set up Kennedy as a target.

Others, like investigative journalist Dan Moldea—author of a book on the RFK assassination—insist on the innocence of Cesar, who is still alive. "Gene Cesar is an innocent man who has been wrongly accused in the Robert Kennedy murder case, and any claim to the contrary is simply not true," Moldea e-mailed the author in 2015, adding that he now acts as the reclusive Cesar's spokesman and has his power of attorney.

John Meier—a former executive in Howard Hughes's Las Vegas organization—has tied Cesar to CIA contractor Bob Maheu, who was hired by Hughes to run his Vegas operation in the 1960s. Meier claims he was introduced to Cesar in Las Vegas before the RFK assassination by Jack Hooper, Maheu's security chief. Meier also stated that after Kennedy's murder, he was warned by Maheu and Hooper never to mention Cesar's name or his connection to Maheu.

But Maheu strongly denied the accusations. "Everything about [Meier] was a lie," he snarled during an interview at his Las Vegas home before his death in 2008. "He was a 14-carat phony." Cesar, too, has rejected Meier's accusations, with Moldea—speaking on behalf of the former security guard—dismissing them as "just more garbage being peddled by Meier."

Maheu pointed out that Meier was accused of evading taxes on money he allegedly skimmed from Hughes mining deals and was convicted on a related charge of forgery. But it was Maheu himself who was the biggest crook in his Nevada organization, Hughes told the press after fleeing Las Vegas in 1970. Maheu was "a no-good, dishonest son of a bitch [who] stole me blind," fumed the eccentric billionaire. While running Hughes's gambling casinos, Maheu had made sweetheart deals with mobsters and allowed the CIA to pay off politicians with Hughes cash and to exploit Hughes's corporate empire as a front for spy activities. While Maheu was being paid over $500,000 a year by Hughes as his Las Vegas overseer, he still treated the CIA like his top client.

Maheu never concealed his hatred for the Kennedys. He even accused JFK of homicide during his testimony before the Church Committee, for withholding air support from the Bay of Pigs invaders. "As far as I'm concerned," he said, "those volunteers who got off the boats that day were murdered." But Maheu denied playing a role in the Kennedy assassinations.

As with his brother's death, the investigation into Robert Kennedy's murder would become clouded with murky agendas. There were hints of CIA involvement, Mafia corruption—and once again glaring displays of official negligence. Sirhan Sirhan's prosecution was a streamlined process, with the defendant often seeming like a confused bystander at his own trial. Just like the JFK inquest, the outcome was never in doubt. Sirhan has spent the bulk of his life in prison, with his periodic requests for a retrial routinely denied.

Allen Dulles, who turned seventy-five in April 1968, kept up a busy schedule all that year, despite Clover and Mary's concerns about his health. Dulles continued attending meetings of the Council on Foreign Relations intelligence study group and the Princeton Board of Trustees; there were luncheons at the Alibi Club, embassy parties and regular get-togethers with old CIA comrades like Angleton, Jim Hunt, and Howard Roman. And he continued to appear as a special guest on radio and TV shows.

Not even the civil unrest in Washington ignited by the assassination of Martin Luther King Jr. that April seemed to faze Dulles. After King's assassination, his followers took their fallen leader's Poor People's Campaign to the nation's capital, erecting a protest encampment on the National Mall that they christened Resurrection City. On June 24—after more than one thousand police officers swept into the camp, dispersing the protesters—riots again broke out in the streets of the capital, prompting officials to call out the National Guard and declare a curfew. But Dulles did not let the disturbances affect his social life. "Lest you worry at the news of a curfew in Washington," Dulles wrote the following day to Clover, who was visiting Allen Jr. and Joan in Switzerland at the time, "you can rest assured that everything remains quiet here." Dulles had invited their old friend, Helen Magruder—the widow of OSS deputy director, Brigadier General John Magruder—for dinner at Q Street. After supper, he wrote, "We were able to get a taxi shortly, and Helen returned home in safety."

That afternoon, Dulles continued, he planned to go to a CIA social gathering with Jim Hunt and his wife. "I am afraid I will have to pass up [family friend] Marion Glover's afternoon affair, as I cannot get to both," he told Clover. There was always too much for Dulles to do in his leisure years.

That same month, Dulles found time to sit down and write a condolence letter to the brother of another murdered Kennedy. "Dear Ted," he wrote the last Kennedy brother, "I join with a multitude of others in expressing to you my deep sorrow. I had the opportunity of working with Bobby on many occasions and had great respect for his dynamic approach to our national problems and for his vigor and forthrightness in dealing with them. His death is a great loss to the country and especially to those like yourself who were so close to him. I send you my profound sympathy." Once again, Dulles's flawless civility is chilling to behold.

Ted Kennedy responded warmly to Dulles's letter, in a way that the spymaster must have found reassuring. "Joan and I want you to know how grateful we are for your message," the senator wrote on his personal stationery. "At a time of sadness, nothing is more helpful than hearing from a friend. . . . I hope we will see each other soon." It was clear that there would be no trouble from the youngest Kennedy brother.

On July 8, according to his day calendar, Dulles made time to meet with Dr. Stephen Chowe, an American University professor who was an expert in Chinese and Russian brainwashing techniques. Dulles had known Chowe, a former CIA researcher, for some time. The mind control expert had reached out to Dulles in June, arranging a time to discuss his latest work on "political psychology." Then, on July 13, 1968—a few days after his meeting with Chowe—Dulles met with Dr. Sidney Gottlieb, the CIA's pharmaceutical wizard, who was involved in the agency's assassination and MKULTRA mind control programs. These meetings on the Dulles calendar are particularly intriguing, coming just weeks after the assassination of Robert Kennedy and the arrest of Sirhan Sirhan—a man who appeared to be in a hypnotic or narcotic state when he was taken into custody and, to some mind control experts, seemed to fit the mold of an MKULTRA subject.

That summer, Dulles also continued to keep a close watch on Jim

Garrison's investigation. In July, Angleton deputy Ray Rocca phoned Dulles to discuss an article about the New Orleans prosecutor by Edward Jay Epstein in *The New Yorker*. In September, CIA mole Gordon Novel called Dulles to give him another inside report on the Garrison probe.

The Old Man's main social event of the fall season was the Washington fête in honor of Reinhard Gehlen, the West German spy chief Dulles had resurrected from the poison ashes of the Third Reich. On September 12, Gehlen's U.S. sponsors threw a luncheon for him, and that night there was a dinner for Hitler's old spy chief at the Maryland home of Heinz Herre—Gehlen's former staff officer on the eastern front, who had become West Germany's top intelligence liaison in Washington.

That fall, Dulles eagerly anticipated the long-delayed presidential election of Richard Nixon, the Dulles brothers' former disciple. He got involved in the Nixon campaign, joining fund-raising committees and contributing his own money. On Halloween, Nixon sent Dulles a telegram, thanking him for his support and appointing him vice chairman of the "Eisenhower Team" for the Nixon-Agnew ticket. The Old Man had visions of returning to the center of official Washington, perhaps with a prominent appointment in the new Nixon administration.

But Clover and others close to him knew the truth—he was slowly fading away. At times, in the midst of his frenetic schedule, Dulles would suddenly seem lost. "Uncle Allen would go off to lunch at the Metropolitan Club or Alibi Club and forget how to get home," said his cousin, Eleanor Elliott. "Sometimes he would just get lost in the neighborhood, and people who recognized him would bring him back. Clover was so worried."

In December—working with Howard Roman, his longtime collaborator—Dulles finished editing a collection of espionage yarns, *Great Spy Stories*, featuring selections by masters of the genre such as Eric Ambler, Graham Greene, Ian Fleming, and John le Carré. In the book's foreword, Dulles offered his final observations on the stealthy profession to which he had dedicated himself. In the past, he wrote, "the spy was generally thought of as a rather sneaky and socially unacceptable figure." But World War II and the Cold War, he observed, had turned spies into dashing heroes. "The spy has the muscle and the daring to take the place of the discarded hero of yore. He is the new-model musketeer." None of the blood and sorrow that had flowed all around him had left a mark on Dulles. He continued to have the highest esteem for himself and his "craft." As he neared the end of his life, there was no self-reflection, only more tale spinning for a public that could not get enough of the cool romance of 007.

Soon after finishing the book, Dulles came down with a bad case of the flu, which confined him to bed. By Christmas Eve, the infection had settled in his chest and turned to pneumonia, and Dulles was admitted to Georgetown University Hospital. Over the following month, he struggled to recover, rallying at one point to write a congratulatory note to Nixon on his inauguration. But on January 29, 1969, Dulles died of complications from his illness.

Even after his death, the secret organism that Dulles had created continued to pulse. A team led by Angleton swept into the Old Man's home office, while Clover lay in bed upstairs, and rifled through his files. CIA technicians installed secure phone lines to handle the flood of condolence calls. An effusive eulogy was crafted for his memorial service at Georgetown Presbyterian Church. The soft-spoken church minister, who was used to writing his own funeral orations, balked at reading the bombastic address that had been written by longtime Dulles ghostwriter Charles Murphy, with input from Angleton and Jim Hunt. But the Dulles team quickly set the cleric straight. "This is a special occasion," the minister was informed by an official-sounding caller the night before the funeral. "The address has been written by the CIA."

The next day, the minister stood up in his church—whose pews were filled with the solemn ranks of CIA spooks and political dignitaries—and recited the eulogy as instructed. "It is as a splendid watchman that many of us saw him," he declared, "a famous and trusted figure in clear outline on the American ramparts, seeing that the nation could not be surprised in its sleep or be overcome in the night.

"It fell to Allen Dulles to perfect a new kind of protection," continued the preacher, not knowing how ironic the words he spoke were. "[F]or us, as for him, patriotism sets no bounds on . . . the defense of freedom and liberty."

Dulles's funeral oration was a celebration of the lawless era that he had inaugurated. Under Dulles, America's intelligence system had become a dark and invasive force—at home and abroad—violating citizens' privacy, kidnapping, torturing, and killing at will. His legacy would be carried far into the future by men and women who shared his philosophy about the boundless authority of the national security system's "splendid watchmen." Dulles had personally shaped and inspired some of these watchmen, including Helms and Angleton—as well as the power players of future administrations, like William Casey, President Reagan's defiantly lawbreaking CIA director, and Donald Rumsfeld, President George W. Bush's smugly confident conqueror of desert sands. And though they never met, Dulles also provided a template for Bush regent Dick Cheney's executive absolutism and extreme security measures in the name of national defense. These men, too, firmly believed that "patriotism set no bounds" on their power.

Today, other faceless security bureaucrats continue to carry on Dulles's work—playing God with drone strikes from above and utilizing Orwellian surveillance technology that Dulles could only have dreamed about—with little understanding of the debt they owe to the founding father of modern American intelligence. Dead for nearly half a century, Dulles's shadow still darkens the land.

Those who enter the lobby of CIA headquarters are greeted by the stone likeness of Allen Welsh Dulles. "His Monument Is Around Us," reads the inscription underneath the bas-relief sculpture. The words sound like a curse on the men and women who work in the citadel of national security, and on all those they serve.

Epilogue

After Dulles, James Angleton soldiered on for several more years in
the CIA's counterintelligence department until his gloomy paranoia seemed to threaten the gleaming efficiency of a new espionage era
and, in 1975, he was forced to retire. Angleton remained a loyal sentry
of the Dulles legacy for many years. He had carried the master's ashes in
a wooden urn at Dulles's funeral. Their stories had been long entwined,
from the days of the Nazi ratlines in Rome through the assassinations of
the 1960s. Dulles was Angleton's revered monarch, and he was Dulles's
ghostly knight.

When Angleton's successors cracked open his legendary safes and
vaults, out spilled the sordid secrets of a lifetime of service to Allen
Dulles. Among the trove of classified documents and exotic souvenirs
were two Bushmen bows and some arrows—which the CIA safecrackers wisely tested right away for poison, knowing Angleton's reputation.
The safecracking team was also horrified to find files relating to both
Kennedy assassinations and stomach-turning photos taken of Robert
Kennedy's autopsy, which were promptly burned. These, too, were mementoes of Angleton's years of faithful service to Dulles.

But as he crept toward death in 1987, Angleton was less bound by
the loyalty oaths of the past, and he began to talk about his career with
a surprisingly raw clarity. By then, his lungs were cancer-ridden from a
lifetime of incessant smoking, and his sunken cheeks and receding eyes
gave him the look of a fallen saint. The Catholic Angleton had always

needed to believe in the holiness of his mission. And now, as he faced the final judgment, he felt compelled to make confessions, of sorts, to visiting journalists, including Joseph Trento. What he confessed was this. He had not been serving God, after all, when he followed Allen Dulles. He had been on a satanic quest.

These were some of James Jesus Angleton's dying words. He delivered them between fits of calamitous coughing—lung-scraping seizures that still failed to break him of his cigarette habit—and soothing sips of tea. "Fundamentally, the founding fathers of U.S. intelligence were liars," Angleton told Trento in an emotionless voice. "The better you lied and the more you betrayed, the more likely you would be promoted. . . . Outside of their duplicity, the only thing they had in common was a desire for absolute power. I did things that, in looking back on my life, I regret. But I was part of it and loved being in it."

He invoked the names of the high eminences who had run the CIA in his day—Dulles, Helms, Wisner. These men were "the grand masters," he said. "If you were in a room with them, you were in a room full of people that you had to believe would deservedly end up in hell."

Angleton took another slow sip from his steaming cup. "I guess I will see them there soon."

Notes

Abbreviations Used

AMD	Allen Macy Dulles Jr.
AS	Arthur M. Schlesinger
AWD	Allen W. Dulles
AWD calendars	Allen W. Dulles calendars, Seeley Mudd Library, Princeton University
AWD correspondence	Allen W. Dulles correspondence, Seeley Mudd Library, Princeton University
AWD interview, JFD OH	Allen W. Dulles interview, John Foster Dulles oral history project, Seeley Mudd Library, Princeton University
AWD OH, JFK Library	Allen W. Dulles oral history, John F. Kennedy Presidential Library and Museum, Boston
AWD OH, Mudd Library	Allen W. Dulles oral history, John Foster Dulles collection, Seeley Mudd Library, Princeton University
AWD papers, Mudd Library	Allen W. Dulles papers, Seeley Mudd Library, Princeton University
DCI	Director of Central Intelligence, Central Intelligence Agency
ELD	Eleanor Lansing Dulles
ELD interview, JFD OH	Eleanor Lansing Dulles interview, John Foster Dulles oral history project, Seeley Mudd Library, Princeton University
ELD memoir	Eleanor Lansing Dulles, *Eleanor Lansing Dulles, Chances of a Lifetime: A Memoir* (Englewood Cliffs, NJ: Prentice-Hall, 1980)
ELD OH	Eleanor Lansing Dulles oral history, John Foster Dulles Collection, Seeley Mudd Library, Princeton University
Fraleigh OH	William Fraleigh oral history, John F. Kennedy Presidential Library and Museum, Boston
JFD OH	John Foster Dulles oral history project, Seeley Mudd Library, Princeton University
JFK Library	John F. Kennedy Presidential Library and Museum, Boston
MB	Mary Bancroft
MB journal	Mary Bancroft journal, Schlesinger Library, Radcliffe Institute, Harvard University

MB papers	Mary Bancroft papers, Schlesinger Library, Radcliffe Institute, Harvard University
MCD dream journal	Martha Clover Dulles dream journal, Schlesinger Library, Radcliffe Institute, Harvard University
MCD journal	Martha Clover Dulles journal, Schlesinger Library, Radcliffe Institute, Harvard University
MCD papers	Martha Clover Dulles papers, Schlesinger Library, Radcliffe Institute, Harvard University
McKittrick interview	Thomas McKittrick interview, July 30, 1964, John Foster Dulles oral history project, Seeley Mudd Library, Princeton University
Mudd Library	Seeley Mudd Library, Princeton University
NARA	National Archives and Records Administration
NYPL	New York Public Library
OH	Oral history
Pell OH	The reminiscences of Herbert C. Pell, Columbia University oral history collection
Pell papers	Herbert Clairborne Pell papers, Franklin D. Roosevelt Library
RFK	Robert Francis Kennedy
Schlesinger Library	Schlesinger Library, Radcliffe Institute, Harvard University

Prologue

1 "That little Kennedy": Willie Morris, *New York Days* (Boston: Back Bay Books, 1993), 36.

2 "the blackest day of my life": James Srodes, *Allen Dulles: Master of Spies* (Washington, DC: Regnery Publishing, 1999), 532.

2 "the secretary of state for unfriendly countries": David Atlee Phillips, *Secret Wars Diary: My Adventures in Combat, Espionage Operations and Covert Action* (Bethesda, MD: Stone Tail Press, 1989), 125.

4 chess master of the free world: Townsend Hoopes, *The Devil and John Foster Dulles* (Boston: Little, Brown, 1973), 143.

4 "Do not comply": Nancy Lisagor and Frank Lipsius, *A Law Unto Itself: The Untold Story of the Law Firm Sullivan & Cromwell* (New York: William Morrow & Co., 1988), 115.

5 "a legacy of ashes": Tim Weiner, *Legacy of Ashes: The History of the CIA* (New York: Anchor Books, 2008), 194.

6 "My Answer to the Bay of Pigs": AWD papers, Mudd Library.

6 "The 'Confessions' of Allen Dulles": Lucien S. Vandenbroucke, "The 'Confessions' of Allen Dulles: New Evidence on the Bay of Pigs," *Diplomatic History* 8, no. 4 (October 1984): 365–76, www.intelligencedeclassified.org.

7 "a very tragic man": Stephen Ambrose, *Ike's Spies: Eisenhower and the Espionage Establishment* (Jackson: University Press of Mississippi, 1999), 318.

7 He soon began meeting with a surprising range of CIA officers: AWD calendars 1962–63, digital files series.

7 He met with a controversial Cuban exile leader: Declassified CIA document, Mary Ferrell Foundation, www.maryferrell.org; G. Robert Blakey and Richard N. Billings, *Fatal Hour: The Assassination of President Kennedy by Organized Crime* (New York: Berkley Books, 1992), 194–99.

8 the Kennedy presidency suffered from a "yearning to be loved": From Oct. 21, 1963,

draft of speech, "The Art of Persuasion: America's Role in the Ideological Struggle," AWD papers, Mudd Library.

8   And on the weekend of the assassination: AWD calendars.

9   "Our faults did not often give us a sense of guilt": ELD memoir, 10.

10   Democracy . . . was "cowed in mind": I. F. Stone, *The Trial of Socrates* (Boston: Little, Brown and Company, 1988), 143.

10   "It seems we just went wild": Author interview with Joan Talley.

Chapter 1: The Double Agent

15   He later told the story of his border crossing with pulse-racing, dramatic flair: Allen Dulles, *The Secret Surrender* (New York: Harper & Row, 1966), 16–17.

16   One of his affairs . . . had a brutal ending: James Srodes, *Allen Dulles: Master of Spies* (Washington, DC: Regnery Publishing, 1999), 81.

17   "the personal representative of President Roosevelt": Dulles, *Secret Surrender*, 18.

17   "Too much secrecy can be self-defeating." Peter Grose, *Gentleman Spy: The Life of Allen Dulles* (Boston: Houghton Mifflin Co., 1994), 154.

17   Donovan . . . wanted to station Dulles in London: Dulles, *Secret Surrender*, 14.

18   He thought he could do a better job than Donovan: Douglas Waller, *Wild Bill Donovan: The Spymaster Who Created the OSS and Modern American Espionage* (New York: Free Press, 2011), 146.

18   Switzerland was a financial haven for the Nazi war machine: See Adam LeBor, *Tower of Basel: The Shadowy History of the Secret Bank That Runs the World* (New York: Public Affairs, 2013).

18   Sullivan and Cromwell, the Dulles brothers' Wall Street law firm, was at the center: See Nancy Lisagor and Frank Lipsius, *A Law Unto Itself: The Untold Story of the Law Firm Sullivan & Cromwell* (New York: William Morrow & Co., 1988); and Christopher Simpson, *The Splendid Blond Beast: Money, Law, and Genocide in the Twentieth Century* (Monroe, ME: Common Courage Press, 1995).

19   he broke down in tears: Lisagor and Lipsius, *A Law Unto Itself*, 134.

19   Foster still could not bring himself: Grose, *Gentleman Spy*, 134.

19   he had the gall to throw a gala party: Reinhard R. Dorries, *Hitler's Intelligence Chief: Walter Schellenberg* (New York: Enigma Books, 2009), 92.

20   "who from humble beginnings": Grose, *Gentleman Spy*, 125.

20   "Germany's position is morally superior": Ibid., 133.

20   "rather impressed" with Joseph Goebbels's . . . "sincerity and frankness": Ibid., 116.

20   "*Juden*" scrawled crudely on the door: Harold Bartlett Whiteman Jr., "Norman H. Davis and the Search for International Peace and Security" (unpublished dissertation, Sterling Library, Yale University, 1958).

20   "those mad people in control in Germany": Lisagor and Lipsius, *A Law Unto Itself*, 138.

21   "somewhat similar views": Charles Lindbergh, *The Wartime Journals of Charles A. Lindbergh* (New York: Harcourt Brace Jovanovich, 1970), 283.

21   Monitoring Dulles proved an easy task: Srodes, *Allen Dulles: Master of Spies*, 200–201.

22   Stephenson was also willing to do the dirty work of espionage: See H. Montgomery Hyde, *Room 3603: The Incredible True Story of Secret Intelligence Operations During World War II* (New York: The Lyons Press, 1962).

22   Stephenson was even authorized to kill: John Loftus, *America's Nazi Secret* (Walterville, OR: Trine Day, 2010), 5; and author interview with Loftus.

22   they sought advice from a British colleague named Peter Wright: Peter Wright,

Spycatcher: The Candid Autobiography of a Senior Intelligence Officer (New York: Dell, 1988), 204.

23 Douglas's hatred for the "unctuous and self-righteous" senior Dulles: William O. Douglas, *Go East Young Man: The Early Years* (New York: Random House, 1974), 259.

24 "I turned and gave him a quarter tip": Ibid., 146.

24 Roosevelt grew so fond of Douglas: Doris Kearns Goodwin, *No Ordinary Time: Franklin and Eleanor Roosevelt—The Home Front in World War II* (New York: Touchstone, 1995), 526.

24 "You stood me on my head": Ibid., 257.

25 resulted in at least two abortive coups: See David Talbot, *Devil Dog: The Amazing True Story of the Man Who Saved America* (New York: Simon & Schuster, 2010).

25 Vanderbilt . . . tipped off Eleanor Roosevelt: Cornelius Vanderbilt Jr., *Man of the World: My Life on Five Continents* (New York: Crown Publishers, 1959), 264.

25 "He was a dangle": Author interview with John Loftus.

26 The secretive BIS became a crucial financial partner: See LeBor, *Tower of Basel*, 78–85; and first chapter of Charles Higham, *Trading with the Enemy: The Nazi-American Money Plot, 1933–1949* (New York: Authors Guild Backprint Edition, 2007).

26 "Somebody grabbed me from behind": McKittrick interview.

27 "an American [bank] president doing business with the Germans": LeBor, *Tower of Basel*, 122.

27 the "nasty crew in the Treasury": McKittrick interview.

27 Project Safehaven that sought to track down: Martin Lorenz-Meyer, *Safehaven: The Allied Pursuit of Nazi Assets* (Columbia: University of Missouri Press, 2007), 178; and Donald P. Steury, "The OSS and Project Safehaven," CIA online library: www.cia.gov/library/center-for-the-study-of-intelligence/csi-publications/csi-studies/studies/summer00/art04.html.

28 lacked "adequate personnel": Neal H. Petersen, ed., *From Hitler's Doorstep: The Wartime Intelligence Reports of Allen Dulles, 1942–1945* (University Park: Pennsylvania State University Press, 1996), 420.

28 "The Treasury [Department] kept sending sleuth hounds": McKittrick interview.

28 By playing an intricate corporate shell game: See Lisagor and Lipsius, *A Law Unto Itself,* 136–37 and 146–52.

28 "Shredding of captured Nazi records": Loftus, *America's Nazi Secret,* 10.

30 "In our uncompromising policy": President Franklin D. Roosevelt radio address, Feb. 12, 1943, the public papers of FDR, vol. 12, p. 71, http://www.ibiblio.org/pha/policy/1943/430212a.html.

30 "merely a piece of paper": Hal Vaughan, *Sleeping with the Enemy: Coco Chanel's Secret War* (New York: Alfred A. Knopf, 2011), 178.

31 Perhaps the most bizarre was Stephanie von Hohenlohe: See Martha Schad, *Hitler's Princess: The Extraordinary Life of Stephanie von Hohenlohe* (Stroud, Gloucestershire, UK: Sutton Publishing, 2004).

31 "If news of such a meeting became public": Martin Allen, *Himmler's Secret War: The Covert Peace Negotiations of Heinrich Himmler* (New York: Carroll & Graf Publishers, 2005), 131.

32 a "flagrant" liar: Grose, *Gentleman Spy,* 157.

32 Royall Tyler . . . was cut from similar cloth: See "Royall Tyler" entry, *Dictionary of Art Historians,* www.dictionaryofarthistorians.org/tylerr.htm; and "Royall Tyler" entry in *Dictionary of American Biography,* 1977. See also Grose, *Gentleman Spy*; and Srodes, *Allen Dulles: Master of Spies.*

33 Dulles broke the ice: Charles Higham, *American Swastika: The Shocking Story of Nazi Collaborators in Our Midst* (New York: Doubleday & Co., 1985), 190.

33 Hovering over the tête-à-tête: See Allen and the Himmler profile in the United States Holocaust Memorial Museum, www.ushmm.org.

35 Himmler even recruited fashion designer Coco Chanel: Vaughan, *Sleeping with the Enemy*, 188–89.

35 he never lost faith in Dulles: Allen, *Himmler's Secret War*, 275.

Chapter 2: Human Smoke

37 The boys would rise early: AWD interview, JFD OH.

38 the children would put small candles in paper balloons: ELD interview, JFD OH.

38 "I never feared hell": ELD memoir, 19.

38 Once Allen flew into a rage: Ibid., 15.

38 One summer incident: Ibid., 16; and Leonard Mosley, *Dulles* (New York: Doubleday, 1978), 27.

40 The minister was a compassionate man: ELD memoir, 25.

40 Edith Foster Dulles was "a doer": ELD interview, JFD OH; and ELD memoir, 8–9.

40 Foster's callousness came into stark relief: ELD interview, JFD OH.

41 "a very sensitive mouth": ELD memoir, 104.

41 Her brother's letter stunned and infuriated Eleanor: Ibid., 138.

41 "We can't have too many Jews": ELD interview, JFD OH.

41 the fragile Blondheim . . . killed himself: Mosley, *Dulles*, 122.

43 The doomed voyage of the *St. Louis*, see Gordon Thomas, *Voyage of the Damned* Minneapolis: Motorbooks International Publishers, 1994). See also the United States Holocaust Memorial Museum Web site, http://www.ushmm.org/wlc/en/article.php?ModuleId=10005267; and the Jewish Virtual Library Web site, http://www.jewishvirtuallibrary.org/jsource/Holocaust/stlouis.html.

43 Morgenthau was so integral: Herbert Levy, *Henry Morgenthau, Jr.: The Remarkable Life of FDR's Secretary of the Treasury* (New York: Skyhorse Publishing, 2010), 320.

43 Roosevelt . . . was the first presidential candidate to campaign against anti-Semitism: Richard Breitman and Allan J. Lichtman, *FDR and the Jews* (Cambridge, MA: Harvard University Press, 2013), 42.

44 "He never let anybody around him": Levy, *Henry Morgenthau, Jr.*, 203.

44 Roosevelt began discussing a plan to rescue millions of German Jews: See Richard Breitman, Barbara McDonald Stewart, and Severin Hochberg, eds., *Refugees and Rescue: The Diaries and Papers of James G. McDonald, 1935–1945* (Bloomington: Indiana University Press, 2009).

45 In June 1940, he circulated a memo: The Long memo can be found on the PBS *American Experience* Web site, in the archives for its "America and the Holocaust" program, http://www.pbs.org/wgbh/amex/holocaust/filmmore/reference/primary/barmemo.html.

45 One Morgenthau aide later called the Long cabal: Ibid.

45 "Breck, we might be a little frank": Levy, *Henry Morgenthau, Jr.*, 357.

45 Long was convinced that he was being persecuted: *American Experience*.

45 he fell for the most notorious anti-Jewish fabrication: Robert Dunn, *World Alive: A Personal Story* (New York: Crown Publishers, 1956), 421.

47 Heinrich Himmler's luxurious private train: Walter Laqueur and Richard Breitman, *Breaking the Silence: The German Who Exposed the Final Solution* (Hanover, NH, and London: Brandeis University Press, 1994), 13–14.

49 Heydrich, who called himself "the chief garbage collector": Robert Gerwarth, *Hitler's Hangman: The Life of Heydrich* (New Haven, CT, and London: Yale University Press, 2011), 196.

50   "These are lies!": Christopher Simpson, *The Splendid Blond Beast: Money, Law, and Genocide in the Twentieth Century* (Monroe, ME: Common Courage Press, 1995), 81.

50   Schulte was not one of those men: Laqueur and Breitman, *Breaking the Silence*, 115.

51   Leland Harrison . . . took a decidedly skeptical view: Ibid., 148–49.

52   "Germany no longer persecutes the Jews": Breitman and Lichtman, *FDR and the Jews*, 197.

53   The OSS agent sized him up as "somewhat naïve": Lucas Delattre, *A Spy at the Heart of the Third Reich* (New York: Grove Press, 2005), 111.

54   One German cable reported that 120,000 Jews: Ibid., 194.

55   "Why did Dulles choose not to emphasize": Neal H. Petersen, ed., *From Hitler's Doorstep: The Wartime Intelligence Reports of Allen Dulles, 1942–1945* (University Park: Pennsylvania State University Press, 1996), 570.

55   Rudolf Vrba . . . escaped from the camp: For Vrba's and Wetzler's miraculous escape and report on Auschwitz, see Rudolf Vrba, *I Escaped from Auschwitz* (Fort Lee, NJ: Barricade Books, 2002); and the PBS program *Secrets of the Dead*, "Escape from Auschwitz" episode, http://www.pbs.org/wnet/secrets/episodes/escape-from-auschwitz/8/.

56   "He was profoundly shocked": Walter Laqueur, *The Terrible Secret: Suppression of the Truth About Hitler's Final Solution* (New Brunswick, NJ, and London: Transaction Publishers, 2012), 98–99.

Chapter 3: Ghosts of Nuremberg

58   she was forced to hold her breath: Rebecca West, *A Train of Powder: Six Reports on the Problem of Guilt and Punishment in Our Time* (Chicago: Ivan R. Dee, 2000), 10.

59   "I can't imagine that!": Richard Overy, *Interrogations: The Nazi Elite in Allied Hands, 1945* (New York: Penguin Books, 2002), 499.

60   "I have no conscience": Ibid., 500.

60   His first hours in captivity surely encouraged his optimism: Brigadier General Robert I. Stack's OH: "Capture of Goering," 36th Infantry Division Association Web site.

60   "you will say I have robbed you of your sleep": Michael Salter, *Nazi War Crimes, U.S. Intelligence and Selective Prosecution at Nuremberg* (Abingdon, UK: Routledge-Cavendish, 2007), 266.

61   "This was a woman": U.S. War Department documentary, *Death Mills* (1945). https://www.youtube.com/watch?v=vdba86U2g68.

61   "The hilarity in the dock suddenly stopped": Gerald M. Gilbert, *Nuremberg Diary* (New York: Signet, 1947), 45.

61   "These were crocodile tears": Salter, *Nazi War Crimes*, 272.

61   "It was such a good afternoon": Gilbert, *Nuremberg Diary*, 46.

62   Churchill estimated the number: Overy, *Interrogations*, 6.

62   "U[ncle]. J[oe]. took an . . . ultra-respectable line": Ibid., 8.

62   George Kennan . . . was one of those: Christopher Simpson, *The Splendid Blond Beast: Money, Law, and Genocide in the Twentieth Century* (Monroe, ME: Common Courage Press, 1995), 151–52.

63   "piglike rush for immediate profits": Ibid., 134.

63   "I am almost the last capitalist": Letter from Pell to President Roosevelt, Feb. 17, 1936, Pell papers.

63   "Your administration has made possible": Letter from Pell to President Roosevelt, Sept. 18, 1937, Pell papers.

64   "Hackworth was well named": Pell OH.

64 "to make clear to every last German in the world": Quoted in Simpson, *The Splendid Blond Beast*, 140.

65 Pell arrived in a frigidly cold, war-torn London: Leonard Baker, *Brahmin in Revolt: A Biography of Herbert C. Pell* (Garden City, NY: Doubleday & Co., 1972), 265.

66 his political enemies were determined to never let him return: Pell OH, 588–93. See also Baker, *Brahmin in Revolt*, 302–3.

66 "His hands shook so": John Morton Blum, *From the Morgenthau Diaries: Years of War 1941–45* (Boston: Houghton Mifflin, 1967), 416–18.

66 There are two reasons he was targeted: Letter from Pell to David Drucker, Sept. 28, 1945, Pell papers.

67 Dulles's offer of assistance . . . was a "God send": Salter, *Nazi War Crimes*, 348.

67 he had fallen into an OSS "trap": Ibid., 374.

68 Jackson stunned the OSS chief: Telford Taylor, *The Anatomy of the Nuremberg Trials: A Personal Memoir* (Boston: Little, Brown & Co., 1992), 184–85.

69 Taylor . . . later called Donovan's actions "ill conceived": Ibid., 186.

70 "Most men of the caliber required": Allen W. Dulles, "That Was Then: Allen W. Dulles on the Occupation of Germany," *Foreign Affairs* 82, no. 6 (November–December 2003): 2–8.

70 the beneficiaries of politically motivated interventions: Salter, *Nazi War Crimes*, 7–8.

70 "The only motive which guided me was my ardent love": Taylor, *Anatomy of the Nuremberg Trials*, 535.

71 "Who in the world is responsible": Ibid., 535–56.

71 it was likely . . . Wheelis, who smuggled the poison capsule: Ibid., 623–24.

71 For the badly conducted Nuremberg hangings, see "The Execution of Nazi War Criminals" by reporter Kingsbury Smith of International News Service, aw2.umkc.edu/faculty/projects/ftrials/nuremberg/NurembergNews10_16_46.html. See also: "Night Without Dawn," *Time*, Oct. 28, 1946; "Hangman's End," *Time*, Aug. 7, 1950; and Taylor, *Anatomy of the Nuremberg Trials*, 611.

72 For more on *Murderers Among Us*, see the DEFA Film Library at the University of Massachusetts Amherst, http://www.umass.edu/defa/filmtour/sjmurder.shtml. See also: "German Rubble Film 1946–49," http://mubi.com/lists/german-rubble-film–1946–49; and "Rotation 1949: Seeing Through Prison Walls," German Cinema, 1946–49, University of Cambridge Web site, http://timescape.mml.cam.ac.uk/users/djw88/.

Chapter 4: Sunrise

75 "To my great and . . . joyful surprise": Jochen von Lang, *Top Nazi: SS General Karl Wolff—The Man Between Hitler and Himmler* (New York: Enigma Books, 2005), 138.

75 "Don't worry": Christopher Hibbert, *Mussolini: The Rise and Fall of Il Duce* (New York: Palgrave Macmillan, 2008), 312.

75 "I am crucified": Ibid., 287.

76 "My hands were tied": Ibid., 312.

76 "there was a great danger": Allen Dulles, *The Secret Surrender* (New York: Harper & Row, 1966), 177.

77 Dulles identified himself as "special representative": From a 1945 interrogation of Wolff by Allied officers, released by CIA under the Nazi War Crimes Disclosure Act; Names file: Karl Wolff, NARA.

78 "I told Gaevernitz that under the strict orders": Dulles, *Secret Surrender*, 177.

79 "I will never forget what you have done": Ibid., 182.

80 "It would have made a lovely headline": "Diary Notes by G.G. on the Rescue of General Wolff," AWD papers, Mudd Library.

80 some historians would identify as the first icy fissures of the Cold War: See, for instance, Bradley Smith and Elena Agarossi, *Operation Sunrise: The Secret Surrender* (New York: Basic Books, 1979), 186–88.

80 some German divisions . . . were told not to lay down their arms: Kerstin von Lingen, "Conspiracy of Silence: How the 'Old Boys' of American Intelligence Shielded SS General Karl Wolff from Prosecution," *Holocaust and Genocide Studies* 22, no. 1 (Spring 2008): 74–109.

80 Truman later wrote in his memoir: Harry S. Truman, *1945: Year of Decisions* (New York: Smithmark Publishers, 1995), 201.

81 "one of the most stunning triumphs": *Time*, Oct. 21, 1966.

81 one of the "dandy officers of the SS": Lang, *Top Nazi*, 119.

82 "Himmler was no businessman": Ibid., 52.

82 For Dulles and Italian Superpower Corp., see Richard Harris Smith, *OSS: The Secret History of America's First Central Intelligence Agency* (Guilford, CT: The Lyons Press, 2005), 107. See also: "Italian Super-Power," *Time*, Jan. 30, 1928; and William J. Hausman, Peter Hertner, and Mira Wilkins, *Global Electrification: Multinational Enterprise and International Finance in the History of Light and Power* (New York: Cambridge University Press, 2008).

83 he was a "moderate": March 9, 1945, Dulles dispatch from Bern, declassified by CIA under Nazi War Crimes Disclosure Act, NARA.

83 "The conclusions . . . must be left to history": Dulles, *Secret Surrender*, 238.

83 "one of the unknown giants": Lang, *Top Nazi*, viii.

84 a highly incriminating letter written by Wolff: Michael Salter, *Nazi War Crimes, U.S. Intelligence and Selective Prosecution at Nuremberg* (Abingdon, UK: Routledge-Cavendish, 2007), 51.

84 Wolff also played a key administrative role: Michael Salter and Suzanne Ost, "War Crimes and Legal Immunities: The Complicities of Waffen-SS General Karl Wolff in Nazi Medical Experiments," *Rutgers Journal of Law and Religion* 4, no. 1 (2004): 1–69, http://lawandreligion.com/sites/lawandreligion.com/files/SalterOst.pdf.

85 Wolff relaxed on the villa's terrace: Eugen Dollmann, *Call Me Coward* (London: William Kimber, 1956), 11–17.

86 had promised him "honorable treatment": For the Dulles team's promises to Wolff, see Salter, *Nazi War Crimes*, 118–21.

87 enjoyed a pleasant summer idyll on the lake: Lingen, "Conspiracy of Silence."

88 Dulles went so far as to bury incriminating evidence: Ibid.

88 it was a way "to prevent me [from] talking": Ibid.

89 he began to have his conversations secretly taped: Salter, *Nazi War Crimes*, 119.

89 Wolff's letters to President Truman and Major General Lemnitzer, and Wolff-related correspondence between Dulles and Lemnitzer: AWD papers, Mudd Library.

89 Wolff insisted that Dulles must come to his aid: Norbert George Barr papers, 1942–1953, Columbia University Rare Books Library.

91 "It seemed like old times": Gaevernitz letter to Dulles, June 18, 1949, AWD papers, Mudd Library.

91 "KW doesn't realize what a lucky man": AWD letter to Waibel, June 12, 1950, AWD papers, Mudd Library.

92 Hitler . . . "completely approved" of his Operation Sunrise machinations: Lang, *Top Nazi*, 339.

93 Wolff had developed a side business: Christopher Simpson, *Blowback* (New York: Collier Books, 1989), 236.

93   Wolff . . . "was most polite": Wolff file, NARA. All of Names files released under Nazi War Crimes Disclosure Act courtesy of Freedom of Information Act attorney James Lesar.

Chapter 5: Ratlines

95   "At least in Dachau they had wooden huts": Eugen Dollmann, *Call Me Coward* (London: William Kimber, 1956), 46.

95   "a delicate alabaster statue": Ibid., 58.

96   His wife, Cicely, would rhapsodize about his "El Greco face": Tom Mangold, *Cold Warrior: James Jesus Angleton, the CIA's Master Spy Hunter* (New York: Touchstone, 1991), 37.

97   In Rome, the two men conferred: Burton Hersh, *The Old Boys: The American Elite and the Origins of the CIA* (St. Petersburg, FL: Tree Farm Books, 2002), 166.

97   "He was talking like a young university lecturer": Dollmann, *Call Me Coward*, 85.

97   "a leather-faced Puritan archangel": Ibid., 30.

98   "We were all afraid you had been killed": Ibid., 93.

99   In Naples, he was invited: Eugen Dollmann, *The Interpreter* (London: Hutchinson, 1967), 37–41.

100   Dollmann later tried to make sense: Ibid., 76–78.

101   "She loved crocodile in every shape and form": Ibid., 117.

101   by reading selections from Hitler's thick police dossier: Robert Katz, "The Talented Doktor Dollmann," The Boot.it, http://www.theboot.it/dollmann's_talent.htm.

102   Heydrich demanded that Dollmann take him: Dollmann, *The Interpreter*, 94–95.

102   "a self-serving opportunist": Michael Salter, *Nazi War Crimes, U.S. Intelligence and Selective Prosecution at Nuremberg* (Abingdon, UK: Routledge-Cavendish, 2007), 73.

103   "one of my most disagreeable acquaintances": Dollmann, *Call Me Coward*, 48.

103   For more on Rauff's mobile crematoria, see Ernst Klee, ed., *"The Good Old Days": The Holocaust as Seen by Its Perpetrators and Bystanders* (Old Saybrook, CT: Konecky and Konecky, 1991), 68–74; "Walter Rauff: Letters to the Gas Van Expert," Holocaust Education and Archive Research Team, http://www.holocaustresearchproject.org/einsatz/rauff.html; and "The Development of the Gas-Van in the Murdering of the Jews," Jewish Virtual Library, www.jewishvirtuallibrary.org/jsource/Holocaust/vans.html.

104   Dollmann felt a firm hand: Dollmann, *Call Me Coward*, 108.

105   "Please call this number": Author interview with William Gowen.

105   "a devious and arrogant son of a bitch": Ibid.

106   Rauff would cap his bloody career in Chile: Names file: Rauff, NARA; "Wanted Nazi Walter Rauff Was West German Spy," BBC News, Sept. 27, 2011.

107   "When I got to Rome": Author interview with William Gowen.

112   U.S. surveillance of Dollmann began getting interesting: Names file: Dollmann, NARA.

114   Siragusa had proved very useful to Angleton: Douglas Valentine, *The Strength of the Wolf: The Secret History of America's War on Drugs* (London: Verso, 2004), 109 and 227.

116   "From the little English I know": Katz, "The Talented Doktor Dollmann."

Chapter 6: Useful People

119   But, still, the imposing figure struck her as "arrogant": Author interview with Joan Talley.

120 "I want you to know I can see how much you and Allen care for each other": Peter Grose, *Gentleman Spy: The Life of Allen Dulles* (Boston: Houghton Mifflin Co., 1994), 224.

120 "the most complex and overwhelming": MB journal, Feb. 23, 1978, MB papers.

120 "those cold, blue eyes of his": Ibid.

120 "that rather peculiar, mirthless laugh": Mary Bancroft, *Autobiography of a Spy* (New York: Morrow, 1983), 133.

120 "in the presence of superior possibilities": William McGuire and R. F. C. Hull, eds., *C. G. Jung Speaking: Interviews and Encounters* (Princeton, NJ: Princeton University Press, 1987), 258.

121 "like a robot, or a mask of a robot": Ibid., 127.

121 "quite a tough nut": Bancroft, *Autobiography of a Spy*, 140.

122 "was constantly on his lips": Ibid., 134.

122 "I married Allen": Grose, *Gentleman Spy*, 75.

123 "some poor convicts": Ibid., 74.

123 Her mother would make "fairy circles": "Parents Journal," MCD papers.

123 "We simply weren't ready for Latin yet": Ibid.

124 "To me it was a terrible strain": Ibid.

125 "I suppose I did kill [Paul]": MCD journal, Feb. 17, 1947.

125 "his life was somewhere else": Author interview with Joan Talley.

126 "As for Allen, . . . when anyone was in trouble": MB journal, Feb. 23, 1978.

127 "Dad asked for news": Clover Dulles letter to Joan Talley, Feb. 18, 1945, MCD papers.

127 "My husband doesn't converse with me": Grose, *Gentleman Spy*, 246.

128 "My wife is an angel": Bancroft, *Autobiography of a Spy*, 241.

128 Clover drew herself as a crying, forlorn donkey: Ibid., 246.

128 "nothing short of a miracle": "Freudian Analysis, Jungian Analysis," May 7, 1947, MCD papers.

129 "My whole stomach had collapsed": MCD dream journal, Nov. 25, 1945.

130 "no solution but for you and me to be killer whales": Bancroft, *Autobiography of a Spy*, 244.

131 "at the height of my sexual prowess": Deirdre Bair, *Jung: A Biography* (Boston: Little, Brown and Co., 2003), 488.

132 "He actually shimmered with it": MB journal, Feb. 23, 1978.

132 "I longed for a life of adventure": Bancroft, *Autobiography of a Spy*, 7.

132 "One of my [OSS] colleagues was frantic": MB, Columbia University oral history project, Schlesinger Library.

133 "What do those people actually *do*?": Bancroft, *Autobiography of a Spy*, 132.

133 he gave the psychologist an OSS number—Agent 488: Bair, *Jung: A Biography*, 492.

133 "Quick!" he barked: Bancroft, *Autobiography of a Spy*, 152.

134 "Why the hell didn't you go?" Ibid., 191.

134 "saturated with Nazi ideology": Bair, *Jung: A Biography*, 494.

134 "Power was my natural element": Bancroft, *Autobiography of a Spy*, 112.

135 by Mary's standards, he was by no means sexually reckless: MB journal, Feb. 23, 1978.

135 "In order to engage in intelligence work": Bancroft, *Autobiography of a Spy*, 89.

135 "I like to watch the little mice": MB journal, Feb. 23, 1978.

136 "just like music": Author interview with Joan Talley.

137 the spymaster kept asking the young man to "prove himself": See Fritz Molden, *Exploding Star: A Young Austrian Against Hitler* (New York: William Morrow & Co., 1979), 203.

137 Joan found Fritz a "very erratic character": Author interview with Joan Talley.

138 "would have gone on trying endlessly": Letter to AWD, July 3, 1959, MCD papers.

139   The opposite of love is not hate: Bancroft, *Autobiography of a Spy*, 95.

Chapter 7: Little Mice

142   she christened her "house of horrors": Erica Wallach, *Light at Midnight* (New York: Doubleday, 1967), 4.

142   "This business of nothing to look at": *Philadelphia Inquirer*, March 29, 1987.

143   "Horror, fear, mental torture": Wallach, *Light at Midnight*, 6.

143   "A person living a normal life": Hermann Field and Kate Field, *Trapped in the Cold War: The Ordeal of an American Family* (Stanford, CA: Stanford University Press, 1999), 101.

144   "I must admit that these days I find it hard to concentrate": Peter Grose, *Gentleman Spy: The Life of Allen Dulles* (Boston: Houghton Mifflin Co., 1994), 257.

145   "Our war is over": Joseph Trento, *The Secret History of the CIA* (Roseville, CA: Prima Publishing, 2001), 44.

146   "The difference between us": Grose, *Gentleman Spy*, 267.

146   "that bastard": Leonard Mosley, *Dulles* (New York: Doubleday, 1978), 251.

147   The CIA . . . "has the duty to act": *The Central Intelligence Agency: A Report to the National Security Council*, Allen Dulles, chairman, January 1949, http://www.foia.cia.gov/sites/default/files/document_conversions/45/dulles_correa.pdf.

147   Dulles scrutinized the election tallies from Rome: Grose, *Gentleman Spy*, 285.

148   At least $2 million of the money: Christopher Simpson, *Blowback* (New York: Collier Books, 1989), 126.

151   "I want to work for world peace": Mosley, *Dulles*, 49.

151   dedicate his life to becoming a "saint": Tony Sharp, *Stalin's American Spy: Noel Field, Allen Dulles and the East European Show Trials* (London: Hurst & Company, 2013), 16.

151   "by far the most practical field": Ibid., 20.

152   "a stupid child in the woods": Ibid., 29.

153   Schlesinger took a strong disliking to Field: Arthur Schlesinger Jr., *A Life in the Twentieth Century* (Boston: Houghton Mifflin Co., 2002), 334. See also Schlesinger's review of *Red Pawn: The Story of Noel Field* by Flora Lewis in *The New York Review of Books*, Feb. 11, 1965.

154   Hermann was taken from his cell for another round of grilling: Field and Field, *Trapped in the Cold War*, 155–70.

155   Operation Splinter Factor succeeded beyond the OPC's wildest dreams: See Stewart Steven, *Operation Splinter Factor: The Untold Story of the West's Most Secret Cold War Intelligence Operation* (London: Hodder and Stoughton, 1974).

155   "The comrades are merrily sticking knives": Mosley, *Dulles*, 277.

155   "Dulles wished to leave Eastern Europe devoid of hope": Steven, *Operation Splinter Factor*, 146.

156   "He would never talk to me about his years in prison": Schlesinger, *Life in the Twentieth Century*, 502.

157   "I was continuously interrogated": *Philadelphia Inquirer*, March 29, 1987.

157   "From a European point of view": Wallach, *Light at Midnight*, 396.

157   "Allen Dulles's motives are easy to imagine": From Erica Wallach interview with James Srodes, Feb. 10, 1993, courtesy of the George C. Marshall Foundation Library.

Chapter 8: Scoundrel Time

159   "one of the greatest thrills of my life": Peter Grose, *Gentleman Spy: The Life of Allen Dulles* (Boston: Houghton Mifflin Co., 1994), 280.

159 "the hangover philosophies of the New Deal": Roger Morris, *Richard Milhous Nixon: The Rise of an American Politician* (New York: Henry Holt & Co., 1990), 363.

160 "This will be no junket": Ibid.

161 he spent a frigid Christmas week: Ibid., 179–80.

162 "we have worked together": AWD letter to Nixon, Feb. 20, 1961, AWD papers, Mudd Library.

162 "Allen Dulles . . . told him to keep quiet": John Loftus and Mark Aarons, *The Secret War Against the Jews: How Western Espionage Betrayed the Jewish People* (New York: St. Martin's Griffin, 1994), 221; and author interview with John Loftus.

163 by demanding a congressional investigation of the controversial Bank for International Settlements: Charles Higham, *Trading with the Enemy: The Nazi-American Money Plot, 1933–1949* (New York: Authors Guild Backprint Edition, 2007), 11.

164 by calling for the nationalization: See Jerry Voorhis, *Beyond Victory* (New York: Farrar & Rinehart, Inc., 1944).

164 "typical representatives of the Southern California middle class": Anthony Summers, *The Arrogance of Power: The Secret World of Richard Nixon* (London: Victor Gollancz, 2000), 46.

164 "young man fresh out of the Navy": Ibid., 47.

166 "This is a friend of yours": Stephen E. Ambrose, *Nixon: The Education of a Politician, 1913–1962* (New York: Touchstone, 1988), 138.

166 "Of course I knew": Ibid., 140.

167 "We've been had!": Richard Nixon, *Six Crises* (New York: Touchstone, 1990), 10.

168 Chambers was "short and pudgy": Ibid., 2.

168 "I am a graduate of Harvard Law School": Summers, *Arrogance of Power*, 67.

168 "It absolutely ripped Nixon apart": Ibid.

169 "One of the most trying experiences": Nixon, *Six Crises*, 19.

170 "an orgy in unconscious self-revelation": Arthur Schlesinger Jr., *Journals: 1952–2000* (New York: Penguin Press, 2007), 153.

170 Nixon was a "sick" man: Ibid., 154.

170 "It was clear he did not want to proceed": Ambrose, *Nixon: The Education of a Politician*, 178.

171 Some of this confidential information about Hiss: Summers, *Arrogance of Power*, 78.

171 The HUAC investigation could have been "acutely embarrassing": Nixon, *Six Crises*, 21.

172 "He was no more concerned about whether Hiss": Summers, *Arrogance of Power*, 67.

173 "We built [the typewriter]": John Dean, *Blind Ambition: The White House Years* (New York: Simon & Schuster, 1976), 57.

173 "unparalleled venom": Nixon, *Six Crises*, 67.

174 "not a revolution by violence": Whittaker Chambers, *Witness* (Washington, DC: Regnery Publishing, 2001), 472.

174 "it was a call to arms": Interview with Hiss conducted by Judah Graubart and Alice V. Graubart for their book, *Decade of Destiny* (Chicago: Contemporary Books, 1978). Available on "The Alger Hiss Story" Web site, iles.nyu.edu/th15/public/home.html.

176 "We looked at each other": Chambers, *Witness*, 73.

176 "his attitude to me": Summers, *Arrogance of Power*, 69.

176 "The true story of the Hiss case": Ibid., 68.

177 "the most important U.S. government economist": James M. Boughton, "The Case Against Harry Dexter White: Still Not Proven" (working paper, International Monetary Fund, 2000).

177 a "New Deal for a new world": R. Bruce Craig, *Treasonable Doubt: The Harry Dexter White Spy Case* (Lawrence: University Press of Kansas, 2004), 144–45.

179 "Allen Dulles's mouthpiece in Congress": Loftus and Aarons, *Secret War Against the Jews*, 222.

179 Bentley, however, proved a highly problematic witness: See Craig, *Treasonable Doubt*; also Kathryn S. Olmsted, *Red Spy Queen: A Biography of Elizabeth Bentley* (Chapel Hill: University of North Carolina Press, 2004).

180 "I cannot say he was a Communist": Chambers, *Witness*, 431.

180 even . . . Clyde Tolson: Craig, *Treasonable Doubt*, 73.

180 "the American creed": Harry Dexter White testimony before the House Un-American Activities Committee, Aug. 13, 1948, courtesy of Hoover Institution Library and Archives, Stanford University.

185 Drew Pearson . . . dropped a bombshell: Drew Pearson, Washington Merry-Go-Round, Sept. 29, 1952; see also Mark Feldstein, *Poisoning the Press: Richard Nixon, Jack Anderson, and the Rise of Washington's Scandal Culture* (New York: Picador, 2010), 46–47.

186 He sent a photostatic copy: Summers, *Arrogance of Power*, 133.

186 "We'd better see Allen Dulles": Ibid.

187 Wisner had even urged that Malaxa . . . be deported: Declassified March 14, 1951, CIA memo, Names file: Malaxa, NARA.

187 The Malaxa money trail: Ibid.

188 "mutilated them in a vicious parody": United States Holocaust Memorial Museum, Romania exhibit, http://www.ushmm.org/wlc/en/article.php?ModuleId =10005472.

189 "perhaps the most concise appraisal": Names file: Malaxa, NARA.

190 Walter Winchell exposed the notorious collaborator: Winchell's syndicated column, "A Balkanazi on Broadway," May 21, 1948.

190 "strategically and economically important": Summers, *Arrogance of Power*, 132.

191 "Smith was a man who could cuss": Ibid., 133.

192 Malaxa reached out the hand of friendship: Declassified CIA memo, Jan. 16, 1953, Names file: Malaxa, NARA.

Chapter 9: The Power Elite

193 "a goddamned anarchist": Kathryn Mills, ed., *C. Wright Mills: Letters and Autobiographical Writings* (Berkeley: University of California Press, 2000), 218.

194 "not adequate even as an approximate model": C. Wright Mills, *The Power Elite* (New York: Oxford University Press, 2000), 300.

194 "the fraternity of the successful": Ibid., 281.

195 America's "invisible elite": Ibid., 289.

196 "I look forward to the time": Quoted in John H. Summers, "The Deciders," *New York Times*, May 14, 2006.

196 "I am a politician without a party": Kathryn Mills, *C. Wright Mills*, 303.

196 the CIA continued to identify him: Summers, "The Deciders."

196 "The men of the higher circles": C. Wright Mills, *Power Elite*, 361.

197 "most of these politicians": Lisagor and Lipsius, 127.

197 "There can be no question": Richard Helms, *A Look over My Shoulder: A Life in the Central Intelligence Agency* (New York: Ballantine Books, 2003), 63.

197 "The real truth": Peter Dale Scott, *The Road to 9/11: Wealth, Empire and the Future of America* (Berkeley: University of California Press, 2007), 1.

197 "but it did create within the political arena": C. Wright Mills, *Power Elite*, 272.

198 "For the first time in American history": Ibid., 184.

198 "Such men as these": John H. Summers, ed., *The Politics of Truth: Selected Writings of C. Wright Mills* (New York: Oxford University Press, 2008), 134.

199   "It would be unfair to say": C. Wright Mills, *Power Elite*, 235.

200   "What reason have you to think I have ever been a Democrat?": Stephen E. Ambrose, *Eisenhower: Soldier and President* (New York: Touchstone, 1991), 259.

200   "save this country from going to Hades": Ibid., 247.

200   The two men did not immediately hit it off: Townsend Hoopes, *The Devil and John Foster Dulles* (Boston: Little, Brown, 1973), 137.

200   "Dull, Duller, Dulles": Jim Newton, *Eisenhower: The White House Years* (New York: Doubleday, 2011), 86.

201   "We should be dynamic": John Foster Dulles, "A Policy of Boldness," *Life*, May 19, 1952.

201   he frantically paced the room: Hoopes, *Devil and John Foster Dulles*, 129.

202   a "solid tree trunk of a man": Ibid., 3.

202   a "tough-fibered individual": Ibid., 140.

203   soon had Eisenhower "in his palm": Ibid., 138.

203   "The general was in fine form this morning": Peter Grose, *Gentleman Spy: The Life of Allen Dulles* (Boston: Houghton Mifflin Co., 1994), 325.

203   Dulles proved his loyalty to the Eisenhower-Nixon campaign: Howard Kohn, "The Hughes-Nixon-Lansky Connection: The Secret Alliances of the CIA from World War II to Watergate," *Rolling Stone*, May 20, 1976.

203   "Smith lacked confidence in Dulles's self-restraint": Ludwell Lee Montague, *General Walter Bedell Smith as Director of Central Intelligence* (University Park: Pennsylvania State University Press, 1992), 264.

204   he found himself outmaneuvered by the Dulles brothers: Hoopes, *Devil and John Foster Dulles*, 145.

205   "America's most covert president": Blanche Wiesen Cook, *The Declassified Eisenhower* (New York: Penguin Books, 1984), xv.

205   "The national security complex became": David Halberstam, *The Fifties* (New York: Ballantine Books, 1994), 371.

205   Senator Joseph McCarthy married his office aide: *Washington Post*, Sept. 30, 1953.

206   there was a "conspiracy" to sabotage Eisenhower's presidency: Curt Gentry, *J. Edgar Hoover: The Man and the Secrets* (New York: W. W. Norton & Co., 1991), 436.

208   a troubled Truman wrote to Eleanor Roosevelt: Ted Morgan, *Reds: McCarthyism in Twentieth-Century America* (New York: Random House, 2003), 321.

208   "I'm going to say that I disagree with you": Ibid., 421.

208   "would continue the suicidal Kremlin-shaped policies": Ibid., 423.

209   "The thing that has puzzled me a great deal": ELD OH.

210   "I felt it in Allen": Ibid.

210   "Every once in a while we were teased": AWD OH, Mudd Library.

211   instructed his brother to arrange a secret CIA payment: David Atlee Phillips, *Secret Wars Diary: My Adventures in Combat, Espionage Operations and Covert Action* (Bethesda, MD: Stone Tail Press, 1988), 126.

211   s speech he planned to deliver on the Soviet Union was "rotten": Ibid.

212   "just how cozy the Dulles brothers' arrangement": Joseph B. Smith, *Portrait of a Cold Warrior* (New York: Putnam, 1976), 102.

212   McLeod was "anti-intellectual": Hoopes, *Devil and John Foster Dulles*, 153.

214   "I went over to New York": ELD OH.

215   "McCarthy with a white collar": Stephen E. Ambrose, *Nixon: The Education of a Politician, 1913–1962* (New York: Touchstone, 1988), 312.

216   "one obsession: to remain secretary of state": Hoopes, *Devil and John Foster Dulles*, 160.

216   "My brother was never a witch hunter": AWD OH, Mudd Library.

217   "Schine was Cohn's dumb blonde": Morgan, *Reds*, 429.

218   "a book burning": Ibid., 441.

218   found other ways to embarrass their country: Ibid., 443.

219   suspected Dulles of "secret communist leanings": Mark Riebling, *Wedge: How the Secret War Between the FBI and CIA Has Endangered National Security* (New York: Touchstone, 2002), 120.

219   "Penetration begins at home": Quoted in James DiEugenio and Lisa Pease, eds., *The Assassinations* (Port Townsend, WA: Feral House, 2003), 141.

219   rumored to occasionally show off photographic evidence of Hoover's intimate relationship: See Anthony Summers, *Official and Confidential: The Secret Life of J. Edgar Hoover* (New York: Putnam, 1993).

219   "that Virgin Mary in pants": Gentry, *J. Edgar Hoover: The Man and the Secrets*, 418.

220   "Joe McCarthy is a bachelor of 43 years": Ibid., 433.

220   The senator was as surprised as many others: See George Washington University Historical Encyclopedia entry on Jean Fraser Kerr: http://encyclopedia.gwu.edu/index.php?title=Kerr,_Jean_Fraser.

220   McCarthy's habit of drunkenly groping young girls' breasts: Gentry, *J. Edgar Hoover: The Man and the Secrets*, 434.

221   "Roy was furious": Walter Pforzheimer interview, CIA Web site: www.cia.gov/library/center-for-the-study-of-intelligence/kent-csi/vol44no5/html/v44i5a05p.htm.

221   "blatant attempt to thwart the authority of the Senate": *New York Times*, July 10, 1953.

221   "I'd kick them out": *Washington Post*, Aug. 8, 1954.

222   "McCarthy has just suffered his first total . . . defeat": *New York Herald-Tribune*, July 17, 1953.

222   "'John Foster Dulles's tougher, younger brother'": *Buffalo Evening News*, July 15, 1953.

222   Not all of the press reaction . . . was so enthusiastic: Grose, *Gentleman Spy*, 346.

223   "I emerged from my [FBI] ordeal": Cord Meyer, *Facing Reality: From World Federalism to the CIA* (Lanham, MD: University Press of America, 1980), 80.

223   "It may be necessary to liquidate Senator McCarthy": Morgan, *Reds*, 475.

224   "take a firm stand, like Allen Dulles": Ambrose, *Nixon*, 316.

224   "We'll wreck the Army": Morgan, *Reds*, 468.

Chapter 10: The Dulles Imperium

227   the Iranian royals looked "worn, gloomy and anxious": Stephen Kinzer, *All the Shah's Men* (Hoboken, NJ: John Wiley & Sons, 2008), 177.

227   "We do not have much money": Abbas Milani, *The Shah* (New York: Palgrave Macmillan, 2011), 189.

228   "Who is going to play tennis with me": "Iran: The People Take Over," *Time*, Aug. 31, 1953.

228   "I took her on the staircase": Scott Eyman, *John Wayne: The Life and Legend* (New York: Simon & Schuster, 2014), 483.

229   Frank Wisner insisted the simultaneous arrival: Tim Weiner, *Legacy of Ashes: The History of the CIA* (New York: Anchor Books, 2008), 102–3.

229   "By the end of the 1980s, most countries in the Middle East": Ervand Abrahamian, *The Coup: 1953, the CIA, and the Roots of Modern U.S.-Iranian Relations* (New York: The New Press, 2013), 82.

230   "This would be the largest overseas development project": Stephen Kinzer, *The Brothers: John Foster Dulles, Allen Dulles, and Their Secret World War* (New York: Times Books/Henry Holt & Co., 2013), 120.

231 "break the back of future generations": Ibid., 123.

231 "delightfully childlike way": Peter Grose, *Gentleman Spy: The Life of Allen Dulles* (Boston: Houghton Mifflin Co., 1994), 364.

231 Mossadegh, who sent the president-elect a heartfelt note: The Mossadegh-Eisenhower Cables, http://www.mohammadmossadegh.com/biography/dwight-d-eisenhower/cables/.

232 suggesting that . . . Mossadegh's government: Weiner, *Legacy of Ashes*, 96.

232 "a maturing revolutionary set-up": Ibid.

232 the global crisis over Iran was not a Cold War conflict: Abrahamian, *The Coup*, 4.

233 "I dubbed [Roosevelt] 'the quiet American'": Leonard Mosley, *Dulles* (New York: Doubleday, 1978), 354.

234 "This was a grave decision": Kermit Roosevelt, *Countercoup: The Struggle for the Control of Iran* (New York: McGraw-Hill, 1979), 18.

234 The general's mangled corpse: Abrahamian, *The Coup*, 179.

235 Mossadegh "lost his nerve": Ibid., 190.

236 He was "a wimp": Evan Thomas, *The Very Best Men: The Early Years of the CIA* (New York: Touchstone, 1996), 109.

236 the shah and Queen Soraya were photographed on a shopping: "Iran: The People Take Over," *Time*, Aug. 31, 1953.

236 the anything goes "new morality" toward sex: Peter Schweizer and Wynton C. Hall, eds., *Landmark Speeches of the American Conservative Movement* (College Station: Texas A&M University Press, 2007), 55.

236 While Dulles was dallying with Luce's wife: Kinzer, *The Brothers*, 202.

237 His "jaw dropped": *Time*, Aug. 31, 1953.

237 "Four times a night": Mosley, *Dulles*, 355.

238 "The shah is living in a dream world": Abrahamian, *The Coup*, 198–99.

238 "Allen would give his left": Miles Copeland, *The Game Player: Confessions of the CIA's Original Political Operative* (London: Aurum Press, 1989), 127.

238 "no one paid any attention to him": "Will Iran Be Another Korea?" *Newsweek*, Aug. 31, 1953.

238 he convinced them to share his exuberance: See William A. Dorman and Mansour Farhang, *The U.S. Press and Iran: Foreign Policy and the Journalism of Deference* (Berkeley: University of California Press, 1987), 31–62.

231 "basically a hollow man": *New York Times*, Jan. 7, 1979.

239 Kim Roosevelt was among those who cashed in: William Blum, *Killing Hope: U.S. Military and CIA Interventions Since World War II* (Monroe, ME: Common Courage Press, 2004), 71.

239 "It was a day that should never have ended": *New York Times*, April 16, 2000. For more about internal CIA reports on Iran coup, see the National Security Archive, http://www2.gwu.edu/~nsarchiv/NSAEBB/NSAEBB435/.

240 more like listening to a rousing "dime novel": David Atlee Phillips, *Secret Wars Diary: My Adventures in Combat, Espionage Operations and Covert Action* (Bethesda, MD: Stone Tail Press, 1988), 131.

240 "purring like a giant cat": Thomas, *Very Best Men*, 110.

240 the shah unleashed his secret police: Ervand Abrahamian, *Tortured Confessions: Prisons and Pubic Recantations in Modern Iran* (Berkeley: University of California Press, 1999), 88–101.

241 Even in death, Mossadegh was taunted by the U.S. press: See "Mossadegh Gets Quiet Iran Burial," The Mossadegh Project, http://www.mohammadmossadegh.com/news/ap-associated-press/march-6-1967/.

242 "He was as nervous as I had ever seen him": Evan Thomas, *Ike's Bluff: President Eisenhower's Secret Battle to Save the World* (New York: Little, Brown & Co., 2012), 7.

243 "I'll just confuse them": Ibid., 160–61.

244 the United States must overcome the "taboo" against nuclear weapons: Ibid., 71.

245 "a curious juncture in the history of human insanity": C. Wright Mills, *The Causes of World War III* (New York: Simon & Schuster, 1958), 113.

245 he offered to give two "A-bombs" to French foreign minister: John Prados, *Operation Vulture* (New York: iBooks/Simon & Schuster, 2004), 208.

245 Foster was surprised to learn: Thomas, *Ike's Bluff*, 158.

246 "doctrinaire and murderous rigidity": Mills, *The Causes of WW III*, 112.

246 "I watched Dulles making notes": Nikita Sergeevich Khrushchev, *Khrushchev Remembers* (Boston: Little, Brown, 1970), 397.

246 Foster sent out a long cable: Townsend Hoopes, *The Devil and John Foster Dulles* (Boston: Little, Brown, 1973), 302.

248 "Allen, can't you find an assassin?": Richard Harris Smith, "Allen Dulles and the Politics of Assassination," *Washington Post*, Dec. 2, 1975.

248 The secretary of state assured the oilmen: Mills, *The Causes of WW III*, 65–66.

249 "takes a strange kind of genius to run it": Weiner, *Legacy of Ashes*, 156.

250 Bush "was the day-to-day contact man for the CIA": Joseph J. Trento, *Prelude to Terror: The Rogue CIA and the Legacy of America's Private Intelligence Network* (New York: Carroll & Graf Publishers, 2005), 8–9.

250 "Walter, you tell Mr. Dulles that he had his hearing": James Srodes, *Allen Dulles: Master of Spies* (Washington, DC: Regnery Publishing, 1999), 486.

250 "The things we did were 'covert'": Jim Newton, *Eisenhower: The White House Years* (New York: Doubleday, 2011), 108.

250 "Dad could be fooled": Thomas, *Ike's Bluff*, 142.

251 "scared the hell out of us": Grose, *Gentleman Spy*, 446.

251 "ardent disciples of Allen Dulles": L. Fletcher Prouty, *The Secret Team: The CIA and Its Allies in Control of the United States and the World* (New York: Skyhorse Publishing, 2008), 368.

251 Arbenz was showered with abuse: "Guatemala: Battle of the Backyard," *Time*, Sept. 20, 1954.

252 Hunt claimed that he had spread the word: Ann Louise Bardach, "Scavenger Hunt," *Slate*, Oct. 6, 2004.

252 "They were trying to break him down": Author interview with Erick Arbenz.

253 The agency's disinformation campaign began immediately: See Roberto Garcia Ferreira, "The CIA and Jacobo Arbenz: History of a Disinformation Campaign," *Journal of Third World Studies* 25, no. 2 (Fall 2008): 59–81.

254 The tragedy was "trapped in his head": Ibid.

254 Hunt . . . continued to track closely the man: Ann Louise Bardach, "Scavenger Hunt."

255 Arbenz's beloved daughter, Arabella: Rich Cohen, *The Fish That Ate the Whale: The Life and Times of America's Banana King* (New York: Macmillan, 2012), 206.

256 But Maria Arbenz always believed that her husband had been assassinated: Author interview with Erick and Claudia Arbenz.

257 Jacobo and Maria Arbenz were the Kennedys of Guatemala's fledgling democracy: Piero Gleijeses, *Shattered Hope: The Guatemalan Revolution and the United States, 1944–54* (Princeton, NJ: Princeton University Press, 1991), 134–47.

259 The powerful influence of the United Fruit Company: Stephen Schlesinger and Stephen Kinzer, *Bitter Fruit: The Story of the American Coup in Guatemala* (Cambridge, MA: Harvard University Press, 2005), 102–7.

260 Foster made a discreet tour of Central America: Peter Chapman, *Bananas: How the United Fruit Company Shaped the World* (Edinburgh: Canongate, 2007), 84–85.

260 a "Communist-type reign of terror": *New York Times*, June 16, 1954.
261 Dulles assembled his Guatemala task force in the White House: David Atlee Phillips, *The Night Watch* (New York: Atheneum, 1977), 49–51.
262 an "opéra bouffe": *New York Times*, June 22, 1954.
262 Arthur Hays Sulzberger was extremely accommodating: *New York Times*, June 7, 1997.
263 the CIA had no qualms about compiling a "disposal list": Kate Doyle and Peter Kornbluh, eds., "CIA and Assassinations: The Guatemala 1954 Documents," National Security Archive, http://www2.gwu.edu/~nsarchiv/NSAEBB/NSAEBB4/.
264 the CIA began pressuring him to purge Guatemala: Stephen M. Streeter, *Managing the Counterrevolution: The United States and Guatemala, 1954–1961* (Athens: Ohio University Press, 2000), 37–57.
265 The worst massacre . . . took place in Tiquisate: Cindy Forster, *The Time of Freedom: Campesino Workers in Guatemala's October Revolution* (Pittsburgh, PA: University of Pittsburgh Press, 2001), 219.
265 "turn the country into a cemetery": *New York Times*, Aug. 9, 1981.

Chapter 11: Strange Love

267 "It was a dream come true": Mary Kay Linge, *Willie Mays: A Biography* (Westport, CT: Greenwood Press, 2005), 42.
267 "He quit because he wasn't Joe DiMaggio anymore": Mark Zwonitzer, prod., *Joe DiMaggio: A Hero's Life*, PBS, *American Experience*, 2000.
268 His skin was so pale: James H. Critchfield, *Partners at the Creation: The Men Behind Postwar Germany's Defense and Intelligence Establishments* (Annapolis, MD: Naval Institute Press, 2003), 82.
268 Most of the intelligence gathered by Gehlen's men: Christopher Simpson, *Blowback* (New York: Collier Books, 1989), 44.
268 Herre, who was the rabid baseball fan: Critchfield, *Partners at the Creation*, 96.
269 The German spymaster then leveraged his expertise: See Mary Ellen Reese, *General Reinhard Gehlen: The CIA Connection* (Fairfax, VA: George Mason University Press, 1990); and E. H. Cookridge, *Gehlen: Spy of the Century* (New York: Random House, 1971).
269 after a heated internal debate, the CIA decided to take over: See Kevin C. Ruffner, ed., *Forging an Intelligence Partnership: CIA and the Origins of the BND, 1945–49: A Documentary History* (CIA History Staff, Center for the Study of Intelligence, 1999).
270 some of the most notorious figures of the Nazi regime, such as Dr. Franz Six: Simpson, *Blowback*, 48.
270 Hillenkoetter . . . strongly urged President Truman to "liquidate": Ruffner, *Forging an Intelligence Partnership*, xxii.
270 calling it an old boy's network of ex-Nazi officers: Ibid., xxiii.
271 "reasonably clean slates": Critchfield, *Partners at the Creation*, 86.
272 watched in "shocked silence": Ibid., 6.
272 "impressed us as being unusually intelligent": Ibid., 93.
272 a three-hour "harangue": Memo from Pullach base to CIA special operations, Dec. 30, 1950, Names file: Gehlen, NARA.
272 "He had a high standard of morality": Critchfield, *Partners at the Creation*, 109.
273 "There's no doubt that the CIA got carried away": *Washington Post*, April 24, 2003.
273 at least 13 percent of the Gehlen Organization: Memo to CIA East European station from unnamed official, 1954, NARA.
273 "I've lived with this for [nearly] 50 years": *Washington Post*, March 18, 2001.

274   "a runt": Memo from chief of CIA Foreign Division M to chief of station, Karlsruhe, Oct. 30, 1950, NARA.

274   "a variety of political embarrassments": Memo for CIA deputy director of plans from assistant director, special operations, June 28, 1951, NARA.

274   "Gehlen will be somewhat difficult to control": Memo from Critchfield to unnamed CIA official, undated, NARA.

274   "we were greeted by a famous member of the Mafia": Critchfield, *Partners at the Creation*, 159.

274   "We looked out on the Rockies": Ibid.

275   "the Americans had sold their souls": Memo from chief of CIA Eastern European division to CIA director Dulles, Aug. 8, 1955, NARA.

275   "I don't know if he's a rascal": Simpson, *Blowback*, 260.

275   a small wooden statuette . . . that the German spymaster described as "sinister": Reinhard Gehlen, *The Service: The Memoirs of General Reinhard Gehlen* (New York: Popular Library, 1972), 196.

276   "a symbol of our work against bolshevism": Letter from Gehlen to AWD, Nov. 12, 1956, NARA.

276   Radcliffe . . . made it clear: Memo from chief of CIA Eastern European division to chief of base, Pullach (Critchfield), Feb. 13, 1955, NARA.

276   "below a layer of soiled feminine niceties": Memo from Munich representative of commander, U.S. Naval Forces, Germany to director of Naval Intelligence, Oct. 12, 1955, NARA.

276   a gift from Dulles that was worth as much as 250,000 DM: *Moscow New Times*, May 1972.

276   "I had no personal disputes with Dulles": Gehlen, *The Service*, 196.

277   "UTILITY was blunt in his criticism": Notes for "letter from the field" by unnamed CIA officer, Aug. 5, 1955, NARA.

277   "one will see the cloven hoof of the devil": Memo from CIA Munich station to Bonn station chief, Nov. 17, 1966, NARA.

277   "Allen Dulles had a soft spot": Thomas L. Hughes OH, Association for Diplomatic Studies and Training, Foreign Affairs Oral History Project, interviewed July 7, 1999, http://www.adst.org/OH%20TOCs/Hughes,%20Thomas%20L.toc.pdf.

278   "in an age in which war is a paramount activity": Gehlen, *The Service*, 17.

278   "that spooky Nazi outfit": Simpson, *Blowback*, 260.

279   "John is the more moral of the two": Memo by unnamed CIA official, Feb. 20, 1952, NARA.

279   only if it was done in a grassroots, democratic way: Otto John, *Twice Through the Lines* (New York: Harper & Row, 1972), 226.

279   "My whole impression of John": Memo by AWD, Dec. 6, 1954, NARA.

280   "Once a traitor": Hugh Trevor-Roper, "Why Otto John Defected Thrice," *The Spectator*, April 12, 1997.

281   "a matter of some importance": Memo from James Critchfield to AWD, March 15, 1956, NARA.

282   investigators revealed that the CIA-backed group had compiled a blacklist: Jonathan Kwitny, "The CIA's Secret Armies in Europe," *The Nation*, April 6, 1992.

282   Code-named Operation Gladio: See Daniele Ganser, *NATO's Secret Armies: Operation Gladio and Terrorism in Western Europe* (London: Frank Cass, 2005).

283   implemented wide-ranging surveillance of West German officials and citizens: Heinz Hohne and Hermann Zolling, *The General Was a Spy* (New York: Coward, McCann & Geoghegan, Inc., 1972), 166–83.

283   Gehlen . . . "has let himself be used": CIA dispatch from Bonn, July 9, 1953, NARA.

283 Globke paid a visit to Gehlen's Pullach headquarters: Memo by unnamed CIA official, December 1974, Names file: Globke, NARA.

284 Adenauer asked Dulles point-blank what he thought of Gehlen: Memo from chief of CIA Bonn station to chief of Munich liaison base, June 6, 1963, Names file: Gehlen, NARA.

285 Gehlen "is and always was stupid": Memo from CIA Bonn station to CIA director John McCone, July 12, 1963, NARA.

285 "more in sorrow than anger": Internal CIA memo, Nov. 22, 1963, NARA.

285 thanking Helms for including him in the Gehlen dinner: Letter from AWD to Richard Helms, Sept. 11, 1968, NARA.

286 "I can only be grateful to fate": *Copenhagen Politiken*, July 7, 1974.

Chapter 12: Brain Warfare

287 Dulles delivered an alarming speech: Allen W. Dulles, "Brain Warfare: Russia's Secret Weapon," *U.S. News & World Report*, May 8, 1953.

288 "reluctant to enter into signed agreements": Alfred McCoy, *A Question of Torture: CIA Interrogation, from the Cold War to the War on Terror* (New York: Henry Holt & Co., 2006), 28.

289 "modernized the idea of demonic possession": Timothy Melley, "Brain Warfare: The Covert Sphere, Terrorism and the Legacy of the Cold War," *Grey Room* 45 (Fall 2011): 18–39.

289 a "living puppet": Ibid.

289 largely debunked the brainwash panic: Robert A. Fein, "Prologue: U.S. Experience and Research in Educing Information: A Brief History," in *Educing Information: Interrogation: Science and Art—Foundations for the Future* (Washington, DC: National Defense Intelligence College, 2006).

291 "augmenting the usual interrogation methods": AWD memo to Frank Wisner, Feb. 12, 1951, NARA.

291 a stockade for notorious Nazi POWs: Arnold M. Silver, "Questions, Question, Questions: Memories of Oberursel," *Intelligence and National Security* 8, no. 2 (April 1993): 81–90.

291 the camp was operating as an extreme interrogation center: Annie Jacobsen, *Operation Paperclip* (New York: Little, Brown & Co., 2014), 317–21.

292 Beecher even began drawing on the work done by Nazi doctors: Alfred McCoy, *Torture and Impunity: The U.S. Doctrine of Coercive Interrogation* (Madison: University of Wisconsin Press, 2012), 75–80.

293 "I never gave a thought to legality": John Marks, *The Search for the Manchurian Candidate: The CIA and Mind Control* (New York: W. W. Norton & Co., 1991), 49.

293 "He had a tough time": Jacobsen, *Operation Paperclip*, 367.

294 Olson was suffering a "moral crisis": Family Statement on the Murder of Frank Olson, Aug. 8, 2002, http://www.frankolsonproject.org/Statements/Family Statement2002.html.

294 "fear of a security violation": Ibid.

295 dosed with acid for seventy-seven straight days: Marks, *Search for the Manchurian Candidate*, 67.

295 "We were in a World War II mode": Sidney Gottlieb obituary, *New York Times*, March 10, 1999.

295 "Well, he's gone": H. P. Albarelli Jr., *A Terrible Mistake: The Murder of Frank Olson and the CIA's Secret Cold War Experiments* (Walterville, OR: Trine Day, 2009), 24.

296 "I am exceedingly skeptical": *Los Angeles Times*, Nov. 29, 1994.

297　Dulles invited an old friend and protégé: William Corson, Susan Trento, and Joseph Trento, *Widows* (New York: Crown Publishing, 1989), 19–30.

300　"Allen probably had a special potion": Joseph Trento, *The Secret History of the CIA* (Roseville, CA: Prima Publishing, 2001), 89.

300　"Both my sister and I would have liked my father": Interview with Joan Talley by Mark DePue, Nov. 28, 2007, Abraham Lincoln Presidential Library and Museum oral history program.

300　"I would imagine": Author interview with Joan Talley.

301　"there could have been all kinds of experimentation": Ibid.

301　filled with a new assertiveness: AMD letters to AWD, Mudd Library.

301　which he signed "Affectionately": Letters to AMD, Jan. 8, 1952, and Sept. 13, 1952, from AWD, Mudd Library.

302　"He didn't have to do any of that": James Srodes, *Allen Dulles: Master of Spies* (Washington, DC: Regnery Publishing, 1999), 448.

302　"How do you feel, son?": *New York Times*, Feb. 1, 1953.

303　Dulles wrote an apologetic letter: Letter to Richard P. Butrick, Aug. 3, 1953, AWD correspondence.

303　"My son was very severely wounded": Letter to United Services Automobile Assoc., May 23, 1954, AWD correspondence.

303　"a lovely, old brownstone": DePue interview with Joan Talley.

303　"He couldn't really think": Ibid.

304　The family's finances were soon stretched: Srodes, *Allen Dulles: Master of Spies*, 449.

304　Sonny would stare at his father: Leonard Mosley, *Dulles* (New York: Doubleday, 1978), 374.

304　his father as a Hitler-lover: Author interview with Joan Talley.

304　"I don't know what we're going to do with him": Mosley, *Dulles*, 374.

305　"relentless drive for accomplishment": Donald J. Dalessio and Stephen Silberstein, eds., *Wolff's Headache and Other Pain* (New York: Oxford University Press, 1993), 3.

305　a "mixture of greatness and narrowness": J. N. Blau, "Harold G. Wolff: The Man and His Migraine," *Cephalalgia* 24, no. 3 (March 2004): 215–22.

305　"But who would test me?": Dalessio and Silberstein, *Wolff's Headache and Other Pain*, 4.

306　"potentially useful secret drugs": McCoy, *A Question of Torture*, 45–46.

306　Joan has disturbing memories: Author interview with Joan Talley.

307　"I have just understood the nature": AMD letter to father, AWD correspondence.

308　Cameron saw himself as an iconoclastic innovator: Rebecca Lemov, "Brainwashing's Avatar: The Curious Career of Dr. Ewen Cameron," *Grey Room* 45 (Fall 2011): 61–87.

308　"shock and awe warfare on the mind": Naomi Klein, *The Shock Doctrine: The Rise of Disaster Capitalism* (New York: Metropolitan Books, 2007), 31.

308　"he was a genius at destroying people": Ibid., 47.

309　"like prisoners of the Communists": Ibid., 37.

309　Kastner would come to think of the doctor: Ibid., 26.

309　Orlikow could not remember her husband: *The Scotsman* (Edinburgh), Jan. 6, 2006.

310　"a terrible mistake": Klein, *Shock Doctrine*, 42.

310　the work of Cameron . . . lives on at the agency: Ibid., 39.

310　"He thought my brother could do better": Author interview with Joan Talley.

310　"I wish I could help him": Penfield letter, Feb. 22, 1959, AWD correspondence, Princeton.

310　She felt "joy": Letter to MB, Nov. 1, 1961, Clover Dulles papers, Schlesinger Library.

311　"endlessly patient in general": DePue interview with Joan Talley.

311 "the hands of a person who thinks": Clover Dulles journals, Schlesinger Library.

312 Dulles arranged for his niece: Author interview with Joan Talley.

312 "walking on the bottom of the sea": Letter to MB, Clover Dulles correspondence, Schlesinger Library.

312 recommended that she see Dr. Cameron: Gordon Thomas, *Journey into Madness: The True Story of Secret CIA Mind Control and Medical Abuse* (New York: Bantam Books, 1990), 91–92.

313 "It is a difficult case": Letter to Heinrich Fierz, March 15, 1962, AWD correspondence.

313 "beautiful, great, old estate": DePue interview with Joan Talley.

314 Willeford later recalled that he made a "connection" with Sonny: Karen Croft interview with William Willeford.

314 "Whether the son comes to experience his father": William Willeford, *Feeling, Imagination and the Self* (Evanston, IL: Northwestern University Press, 1987), 94.

314 "Never!" he shouted: Mosley, *Dulles*, 517.

314 arranged to take him out of the sanitarium: Author interview with Joan Talley.

Chapter 13: Dangerous Ideas

316 "left Franco's frying pan": Stuart A. McKeever, *The Galindez Case* (Bloomington, IN: Author House, 2013), 15.

317 their bodies displayed in macabre festivals: Lauren Derby, *The Dictator's Seduction: Politics and the Popular Imagination in the Era of Trujillo* (Durham, NC: Duke University Press, 2009), 2–3.

317 "a method of [execution] that was slower": Mario Vargas Llosa, *The Feast of the Goat* (New York: Picador USA, 2001), 90.

317 "sensation that Trujillo was always watching": Derby, *Dictator's Seduction*, 2.

317 At his 1929 wedding: Ibid., 193.

318 a strutting style of masculinity known as *tigueraje*: Ibid., 186.

318 "one of the hemisphere's foremost spokesmen against the Communist movement": Stephen G. Rabe, "Eisenhower and the Overthrow of Rafael Trujillo," *Journal of Conflict Studies* 6, no. 1 (Winter 1986): 34–44.

318 "Spaniards had many talents": Ibid.

318 The leading symbol of Dominican masculinity: Derby, *Dictator's Seduction*, 175–84.

319 delivering suitcases stuffed with cash: McKeever, *Galindez Case*, 102–3.

320 His own people's doomed crusade: Josu Legarreta, "Jesús de Galíndez: Martyr for Freedom," *Current Events*, issue 72 (2006): 23.

321 Galíndez was "an invaluable informant": McKeever, *Galindez Case*, 111.

321 the Basque exile was strongly critical of U.S. foreign policy: Ibid., 114–16.

321 "may involve informant in personal difficulties": Ibid., 116.

322 Trujillo . . . confronted the traitor: Bernard Diederich, *Trujillo: The Death of the Goat* (Boston: Little, Brown, 1978), 8–9.

323 Joy felt "horrified": *Columbia Daily Spectator*, May 3, 1956.

323 the case worked its way into President Eisenhower's press conference: McKeever, *Galindez Case*, 101–2.

323 Dulles himself communicated the importance of the Galíndez case: Ibid., 92–93.

324 Frank . . . was not part of the CIA's Georgetown inner circle: Jim Hougan, *Spooks* (New York: William Morrow & Co., 1978), 312–25.

325 The CIA used Maheu and Associates as a front: See Hougan, *Spooks*, and Robert Maheu, *Next to Hughes* (New York: Harper Paperbacks, 1992).

325 "Call it my personal Rosebud": Ibid, 19.

325   "I always resented the fact": Author interview with Maheu.

326   Grayson Kirk . . . a trustee of several foundations: "Who Rules Columbia?" original 1968 student strike edition, http://www.democracynow.org/pdf/who-rules-columbia.pdf

326   Galíndez was "suffering from a persecution complex": *Columbia Daily Spectator*, May 3, 1956.

327   the CIA disseminated other disinformation about Galíndez: McKeever, *Galindez Case*, 145–47 and 159–60. See also: Drew Pearson, Washington Merry-Go-Round, June 9, 1960.

327   Murphy's life took a fateful turn: See Hougan, *Spooks*; McKeever, *Galindez Case*; and Diederich, *Trujillo*.

328   even Stuyvesant Wainright . . . waded into the growing controversy: Wainright letter to Dulles, March 6, 1957; Dulles reply, March 15, www.foia.cia.gov.

328   *Life* magazine ran a dramatic version: *Life*, Feb. 25, 1957.

329   "the information given to you by the CIA is vague": McKeever, *Galindez Case*, 212.

329   "like hitting a man with a feather": Ibid., 214.

330   "The production of souls": Nick Romeo, "Is Literature 'the Most Important Weapon of Propaganda'?" The Atlantic.com, June 17, 2014.

330   "a kind of cultural NATO": James Petras, "The CIA and the Cultural Cold War Revisited," *Monthly Review* 51, no. 6 (Nov. 1, 1999): 47–56.

331   "These stylish and expensive excursions": *Salon*, April 16, 2000.

331   Many leading artists and intellectuals fell into the ranks: See Francis Stonor Saunders, *The Cultural Cold War* (New York: New Press, 2001); and Hugh Wilford, *The Mighty Wurlitzer: How the CIA Played America* (Cambridge, MA: Harvard University Press, 2008).

331   "Wright is fortunate in his enemies": Norman Birnbaum, "The Half-Forgotten Prophet: C. Wright Mills," *The Nation*, March 11, 2009.

332   Macdonald . . . broke out of the Cold War thought bubble: Saunders, *Cultural Cold War*, 266.

332   "obviously published under American auspices": Wilford, *Mighty Wurlitzer*, 115.

332   "What did you think of the dominance of poetics by the CIA?": Ibid.

333   "I remember Jim as one of the most complex men": Richard Helms, *A Look over My Shoulder: A Life in the Central Intelligence Agency* (New York: Ballantine Books, 2003), 276.

333   Angleton would report to Dulles on the results of his "fishing expeditions": Michael Howard Holzman, *James Jesus Angleton: The CIA and the Craft of Counterintelligence* (Amherst: University of Massachusetts Press, 2008), 131.

333   "You know how I got to be in charge": Joseph Trento, *The Secret History of the CIA* (Roseville, CA: Prima Publishing, 2001), 478.

334   "They'd start chasing each other": Author interview with Siri Hari Angleton.

335   the exposure of Kim Philby was lodged in the deepest recesses: Helms, *A Look over My Shoulder*, 278.

335   If he were the sort of chap who murdered people: Tom Mangold, *Cold Warrior: James Jesus Angleton, the CIA's Master Spy Hunter* (New York: Touchstone, 1991), 68–69.

335   "I couldn't find that we ever caught a spy": Ibid., 313.

335   "'I'm not a genius'": Author interview with Siri Hari Angleton.

335   "Jim . . . is the apple of my eye": Ibid.

335   "Angleton was fascinating": Author interview with Joan Talley.

336   Clover suspected that the aesthetic spy was "in his cups": Clover Dulles letter to Joan Talley, May 8, 1961, MCD papers.

336   "It is inconceivable that a secret intelligence arm": Robin W. Winks, *Cloak and*

Gown: Scholars in the Secret War, 1939–1961 (New Haven, CT: Yale University Press, 1996), 327.

337   He summoned two Jewish CIA officers: Author interview with confidential source.

338   "I am not Christ": Jon Lee Anderson, *Che Guevara: A Revolutionary Life* (New York: Grove Press, 1997), 199.

339   "This is like prison": *New York Times*, April 25, 1959.

339   "Castro is not only not a Communist": Tad Szulc, *Fidel: A Critical Portrait* (New York: Perennial, 2002), 490.

339   a "pathological hatred for Castro": Anthony R. Carrozza, *William D. Pawley: The Extraordinary Life of the Adventurer, Entrepreneur and Diplomat* (Washington, DC: Potomac Books, 2012), 224.

342   "We Negro people have enough problems": *New York Times*, Sept. 26, 1960.

342   "We don't discriminate against anybody": *New York Times*, Sept. 21, 1960.

342   The gangster was not "a communist": Rosemari Mealy, *Fidel and Malcolm X: Memories of a Meeting* (Baltimore: Black Classic Press, 2013), 36.

342   Wilcox saw a "spiritual connection": Ibid., 37.

343   "told white America to go to hell": Ibid., 48.

344   "Colonies do not speak": Fidel Castro speech to the UN General Assembly, Sept. 26, 1960, http://www.school-for-champions.com/speeches/castro_un_1960.htm#.UalVYBdUa4.

344   I. F. Stone pronounced Castro's oration: D. D. Guttenplan, *American Radical: The Life and Times of I. F. Stone* (New York: Macmillan, 2009), 351.

345   Robert Taber . . . stirred liberal circles: Bill Simpich "Fair Play for Cuba and the Cuban Revolution," *CounterPunch*, July 24, 2009, www.counterpunch.org.

345   "addicted to the habit of conversation": Introductory essay by Gabriel García Márquez, "A Personal Portrait of Fidel," in Fidel Castro, *My Early Years*, ed. Deborah Shnookal and Pedro Álvarez Tabío (Melbourne: Ocean Press, 1998), 13.

346   "the people in Harlem are not so addicted to the propaganda": *New York Citizen-Call*, Sept. 24, 1960.

346   "The only white person that I have really liked was Fidel": Mealy, *Fidel and Malcolm X*, 57.

347   "usually when one sees a man": Confidential FBI memo, Nov. 17, 1960, file # 105–8999, http://vault.fbi.gov/Malcolm%20X/Malcolm%20X%20Part%207%20of%2038.

347   Maheu recounted a long night of soul-searching: Author interview with Robert Maheu.

347   Maheu realized that he would "have blood on [his] hands": Maheu, 138.

348   "What do you want us to do?": Fidel Castro press conference, YouTube, https://www.youtube.com/watch?v=8mqAEslLB3M.

349   "Fidel Castro is part of the legacy of Bolivar": John F. Kennedy, *Strategy of Peace* (New York: HarperCollins, 1960), 167.

349   "betrayed the ideals of the Cuban revolution": JFK campaign speech, Cincinnati, Ohio, Oct. 6, 1960, JFK Library.

350   "I am happy to come to this hotel": JFK campaign speech, Hotel Theresa, New York City, Oct. 12, 1960, JFK Library.

Chapter 14: The Torch Is Passed

352   "Democracy works only": Peter Grose, *Gentleman Spy: The Life of Allen Dulles* (Boston: Houghton Mifflin Co., 1994), 127.

353   "broad social aims": *New York Times*, Sept. 16, 1938.

353 "selling out" his country: *New York Times*, Sept. 20, 1938.

353 "I'm not a political type": Ted Widmer, ed., *Listening In: The Secret White House Recordings of John F. Kennedy* (New York: Hyperion, 2012), 30.

354 "I knew just about everybody": *Newsweek*, April 23, 1962.

354 "aggressively shy": Dave Powers interview, Clay Blair Jr. collection, American Heritage Center, University of Wyoming.

355 "It was great": Ibid.

356 "I just don't think you have to have that type of personality": Widmer, *Listening In*, 39.

356 "All war is stupid": Thurston Clarke, *Ask Not: The Inauguration of John F. Kennedy* (New York: Henry Holt, 2004), 109.

356 "He was very close to my brother": Author interview with Edward M. Kennedy.

356 Dulles first met Kennedy: Dulles OH, JFK Library.

357 "At least one half of the days": Pierre Salinger and Sander Vanocur, *A Tribute to John F. Kennedy* (New York: Encylopaedia Britannica, 1964), 156.

357 Kennedy recited his favorite poem: Arthur M. Schlesinger, *A Thousand Days: John F. Kennedy in the White House* (New York: Mariner Books, 2002), 98.

357 Wrightsman was a globe-trotting oil millionaire: Francesca Stanfill, "Jayne's World," *Vanity Fair*, January 2003.

358 "Jayne and I are leaving Paris": Wrightsman letter to Dulles, July 31, 1953, AWD correspondence, Mudd Library.

358 "The mere mention of the Wrightsmans": MB journal.

359 "He was suffering a good deal of pain": Dulles OH, JFK Library.

360 "At Antibes, we did the usual thing": Clover Dulles letter to Allen Dulles Jr., Sept. 1, 1955, MCD correspondence, Schlesinger Library.

361 Kennedy met with an astute American embassy officer: Seymour Topping, *On the Front Lines of the Cold War* (Baton Rouge, LA: Louisiana State University Press, 2010), 152.

361 "to pour money, materiel and men into the jungle": Remarks of Sen. John F. Kennedy before Senate, April 6, 1954, JFK Library.

362 "The most powerful single force": Remarks of Sen. John F. Kennedy before Senate, July 2, 1957, JFK Library.

363 "That's fine—everybody likes independence": William B. Ewald OH, JFK Library.

363 "that little bastard": AS journals, June 20, 1973, NYPL archives.

363 "He is a terribly cold man": Schlesinger, *A Thousand Days*, 18.

363 While Kennedy's denunciation of French colonialism: Richard D. Mahoney, *JFK: Ordeal in Africa* (New York: Oxford University Press, 1983), 20–21.

364 "Some of the peoples of Africa have been out of trees": Philip E. Muehlenbeck, *Betting on the Africans: John F. Kennedy's Courting of African Nationalist Leaders* (New York: Oxford University Press, 2012), 6.

364 "those niggers": Ibid., 5.

364 "I could see that my brother was in great pain": AWD OH, Mudd Library.

365 "formidable and ruthless challenge": Ibid.

365 "Foster had only days": Grose, *Gentleman Spy*, 461.

366 one of the most "soul-searching questions": White House memorandum for the record, written by A. J. Goodpaster, Feb. 8, 1960, U-2 spy plane files, Eisenhower Library.

366 "a most unusual event": L. Fletcher Prouty, *The Secret Team: The CIA and Its Allies in Control of the United States and the World* (New York: Skyhorse Publishing, 2008), 422.

366 "yelling at the top of his voice": Evan Thomas, *Ike's Bluff: President Eisenhower's Secret Battle to Save the World* (New York: Little, Brown & Co., 2012), 380.

366   never wanted to set eyes on Dulles again: Ibid.

367   "I cannot change Allen Dulles": Tim Weiner, *Legacy of Ashes: The History of the CIA* (New York: Anchor Books, 2008), 193.

367   "a body floating in thin air": Ibid., 194.

367   a "legacy of ashes": Ibid.

368   Bancroft wrote Kennedy a gushing letter: Bancroft letter to JFK, July 14, 1959, MB papers, Schlesinger Library.

368   add his late brother's name: AWD letter to JFK, June 21, 1959, JFK Library.

368   It was Jackie Kennedy who tipped off Dulles: AWD OH, JFK Library.

369   Nixon accused Kennedy: Richard Nixon, *Six Crises* (New York: Touchstone, 1990), 353.

369   "Nixon indicated he thought he'd been double-crossed": AWD OH, JFK Library.

369   Robert Kennedy . . . phoned Dulles at home: AWD memorandum for the record, Sept. 21, 1960, AWD papers, Mudd Library.

370   "As I mentioned to you": AWD memorandum for Gen. Andrew J. Goodpaster, Sept. 25, 1960, Mudd Library.

371   The first thing he should do: Schlesinger, *A Thousand Days*, 125.

371   "He used to be a liberal": AS journals, Aug. 31, 1962, NYPL.

372   "but they shouldn't worry": Schlesinger, *A Thousand Days*, 143.

372   "I'm your basic man-eating shark": Thomas, *Ike's Bluff,* 405.

373   "There must be someone you really trust": Ibid.

373   maintaining a warm correspondence: See AWD papers, Mudd Library.

373   he used his post to identify future prospects: David Atlee Phillips, *Secret Wars Diary: My Adventures in Combat, Espionage Operations and Covert Action* (Bethesda, MD: Stone Tail Press, 1988), 149.

373   "the Pentagon's secretary of state": *Time*, Nov. 15, 1963.

374   secretary, Letitita Baldrige, had worked for the CIA: *New York Times*, Nov. 2, 2012.

374   "After dinner, the men sat around": William Walton OH, JFK Library.

375   "the vilest scramble for loot": Adam Hochschild, *King Leopold's Ghost* (Boston: Houghton Mifflin, 1998), 4.

376   "much too painful to be forgotten": Lumumba's Independence Day speech, June 30, 1960, www.marxists.org/subject/africa/lumumba/1960/06/independence.htm.

376   "marred the ceremonies": *New York Times*, July 1, 1960.

377   "mortgage the national sovereignty": *New York Times*, Oct. 3, 1960.

377   "[Father] seemed uncomfortable": Adam Hochschild, *Half the Way Home: A Memoir of Father and Son* (Boston: Mariner Books, 2005), 155.

378   stuffed full of the imbecilities: See Wendy Burden, *Dead End Gene Pool: A Memoir* (New York: Gotham Books, 2010).

378   Everything was "marvelous": Ibid., 54.

378   "Dear Allan": Cable from Burden to Dulles, Nov. 27, 1959, www.foia.cia.gov.

379   "We want no part": *New York Times*, Aug. 4, 1960.

379   "a Castro or worse": Muehlenbeck, *Betting on the Africans*, 22.

379   "would fall into a river of crocodiles": Ludo De Witte, *The Assassination of Lumumba* (London: Verso, 2001), xiii.

379   "There was a stunned silence": *London Guardian*, Aug. 9, 2000; see also the Church Committee Report, *Assassination Planning and the Plots: Congo*, 55–56.

379   "would remain a grave danger": Church Committee Report, *Assassination Planning and the Plots: Congo*, 52–53.

380   "give [sic] every possible": Ibid., 62.

380   "He had this tremendous": Ibid., 63.

380   "unsavory": Ibid., 46.

381 "Our program is clear": Lev Volodin, *Patrice Lumumba: Fighter for Africa's Freedom* (Moscow: Progress Publishers, 1961), 104–10.

381 "the life of the whole nation is at stake": Andrée Blouin, *My Country, Africa: Autobiography of the Black Pasionaria* (New York: Praeger Publishers, 1983), 272.

381 "When one struggles": Madeleine G. Kalb, *The Congo Cables: The Cold War in Africa* (New York: Macmillan, 1982), 162.

382 "On Lumumba's dazed face": Blouin, *My Country, Africa*, 273.

383 a Democratic fact-finding delegation: *New York Times*, Dec. 24, 1960.

383 he became closely associated with Jim Angleton: Author interview with William Gowen.

384 "inexperienced and irresponsible": *New York Times*, Aug. 19, 1960.

384 "virtual dictator": *New York Times*, May 18, 1960.

384 "the weirdest character": *New York Times*, Oct. 16, 1960.

384 "three houseboys at his service": *New York Times*, Dec. 11, 1960.

385 "The CIA was not the innocent bystander": Stephen R. Weissman, "An Extraordinary Rendition," *Intelligence and National Security* 15, no. 2 (April 2010): 198–222.

385 "his goose was cooked": Church Report, *Assassination Planning*, 50.

385 Devlin sealed Lumumba's fate: See Weissman, "What Really Happened in the Congo," *Foreign Affairs* 93, no. 4 (July–August 2014): 14–24; see also: Kalb, *Congo Cables*, 189–96.

386 even Tshombe and his ministers: De Witte, *Assassination of Lumumba*, 105–6.

386 "Eventually he was killed": Mahoney, *JFK: Ordeal in Africa*, 71.

386 Stockwell fell into conversation: John Stockwell, *In Search of Enemies: A CIA Story* (New York: Norton, 1978), 105.

386 The old Congo hands were alarmed: Larry Devlin, *Chief of Station, Congo* (New York: Public Affairs, 2007), 133–50.

387 "stick around": Jacques Lowe Web site, jacqueslowe.com.

387 "I was alone with the president": Jacques Lowe, *Kennedy: A Time Remembered* (Northampton, MA: Interlink Publishing, 1983).

388 *Time* magazine snickered: "Congo: Death of Lumumba—and After," *Time*, Feb. 24, 1961.

388 *The New York Times* continued to demean: *New York Times Magazine*, Oct. 29, 1961.

388 "Our strong leader is gone": *New York Times*, Feb. 15, 1961.

388 his final letter to his wife: "The Last Letter of Patrice Lumumba," http://ziomania.com/lumumba.

389 "I think we overrated": Weissman, "What Really Happened in the Congo."

Chapter 15: Contempt

394 "I'm Dick Drain": Peter Wyden, *Bay of Pigs: The Untold Story* (New York: Simon & Schuster, 1979), 265.

396 "I knew I could get back": AWD OH, JFK Library.

396 "inexcusable": Jack B. Pfeiffer, *Official CIA History of the Bay of Pigs Operation*, vol. 4, http://nsarchive.gwu.edu/NSAEBB/NSAEBB355/

396 Drain vented: Ibid., vol. 3, 128.

397 staffed largely by the agency's losers: Lyman B. Kirkpatrick, *Inspector General's Survey of the Cuban Operation*, October 1961, 41–43.

397 "a bunch of guys": Ralph E. Weber, ed., *Spymasters: Ten CIA Officers in Their Own Words* (Wilmington, DE: Scholarly Resources, 1999), 173.

398 "When the project became blown to every newspaper reader": Kirkpatrick, *Inspector General's Survey of the Cuban Operation*, 62.

398   "status of puppets": Ibid., 143.

398   "badly organized": Ibid., 144.

398   "so wrapped up in the military operation": Ibid., 143.

398   "doomed" from the start: Ibid., 34.

398   "now seen to be unachievable": Quoted in *Miami Herald*, Aug. 11, 2005.

399   "Kennedy's election has given rise": AS journals, Feb. 2, 1961, NYPL archives.

399   "a grenade with the pin pulled": Jim Rasenberger, *The Brilliant Disaster: JFK, Castro and America's Doomed Invasion of Cuba's Bay of Pigs* (New York: Scribner, 2011), 114.

399   "invading Cuba without actually invading it": Ibid., 140.

400   "I was prepared to run it": Ibid., 216.

401   "a little bit trapped": Weber, *Spymasters*, 175.

401   Admiral Burke was especially gruff: Wyden, *Bay of Pigs*, 270.

402   "They were sure I'd give in": Kenneth P. O'Donnell and David F. Powers, *"Johnny, We Hardly Knew Ye"* (Boston: Little, Brown, 1972), 274.

402   "Nobody is going to force me": Paul B. Fay Jr., *The Pleasure of His Company* (New York: Popular Library, 1977), 161.

403   "great emotional stress": Wyden, *Bay of Pigs*, 294.

403   "One ought never to sell": AWD OH, JFK Library.

403   "I stood right here": Theodore C. Sorensen, *Kennedy* (New York: Bantam Books, 1966), 332.

403   Dulles "didn't really feel comfortable": Weber, *Spymasters*, 158.

403   "Mr. Houston says [Yarmolinksy]": Declassified CIA memo to Dulles, Feb. 21, 1961, www.MaryFerrell.org.

404   Kennedy "was not very impressed": John Helgerson, "Getting to Know the President: Intelligence Briefings of Presidential Candidates, 1952–2004," Center for the Study of Intelligence/CIA monograph, May 2012.

404   "There was never any recrimination": AWD OH, JFK Library.

405   Dulles convened a private meeting of CEOs: Declassified CIA document, April 18, 1961, www.foia.cia.gov.

405   "I have the greatest admiration": Letter from Charles D. Hilles Jr. to AWD, May 4, 1961, AWD papers, Mudd Library.

405   "This would be mere child's play": Letter from Watson Washburn to AWD, June 6, 1961, AWD papers, Mudd Library.

405   "implied that had events taken their planned course": Ralph W. McGehee, *Deadly Deceits: My 25 Years in the CIA* (Melbourne: Ocean Press, 1999), 54.

406   when a Harvard Business School student named L. Paul Bremer III: Letter from AWD to Paul Bremer, April 28, 1965, AWD papers, Mudd Library.

406   "you have honored me": Letter from Charles Murphy to AWD, July 9, 1960, AWD papers, Mudd Library.

407   "I probably made a mistake": Arthur Schlesinger Jr., *Journals: 1952–2000* (New York: Penguin Press, 2007), 112.

407   "splinter the CIA": "CIA: Maker of Policy, or Tool?" *New York Times*, April 25, 1966.

407   "We not only look like imperialists": Schlesinger, *Journals*, 120.

407   "there would be serious difficulties": AS journals, May 23, 1961, NYPL archives.

407   Dulles "actually had more misgivings": Schlesinger, *Journals*, 113.

408   Taylor's "strongest tilts": Pfeiffer, *Official CIA History of the Bay of Pigs Operation*, vol. 4, 8.

408   "crossed all lines": Ibid., 4.

409   "a chain reaction of success": Letter from AWD and Arleigh Burke to Gen. Maxwell Taylor, June 9, 1961, www.MaryFerrell.org.

409 "were headed for the elephants' burial ground": Pfeiffer, *Official CIA History of the Bay of Pigs Operation*, vol. 4, 8.

410 he demonstrated integrity as IG: Kirkpatrick obituary, *New York Times*, March 6, 1995.

410 opposing the assassination of Lumumba: Ibid.

410 arranged for one finally to be hung: Kirkpatrick OH, JFK Library.

410 a "hatchet job": Weber, *Spymasters*, 137.

410 "basically Kirk's vendetta": *Miami Herald*, Feb. 28, 1998.

410 "When you speak honestly": Author interview with Lyman Kirkpatrick Jr.

411 a "stuttering rage": Joseph B. Smith, *Portrait of a Cold Warrior* (New York: Putnam, 1976), 327.

411 "It seemed [to us] that the RIF program was aimed more at the CIA": McGehee, *Deadly Deceits*, 54.

411 "Pulling out the rug": Harris Wofford, *Of Kennedys and Kings* (Pittsburgh, PA: University of Pittsburgh Press, 1992), 350.

411 "Mr. Kennedy . . . was a very bad president": Arleigh Burke OH, U.S. Naval Institute.

412 "He thought Lemnitzer was a dope": Author interview with AS.

412 "Johnson was a great admirer of the military": Jack Bell OH, JFK Library.

413 two units of paratroopers: Alistair Horne, *A Savage War of Peace: Algeria 1954–1962* (New York: New York Review Book, 2006), 454.

413 "government of capitulation": Ibid., 450.

413 De Gaulle quickly concluded: *London Observer*, May 2, 1961. See also Vincent Jauvert, *L'Amérique contre de Gaulle: Historie secrète (1961–1969)* (Paris: Éditions du Seuil, 2000), 198–99.

414 had a luncheon meeting with Richard Bissell: *New York Times*, May 4, 1961.

414 De Gaulle's foreign ministry was the source: Jauvert, *L'Amérique contre de Gaulle*, 192–93.

414 "because he was convinced he had unqualified American support": *Washington Post*, April 30, 1961.

414 Dulles was forced to issue a strong denial: *New York Times*, May 2, 1961.

415 "To set the record straight": *New York Times*, May 1, 1961.

415 "Young Cy Sulzberger had some uses": Carl Bernstein, "The CIA and the Media," *Rolling Stone*, Oct. 20, 1977.

415 "involved in an embarrassing liaison": *New York Times*, April 29, 1961.

415 a long history of acrimony: See Robert Belot and Gilbert Karpman, *L'affaire suisse: La Résistance a-t-elle trahi de Gaulle?* (Paris: Armand Colin, 2009).

415 de Gaulle accused Dulles: Charles de Gaulle, *The Complete War Memoirs* (New York: Carroll & Graf Publishers, 1998), 630.

416 the spymaster would set himself up at a suite: Frédéric Charpier, *La CIA en France: 60 ans d'ingérence dans les affaires françaises* (Paris: Éditions du Seuil, 2008), 102–5.

416 determined to shut down the secret "stay-behind army": Jonathan Kwitny, "The CIA's Secret Armies in Europe," *The Nation*, April 6, 1992.

416 Dulles flew to Paris for a face-to-face meeting: Charpier, *La CIA en France*, 219–28.

417 At a National Security Council meeting: Jauvert, *L'Amérique contre de Gaulle*, 190–91.

417 "A pre-revolutionary atmosphere": Ibid.

418 "the CIA is such a vast": Ibid., 197–98.

418 to offer the French leader "any help": *Le Monde*, May 10, 1961.

419 a "reactionary state-within-a-state": *New York Times*, May 4, 1961.

419 "He thought that harmonious relations": Hervé Alphand OH, JFK Library.

419 "In this grave hour": *Washington Post*, April 25, 1961.

420 "I am surprised that you are still alive": Anne and Pierre Rouanet, *L'Inquietude outré-mort du General de Gaulle* (Paris: Éditions Grasset, 1985), 219.

420   "there was not much to stop them": Horne, *A Savage War of Peace*, 455.

420   "by men whose duty": Ibid.

420   Over ten million people: *New York Times*, April 25, 1961.

421   handing out helmets and uniforms: Horne, *A Savage War of Peace*, 456.

421   Police swooped down: *Washington Post*, April 29, 1961.

421   "carrying his own suitcase": *Time*, May 5, 1961.

422   de Gaulle launched a new purge: Charpier, *La CIA en France*, 224–25.

422   "liquidations [were] an almost daily routine": Philippe Thyraud de Vosjoli, *Lamia* (Boston: Little, Brown & Co., 1970), 261.

422   "I can testify": Constantin Melnik, *Politiquement incorrect* (Paris: Éditions Plon, 1999), 84.

422   offered to hire him for a new private intelligence agency: Charpier, *La CIA en France*, 226.

423   recruited their own secret assassins: De Vosjoli, *Lamia*, 266–69.

424   "Why wake up old demons": Jauvert, *L'Amérique contre de Gaulle*, 202.

424   "Kennedy will not begin to be President": AS journals, March 23, 1961, NYPL archives.

424   The president was "disgusted" by Wrightsman's disloyalty: Arthur M. Schlesinger, *Jacqueline Kennedy: Historic Conversations on Life with John F. Kennedy* (New York: Hyperion, 2011), 188.

425   "scapegoats to expiate administration guilt": E. Howard Hunt, *Give Us This Day* (New Rochelle, NY: Arlington House, 1973), 215.

426   "We tried to make a pleasant evening of it": Senator Prescott Bush letter to Clover Dulles, undated, AWD papers, Mudd Library.

426   "The Allen Dulles Memorial Mausoleum": David Atlee Phillips, *Secret Wars Diary: My Adventures in Combat, Espionage Operations and Covert Action* (Bethesda, MD: Stone Tail Press, 1988), 162.

426   "I regard Allen Dulles as an almost unique": Remarks upon presenting National Security Award to AWD, Nov. 28, 1961, JFK Library.

427   who's who list of Fortune 500 executives: CIA memo, Nov. 28, 1961, AWD papers, Mudd Library.

427   "It is almost unbelievable": J. Peter Grace letter to Dulles, AWD papers, Mudd Library.

427   "Clover, I'll be home later": Phillips, *Secret Wars Diary*, 165.

427   "His morale . . . was pretty low": Ibid.

427   "I don't want any more of the Dulles family": Leonard Mosley, *Dulles* (New York: Doubleday, 1978), 510.

427   "It was silly": Ibid.

428   "He had a very difficult time": Angleton testimony, Church Committee, Feb. 6, 1976.

428   "As you know": Jan. 16, 1962, AWD letter to colleague whose name was deleted by CIA upon release of document, Mudd Library.

Chapter 16: Rome on the Potomac

429   The astronaut succeeded in staying dry, but: Arthur Schlesinger Jr., *Journals: 1952–2000* (New York: Penguin Press, 2007), 158.

430   "a huge, dripping mass": Ibid., 122.

430   "Southern congressmen were especially interested": Drew Pearson, *Washington Merry-Go-Round*, June 24, 1962.

430   the president shared some of his own . . . movie opinions: Schlesinger, *Journals*, 137.

431   *Time* magazine, which poked fun: "The Administration: Big Splash at Hickory Hill," *Time*, June 29, 1962.

431   "I scent a manhunt": AS journals, July 1, 1962, NYPL archives.

431   "Don't worry about it": Ibid.

432   Schlesinger endorsed a crude effort: Michael Wreszin, "Arthur Schlesinger, Jr., Scholar Activist in Cold War America: 1946–1956," *Salmagundi*, nos. 63–64 (Spring–Summer 1984): 255–85.

433   "like the brightest student in the class": *New York Times*, March 1, 2007.

433   the Soviet Union was a "messianic state": Arthur Schlesinger Jr., "Origins of the Cold War," *Foreign Affairs* 46 (October 1967): 22–32, 34–35, 42–50, 52.

433   "the notion of American spooks": Arthur Schlesinger Jr., *A Life in the Twentieth Century* (Boston: Houghton Mifflin Co., 2002), 350.

433   "The Dulles brothers . . . were self-righteous": Author interview with Marian Schlesinger.

434   Schlesinger made an effort to maintain cordial relations: AS-AWD correspondence, AS papers, JFK Library.

435   Kennedy was nervous about meeting the formidable New York intellectual: AS journals, July 28, 1961, NYPL.

435   JFK was at his dazzling best: Ibid., Aug. 1, 1961.

435   "And I still believe": Ibid., April 8, 1962.

436   "Now Arthur, cut it out": "The Historian as Participant," *Time*, Dec. 17, 1965.

436   "You can be damn sure": Ibid.

436   C. Wright Mills denouncing "Kennedy and company": Arthur M. Schlesinger, *A Thousand Days: John F. Kennedy in the White House* (New York: Mariner Books, 2002), 286.

437   "That's a great idea, Arthur": Kenneth P. O'Donnell and David F. Powers, *"Johnny, We Hardly Knew Ye"* (Boston: Little, Brown, 1972), 282.

437   "I have the feeling that the president": Schlesinger, *Journals*, 166.

438   "Dulles stooges": AS journals, July 9, 1961, NYPL archives.

438   "a man of limited interests and imagination": Ibid., July 15, 1961.

439   "I served in the OSS": AS memo for the president, April 21, 1961, AS White House files, JFK Library.

439   "The Central Intelligence Agency is sick": Confidential memo, author unidentified, AS White House files.

439   "implies a fairly drastic rearrangement": AS memo for the president, June 30, 1961, AS White House files.

440   Taylor argued forcefully against the Schlesinger plan: AS journals, July 9, 1961, NYPL archives.

440   Schlesinger gave the choice his blessing: Ibid., July 15, 1961.

441   "The possibly consoling thought": Ibid., Oct. 8, 1961.

441   "He was very critical of Dulles": Ibid., Oct. 17, 1961.

442   "systematically sabotaged by the military and the CIA": Ibid., May 14, 1962.

442   "McCone has no business": Ibid., March 21, 1963.

442   a "sick elephant": Syndicated column by Henry Taylor, *New York World-Telegram*, Jan. 17, 1964.

443   "a direct attack on me": AWD letter to Henry Taylor, Jan. 21, 1964, declassified by CIA, www.foia.cia.gov.

443   "there is no such thing as the New Frontier": AS journals, Nov. 12, 1961, NYPL archives.

443   "Eisenhower-Dulles continuities": Schlesinger, *Journals*, 164.

444   "Every time steel prices jump": *Kansas City Times*, March 9, 1959.

445 "the most painfully embarrassing": O'Donnell and Powers, "*Johnny, We Hardly Knew Ye*," 406.

445 "We were going to go for broke": Edwin O. Guthman and Jeffrey Shulman, eds., *Robert Kennedy in His Own Words* (New York: Bantam Books, 1988), 333.

445 "I told him that his men could keep their horses": Schlesinger, *A Thousand Days*, 637.

446 "a display of naked political power": Ibid., 638.

446 "I understand better every day why Roosevelt": Schlesinger, *Journals*, 157.

446 "ass-kissing posture": AS journals, June 17, 1962, NYPL archives.

446 "I have rarely seen a man": Ibid., July 1, 1962.

446 he "only wished there were no Cold War": Schlesinger, *Journals*, 137.

447 "I was their man of the year": O'Donnell and Power, "*Johnny, We Hardly Knew Ye*," 407.

447 "I do feel an immense relief": Clover Dulles letter to MB, Jan. 3, 1962, Schlesinger Library.

448 "It was a memorable moment in my life": Henry Luce OH, JFK Library.

449 "I wrote this book as an antidote": E. Howard Hunt letter to AWD, Aug. 28, 1962, www.foia.cia.gov.

449 "I have always thought well of Hunt": AWD letter to Richard Helms, July 27, 1962, www.foia.cia.gov.

450 Shef Edwards . . . even stepped in: AWD letter to Sheffield Edwards, Jan. 31, 1963, www.foia.cia.gov.

450 Rumsfeld arranged for Dulles to speak: Correspondence between Donald Rumsfeld and AWD in February–March 1963, Mudd Library.

451 "The President believed he was President": Robert F. Kennedy, *Thirteen Days: A Memoir of the Cuban Missile Crisis* (New York: W. W. Norton & Co., 1969), 72.

451 "At the climax of the events around Cuba": Schlesinger, *A Thousand Days*, 690.

451 "He didn't let himself become frightened": Nikita Sergeevich Khrushchev, *Khrushchev Remembers* (Boston: Little, Brown, 1970), 500.

452 his Georgetown neighbors poured into the street: AS journals, July 21, 1963, NYPL archives.

452 "I am almost a 'peace-at-any-price' president": Ibid., Sept. 5, 1961.

453 "There was virtually a coup atmosphere": Author interview with Daniel Ellsberg.

453 LeMay and his top Air Force generals: *Strategic Air Warfare: An Interview with Generals Curtis LeMay, Leon Johnson, David Burchinal and Jack Catton* (Washington, DC: Office of Air Force History, U.S. Air Force, 1988).

454 "He said to get out of that boat business": Anthony R. Carrozza, *William D. Pawley: The Extraordinary Life of the Adventurer, Entrepreneur and Diplomat* (Washington, DC: Potomac Books, 2012), 255.

454 Pawley wrote a long letter: Ibid.

456 "He's a real bastard": Ted Widmer, ed., *Listening In: The Secret White House Recordings of John F. Kennedy* (New York: Hyperion, 2012), 77.

456 he "doubted" he would ever be willing to work: *Newsday*, June 22, 1963.

457 the conversation . . . soon grew heated: Peter Dale Scott letter to author.

458 Sierra arranged to meet with Dulles: Internal CIA document, www.maryferrell.org.

458 Dulles and Clay were unusual company for a man who: For Sierra biographical background, see House Select Committee on Assassinations Report; see also Robert Blakey and Richard N. Billings, *Fatal Hour: The Assassination of President Kennedy by Organized Crime* (New York: Berkley Books, 1992), 194–99.

460 local Secret Service officials foiled: See Lamar Waldron, *The Hidden History of the JFK Assassination* (Berkeley, CA: Counterpoint Press, 2013), 301–9; and Abraham Bolden, *The Echo from Dealey Plaza* (New York: Broadway Books, 2009).

461   "Father's patriotism . . . made him go a little overboard": Author interview with Paul Sierra.

Chapter 17: The Parting Glass

463   Segni paid tribute: Fraleigh OH.

463   "war is not inevitable": Remarks of the President at Dinner Hosted by President Antonio Segni, July 1, 1963, JFK Library.

464   Even *L'Unità* . . . appreciatively noted: *L'Unità*, July 2, 1963.

465   "My impression is that [Nenni] has honestly broken": AS memo to President Kennedy, March 5, 1962, AS papers, JFK Library.

465   former ambassador Luce lobbied frantically: Spencer M. Di Scala, *Renewing Italian Socialism* (New York: Oxford University Press, 1988), 131.

466   "Lest you think": Arthur Schlesinger Jr. lecture, "The Kennedy Administration and the Center Left," delivered at JFK Library, March 18, 1993.

466   he arranged for United Auto Workers leaders: Leopoldo Nuti, "Missiles or Socialists: The Italian Policy of the Kennedy Administration," in *John F. Kennedy and Europe*, ed. Douglas Brinkley and Richard T. Griffiths (Baton Rouge: Louisiana State University Press, 1999), 133–34.

466   When an Italian news photographer: Fraleigh OH.

466   "They have spent hundreds of millions of dollars": Pietro Nenni, "Where the Italian Socialists Stand," *Foreign Affairs* 40, no. 2 (January 1962): 213–23.

467   Nenni was "absolutely enraptured": Fraleigh OH.

467   The president, too, thought his trip to Rome was a "considerable success": AS journals, July 5, 1963, NYPL.

468   The secret meeting between Pionzio and Freato: Author interview with Carlo Mastelloni, a former investigating magistrate in Venice and a leading expert on the secrets of the First Italian Republic

469   Guy Burgess . . . drew a lewd . . . caricature: David C. Martin, *Wilderness of Mirrors* (Guilford, CT: The Lyons Press, 2003), 48.

469   "the poet and the cop": Ibid., 11.

470   a "very esteemed [and] really reliable friend": Reinhard Gehlen letter to CG Harvey, Jan. 4, 1977, Bayard Stockton papers, University of California, Santa Barbara Library, Special Collections.

470   "one of the most daring": Bayard Stockton, *Flawed Patriot: The Rise and Fall of CIA Legend Bill Harvey* (Washington, DC: Potomac Books, 2006), 92.

470   One of CG Harvey's secret assignments: *Indianapolis Star*, Oct. 3, 2000.

471   Harvey made a trip to Europe: Stockton, *Flawed Patriot*, 114.

471   Harvey was put in charge of the top secret operation: Ibid., 123.

471   Rosselli was a man of "integrity": William Harvey testimony before the Church Committee, June 25 and July 11, 1975.

471   "I loved Rosselli": Interview with CG Harvey, jfkfacts.org., Nov. 6, 2014.

472   Harvey kept much of the operation . . . a secret from President Kennedy: William Harvey testimony, Church Committee.

472   and let loose a fart: Martin, *Wilderness of Mirrors*, 137.

472   "that fucker": Ibid., 136.

473   Giving him Rome was Angleton's idea: Ibid., 183.

473   Helms and Angleton did not tell McCone: Ibid., 186.

473   "goddam wops": Ibid., 182.

473   "I just don't understand": Author interview with Susan Wyatt.

473   would throw rats over the wall: Stockton, *Flawed Patriot*, 237.

475　The CIA station chief urged Colonel Renzo Rocca: Philip Willan, *Puppetmasters: The Political Use of Terrorism in Italy* (San Jose, CA: Authors Choice Press, 2002), 38.

475　stunned to hear his boss propose recruiting Mafia hit men: Author interview with Alan Wyatt.

475　Harvey pulled a gun on Wyatt: Author interview with Susan Wyatt.

475　General Giovanni de Lorenzo . . . threatened to: Di Scala, *Renewing Italian Socialism*, 152–54; Daniele Ganser, *NATO's Secret Armies: Operation Gladio and Terrorism in Western Europe* (London: Frank Cass, 2005), 71–72; see also: "Twenty-Six Years Later, Details of Planned Rightist Coup Emerge," Associated Press, Jan. 5, 1991.

476　to give the old man the "chilling" truth: Di Scala, *Renewing Italian Socialism*, 143.

476　Wyatt found Harvey collapsed in bed: Stockton, *Flawed Patriot*, 208–9.

476　"My dad would sometimes talk about Harvey": Author interview with Tom Wyatt.

477　" 'I always wondered what Bill Harvey was doing in Dallas in November 1963' ": Author interview with Fabrizio Calvi. Susan Wyatt believes that Calvi must have misunderstood her father, whom she doubts took a flight to Dallas in November 1963. She thinks that her father's suspicions about Harvey were based on remarks that the Rome station chief made to Wyatt after Kennedy's assassination.

478　"It would be a waste of time": Kenneth P. O'Donnell and David F. Powers, *"Johnny, We Hardly Knew Ye"* (Boston: Little, Brown, 1972), 358.

479　he looked "very tired": Thomas Maier, *The Kennedys: America's Emerald Kings* (New York: Basic Books, 2003), 432.

479　"From the time he stepped off that plane": *President Kennedy in the Island of Dreams* documentary, http://www.youtube.com/watch?v=cznNVmdXqmk.

479　"Here he was": Ibid.

479　"When my great-grandfather left here": Ibid.

480　"There is an impression": Maier, *Kennedys: America's Emerald Kings*, 437.

480　"He never would have been President": Ryan Tubridy, *JFK in Ireland: Four Days That Changed a President* (London: Collins, 2010), frontispiece.

481　"But there were many times when the key": O'Donnell and Powers, *"Johnny, We Hardly Knew Ye,"* 368.

481　The indomitable people of Ireland: President Kennedy's address before the Irish Parliament, June 28, 1963, JFK Library.

482　"JFK accomplished an Americanization": AS papers, JFK Library.

482　Kennedy had come under the spell: Maier, *Kennedys: America's Emerald Kings*, 431.

483　"The trip meant more to him": Tubridy, *JFK in Ireland*.

Chapter 18: The Big Event

484　"a little tepid": AS journals, Oct. 2, 1963, NYPL archives.

484　The Soviet spy "has been fully indoctrinated": Allen W. Dulles, *The Craft of Intelligence* (New York: Harper & Row, 1963), 91.

485　"our desire to be 'loved' ": Ibid., 165.

485　"massive recruitment" of Nazi war criminals: Ibid., 106.

485　he sat for a remarkable interview: NBC News special, *The Science of Spying*, Internet archive, www.archive.org.

486　"We'd kill him": *Bridgeport* (CT) *Telegram*, Jan. 14, 1975.

486　"I shall have to persuade myself": AWD letter to Cass Canfield, Oct. 15, 1961, www.foia.cia.gov.

487　"use your potent association": Sherman Kent letter to AWD, Nov. 15, 1962, AWD papers, Mudd Library.

487　"brilliantly selective candor": *New York Times*, Oct. 15, 1963.

487 "the best news I have read in a long time": Julius Ochs Adler letter to AWD, Jan. 26, 1953, Mudd Library.

488 "We can annihilate Russia": Fred Cook, *The Warfare State* (New York: Macmillan, 1962), 29.

489 "He had promised to protect them": Robert Caro, *The Passage of Power* (New York: Vintage, 2013), 269.

490 "Come clean, Lyndon": Sylvia Jukes Morris, *The Price of Fame: The Honorable Clare Boothe Luce* (New York: Random House, 2014), 519.

490 "Lyndon had been very dark": AS journals, March 21, 1963, NYPL archives.

491 "Poor Lyndon": Ibid., Jan. 6, 1963.

491 "like being a cut dog": Caro, *Passage of Power*, 205.

491 "who believes as I do": Evelyn Lincoln, *Kennedy and Johnson* (New York: Holt Rinehart Winston, 1968), 204.

492 Johnson had become a "political liability": *Dallas Morning News*, Nov. 22, 1963.

492 "This guy looks like a bandit": Caro, *Passage of Power*, 298.

493 Johnson made a strange power grab: Ibid., 170.

494 "I need you to do exactly as I say": Saint John Hunt, *Bond of Secrecy* (Walterville, OR: Trine Day, 2012), 10.

496 "open up that whole Bay of Pigs thing": H. R. Haldeman, *The Ends of Power* (New York: Times Books, 1978), 66.

496 "I liked all those men": *Miami Herald*, June 5, 2005.

497 "I can tell you that's the biggest load of crap": Erik Hedegaard, "The Last Confession of E. Howard Hunt," *Rolling Stone*, April 2, 2007.

498 Saint John Hunt flew to Florida . . . to hear his [father's] final testament: Saint John Hunt, *Bond of Secrecy*; also author interview with Saint John Hunt.

500 "Dave Morales did dirty work": Author interview with Wayne Smith.

500 "We all admired the hell out of the guy": Morales entry, www.spartacus-educational.com.

500 "When some asshole needed to be killed": Author interview with Ruben Carbajal.

500 "He did whatever he was told": Author interview with David Morales's daughter.

500 "off-the-board" operation: Saint John Hunt, *Bond of Secrecy*, 43.

501 Harvey and Morales . . . "could have been manufactured": E. Howard Hunt, *American Spy: My Secret History in the CIA, Watergate and Beyond* (Hoboken, NJ: John Wiley & Sons, 2007), 141.

501 "that no good son of a bitch": Gaeton Fonzi, *The Last Investigation* (New York: Skyhorse Publishing, 2013), 389.

501 "You're somebody we all look up to": Saint John Hunt, *Bond of Secrecy*, 45.

502 "We tried to get Harvey's travel vouchers": Author interview with Dan Hardway.

505 "[Hunt's] luck has run out": *The Spotlight*, August 1978.

506 "This is a thing in my mind": Author interview with Victor Marchetti.

507 They "threw him under the bus": Author interview with Sally Harvey.

507 "Bill always had very good opportunities": CG Harvey letter to Bayard Stockton, Stockton papers, University of California–Santa Barbara Special Collections.

507 "It is difficult to prepare a fitness report": William Harvey fitness report, October 1962, www.foia.cia.gov.

Chapter 19: The Fingerprints of Intelligence

510 witness scenes of sexual exploitation: Anthony Summers, "The Secret Life of Lee Harvey Oswald," *Esquire* (British edition), December 1993.

511 he made the thirteen-year-old the subject: Dick Russell, *On the Trail of the JFK Assassins* (New York: Skyhorse, 2008), 252.

511 Hartogs went on to work with Dr. Sidney Malitz: Ibid., 254.

513 "ought to be shot": FBI interview with David Ferrie, Nov. 27, 1963, www.mary ferrell.org.

513 A CIA memo titled "'Truth Drugs'": www.cia.gov.

513 he was one of the young marines: Martin Lee, Robert Ranftel, and Jeff Cohen, "Did Lee Harvey Oswald Drop Acid?" *Rolling Stone*, March 1983.

514 he had taken a "hop": Author interview with JFK assassination researcher Mary La-Fontaine.

514 There was a magical element to Oswald's journey: Anthony Summers, *Not in Your Lifetime* (New York: Open Road, 1998), 111.

515 he never could hit anything: Daniel Schorr, "From the KGB's Oswald Files," *Christian Science Monitor*, Aug. 24, 2001.

515 "an empty person": Ibid.

515 a revealing memoir: Ernst Titovets, *Oswald Russian Episode* (Moscow: MonLitera, 2010).

518 "Everywhere you look": David Talbot, *Brothers: The Hidden History of the Kennedy Years* (New York: Free Press, 2007), 379.

519 "I wondered why": *Newark Star-Ledger*, Nov. 17, 2013.

520 "[Lee] did not know": Russell, *On the Trail of the JFK Assassins*, 205.

520 "a shack near Sears Roebuck": De Mohrenschildt's Warren Commission testimony, April 22, 1964, www.maryferrell.org.

520 "not particularly pretty": Ibid.

523 he manhandled her: Joan Mellen, *Our Man in Haiti: George de Mohrenschildt and the CIA in the Nightmare Republic* (Walterville, OR: Trine Day, 2102), 28.

524 put Byrd's wife on the board: Russ Baker, *Family of Secrets* (New York: Bloomsbury Press, 2009), 111.

525 a "very nice fellow": George de Mohrenschildt, *I Am a Patsy!*, 208, aarclibrary.org.

528 "[He] was there as a distant threat": Ibid., 215.

529 they were invited by Janet Auchincloss: Ibid., 225.

531 "not jealous of [the] Kennedys' wealth": Ibid., 89.

532 "Under dictatorship": Ibid., 121.

532 "My wife and I spent": Ibid., 270.

532 "Our phone [is] bugged": De Mohrenschildt letter to George W. Bush, Sept. 5, 1976, www.maryferrell.org.

533 Gaeton Fonzi rolled up: Gaeton Fonzi, *The Last Investigation* (New York: Skyhorse Publishing, 2013), 189.

535 "In spite of my faulty Russian": Ruth Paine article, Warren Commission exhibit 460, www.maryferrell.org.

535 collaborated with author: Thomas Mallon, *Mrs. Paine's Garage* (Orlando: Harcourt, 2002).

536 "My parents had a name for that": Author interview with Ruth Paine.

536 "as if she were a sister": Warren Commission exhibit 460.

537 Hyde was considered "for a covert use": CIA memo, May 9, 1967, www.maryferrell.org.

537 Ruth's sister, Sylvia, later went to work: See Barbara LaMonica et al., "The Paines," as well as other Sylvia Hyde Hoke documents on www.maryferrell.org.

538 Among those invited to Naushon Island: Author interview with Ruth Paine.

538 "I was always fascinated": MB letter to AWD, March 17, 1964, Mudd Library.

538 "I would only like to point out": MB letter to AWD, Dec. 1, 1963, Mudd Library.

539 The conspiracy-minded would have a field day: George Michael Evica, *A Certain Arrogance* (Bloomington, IN: XLibris, 2006), 230.

539 the millionaire took the odd step: *Wall Street Journal*, Feb. 21, 2009.

540 He also belonged to the Suite 8F Group: www.spartacus-educational.com.

540 LeMay bestowed a glowing: Scroll of appreciation presented to D. H. Byrd, May 24, 1963, www.spartacus-educational.com.

540 the target of such heavy FBI and CIA pressure: Bill Simpich, "Fair Play for Cuba and the Cuban Revolution," *CounterPunch*, July 24, 2009, www.counterpunch.org.

541 "to create an incident": Jefferson Morley, *Our Man in Mexico* (Lawrence: University Press of Kansas, 2008), 172.

541 Oswald and Phillips were observed talking together: Author interview with Veciana. See also: Fonzi, *Last Investigation*, 141.

541 "I was trained by the CIA": "Antonio Veciana Comes Clean," Oct. 26, 2014, www. jfkcountercoup.blogspot.com.

542 "a keen operational interest": John Newman, *Oswald and the CIA* (New York: Skyhorse Publishing, 2008), 392.

543 had a "maturing effect": CIA memo from DCI to Mexico City station, Oct. 10, 1963, www.maryferrell.org. For discussion of memo, see Jefferson Morley, "Did the CIA Track Oswald Before JFK Was Killed?" Feb. 4, 2014, www.jfkfacts.org.

543 "I had never thought of him as a violent man": Ruth Paine's Warren Commission testimony, March 19, 1964, www.maryferrell.org.

543 "I never did discover": Michael Paine's Warren Commission testimony, March 18, 1964, www.maryferrell.org.

545 "I thought of going over": Author interview with Michael Paine.

547 "The Farm was basically": Author interview with Dan Hardway.

547 "Oh, I rated him high": AWD OH, JFK Library.

Chapter 20: For the Good of the Country

549 penciled in an interesting appointment: AWD calendars. Dulles placed a question mark next to Dillon's name, perhaps indicating that the meeting—or its scheduled time—was not definite.

550 "When I appeared before them": NBC News, *The Science of Spying*.

552 ran his own private intelligence network: See Gerard Colby, *Thy Will Be Done: The Conquest of the Amazon—Nelson Rockefeller and Evangelism in the Age of Oil* (New York: HarperCollins, 1995); and Richard Norton Smith, *On His Own Terms: A Life of Nelson Rockefeller* (New York: Random House, 2014).

552 David Rockefeller served with a special Army intelligence unit: David Rockefeller, *Memoirs* (New York: Random House, 2002), 112–21.

553 David took him to lunch in Manhattan: Frances Stonor Saunders, *Who Paid the Piper? The CIA and the Cultural Cold War* (London: Granta Books, 1999), 141.

553 "I often briefed David": Ibid., 145.

554 "I can't begin to tell you": Nelson Rockefeller letter to AWD, Dec. 21, 1955, Mudd Library.

554 "To say that I appreciate": AWD reply, Jan. 16, 1956, Mudd Library.

554 asking him to pull strings: AWD letter to Laurance Rockefeller, Aug. 5, 1959, Mudd Library.

555 he dismissed Kennedy as a lightweight: Kai Bird, *The Chairman: John McCloy and the Making of the Establishment* (New York: Simon & Schuster, 1992), 496.

555 "as a means of forcing you to come to terms with business": Kennedy press conference, June 14, 1962, JFK Library video.

556 "Who is this upstart president": Nomi Prins, *All the Presidents' Bankers: The Hidden Alliances That Drive American Power* (New York: Nation Books, 2014), 246.

556 "an eloquent and logical articulator": "What to Do About the Economy," *Life* magazine, July 6, 1962.

557   "even if Standard Oil and David Rockefeller objected": Richard Goodwin, *Remembering America* (Boston: Little, Brown, 1998), 167.

557   "Neither U.S. nor Latin American businessmen": Ibid., 204.

557   America's reputation in Latin America as an imperial bully: David Talbot, *Brothers: The Hidden History of the Kennedy Years* (New York: Free Press, 2007), 62–64.

558   "We Kennedys eat Rockefellers": Goodwin, *Remembering America*, 439.

558   "we moved in very different circles": Rockefeller, *Memoirs*, 427.

558   "ever since I was a kid": *New York Times*, Nov. 4, 1970.

558   "losing our property": Colby, *Thy Will Be Done*, 313.

559   Rockefeller lashed into the president: *Dallas Morning News*, Nov. 14 and 17, 1963.

559   echoed in the pages of the business press: Donald Gibson, *Battling Wall Street* (New York: Sheridan Square Press, 1994), 64–68.

559   "in their luxury bunker": Talbot, *Brothers*, 275.

560   Dillon notified the president: C. Douglas Dillon memo to President Kennedy, Oct. 28, 1963, JFK Library.

561   He was supposed to be killed: Author interview with G. Robert Blakey.

561   "He was real calm": William Weston, "The Interrogation of Oswald," *JFK/Deep Politics Quarterly* 1, no. 2 (January 1996): 9–16.

561   "I was amazed": Summers, *Not in Your Lifetime* (New York: Open Road, 1998), 128. by trying to make an intriguing phone call: Randolph Benson, "JFK, Oswald and the Raleigh Connection," *Indy Week* [Raleigh, NC], Nov. 14, 2012.

562   As Simpich has detailed: Bill Simpich, "How the Warren Commission Covered Up JFK's Murder," Op-Ed News.com, Nov. 19, 2014.

563   "I was interrogated": *Richmond Times-Dispatch*, Nov. 17, 2013.

563   As many as twenty-one law enforcement officers: JFK Facts.org, Sept. 24, 2013.

564   "The surgeons who labored": See Charles Crenshaw, *JFK: Conspiracy of Silence* (New York: Signet, 1992); see also "Surgeon Who Treated JFK Remembers," Philadelphia .cbslocal.com, Nov. 19, 2013.

564   "The list [of names] was almost a duplicate": Talbot, *Brothers*, 21.

565   "What is this": Ibid., 19.

565   Eisenhower . . . had the same reaction: Ibid.

566   The foreign press was filled with commentary: United Press International wire story, "European Press Doubts Entire Truth Revealed," Nov. 27, 1963.

567   "What happened to Kennedy": Alain Peyrefitte, *C'était de Gaulle* (Paris: Fayard, 1997), 42–45.

568   Khrushchev . . . broke down weeping: William Taubman, *Khrushchev: The Man and His Era* (New York: Norton, 2003), 604.

568   "This is bad news": Jean Daniel, "When Castro Heard the News," *New Republic*, Dec. 7, 1963.

569   "a cloudy organism": *Washington Daily News*, Jan. 3, 1964.

569   "The CIA Is Getting Out of Hand": Sen. Eugene McCarthy, *Saturday Evening Post*, Jan. 4, 1964.

570   The CIA "was really HST's baby": AWD letter to Clark Clifford, Jan. 22, 1964, Mudd Library.

570   "deeply disturbed": AWD letter to Truman, Jan. 7, 1964, Mudd Library.

571   "quite astounded": AWD letter to Houston, April 21, 1964, Mudd Library.

571   "I think it was a mistake": Merle Miller, *Plain Speaking: An Oral Biography of Harry S. Truman* (New York: Berkley Publishing, 1986), 391.

571   "I am happy as I can be": Hayden Peake, "Harry S. Truman on CIA Covert Operations," *Studies in Intelligence* 25, no. 1 (Spring 1981): 31–41.

572   "The CIA was set up by me": Ray McGovern, "Are Presidents Afraid of the CIA?" CommonDreams.org, Dec. 29, 2009.

572   "the two men Bobby Kennedy asked me": Lyndon Johnson, *The Vantage Point* (New York: Holt, Rinehart, 1971), 27.

573   "lay the dust": Warren Commission executive session, Dec. 5, 1963, www.maryferrell.org.

573   "personally persuaded": Michael Kurtz, *The JFK Assassination Debates* (Lawrence: University Press of Kansas, 2006), 173.

573   "wanted to make sure": Author interview with Michael Kurtz.

574   "lobbied hard for the job": Joseph Trento, *The Secret History of the CIA* (Roseville, CA: Prima Publishing, 2001), 269.

574   establishment allies like . . . Dean Rusk: Peter Grose, *Gentleman Spy: The Life of Allen Dulles* (Boston: Houghton Mifflin Co., 1994), 541.

574   Alsop deftly maneuvered Johnson: LBJ audiotapes, www.maryferrell.org.

575   "Whitewash": Richard D. Mahoney, *JFK: Ordeal in Africa* (New York: Oxford University Press, 1983), 235.

575   "I don't think Allen Dulles ever": Earl Warren OH, LBJ Library.

576   Dulles had "heartily" recommended: AWD letter to J. Lee Rankin, March 8, 1958, Mudd Library.

577   "A great deal of the description": AWD memo to J. Lee Rankin, July 27, 1964, Mudd Library.

578   Rocca . . . met with Dulles: Memo from Raymond Rocca to Richard Helms, March 23, 1964, www.maryferrell.org.

578   Marguerite Oswald declared that her son: *Washington Post*, Feb. 13, 1964.

579   McCone . . . brought along Helms: Testimony of John McCone and Richard Helms, Warren Commission, May 14, 1964, www.maryferrell.org.

580   "one of the most fluent and self-confident": Howard Willens, *History Will Prove Us Right* (New York: Overlook Press, 2013), 112.

580   "I came to like and trust": Philip Shenon, *A Cruel and Shocking Act* (New York: Holt, 2013), 119.

581   a disturbing phone call: Ibid., 537.

581   "There have been many": AWD letter to unidentified friend, May 26, 1964, Mudd Library.

581   "By George": *U.S. News & World Report*, Aug. 17, 1992.

582   "I wish sometime": AWD letter to Rebecca West, March 24, 1964, Mudd Library.

582   Mary relayed a news report: MB letter to AWD, April 7, 1964, Mudd Library.

582   was set to "unequivocally reject": *New York Times*, June 1, 1964.

583   a dinner table conversation: Leon Hubert Jr. and Burt Griffin memo to Howard Willens, Feb. 28, 1964, Mudd Library.

583   Dillon was treated to a kid-gloves: C. Douglas Dillon testimony, Warren Commission, Sept. 2, 1964, www.maryferrell.org.

583   Willens believed that "the Secret Service": Willens, *History Will Prove Us Right*, 114.

584   "Dillon was a very shrewd guy": Author interview with Howard Willens.

585   "Without exception": John Jay Iselin letter to AWD, Sept. 28, 1964, Mudd Library.

585   "I think he accepted the Warren Report": Author interview with Carol Bundy.

Chapter 21: "I Can't Look and Won't Look"

587   "a princely sum": David Lifton, *Best Evidence* (New York: Carroll & Graf, 1988), 33.

588   "For similar reasons": Ibid., 4.

588   warned Lifton not to "badger": Lifton's notes on his debate with Dulles, Dec. 7, 1965, courtesy of Vincent Salandria.

591   in the presence of "evil": Author interview with David Lifton.

592   "happy to note": AWD letter to Gerald Ford, Feb. 1, 1965, Mudd Library.

592   how to convince: Clover Dulles letter to MB, Feb. 11, 1966, Schlesinger Library.

594   "an old and close friend of mine": AWD letter to J. Lee Rankin, Sept. 9, 1966, Mudd Library.

594   "a matter of concern to the U.S. government": "More Material on the Assassination of President Kennedy," *Propaganda Notes*, CIA bulletin, May 15, 1967.

594   a particularly "terrible nuisance": AWD letter to MB, July 22, 1964, Mudd Library.

595   "I have been told that his wife": Letter from unidentified source to AWD, Jan. 7, 1964, Mudd Library.

595   the CIA went beyond spreading ugly gossip: Author interview with Mark Lane.

596   "After listening to him": MB letter to AWD, July 25, 1964, Schlesinger Library.

596   agree to disagree: AWD letter to MB, Nov. 9, 1966, Mudd Library.

596   "At the beginning of the investigation": Jim Garrison, *On the Trail of the Assassins* (New York: Sheridan Square Press, 1988), 175.

597   Gordon Novel—phoned the spymaster: AWD calendars, 1968.

597   "This is what happens to you": Garrison, *On the Trail of the Assassins*, 283.

597   "I hope you had a chance": William Small letter to AWD, July 5, 1967, Mudd Library.

598   "a single communication from the [new] president": Arthur Schlesinger Jr., *Journals: 1952–2000* (New York: Penguin Press, 2007), 218.

598   "absence of intellectual curiosity": Ibid., 224.

599   a harrowing account of "that ghastly afternoon": Ibid., 227.

599   "we did not control the Joint Chiefs": Author interview with AS.

600   a raucous Norman Mailer party: Earl Wilson column, *New York Post*, Feb. 1, 1967.

600   "I can't look and won't look": David Talbot, *Brothers: The Hidden History of the Kennedy Years* (New York: Free Press, 2007), 287.

600   "disgraceful piece": AS letter to AWD, Dec. 29, 1964, NYPL archives.

601   "I was so irritated": Andrew and Stephen Schlesinger, eds., *The Letters of Arthur Schlesinger* (New York: Random House, 2013), 323.

602   "Turner obviously regards Angleton": AS journals, 1978, NYPL archives.

602   a "rather wary friendship": Ibid., 1991.

602   "feeling kind of weird": Author interview with AS.

602   "a terrible story of CIA recklessness": AS journals, 1991, NYPL archives.

603   "a charming, earnest man": Ibid.

604   "he wished he'd written a book": Author interview with AS.

Chapter 22: End Game

605   "He was sad most of the time": Karen Croft interview with Angelina Cabrera.

605   "The senator dearly loved": Peter Edelman OH, JFK Library.

606   "As I walked in": Karen Croft interview with Angelina Cabrera.

607   For RFK's awkward balancing act on the Warren Report, see David Talbot, *Brothers: The Hidden History of the Kennedy Years* (New York: Free Press, 2007).

608   "One of the things you learned": Author interview with Adam Walinsky.

609   "Something bad is going to come of this": John Ehrlichman, *Witness to Power* (New York: Simon & Schuster, 1982), 24.

609   "Do you know what I think will happen": Arthur Schlesinger, *Robert Kennedy*, 857.

609   "if you believe that Johnson's reelection": Arthur Schlesinger Jr., *Journals: 1952–2000* (New York: Penguin Press, 2007), 274.

609 "Living every day is like Russian roulette": Jack Newfield, *RFK: A Memoir* (New York: Nation Books, 2009), 31.

610 "You have been much in my thoughts": AWD letter to RFK, Mudd Library.

611 including one of the men who subdued Sirhan: Talbot, *Brothers: The Hidden History of the Kennedy Years*, 373.

611 "Thus I have never said": Thomas Noguchi, *Coroner* (New York: Simon & Schuster, 1983), 108.

611 He struck many observers . . . as a "Manchurian candidate": See Shane O'Sullivan, *Who Killed Bobby?* (New York: Union Square Press, 2008); William Turner, *The Assassination of Robert F. Kennedy* (New York: Thunders Mouth Press, 1993); Robert Blair Kaiser, *RFK Must Die!* (New York: Grove Press, 1970).

611 "Gene Cesar is an innocent man": E-mail communication from Dan Moldea.

612 Meir claims he was introduced to Cesar: Author interview with John Meier.

612 "Everything about [Meier] was a lie": Author interview with Robert Maheu.

612 "just more garbage": E-mail from Dan Moldea.

612 "a no-good, dishonest son of a bitch": Michael Drosnin, *Citizen Hughes* (New York: Broadway Books, 2004), 424.

612 Maheu had made sweetheart deals with mobsters and allowed the CIA: See ibid.; see also Larry DuBois and Laurence Gonazales, "Hughes, Nixon and the CIA," *Playboy*, September 1976; and Gerald Bellett, *Age of Secrets* (Maitland, Ontario: Voyageur North America, 1995), 28.

612 "As far as I'm concerned": Robert Maheu testimony to Church Committee, Sept. 23, 1975.

613 "Lest you worry": AWD letter to Clover Dulles, June 25, 1968, Mudd Library.

614 "Dear Ted": Correspondence between AWD and Edward Kennedy, Mudd Library.

615 "Uncle Allen would go off": James Srodes, *Allen Dulles: Master of Spies* (Washington, DC: Regnery Publishing, 1999), 560.

616 "the spy was generally thought of": Allen W. Dulles, *Great Spy Stories* (Secaucus, NJ: Castle, 1969), xi.

616 "This is a special occasion": David Atlee Phillips, *Secret Wars Diary: My Adventures in Combat, Espionage Operations and Covert Action* (Bethesda, MD: Stone Tail Press, 1988), 172.

Epilogue

620 "the founding fathers of U.S. intelligence were liars": Joseph Trento, *The Secret History of the CIA* (Roseville, CA: Prima Publishing, 2001), 478.

Index

About the Author

DAVID TALBOT is the author of the *New York Times* bestseller *Brothers: The Hidden History of the Kennedy Years* and the acclaimed national bestseller *Season of the Witch: Enchantment, Terror, and Deliverance in the City of Love*. He is the founder and former editor in chief of *Salon*, and was a senior editor at *Mother Jones* magazine and the features editor at the *San Francisco Examiner*. He has written for *The New Yorker, Rolling Stone, Time, The Guardian*, and other major publications. Talbot lives in San Francisco, California.